CITY
ROOM

CITY
ROOM

ARTHUR GELB

A Marian Wood Book

*Published by G. P. Putnam's Sons
a member of
Penguin Group (USA) Inc.
New York*

A Marian Wood Book
Published by G. P. Putnam's Sons
Publishers Since 1838
a member of
Penguin Group (USA) Inc.
375 Hudson Street
New York, NY 10014

Library of Congress Cataloging-in-Publication Data

Gelb, Arthur, date.
City room / Arthur Gelb.
p. cm
"A Marian Wood book."
Includes index.
ISBN 0-399-15075-7
1. Gelb, Arthur.   2. Journalists—United States—Biography.
1. Title.
PN4874.G347A3   2003   2003043154
070.92—dc21
[B]

Printed in the United States of America
1   3   5   7   9   10   8   6   4   2

This book is printed on acid-free paper. ∞

Book design by Amanda Dewey

*To Barbara, who won my heart
in the old city room*

ONE

As I ENTERED THE LOBBY of *The New York Times* at 10:30 P.M., normally deserted at that late hour, I found myself in step behind a lissome woman with wavy ash-blond hair, wearing a snug-fitting black dress.

It was late May 1944, my first week as a copyboy, the humblest rank on the newspaper's staff. I was on my way back to the city room, second home to a legion of reporters and editors, all collaborators in the daily ritual of getting the paper out in time to meet truck, mail and rail schedules.

Sammy Solovitz, also a copyboy, and I—both of us just turned twenty— were balancing bundles of newspapers on our shoulders. They were early editions of competing New York dailies, and the ink, still damp, smudged our hands and clothes. We had been sent to fetch the papers from a newsstand around the corner in Times Square, so that the editors could check whether *The Times* had missed any important stories.

I was uneasily aware of the odd couple Sammy and I made—he an elfin four-foot-nine and I a gangling six-foot-two. Despite the bundle weighing him down, Sammy nonchalantly blew smoke rings, mimicking the soldier in Times Square's bigger-than-life Camel cigarette ad. By contrast, I must have appeared self-consciously earnest as I stared straight ahead through horn-rimmed glasses. My discomfort galloped nearly out of control when the woman we had followed into the elevator turned around, and I gazed into the sapphire eyes of Madeleine Carroll—for me, the screen's most beautiful actress.

Among the films in which she had starred were *The 39 Steps,* the Hitchcock thriller, and *My Favorite Blonde,* with Bob Hope, and I had spent a good part of my adolescence fantasizing about her. When the elevator door opened onto the reception area of the third-floor city room, I was frozen. Sammy had to tug my arm and lead me out. Instead of following him into the city room, I rang for the ascending elevator and, when it returned, I asked my new friend, Herman, the white-gloved elevator operator, where he had taken Miss Carroll.

"Kid, keep your shirt on," he said, and snapped the elevator gate shut.

Sharing Madeleine Carroll's aura was beyond anything I had expected during my first week at *The Times,* but I realized I would have to restrain my curiosity at least temporarily. The last thing I wanted was to do anything to jeopardize my new job on this titan of newspapers.

The city room was in full cry, with the paper going into extra editions through much of the night due to the breaking war news. Reporters, virtually all men in those days, unwound with drink and camaraderie in nearby saloons, and wives and girlfriends were expected to understand and not scold when their men broke dates or came home late.

That night, after the next edition was locked up, a reporter invited me to join him and two of his colleagues for drinks at Bleeck's, a legendary hangout for newspapermen three blocks south of *The Times.* While a wide gulf existed between reporters and copyboys, the invitation was my reward for having delivered a note the night before to my host's girlfriend, a chorus girl at the Latin Quarter.

Named for its curmudgeonly proprietor, Jack Bleeck (pronounced "Blake"), the saloon, a former speakeasy, adjoined the rear entrance of the *New York Herald Tribune* building. Odd mementos adorned its walls and a suit of armor stood in an inside room, a donation from the old Metropolitan Opera House a block away. The pub was a warm haven and, at the elongated front-room bar, shop talk resounded into the wee hours. Among the regulars at the bar that night were Wolcott Gibbs, *The New Yorker*'s theater critic, and Richard Maney, dean of Broadway press agents—the only one of his tribe regarded as talented enough to write now and then for *The Times*'s Sunday *Magazine.* Also present was Ralph Ingersoll, the publisher and editor of the muckraking afternoon tabloid *PM,* the man I had most wanted to work for before I landed at *The Times.*

I was still puzzling over Madeleine Carroll's presence at *The Times,* having read that she'd put her career on hold to join the Red Cross in Italy soon after American forces landed there. I also remembered reading she recently had been voted by Columbia University students for three successive years "the blonde with whom we would most like to be stranded on a desert island. She and two other actresses were asked whom *they* would most like to be stranded with. One said Clark Gable. The second chose Albert Einstein, as his conversation would never bore her. Madeleine Carroll's pert response was, "An obstetrician."

During a lull in the banter, I quietly asked one of the reporters if he was aware that Madeleine Carroll had been in the *Times* building earlier that night. With a knowing grin, he told me it was an open secret that she made occasional visits to the publisher, Arthur Hays Sulzberger, and had doubtless been on her way up to the fourteenth floor, where he maintained a suite and sometimes spent the night.

The disclosure that the publisher was having a liaison with the object of my most ardent fantasies convinced me I was working at the most glamorous place in the world. If the headiness of the job so far hadn't been enough, if there had been the slightest doubt in my mind, all hesitation vanished. I felt I might implode with joy.

I remembered this episode some forty-five years later, as I was preparing for my retirement as managing editor. I was cleaning out my desk and happened upon an old photo of Madeleine Carroll. The memories came rushing back—what it had been like for a kid raised by hardworking immigrant parents in a provincial Bronx neighborhood to enter the cosmopolitan world of *The New York Times*. Sadly, I pondered how little was left of that raffish, freewheeling old city room.

When I began at the paper, out-of-town correspondents telegraphed their stories to a clicking battery of Morse code operators, and foreign dispatches usually arrived by cable. Now out-of-town stories flowed in accompanied by the faint hum of computer monitors. And instead of the rattle of typewriters, there was the barely perceptible percussion of computer keyboards.

As I continued to toss clippings and ephemera into a shopping bag, I came across a packet of letters from my first mentor at *The Times*, Wilson L. Fairbanks, the former telegraph editor (a title later changed to national editor). He was a stalwart eighty-one when he appointed me as his clerk a few weeks after I started in the city room, and I might never have had the privilege of learning from him had I not come to the paper during those more tolerant earlier days. The notion of mandatory retirement at sixty-five for top editors did not evolve until the 1960s.

The Times in 1944 was determinedly paternalistic. The only way you could lose your job was through a serious lapse in taste or ethics. I saw this happen to three people during my apprentice years. The first was a reporter on the transportation staff who wrote to an automobile manufacturer about a "lemon" he had purchased, asking that it be replaced. He was dismissed because he used stationery with *Times* letterhead to complain about this personal matter. Another wrote to the city's chief magistrate asking that his parking ticket be excused. He too was dismissed.

The most bizarre case involved the photo editor, John Randolph. When Arthur Hays Sulzberger saw, in the first edition of January 15, 1954, a two-column picture of Marilyn Monroe, mouth slightly open, about to kiss Joe DiMaggio before their marriage ceremony, he deemed the picture a breach of taste and ordered it killed for the last edition. Randolph was demoted. He was reassigned to the national copy desk and later moved to the sports department, where he wrote the "Wood, Field and Stream" column. The beat took him on fishing excursions on the best boats, and hunting in fecund game forests with the best guides. Randolph never complained about his demotion.

Many editors still holding sway in the city room when I arrived had been hired by Adolph S. Ochs himself, the paper's early visionary publisher, or by his managing editor, Carr Van Anda, who had come from the *Sun* in 1904. Van Anda, who could read hieroglyphics, was responsible for *The Times*'s exclusive American coverage of such milestones as the opening of King Tutankhamen's tomb in Egypt—as well as Robert E. Peary's voyage to the North Pole and Richard E. Byrd's exploration of the Antarctic. Van Anda was so astute a mathematician that he once found a flaw in an equation that Albert Einstein had hastily scribbled on a blackboard during a lecture.

From the day in 1896 when the thirty-eight-year-old Ochs, publisher of the *Chattanooga Times,* took control of the failing *New York Times* on Park Row near City Hall, he sparkled with faith, imbuing his new acquisition with a decisive moral stance. With Napoleonic nerve, he had talked J. P. Morgan and others into backing his financial plan to take over the paper. ("I am impelled by only one desire in these negotiations," he told Morgan, "and that is to secure permanent control of *The New York Times,* which I believe I can make a successful and very profitable business enterprise, and at the same time make it the model American newspaper.") He then lured the cream of reporters and editors to his staff, and they in turn drew the elite of readers—and advertisers.

Ochs never commissioned polls to determine what readers wanted, relying instead on his own instincts. He believed, for example, that a civilized person should care about the world. Unlike most of his rivals, who gave primary position to local coverage, he mandated that news from abroad lead the paper's inside pages. He enriched the foreign and national bureaus, despite the cost of maintaining a highly qualified staff and the expense of cable and telegraph dispatches. Unhesitantly, he reinvested much of his profits into strengthening the paper.

It was Ochs who encouraged a benevolent attitude toward the staff, which in turn responded with intense fidelity. He had died only nine years before I came to the paper, and his presence was still palpable. He was remembered with both affection and awe, especially by those he had personally hired; indeed, they held a unique status as members of the "Ochs Plan," entitling them to an additional pension whenever they opted to retire.

With the precedent set by Ochs, it was not unusual for someone past seventy to continue working forty or fifty hours a week. The copy desk that handled obituary, society and cultural stories was led, for example, by another spry octogenarian, William D. Evans, known as "the Judge," a title bestowed in part because of his courtly bearing, accentuated by his gray Vandyke and thatch of pure white hair. In 1885, soon after graduating from Yale, the Judge headed for a newspaper in Duluth, Minnesota, at a time, he would reminisce, when typewriters and telephones were considered "newfangled."

As a young reporter he was stricken with a lung ailment, and his doctor gave him only six months to live. ("Doctors be damned," he would tell each new copyboy, laughing merrily.) At his desk he wore a dark fedora in even the most sweltering weather. "It's to prevent drafts," he once confided to me, "a scourge that could give me a head cold and send me to an early grave." The Judge retired at ninety, in 1952.

Even older than Judge Evans and Wilson Fairbanks was ninety-year-old Edward M. Kingsbury, one of the most lucid editorial writers in the business. In 1925, his editorial on New York's poor won the Pulitzer Prize, *The Times*'s third. Six months after my arrival, he announced his retirement and turned in his last editorial, which throbbed with nostalgia; it was pegged to the death of Al Smith, that icon of New York grit who had climbed from the sidewalks of the Lower East Side to the Governor's Mansion.

I WAS FIFTEEN when my history teacher at the all-boys DeWitt Clinton High School in the north Bronx opened my eyes (no doubt unwittingly) to the course my life was to take. Irwin Guernsey, called "Doc" by his students, had contracted polio as a child, walked with a limp and supported his stocky frame with two canes. Sometimes, to emphasize a point, he'd crack a cane across his classroom desk, alarming us all.

He knew I was stagestruck, for I'd told him about my habit of attending a Broadway matinee practically every Saturday—when I would take the nickel ride on the subway down from the Bronx and buy a fifty-five cent second-balcony seat with money earned from working after school as a delivery boy for a dry-cleaning store.

When I was fourteen, I saw my first Broadway play, a comedy called *What a Life!* I was enthralled by everything about that Saturday matinee: the antics of an actor named Ezra Stone playing a problem-prone teenager, Henry Aldrich. I reveled in the sweet, slightly musty aroma of the playhouse and pored over the shiny, crisp *Playbill*. Many of the illustrious performances I saw as a teenager are alive in my memory: Paul Robeson's rich bass in *Othello* and Laurette Taylor's plaintive cry of "Rise and shine!" in *The Glass Menagerie.*

A theater fan himself, Doc urged me to supplement my playgoing by reading some of the noteworthy plays of the recent past—among others, the Ben Hecht–Charles MacArthur comic masterpiece *The Front Page.* I was mesmerized by this glimpse into the embattled world of Chicago newspapermen, as personified by the cunning, unflappable managing editor, Walter Burns, and his resourceful star reporter, Hildy Johnson. I dreamed of myself as a real-life Hildy, tricking reluctant politicians into spilling the beans, beating the cops to their crime scenes, wheedling confessions out of criminals—and writing the front-page scoop. I had always wanted to be a writer, but as a practical matter, in those Depression years, I knew I would also have to earn a salary. As a newspaper reporter, I could realize my ambition to write, and be paid a weekly wage.

When I turned eighteen, with no end in sight for the war, I found myself up in the air about my draft status. I had, of course, received my draft notice, but my eyesight was poor and the draft board quota for the category I was placed in after my physical exam was "limited service (1A-L)," which was temporarily filled. I was told I would likely be called by the end of the year. With this disconcertingly vague forecast, I dropped out of college and went from one temporary job to another—an airplane washer at Fiorello H. La Guardia Field (recently named for New York's much-loved mayor), a complaint clerk at Gimbel's (the department store at Herald Square) and a soda jerk at a Bronx ice cream parlor—where I was fired within two hours for experimenting with lemon-flavored chocolate malteds. Dispirited, I went home to bed and stayed there.

My mother, the patron saint of my mental well-being, urged me to stop agonizing about forces beyond my control. She felt I ought to apply immediately for a job on a newspaper—that very day. I did.

I made my way to the offices of *PM*. The paper was the brainchild of Ralph Ingersoll, the man who would soon be standing just a few feet away from me at the bar of Bleeck's. Ingersoll had been managing editor of *The New Yorker* and, later, *Fortune*. He had also served briefly as publisher of *Time*, where he had once angered Henry Luce by choosing Hitler as Man of the Year, and then depicting him on the cover as a little man playing a hymn of hate on an organ. Although considered a renegade from his privileged class, Ingersoll was included in the Social Register and was a member of both the exclusive Union Club and the Racquet Club.

He had followed a revolutionary vision of journalism in 1940 with *PM*, his grand experiment (or folly, as some thought it), and originally considered calling it, simply, *Newspaper*. Containing no advertisements, *PM* sought to retain its integrity at a remove from what Ingersoll regarded as the grubby, capitalist interests of sponsors. Its lofty goal to "seek truth" was derided by the mainstream press, which sneered at it as a "Red rag."

One of *PM*'s early copy editors was Dashiell Hammett; Ben Hecht was a prominent, albeit short-lived, member of its writing staff. The paper's premier photographer was Arthur Fellig, better known as Weegee, who night after night, lugging a cumbersome Speed Graphic, managed to capture Gotham's seamiest street life. It was rumored that Weegee's nickname derived from the Ouija board, a tribute to his almost supernatural ability to get to the scene of a crime before the police. His subjects included prostitutes, gang violence, suicides and grisly accidents.

To offset the lack of revenue from advertising, Ingersoll set the price for *PM* at five cents—two cents more than *The Times*. Ironically, the paper was bankrolled by Marshall Field III, the progressive Chicago department store scion; fearful that the country was becoming dangerously conservative, he also had founded the *Chicago Sun*.

When *PM* started publishing, it entered a crowded field of afternoon New York papers: the *Sun,* the *World-Telegram,* the *Journal-American* and the *Post,* then a broadsheet. Among the morning papers, the *News,* with a daily readership of 2,038,634 and 3,724,755 on Sunday, had the largest circulation, followed by the *Mirror, The Times* and the *Herald Tribune. The Times's* circulation was 449,409 daily and 817,960 on Sunday. There were at least fifteen smaller papers, 100,000 or less in circulation, including the *Brooklyn Eagle,* the *Wall Street Journal,* the *Morning Telegraph,* the *Staten Island Advance,* the *Long Island Press* and the *Journal of Commerce.*

Against the backdrop of the war, newspapers played a role in people's lives that was almost as vital as food and water. The correspondents, who provided wrenching descriptions of the military campaigns, were heroes to the average citizen; indeed several were killed on assignment, including Byron (Barney) Darnton, a beloved forty-five-year-old *Times* man who had lost his life in New Guinea less than two years before I started at the paper, and whose death was still being mourned. He had been on a small Australian fishing vessel crammed with soldiers and threading its way through enemy waters when an American B-25, believing the boat was Japanese, strafed it. Barney's wife, Eleanor, worked for *The Times* as women's news editor. Their older son, Robert, who became a noted historian, was three when his father was killed; their younger son, John, eleven months old at the time, was to become a Pulitzer Prize–winning foreign correspondent for *The Times*.

For news and editorial opinion about the war's progress, I turned first to the pages of *PM*. Of the two papers I devoured (*The Times* was the other), *PM* seemed the more unpredictable and definitely more feisty. Ingersoll's iconoclastic staff worked hard at setting the political and business establishments on their ears.

I wasn't as radical as some of my school friends, but I did have a rebellious social conscience, and I often found myself at ideological odds with *The Times*. I respected its eloquent, thorough reporting, but its overall tone on several major issues had seemed to me less than balanced. I was upset, for example, by its decision to endorse Wendell Willkie rather than Franklin D. Roosevelt in his bid for a third term in 1940, and I thought its coverage of the Spanish Civil War had been too pro-Franco. My friends and I—supporters of the Loyalist side and despising Franco as a Nazi ally—had been influenced in our thinking by a letter in *The Times* signed by Archibald MacLeish and Bennett Cerf, among other literary figures, that criticized the paper for allowing its correspondent, William P. Carney, to rely heavily on Franco's propaganda.

Then there was my sense that *The Times*'s coverage of Nazi atrocities— despite the moral loftiness and balance it espoused—was dismayingly thin. While it was true there had been scores of stories about the persecution of European Jews in the paper since 1939, the accounts were brief, rarely appeared on page one and bore no interpretation. Nor did the editorial page express sufficient indignation when our government ignored various proposals by Jewish organizations to rescue those destined for systematic slaughter in what, at the time, were insidiously designated as "reservations."

I can remember, growing up in the Bronx, my parents' anguish upon receiving letters from Europe disclosing the tragic fate of relatives. In my adolescent innocence, I did not want to believe that the timidity of *The Times*'s coverage might have stemmed from the insecurity of its Jewish owners and their dread that *The Times* might be seen as a "Jewish paper." Was it that they—like other powerful assimilated American Jews—feared to raise their voices in outrage over the persecution of their co-religionists because such a stance might threaten their own hard-won social and economic status?

From anecdotal accounts in *PM,* as well as from what my father told me he was reading daily in the Jewish press—together with the preaching I heard on national radio by bigots like Father Charles Coughlin, the Catholic priest in Michigan who felt free to blame the recent Depression on Jews' having cornered all the good jobs—it gradually dawned on me that anti-Semitism must be rampant in America. I had experienced scarcely any discrimination in my own Bronx neighborhood. The mostly Jewish, Irish and Italian families had their own hardships arising from the Depression and, while there were occasional flare-ups, prejudice among the ethnic groups was generally fleeting.

My first shocking encounter with discrimination came when I was seventeen and tried to land a summer job as an office boy at a downtown Manhattan law firm. Answering newspaper ads, I was rejected at one high-toned company after another. I finally went to one of the employment agencies on Sixth Avenue, underneath the El. The man in charge called me into his office. "You're Jewish, aren't you?" he asked. I was surprised and confused. "Let me tell you the facts of life," he said. "The leading downtown law offices generally won't hire Jews. That's just the way it is. I'm sorry."

I had a warmer reception when I tried for a job on a newspaper. At *PM* the friendly woman in charge of personnel told me there were no openings right then but we chatted a bit about theater and politics. She said she happened to know that *The Times* had an opening for a copyboy, and asked if I would be interested in working there. I swallowed my reservations and said I would. She dialed someone she knew at the paper and recommended me. "He's an earnest, curious, enthusiastic young man," she said, winking at me. "I think he'll do well at *The Times.*"

I was told to report there the next evening to be interviewed for a night copyboy post. I had to admit I was somewhat cowed by the possibility of working for what was, after all, the most influential newspaper in the world. My heart began to race as I approached the building on Forty-third Street, a little west of Broadway. Arriving on the third floor for my interview, I had my first glimpse of the city room, the place that was to be my home away from home for nearly half a century.

What I saw was a high-ceilinged room filled with clamor, clutter and cigarette smoke. There was an overwhelming sense of purpose, fire and life: the clacking rhythm of typewriters, the throbbing of great machines in the composing room on the floor above, reporters shouting for copyboys to pick up their stories. Some of the editors wore green eyeshades while others relied on fedoras to block the glare of the suspended lamps as they worked feverishly with pencils, scissors, paste pots and copy paper. Solid brass spittoons were placed strategically around the room and a carpet of cigarette butts all but obscured the gray concrete floor.

A quartet of reporters who had finished their stories played a casual game of bridge at the front of the room, while others were intent on a poker game in the rear. The old city room was compact and cozy, with no partitions (as in later years) separating the rows upon rows of wooden desks. At the desks—some so worn they were splintering—reporters typed at top speed, while cradling the receivers of their upright phones between ear and shoulder.

Almost paralyzed with excitement, I felt as though I had walked into *The Front Page*. I knew instantly this was my element. It was where I wanted to stay forever. I was directed to the desk of the managing editor's secretary, just outside the only enclosed office on the floor. There I was interviewed by Belle Sloane, a plump, no-nonsense woman with a round face and dark reddish hair. She hired me on the spot. My salary, she said, would be sixteen dollars a week, and I went to work that very night. I would happily have worked for lunch money and carfare.

Still reeling with wonder, I watched as the boss of the entire city room, managing editor Edwin L. James himself, emerged from his office. He was a cigar-chomping, dyed-in-the-wool newspaperman with a flashy wardrobe and a reputation for gruffness. He sported a plaid vest, striped shirt with a white collar, and a pearl stickpin in his cravat; yellow spats covered his gleaming black shoes. Despite his rotundity and lack of height, he was a dashing figure and he knew it.

Once, while doing research in the public library for a high school report, I had come across James's classic *Times* account of Charles Lindbergh's flight to Paris. James's imagery gave his readers the sense they were at his side as he described the scene at Le Bourget, scurrying along with a mob of thousands past policemen, pushing through barricades, climbing over fences, finally reaching *The Spirit of St. Louis* as Lindbergh emerged, tousle-haired and triumphant. I read the story over so many times I could recite some passages from memory.

James's uncanny mind for detail was the envy of his peers. In 1915, when he became a *Times* reporter at twenty-five, his first assignment brought him accolades. The city editor had sent him to the Astor Hotel to cover a banquet attended by diplomats and other dignitaries. The host, accompanied by a U.S. Marine Guard, presented himself as "Lieut. Comdr. Ethan Allan Weinberg, K.G.," the new consul general for Romania. In the harbor earlier that day, he had received an eleven-gun salute.

Of the many reporters present at the banquet, only James sensed that something was askew. He noticed that though the consul general's jacket was adorned with medals, his shoes were unpolished and scuffed. James called *The Times*'s Washington bureau, which checked with the State Department. There was no Weinberg listed as the new consul general for Romania. In fact, Romania did not have a consul general. It turned out that the banquet's host was a grand impostor who prided himself on assuming bogus identities purely for the joy of exploiting the gullibility of men of influence. Weinberg was arrested and returned to upstate Elmira to complete a prison term. James had his scoop and was on his way to stardom.

Like other fabled newspapermen of that era, James (known as "Jimmy James" to his peers) was a true eccentric. He had trundled all over the continent as chief European correspondent and, relaxing between stories, had drunk the finest Armagnacs and dined in the best restaurants. In New York, he took long, solitary walks late at night down unfrequented streets and alleys. And, as everybody knew, he was an addicted horse player. He usually came out of his office only to place or collect his bets. Actually, he hated to come out at all. Hiding in his office was the best way to avoid the reporters and editors who sought to badger him for raises.

I watched as James, adhering to what I later learned was a daily routine, ambled past me, oblivious of the tumult surrounding him. *Daily Racing Form* in hand, he headed for a desk in a corner of the room where two bookies presided. Tough and street smart, they were originally hired as copyboys, as were other youths who lived in neighboring Hell's Kitchen—but their particular bent led them to bookmaking as a supplementary career.

James had promoted Angelo Gheraldi and Phil Brennan to clerks' jobs, but taking bets seemed to be their principal duty, and wads of bills always peeked from their pockets. Eventually they graduated to clerical supervisory positions and gave long, loyal service to the paper. But once, when Angelo and Phil were still placing bets for James and other *Times* staffers, two detectives arrived in the city room looking for them.

A reporter's wife had called the precinct station house when her husband came home without his weekly paycheck. He finally confessed he had lost his salary betting with the office bookies. His wife turned up in the city room demanding to see James, who hid. Her next stop was the police station. A copyboy somehow discovered the detectives were on their way, and alerted Angelo and Phil, who quickly beat a retreat. The bookies rewarded their Paul Revere with a week's holiday in Miami.

When the detectives left the city room, James relaxed with a cigar, donned his black derby and prepared to leave for the night, in a ritual anticipated by the city staff. Approaching one of the slow-moving elevators, he would hurl oaths at it. If that didn't bring results he would strike the elevator with his cane.

When at last the elevator door slid open, James departed regally, seemingly oblivious to the fact that the city room, at 6:30 P.M., had begun its climb toward the peak of nightly activity. By now, copy was pouring in by cable and telegraph, and most city-room reporters were putting the finishing touches on their local stories.

I was astonished to see the managing editor turn his back on this crucial phase of producing the paper. "Who's in charge now?" I asked Sammy Solovitz, who had been at *The Times* some months longer than I. "The boss will be here soon," explained Sammy, pointing to a desk in an enclosure known as the bullpen. That was where, Sammy said, James's first deputy, the night managing editor, Raymond H. McCaw, would take charge of putting the paper to bed—his job since 1930. Before joining *The Times* in 1923, McCaw had been part of that wanderlust breed of newspaper tramps journeying from town to town across the country in search of work as reporters or copyreaders, or even typesetters.

As unaffected and down-to-earth as James was self-conscious and foppish, McCaw arrived promptly at seven o'clock. Completely at home in the world of printer's ink and newsprint, he hung his rumpled jacket on a coat rack, rolled up his sleeves and attacked the pile of copy and proofs on his desk awaiting his approval. He also looked at the memos James had left him; since James often made it a point to be gone by the time McCaw arrived, the two rarely spoke.

After each edition, when the paper was delivered to him just off the press, McCaw methodically turned every page and corrected anything amiss. In the staff's view, the "day side," represented by James, and the "night side," represented by McCaw, were separate, autonomous worlds. Turning a blind eye, James, convinced the paper went to press under a remarkably successful system, was content to leave its production entirely to McCaw. Thus, McCaw had final say about editing of stories, their space allotment and position, and, most important, which stories would appear on page one.

Marveling at the hectic but somehow orderly pace of the city-room operation during that first night at *The Times,* I nervously awaited a summons to duty. When McCaw shouted, "Boy!" I rushed to his desk. He handed me a proof and told me to take it to the composing room.

For a moment, I forgot where the composing room was. Seeing my hesitation, McCaw took the trouble to smile reassuringly. "You're new here, son, aren't you? Go up that spiral staircase over there and give this proof to the man at the desk. And watch your step going up." He was the first editor who had said a word to me—and a gracious word, at that. He made me feel I was a bona fide member of *The Times,* and I sprinted joyfully up the narrow iron stairs to the composing room.

TWO

P AT SPIEGEL WAS the first reporter in the city room to befriend me, disregarding the caste system that dictated a haughty distance between reporters and copyboys. He had himself started on *The Times* as a copyboy in 1925, and enjoyed nothing more than satirizing reporters who assumed snobbish attitudes.

Pat was also a racetrack fiend and, not long after I came to *The Times,* he invited me to accompany him to "play the ponies" on my day off. In my insular Bronx neighborhood, I had never met a bookie, nor did I know anything about horses. Pat promised to introduce me to a milieu that I had, up to now, only glimpsed in the movies—a world of big-time bettors and small-time touts. Kinetic and fast-talking, Pat posed as a knowledgeable handicapper, and he tried to teach me how to read the *Racing Form;* but it turned out he didn't know much more about the ponies than I did.

Nonetheless, I soon was putting down $2 bets—"a deuce," in track parlance. His pals at the track considered his system somewhat radical. To have a winner, he would bet on six horses in an eight-horse race. It didn't faze him that he had to invest $12 to arrive at a $2.80 winning ticket. It was the win that was important, not the money. And if he did chance to come out ahead, he would spend his winnings on whomever he happened to be with.

Pat's real name was Irving. The nickname "Pat" stuck when, years earlier, an assistant city editor, Walter Fenton, had assigned him to cover Sunday sermons at St. Patrick's Cathedral; every time Irving returned to the city room, Fenton would announce: "Our Jewish Patrick is back." Later, when he began covering what we all took to calling the "Jewish beat," Pat would occasionally invite me to join him, and we would "schul-hop," going from one congregation to the next, as one might go nightclub hopping. Religious news in those days was a kind of gossipy, neighborhood-oriented staple of the paper, and it was important for a modest-sized synagogue to get a mention in *The Times;* the rabbis at such congregations stood in terror of Spiegel's power.

Pat saw no reason why he shouldn't interrogate a rabbi about parochial ins and outs in the same manner that got results on the police beat. "Now, listen, Rabbi," he'd shout into the phone, "you'd better play straight with me. You mean to tell me you've been sitting on this story for three days? Listen, Rabbi, if you're going to play the game that way, I'll get the story from someone else. And you won't like that, Rabbi, will you?"

Pat was a self-taught pianist. No less an authority than *The Times*'s music critic, Harold Schonberg, evaluated his musicality: With a twinkle of mock envy, he told me: "Once, and only once, did I hear Spiegel *auf dem Flügel*. It was at a *Times* party, and he was sitting at the piano. He was quietly amusing himself with the first movement of Mozart's Coronation Concerto. Landowska used to play it, and Casadesus once or twice. Not many others. There was Spiegel, hands in classic position, fingers nicely curved, rippling out D Major phrases with perfect equilibrium, articulation and weight placement. He saw me coming and suddenly got bashful. I did not ask him to continue. It's not fair that a man should play pinochle like Moorhead, gin rummy like Goren, and Mozart like Artur Schnabel."

Wherever he happened to be, Pat drew an audience. He loved to translate Hamlet's famed soliloquy into Yiddish, interspersing it with double-talk in both languages. A popular lecturer, he once invited me to a talk he gave at City College about police reporting. He described walking beside Dutch Schultz as he was marched in handcuffs to Police Headquarters. "How do you think you'd look with daylight streaming through holes in your body?" the gangster slyly joked to Pat. A humorless *Daily Mirror* reporter misinterpreted the remark as a threat and filed a story. Pat recalled his anxious efforts to persuade Schultz's pals he had nothing to do with the *Mirror*'s report.

Pat's talent for instant camaraderie was a big help on assignments. Once, covering a train wreck upstate, he secured exclusive access to the only telephone in the vicinity by flattering the elderly woman who owned a house near the site. The woman told competing reporters trying to reach their city desks that she would allow no one to use the phone except "that nice, kissing reporter."

Pat was at his most relaxed when Emanuel Perlmutter, his closest ally in the city room, joined us at the track. Manny, who had grown up in the Brownsville–East New York section of Brooklyn that had spawned a generation of mobsters, came to *The Times* in the early thirties. Like so many other reporters in the Depression years, he had come of age in a working-class family and believed a glamorous job on a newspaper, despite the low pay, would rescue him from the sort of drab existence endured by relatives and friends in his Brooklyn neighborhood. Although he had a bachelor's degree from New York University, he was happy to begin as a copyboy, and, like Pat, he was promoted to reporter after several years of demonstrating he had the right stuff.

There were other ways, of course, to make reporter: You could come to *The Times* after gaining a reputation on another paper; you could establish a journalistic knack as a college correspondent for *The Times* and be hired upon graduation; or you could be related to someone important.

I hoped to follow the route taken by Manny and Pat: climbing from copyboy to desk clerk, thence to desk news assistant, wangling some short writing assignments and hoping to demonstrate my ability and motivation. Many of the top reporters and editors, including a number of Pulitzer Prize winners, had also started out as copyboys—including the paper's premier reporter, Meyer Berger.

While Manny talked tough, wore a fedora slouched over his eyes, dangled an unlit cigarette from the side of his mouth and jabbed his forefinger at you for emphasis, he didn't intimidate anyone, for we all knew he was soft at heart. Manny and Pat were inseparable in the city room, checking each other's copy, relishing the stories behind each other's assignments and supplying one another with hot track tips.

"When I started as a night office boy," Manny once recalled, "young Spiegel was already showing other copyboys how to make the tough points on dice—ten and four. He was the best craps shooter on the night shift. When he went out to cover police districts a few years later, the cops who wandered into the West Side, East Side and Centre Street reporters' shacks were just as easy marks."

At times Sammy Solovitz joined us at the track. Before starting at the paper, he had been a messenger for Western Union, and had taken pride in the cap and uniform he wore when delivering telegrams to *The Times*. When Steve Moran, the assistant head of the copyboys, first saw him, he groaned: "Is Western Union running a kindergarten now?" Sammy put his hands on his hips and jutted out his chin: "Shut your trap, you big fathead." James, overhearing the exchange, promptly hired Sammy as a copyboy. Sammy, who had "resigned" from Brooklyn Automotive High School after his sophomore year, was soon bossing a group of copyboys all taller, older and better educated than he.

The actual chief of the copyboys was Tim Connery, a cheerful man in his mid-thirties, who looked like a prizefighter because of his broken, flattened nose. Adolph Ochs had given him the job some years earlier after Tim was injured working as a flyboy in the press room and lost his right arm. Tim and Moran kept watch over the city room, standing like sentinels at a post near the city desk. Moran's nose glowed nightly after he consumed pitchers of beer fetched by Sammy from a nearby saloon.

Along the Forty-third Street side of the city room, directly in front of a wall of tall casement windows, stood a large desk for the city editor and smaller ones for his secretary and three assistants. These desks, known collectively as the "city desk" (later the metropolitan desk), were flanked on the west side by the managing editor's office; on the east side was the bullpen, containing, along with McCaw's desk, seating for three assistant night managing editors.

From his command site, the city editor looked out into the city room, where his staff of almost a hundred reporters—an all-white and virtually all-male domain—sat at their battered desks, fourteen rows with six desks in each, connected like Siamese twins. Also within his view were the fifteen copyreaders seated around the long, wooden horseshoe-shaped city copy desk. And nearby were the other two horseshoe copy desks: telegraph and cable (later renamed national and foreign).

The room had undergone no major change since the building, which opened in 1913, had been somewhat enlarged in 1924. (The paper had previously been published from its cramped 1905 structure in the trapezoidal Times Square island.) While the additional space allowed more elbow room, there was still a sense of intimacy. And not least among the room's unplanned perks was its view from a rear window of the dressing-room windows across an alley of the Forty-fourth Street Theater. Copyboys took up nightly vigils to watch the chorus girls changing costumes, an entertainment that ended when the theater (which housed the Stage Door Canteen in its basement for soldiers and sailors) was torn down to make room for *The Times*'s new annex.

No one felt more at home in that city room than Sammy Solovitz as he bantered with reporters and editors through the long night. Sammy wore his hair in a crew cut. He was a chain-smoker, though he never bought his own cigarettes, preferring to cadge them, regardless of brand. Under pressure, he'd shout curses, sometimes in the obscure Yiddish he had picked up in the Williamsburg neighborhood of Brooklyn, where his parents owned a candy store.

Eventually, Sammy ascended to bona fide boss of the copyboys, many of whom were destined to be correspondents in bureaus all over the globe. One of his charges was Al Gore, who had himself worked as a copyboy during a summer in the late 1960s, and went on to become a reporter on the *Nashville Tennessean*. Once, on a visit to *The Times* during his vice presidency, he recalled Sammy fondly as a "hard taskmaster."

I had not known Sammy for more than half an hour when he suddenly grabbed my arm, squeezing it so hard his eyes seemed to pop out under his heavy lids. His long, sharp nose quivered as he muttered furtively, "There she is. I have to have her! I have to have that Lucy Greenbaum!"

The object of his lust was a generously rounded young reporter whose low-cut dresses drew all eyes in the city room. Lucy belonged to the female vanguard of four, all hired to replace men who had been drafted or become war correspondents. She had a gracious smile that masked a tough, spirited core, and it was surely her competitive training as a catcher on school and neighborhood baseball teams that provided her with ideal seasoning for survival in this male jungle. She boasted she could catch the fastest ball thrown, but "I gotta have the right kind of mitt." No one doubted her.

"Sammy," I said in disbelief, "that woman could squash you! She's twice as tall as you and three times as wide!" Sammy was not to be dissuaded, especially when Lucy drew close to him and spoke his name in the whisper she affected. "I must have her!" he cried, a refrain I heard month after month.

As tokenism, *The Times* had been hiring women reporters since 1869, when Midy Morgan, an Irish-born expert on livestock, was engaged as a business staff reporter to cover the cattle-market beat. But it wasn't until 1935 that the paper hired a woman, Kathleen McLaughlin of the *Chicago Tribune,* to cover breaking news for the city staff.

Lucy was the second woman engaged to write about hard local news. She was the niece of the Sulzberger family's attorney, General Edward S.

Greenbaum, and after her graduation from Bennington in 1940, she persuaded her uncle to ask the publisher to grant her a chance to try out. At that time, women reporters were generally known as "sob sisters," mostly relegated to writing sentimental human-interest stories, or contributing columns on the "Four F's": Family, Food, Fashions, Furnishings. This was an era when newspapering was considered a rough trade, when almost all editors thought it unthinkable for a woman on *The Times* to cover stories of violence and mayhem. Women staffers were considered delicate, breakable objects, to be treated with chivalry to their faces—and often with scorn behind their backs.

Reversing that kind of thinking over the years was a hard struggle—and pity the woman reporter who rejected an assignment because it was dangerous. (Once in the early 1970s, during my tenure as metropolitan editor, I assigned several reporters to cover the celebration of Earth Day in Union Square, at that time a deteriorating neighborhood. As night fell, the crowds became rowdy and one of the reporters, a young, attractive woman, phoned me from a sidewalk booth; she complained she was being harassed by some youths and asked, "Could you please send a man to replace me?" Linda Charlton, one of the stars on the rewrite battery, happened to be standing nearby and picked up the drift of the conversation. "How can you let her come back?" she demanded. "If you do, I insist you send me out to replace her." I did.)

An outstanding exception in my early days at the paper was Anne O'Hare McCormick, the first female columnist and one of the most influential writers on the editorial staff. In 1921, after having submitted several notable articles to the Sunday *Magazine,* she wrote to Carr Van Anda asking if she could send him an occasional story from Europe, when she accompanied her husband, Francis J. McCormick, an importer and engineer, on a business trip. Van Anda replied, "Try it." Her assessment of Mussolini's rise was in astute contrast to the dispatches from other correspondents who tended to dismiss him as a poseur, and her place at *The Times* was assured.

She wrote about domestic and foreign policy events and obtained exclusive interviews with European heads of state, including Hitler as well as Mussolini. She rarely took notes, once explaining that, "It makes people too cautious." She relied on her flawless memory and ability to sense the mood of a situation. Despite her renown, Adolph Ochs refused to employ her—or any woman—for the foreign or national staffs.

It wasn't until a year after Ochs's death in 1935 that his successor, Arthur Hays Sulzberger, offered Anne McCormick a job on *The Times*'s editorial board. Only one year later, she became the first *Times* woman to win a Pulitzer Prize. Sulzberger later said of his decision: "It's a pretty scary thing to be a brand-new publisher of *The New York Times* and to score a bull's-eye when your trigger finger is still trembling."

Mrs. McCormick, as she preferred to be known, spent months at a time reporting on military and political developments in war-torn Europe. One night she and her husband were invited to dine with General George S. Patton. The road to his headquarters was under bombardment, washed out in places. The officer who served as their driver and guide suggested it was too dangerous to make the trip in the dark, especially under enemy fire. But Mrs. McCormick was undeterred. When they arrived at Patton's camp, the general was amazed to see them.

It appeared that commanders at the front were more at ease with Mrs. McCormick than with her male counterparts. Patton, for example, allowed her to witness his blunt briefing of his officers. She complimented him on putting on "such a good act." Responding good-humoredly, he said, "The American stage lost a great actor when Geeorge S. Patton joined the Army."

I had heard many such stories about Mrs. McCormick's exploits, and imagined her as a kind of Rosalind Russell playing the wisecracking, flirtatious star reporter in *His Girl Friday*. I was confounded when I first delivered copy to her to find a matronly woman in her sixties, sitting at her desk wearing a lacy hat.

FROM MY VERY FIRST DAY at the paper, I had savored working in Times Square. Even before reaching the city room, I breathed in the exotic aura of nighttime Broadway, the pulsing, gritty essence of the city. Broadway's lights were now dimmed for the war. But on dark, cloudy days during my boyhood, the lights in Times Square were switched on early and the gray haze magically vanished. Often, I left the subway from the Bronx at Columbus Circle to walk down Broadway, sometimes lingering to listen to the speakers in the Circle as they ranted from their soapboxes, American flags at their sides.

Below the Circle, the island enveloping Times Square was incandescently white, an effect achieved by tens of thousands of glittering electric bulbs in gigantic advertising signs, along with the beckoning movie palace marquees that lined both sides of Broadway. I felt myself transported to another world. Jewel-like in its iridescence, the light flew skyward, visible for miles. It was enhanced by the relatively new neon signs, which were introduced in a big way in 1925 when the George M. Cohan Theater heralded "Ben-Hur" in red letters five feet high.

In 1936, I was taken by my uncle to see the dazzling multicolored Wrigley's Spearmint sign, erected to a height of five stories above the Criterion movie theater. A forerunner of the neon spectaculars, the sign provided free sidewalk entertainment; people stopped, sometimes for as long as half an hour, to gaze at the animated electric aquarium of eleven vari-sized green, red, purple and yellow fish swimming up and down and blowing neon bubbles.

Polished brass everywhere along Broadway reflected the lights. All the movie theaters and restaurants were plated with brass, and brass buttons dotted the smart uniforms of ushers standing under their marquees, erect as soldiers on parade, staring straight ahead. With rare exceptions, these ushers were fair-skinned all-American boys, drilled daily on the roofs of the movie houses.

One of Times Square's enticements was the stage show, often featuring big bands, that followed the film presentation in the larger movie houses. When Sinatra made his bow at the Paramount not long after my arrival at the paper, some twenty-five thousand screaming teenage girls, all wearing the requisite bobby socks, snaked around three city blocks trying to buy tickets—or at least get a glimpse of their idol—causing traffic snarls and requiring a detail of two hundred policemen. Since the entrance to *The Times* was a short distance up Forty-third Street from the Paramount's stage door, my colleagues and I had to force our way through the crazed mob. Sammy Solovitz flirted with the girls as he shoved through their ranks, confiding that he was a close friend of Frank's.

I spent part of my dinner break people-watching in Times Square. There was a flower shop above the front steps of the Astor Hotel where gigolos bought corsages for the matrons they escorted. Young couples crowded the barroom of the Taft Hotel to hear Charlie Drew at the piano singing risqué ditties, and I became an expert at nursing a single beer for the duration of the hourlong show. Dinner at times consisted of an outsize hot dog and a small beer at a bar called McGuiness that set me back a quarter, but for no extra charge I could watch ribald cartoons revolving above the bar.

Returning from my dinner break during my first week at work, I was just in time to hear a reporter yell, "Copy!" I ran to his desk as he pulled a page from his typewriter. Copy paper, on which all stories were written, was shiny, cheap, lightweight newsprint cut into sheets eight by ten inches and stacked high in the city room.

Grabbing the page, I turned to carry it to the copy desk when suddenly I heard a loud whistle. I spun around in time to see the reporter, lanky, balding and bespectacled, stand up from his chair, rub his hands together and blow into his closed-knuckled thumbs, again creating the piercing noise. He then leaped onto his desk and began a lap around the city room, jumping from desktop to desktop. Reporters sensing his arrival nonchalantly ducked their heads and then went about their business. I was bewildered.

"Sammy, what is he doing?" I asked.

"Oh, that's just his way of blowing off steam when he finishes a story. That's Mike Berger." Meyer Berger, who occupied the first desk in the first row, was the preeminent stylist on the staff and arguably the best writer on any newspaper. When the paper—which generally shunned frills—boldly inaugurated a column of whimsical, human-interest anecdotes, no one doubted the assignment would go to Berger. The column, which grew out of a feature launched at the 1939 World's Fair, was called "About New York," but because it focused on the lighter side of life, it was discontinued with the onset of the war (and didn't reappear under Berger's byline until 1953).

Born in 1898, Berger had left grammar school at twelve to take a job as a messenger for the *New York World*. But when he finally tried out as reporter, it was clear he was a natural. After starting at *The Times* in 1928, he was invariably assigned to the front-page story about the St. Patrick's Day parade, in an era when there were more Irish in New York than Dublin. He always wrote his story in metrical prose. One paragraph went like this: "Shrill blew the pipes and shriller the fifes, and shrill were the million wind-whipped at the curb. Bright sun spread pale gold on the pavements and turrets, and in late afternoon the marching phalanxes clumped through barred shadows."

Raymond McCaw made only one correction in his story. "I wrote that the leader of the Ancient Order of Hibernians 'marched stiff as a ramrod,'" Berger later told me. "The slanderous implication was fixed by his substituting the word 'straight.'" McCaw was sensitive to the word "stiff"; he himself consumed a three-martini dinner most nights, and occasionally, when an important story broke, I was sent to fetch him from Kieran and Dineen, his favorite Eighth Avenue haunt.

The Irish called Mike "Meyer O'Berger," and his parade stories were must reading in classrooms all over New York. Berger was also an authority on bootleggers and gamblers of the Prohibition and Depression years. They confided in him, for he understood their patois and habits, and could be trusted with their secrets.

He liked to tell copyboys about the gangsters he knew, and we all read his book *The Eight Million* to learn more about the murderers he had covered. He described some of them as "rather merry-looking fellows"—for example, Al Capone, who resembled "any head barber who hadn't watched his diet. In repose, his face was fat and smiling." Then there were the less merry ones, like Jack "Legs" Diamond, who was "sinister and ratty," and Vincent "Mad Dog" Coll, who had killed fifteen men and two women and was finally gunned down in a phone booth; he had "eyes the texture of cubes fresh from the ice tray."

When Berger was first introduced to Dutch Schultz, the beer baron stared at him (in no mood for the kind of humor he had once directed at Pat Spiegel). "Ain't you the one who wrote I was a pushover for blondes?" he asked. "Didn't you write that in *The Times?*" Berger, a whiz at shorthand, prided himself on the accuracy of his quotes. He had the quote from a good source, he said. That was beside the point, Schultz argued. "I only remember it made me feel bad when I saw it in *The Times.* I don't think 'pushover for blondes' is any kind of language to write for a newspaper like *The Times.*"

Most of Berger's peers found it hard to believe that with so little schooling he could write so articulately, and credited his wife, Mae, a teacher at P.S. 1, with encouraging his self-education. I once tried to talk Sammy Solovitz into going back to school. "Why?" he asked. "School never did anything for Mike Berger."

The newspaper business was considered just that—a business, not a profession. "Journalism" was a dirty word, thought to be highbrow, and when college graduates first began entering the field in large numbers, flaunting their journalism degrees, veterans like Berger were disgusted. He felt they should be exposed to the old-style methods of newspapering, that their soft brand of writing with delayed leads would spell the end of the great, hard-nosed tradition of American reporting as it had evolved.

The New Yorker's editor Harold Ross once lured Berger away from *The Times,* but it was not long before he returned. Although the job at *The New Yorker* paid more, Berger couldn't abide the idea of waiting, sometimes months, for publication of his stories at the weekly magazine. He told me the true pleasure of being a newspaperman was seeing a story in type often within an hour or less of writing it.

Like Berger, most *Times* reporters held the belief that their paper was the pinnacle and they embraced its tradition of building a career methodically, always sharpening the essential tools of their trade. This arsenal included, at its best, a crisp curiosity about everyone and everything; a detective's obsession to probe for facts; a rational mind to interpret them and write them up speedily in a logical sequence; and finally, the gift to imbue these facts with imagery, suspense and—if possible—wit.

A year on the police beat was typically a reporter's first assignment in those days. There he learned by trial and error, working alongside veteran, street-smart legmen, who were not expected to write their stories and never received a byline, but who knew everything about pinning down the facts. They phoned in their information to rewrite men in the city room, who stitched them into stories, often in a race against the clock. Then came a period of "general assignment," when the reporter might be sent out by the city editor to cover just about any kind of story—a labor demonstration in Union Square, a political rally in Brooklyn, a building collapse in Queens, a charity banquet at the Astor Hotel, a brawl on the Staten Island Ferry.

There was additional seasoning to come before a reporter was considered truly rounded—often an assignment to the rewrite battery, doubtless the most pressured job in the city room; and then possibly a stint at City Hall or in Albany, or a specialized beat such as the courts or the hospitals department. Finally, for some, there was the prize of a national bureau, Washington or an overseas assignment.

Sometimes there was a refresher period back in the city room. In this way, traditions were baked into a reporter's marrow, and by the time he was offered a promotion to editor he was in no doubt about what his paper stood for, and how and why its standards had to be fiercely protected. (It is true that aspects of this process remain in effect today, but all too often the successive roads are traveled at dizzying speeds.)

In my early days at the paper, I was struck by the fact that most reporters were poor typists, often using a two-fingered technique, yet their speed and concentration were remarkable when up against deadline. After completing each paragraph, the reporter would yell for a copyboy, who dashed over and took the page to the city copy desk.

There sat a dozen or so copy editors clutching thick, soft, black pencils (stamped "Ebony 6325"); also at hand were a paste pot, scissors and a stack of copy paper. Swiftly and often ruthlessly, they pencil-edited a reporter's copy, cutting out and rearranging paragraphs, pasting them up on a clean sheet of copy paper. The discarded portion of a story was impaled on a small green spike, positioned at each editor's elbow.

Edited copy was dispatched to the floor above where a squad of Linotype operators, schooled at translating the editors' hurried marks and scribbles, typed the day's stories onto hot metal slugs. With everyone racing against the clock, mistakes were often made in the hot type, to be subsequently corrected on proofs. I remember the first time I picked up a newspaper that had arrived directly from the basement press room—it was still warm and the ink rubbed off on my hands and stained the cuffs of my shirt. I learned to turn up my sleeves and secure them with rubber bands. In those days, even copyboys wore long-sleeved shirts with ties and often jackets.

Every day we filled glass jars with paste, and I can still smell its pungent sweetness. Other of our routine chores included sharpening pencils, preparing towers of copy and mimeo paper and, at night's end, rolling up the discarded copy from the spikes to be retained for its background information in case of a libel charge.

Many years later, in the aftermath of the assassination of Martin Luther King, Jr., in Memphis in 1968, I experienced an instance of city-room pressure at its most extreme. As the then metropolitan editor, I had assigned my top rewrite man, Sylvan Fox, to piece together the breaking page-one story about the burst of looting and violence by bands of young black men in parts of Manhattan and Brooklyn, the details of which were being updated by the minute. A reporter sat by Fox's side, feeding him facts phoned in by reporters in the field. I scrutinized every page of Fox's story as it was brought to me, and several times interrupted his typing to request changes.

I thought Fox had buried a facet of the lead in the second paragraph, but I didn't want to bother him about it until he'd finished the entire story. We were right up against edition time. Fox was hugely admired for his speed and organizational skills. No story, no matter how big or complex, ever seemed to ruffle him, and I had little doubt that he would be able to handle this last-minute change.

Red in the face and perspiring, Fox finished the story, leaned back in his chair, and let out a sigh. I gestured to him—"May I see you for a second?" He came to my desk and I suggested how he could change the lead. "How much time do I have?" he asked. I told him, "Five minutes."

Fox went back to his chair, sat down and keeled over. The reporter who had been feeding him the phoned-in facts shouted: "Arthur, you killed him!"

I ran to Fox and found him still breathing. The medical department was summoned and he was carried out on a stretcher and taken by ambulance to St. Vincent's Hospital. I was devastated. My assistant editor, Sheldon Binn, suggested I phone Fox's wife, Gloria. I tried to sound reassuring as I relayed the story of her husband's collapse.

Gloria was a nurse and asked for additional details, then offered a diagnosis. "Don't worry," she said. "He'll be fine." And he was. He had simply fainted from the stress and, Gloria said, it wasn't the first time that had happened. We never did get around to changing the lead of his story.

I HAD BEEN AT THE PAPER roughly a week when we were electrified by the arrival of D-Day—the opening of a second front in Europe by Allied forces. We had known something momentous was brewing; rumors of an invasion were rife. Advance stories were being written, and set in type, and we had stayed up several nights until six A.M.

On Tuesday, June 6, shortly after midnight, a bulletin arrived from the Associated Press in London relaying reports picked up from Berlin radio dispatches that the Allies were storming the beaches: "Combined British–American landing operations against the western coast of Europe from the sea and air are stretching over the entire area between Cherbourg and Le Havre." But there was no confirmation from Allied headquarters. We wondered if this was some sort of Nazi disinformation.

The cable editor, Theodore M. Bernstein, who had left for the night, was summoned back to the city room. As the bulletins flew in over the wires, I delivered them to Raymond McCaw. I still have the original bulletins, which I've kept all these years. McCaw regarded the bulletins with suspicion as there had yet been no confirmation from Allied sources. *The Times*'s Washington bureau, asked to check with the Office of War Information, telegraphed the following to McCaw:

"Washington is still quiet. OWI [Office of War Information] and the War Department continue to say they have no information, although Elmer Davis of OWI rushed to his office to await further developments, showing the reports to be true or not. Anything new up there?"

Despite the lack of confirmation, McCaw decided to put out an extra at 1:30 A.M. based solely on the reports from Berlin.

As the city room grew tense with speculation, McCaw and the cable desk leaped into action. War maps were consulted. Theories attempting to pinpoint the area of invasion were debated. The foreman of the composing room had begun planning with McCaw the paper's makeover and two forty-eight-point headlines were set in type as a precaution—one heralding the invasion of southern France and the other of northern France. Knowing we would all be in the city room until dawn, McCaw sent Sammy and me out to buy sandwiches and coffee. We appropriated a mail-room cart and, wheeling it at high speed, stalked the delis of Broadway and Eighth Avenue. Finally, at 3:42 A.M., when the suspense had grown all but unbearable, confirmation came over the wires from the United Press: "FLASH FLASH LONDON — OFFICIALLY ALLIED TROOPS LAND IN FRANCE."

With all eyes focused on the machines, the UP ticked out: "Supreme Headquarters, Allied Expeditionary Forces, Somewhere in Great Britain, Tuesday, June 6—Gen. Dwight Eisenhower's Supreme Allied Expeditionary Headquarters announced today that Allied Armies were landing on the northern coast of France."

Within a short time, *The Times*'s chief correspondent in London, Raymond Daniell, began filing from Supreme Headquarters: "The invasion of Europe from the West has begun. In the gray light of the summer dawn Gen. Dwight Eisenhower threw his great Anglo-American force into action today for the liberation of the Continent."

The Times was the first New York—and the only morning—newspaper that carried the early reports so long awaited, a major coup I was fortunate enough to experience firsthand.

Advertisements were killed by McCaw to open additional space for dispatches from war correspondents—which, I was impressed to learn, was an undisputed rule when important news broke suddenly. The last extra was off the presses at six A.M. All of us in the city room were too highly charged to go home to sleep. After a while some of us headed for Hector's, the all-night Broadway cafeteria, for breakfast and talk. When we emerged at eight o'clock, we were startled to see groups of people on their way to work, gathered on the sidewalk, gazing upward at *The Times*'s "zipper," the horizontal ribbon of electric lights that displayed war headlines on its revolving screen between the third and fourth floors of The Times Tower, the paper's earlier headquarters in Times Square.

Powered by almost 15,000 amber bulbs, the headlines were written by *Times* reporters at regular intervals and dispatched by copyboys (later by teletype) to the technicians in the Tower. The zipper's design made it possible to get a bulletin moving around the Tower within three minutes of the time the story broke. The zipper had its start on election eve of November 6, 1928, and had been running continuously ever since, except for recent breaks caused by wartime blackouts and dimouts. Only a month before, the zipper had resumed operation daily from four P.M. to midnight.

As I later discovered, permission had been granted to turn on the zipper at eight that morning in response to the Normandy invasion. A cheer went up from the street when one of the bulletins flashed: "PRIME MINISTER

CHURCHILL REPORTS ALLIED AIRBORNE TROOPS HAVE CAPTURED SEVERAL STRATE-
GIC BRIDGES IN FRANCE BEFORE NAZIS COULD DESTROY THEM." Another bulletin
followed quickly: "THE LANDINGS ON THE BEACHES ARE PROCEEDING AT VARIOUS
POINTS AT THE PRESENT TIME. THE FIRE OF SHORE BATTERIES HAS BEEN LARGELY
QUELLED . . . OBSTACLES WHICH WERE CONSTRUCTED IN THE SEA HAVE NOT PROVED
SO DIFFICULT AS WAS APPREHENDED."

My colleagues and I were, naturally, elated. But just about all of us who
were gathered in Times Square that morning had a relative or close friend in
the service, and we were sure that when the cost in lives of that heroic invasion was added up, the numbers would be devastating.

At last, exhausted, we called it a night, and I took the subway home,
reading and rereading my copy of *The Times*'s Extra. I knew the edition
would be devoured nationwide and filed away for future historians. Heading to my Bronx neighborhood, I couldn't help feeling a surge of pride for
the role I had played, insignificant as it was, in helping to proclaim this
world-shaking event.

THREE

DURING THE EVENING CITY-ROOM HOURS, copyboys warmed a
wooden bench, anticipating various commands. After a few weeks on
the bench, I was tapped for my first promotion by the telegraph editor. Wilson L. Fairbanks had evidently taken note of the speed with which my long
legs enabled me to whisk copy up the spiral staircase to the composing room.
He beckoned to me, and I approached him with trepidation, for he was a
presence to be reckoned with.

Everyone addressed him as Mr. Fairbanks—including the managing editor and the publisher. A gentleman of the old school, he was an unrecon-
structed Victorian—wiry, proud and upright, wisps of white hair falling
over his ears and forehead. The deep pouches under his eyes were a testament to the puritanical fervor with which he attacked his work, reminders
of triumph over slovenly copy thrust on him by careless writers.

Mr. Fairbanks's intimidating air, combined with his age and his reputation as a teetotaler, kept him at a certain remove from the rest of the staff.

When he shouted "Copy!" the boy whose turn it was rose like a private saluting a four-star general. Orders would be muttered, and if a mission was not completed with speed and exactitude, his accusing stare was enough to make a grown newspaperman tremble. Because he mumbled his commands, head down into his chest, he was often hard to understand, and this was what got copyboys into trouble. One of them walked out of the city room one night rather than face Mr. Fairbanks's anger, and was never heard from again.

Mr. Fairbanks's desk clerk had to leave when he developed a facial tic, and I was chosen to fill the vacancy. I didn't know whether to celebrate. The promotion to the telegraph desk meant a weekly salary increase from sixteen dollars to twenty-two. What concerned me was having to sit at the copy desk in a swivel chair at Mr. Fairbanks's immediate right. This proximity, at first, threw me into heart-pounding anxiety. But I was determined to decipher his mumblings, and I finally found the key. It was almost like learning a foreign language.

My eagerness to conform to his finicky ways was recognized and, to my shock, he appeared to take to me. Like virtually all the paper's senior editors and reporters, Mr. Fairbanks was rooted in the long-established tradition of mentoring, and he became, in effect, my first newspaper tutor. Every night, after the edition, he swiveled his chair to face me and talk about the old days. The pre–World War I era of anarchists and socialists came alive in his stories, as did the postwar period of our country's growth as a prosperous nation, the tragedies of the recent Depression and what he condemned as hypocritical party politics in Washington.

Mr. Fairbanks's worship of the paper was evangelical—and he was the first to instill that reverence in me. Through our informal conversations, I began to understand the attachment that senior editors and reporters had for *The Times.* I also absorbed some of the paper's stringent ideals, chiefly its insistence on factual accuracy, its demand for fairness and its intolerance of trendiness and triviality.

"We record the deeds of men in all their multicolored shades of good and evil," Mr. Fairbanks was apt to pronounce. "Here in the night's copy are the sins—and the glories, too. But we must not gaze too long on these things. We must keep the record straight and without prejudice." Mr. Fairbanks guarded these principles with a ferocity that surpassed the merely professional. For him, it was a lifelong commitment.

Mr. Fairbanks was merciless in trimming inflated stories to their lean essence. Some of his theories about writing were documented in the letters I was to hold in my hand close to five decades later. These letters, in an ornate scrawl, were mailed to me at intervals from his hilltop farm in Newfane, Vermont, following his retirement in 1946. He was too preoccupied with inspirational advice to bother with tidy penmanship. He was upholding his duty to bestow his wisdom on those who, like me, would one day inherit the mantle of responsibility and trust.

In the city room, Mr. Fairbanks enjoyed analyzing and dissecting for me the mystical power of *The Times*'s front page—in those days set in an eight-column format. He described how the page, over more than nine decades, had evolved into the most carefully crafted, authoritative daily summary of major news events—foreign, national and local. Day after day, knowledgeable and sophisticated readers, including the president himself, relied on that balance.

"Page one must always reflect the most significant occurrences in yesterday's world," Mr. Fairbanks said. "Deciding which stories go there is based on the intuitive wisdom of editors with a solid work foundation, both out in the field and for the various news desks. Those of us who managed to come through it all now know in our bones why a story belongs on the front page, whether it deserves to lead the page in the top right position, or in the second most important placement on the top left, or in the top positions in the middle of the page, or above or below the paper's fold." He chuckled. "I have to admit that the only editors who can compete with our own decision-making process are those over at the *Herald Tribune*." Although he regarded the *Tribune* as a serious newspaper, he disapproved of its efforts to achieve a livelier makeup and snappier writing style than *The Times*—which might have made the paper an easier read but at "a cost in dignity."

With restrained amusement, Mr. Fairbanks alerted me to a bizarre practice about which I already had my suspicions: If the night bullpen editors discovered that the *Tribune,* in its first edition, had positioned a spot news story on page one that *The Times* had consigned to an inside page, *The Times* often switched its story to page one for the second edition; conversely, upon examining the front page of *The Times*'s first edition, the *Tribune* might well move its story from page one to an inside page. When the second edition came up, it was not unheard of for both papers to reverse positions again.

Several times Mr. Fairbanks went so far, in his letters, as to write out for me variations on his own credo of good newspapering. In one entitled "Some Essentials of Good Leads," he advised:

Introductions rank high among the essentials of newspaper writing even if we call them nothing but leads. Many a story is saved by its lead and by the same token many a story is sunk by its lead—dull, heavy-witted, inadequate for its subject which may be itself very interesting.

In essence, I should say the very first requisite for a lead is directness. Directness means going straight to the 'it' of the news—the one fact that makes your story worthwhile writing and perhaps fit for the front page. So far as The Times is concerned, it wants to know (first of all) in every important story "what happened." And this one thing should be told right away without elaboration.

Directness is the most natural method of expression by a normal human being. If a man, coming from a railroad wreck, met a friend, would he say to him, "A horrible event has just occurred downtown?" Or would he say, "The chief of police has just announced that," etc.? Would he say, "Much grief has been caused to the people of the city as a result," etc.? Of course, he will say nothing of the sort. He will assert in imperative words that "ten persons have been killed in a head-on collision" and then the details as he knows them. As a rule, one sentence can convey the essence of the story it is your privilege to tell. It is real art to make every word count weightily in producing the final effect.

Another relative of directness (perhaps a first cousin) is concreteness. This is the summons for a sharp and distinctive statement which abhors generalities as a pestilence (which they are). I suppose there are more failures in fashioning a good lead, due to wandering off into the byways of generalities, than can be blamed on almost any other way of writing. . . . Simplicity has always had a charm for me as a news element worth the striving for. . . . Then you are kindred in spirit, even if only a humble disciple, of the Bible, and on to Abraham Lincoln, Woodrow Wilson and Winston Churchill.

No one could accuse Mr. Fairbanks of not speaking with concrete directness, or of pandering to petty diplomacy. A crusty New Englander to his core, he was the descendant of Yorkshire pioneers. His family had settled in Dedham, Massachusetts, in 1636, establishing a permanent and respected presence near Boston, that bastion of Yankee tradition. Born on Washington's birthday in 1865 in the town of Natick, Mr. Fairbanks graduated from Tufts College (majoring in Greek and Latin) before embarking on his newspaper career.

His background in the classics was the bedrock of his standards as copy editor nonpareil. Virtually every member hired to his staff had studied

Latin. He insisted on grammatical perfection, and the improper use of a word, or a flowery adjective, could cause him almost physical discomfort. On such occasions, he would lean back in his swivel chair (for once not mumbling), thrust out his chin and declaim arcane epithets in one of the dead languages. If a reporter handed him a story containing a sloppy phrase or imprecise use of a preposition, it could drive him to despair, eliciting a lecture about the "grotesque state" of the American intellect and the evils of mental laziness in the young.

One night, the picture editor asked him to check the accuracy of a caption. The word "homes" was used in the caption to describe new buildings for war veterans. Mr. Fairbanks growled that "houses," not "homes," was the correct word.

"What's the difference?" asked the picture editor.

"Houses are built of wood and brick," Mr. Fairbanks snapped, "but it takes a woman to make a home."

Mr. Fairbanks was always confident that such an "error" would be caught by *The Times*'s trusted proofreaders, and he often assured all sixty of them that they held a special place in his heart. In those days, they were highly educated grammarians—both men and women—who combed through every story after it was set in type to make certain it was free of typographical errors and lapses in style. Ensconced in offices off the composing room, the proofreaders worked in pairs, one reading the copy aloud to the other, who made the corrections in the proof. About fifteen minutes was devoted to each column of type.

Every night as the first edition went to press, George, the cafeteria waiter, brought Mr. Fairbanks a tray with a sandwich, a small salad and tea. He would gulp down his food, never taking his eye from the copy as it poured onto his desk from *Times* bureaus around the nation. Sometimes at this point, briefly leaning back in his chair, he would mutter a sort of apology to no one in particular: "The sharp words that pass in the headlong plunge toward edition time are forgotten with the tick of the clock."

No matter how acerbic he was during the processing of copy, he instantly became a courtly New England gentleman on those rare occasions when one of the few women on the staff approached his desk. I used to watch in astonishment as he rose from his chair, nodding graciously, a genteel smile warming his face.

One such visitor was likely to be Rachel Kolloch McDowell, the religion editor. Whenever she had a problem with a story, she cautiously crept from her tenth-floor office to seek Mr. Fairbanks's guidance. Lantern-jawed and slouching sideways, she created the impression that one leg was shorter than the other. She would slip between Mr. Fairbanks's chair and my own to make her presence known and, no matter how harried he was, he quickly stood to inquire: "How may I be of service to you?"

As she grew older, Rachel McDowell became ever more distrustful of the male sex, to the point of near-delusion. She was the only editor in the building who locked her office door, fearful of being attacked. Sammy had given me a scenario for the procedure to be followed when I knocked on her door to pick up her copy:

"Who is it?" Miss McDowell would call.

"A copyboy, Miss McDowell."

"What's your name?"

"Arthur Gelb."

"Who sent you?" she would ask, thinking (as Sammy had warned) that I had designs on her.

"Mr. Fairbanks, Miss McDowell."

After a few seconds of silence, presumably spent tiptoeing across the room, she would unlock the door and slowly open it—but only a crack. She would thrust her copy at me, while giving me a hard look.

"I've heard you talk downstairs," she would scold, "and you should be ashamed of yourself!" The door would be slammed in my face.

There was a story afloat that a newly hired copyboy once came to her door and, when she opened it to hand him her copy, he moved toward her too quickly. She screamed, and the boy turned and ran, pages spilling to the floor. Those few copyboys to whom she took a liking, she would compliment by saying, perversely, "You're a good little girl."

When she took her clothes to be dry-cleaned, she specified that they were to be processed separately from the men's garments. The dresses she wore were lopsided, one side of the hem hanging lower than the other, and they were buttoned up to her chin. She always wore a feathered hat. Once, when a *Times* physician removed her shoe and stocking in a corner of the city room, so that he could examine the ankle she had sprained on assignment, she almost fainted with embarrassment.

She was known to all as "Lady Bishop," and her utter lack of worldliness often drew peals of laughter from the copy editors. On one occasion, when she was covering a religious convention in Atlantic City, she sent an apologetic telegram to the desk: "Copy a little late. Have been on the Boardwalk all day. Am hustling."

Despite her eccentricities, Miss McDowell was a good reporter, respected by clergy everywhere, and was the only reporter in the city to have the cardinal's private telephone number. "Quite often," she once said, "I have made a friend of the preacher's wife before knowing the preacher. In this way, I have an advantage over a man reporter because he cannot do this. When the preacher's wife is my friend, the preacher also is."

When she ventured into the city room, she moved very slowly, eavesdropping for evidence of the foul language against which, as president and founder of the Pure Language League, she waged a ruthless campaign. The managing editor gave her permission to have the cashier distribute small leaflets on League letterhead with everyone's paycheck, urging employees to eliminate profanity from their conversation.

On several occasions, she caught me saying "damn it." Her eyes blazed as she told me my soul would be consigned to the devil if I persisted. She conducted informal lectures on the evils of liquor, gambling, dancing, and smoking by women. Strangely enough, she chose to reside at the Times Square Hotel, just yards west of the Times building. This somewhat run-down establishment was home to traveling salesmen and assorted Broadway characters, some down on their luck, all of whom received complimentary lectures in the lobby from the one-woman Pure Language League.

One of her principal targets for conversion in the city room was a friendly man with a salty vocabulary to whom smoking, drinking and a lust for life were second nature. His repertoire of funny, off-color stories drew listeners from all corners of the city room. He was a second-string movie critic, A. H. Weiler, known to everyone as "Abe," a slight, urbane man with a brush mustache.

Soon after his birth in Russia in 1908, Abe settled with his parents on the Lower East Side. While taking night courses at City College, he was hired by *The Times* in 1927 as a clerk in the morgue (the voluminous archives containing clippings about people and other subjects that had been mentioned in *The Times* or other major journals). He had longed to study medicine but grew discouraged when told that medical schools would probably not accept him because of his religion. (Many Jews seeking medical degrees at that time were forced to apply to schools in Scotland or Mexico.)

One night Abe, after having dinner with another clerk from the morgue, bade his friend good night and, with thirty dollars in his pocket, he bought a ticket for the first bus out of town. It was June of 1930, early in the Depression, and Abe lived in a Chicago flophouse for ten cents a night. Traveling west and south, he witnessed streams of jalopies headed to California from the Dust Bowl.

Abe had left New York without saying good-bye to his parents. Devastated, they called the police, but they were unable to trace him. A year later he was back, and promptly reported for work at *The Times*. The assistant managing editor, the dignified Osgood Phillips, walked Abe to his old desk in the morgue and Abe set back to work at once as if nothing had happened. Mr. Phillips went to Mr. Ochs to inform him of Abe's wanderings and his return. "What a silly thing to do," said the publisher. "But tell him he's always welcome here." After hearing this story, I remember saying to myself, "This is a place that will shelter you for the rest of your life."

ONE OF THE BEST LESSONS I ever received about newspapering was through watching Mr. Fairbanks's herculean feat on the night of August 29, 1945. The long-awaited Pearl Harbor Investigation Report, with little advance notice, was flown in from Washington at 5:45 P.M.—only four hours before the first edition deadline.

The report contained 130,000 words, the equivalent of a 400-page book. Mr. Fairbanks and managing editor James, after scanning the document, decided it was of such major significance that every word of it should appear in the paper. *The Times*'s reputation as "the paper of record" stemmed from its long-held practice of running complete texts of documents and speeches, but no text up to that time had ever run this long. It would take up fifteen full pages, and numerous ads would have to be killed to make room for it, at great expense to the paper. Mr. Fairbanks, his jacket off and his sleeves rolled up, instructed me to divide the report into roughly twenty sections.

He summoned copy editors whose day off it was and recruited others from disparate city-room operations, and the composing room foreman called in additional Linotype operators and compositors. Mr. Fairbanks then distributed the sections of the text to his editors to check for misspellings and incorrect punctuation and to write heads and subheads. He kept the edited pages flowing to the composing room at an ever-quickening pace. Glancing often at the large, round wall clock and muttering oaths at editors who were falling behind, he himself pitched in, editing portions of the copy and occasionally handing me pages to check.

Without air-conditioning and with no breeze coming from the open windows, the city room was stifling. Electric fans whirring nearby offered little relief. The editors, their faces flushed and perspiring, were under fearsome pressure, while Mr. Fairbanks somehow managed to stay dry and collected. I heard one of the editors whisper to another, "He has no blood."

Although most of the report reached the composing room just before deadline and made the first edition, a few final pages had to be held for the second. Nevertheless, *The Times* was the only paper to publish the entire report that morning. Mr. Fairbanks did not leave the office until after the 3:20 A.M. closing time, wanting to be certain the report was free of error. The desk editors—some of them half his age—were bent and weary as they headed for home. Mr. Fairbanks stood tall and unruffled as he bade us all good night.

Prominently seated at Mr. Fairbanks's left that night had been his chief assistant, Frederick A. Austin, a man whose habits and idiosyncrasies I also became privy to at my new post. Lean and angular, with inquisitive eyes behind steel-rimmed glasses, Austin was one of the sharpest copy editors in the business. He was a second-generation *Times* man, his uncle having joined the paper in 1878 after working in Nevada with Mark Twain. His mother was said to be descended from the Indian tribe that welcomed Roger Williams into Rhode Island after his expulsion by the Puritans in Massachusetts. Austin never tired of reminding us that he had Indian blood.

He had joined *The Times* in 1919, and his background as a grammarian led to his recruitment to Fairbanks's telegraph desk. He was a close friend of Frank Vizetelly, editor of *Funk & Wagnalls Standard Dictionary,* an association that inspired a series of *Times* articles on Mr. Vizetelly and uses of the English language. Austin went dancing on his days off, and it was at his behest that *The Times* gave dance reviews a respectable status almost on a par with that of its theater criticism.

He was one of the best-tailored and best-natured men to grace the city room. A conspicuous imbiber as well, he didn't always manage to keep his habit from interfering with his work. Often, by the time he was ready to take his departure from the city room, his balance was not quite steady. He drank one green-tinted bottle of ale after another throughout the course of the night, lining the bottles up on his desk as he emptied them.

All of us watched with concealed mirth as the night progressed. I expected him to fall out of his chair at any moment—and occasionally he did. I tried to be there in time to catch him, but when I didn't make it, he landed on the floor. Mr. Fairbanks disapproved of this, naturally, but Austin was never, in so many words, asked to stop.

There was a popular saying, "Liquor is the curse of the *Herald Tribune* and sex is the bane of *The Times,*" but liquor seemed to play as much a role as any other vice in the *Times* city room. Two or three drinks during a lunch or dinner break at a nearby eatery or saloon were not uncommon, and there were reporters and editors other than Austin who drank openly in the city room. (Beer, in fact, was sold in the *Times* cafeteria until the 1970s.) While some kept whiskey in their desks, others would sneak off to their lockers. Open or concealed, this behavior was usually overlooked.

A goodly amount of off-the-job drinking was done at Schrafft's, a restaurant on the east side of Broadway at Forty-third Street that was traditionally the territory of middle-aged dowagers. A table was regularly reserved for the Sunday department editors in the back part of the restaurant, which contained the bar. One of the stars of the Sunday department was Charlie Palmer, who invariably downed three martinis before returning to his *Times* desk. One day he chose to have four, and a colleague complained to Sunday editor Lester Markel, a sour disciplinarian. "I'd rather have Charlie around here drunk than the lot of you sober!" came the reply.

Alcoholic or not, just about everyone at *The Times* smoked. Though there were spittoons for the tobacco chewers, ashtrays were nonexistent. Cigarette butts were swept up nightly by porters. Now and then someone threw a cigarette butt into a wastebasket and copyboys had to stamp out the fire. The only spittoon preserved from those olden city-room days was appropriated by the publisher's son, Arthur Ochs Sulzberger, known to everyone by his nickname, "Punch," who later housed the polished, proud relic in the den of his New York apartment.

While certain behavior was condoned, other behavior was not. The rules seemed to be that quirky habits were permitted if they did not impede the sacred task of getting the paper out on time. Those who dared cross the line between eccentricity and insubordination, however, were dealt with severely.

At the end of the day shift, at around seven P.M., reporters customarily began lining up at the night city editor's desk, in conformance with an unspoken rule that you did not go home until you received a "Good night" from the editor. Only when he looked up and said "Good night" was it permissible to leave. If you left without a "Good night," it was tantamount to a felony. The ritual was not unreasonable, since it gave the editor an opportunity to raise questions about a reporter's copy before he departed for the night.

Once, Pat Spiegel neglected to wait for his "Good night" and had to face the ire of the night city editor Bruce Rae. Another such victim was A. J. Gordon, a reporter known as the "gumshoe." He served as in-house informer and, whenever a suit was filed against *The Times* or when an employee was perceived as causing trouble, Gordon would be assigned to dig up unsavory and potentially damaging details from that person's past.

Everyone on the paper was aware of the gumshoe and, of course, he was universally despised. But there was one aspect of his behavior that provided endless amusement: When he received his weekly pay from the cashier, he hurried to his bank to trade in his bills for crisp new ones. He was convinced old bills carried germs.

When Bruce Rae discovered that Gordon had gone home without his "Good night," he could not restrain his pleasure in pursuing the matter. Rae's background was similar to Mike Berger's; he had left school at an early age and received his real education in the city room of *The Times*. Always reading, he could quote long passages from his beloved Dickens and Thackeray. He had started as a copyboy at five dollars a week in 1909, and was steeped in *Times* tradition. Known for his wit and a tongue that spared few, he had particular disdain for those who shirked responsibility.

After calling the local bars, Rae's clerk finally, at around ten P.M., found Gordon at home. He told him the boss wanted him to come back to work immediately.

"What's it about?" Gordon asked, assuming there was some hot story or other breaking. "I don't know," said the clerk, "but you'd better get back, quick!"

Gordon dashed for the subway and started the long commute from his home to Times Square, raced to the city room and presented himself at Rae's desk, breathless. "What's up?" he asked of what seemed to be a strangely calm city editor perusing some paperwork. Without looking up, Rae paused a moment and said, simply, "Good night."

THE TELEGRAPH DESK became my classroom and gave me a sense of belonging. The other great copy editor on the desk was Grover Cleveland Loud. Like Fairbanks and Austin, he carried on the tradition of mentoring young staffers he thought showed promise. On my first day on the desk, Loud watched with amusement my bewildered reaction to some of the city room's antics. "Newspapermen are strange," he said wryly. "There is a bond which unites them in a noncompetitive fraternity, and if you don't belong on a newspaper it won't be long before you realize it. After twenty or thirty years, a person may receive a salary of only sixty or seventy dollars, but that's of little consequence. People work on newspapers for the fun of it."

Grover Loud was a tall, thin man with a shock of red hair and a flair for the dramatic. One of the stories he loved to tell involved his introduction to reporting. While still in high school, in his home state of New Hampshire, he was witness to a train accident and took it upon himself to contact the region's largest paper. He related the details of the disaster, and the story made the front page. The editor was so impressed with Loud's reporting skills he offered him a stringer's job.

Loud also reminded me frequently that, like Austin, he had Indian blood. And he was forever talking about his experiences in combat during World War I as a captain in the infantry. "Here, feel the shrapnel I still have in my back," he would say. He smoked a corncob pipe, always wore a vest and a polka-dot blue bow tie, and carried a cane. When I occasionally left the city room with him at the end of the shift, he would twirl his cane in the midst of telling a story.

"Someday, young feller," he once said, "you will be amazed to discover that behind your back you are being called the 'Old Man.' That's the way it is on the timeless *Times*. The best of it is how all of us can go forward with the living personality of a newspaper into everlasting remembrance. Achievements and peccadilloes alike become legendary. Human qualities survive. Beneficent ghosts tread the paths trod by their successors."

Loud chewed tobacco. Mr. Fairbanks, when in a playful mood, would wait for Loud's mouth to be stuffed with chaw and then ask an urgent question about a headline that Loud had just begun to write. Loud, whose great pride was as a headline writer, would speechlessly point at his mouth, rise from his seat and head for the nearest spittoon. In his momentary absence, Mr. Fairbanks would himself compose the headline and send it up to the composing room. Mr. Fairbanks's mind worked so fast that he never had to count the units of a headline to make sure they would fit a column's width—the only city-room editor capable of such a feat. When Loud returned to the desk and looked for the story, he was informed of Mr. Fairbanks's meddling. It was painful to witness his fury.

Loud's bred-in-the-bone New England manner, like that of Mr. Fairbanks and Austin, led him always to speak his mind. When reading particularly bad copy, he would blow through his teeth, whistle low and say, "Jesus wept, and well he might!"

When the mandatory retirement policy was introduced some years later, Loud, who had been growing increasingly crotchety, wrote his own advance obituary and filed it in the morgue. It was succinct, and at its conclusion stated: "Spare me the obscene hypocrisy of newspaper management which likes to expand an obituary as compensation for a conscience it never had. And spare my family the ultimate mockery of flowers and condolences." When Loud died in 1968, *The Times,* ignoring his instructions, published a fulsome obit.

FOUR

THE NIGHTLY WHIRLWIND around the telegraph desk gathered force at five o'clock and did not abate until the first edition went to press at ten. Stories from Washington were dispatched by Morse code operators to their New York counterparts in the "wire room," which housed the various news service ticker machines and was adjacent to the telegraph desk.

All the Washington correspondents began filing their stories at about the same time. The New York operators decoded the telegraphed copy and typed each page onto a stencil for mimeographing. The unsorted mimeographed pages were then routed to my station at the telegraph desk. As the deadline approached, I was half buried in a blitz of paper. It was my job to put each page of every story in its proper order as it flew onto my desk; I felt like a frantic Charlie Chaplin struggling to prevent a pileup on his assembly-line conveyor belt.

Mr. Fairbanks gave me a copy of the assignment schedule at the start of each evening, and I was required to distribute the stories, page by page, to the copy editors assigned to read them. The copy editors, in turn, sent the stories, a page or two at a time, to the composing room. I had to keep a duplicate of every page, assembled in sequence, in case Mr. Fairbanks or a bullpen editor needed to check back. I knew that my new job would evaporate if by some horrible mischance I gave the wrong page to the wrong editor, thus disrupting the smooth running of the conveyor belt.

One evening, after I had endured a nerve-wracking two weeks, Mr. Fairbanks turned to me after the edition had gone to press: "Well, young man, what of importance have you learned in your job thus far?"

I hesitated briefly, then decided to be forthright: "Mr. Fairbanks, I've been surprised to learn President Roosevelt has an understanding with the White House press corps that prevents them from quoting him directly unless he gives his permission."

"So, you've caught that, have you?" remarked Mr. Fairbanks, and went on to express his own irritation with the agreement. He said that Roosevelt had insisted upon those terms at his initial press conference in 1933, and it had been blithely accepted by the Washington reporters. "Personally, I don't like it," added Mr. Fairbanks with a dismissive shrug. Then abruptly changing the subject, he praised my work and, to my joy, offered me a promotion from clerk to news assistant and a ten-dollar raise (bringing my weekly salary to thirty-two dollars!).

Later that night, Grover Loud told me I was the first person in the job to keep nightly copy flowing without error. But, he pointed out, good-humoredly, surely I must realize it didn't take a mental giant to assemble and distribute copy, no matter how severe the pressure, and I mustn't let the accolades go to my head. He said I was doubtless capable of rising to higher challenges, and invited me to meet him at the Harvard Club the next afternoon at three o'clock to celebrate my raise.

The Harvard Club was a short walk from *The Times*. I had never been inside, nor for that matter inside any private club. I was awed by the climate of subdued orderliness and studied the punctilious staff as they served a mostly graying male membership plainly beyond draft age. (I myself was still awaiting notification from my draft board.)

Loud asked me what I would like to drink. "A Manhattan," I said, with all the insouciance I could muster. I knew from the movies about Manhattans, a mixture of Canadian rye and sweet vermouth, stirred with ice, poured into a stemmed glass and garnished with a maraschino cherry. Elegant sophisticates like Cary Grant, Clark Gable, Ronald Colman, Gary Cooper, William Powell and James Stewart sipped what I believed to be Manhattans in their penthouses or country estates in the company of seductive but virginal women (Katharine Hepburn, Carole Lombard, Myrna Loy, Irene Dunne, Claudette Colbert, Jean Arthur and, of course, Madeleine Carroll).

"A Manhattan?" exclaimed Loud in mock horror. "A mixed concoction like that will turn your brain to the white of egg. Drink only Scotch with water. At least it won't give you a hangover—unless you drink too many." The waiter brought us each a Scotch and water.

"Well, young man," said Loud. "Now that you've reached the first rung upward, I'd like to know why someone as well-read as you does not have a college degree?"

I explained that I had left CCNY in my junior year because I was waiting to be drafted and simply could no longer concentrate on my course load. Formally called the City College of New York, CCNY was an exemplary tuition-free school that mainly served the underprivileged children of European immigrants, who shared the conviction that the only escape from financial struggle was through education. CCNY was so highly regarded that it was jocularly referred to as the Harvard of New York.

When I first arrived at the gates of the campus in Harlem at sixteen, the tumultuous scene startled me. Students confronted me with leaflets espousing every conceivable cause. There were petitions against bigotry, members of Congress, the president, landlords, socialists, communists, bosses. Among my fellow undergraduates—at least during the tail end of the Depression—were several future Nobel Prize laureates. Admission was based solely on high school grades, a minimum average in the high 80s being required. Two of my friends from affluent families, whose high school grades were among the highest, were students at CCNY; they had been rejected by Ivy League colleges because of the so-called "New York quota," a euphemism for limiting admission to a few token Jews.

Savoring the unfamiliar but admittedly clean taste of my Scotch and water, I told Loud I was proud of being among the youngest freshmen. The money I earned from after-school jobs I spent primarily on books and theater tickets. I skimped on lunches, relying on an invention of my fellow students in the cafeteria: the ketchup sandwich. Bread was a nickel and ketchup was free—not bad at all, especially when washed down with a nickel cup of coffee.

"Go back to school," Loud commanded. "You may become a reporter without a college degree, but that era is fast disappearing. And you certainly don't want to stay around here in a clerical job the rest of your days like some of the human fixtures in our city room. Do what I did. Keep your newspaper job while you finish your college credits. If CCNY is too tough a school to attend while holding down a full-time job, what about NYU?"

I told him I would seriously consider his advice. If nothing else, it would make my mother happy. Then Loud asked about my parents. He seemed absorbed as I diffidently described my roots. Perhaps it was the sense of being accepted by so formidable a member of *The Times,* or maybe it was the Scotch. Whatever the reason, I regaled Loud with my family history, which had its beginnings in Eastern Europe.

Both my parents, Daniel and Fannie, came from the same small town in the Carpathian Mountains, in what is now Ukraine—a border town called Kimyat. The town was then part of Czechoslovakia (and before that Hungary). My paternal grandfather owned a flourishing tavern there, which he operated with the help of his second wife and his twenty-year-old son—my father, Daniel.

Daniel did not get along with his difficult stepmother. One day, when he talked back to her, he was reprimanded severely by his father, who raised a threatening fist. My father ran out of the tavern and, feeling misunderstood and maligned, decided to take dramatic action. He returned to the tavern after it had closed, helped himself to money from the cash drawer and took a train to Prague, where his younger brother, Joseph, was studying. When he told his brother he was going to America, Joseph made a quick decision to leave school and accompany him.

New York was their destination, and they arrived filled with hope. My father settled into a tenement on the Lower East Side and found work as a cigar maker, a trade that had attracted other recent immigrants from his area. Joseph found lodgings in Brooklyn, and a job there driving a horse-drawn laundry wagon.

Making his rounds in foul weather, Joseph caught a cold that turned into pneumonia, and he died in a matter of days. My father, who had not at once received word of his brother's illness, reached his Brooklyn rooming house too late. By the time he got there, Joseph was dead. My father never recovered completely from the shock. His faith and optimism evaporated, and his life began to spiral downward.

My father was haunted by guilt over his brother's death for the rest of his days. He blamed himself for having encouraged Joseph to leave a promising life as a scholar in Europe for the uncertainty of life in America. In his mourning, he did not shave for months. Within the next year, he embarked on a period of restless drifting, spending his time gambling at cards and drinking.

In Kimyat, my grandfather grieved over both lost sons. He was a leading figure of the town, respected and well-to-do. From the closely knit immigrant community in Manhattan, he received word that his prodigal son was living somewhere on the Lower East Side. When he was told that a young woman from his town was preparing to embark for a new life in America, he sent for her. If she should ever run into Daniel, he pleaded, would she ask him to write to his father, who loved and forgave him.

My mother was seventeen when she set out alone in 1913 in steerage, the first member of her family of ten to travel to America. Her father, Eliezer, was a Talmudic scholar, and he and his wife, Hannah, eked out a living operating a small general store. When Fannie left home, the town and the farming area surrounding it were experiencing a depression. She was determined to make good in America so that she might provide at least a small measure of support for her family.

Fannie found room and board on the Lower East Side among the now thriving community of European immigrants, and landed a job in a large children's dress factory. It did not take long for her employer to recognize her ambition and ability and decide she should study designing. When I met him years later, he told me my mother had been his most talented employee. He wanted her to ascend in rank, but fate intervened.

One day in Tompkins Square Park, Fannie was with a friend who pointed out a lanky, melancholy, but quietly dignified man. "I think he's from your town in Europe," the friend said. It was, of course, my future father, Daniel Gelb. Somewhat shyly, Fannie and her friend introduced themselves. As surprised as she was to find the man for whom she carried a message from across the ocean, he was equally astounded to hear news of his estranged father.

More than anything, he was captivated by Fannie. Tall for that era—five-foot-seven—she was striking, with long black hair and green eyes. Daniel's melancholy seemed almost instantly to lift. He asked to see her again and she—equally attracted—agreed. As she later told the story to my brother and me, she persuaded him to marry and settle down.

As I continued the narrative, Grover Loud, who at times interrupted with a question, seemed genuinely interested. My parents, I told him, were an ideal match; my father loved to listen and my mother loved to talk. Fannie gave up her job at the dress factory to have children. Not long after, the cigar workers' union, of which my father was a member, was called out on strike by its leader, Samuel Gompers. My father was out of work for a long, hard year. Finally, my mother suggested they open a shop specializing in custom-made children's dresses. She would make the dresses and he would run the business.

My parents' first child, Harold, was born in an apartment behind their store in Harlem, at 205 East 102nd Street, near Second Avenue, and I was born there four years later. On the cold February day she gave birth to me, my mother was at work at her sewing machine until the last minute. She had been feeling uncomfortable all day, but needed to finish a dress for a customer's daughter, who was to wear it for her birthday party. She did finish it, and went into labor. My father called our postman's son, a newly graduated medical student, with whom he had earlier made arrangements. I was the first baby that the young doctor delivered. He later went on to a practice on Park Avenue, and became our family physician.

At first, my parents used to open their shop very early in the morning and did not close it until late at night. They struggled through times of economic uncertainty, but somehow we always had enough to get by and our home glowed with hope. My parents were extraordinarily loving—I can't remember either of them ever raising a voice to the other. The bond between them seemed so unassailable that, in my youth, I honestly believed all marriages were made in heaven.

The store was a happy place, so happy that I loved falling asleep there, under the counters on top of bolts of fabric. I loved the shop life and the comings and goings of customers and tradesmen. People constantly sought out my mother, who became the neighborhood sage. The store was an informal therapeutic center. I used to listen intently, absorbing the advice my mother dispensed to customers and friends.

From the time I was four, I looked forward to each day's adventure on the block outside my parents' store. From early morning until nightfall, I went back and forth between the store and the sidewalk. The sidewalks were absolutely safe, and we kids—not unlike the Our Gang rascals—were basically on our own, exploring and making friends under the minimally watchful eyes of our mothers, who never seemed to find it necessary to interfere with our social interactions. Looking back, I see myself as a blissful urchin, dressed in short pants, playing until my face and knees were black with grime. I was so deeply engrossed in my street activity that my mother had a hard time persuading me to come in at last, to scrub my face and knees and eat my dinner. When I started school my street life, to my regret, was postponed until after the three-o'clock bell.

When I was almost five, my parents decided to move from East Harlem to the Bronx, convinced that the high hills and abundance of trees would provide clean, healthy air for my brother and me, and that the endless vacant lots would serve as our playing grounds. They leased a shop close by the Grand Concourse, less than a mile from Yankee Stadium, and rented a sun-drenched apartment nearby on a tree-lined street.

The Grand Concourse was the Bronx equivalent of Manhattan's Park Avenue. It was a broad, three-mile-long boulevard that cut across the borough from 138th Street to Mosholu Parkway. Its expansive middle lane was reserved for fast-moving automobiles, while narrower lanes on each side, bordered by large shade trees, carried buses and slower vehicles. Hugging both sides of the avenue were row after row of tidy five-story walk-up tenements, occasionally interrupted by a sleek art deco apartment building that boasted a uniformed doorman and elevator operator.

For Sunday strolling, there was no more inviting avenue in the city than the Grand Concourse. Jewish families lived mainly on the west side and Irish families on the east, and it seemed perfectly natural for Jews to do their strolling on their side and the Irish on theirs. The Irish appeared to enjoy jogging (then called "running"), and "foot races" were a weekly occurrence along the Concourse's side lanes.

Most of the Irish children attended parochial school, but there were several older Irish boys in my school with whom I teamed up to play basketball after class in the schoolyard. I had the height for basketball and I was good at it, and our camaraderie helped protect me from the schoolyard bully, who also happened to be Irish.

On Halloween, my friends and I sometimes filled old silk stockings with flour and swung them across each other's legs and back, the flour leaking through the stockings onto our clothes. One year the bully added rocks to the flour and, when he struck, his principally Jewish victims howled in pain. My Irish friends knocked him to the ground and dumped the contents of his stocking over his face and body—a satisfying finale if there ever was one.

My parents eventually moved their shop a little farther north, elevating the business to the Concourse itself and settling into an apartment above the shop. As I was growing up, I explored what seemed to me every inch of that boulevard and three of its landmarks will forever be etched in my memory.

The 4,000-seat Loew's Paradise was the Concourse's palatial movie house and a beacon for everyone who yearned to escape to a romanticized world; it was an essential pleasure of my life. The marbled grand lobby, lofty ceilings, fat columns and grandiose, spotlighted statuary wrung sighs from patrons not long since arrived from the Old Country. The lobby's magnificent fountain and its pool of giant goldfish delighted the neighborhood children. The auditorium was crowned by a realistically painted azure sky with slow-moving fluffy white "clouds" and twinkling lights that looked like stars.

The Paradise was as much an addiction for my mother as for me. It took her mind off the confined and drab world of the Depression years that seemed to go on and on. Every Friday night after dinner, my mother and I rushed off to the Paradise. My father preferred to stay home devouring his newspapers, and my brother was happier in the company of his friends. On Saturday mornings, my brother and I went to the Avalon, a much smaller, cozy movie house that showed third-run double features, a weekly chapter of a cliff-hanging serial and two or three comedy shorts. Sometimes on Sundays, my mother succeeded in persuading my father to take the entire family on an outing—to the RKO Fordham on the bustling throughfare of Fordham Road.

Edgar Allan Poe's cottage, modest and cramped, was another Concourse landmark significant in my life. Situated at the edge of Poe Park north of

Fordham Road, it was where Poe had written "Annabel Lee" and "The Bells" almost a hundred years earlier, and I liked to linger there, envisioning the impoverished poet at his tiny desk scribbling by candlelight as his ailing wife, Virginia, lay in her bed upstairs.

Toward the southern end of the Concourse and not far from Yankee Stadium was the pride of Bronx hotels, the Concourse Plaza. Flag-bedecked, it stood tall and gleaming among the neighborhood tenements. Upper-crust weddings and bar mitzvahs were celebrated there, and it housed the Yankees when they were in town, as well as visiting teams. Now and then my friends and I would take the trek down the Concourse to the hotel's entrance, hoping for a glimpse of Babe Ruth or Lou Gehrig.

One night during the depth of the Depression, at the time our apartment was above the store, the doorbell rang loudly after midnight. The policeman at the door told my father that the store had been burglarized. Several thousand dollars' worth of dresses had been stolen—to us, a fortune.

My mother had refused to pay some mobsters who demanded a hard-earned two dollars a week to "protect" the store, and the police were convinced that the burglary was intended to teach her a lesson. By early morning, my mother was at her sewing machine in the empty store, beginning work on a new dress. When one of her friends appeared, asking, "How can you start all over again?" my mother said, "There's no other way. I have my children to look after. No one will do it for me." So, with some borrowed money and much courage, she and my father began anew.

Loud was curious about the cultural influences of my early childhood. Self-consciously, I began to describe some of the religious rituals we practiced, such as the lighting of candles on Friday night before dinner. I feared he would find my background so alien, it would threaten our newly forged bond.

Nonetheless, I did tell him about the traditional Friday-night dinner enjoyed by all the neighborhood Jewish families, and how on Friday morning every butcher store was packed with housewives. My mother, a natural cook, taught my father the rudiments.

On Friday afternoons, they took turns dashing from the store to our apartment to prepare the elaborate evening feast, usually consisting of a cold fish loaf (gefilte fish), spicy chopped chicken liver, chicken soup with thin homemade egg noodles, roast chicken accompanied by a mixture of carrots, peas, sweet potato and stewed prunes, and an assortment of cakes and pies that my mother had baked early that morning before leaving for work. The aroma of the baking sweets—apple, nut and raisin, cheese, sponge and honey—was the alarm clock that woke me for school every Friday.

On all mornings, in fact, my mother was already at her command post in the kitchen when I awoke. By then, my father had brought in the two bottles left outside our apartment door by the milkman, who had arrived at dawn by horse and wagon. Milk came in two grades, A and B, and my family's standing order was for one of each. The richer Grade A was for my brother and me. In those days before homogenization, the cream in the Grade A would rise to the top and the bottle had to be vigorously shaken before pouring. The bottles were stored in a wooden icebox, whose top compartment was regularly filled with a block of ice carried up the stairs of our apartment house on the back of the iceman.

As the Friday-night meals were being cooked throughout the neighborhood, I and the other hungry kids playing in the streets would shout up to our respective tenement windows for a snack. The indulgent mothers would toss down brown paper bags containing sandwiches, usually an onion roll cut in half, lathered in chicken fat and spread with chopped liver and something called gribenes, bits of fried chicken skin that tasted like bacon. The sandwiches were nutritionally appalling and absolutely delicious. As dusk descended on Friday evenings, you might look up and see half a dozen paper bags flying out of windows.

Loud seemed to delight in this sort of ethnic flavor, and I felt encouraged to go on.

What bound my friends and me together were the streets, where we played stickball; the empty lots, where we played baseball; and the schoolyard, where basketball was the attraction. We ingeniously fashioned guns out of wood and rubber bands that shot small squares of cardboard cut out of discarded movie posters. We made wagons from wooden fruit crates dumped by grocery stores, old baby carriage wheels and old roller skates.

We stole potatoes from produce stands and baked them in fires we made in the lots until they were charcoal-black. Nothing tasted better. At the end of the day, our faces would be caked with dirt and ash. We were learning how to live together, what friendship meant, and how to get along with people who were different from us.

There was no air-conditioning, so when it was too hot to sleep, my parents took my brother and me to the park—Central Park (near the 110th Street lake) when we lived in Harlem, and Echo Park (a quiet neighborhood oasis) when we lived in the Bronx. We brought a basket of food and spread a blanket on the grass, where we slept until it grew cool enough to return to our apartment. Summer's end was heralded by a ritual in which the older boys went around grabbing straw boaters from the heads of strolling or loafing male pedestrians, and burning them in empty-lot bonfires. Anyone who wore a straw hat after Labor Day was fair game.

Every square block contained its own tribe. At the corner candy store, a meeting place after school, you could get a ten-cent malted, a two-penny glass of seltzer, or a strip of sweet, crunchy halvah for two cents. Vendors proliferated on the streets, selling flavored shaved ice and corn-on-the-cob in summer, baked sweet potatoes and hot salted chickpeas in winter. Peddlers, too, were common, walking up and down the street shouting, "I cash clothes!" or whatever it was they were trading in. Troubadours went from backyard to backyard, rewarded with spare change wrapped in strips of newspaper and tossed from windows. An Italian man cranked up his hurdy-gurdy while his monkey on a string danced and begged for pennies.

On Sunday nights during the Depression, radio provided a free comic marathon to households in all neighborhoods. Families gathered around their sets to listen to three consecutive hours of shows starring Eddie Cantor, Fred Allen, and Jack Benny. The streets on those nights were deserted. If someone happened to be walking in my neighborhood on a Sunday night, he was likely to hear the same programs blaring forth from scores of apartment windows.

Loud asked me about my brother, and I told him that Harold was very important to me as I was growing up. Both my parents had a profound regard for education and constantly urged us to do well in school. My brother helped me with my schoolwork and encouraged me to read. Every Saturday after the movies we went to the library together, where he amassed an impressive armload of books. I was sure he would grow up to be a writer. The more educated my brother and I became, the more educated my parents became as well.

Harold was almost ten years old when the Depression descended. Every few blocks, there was a jobless man, always neatly attired—sometimes in tie and jacket—selling apples for a nickel apiece; long "bread lines" were set up by the city and people waited for hours to obtain free loaves.

My brother was traumatized when he accompanied my father to stand on the blocklong line outside the bank where our family savings were deposited. My panic-stricken father prayed that he could retrieve his money before the bank was forced to close, and while on line he kept muttering, "What are we going to do? What are we going to do?"

I was similarly traumatized when my parents took me to Central Park one Sunday to make an offering of cans of food to the hungry and homeless.

Desperate to find shelter, they had set up huts of tin, wood and newspaper on one of the park's spacious lawns, creating what came to be known as a "Hooverville." In contrast to my earliest years in Harlem, I never saw a black person in my Bronx neighborhood. I witnessed only white poverty—which was pervasive. One heartbreaking childhood memory was the sight of bereft parents clutching their infants, huddled on the sidewalk after they had been dispossessed for not paying their rent.

The endless hardships led to frequent protest rallies in the streets. During the 1932 presidential election campaign, the sidewalks resounded to oratory propounding ways out of the Depression. On almost every corner, speakers set up soapboxes and American flags. My father, as a kind of civics lesson, took my brother and me from corner to corner to listen to them. Most of the speakers in that overwhelmingly Democratic neighborhood extolled New York's governor, Franklin D. Roosevelt, in his battle to defeat President Herbert Hoover. Although Hoover was blamed in our neighborhood for the ills of the Depression, there was a scattering of intrepid speakers who tried to rally support for him. But the hostility was so palpable toward the Hoover boosters that I wondered how they would get out of the neighborhood unharmed.

During the Depression, the way my family lived was unpredictable, all depending on the volume of business in my parents' store. There were good times, particularly during the Easter and Christmas shopping seasons. The extra money taken in was put aside for summer vacations in the Catskills or the Rockaways. During the lean times, though—when my mother had to work on her sewing machine past midnight—there was often nothing to spend on entertainment or even on clothes.

But I can never remember my parents skimping on food. Those hard times were endured by almost everyone in the city, many on "home relief." Sometimes I shared my lunch with two of my school friends, Linky and Sammy and, often after school, brought them back with me to my parents' store so my mother could feed them.

It was then that Harold vowed to find a secure job when he grew up. In high school, he was impressed with the lifestyle of his best friend, who lived in an elite building on the Grand Concourse. My teenaged brother soon discovered the source of his friend's wealth: his father was a certified public accountant, a profession about which Harold made inquiries. If being a CPA could do that much for his friend's father, why wouldn't it do the same for him?

By the time I started at *The Times,* Harold had graduated from CCNY, married his college sweetheart, Sylvia, and passed his CPA exams. He eventually became the co-managing partner of one of New York's most prestigious accounting firms. I told Loud I felt I was perhaps more of a dreamer.

Loud appreciated my sharing these intimate details, and said he wanted to help me along. He thought there might be a shortcut to getting me onto the reportorial staff.

"I have an idea," he said. "Why not start an in-house organ in which you interview various staff members about their backgrounds, mixed in with stories about the goings-on in the building? You and a couple of your peers could edit it, and it would be the quickest way to get your skills noticed."

I immediately embraced the idea.

"The sheet might be sent overseas to our foreign correspondents," Loud continued. "And to those on the staff serving in the war. It could provide them with a much-needed taste of home."

But how would I get it published, I wondered.

"Before you begin work tonight, go and wait for James to come out of his office," Loud advised. "Tell him your idea. And remember what I told you about finishing college. Don't worry about sleep—at your age you don't need much. Hard work will keep your imagination flourishing. To smooth your way, make sure to take classes in Latin and Greek. And you will profit from studying Emerson and Thoreau and the other New England Transcendentalists. Never forget, as Emerson taught us, knowledge is transmuted into truth by action. Keep exploring, keep experiencing, keep questioning, until you find the right path here at *The Times* or wherever life may lead you. Above all, never lose your childlike curiosity—the staple of all good reporters in their quest for facts, facts and more facts."

Fortified with the sound of our own words and our Scotches, we walked back to *The Times.* Loud continued to coach me about talking to Edwin James.

As soon as we reached *The Times,* I grabbed several of the news clerks and told them of the idea. Two of them, John Meixner and Gene Davis, quickly grasped the possibilities. When I saw James leave his office, nervous as I was, I surprised myself by boldly blurting: "Mr. James, may I talk to you for a moment?"

As always, he was preoccupied, chewing on a cigar and studying the *Racing Form,* and he recoiled. "Yes?" he asked, feebly.

I made my proposal and requested permission to have the house organ printed in the composing room. He looked bemused.

"What kind of sheet will this be?" he asked. I explained, stressing that it would be good for our men overseas. James finally nodded. "Have it hectographed," he said. Hectographing was a duplication process employing purple ink, cheaper than mimeographing and less efficient. But of course I didn't argue.

"Prepare a sample and let me look at it, and we will go from there," James said.

FIVE

TOWARD THE END OF JUNE 1944, when I'd been at *The Times* for about a month, Gene Davis, John Meixner and I met for lunch at the Blue Ribbon, a vintage rathskeller on Forty-fourth Street near Broadway, to plan our paper's first issue.

Davis was short, curly haired and wore his trousers pegged at the bottom, aping the style of his Brooklyn peers. Meixner was as tall and gangly as I; his black hair was slicked back and his tired eyes peered from behind rimless glasses. Davis and Meixner, both my age, were, like me, waiting to be drafted. They shared my hopefulness and curiosity as well as my sense of the absurd. The three of us had picked up from reporters the habit of parodying the crotchets of editors behind their backs.

We had in common, too, a passion for exploring the city—especially the midtown area—from Professor Heckler's circus of trained fleas on Forty-second Street to the jazz dens along Fifty-second. They also loved to walk and talk, and we often did both after we finished work—sometimes down to Greenwich Village, sometimes up to Harlem.

The streets were safe for nocturnal strolling save for a smattering of dangerous pockets. We generally avoided Central Park, which only recently had been declared off-limits for walking at night; the Bowery; parts of Hell's Kitchen; and a few sections of Third Avenue with its rows of dingy saloons, cringing in the shadow of the El. Street brawls were commonplace there and passersby were occasionally mugged.

Food at the Blue Ribbon was hearty and cheap—Wiener schnitzel, sauerbraten, outsize sausages on heaps of sauerkraut. By the time we got to dessert—giant pancakes smothered in *Preiselbeeren*—Meixner, Davis and I had agreed to function as a triumvirate, each with the masthead title of managing editor—an arrangement no grown-ups would have dreamed of accepting. We christened our paper *Timesweek* and mapped out story ideas for the first issue.

The best part was the recruitment of a dozen or so reporters for our staff. We would select them principally from the clerical pool, which consisted of the appealing young women who, in most cases, had replaced the young men recently drafted. We would have been delighted to date any one of them and, by inviting them to join our staff, we believed we would have an edge on the reporters already taking them out.

Among those I assigned myself to enlist were three I thought particularly congenial and pretty. They all happened to be Irish and reminded me of the Irish girls who lived on the other side of the Grand Concourse and had sat near me in class at P.S. 79. Sometimes, overcoming my shyness, I had talked to them in the schoolyard during lunch recess. I was especially drawn to a girl with long dark hair named Adeline Ryan, but, with the three-o'clock bell, she always vanished, along with the others, across the Concourse into her own neighborhood.

My first recruits for *Timesweek* were Lee McCabe, Sally McKay and Ann Marie Burke. Lee, spunky and iconoclastic with fair skin and reddish-brown hair, could always make me laugh. Sally was an auburn-haired beauty who seemed unconscious of her attractions; she always looked sad and in need of cheering up. Ann, who a few years later was to marry the then United Nations correspondent, A. M. Rosenthal, was golden-haired, with brilliant blue eyes and the most trusting and optimistic nature I had ever encountered.

Now I had the perfect excuse to spend more time with them. As an adolescent I'd had the standard self-consciousness about the opposite sex, but my older brother and his friends had passed on some tips on how to talk to girls. I was also gregarious by nature and it seemed reasonable that since I liked girls, they would like me.

I had already begun my dating career at CCNY, which hosted Friday late-afternoon dances. As there were far fewer female students than male, girls from Hunter College were recruited. My brother, a deft dancer, had shown me some steps that I'd practiced for hours to *Hit Parade* songs on the radio in our living room, using a pillow as a partner.

The Peabody was a tangolike dance calling for close body contact. The Shag was a silly exercise that involved thrusting your head forward, like a chicken, on either side of your partner's head. I counted on my mastery of these steps to impress the girls. Other boys knew only the fox-trot or the

Lindy (also called the jitterbug, and actually quite difficult to do), while I had finessed these more esoteric routines. I'm sure the girls I led around the floor weren't as bowled over as I'd hoped, but some of them agreed to go out with me. Most were from the Bronx.

After calling for them at their apartments, where I underwent a sizing-up by their hovering mothers, I took them to the movie and stage show at the Paradise. Settling into our plush seats in the theater's gilded splendor, I felt a twinge of disloyalty to my own mother—until recently my faithful movie-going companion.

After the movie we strolled north to Poe's Cozy Nook, a barroom hideaway on a quiet Concourse block across from Poe Park. To me, this tiny, nearly pitch-dark lounge, down several steps, seemed the height of cosmopolitanism. To find a table, you more or less had to feel for one. In my most debonair voice, I'd order a Manhattan for each of us. My opening conversational gambit was apt to be a discourse on a recent best-seller, John Steinbeck's *The Grapes of Wrath*.

Light-headed, my date and I ambled home. If all was going well, I might serenade her (somewhat off key) with snatches of "Mandy," the jaunty ballad Paul Robeson had recorded in Europe (along with such other renditions as "Shenandoah" and "Dere's a Man Goin' Roun' Takin' Names"). I had a 78 recording and played it obsessively at home. When I got to the lyric "Me and Mandy, hand in hand, down de lover's lane," I would slip an arm around my date. If she leaned in toward me I was reasonably sure she would let me take her to the roof of her apartment house to watch the moon and stars over the Bronx, and that she would accept a kiss or even, on a rare lucky occasion, more exploratory maneuvers.

They were nice girls, all of them, sweet natured and soulful. But the Irish girls in the *Times* city room seemed worldlier and smarter, and they didn't have that dampening preoccupation with getting married. I flirted relentlessly, eventually taking Lee and Sally on dates. We drank at Bleeck's or at Childs on Forty-third Street, the combination restaurant and barroom diagonally across the street from *The Times,* where an affable Irish magician-turned-bartender named Bill McKinney demonstrated his trick of making a coin fall through the bottom of a beer glass.

When I first found myself standing at the bar at Childs, I felt eerily at home; the establishment—with its distinctive nameplate painted in script across the windows—was part of the same genteel chain of family restaurants familiar to me while I was growing up. For a very special Sunday treat, my parents took my brother and me to one or another Childs in Manhattan for pancakes—the chain's specialty—where waitresses in pleated black uniforms and starched white caps made us feel we counted. But I remember no trace of a bar at any Childs my family patronized.

Actually, there was a second Childs on Forty-third Street, this one in the basement of the Paramount building, and I occasionally took my girlfriends tea-dancing there. A five-piece band played fox-trots and, when we got tired of squeezing around the other couples on a dance floor not much larger than a pocket handkerchief, we sipped our drinks at tiny tables and tried not to gobble the platefuls of watercress sandwiches that were my cheap substitute for dinner.

Only rarely could I afford to treat a date to a real meal. I managed to supplement my meager income with filler copy—or, as it was known, "CGO," as in "can go over." Since you were paid by the word, you padded the stories to make them as long as possible. The paper in those days rarely ran house ads and so was in constant need of such copy, mainly to hold space for stories that would break in later editions.

I rewrote press releases from the National Park Service—about, say, the decline of the bear population in Yosemite, or precautionary bulletins from the Department of Health. Once in a while I was flush enough to buy my date roast chicken at Bleeck's, or ham with raisin sauce at Toffenetti's on the southeast corner of Forty-third and Broadway, but these were special occasions.

WHEN DAVIS, MEIXNER AND I got back to the office after lunch at the Blue Ribbon, fired with dreams of success, we ran into Mike Berger. Meixner, a clerk on the city desk, had come to know Berger fairly well, and began describing our new venture. Berger congratulated us and offered to help in any way he could.

During the week we scrambled to prepare *Timesweek,* commandeering reporters' desks on their days off. We more than once stopped by Berger's desk to ask his advice—an excuse, really, to listen to him talk. Although Berger at his most unrestrained not only desk-hopped but also stood on his head while the change in his pockets rained onto the floor, much of the time he was a quietly intense presence.

His speech was rapid, but soft as a librarian's, and he stammered slightly when excited. He rarely barked "Copy!" or "Boy!" as was habitual with other reporters, preferring to walk his own copy to the city desk. And even the newest copyboy was invited to address him on a first-name basis. He was "Mike" to everyone.

Then forty-five years old, he was often surrounded at his desk by a cluster of admiring young reporters, clerks and copyboys who came to him with questions about newspapering or with personal problems. Like most reporters, Mike was proud of his calling, and pleased to bring along its neophytes. Of all the seasoned reporters, he was the most generous with his time. He listened patiently to all cub reporters who sought him out, and suggested fixes on their copy. A dead-on mimic, he told ribald stories about his exploits on assignments. And he even offered advice on how to take care of a cold and other ailments (he himself suffered from a stomach ulcer).

Murray Schumach, who as a young reporter had been a Berger disciple, later recalled the pride he felt at being permitted "as a man among men" to join the circle around his desk—especially when Mike came back from an out-of-town assignment "bubbling with tales not fit for a family paper." Ending an anecdote, Mike might abruptly confront an acolyte and ask, "Do you believe in God?" "Do you think it's all worthwhile?" or "Are you a good boy?"

The graphic and uncensored details of criminal trials related by Mike in a casual city-room chat would surely have enriched his published stories had he felt free to include them. Sometimes these unsavory details carried significant information that would have made a jury's verdict more comprehensible to readers. But all reporters practiced self-censorship. In those days, such facts were not perceived as fit to print. It wasn't until much later that, for example, the quaint "woman of ill repute" emerged boldly as "prostitute"—and in some cases even as "whore." Murray Schumach once told me about a trial he had covered in Bridgeport, Connecticut, in the 1930s, of a black man accused of raping a white woman.

It was extraordinary for *The Times* to cover a rape trial in the first place, but this was an unusual case—the woman was the wife of a prominent advertising executive. The defendant insisted she had invited his advances and, at her request, he had ejaculated into her handkerchief during their assignations.

The man was found not guilty, but the crucial evidence on his behalf, a semen-stained handkerchief produced on cross-examination, was not described in Murray's story. The reader was left wondering on what basis the jury had made its decision. Murray had actually included the vital evidence in his account, pleading in a note penciled at the bottom that the copy editor find a way of getting the handkerchief into the story—but to no avail.

When I became deputy metropolitan editor in 1963, reporters were still straitjacketing themselves, despite a loosening in both the paper's and the public's perception of what was appropriate to publish. Intimidated by the aura of *The Times,* they saw the paper as more prudish than it actually was. I cautioned young reporters not to save their best stories to tell around the office, and not to assume that their editors would necessarily excise juicy facts in the interest of good taste.

Davis and I, new to the paper, were at first too shy to join the group around Mike Berger's desk. But we were gradually emboldened by Meixner's acquaintance with him, as well as by our brand-new positions as managing editors of our own newspaper. One day I found myself telling Mike I was planning to go back to college. Why? asked Mike, whose attitude was exactly the opposite of Grover Loud's. Peering dubiously at me, he asked if I thought there was anything college could possibly teach me about reporting.

"And if you do go back," he said, "for God's sake, don't take any journalism courses. Forgive me for sounding like a crusty old man, but the only way to learn newspapering is by doing it."

He told me about his childhood—how he'd left school in 1910 when he was twelve, to work full-time helping support his immigrant parents and ten siblings, and about his first job at the Brooklyn office of the old *Morning World,* running copy over the bridge to the main office on Park Row.

When there was no copy to deliver, he fetched pints of cold beer and hot bean sandwiches from Dinty Moore's for the office poker games. While the reporters played, he listened to them swap stories—the tricks they'd used to cajole information from balky subjects or to scoop rivals, the telling tidbits of color they'd finagled from cops at crime scenes. These sessions had formed his basic education and engendered his love affair with newspapering. ("I contracted newsprint fever," he wrote years later, recalling those poker-playing reporters. "The men from whom I caught this fever have, for the greater part, long since died of it.")

"You wouldn't get that foundation in any classroom," Mike told me, "and you'd never get it in journalism school—especially now, with such a well-oiled public-relations industry out there." Between slick publicists and the news services, he explained, rookie reporters were failing to rely on their own resources. Only hanging around veteran reporters, being exposed to some of the old-time methods of reporting, would teach me to stand on my own pins.

He told me that Adolph Ochs had never finished high school, going to work full-time at fourteen as an apprentice, or printer's devil, in the composing room of his hometown newspaper in Tennessee, the *Knoxville Chronicle,* and had bought the *Chattanooga Times* when he was only twenty. "As his daughter once said," Mike added, "he had 'newsprint in his fingers.' And what more do you need to be a good newspaperman?"

It was not a scolding speech and, as he talked, he filled a page in a stenographer's notebook with little leprechauns, his habitual doodle.

"Tell me," he said, "did you say why you're going back to school?"

I could think of only one reason. "I'm doing it for my mother," I answered sheepishly. It was the truth: My mother, still upset over my dropping out of CCNY, longed to see me graduate.

He shrugged, smiling gently. "Oh, well, in that case you have to go. Read some good books for me while you're there—and don't forget what I told you about those journalism classes."

ON THE AFTERNOON OF JULY 18, 1944, flanked by Davis and Meixner, I set a stack of *Timesweeks* on an empty desk in the city room, where the staff was sure to see them as they straggled in after lunch. We retreated to the back of the room, where we stood nervously sneaking looks to see if we were being read.

Restricted to cheap paper and condemned to fuzzy printing, *Timesweek* looked even more amateurish than my high school weekly. It consisted of five eight-by-eleven-inch pages that we had stapled together, after having stayed up all night typing copy onto purple carbon stencils and then hand-cranking the hectograph machine to produce the copies. Our fingers were stained purple from the carbons and our heads were woozy with the fumes from the alcohol toner the machine required.

Timesweek's unpolished appearance was at odds with its high-minded goals. "We intend to be a serious, energetic and intelligent publication," we wrote in our page-one editorial. "And though this might suggest dullness to some, we believe they are important virtues—the elements necessary for a successful and interesting newspaper." Our first issue was an earnest, eager-to-please statement of purpose—containing the very same qualities associated with *The Times* itself.

Our lead story, as befitted a publication produced by three freshly promoted copyboys, was about an ex-copyboy named Richard J. H. Johnston, who had been posted to the paper's London bureau the previous week. We continued, in subsequent issues, to take a proprietary interest in Johnston's career, reporting when he was wounded by a piece of shrapnel in France, and eventually quoting him on his return home from Germany: "Patton is a good soldier, a helluva good actor and a bit of a swami who hypnotizes correspondents."

At the bottom of the front page, as a thank-you for suggesting the idea of *Timesweek,* we featured a profile of Grover Loud that I had written, leading with a description of "his nightly scrap" over copyediting with Wilson Fairbanks, who, Loud conceded, "is always ninety-nine-point-nine percent correct." Other stories included the trouncing by *The Times*'s softball team of the *Herald Tribune.* A reference to a *Times* second baseman, a file clerk named Kathleen Burke—Ann's sister, soon to enlist in the WAVES—was smugly sexist, in the manner of the era: "She'll fill a uniform nicely," we commented.

Exhausted, bleary-eyed, but pumped full of coffee and adrenaline, we watched as reporters, editors, clerks and others took copies back to their desks where, to our delight, they appeared to read the issue cover to cover.

By the second issue I had begun "Talk of the Times," a column with facts and anecdotes about *Times* personnel—with priority given to excerpts from letters to friends from homesick staffers fighting overseas. "Times Square is shown often in the movies and makes me wish I was back working in the pressroom," read one missive from New Caledonia. "Some day when all this is over I'll be back printing a paper for you again."

Also noted were weddings, parties (though downplaying the liquor that flowed freely), promotions, vacations, retirements, babies born. *Timesweek* often read like a small-town newspaper. We recorded the comings and goings of its prominent citizens—correspondents and bureau chiefs—and profiled its favorite sons. With experience, we began doing pieces on significant developments at the paper, especially stories about how reporters got their scoops—the exclusive account, for example, by Brooks Atkinson about General Joseph W. Stilwell's recall from China.

The Times had sent Atkinson, its famed drama critic, to Chungking when he became restless during the course of the war and told Arthur Hays Sulzberger he could no longer stick it out as drama critic, which he labeled "a job for little boys" in wartime. Soon after his arrival in Chungking, Atkinson could not resist evaluating a performance of *Hamlet* in a theater crowded with soldiers, students, women with babies, and "intellectuals in Western attire." In the dispatch, which ran on December 8, 1944, on page one, Atkinson jested that the production was not yet quite ready for Broadway."

But it did not take long for Atkinson to demonstrate his superb reportorial talent. He took the measure of the hidden animosity between Generalissimo

Chiang Kai-shek and General Stilwell. Although stricken with jaundice from malaria, he managed to get an exclusive interview with Stilwell, who had been quietly relieved of his command by General George C. Marshall. Atkinson flew back to the United States with his great scoop, thereby ducking the Chungking censors controlled by Chiang Kai-shek. The story received prominent display on the front page.

Years later, Theodore White, *Time* magazine's correspondent in China, told me that being beaten by a drama critic was the most humiliating professional experience in his career. In any event, when Atkinson returned home, it was *Timesweek* that allowed me access to him; weak from his illness, he nevertheless managed to answer a few questions from his hospital bed—an introduction that began our long association at the paper.

A year after we began publishing, the trade magazine *Editor & Publisher* ran a piece about us, calling *Timesweek* "well-written and dignified," not like other house organs, which were "full of such coy items as 'Telephone Room Office Boy Ernie Hicks . . . has been getting sand in his ball bearings passing the desk of Jennie Lee Goon. Could it be . . . ?'"

The response to our second issue was even more encouraging. Front-page stories included an account of coverage of the Democratic convention in Chicago by "*Times* staff men" (though the paper's twenty representatives included *Times* staff woman Anne O'Hare McCormick). They had found, we reported, that the vice-presidential contest between Henry Wallace and Harry Truman "made the gathering lively" but that "eight newspapermen for five seats does not make for comfort." Mike Berger acted as quartermaster for the group, foraging for "120 bottles of Coca-Cola and two dozen chocolate bars besides a three-day supply of fruit which included a crate of plums and one basket of peaches."

Edwin L. James approved of us, too. H. K. Tootle, the head of the personnel department, who was big-hearted over small matters, wrote James a memo recommending that *Timesweek* be mimeographed outside the building. If not as good as printing, mimeographing was far clearer and less odoriferous than hectographing. Tootle urged that *The Times* take over the cost: $15 to run off four hundred copies.

"I would be very much in favor of doing it," James wrote Sulzberger. "I like to encourage this sort of thing." And so it was done, though apparently not quite as cheaply as Tootle had promised. "The mimeograph people now say it will cost $35 a week," James wrote in August to Orvil E. Dryfoos, Sulzberger's son-in-law, who was later to succeed him as publisher. "What will we do now?"

Memos flew back and forth in an effort to solve this momentous question. One from Dryfoos read, "You authorized the $15 and it seems a mistake was made and the boys were told *The Times* would pay for the mimeographing. I think we should go to the $35." Sulzberger agreed.

Other affirmations came our way as well. In late September, Sulzberger suggested to Dryfoos that *Timesweek* be sent to the news staff abroad. Dryfoos agreed: "There is a lot in it, besides which, it would show the staff what is being done here." In January, Dryfoos asked Sulzberger if *Timesweek* could be sent (at $20 per mailing) to employees in the armed services, and again Sulzberger gave his consent.

By year's end, I was given the best encouragement yet: James decided that one of *Timesweek*'s trio of editors should devote a full day each week to putting out our publication. I was chosen, and my duties were rearranged to widen my experience during the remaining four days. For two days each week I would continue working on the telegraph desk as a news assistant. For the other two days I would work in the same capacity on the cable desk, sitting at the end of the horseshoe table next to cable editor Theodore Bernstein. Wilson Fairbanks and Grover Loud, my staunch supporters, readily went along with my broadened schedule.

I welcomed the arrangement because under Bernstein I would have the chance to learn how foreign news was edited. The youngest of the major editors in the city room, he was a mild man whom everyone called Ted. He had arrived at *The Times* in 1925, fresh out of the Columbia School of Journalism. Ten years later, after having served as assistant to the cable desk editor, he was named night cable editor. Now, at forty, he was still a neophyte compared with the editors who had slipped into old age on the job.

The desk men under Bernstein's command, most of them youthful like himself, were a contentious bunch, prone to endless debate over everything, from predicting the war's outcome to which office girl had the shapeliest legs. This rambunctiousness was in sharp contrast with Wilson Fairbanks's desk men—most of them elderly like their boss—who worked in near-silence. Virtually all of them had been top reporters whose legs gave out and who no longer wanted to chase stories. Many of Bernstein's men were not long out of journalism school, and preferred copyediting to reporting. But Bernstein had the unquestioned respect of his colleagues. Even on nights when blizzards of copy flew around the cable desk, he could quell all bickering with a firm "We must get the copy up."

Bernstein was evolving into *The Times*'s official grammarian—a position that became increasingly valued when tight editing was made a premium at the paper. He eventually assumed the role of in-house arbiter of grammar and usage, *The Times*'s resident Fowler. For years, he and night city editor Robert E. Garst had taught a popular copyediting course at the Columbia School of Journalism, their common alma mater. "Garstein," as their students called them, had collaborated on *Headlines and Deadlines,* a copyediting manual that was a bible in the field.

Foreign correspondents, often prickly about Bernstein's changes in their copy, would grouse that he had no reporting experience, that he was strictly a desk man. When in New York, they rarely invited him to join their drinking sessions at Bleeck's. However, Mike Berger, even with his contempt for journalism schools, never belittled Bernstein on this account, perhaps understanding it was enough to be an intuitive grammarian—and that the street smarts that couldn't be learned in school might be essential for a reporter but not for a copy editor. As for Bernstein, he was unperturbed by the correspondents' attitude. A man of reserve and routine, he eagerly returned home after work to his lower Fifth Avenue apartment, his wife, Beatrice, and his nightcap.

Even under deadline pressure Bernstein was cordial and considerate to me, occasionally ribbing me about having enrolled at CCNY instead of Columbia, and reminiscing about DeWitt Clinton, the high school we had both attended. When we published a grammatical blunder in *Timesweek,* he pointed it out, but gently. After a while he became *Timesweek*'s arbiter of grammar and style. I dreaded his reading each new issue, sure he would find something to criticize. He once circled the word "asserted" four times in a four-page issue. "What's wrong with 'said'?" he asked. He then gave me a copy of his manual with the following passage underlined:

"Discrimination in the use of words is an art. The synonym is convenient but dangerous, and it should be employed with great care. If the copy editor substitutes 'assert' for 'say,' a common practice to obtain variety, he has altered the meaning perceptibly. Variety can be achieved in many other ways than by abusing the synonym."

The show I most anticipated nightly before deadline was enacted by Bernstein and the art department's cartographers, who were responsible for creating the front-page war map, a highlight of *The Times*'s daily coverage. Before turning to any story in the paper, readers often studied this precisely delineated map to see whether our troops had advanced in the past twenty-four hours and by precisely how much.

By eight o'clock, I had prepared the cables for Bernstein from the half-dozen press services as well as from *The Times*'s correspondents. Chain-smoking and oblivious to the clatter around him, he completed his reading of the data just as the two cartographers walked briskly into the city room, one of them carrying cardboard "base" maps of the European and Pacific theaters.

Huddling at a table to one side of the cable desk, Bernstein and the two men updated each of the maps, drawing in—on tissue paper overlaid on the base maps—battle lines, arrows and numbers to show cities under siege. When he was certain of the changes, Bernstein allowed the cartographers to copy the additions onto strips of celluloid, which were then placed over the maps.

While the finished maps were whisked off to the engraving room, Bernstein returned to his desk to compose, in his own clear handwriting, meticulously worded captions to accompany the maps, concentrating so intently that the cigarette he had laid down at the edge of the desk burned its way into the wood. "In the past five years," he said to me once, after finishing his nightly stint, "I've learned more about cartography, geography and military strategy than I thought it was possible to know." For me, observing the mapmaking process was a journalism lesson no school could have taught.

Despite the grant of a day each week to work on *Timesweek*, I still stayed late at the office some nights, napping on reporters' desks. Around dawn, I would awake in a dark and empty city room, silent except for a porter or two carting away discarded copy paper from rows of wastepaper baskets.

I was so sleep-starved that I often nodded off halfway through eating a sandwich, but I didn't much care. My *Timesweek* obligations brought rich dividends: I had entrée to everyone at the paper, from the publisher to the managing editor, to all the city-room editors, reporters and rewrite men, to the mallet-swinging typesetters in the composing room, to delivery truck drivers. I learned about the daily problems of getting *The Times* out on time, and about the process of replating the paper for breaking news stories.

I called whomever I pleased—and no one refused to speak to me. On the contrary: Reporters wanted their names in *Timesweek*, to show off to their friends and families, and they enjoyed being asked about their work, a welcome break from asking others about theirs. Correspondents in Washington talked to me collegially about everything from national politics to backbiting antics in the bureau and, by telegraph and cable, I was in touch with correspondents all over the globe.

No one treated me like the raw youth I was. Even the formidable, high-handed chief of the Washington bureau, Arthur Krock, came to the phone to answer my questions. Soon some of the reporters and editors, including

Berger, Loud and Fairbanks, were writing feature articles for *Timesweek* and graciously allowing Davis, Meixner and me to fact-check and edit them.

One of the staffers I met through *Timesweek* was A. M. (Abe) Rosenthal. A couple of years older than I, he had been two years ahead of me at CCNY. And while I'd been aware of Abe's reputation as editor of the college newspaper, the *Campus,* and as *The Times*'s college correspondent, our paths had never crossed in college. More than any other New York college except Columbia, CCNY had been an incubator for *Times* reporters. The job of college correspondent, which often led to a full-time position at *The Times,* was a coveted one, bestowed only on a school's most promising would-be journalists. The correspondent was paid a small fee for each story he filed.

Abe had left CCNY in 1943, a few months before graduating, when the city editor, short of gifted reporters because of the war, offered him a job. (Seven years later, he was awarded his diploma, with his reportorial experience credited toward his degree.) Mike Berger recognized Abe's talent at once and treated him less as a rookie than as a peer—enviable attentions not lost on the rest of us. Abe from the first believed he was destined to become a great foreign correspondent. But never—despite his unswerving faith in his own journalistic gifts—did it cross his mind that he would one day be executive editor of *The Times,* arguably the most powerful newspaper job in the world.

Abe's childhood, I discovered after we became close friends, had been haunted by hardship and death. Abe's father, Harry Shipiatsky, a socialist and a farmer in Byelorussia and the son of an Orthodox rabbi, had loathed the czar with a passion. He and Abe's mother fled his despotic rule for Ontario, Canada, where he changed his surname to Rosenthal, the name of a maternal uncle, and drew away from his Orthodox roots.

The darling of five older sisters, Abe was born in Sault Sainte Marie, where Harry traded farming for fur trapping. But he later decided to move his family to New York, to a cooperative union housing project in the north Bronx on the edge of an expansive stretch of greenery, Van Cortlandt Park. In New York, Harry became a housepainter.

Abe adored his father. He saw him as physically powerful, charismatic and a spellbinding storyteller. Just before Abe's thirteenth birthday, Harry died after a fall from a ladder. More tragedies followed while Abe was still a child: One of his beloved sisters died of pneumonia, and another, who had married George Watt, a commissar of the volunteer Abraham Lincoln Brigade that fought on the Loyalist side during the Spanish Civil War, died of encephalitis after giving birth in a crowded city hospital. Two other sisters died of cancer.

At seventeen, Abe was stricken with terrible pains in his leg. Unable to diagnose the illness, doctors at the Hospital for Joint Diseases in Harlem ordered him placed in a body cast from the neck down, telling him he would never be able to walk again. For weeks, he lay in a ward of forty sick and dying men—an experience, he later said, that was no less than a living hell. One of his sisters was his salvation. She got in touch with the Mayo Clinic in Minnesota and arranged for Abe to be sent there as a charity case—where he was, at last, diagnosed with osteomyelitis, a degenerative bone marrow disease. A complicated operation finally corrected the problem.

These punishing early traumas did not break his spirit, but instead gave him a fiery desire to excel, as if to make the ghosts of his lost loved ones proud of him. He hadn't smothered his sadness. He seemed in constant touch with it, unable to talk about his childhood and his father and sisters without tears welling in his eyes—a far healthier adaptation, it seemed to me, than burying it. And when Abe cried, I cried. The two of us in later years would sit at a bar, wiping away our tears.

But these disclosures—and my close identification with Abe as the son of immigrants, as a Bronx boy, a DeWitt Clinton High School graduate, and as a CCNY student—all came later. To those of us who wanted desperately to become reporters, Abe seemed totally self-possessed and mature. He smoked a pipe, looked intellectual in his dark-rimmed glasses, and his lighthearted quips made us laugh. But he kept a tentative distance.

If Abe's writing style was imposing, his physique was not. He had an indoor pallor and slight build, and the differences in our heights irked him no end. He was utterly indifferent to clothes. One shirttail sometimes hung outside his rumpled trousers, which rode low on his narrow hips, seemingly about to slide to the floor. He looked hip-hop before hip-hop. It was years before he began taking even a minimal interest in what he wore, claiming to be more than satisfied with the bargain suits he bought at a downtown discount clothier—which gave me something to needle him about:

Abe (looking at me looking at his suit): "What's the matter with it? It was a bargain!"

Me: "That's great, Abe. If you don't know the difference between a bargain suit and a good suit, then a bargain suit is fine for you."

And so forth, while those around us rolled their eyes, having heard the routine before. As a dressmaker's son, I had a fondness for fine fabrics and good tailoring, a trait of which Abe was contemptuous. He sneered when I began buying my suits at Paul Stuart on Madison Avenue. In the early 1980s, while Abe was executive editor, and Seymour Topping was managing editor, I came to work one day in a new suit of Canadian wool.

Abe and Top promptly decided to make an expedition during lunch to Paul Stuart—which neither had ever patronized. As it happened, a big story broke while they were shopping, and I had to find Abe. I called Paul Stuart and explained to the salesman who came to the phone that I was looking for two customers. "Since the store is very crowded at the moment," said the voice at the other end, "that will be difficult." "Try looking for two men who don't belong there," I said. Abe and Top were delivered to the phone within seconds.

Actually, it was Abe's obliviousness to his appearance that gave me an excuse to approach him for the first time. A story had circulated in the city room about a curious remark he had made while covering a press luncheon hosted by the writer Christopher Morley. It had been a sweltering day, and Morley had suggested that each of the reporters at the small gathering introduce himself and remove his jacket. "I am a reporter from *The New York Times*," Abe said when his turn came, "and reporters from *The Times* never remove their jackets."

I walked over to Abe's desk and said I wanted to write up the item for *Timesweek*. He smiled mischievously, and told me that he had made his comment out of desperation. The sleeve of the shirt he had put on that morning had ripped. It was his last clean shirt and he hadn't had time to pick up his freshly laundered ones.

His remark had been the only thing he could think of to keep the torn shirt concealed. Fifty years later, I find a certain poignancy to this story. Abe's statement, although a clever way out of a tight spot, was also a foretaste of his identification with the paper. He grew increasingly sensitive to any criticism of *The Times,* as if he and the paper were one.

He told other stories at his own expense about learning on the job. On his first day as a reporter, he was sent to cover a death—a murder or suicide, it wasn't immediately clear—at the Mayflower Hotel. Abe rang the buzzer of the room where the body had been found. A detective—"twelve and a half feet tall," as Abe put it—opened the door. Abe identified himself as a *Times* reporter and said, "I want to see the body."

"Beat it," said the detective.

"Oh, but there must be some misunderstanding," Abe told him smoothly, flashing his brand-new press card.

The detective studied it and handed it back. "Shove it in your ear," he said.

"But I'm from *The Times*!" Abe protested. "A reporter from *The New York Times*! Don't you want me to get the story right?"

"Listen, Four Eyes," said the detective. "I don't care if you drop dead," and slammed the door.

It was a year or so after Abe's rude initiation that I arrived at *The Times*. For the next year, I and the other clerks never tired of watching him at his typewriter. He was mesmerizing—like a virtuoso pianist or an action painter. He had composed the entire story in his mind before starting to type. He was not so much writing it as copying down, word for word, what was inside his head. His fingers danced over the keys of his typewriter. He didn't pause, either to check his notes or to look up a spelling of a name, until he tapped out the last letter of the last word of his story. Not even Mike Berger wrote with such speed.

Those of us who observed Abe were beyond jealousy. He clearly had a gift that could not be duplicated. As his stories were being edited, I sometimes glanced over the copy editor's shoulder, awed by the clean pages with scarcely any editing marks. But it was not until October 1945 that a story by Abe was signed. Bylines in those days were a rarity, and only given as a reward for a scoop or a story written with special flair. They were bestowed with no prior notice by the city editor, a tormenting tradition that all local reporters believed had been designed to make their lives a misery and drive them to drink.

As Abe later said, when reminiscing about his first bylined story, he had a feeling he would make his bones on this one. And snatching a peek at his typically clean copy—not a single word crossed out—I had the same feeling. That night, the article was one of only two city stories on page one. Dated October 20, it carried the headline:

THE *NEW YORK* HERE ON LAST TRIP HOME
First Battleship of Fleet to Arrive
Is to Be Scrapped or Made Atom Bomb Target

The story began:

The battleship New York, sixth of her name, arrived here yesterday, thirty-one months and four battles out of home port. It was her last homeward run. In a matter of weeks the New York will be given over to the cutter's torch or sacrificed in research to a test of the atomic bomb.

Aboard the New York were 1,400 crewmen and 1,050 other Pacific veterans returning to a life of peace, and one of the proudest and longest battle logs in the fleet. The latest volumes in the neatly written records of thirty-one years at sea tell in laconic Navy fashion of three days of sharp triumph off North Africa, of slow, tense months in the Atlantic, of bitter weeks in Iwo's waters and seventy-eight days of hell and glory off Okinawa.

It was superb newspaper writing under deadline pressure—eloquent and authoritative. Abe, usually after a few drinks, loved to recite these two paragraphs. He quoted them so often over the years that friends would groan in theatrical agony:

"No, Abe, not the battleship again! Enough already with the days of hell and glory!"

But all of us knew the truth: This was the bylined piece that marked the rightful beginning of his brilliant career—the one that made his name at the paper as a rising star. No wonder he loved to recite it. It was his birth announcement.

SIX

To my relief, *The Times* decided to support President Roosevelt for a fourth term, maintaining he was far better qualified than Governor Thomas E. Dewey to bring the war to a victorious end. The coverage of the campaign had to be planned with extra care because wartime restrictions made newsprint scarce.

Early the previous March, James had counted the number of columns used to cover the 1936 and 1940 presidential elections. Estimating that 160 tons of paper would be needed this time, he set up a newsprint reserve. (The columns for the 1944 campaign, when added up, came to 158.6 tons—a variance of only 1.4 tons from James's forecast.)

Determined to demonstrate that our *Timesweek* staff was every bit as professional as that of *The Times* itself, Davis, Meixner and I decided to publish our seventh issue as a special election report. It was a self-imposed trial by fire.

In those pre-polling, pre-electronic days, newspapers tried to predict winners on election night by evaluating the ongoing tallies in election districts in certain bellwether states (or, for local elections, counties). Even though they strove for caution in projecting winners, occasionally there were embarrassing errors. *Times* editors, however, took pride in knowing their scores in the guessing game were the best in the field.

Every reporter assigned to a story about the election had a small numbered flag on his desk. A crew of editors sorted and marked the tallies of the evolving votes in the various local and national races with numbers corresponding to those on the reporters' desks. The tallies, distributed by copyboys throughout the night, were studied by the reporters as edition after edition went to press.

Arthur Krock, as usual on the night of a national election, came up from Washington to write the lead story. His command post, set up close to Wilson Fairbanks's desk, was somewhat removed from the rest of the political writers. Grover Loud had told me Krock never lost his cool, no matter how severe the pressure as deadline approached. Since I was to take my regular position next to Mr. Fairbanks that night, I looked forward to meeting Krock at his typewriter.

He had won two of his four Pulitzers by then and, in a recent poll of the congressional press gallery conducted by the *Saturday Review of Literature,* had been voted the correspondent who exerted the most influence in Washington. Because he was so widely read and projected a voice of such authority, he was more powerful than many members of the Cabinet.

His austere, aloof manner signaled his sense of self-importance. He wore a vest and a flawlessly pressed white silk shirt. When I handed him a sheet of AP copy with the latest tallies, he snatched it without looking up. He had always been polite, if distant, to me on the phone when I had called to check items for *Timesweek,* and I felt affronted.

Like Wilson Fairbanks, Krock was addressed as "Mister" by everyone in the city room. A Kentuckian by birth, he had served as chief correspondent of the Washington bureau since 1932, at the start of Roosevelt's New Deal presidency. He was narrowly watched by his peers to see whether he could live up to his predecessor, the great Richard V. Oulahan, the paper's first Washington correspondent whose dispatches were signed on a regular basis, usually the only byline in those days to appear on page one.

Krock's Washington expertise eventually superseded even Oulahan's, and *The Times* came to regard him as indispensable in directing the behind-the-scenes coverage of the Roosevelt administration. Despite Adolph Ochs's often voiced disdain of opinionated political columns, he finally, in 1933, allowed Krock to launch such a column for the editorial page.

Roosevelt, however, grew annoyed with Krock's arrogance and was unsympathetic to his conservative political leanings. He had also become increasingly concerned that Krock probed too deeply into clandestine presidential matters. Believing there were too many loose-tongued sources on his White House staff, Roosevelt cautioned his aides about seeing "too much of A.K."

By contrast, the gaunt, stooped James A. Hagerty, a treasured veteran of local political reporting, pecked away at his typewriter with no dramatic flourishes whatever. Every copyboy glowed when he looked up in a gesture of thanks. His predictions on how the vote would go in New York State during presidential elections had been on the mark since 1928, when Governor Al Smith ran against Herbert Hoover. Though it was widely believed that the popular governor would carry New York State, Hagerty insisted Hoover would win by 100,000 votes. Hoover did win—by 103,481.

No one covering politics had more reliable sources among the county bosses, not only in the city itself but in the outlying areas. When Hagerty phoned, no party official failed to take his call. His integrity was absolute. "Give this story to Jim Hagerty," President Roosevelt once told Jim Farley, his Democratic Party chief. "If it appears under his name no one will doubt its accuracy." Like everyone else in the city room, I thought it was unfair that Krock had been awarded two Pulitzers, while Hagerty, just as talented, had never received one.

Soon after Hagerty was hired by the *New York Herald* in 1910, he was asked to head its new Harlem–Bronx section. The Bronx had recently become a separate county, and Hagerty got to know Ed Flynn, the Bronx leader. Flynn was not only the most potent Democratic political boss in the state but also in the country. The only reporter he talked to was Hagerty.

Hagerty came to *The Times* in 1920, when the publisher Frank Munsey bought the *Herald*. Four years later, he sold it to the *Tribune,* and the newly merged *Herald Tribune* eventually became *The Times*'s chief competitor. Hagerty scored so many scoops while covering the 1932 Democratic presidential convention in Chicago at which Roosevelt was nominated that the *Herald Tribune* sent its bureau chief a desperate wire that arrived at *The Times* office by mistake. "*The Times* has beaten us again on everything tonight," the wire said. "Can't you do something?" It was Hagerty, however, who did something. He discovered that a California–Texas switch to Roosevelt had been fixed so that Roosevelt would be nominated that night, giving *The Times* yet another scoop.

The city-room audience for the current election-night display included the after-dinner guests of Arthur Hays Sulzberger and his wife, Iphigene. The Sulzbergers enjoyed showing off the city room when it was operating at full tilt, and their guests seemed delighted to witness the making of the newspaper they would read at breakfast only a few hours later. We in the city room, aware we were onstage, enjoyed it too, shouting a bit louder than usual, dashing about a bit more purposefully.

Sulzberger often dropped into the city room at night to chat with Raymond McCaw, but this was the first time I saw him close-up. In his early fifties, he was handsome and charming enough to be taken for the kind of movie star who might have played opposite Madeleine Carroll: ruddy-complected, with alert blue eyes, a strong jaw, graying hair parted just slightly off-center, and a lean, determinedly erect carriage.

Iphigene was Adolph Ochs's only child, and when Arthur Sulzberger married her during World War I, he was destined to succeed his father-in-law as publisher. Iphigene, who had dark hair and a slim, distinguished bearing, was hardly ever seen in the city room. That election night she seemed shy. But as I discovered years later, she was not at all as she had appeared. In public she never stepped to center stage. Privately, she was strong-willed with a firm social conscience, and did not hesitate to phone me and other editors with suggestions for story ideas, especially concerning philanthropic causes and her pet project, the preservation of the city's parks.

She grew up with an unfaltering adoration of *The Times,* and if her possessive, Victorian-minded father had not been convinced that journalism was a career unsuitable for women, she surely would have worked at the paper following her graduation from Barnard, where she majored in history. She met Arthur Sulzberger while he was a student at Columbia and, some time later, they began their courtship—Iphigene taken with Arthur's self-confidence and humor, and he with her wit and intellect.

Arthur Hays Sulzberger had been born into a prosperous Jewish New York family with pre–Revolutionary War roots on his mother's side, and joined his father's thriving cotton goods business after college. At first, Adolph Ochs opposed the marriage, but he finally gave his consent on condition that Arthur leave his father's business and join *The Times.* It was his way of solving the problem of his succession.

Sulzberger learned from his father-in-law how to run the paper and protect its traditions. When Ochs died in 1935, Sulzberger, at forty-four, took full control of the paper, not only upholding Ochs's standards with a strong hand but also imposing his own ideas with a self-assurance quickly noted by city-room editors as well as the paper's business department executives.

In an editorial eulogizing Ochs, Sulzberger wrote: "I pray that some of the qualities of heart and mind which he possessed in such amazing strength may be vouchsafed to me, and that I may never depart from the principles of honest and impersonal journalism which he, with such force and courage, impressed upon our land." He assured his readers he had inherited Ochs's strong opposition to crusading journalism: "With a crusading editorial policy you run a risk of wrecking impartiality in the news columns. Without realizing it, reporters would look for that issue in the story they were covering and neglect other factors equally important."

Besides the visit by the Sulzbergers on election night, a welcome diversion for the staff was the $1 office pool. The participant whose estimate came closest to the actual plurality of New York State votes cast for the winning candidate would be proclaimed the victor. Hagerty invariably won the pool and donated his winnings to the copyboys, to be split among them. But this time the winner was a newly hired rewrite man, Douglas Dales, who later spent many years as head of our Albany bureau. Like Hagerty, he was a shrewd observer of state politics, and he guessed the plurality would be 315,000—only 1,013 votes less than the actual total. Dales, too, gave his winnings to the copyboys.

After Krock and Hagerty had evaluated the election results, the editors sent the signal to the Times Square zipper sign: "THE NEW YORK TIMES ANNOUNCED AT MIDNIGHT THE PROBABLE ELECTION OF PRESIDENT ROOSEVELT FOR A FOURTH TERM." From the open windows of the city room I could hear the jubilant collective roar of thousands in the square.

At 3:15 A.M., Dewey conceded Roosevelt's reelection, and at five o'clock the paper was put to bed. The election staff staggered to their homes or hotels to catch a few hours of sleep, and that was when *Timesweek*'s staff went to work. Fortifying ourselves with coffee and doughnuts, we took over a corner of the city room, reveling in our own small-scale duplication of the previous hours' frenzy.

John Meixner and Donald Paneth, a star *Timesweek* reporter, speedily typed out their front-page pieces. Gene Davis and I grabbed their copy for editing page by page and composed the headlines. At noon the next day our election issue was distributed around the city room. We reported not only on the coverage of the presidential election—including the staff's ravenous consumption of "1,800 sandwiches, made of liverwurst, bologna, salami, Spam, roast beef, chicken, and egg salad"—but also on the Democratic battle to unseat the Republican, Clare Boothe Luce (wife of Henry Luce of *Time*), as the congressional representative from Connecticut's Fairfield County.

A telegraphed dispatch from Hartford, where Luce's victory had been predicted, arrived just before the third edition, carrying the report that she was trailing by 300 votes. But she finally prevailed and we wrote that Arthur Krock "got the news soon enough" to change his front-page lead story for the last edition to include the fact that Roosevelt had been wrong in rejoicing earlier in Mrs. Luce's defeat.

Collapsing in a chair to steal some sleep, I wasn't thinking about Roosevelt or Clare Boothe Luce, and certainly not about liverwurst sandwiches. All I could think about was that we had pulled off our high-wire act.

THAT SEPTEMBER, still not having heard from my draft board, I signed up for college classes. My mother was pleased, but my own heart wasn't in it. My life now was at *The Times,* not in a classroom. I loved being a member of the large, eccentric *Times* family. Attuned to its jittery pace, I wouldn't for anything have traded my role, however minor, in getting the paper out. The notion of sitting in a lecture hall again was as appealing as doing sit-ups— good for me but tedious.

Following Grover Loud's advice, I had jettisoned the idea of going back to CCNY, knowing I wouldn't be able to keep up with its rigorous academic demands while also working full-time. I enrolled instead at New York University in Greenwich Village. Unlike CCNY, NYU charged tuition, which I had to pay out of my meager salary. At times, I felt I was buying a diploma; though NYU is now an esteemed school with high academic standards, it was known then as a place you could glide through. Work at C level could get you a B or even an A, which was exactly what I had in mind.

Being back at school wasn't quite as dull as I had dreaded. While CCNY's faculty had been for the most part formal and distant, my professors at NYU were friendly and approachable, easy to chat with after classes or even to join for coffee at a nearby café. Although my courses, mostly literature and politics, were not uninteresting, I attended classes only for major lectures and to hand in papers. I didn't mingle much with the other students, since campus life seemed shallow to me. I had already begun my professional life, while most undergraduates were on the thresholds of theirs.

If I had an hour or two to kill between classes I explored the Village's crooked streets, stopping for a beer and a bacon-and-egg sandwich at a snug saloon on Sheridan Square called Louie's. I was a literature junkie, in love with writers and the idea of writing, so I paid dreamy homage at the houses where some of my idols had lived and worked: the brownstone at 60 Washington Square where Willa Cather and Theodore Dreiser had rented flats, and a neighboring brownstone that had housed both John Reed and Lincoln Steffens, whose muckraking radicalism captivated me as far back as high school. I traced the footsteps of e. e. cummings and Edna St. Vincent Millay and, on the west side of the square, found the site of the vanished rooming house of Eugene O'Neill, whose plays I had eagerly borrowed from the library.

Café Society, on Sheridan Square off Christopher Street, became my Village oasis on my nights off from *The Times*. The club had been opened a few years earlier by Barney Josephson, a left-leaning impresario who couldn't abide the segregation in midtown cabarets. Benny Goodman, likewise fed up with color barriers in entertainment, invested $5,000 in the club, which welcomed blacks in the audience as well as onstage. Billie Holiday had first sung "Strange Fruit" at Café Society, and Josephson had persuaded Lena Horne to drop "When It's Sleepytime Down South" from her repertoire, a song he felt was demeaning.

The club was a favorite with young intellectuals who shared the avant-garde outlook of many of its performers, but none of my friends went there. I happened on it by chance, and found it a welcoming refuge. There wasn't a middle-aged tourist in sight, which was quite a contrast with the midtown clubs.

As a teenager, I'd been a regular customer at a small record shop on the Grand Concourse, whose young husband-and-wife owners had made me a passionate fan of folk ballads, jazz and blues. "Listen to Woody Guthrie," the wife told me one day. "He sings songs with his guitar in a kind of talking rhythmic patter." And she played Guthrie's "Talkin' Dust Bowl Blues." It was here, on another idle afternoon, that I first heard Paul Robeson's majestic voice. Soon I had a sizable collection of 78s stacked in piles under my bed and had started a neighborhood craze for the prison songs of Huddie Ledbetter, known as Leadbelly, that he performed with the Golden Gate Quartet; the Revolutionary War ballads of John and Lucy Allison, and Joseph Marais's songs of the South African veld.

Café Society was a haven for fans of blues and folk music. At last, I was hearing in person some of the singers I'd listened to on my 78s: Josh White's melancholy chain-gang songs and Burl Ives's poignant American folk songs and traditional English ballads.

How could one year encompass so many events? For weeks after D-Day, many of those in the city room continued to stay up all night to track the battle news from Europe and the Pacific. *Timesweek* gave me an excuse to stay through some of the nights too, watching editors and rewrite men working at top form as they rushed to give readers news of the V-2 rocket attacks on London, the liberation of Paris, the Battle of the Bulge. I hated going home, afraid I'd miss something.

And what wasn't happening inside the building was happening just outside. New Year's Eve 1944 was my first in Times Square. A half-hour before midnight I bolted from the office and joined the crowd, whose random shouts and noisemakers I had been hearing all evening. I was there not only to do requested legwork for the reporters, picking up quotes and color, but also as a happy member of the mob.

The evening's drizzle had stopped, leaving the air unseasonably muggy. Five minutes before 1945 arrived, a radio announcer broadcast a request that the thousands in the Square sing the national anthem, so that the "boys on the far-flung battlefields may hear us." I sang too, moved to be part of the vast chorus. A few in the crowd looked up when flashbulbs from photographers on the catwalk above the zipper sign began popping, but most kept their eyes straight ahead as they sang, unwilling to sully the moment.

We sang for those killed in action, and to show our support for a war meant to keep us free. D-Day had given us reason to hope, but we had lost many thousands of young men and knew we would lose many more. Then the zipper flashed out the paper's message from the Times Tower: "IT IS NOW 12 O'CLOCK. THE NEW YEAR IS HERE. LET US MAKE IT A YEAR OF VICTORY. LET US NOW PLEDGE OURSELVES TO GET ON WITH THE JOB SO THAT THOSE WE LOVE MAY SOON BE HERE WITH US AGAIN."

The lighted ball floated down from the tower for the first time in two years, followed by the riotous bleating of horns, and en masse smooching.

A couple of weeks after the New Year, Edwin James suggested that I might want to do a story for *Timesweek* about a speech he planned to deliver to the New York State Publishers Association. I was glad I did take note of his speech, for he expressed forcefully some of the concerns about war coverage that all of us in the city room had been discussing. But I was puzzled about one aspect of James's talk, which ran counter to what I had been hearing. James, like many of the top editors in the press, did not object to most instances of military censorship; acutely aware of the harrowing consequences should Hitler prevail, editors generally cooperated with the government in withholding any information that would give the enemy an advantage.

James's point was that this war's censorship was "infinitely more intelligent" than that of World War I, when mention of American casualties was banned. "We could kill a million Germans before breakfast," he continued, "but we could never mention that an American had received a scratch. That of course was quite stupid and accounted for the terrific shock to the country when General Pershing's first casualty list of 35,000 came through."

The correspondents in the field generally did not agree with James's line of thought. Foster Hailey, a respected *Times* editorial writer, spoke for many correspondents when he addressed a group of schoolteachers in a *Times* auditorium and lashed out at the excesses of censorship. "Censorship sharply curtails during wartime one of the attributes of the good reporter, the inquiring mind," he said. "After you have met several rebuffs from gold-braided officials from whom you have sought information or had ruthlessly eliminated from your copy facts you have spent much time searching out or, perhaps, have risked your life to get, you are often inclined to say, the hell with it all, and write only what you are told in the communiqués or what you are pretty sure will get by. When you reach that stage, it's time to come home. Fortunately for the American public, or it would not have had as much information as it has had, the majority decided they didn't like censorship of any variety, even the American, and have continued to fight it out on every battlefront."

Anne O'Hare McCormick, who had returned to New York in February 1945 after a six-month tour of the Western Front to collect material for her editorial page columns, was one of the most outspoken on the subject. The foreign correspondent, she said in a speech, is "an up-to-the-minute reporter struggling in a slowed-down, broken-down world." As an example, she cited her coverage of a press conference given by General Eisenhower, at which he specifically asked reporters to quote him, because he wanted to send a message to Americans at home. It took three days for the censors to clear the words that the supreme commander himself wanted published. Moreover, the censors arbitrarily deleted innocuous background material Mrs. McCormick had written to give Eisenhower's message a context.

The incongruity was that many censors in the armed forces had been newspapermen in civilian life. One of them, Will Weng, a copy editor on *The Times*'s city desk drafted into the Navy (and who years later became the crossword puzzle editor), recently had written a letter to *Timesweek* that took a more ironic view of the censorship controversy: "If there had been no censors around, the correspondents would have had no one to blame for the lousy stories they wrote. As it was, they could always explain that censorship had ruined what originally was a masterpiece."

While I could comprehend the difficulties of being a war correspondent, it never occurred to me that anyone would regard the job as tedious. But Warren Moscow, a *Times* correspondent in Guam, soon to return to his city-room political beat, wrote, in a piece I ordered for *Timesweek,* that he was "just plain bored."

"Did I say 'plain' bored? That is an error. I will back the Guam type of boredom against any around." His chief complaint was that correspondents were spoon-fed stories by an Army public relations officer, who thwarted interviews with pilots returning from sorties. Attempts to garner facts from primary sources were quashed. This situation might have been bearable, said Moscow, if the bar on the base stayed open all day and served a better grade of spirits. Moscow was grateful to return to New York, where he could once again do "some real reporting and some real drinking."

ANTICIPATING THE END of the long war in Europe, Arthur Hays Sulzberger began planning a *Times* that could deal with the complexities of a new era. This postwar *Times* would have to be strictly on its toes: better run, better written, better-looking. The paper would need additional bureaus both in this country and abroad, with correspondents ever more attuned to the political, social and economic nuances of the areas they covered. And more emphasis on photography would be required, particularly in a world that was soon to introduce television.

In December, Sulzberger had named Turner Catledge, the forty-three-year-old national correspondent, as assistant managing editor, so that he would be directly in line to replace James, who was thinking of retiring. Sulzberger completed his blueprint for succession by appointing James B. Reston, one of the paper's most respected correspondents, who had served in the London and Washington bureaus, to succeed Catledge as national correspondent based in the capital.

Sulzberger had come to appreciate the advice and wisdom of both Catledge and Reston, who was nine years younger than the new assistant managing editor. He had toured battle areas with each of them—with Reston in Moscow and with Catledge in the Pacific—and had found both of them compatible traveling companions. Though few of us had any inkling at the time, these were the seeds of change that would, in the decades to come, reshape the paper and assure its ability to compete.

Catledge's honeyed southern accent and cherubic face belied a steely will. He had a knack for mimicry and his lively anecdotes about newspaper and political friends, past and present, amused the publisher. While still in school, Catledge had assisted printers at the *Neshoba Democrat,* a hand-set weekly in his hometown of Philadelphia, Mississippi. After graduating from Mississippi State University, he worked on a series of small papers in the South and, at twenty-six, was a star reporter for the Memphis *Commercial Appeal.*

In the spring of 1927 he covered the disastrous Mississippi River flood, and Herbert Hoover, then secretary of commerce, sought Catledge's advice about flood relief. Catledge so impressed Hoover that he wrote to Adolph Ochs, suggesting *The Times* hire him. But Catledge went to the *Baltimore Sun* instead, and did not join *The Times* until two years later, in the spring of 1929.

As a correspondent in the *Times* Washington bureau, Catledge gradually accumulated more sources in the seats of power than even Arthur Krock. Catledge covered every kind of assignment from the White House to Congress, the Supreme Court and various governmental agencies. His insider's book, written with Joseph Alsop of the *Herald Tribune* and called *The 168 Days,* about President Roosevelt's attempt to pack the Supreme Court in 1937, was essential Washington reading, filled with tales of clandestine political shenanigans.

In 1941, Catledge was lured to the *Chicago Sun;* yet he was not happy in his post as chief correspondent and later editor in chief there. "I was attuned to *The Times* and its way of doing things," he said, and less than two years later, he gladly accepted an offer to return to *The Times* in the newly created post of national correspondent, under Arthur Krock. His headquarters was Washington but there were no boundaries to his coverage. He regarded the assignment as the most strategic on the paper.

National news was beginning to dominate journalism, he said when I interviewed him for *Timesweek.* When he first joined *The Times,* he explained, "Washington was nothing like it is today; New York was the center of the country in every way except for being the seat of the government. But since the New Deal, more and more national functions have moved there, and today one-fifth of *The Times*'s coverage is devoted to Washington news."

Sulzberger might have chosen Reston as James's heir, but he saw him, rather, as the eventual successor to Krock. To run the paper, he valued

Catledge for his longer experience. Besides, he was more comfortable in Catledge's company, prizing him as a good storyteller and sharing his fondness for bourbon and Scotch.

Reston had won the Pulitzer Prize in 1945 for a coup much envied by competing journalists—a series of exclusive stories revealing the secret proposals for the United Nations Charter that were being hammered out by the United States, England, the Soviet Union, France and China at a conference at Dumbarton Oaks, a mansion in Georgetown. No one at the time knew Reston's obviously impeccable source (identified years later in his memoir as a Nationalist Chinese delegate he had met through the Sulzbergers) and, driving the world's press up the wall, he filed one fact-studded daily page-one exclusive report after another as the conference progressed.

Grover Loud, after editing one of Reston's Dumbarton Oaks dispatches, suggested I study it as "a lesson in flawless, crystal-clear newspaper writing." When Reston visited the telegraph desk shortly thereafter to express his appreciation for the delicate handling of his stories, I was glad to see he was a far cry from the autocratic Arthur Krock. Looking relaxed in his tweed sports jacket, speaking softly and puffing on his pipe, he put me at ease when Mr. Fairbanks introduced us. He volunteered a kind word for *Timesweek* and took the time to answer a few questions for our next issue.

Like Catledge, Reston had a book to his credit—*Prelude to Victory,* a popular account of the war. Born in Scotland, he had been raised in poverty and crossed the Atlantic in steerage with his parents when he was eleven. While attending high school in Dayton, Ohio, he covered sports for a local daily. After graduating from the University of Illinois, he began working for the AP in New York, and in 1939 he joined *The Times's* London bureau. Two years later, he was transferred to Washington, where everyone in the bureau felt privileged to call him "Scotty."

IN EARLY 1945, Sulzberger also made a startling change in the paper's war coverage, sending two women abroad as correspondents in addition to Anne O'Hare McCormick, who had been filing her columns from the front since July 1944. They were Kathleen McLaughlin, assigned to Supreme Allied Headquarters in London, and Virginia Lee Warren, who joined her husband, Milton Bracker, in the Rome bureau.

Hitler's collapse seemed increasingly imminent, and once again the *Times* city room was staffed around the clock as Allied forces pounded their way into Germany. But our exhilaration about battles won—especially General Patton's heroic crossing of the Rhine on March 23—turned to shock when, a week later, Allied soldiers reached the first of the German concentration camps and invited American reporters to witness the inhuman horrors that the Nazis had wrought.

The coverage of the liberation was frustratingly inconsistent from the start. *The Times* and other papers had already reported on the Russian liberation in August 1944 of the Majdanek extermination camp in Poland, with its gas chambers and crematoria, and the paper had given page-one display as well to the death camp at Auschwitz. While Jews were predominant among the inmates, they weren't singled out as victims until the story jumped to an inside page. Even in the most detailed account thus far of the German atrocities—related in a story that started at the bottom of page one on November 26—the "millions of innocent civilians" who were "systematically murdered" in the death camps were reported to be "Jews and Christians alike."

And now, with the liberation by American soldiers of the camps in Germany, descriptions of barbarism trickled out day by day, one horrifying revelation following upon another. Many Americans began to feel they had not been adequately informed over the years by their newspapers about the torture and slaughter of innocent people who, as it turned out, were mostly Jews.

Indeed, by any journalistic measure, most of the early reports in *The Times* were insufficient. Unfortunately, the country's mainstream press generally followed *The Times*'s lead. To my dismay and that of many of my colleagues, the stories about the American liberation of prisoners that began appearing in early spring of 1945—with only a couple of exceptions—were not displayed on the front page. And there was scarcely any attempt early on to put into perspective what was emerging as the genocidal epic of modern times.

Among the most egregious examples of news misjudgment by *The Times* was the story it ran on April 13 announcing that American troops of the Third Army had freed the inmates at Buchenwald. *The Times* used only three brief paragraphs from the AP dispatch, which was placed at the bottom of page eleven among several other short items, including one headed "War Dog Honored Here."

It was as though the top editors, in the beginning at least, simply could not bring themselves to entirely accept the reports filed by seasoned war correspondents. Since the stories tended to describe the liberated inmates as "victims" and "prisoners," rarely as "Jews," many of us in the city room simply couldn't fathom what was in the minds of our editors. One or two of the established reporters—even though aware that in those days a decision made by a top editor was understood to be unassailable—did try to elicit an answer to the inscrutable news judgment. Pat Spiegel for one told me he actually received a partial explanation from an assistant foreign editor, who said the paper had to proceed with caution for fear the reports might be exaggerated. "Remember what was falsely reported about German soldiers bayoneting babies in World War I," he told Pat.

Readers of *The Times* expressed their outrage and five days later, on April 18, the paper finally gave the coverage of Buchenwald the two columns of space it deserved, even though the story received only a modest display on page one below the fold. It was an eyewitness account of unbelievable cruelty unmasked with excruciating detail by our correspondent Gene Currivan, who had been traveling with Patton's Third Army.

Currivan described the "gallows, torture rooms, dissection rooms, modern crematoria [manufactured, Currivan pointed out, by the same company that provided German bakers with their ovens], laboratories where fiendish experiments were made on living human beings and sections where people were systematically starved to death," as well as such items as table lamps with parchment shades made of human skin.

But even in this devastating account, none of the "prisoners" were identified as Jews until, far down in the story, a nine-year-old Hungarian Jewish boy, part of a typhus experiment, told Currivan he had been in the camp three years. When asked where his parents were, he said without emotion, "My father was killed and my mother was burned to death."

What I found incomprehensible was the stunted editorial the following day. I opened the paper expecting a cry of anger, but the hollow editorial— the third in sequence on the page—contained only three brief paragraphs, with no mention of Jewish victims. Equally disturbing was the reserved manner in which the paper, two weeks later (April 26), handled its second account of Nazi extermination strategy at Buchenwald—although this eyewitness report had been filed by *The Times*'s own general manager, Julius Ochs Adler, a nephew of Adolph S. Ochs. The gruesome facts obviously belonged on page one, but they appeared instead under a constrained single-column headline on page six that read: "Buchenwald Worse Than Battlefield."

Adler, a retired Army general who had received a medical discharge after four years of active service, was among a group of top newspaper executives invited by General Eisenhower to survey the liberated camps. Apparently surprised by the paucity of continuing press coverage, Eisenhower wanted the executives to witness the barbarism for themselves.

"The story of Buchenwald has been told," Adler wrote, "but it cannot be told too often to the people of the United States. The skinny corpses of Buchenwald should remind us of what the loss of human freedom entails." About halfway through the story, Jews were mentioned as being among the victims: a "half-dead Polish Jew" told Adler about prisoners in midwinter forced to stand under a hose for half an hour. Adler witnessed "corpses piled in squares with twenty to twenty-four bodies in each square" who "had starved to death."

The Times continued giving only cautious display to the stories that followed, even when a group of congressmen officially verified the reports after touring Buchenwald in late April; a seven-paragraph story on page five quoted the influential Representative Henry M. Jackson of Washington, who described the camp's atrocities as "the most sordid I have ever imagined."

Times readers erupted and, on May 1, the story of the liberation of Dachau by American troops made it onto page one—although it was anchored at the bottom of the page. But as had become something of a ritual, nowhere did the word "Jew" appear; the freed inmates were described as "Russians, Poles, Frenchmen, Czechs and Austrians."

The next day, however, an article appeared on page nine, written (but not signed) by Pat Spiegel, that made specific reference to the mass murder of Jews in the concentration camps. Pat, who told me he had gathered the details of his story from sources on his Jewish beat, fought to keep his own emotions from spilling into his copy, and thus managed to produce a column-length factual liturgy of the Jewish slaughter that was left virtually intact by the desk editors.

The story presented an early estimate that "more than 3 million men, women and children of the Jewish faith" (a figure that not long after was amended to 6 million) had been exterminated: "Hitler's all-European pogrom against the Jews, whom he held responsible for Germany's plight and for the woes of the world, marked the greatest catastrophe in the history of the Jewish people. Even Jews in the most advanced countries of Europe did not escape. In France, Holland, Belgium, Norway, Denmark, wherever the heel of the Nazi conqueror was planted the Jews suffered the fate imposed upon them in Germany. They were his first victims and remained his most hated enemies to the last."

It was clearly the kind of story that should have evoked a powerful commentary on the editorial page. But nothing appeared. In my own mind, over the years, I periodically returned to the question of why *The Times* had failed to take a strong editorial position on the early reports of the death camps. I had learned by 1945 from Jewish reporters on the staff that Arthur Hays Sulzberger had serious conflicts about his Jewish roots, believing that Judaism was a religion and not a national or ethnic identity. As a result, he opposed the American Zionist movement for a Jewish homeland in Palestine. He was uncomfortable when reporters dwelled too long on the Jewish backgrounds of personalities who figured in their stories. And it was only a year before I arrived at the paper that Sulzberger had complied with the district attorney's warning that it was illegal to publish real estate ads for house sales or rentals in neighborhoods described as "restricted," the code word for the barring of Jews.

In 1993, shortly after the United States Holocaust Memorial Museum opened in Washington (by which time I had become president of The New York Times Foundation), I was having dinner with Arthur (Punch) Sulzberger, who had succeeded his father as publisher. We had both made it a point to visit the museum and had been disturbed by the display of *The Times*'s scanty initial reports of the Jewish slaughter in the death camps. Why had a newspaper published by Jews given such short shrift to German inhumanity against Jews? What had his father and the editors been thinking? Punch was genuinely upset. He did not suffer from his father's insecurities about being Jewish, and he was flabbergasted by what could only be regarded as a nadir of *Times* news coverage and commentary. In no way could this have occurred on Punch's watch.

Very possibly, Arthur Hays Sulzberger was haunted by the events that had sent his father-in-law, Adolph Ochs, into a nervous breakdown in 1916. Long before coming north to buy *The New York Times,* Ochs had been a thoroughly assimilated southerner as publisher of the *Chattanooga Times.* And as publisher of *The New York Times,* Ochs, from the start, set an example of shying away from Jewish causes, always wary of calling attention to his own ethnic origins. It was he who determined that *The Times* must never be viewed as a "Jewish paper," which he believed would undermine its image as an objective source of news.

Uncharacteristically, he allowed himself and *The Times* to become deeply embroiled in a cause célèbre in 1913, involving the murder of a fourteen-year-old female employee of the National Pencil Company in Atlanta. When Leo Frank, the Jewish manager of the factory, was convicted of the crime and sentenced to death, Ochs, convinced that Frank had been railroaded, used *The Times* to drum up support for an appeal. Georgia's governor commuted the sentence to life imprisonment but, ultimately, a lynch mob hanged Frank. Ochs's worst nightmare became reality. *The Times* was widely accused of taking up Frank's cause because he was Jewish and because *The Times* was, indeed, a "Jewish paper." Clearly, Sulzberger wanted no such reprise.

FIVE MINUTES AFTER I arrived at work at 4:30 p.m. on April 12, amid reports of concentration camp atrocities and news about our army's advances toward Berlin, a brief bulletin announcing the death of President Roosevelt cast a pall over the city room. He had been visiting his retreat in Warm Springs, Georgia, when he was stricken by a massive cerebral hemorrhage. His last words, we were informed, were, "I have a terrific headache." Vice President Truman was sworn in as president a few hours later.

In the month before Roosevelt died, my friends and I had noticed how weary he looked in the photos arriving in the city room. When he addressed Congress after returning from the Yalta conference, he delivered his speech sitting down, for the first time; he asked Congress's pardon, explaining it was easier for him "not having to carry about ten pounds of steel around the bottom of my legs." This was the only time he talked about the braces he had been obliged to wear since having contracted polio.

Many of us were in tears, mourning a man we regarded as a true hero. We were struck by the irony of the timing, for at that very moment the American Army was crossing the Elbe, with Berlin only fifty miles distant. Roosevelt was not to savor the European war's victorious end. And, along with many of my colleagues, I worried about Truman. Was he resolute enough to finish the war with Japan? And what kind of postwar leader would he be?

Good news poured in from Europe by the hour. On April 29, word spread throughout the city room that *The Times* had achieved an amazing coup: Benito Mussolini had been executed that morning, and Dan Brigham, our man in Bern, obtained exclusive photos of the grisly event.

"Boy, oh boy, what a picture!" Brigham had shouted over the phone when he got through to the New York office. The images were radiophotoed by 11:30 that night and were in *The Times*'s darkroom for printing fifteen minutes later. I waited at the paper until the closing of the second edition—the earliest that the pictures could be published.

There they were, clearer and more gruesome than I'd imagined: On page one, with McCaw's caption, "Inglorious end of a dictator," were the battered bodies of Mussolini and his mistress, Clara Petacci, lying side by side, surrounded by armed Italian partisans; they had been executed and their corpses pummeled in a square in Milan.

Inside, on page three, were two more pictures—one of Mussolini's and Petacci's bodies hanging upside down from a gas station girder, and one of a general being led to his execution. The photographs were published world-wide, thanks to Arthur Sulzberger, who responded instantly to the flood of requests to purchase them. He announced that *The Times* would give them without charge to any publication that wanted them. "I think it will be a public service to give them maximum circulation," he said.

The story behind the pictures was the talk of the city room in the days that followed, a tale of journalistic adventure. The Italian photographer who had taken them hitchhiked from Milan to the Italian–Swiss border, where he had put them on a train to Bern; after picking them up, Brigham drove 125 miles on narrow, slippery mountain roads in a blinding blizzard to Geneva, the only place in Switzerland from where the pictures could be transmitted. *Timesweek* managed to squeeze a short story about the caper onto the first page of the issue just before it went to press.

On April 30, 1945, the city room greeted the bulletins announcing that Hitler had taken his own life—an event celebrated by Sammy Solovitz with an impromptu jig on Mike Berger's desk. It took a while for the stunning news to sink in. Hitler, who had epitomized evil to my family and friends since my early childhood, who had terrified us over the years with his guttural pronouncements of victory, was dead at last.

On May 7, the German military leaders signed the unconditional surrender in a little French schoolhouse in Reims. The city room received official word of the surrender early in the day. Within minutes, the entire staff, from the most senior editors to every last copyboy, fled the building for the V-E Day festivities in Times Square. The daytime city room—as far as I know for the only time in the paper's history—was deserted.

I suddenly was overcome with a wish to be with my parents, to share with them this glorious moment that had long been in our prayers. Always, just below the surface, was my consciousness of the heartaches endured by them as they had periodically received reports of the imprisonment and death of the brothers and sisters they had left behind in Europe.

I hurried to Madison Avenue and Sixty-seventh Street, to where my parents had recently moved their dress shop from the Grand Concourse. I found them in the store listening to the radio bulletins. When my mother saw me, she wept uncontrollably, expressing joy and releasing sorrow with the same tears. My father and I tried to comfort her, and I thought it would soothe us all to bond with other New Yorkers. I persuaded my parents to close the store and come with me to Times Square.

We watched in astonishment as hordes converged on the square from office buildings and movie houses. The sound was unbelievable—whistles, whooping, cheering. Paper flung from windows swirled in the air like pillow feathers, in defiance of Mayor La Guardia's pleas by loudspeaker not to waste the precious commodity while the country was still at war with Japan. People danced in conga lines, stood on their heads, kissed and hugged strangers.

"I want all the people who have thoughtlessly left their jobs to return to their jobs," La Guardia scolded, "and not to do it again." The crowd ignored this second directive and continued to swell. My parents, considerably cheered, finally went home to the Bronx. (They had been unable to find a place to live near their new store, because of the severe wartime shortage of apartments.)

I returned to the city room, but I have no recollection of how *The Times* got published that day. Nor do I remember why we didn't make more of that extraordinary celebration in our June issue of *Timesweek*—unless, possibly, we considered it old news by the time the edition went to press. *Timesweek* may have missed the boat in its coverage of the V-E Day celebration, but we did better with our stories about two of the first correspondents to return from the war. Gene Currivan's and Harold Denny's overseas dispatches had dominated *The Times*'s front page for several years.

In March, Currivan had written a letter to Mike Berger from Germany that was passed around the city room: "It seems strange, but you never get used to shellfire. I've been up against everything the Germans could dream up, including V-2's, dive bombers, mines, snipers and all the rest, but artillery gets me down. I don't mean that those other things don't scare me, but I became accustomed to them to some degree. Frankly, I'm all worn out. I'm really tired mentally and physically and I think my copy is beginning to show it." When he returned in late May, I interviewed him for *Timesweek* about his travels with Patton's Third Army in its epic drive through France, Germany and Austria to its linkup with the Russians as they advanced into Berlin.

In the same issue we announced Harold Denny's return. He looked snappy in his immaculately pressed correspondent's uniform as he made his way through the city room to greet Ted Bernstein and the other men at the cable desk who had edited his copy. At fifty-six, he had been chasing world conflicts for two decades—in Morocco, Nicaragua, Cuba. In Europe, he had barely escaped capture by the Germans near Malmedy, when he "left a little town by one road and they came in from another." Fueled by the drama of combat, Denny had no domestic life, and essentially no home.

"I wish I could live in America," he confided to city-room friends, "but I'm afraid I wouldn't know how to." He had been captured once by Germany's Afrika Korps and held prisoner for six months. The caption on a German photograph of him read, "A correspondent who will send no more dispatches." "I wanted to go to Berlin and file from there," he said. "That would have been very satisfactory revenge. I was sore when politics kept us from marching in."

A short time later, Denny, who had been away from the country virtually all his adult life, returned for a visit to Iowa, his home state, where he died of a heart attack. But he left behind his own epitaph—in the form of a testimonial he had pasted onto one of the two typewriters he brought back from Europe: "This typewriter fought its way through the Normandy beachhead, St. Lo, Paris, Belgium, the Siegfried Line, the Ruhr River valley and the Rhineland; it captured Leipzig and got drunk with the Russians at Torgau on the Elbe. It was wounded in action in the German dive-bombing of the First Army press camp near Liege on Dec. 23, 1944. It thus rates five campaign stars and the Purple Heart."

Now that the country was bent on defeating Japan, there was a call for more draftees, and the small "limited service" quota—the category to which I had been assigned—was suddenly raised. Abruptly, my draft board in the Bronx was no longer concerned about my poor eyesight and at last, in early July, summoned me for induction into the Army. My *Timesweek* colleagues threw a party for me at Childs the day before I was to leave.

I said good-bye to my friends in the city room. But the next day, when I appeared at my draft board to be briefed about my departure, I was notified that the Selective Service administrators—for reasons I will never know—had, that very morning, reinstated the original limited service quota. I was told I would not be called up for at least six more months.

During the next two years, I was summoned twice more by my draft board. On each occasion, when I reported for duty, I was informed that my category had just been filled. As Joseph Heller, who later became my good friend, might have said (and often did), Go figure.

SEVEN

WHEN THE CITY ROOM finally quieted down a few days after V-E Day, Jack Tell, recently a copyboy and now a clerk on the picture desk, handed me a piece of paper. "I thought you might want to run this," he said.

My fellow *Timesweek* editors and I had put the word out around the city room that we needed additional reporters, and Tell was one of the first to respond. What he gave me was a poem, which began: "That face of joy, who answers to 'boy!' / Is really a decent chap / He's yours to command, please don't reprimand / Consider him not a 'sap.'"

Jack Tell was not a man you felt comfortable turning down. Thickset and with a permanent five-o'clock shadow, he looked vaguely menacing. He was ten years older than the rest of us clerks and news assistants, and usually wore a double-breasted suit, no matter how warm the day. He walked with a slight swagger, spoke out of the side of his mouth and was a habitué of the racetrack.

I told him I would think about his poem, and every day for a week he stopped by my desk to ask me what I had decided. Worn down, I said I would run it. During these visits he told me he was a "dese, dem and dose kind of guy" who was seeking self-improvement. His dream was to write for *The Times*. If he tried his hand at a few *Timesweek* pieces, would I go over his copy and give him some pointers? I was touched by his ambition. And so we began our sessions, Jack sitting by patiently while I combed through his prose. After I had wrestled it into some sort of shape, he would ask me what books he should be reading.

Between tutorials, he filled me in on his background. He said he had managed the International Casino in Philadelphia in the 1930s, and had owned a few nightclubs as well, including Mother Kelly's in Saratoga Springs. He had also operated pinball concessions at the 1939–1940 New York World's Fair. Green as I was, I knew that such careers were sometimes conducted to the left of the law, and I was beguiled. Here was a character straight out of Damon Runyon. Jack Tell even spoke in a Runyonesque patois—palooka, scram, scratch, plug. I started taking surreptitious notes on what he said, thinking he'd make a terrific character in a play.

"Come on," Jack said as his shift ended one midnight. "I want you to meet a friend of mine." We walked the few blocks north along Broadway to Forty-eighth Street, then turned east. On the way, he told me about his friend, Eddie Jaffe, a press agent. He was a nutsy little guy, said Jack, a hypochondriac and in analysis with a head doctor who didn't like him and thought he should get into a more respectable line of work.

But in spite of everything, Eddie had a sweet nature. His mother had died when he was a young child, and his father had placed him in an orphanage. Living with five hundred other deprived kids had given Eddie a compulsion to be surrounded by crowds, and he found his calling as a press agent. Jack had met him while running the hat-check concessions for Fifty-second Street clubs—the Three Deuces, Minsky's and a half-dozen others. He told me Eddie's clients included the nightclub comedian Joe E. Lewis, and Jimmie Davis, the popular troubadour who composed "You Are My Sunshine" and eventually became Louisiana's governor. But what most impressed Jack was that Eddie numbered among his clients two nationally known strippers, Ann Corio and Margie Hart.

Margie Hart, jocularly awarded a "four G-string" rating by the eminent drama critic George Jean Nathan, was also a favorite of mine. Before Mayor La Guardia outlawed burlesque in 1942, my friends from CCNY and I had attended her act at Broadway's Gaiety Theater. She revealed far more than the staged nudity I had first encountered during the World's Fair in New York, which I frequented with cut-rate tickets sold at my high school. I lied about my age to gain entrance to a sideshow where "mermaids" swam in a glass tank, wearing see-through fishnet tops. To an adolescent for whom a celluloid Rita Hayworth in a low-cut, skin-tight gown was the height of sensuality, those live, seminude mermaids gliding by, almost close enough to caress, became an ecstatically charged experience.

Margie Hart would sashay onstage in a demure picture hat and a puffy Scarlett O'Hara gown, then daintily disrobe down to her G-string. Margie credited Eddie with building her reputation. He had masterminded a four-page spread in *Life* and pulled one stunt after another that the tabloids seized upon. Trading on her Missouri farm-girl roots, he posed her in overalls and quoted her on the nation's agricultural issues, and once he drew widespread press attention by planting her in the Senate gallery, insinuating to reporters that a certain unnamed senator was gone on her.

By now Jack Tell and I had reached Eddie's place, a five-story brick building between Sixth and Seventh Avenues. Walter Winchell, the potentate of the gossip columns, whose one-liners could make or break a reputation, had lived here once, Jack said reverently, and also Winchell's buddy Runyon, and Jack Dempsey, and Ed Sullivan. On the street level was a saloon called Duffy's Tavern, once owned by a gangster named Bill Duffy, who had trained boxers in Jaffe's fifth-floor walk-up apartment.

We climbed to Eddie's quarters, up a steep, creaky wooden staircase. We were midway on the second flight when two very tall, giggling women descending from above tried to squeeze by us. They each had on big glittering paste earrings, and wore heavy stage makeup—false eyelashes, pencil-thin eyebrows, fire-engine-red lips. Their proximity was pretty intoxicating. "Have fun!" one of them purred to me as they squeezed by us. "Tootle-ooo!"

"Showgirls," muttered Jack. "Crazy dames."

Out of breath but upstairs at last, Jack opened a door to a large room. The scene inside reminded me of a kindergarten classroom, where clusters of children are simultaneously pursuing separate activities—some building block towers in one corner, some finger painting in another, a group being read aloud to in yet another. Only this was a wonderfully dissolute kindergarten, for grown-ups.

Four men in shirtsleeves played poker inside a blue cloud of cigar smoke. Two leggy girls slumped at one end of a sofa, one languidly painting the other's toenails. Two men spun wildly around on barstools against a montage of glossy photographs of showgirls. Next to the bar, sunk into the floor, was a small pond filled with fish. A man and woman in evening dress stood a few feet back from the pond, spitting olive pits into it in some kind of contest. Another group was gathered around a piano raucously singing a war ditty: "Hitler has only got one ball, Goering has two but they are small, Himmler has something sim'lar, and Goebbels has no balls at all."

Jack got us each a whiskey and led me into an adjoining room. There, propped up on pillows, looking tiny on an enormous bed strewn with papers and within easy reach of a pill-laden nightstand, was a scrawny, pallid man wearing glasses and talking on the telephone. "Terrific!" he was saying in a high, reedy voice. "It's gonna be terrific!" This was Jaffe himself, still in his early thirties. I later read that someone had dubbed Eddie "a twenty-nine-cent version of the story of mankind" and that Eddie called himself "the ugliest man alive," but to me he looked appealingly frail.

Eddie nodded pleasantly to Jack, who introduced me as "Mr. Gelb of

The New York Times." Eddie, with his press agent's instinct, responded to the name of the paper like a hunting dog to the scent of a fox. I shook his hand and told him I was a great fan of Miss Hart.

"Margie Hart," Eddie responded. "Greatest tits in show business. Sleeps with 'em on ice every night. Nice to meet you." He returned to the telephone.

I was in heaven. Here, before my eyes, were the actual guys and dolls of Runyon's demimonde. The cast of characters drank Eddie's whiskey and wolfed down platters of cold cuts sent up from the tavern below. Among the regulars were the tall girls from the Latin Quarter, who arrived between and after shows and brought Eddie terrific items to peddle to columnists; several correspondents from *Time* and *Life,* who stopped by when they were in town, bringing Eddie juicy items unfit for Henry Luce's publications; enlisted men and officers; diplomats; debutantes seeking novel ways to misbehave; actresses; models; photographers—and later, even a few reporters from *The Times,* whom Jack Tell introduced to the place and who seemed surprised and not especially pleased to find me there.

The poker-playing bunch was made up of press agents, part of a neverending flood that came to Eddie's looking for business from actresses and strippers and producers, as well as in search of a card game. Two of the regulars lived in the building, on the same floor as Eddie. Joe Russell handled Mafia nightclubs in New York and elsewhere, and was so cheap that when he had a fire in his apartment he used Eddie's phone to call the Fire Department. Jack Tirman, who represented actors and producers, was nice enough but had been known to toss the poker table out the window after being dealt a series of bad hands.

Tirman and Russell and the other agents took to me, perhaps misguidedly thinking I might be able to get something about their clients into *The Times,* and sometimes they showed me their copy. "Hey, kid," one of them asked as he pointed to a sentence, "is 'splendifleurus' a word?"

Revered by Jaffe and everyone in the building, Irving Hoffman lived on a floor below. Stocky, with an open, pleasant face, he wore the thickest glasses I'd ever seen. Because he was well-read, he was regarded as an intellectual by Jaffe's ménage. He was the senior statesman in the world of press agents and columnists, occupied a Park Avenue office and was on the payroll of just about every movie company. He not only plugged his clients in his own column in *The Hollywood Reporter,* but also wrote many of Winchell's movie items. His influence was such that he never had to court Hollywood or Broadway clients; they flocked to him. He had been known to fire clients he didn't like, which was against every press agent's religion.

It was the golden age of the Broadway gossip column. Not only Winchell but also Leonard Lyons, Ed Sullivan, Earl Wilson, Lee Mortimer, Danton Walker and Cholly Knickerbocker were having their heyday. The columnists needed items and it was the press agents who supplied them—tattle, quips, gags, rumors. And in return, the columnists provided plugs for the press agents' clients.

For every five items Winchell used, Jaffe was given one plug. When Winchell was particularly pleased with a press agent's offerings, he would pay off with an "orchid" to the press agent's client. The "orchid" was the sine qua non of plugs.

I CONTINUED TO CULTIVATE my symbiotic relationship with Jack Tell. He needed me to show him how to write and tell him what books to read, and I needed him to satisfy my enormous, indiscriminate curiosity, to educate me in the ways of Broadway nightlife.

On nights when we didn't go to Eddie's, we might pick up hot dogs at McGuiness, then stroll along Broadway to listen to a singer or some jazz quartet at one of the Fifty-second Street clubs or stop in at the "little" Lindy's at Forty-ninth and Broadway, which was the model for Mindy's in Runyon's stories (not the newer, bigger Lindy's diagonally across Broadway at Fifty-first Street).

It was at the little Lindy's—in an old, two-story structure—that Runyon, who lived nearby at Broadway's Buckingham Hotel, gorged over the years on gefilte fish, Hungarian goulash, pickled herring, corned beef, potato pancakes, smoked sturgeon and salmon and, of course, the famous cheesecake. Leo Lindemann and his wife, Clara, were ever present to care for their loyal patrons, and Runyon dubbed them "Mr. and Mrs. Broadway." When Runyon was seriously ill, Clara herself took meals to him at his hotel.

Gamblers and mobsters with a penchant for mouthwatering Jewish dishes were drawn to Lindy's, even though Clara—who had inherited the recipes from her mother—tried to discourage their patronage. No one had savored Lindy's dishes more than Arnold Rothstein, New York's number-one gambler. Known along Broadway during the 1920s as "Mr. Big," he feasted at Lindy's nightly, using his booth as an office. According to Jack Tell, Rothstein's committed attendance had so upset Clara that she had fired a cashier who was taking phone messages for the gambler. When Jack introduced me to Clara one night, she told him she was delighted he finally seemed to be in good company and was trying to make something of himself at *The Times*.

On our Broadway route, we passed the While-U-Wait photo shops, corner drugstores, penny arcades, taxi dance halls, chop suey joints, tropical fruit juice stands and all-night diners, and Jack seemed to know everyone: streetwalkers having a smoke in front of hotels, zoot-suited petty gangsters shooting the breeze in front of a cigar store. He even knew many of the panhandlers, of whom there were scores in midtown, some feigning blindness or other handicaps. Occasionally, he'd give one of them a quarter—even though Mayor La Guardia had pleaded with the public not to offer handouts.

In the Runyon stories, New York was a small town where all the characters knew one another, and they all lived on Broadway or its side streets. At times during our strolls, Jack might introduce me, sonorously, as his "colleague from *The New York Times*." He hardly ever called anyone by his real name, aping Runyon's habit of bestowing monikers like Regret, Harry the Horse and Rusty Charlie. Most of his acquaintances had monikers: "Benny, I would like you to know Arthur Gelb of *The New York Times*," Jack would say as we approached a doughy-faced man scratching himself on a street corner. "Arthur, this here is Benny the Bug."

Jack couldn't resist trying to impress me.

"Did you really once meet the guy who shot the guys in Chicago in the Valentine's Day massacre?" I might ask.

"Sure—he's the guy that went to jail for Owney Madden."

"Owney Madden, the Gopher Gang Owney Madden?"

"Sure, that Owney Madden. You know another?"

"Why'd he go to jail for Owney Madden?"

"He confessed to a murder Owney Madden committed."

"Who else did you meet?"

"Well, I met a guy who was a pal of the guy who machine-gunned Vincent Coll."

"Gee, Mad Dog Coll! The guy who kidnapped Sherman Billingsley! I thought they never found the guy who killed Coll."

"They didn't."

"But Owney Madden was behind it, right?"

"I didn't say it, you did."

"Owney Madden's a pal of Winchell's, isn't he?"

"Gave him his Stutz Bearcat."

"You know Winchell too, right?"

"I give him items now and then."

"Who else did you meet?"

"Oh, I dunno. Guys. Lepke."

"Murder Incorporated Lepke? No fooling?"

"Yeah, me and Lepke got a lot in common. We're both Jews. Hah-hah."

"Did you ever see anyone murdered? You don't have to answer that if you don't want to."

"I don't want to. Let's just say I know someone who could get someone rubbed out."

"How?"

"Never mind how."

"Sorry."

"That's okay, kid."

WHEN THE PONIES PAID OFF, Jack invited me to join him at a high-end nightclub. Big, splashy clubs had replaced the smaller speakeasies of Prohibition; their impresarios conducted a volume business, offering shows and entertainment to conventioneers, out-of-towners as well as locals. And no club was swankier or more vast than the Latin Quarter, on Forty-seventh between Seventh and Broadway, operated by Lou Walters.

Barbara Walters, his daughter, once reminisced with me about the elaborate showgirl production numbers at the Latin Quarter, insisting there was a wholesome quality to the entertainment. She remembered that the comics were not risqué, and that families came for holiday shows. My memory was slightly at odds with hers. I remembered the Latin Quarter chiefly as the place to watch statuesque showgirls posing languidly in their pasties. When Jack Tell took me backstage to meet them, I tried not to stare at the pasties on their chests.

The chorus girls at the Copacabana weren't as tall as those at the Latin Quarter, and they moved less gracefully. But the Copa featured Joe E. Lewis, to whose bawdy jokes I was attuned. When Jack introduced me to him, I spent our brief encounter trying not to look at the famous facial scar inflicted by Chicago gangsters when he dared switch from one speakeasy to another.

After a while, a combination of exhaustion, my ambitions at the paper and a guilty conscience began to catch up with me, and I tired of my gaudy nightlife. One episode in particular shut the lid on my nocturnal prowlings.

Jack and I had gone to a midtown saloon. Some bookies were after him, which depressed him, and I decided to help him drown his troubles in drink. At one point, two women showed up at the end of the bar. They were not much older than I and very pretty in a dolled-up fashion.

Jack, it turned out, knew them. He began buying us all rounds, Jack cozying up to one of the women and I to the other. When the club closed, the woman who liked me invited us back to her apartment, and we stumbled off to it.

I remember that it held a warren of rooms opening off a long hall, and that the woman whispered she had to tell me something funny: her jockey boyfriend was sleeping in one of the bedrooms. Even in my inebriated fog I knew it was time for this adventure to be cut short. I might possibly have bested the jockey in a fistfight, but not, as seemed likely, a jockey with a pistol or a knife.

Enough, I said to myself, making my way to the front door. Time to be a good boy.

EIGHT

I REFOCUSED ON MY TWIN OBJECTIVES: promotion to reporter and— to appease my mother—earning a diploma at NYU. My favorite college class was "Contemporary American Theater," taught by Professor Bruce Carpenter, whose lectures were spiced with malicious gossip about the luminaries of Broadway.

Carpenter liked to boast about having sat next to Eugene O'Neill in George Pierce Baker's 1914–1915 Harvard course for budding playwrights. Also a member of the class had been William L. Laurence, now the senior science reporter for *The Times,* and when Carpenter discovered I worked for the paper, he asked me to give Laurence his regards.

When I sought out Laurence, he said he wasn't surprised that Carpenter had become a professor: "I always knew he'd never make a playwright. Too sanctimonious." Laurence was the only staffer in the city room to wear his hair long, almost to his shoulders—a style rarely seen in that era except on musicians and artists. At his desk, he sat hidden behind a paper fortress of haphazardly stacked scientific journals that he scrutinized for possible stories. Rarely was he given specific assignments. Editors left him alone to explore the frontiers of human knowledge and chronicle the discoveries of scientific pioneers.

Laurence was the undisputed master in his field. In 1930, he became the first reporter to pound an exclusively scientific beat, and to pursue stories neglected by writers less farsighted. His thorough understanding of disciplines as varied as atomic physics, medicine and psychology was unmatched in journalism, and his ability to simplify complex technical ideas surpassed the capabilities of many scientists.

His reputation earned him access to all the top researchers. He once persuaded Albert Einstein to break his rule against sitting for news photographers. Einstein, dressed in a wrinkled shirt and a shabby gray cardigan, held an animated conversation with Laurence for nearly an hour while a *Times* photographer snapped pictures.

In 1940, Laurence—in terms a plumber could follow—unveiled the process and potential of isolating uranium-235. A feature on the subject that he wrote for *The Saturday Evening Post* so unnerved government officials by its clarity that the FBI requested the magazine halt further distribution of the issue and report anyone who requested copies.

Often during a spare moment, I made my way to Laurence's desk at the rear of the city room. For me, listening to his tales of life and art, recounted in a Russian accent, felt like sitting at wisdom's knee. I hung on his words as he spoke about the theater of bygone days, and we fell into a habit of evening drinks at Childs.

Born in Lithuania in 1888, he joined a revolutionary faction against the czar when he was twelve. At seventeen he fled the political purge of 1905, bumped his way to Germany in a barrel on the back of a cart, and then crossed into Switzerland. He finally came ashore in Hoboken, New Jersey, in June of that year, with fifty cents in his pocket and a copy of Nietzsche's *Thus Spake Zarathustra.*

In the twenty-five years between landing in America and arriving at *The Times,* Laurence had toiled in a sweatshop, studied at Harvard, delivered flowers, seen combat in World War I and earned a law degree. He was invited to try his hand at reporting when, at a dinner party, he defeated Herbert Bayard Swope, editor of the *World,* in a parlor trivia game. Swope gave him a job and from the *World* he moved to *The Times.*

Although Laurence appeared to have seen it all and was immune to surprise, there was one experience to come that would clearly astonish him.

One day in early May, when I went to his desk, he was gone. No one knew where he was and, after a week, I concluded he must be following a story he wanted to keep under wraps. He had left his desk, however, uncharacteristically clean. Others noticed his continuing absence, but our curiosity was met by Edwin James with evasions.

After a time, in light of daily sensational war developments, Laurence's disappearance was forgotten. With the nation's focus shifting to the Pacific Theater following V-E Day, *The Times* provided graphic accounts of the aerial bombardment of Japan. But on July 28 our attention turned briefly stateside—to a disaster in our own backyard. At 9:45 A.M., a B-25 Army bomber en route over Manhattan to Newark Airport in a thick fog slammed into the 102-story Empire State Building. The wreckage of the twin-engine plane careened through the seventy-eighth and seventy-ninth floors, 915 feet above Thirty-fourth Street. Pieces of the motor ripped through the building and out, soaring across Thirty-third Street to land on a neighboring roof. Flames ravaged offices and filled elevator shafts. Eleven people were killed instantly, some burned beyond recognition. If it hadn't been a Saturday, the toll would have been nothing less than catastrophic.

At work on *Timesweek,* I rushed to the scene with the few reporters on hand. It was earlier than the usual working hour for most *Times* men, but emergency calls summoned twenty-five reporters to the disaster site in less than an hour.

To all newspapermen on the scene, the hero of the day was Ernie Sisto. At forty, Sisto was the dean of newspaper photographers, regularly winning awards for his imagination and bravery.

No obstacle was too daunting to deter him from a shot, even when he later lugged a bulky 4x5 Speed Graphic hundreds of feet up an arm of the Whitestone Bridge in the Bronx, or when he wore an oxygen mask aboard a plane to take photos through an open window of a solar eclipse with a six-foot-long instrument he had built himself and affectionately called "Big Bertha." Especially renowned for his sports photos, he befriended Joe DiMaggio and Phil Rizzuto. A great shortstop, Rizzuto would signal Sisto if he was going to bunt, giving him the few seconds he needed to ready his camera.

The morning of the crash, Sisto was in the city room, and he raced by subway to Thirty-fourth Street with his Speed Graphic. After jostling his way through a crowd of hundreds, press card protruding from the band of his bent-brim hat, past police lines and firemen, he entered the Empire State Building. He took an elevator to the sixty-seventh floor, then climbed to the seventy-ninth, where he assessed the scene.

The golden shot, the one that would best convey the hardly imaginable story, could only be taken from a parapet above the point of impact. He continued his climb to the eighty-sixth floor, where he brokered a life-threatening deal. If two other cameramen would hold his ankles while he stretched himself past the ledge, he would make a plate for each of them. Dangling a thousand feet over the concrete chasm, one arm pressed to the parapet, the other extended into the air gripping his heavy camera, Sisto took his daring shot.

The gaping wound torn into the steel-and-cement flesh of this urban behemoth made photographic history. Sisto's angle imparted a vertiginous sense of height, capturing the sheerness of the building as it narrowed to the street below, its upper floors enveloped in smoke.

His courage was rewarded the next morning by a front-page display in *The Times,* reproduced by papers all over the country. This was itself a testament to the picture, since *The Times* was still, in 1945, emphasizing words over images. Photos were the province of the tabloids, especially the *Daily News.* But on that Sunday, July 29, *The Times* photographically carried the day. Aside from the dramatic shot on page one, an inside spread was devoted to other pictures of the crash. The paper hadn't received such praise for its photos since it published the shot of Mussolini's hanging.

The Empire State Building crash marked my professional reportorial debut. Pat Spiegel pulled me aside amidst the chaos of smoke and sirens, emergency crews and bystanders, and asked me to accompany him to Bellevue Hospital to help him gather facts about the injured. I jumped at the opportunity.

Internationally known for its emergency medical team, Bellevue made no pretense to elegance, but its reputation for saving lives was unsurpassed. Doctors had set up a field unit in the lobby of a building near the crash site, transporting those in need of intensive care to the hospital. I managed to talk my way into the emergency room to ask the nurses some simple questions. Because of my youth and obvious inexperience, I guess they felt sorry for me, and they gave me a vivid account of their lifesaving efforts.

My success alerted me unwittingly to a journalistic virtue—naiveté. The best reporters, I began to realize, were masters of feigned innocence; by disarming their subjects, they collected perceptive details. But as I knew there was no chance I'd be allowed to write the story, I turned over my facts to Pat, who phoned them in. In those days it was rare for a clerk or news assistant even to help a reporter with legwork. I felt it was honor enough to have done some reporting for the paper itself rather than for *Timesweek,* and I exulted in every minute of it.

UNBEKNOWNST TO THE STAFF of *The Times,* a confidential letter had arrived for Edwin James a few days earlier, from the long-absent William

Laurence. It was the first contact that Laurence had made in months, and was for the eyes only of James, Turner Catledge and the publisher. Dated Thursday, July 12, 1945, the letter read:

Dear Mr. James:

Forgive me for not writing sooner. I have been busier than the proverbial one-armed paperhanger ever since I left. I have covered lots of ground and seen things that made me dizzy. In fact, I have been in a constant state of bewilderment now for some two months and the biggest surprises are still ahead.

This story is much bigger than I could imagine, fantastic, bizarre, fascinating and terrifying. When it breaks it will be an eighth day wonder, a sort of Second Coming of Christ yarn. It will be one of the big stories of our generation and it will run for some time. It will need about twenty columns on the day it breaks. This may sound overenthusiastic, but I am willing to wager you right now that when the time comes you will agree that my estimate is on the conservative side.

I am going to do my best to arrange to give you sufficient notice in advance (through the proper channels) so that you may have the time to prepare for it. We hope that we can control the timing, but that is in the lap of the gods.

This is not just one big story. There are at least twenty-five individual page one stories to be given out following the break of the Big News. When it does break you will undoubtedly think of many other angles, national, international, political, diplomatic, industrial and what not.

The world will not be the same after the day of the big event. A new era in our civilization will have started, with enormous implications for the post-war period, both from a military and industrial standpoint.

I am expected to stay on the job until the Big Day. As you already know I am going places some distance away. Nobody as yet knows the exact date. Under the circumstances I am figuring on being back on the job sometime between September 15 and October 1. I hope it will be earlier than that, but I will not be told until the last minute and then probably I will not be in a position to let you know until the "break."

I am deeply grateful to you and The Times for giving me this opportunity of a lifetime. In addition to the privilege of writing one of the big stories of our day, it is also a great privilege to be of some service to the nation. The proper handling of this story will be of considerable importance to what happens in the future. I hope I can live up to the responsibility.

I want you to know I am not conceited enough to think that this opportunity was given to me as an individual. The honor of being the one selected to handle the story, I know full well, is due to the fact that I am a staff member of The Times. And I know that when the proper time comes, The Times will be the only one to do the story justice, despite the fact that my services are not to be exclusive. I wish they could be. I will advise the authorities to call you in consultation some time before the release date. I hope you will be in town at the time.

At present, I am one of the few men in the world who knows the complete story, with the exception of dates. The security restrictions are so stringent that I am afraid even to talk to myself. Even my identity is kept a deep secret and I find myself slinking around corners for fear someone will recognize me. While the job is naturally exhilarating and thrilling it has been a tremendous weight on one's shoulders. It goes against the grain to write a big story and mark it "Top Secret" and lock it up in a safe. I am looking forward to the day when I can dig up a good story and dash to the nearest Western Union office.

There is another consolation for my prolonged absence from the staff. After the story breaks I will be the only one with first hand knowledge of it, which should give The Times a considerable edge. Much of it, however, will be kept on ice for some time. I am looking forward to the time when I can see you again. My desk probably looks much too clean at present and that must look unnatural to you. As usual I am in need of a haircut.

The letter was signed: "Faithfully yours, Bill Laurence."

Apart from James, Catledge and Sulzberger, no one at *The Times* had an inkling of Laurence's activities, and even their knowledge of the secret mission's precise details was somewhat vague. It was not until August 7 that his whereabouts were revealed, with an eight-column banner emblazoned across page one of *The Times*:

FIRST ATOMIC BOMB DROPPED ON JAPAN;
MISSILE IS EQUAL TO 20,000 TONS OF TNT;
TRUMAN WARNS FOE OF A "RAIN OF RUIN"

On page five, the headline on one of the sidebar stories read:

WAR DEPARTMENT CALLED TIMES REPORTER
TO EXPLAIN BOMB'S INTRICACIES TO PUBLIC

The reporter, naturally, was Laurence. When he returned to the city room, he graciously made himself available so I could ask questions about the sterling scoop of all time. In a very small way, I am proud to recall, these conversations provided the material for *Timesweek*'s greatest scoop as well.

Major General Leslie R. Groves, head of the Army's atomic efforts, had approached James in April to request Laurence's services. After consulting with Sulzberger, James gave his approval, but neither man knew the exact nature of the assignment. Laurence soon discovered he was to be the sole journalist invited into the secret world of the Manhattan Project.

His role was to record the development, testing and deployment of the world's first atomic weapons—the most momentous beat ever assigned. He was handpicked because of his background and knowledge of atomic science, and for his ability to translate his knowledge into layman's terms.

From May to mid-July, Laurence continuously crisscrossed the country, logging over 40,000 miles between the "invisible" labs at Oak Ridge, Tennessee, Los Alamos, New Mexico, and Hanford, Washington—a witness to activities that astounded him. Concerned that traitorous eyes might decipher his jottings, the Army allowed him to write only in Oak Ridge or Washington, D.C., where they could safeguard his notebooks. While traveling, he had to rely on memory for storing information.

When he finished a story it was filed away in a safe, not to see the light until the project was completed. Notes, drafts, and carbons were taken from him daily by two armed guards, to be burned.

In our interview, Laurence told me he hardly slept during his first weeks on the Manhattan Project: "Here was the biggest story any newspaperman ever had—a dream reality. I thought, 'How could I write my stories so the people would believe and understand them?' I devised dozens of leads, but every one sounded phony. I began to believe that a lead couldn't be written." He often woke in a cold sweat from nightmares set in a Western Union office, from where he was supposed to telegraph his story, which still had no lead.

By July 12, when he sent the letter to James, Laurence had finished most of his writing about the bomb's development. In four days he would cover its first test at the Trinity Site, north of Alamogordo, New Mexico. He knew there was a chance that neither he nor anyone else present would return from the desert alive.

As a precaution against enemy suspicions, Laurence was asked by General Groves to concoct a false news story to be released in case catastrophe simultaneously took the lives of some of the world's most prominent scientists, including J. Robert Oppenheimer and Enrico Fermi. If things went wrong, he wouldn't be able to compose one later. The invented story, he subsequently said, "was a lurid tale of the accidental explosion of a new deadly (and nonexistent) poison gas." He later told me that he had also been assigned to prepare biographical sketches of each scientist for newspaper obituaries in the event of the fatal mishap.

At eleven P.M. on July 15, in Albuquerque, Laurence joined a caravan of scientists en route from Los Alamos to the Trinity Site. The night was black. There were no stars, no moon. Only an occasional flash of lightning eerily illuminated the desert landscape. The group of ninety men reached their destination at approximately two A.M.

The observers gathered to receive safety instructions. Signals would be broadcast to alert them five minutes and again two minutes before the "shot," which was scheduled for 5:30 A.M. At the two-minute warning, they were to lie on the ground, eyes down, their faces covered by their arms until the blast wave passed. Colored glass eye shields of the type used by arc welders were distributed.

In hindsight, many of the precautions taken seem absurdly naive. Not only were the observers encouraged to wear long-sleeved shirts to guard against radiation, but suntan lotion was passed around. The top scientists of the day slathered themselves in sun block to help protect them from the effects of atomic fallout. One wonders now at how little these men knew of the forces they were about to unleash.

Laurence was taken to a post on a hillside 5.7 miles from the blast point. When he complained about being so far away, General Groves reminded him that the project had "a considerable interest in having the eyewitnesses survive."

Tension grew palpably as zero hour approached in the cold of a predawn drizzle. At minus two minutes, Laurence assumed the prescribed position, facedown. Finally, a voice boomed out of the darkness: "Zero minus ten seconds!" and again, "Zero minus three seconds!" When he raised his eyes, he later wrote, "there rose from the bowels of the earth a light not of this world, the light of many suns in one."

For Laurence, it was an event of biblical proportion. "It was as though the earth had opened and the skies had split. One felt as though he had been privileged to witness the Birth of the World—to be present at the moment of Creation when the Lord said: Let There Be Light."

Since the test had been a success, with those present certain that the long, debilitating war would soon be over, Laurence received his next assignment from General Groves—to witness and record the planned atomic attack on Japan. He went briefly home to New York to see his wife and told her he was being sent to London. Then he crossed the Pacific to Tinian Island, where the bomb was being assembled.

In a crushing disappointment, Laurence wasn't allowed to fly over Hiroshima with the *Enola Gay* as planned. There had been an unexplained change in the orders. But he had foresightedly asked one of the crewmen on board to take notes. *The Times* devoted ten full pages of coverage to the bombing and the maneuvers that preceded it. Nearly every story had been based on advance copy written by Laurence, stored in an Army safe and now released to the press.

Three days later, when the Japanese failed to capitulate, the decision was made to unleash yet another atomic storm on the empire. This was Laurence's opportunity to cover the story as an eyewitness; he accompanied the crew of *The Great Artiste,* a B-29 instrument plane, on its mission to measure and photograph the apocalyptic payload delivered to Nagasaki by its sister Superfortress, *Bockscar.*

He saw "a giant ball of fire rise . . . belching forth enormous white smoke rings," then "a giant pillar of purple fire, 10,000 feet high, shooting skyward with enormous speed," which soon reached the height of his aircraft. It seemed to be alive, "carved with many grotesque masks grimacing at the earth." Then "there came shooting out of the top a giant mushroom that increased the height of the pillar to a total of 45,000 feet. The mushroom top was even more alive than the pillar, seething and boiling in a white fury of creamy foam, sizzling upward and then descending earthward, a thousand Old Faithful geysers rolled into one."

While working with the Manhattan Project, Laurence was an employee of the government, not *The Times*. The stories he wrote about the creation of the bomb were distributed by the Army to newspapers nationwide, and he received no byline. But his eyewitness accounts of Nagasaki and the Trinity Site, as well as in-depth articles about the bomb that only he could write, were published exclusively by *The Times* in a ten-part series in late September and early October 1945.

When news of the bombing of Hiroshima reached the United States, jubilation swept the nation, for the end of the war felt near at hand. In pockets of conversation in the city room as well as at Bleeck's and Childs, reporters and editors were of one mind: Using the atomic bomb was clearly justified. In fact, I recall no American in 1945 speaking out in favor of restraining our government from using any means whatever to defeat the Japanese. Even Einstein, an outspoken pacifist, supported the building of the bomb, despite foreseeing the dark consequences.

It was an accepted fact that Emperor Hirohito had no intention of surrendering and, without the bomb, an Allied victory would have necessitated a land invasion of Japan, with an unfathomable loss of American—and Japanese—lives. Americans were weary of the bloodshed and sick at the deaths of so many of our young men. Moreover, the Japanese, in those emotional times, were seen by the Allies—unable to erase the memories of Pearl Harbor and the Bataan death march—as vicious, inhuman enemies.

Once, a Linotype operator for *The Times* intentionally mis-set the name of Emperor Hirohito in a story that led page one, spelling it "Hiroshito." The "error" was caught just after the first edition began to roll and the presses were stopped to make the correction. The Linotypist was called into James's office where he was about to be fired. He collapsed in tears, explaining that he had recently received word that his son had been killed in the Pacific. He kept his job.

In 1995, the fiftieth anniversary of the dropping of the Hiroshima bomb, Japan's preeminent newspaper *Asahi Shimbun* and the Elie Wiesel Foundation for Humanity co-sponsored a conference in Hiroshima to analyze the anatomy of hatred in our time and discuss the possibilities of an idealistic society that might temper that hatred. I was invited to speak about artistic hope—how great artists convey hope through their work

A young Japanese scholar, aware I had been in New York when the bomb was dropped on Hiroshima, asked me whether Americans had not been horrified by the human cost. I found it difficult to tell him the truth, but I tried. It was only in retrospect, I explained, that Americans felt dismay and remorse over the bomb's gruesome aftermath. Most of us were unaware, at first, of the extent of the devastation caused by the bombs, I told him. John

Hersey's excruciatingly detailed account, reported in *The New Yorker* (on August 31, 1946, a year after Hiroshima and Nagasaki), finally brought home to Americans the magnitude of the event. But initially, I had to admit, I knew no one who publicly decried the bombings; most Americans believed it was them or us.

A few days after the mission to Nagasaki, Hirohito raised the white flag. On August 14 at 7:03 P.M., the news was flashed across the zipper sign to throngs that had gathered in Times Square: "OFFICIAL — TRUMAN ANNOUNCES JAPANESE SURRENDER."

An exultant cry burst from the crowd. Once again, strangers embraced, tears flowed, the air rang with cheers for the war's end—"the greatest moment of collective inebriation in American history," as Philip Roth once called it. Unlike celebrants on V-E Day, however, these seemed less to be commemorating a great victory than expressing a blessed release from the strains of war.

Laurence returned to the city room a few weeks later, startling us with his dapper suit and his hair shorn. He was a hero, and everyone applauded him. His manner, however, was modest. He carried himself with the quiet confidence of a man who knew he had nothing to prove.

NINE

THE STAFF OF THE CITY ROOM had almost forgotten what it was like to put out a paper free of wartime restrictions. But the publisher and the top editors quickly readjusted to a peacetime rhythm. Along with the rest of the country, *The Times* readied itself for an era of growth and prosperity.

International telephone lines destroyed in combat were operational again, and lines silenced for fear of being intercepted by the enemy were restored to service. Stories filed from abroad no longer had to pass through censors.

A total of 920 employees had served in the armed forces, seventeen of them killed in the line of duty, and a bronze plaque engraved with their names was mounted in the *Times* lobby. A plaque was all very well, but I was appalled by the way some of the veterans were greeted when they began to reclaim their jobs. "I don't know what we're going to do with you," was the callous welcome proffered one returnee by city editor David H. Joseph, a man not known for his warmth.

Staff shuffling was required, but for the most part accommodations eventually were made for the veterans, whatever their prewar status on the paper. Arthur Neuhauser, for example, a copyboy who had enlisted in the infantry, returned as a much-decorated lieutenant. Concerned that *The Times* might not have a place for Arthur, his father advised him to wear his uniform when he reentered the city room. His medals were so impressive, he was promoted at once from copyboy to clerk on the city desk. (Ultimately he became the editor of the obit/society/arts copy desk, the position once held by "Judge" Evans.)

Then there was the case of Benedict Amato, who reclaimed his post as head watchman after five years in the Army. A true hero, he had stormed the Normandy beaches on D-Day, and was wounded twice; captured by the Germans, he refused to cave in under interrogation and escaped from the stalag a few days later. He smuggled himself to Warsaw, where he was nearly shot by Russian troops who thought he was a spy. *The Times* was only too happy to have a man of Ben's caliber back in charge of security, and entrusted him as the only guard allowed to carry a pistol. (He never had to use it.)

Some new talent was also recruited for the postwar city room and one day toward the end of 1945, to the staff's astonishment, George Walker Streator made a subdued entrance as the lone black reporter. While no one seemed to know much about him, it was rumored that his father-in-law, Brigadier General Benjamin O. Davis (the first black to rise to that rank in the Army), had recommended him to a fellow general, Julius Ochs Adler (now general manager in charge of the paper's business side). The timing coincided with Arthur Hays Sulzberger's edict to James that he wanted a black reporter on the news staff. In a résumé requested by city editor Joseph, Streator found it necessary to assure him that he was a reserved man who had acquired experience working with white people, and thus saw no reason why he couldn't get along with whites at the paper.

We soon learned that Streator, in his early forties, had been born in Nashville, Tennessee, received a B.A. degree from Fisk University, an M.A. from Western Reserve and had recently served as a labor relations representative with the War Production Board. He was notches above most of the street-smart reporters in manner and dress, and better-spoken than many of them. He was light-skinned, wore his graying hair close-cropped and was always attired in an expensively tailored suit, with a gold watch chain dangling from his vest. We also learned that he lived in Sugar Hill, perhaps the most affluent of Harlem neighborhoods.

Streator had contributed articles to *Commonweal* and *America,* and was eager to prove he could make it as one of a handful of black reporters employed by the country's white-owned newspapers. But since Streator was inexperienced as a newspaper reporter and not a naturally stylish writer, his career at the paper languished. He soon intuited that he was regarded as *The Times*'s token Negro, there to trumpet the paper's newfound sense of civic responsibility.

Few of the reporters made any effort to put him at ease, even though most of them prided themselves on being socially progressive. And, while I couldn't prove it, I believed none of them ever invited him to join them in a drink after work. I longed to talk to Streator about his situation, but didn't dare broach what I felt was delicate terrain. He was generous with his praise for *Timesweek,* and for weeks he kept making imaginative suggestions for our coverage. One night, he offered to buy me a drink at Childs, and we stood at the crowded bar, where he was the sole black patron.

A black man and a white man drinking together might not have attracted particular notice at some of the bohemian hangouts in Greenwich Village, but it was far from the norm at a Times Square saloon. Neither Streator nor I could help but be aware that we were being stared at. What I found ironic was that it seemed not to matter to the gawkers that the elegantly dressed Streator was the most imposing figure in the saloon.

After a while, the liquor began talking. "I suppose to them we're as strange as two rare specimens in the zoo," Streator said, smiling bitterly. "Negroes helped win the war, but we're still nowhere. These dumbfounding stares are proof of what I'm saying. So here you are, a nice, decent white kid bravely having a drink with a Negro in this great liberal city."

He was right, of course; midtown was essentially a white enclave. I am still aghast—when I look at photographs of Broadway during that period— by the absence of black faces. On several occasions, I witnessed a disturbing scene: A black man walking in Times Square would pause to look in a window or stand on a corner gazing at the signs and, inevitably, a policeman would approach him, ask if there was a problem and suggest he move along. If the man talked back—no matter how meekly—the policeman was more than likely to swing his club across the back of his legs.

An absence of concern about blacks extended to *The Times*'s city room. Editors seldom ran stories about blacks unless they scored feats as athletes or were featured in vaudeville, Harlem nightclubs or the movies—entertainers like Lena Horne, Bill "Bojangles" Robinson, Louis Armstrong, Ethel Waters, Cab Calloway or the stereotyped, slow-moving Stepin Fetchit. If a reporter phoned in what he believed was an interesting robbery or homicide in which the victim happened to be black, the editor invariably muttered, "Forget it." Reporters, of course, knew better than even to suggest stories about crimes involving blacks against blacks. That was copy more suited for the Harlem-based weekly, the *Amsterdam News*.

For a moment, I considered telling Streator about my own travails with prejudice—the anti-Semitism I had encountered in my high school days when applying for a summer office boy job at law firms. But I was aware that my experience was not really comparable, especially since war's end had brought some signs of a lessening of anti-Semitism in the city; Streator, on the other hand, appeared trapped indefinitely by the color of his skin.

"It's not my intention," he said, "to make you feel more uneasy than you already do, under these barroom stares, but I'm willing to bet you've never invited a Negro boy to your home and that there isn't one Negro kid among all your friends. You must understand that it's young kids like you who are probably our best hope."

Warming to his subject, he went on to make his case. "Wouldn't it be something to cheer about if the paper hired Negro copyboys and gave them the same sort of chance you and your friends are getting in the city room— even letting them prove their talent as members of your *Timesweek* staff?" He reminded me that the pool of qualified Negro journalists in the country was infinitesimal because there was no training ground for them; not only were they unwelcome as copyboys, but talented black students were not encouraged to take journalism courses in college.

Streator was keenly aware that *The Times* disregarded news of the ghettos in the belief that white readers weren't interested. He said this would not be the case if there were well-trained black writers on the staff. They would be able to report on Negro life accurately and with perspective, because they had grown up in black communities, knew the people and their agonizing struggle to emerge from poverty.

With such probing articles, he said, whites would surely find that stories about ghetto life were of interest, in the same way they read any good story involving people about whom they had scant knowledge. But it was a vicious circle, because we would need ranking black editors to encourage such coverage—and, of course, there were none on any white newspapers.

"Opening doors for training Negro kids is the only way to free us from this awful tokenism," he said, looking me straight in the eye. "And now I'm beginning to feel bad for harassing you. It's just that I don't expect to be at the paper much longer. I have a feeling you're going to get someplace at *The Times* someday. I simply want you to remember what I've been telling you."

It gradually occurred to me that the solution required far more than training copyboys. I felt that, as in the case of the negligent coverage of Jews in Nazi concentration camps, the paper's top brass was, consciously or not, insensitive to the plight of minorities. (The number of even token black reporters on New York's white-owned newspapers had not increased in years.)

Pat Spiegel had told me a story that illustrated the stubborn reluctance of mainstream newspapers to hire black reporters—and of one paper's resulting comeuppance. His story was about Ted Poston, who had been hired by the *Post* in 1937; by the time I came to work for *The Times,* he was the most highly regarded of the few black reporters in the city.

When Poston graduated from Tennessee State College, where he wrote for the student paper, the only job he could find was as a sleeping-car porter on the Pennsylvania Railroad. He finally made his way to reporter at the *Amsterdam News,* but was fired for leading a strike against the paper in 1936. After hearing from friends that *The Times* was reluctant to employ a black reporter, he sought a job on the *Post,* boasting that he was the best newspaperman in town. But the *Post* was no more eager than *The Times* to hire a black reporter. Nevertheless, the editor, Walter Lister, challenged him to bring in an exclusive story for the next day's paper.

Discouraged, Poston took the subway home to Harlem. As the train reached his station, he witnessed a crowd of black men chasing a bloodied white man down the subway stairs; the man was a process server and his targets seemed determined to kill him. At last, after a battle that stopped train service on the line for some time, a transit cop rescued the white man. There were no white reporters on the scene and Poston submitted his exclusive story, which led to a job offer by Lister.

As for George Streator, he left *The Times* in 1949, almost four years after he was hired. Both Catledge and Sulzberger had concluded he had not matured sufficiently as a reporter, and Streator himself was unhappy over his routine assignments. After he quit to become editor of the weekly paper published by the National Maritime Union, we lost touch with each other.

LITTLE BY LITTLE, many of the female clerks hired as temporary replacements for male draftees lost their jobs. One who was still hanging on when I met her early in 1945 was an eighteen-year-old clerk for the tenth-floor editorial board, who occasionally stopped by the city room on her way back from the newspaper morgue or some other errand. On this particular January afternoon, she had come down to the third floor before leaving for the day to talk to John Meixner about joining our *Timesweek* staff.

I had just returned from a matinee of a new Broadway hit by one of my favorite writers, S. N. Behrman. *Jacobowsky and the Colonel,* directed by Elia Kazan, was a wry wartime comedy about two mismatched Poles—a Jewish refugee and an autocratic army colonel—who team up to escape from the Nazis.

Still aglow from the performance, I entered the city room and saw Meixner talking to a startlingly pretty girl who could herself have just stepped off the stage. Her complexion reminded me of vanilla ice cream, her reddish-brown hair curled around the edges of a black beret, and she wore a raspberry-pink raincoat that emphasized her slenderness. Meixner introduced me to Barbara Stone, saying he'd asked her to join *Timesweek,* and the three of us headed upstairs to the cafeteria for coffee.

My friends knew I habitually attended matinees, and Meixner asked what play I'd just seen. When I told him, he said, "Well, you'll be interested to know that S. N. Behrman is Barbara's stepfather." I tried to appear unruffled, but my face must have betrayed some amazement.

Behrman, after all, was not only the acknowledged master of the American drawing room comedy, but a contributor of elegant profiles to *The New Yorker,* and a sought-after Hollywood screenwriter.

Of course I wanted to know more about Barbara and her connection to one of my literary idols, and I began to interview her. She wasn't reticent, but she had a somewhat quizzical take on her family background, for reasons that were gradually to become clear. That evening I learned her parents had divorced when she was nine, and that her mother married Behrman a year later. She was sent to boarding school because her stepfather—for whom she had great affection and admiration—required an atmosphere free of domestic disturbance for his writing. He was a middle-aged bachelor when he married Barbara's mother, and he couldn't change his habits. (Barbara's younger brother, as soon as he was deemed old enough, joined her at boarding school.)

Barbara had entered Swarthmore at sixteen in 1943, the youngest girl in the freshman class, and had become so immersed in theatrical and literary activities that she failed to complete her required subjects. The dean advised her to take a year off to "mature," and then reapply. She knew she could not live with her mother. Her biological father was remarried and had a young son, and she felt she would not be welcome with them. So she got a job as a copygirl on *The Times* and found a room in Greenwich Village that she could afford on her own, just barely, asking no financial help from either of her parents.

She did ask her stepfather, whom she called by his family nickname, Berrie, to send her to *The New Yorker* for an interview with its managing editor, William Shawn. Behrman was a true prince of *The New Yorker,* and many years later Shawn captured his immeasurable value to the magazine: "Decade after decade, his brilliant writings kept streaming down from wherever he lived uptown . . . and, for those who were lucky enough to be his friends, his talk flowed along in parallel bounty and with equal brilliance. . . . The world presented itself to him as a comedy, so his literary style was comic. Almost every piece of formal writing he did, like every letter or note he wrote to a friend, bore the Behrman mark: the unexpected inversion or inflection of thought, the surprising placement of a word, the idiosyncratic phrase, the droll shift in tempo, the pure funniness."

Shawn, famous for his pathological shyness, reacted to Barbara strangely. Although she could seem a bit haughty, she made every effort to be winsome with Shawn. Behrman called Barbara the next day, saying Shawn had told him he didn't think there was a job available at the moment. Then, according to Behrman, Shawn added, oddly, "You know, she hated me."

Barbara asked me if she could write a profile for *Timesweek* on Robert L. Duffus, one of *The Times*'s editorial writers for whom she ran copy. By this point, I would have agreed to her writing just about anything. I wondered if there was any chance in the world of dating this pretty, funny, entrancing girl. Her world seemed so remote from mine—and yet there was a vulnerability about her that made me hope.

My best bet, I thought, was to impress Barbara with my talents as an editor. When I received her piece on Duffus, I rearranged some of her sentences and made substitutions for a few phrases—without bothering to show them to her. When the piece ran on February 26, she stalked to my desk in the city room, and asked icily, "How could you change my lead without discussing it with me? Please don't ever again edit anything I write for *Timesweek*!"

I compared Barbara's copy with the edited version and had to admit that her original lead was better than my rewritten one. I sent her a note of apology which she didn't acknowledge. It was a potent lesson: Beware the itchy editor's pencil! But more about that later.

IN THE DECADE AFTER THE WAR, New York, whose growth had been suspended because of material shortages, began to modernize. The beloved cobblestones of my boyhood were gradually replaced by paved streets. Aging tenements along Second Avenue were demolished and tall, gleaming apartment houses sprang up. Eventually, the Third Avenue El was demolished, and the avenue itself, dingy and saloon-infested, was transformed into a sunny—if characterless—thoroughfare.

The Times began expanding soon after peace was declared. With the lifting of government directive L-240, which rationed the supply of newsprint, more space became available for news as well as advertising. The paper's daily run of 555,991 in 1945 was increased by 110,000 copies the next year and the Sunday *Times* soon exceeded a circulation of one million.

Reflecting a surge in public interest, *The Times* pumped up its coverage of national news. The Washington bureau was filing a near record-breaking number of words on a daily basis. Staff reporters were sent to key industrial cities, such as Detroit and Akron, to cover postwar reconversion developments. A new bureau was established in Los Angeles, replacing the services that had been previously provided by the *Los Angeles Times,* and other bureaus were opened in San Francisco and Boston.

Local coverage was expanded as well, and Mike Berger prepared to revive his "About New York" column (discontinued when the war began). After years of neglect, *The Times* assigned a reporter to the Municipal Building. Police reporting, which had slipped off the front pages during the war, was also beefed up; Mike Berger had lamented its disappearance in verse for *Timesweek:* "Where are the tales now on the wires? / Assault and arson, oil plant fires? / Battles, muggings, countless strikes, / Kidnapping of wistful tykes?"

But none of the broadening of national and local reporting was at the expense of foreign news. A battery of the best reporters were assigned to cover the newly forming United Nations. Anne O'Hare McCormick toured postwar Europe for five months and relayed the gratifying results of the Nuremberg trials. New overseas bureaus were created, usually staffed by former war correspondents.

George Jones, for example, who had reported from Guadalcanal, Okinawa, Truk Island and Tokyo, was assigned to reopen the New Delhi bureau. His most memorable postwar moment had been participation in the arrest of Japan's prime minister, Hideki Tojo. When a shot was heard from inside the minister's home, Jones helped a member of the arresting team to break down the door. They discovered the minister slumped in a chair, holding the gun with which he had shot himself. (He was still alive and later was found guilty of war crimes by an international military tribunal and hanged.)

The Times made plans to reopen the Tokyo bureau, closed since the day following the attack on Pearl Harbor, when *Times* man Otto Tolischus was interned by the Japanese. Rousted from bed in the middle of the night, Tolischus spent the next four months in a near-freezing cell, tortured by captors who tried to force him to confess he was an American spy. Every day, one Japanese officer, whom he nicknamed "the Snake," would put a chair on his legs and another officer, "the Rabbit," would sit in it. Then the Snake would slap his face. Tolischus held firm and eventually the torture ceased. He once told me he believed he was singled out for this treatment because he represented *The Times,* and the Japanese thought that his capitulation would lead to the arrest of all foreign correspondents as spies. Though found guilty of the charge in a Tokyo court, Tolischus was allowed to sail for the States a month later.

To help plan *The Times*'s postwar expansion, Arthur Sulzberger, along with other newspaper executives, accepted the Army's invitation to tour areas of American occupation on the continent. Edward Hausner, an Army sergeant photographer from the Bronx, agreed to stay past his discharge date to take pictures of the group as they traveled from country to country, in exchange for permission to fly home with them, rather than cross the Atlantic by troopship. On the flight home, after the twenty-four-day tour, Sulzberger approached Eddie.

"I've been observing you," he said. "Tell me how old you are."

"Twenty, sir."

"That's my son's age. He's in the Marines. Listen, I need someone to open a photo bureau in Europe, and I think you're the man."

Sulzberger cabled Eddie's parents from Paris to meet their son in Washington and reserved a suite for them at the Hay-Adams Hotel. After witnessing Mrs. Hausner's profoundly emotional greeting of her son at the airport, Sulzberger pulled Eddie aside and said, "I think it would be a bad idea for you to go away to Europe again. Let me offer you a job as a staff photographer in New York instead."

Eddie was elated. But when he reported for work in the city room, the other photographers were resentful. They viewed him as the "publisher's pet" and sneered at his lack of experience. The publisher had rightly judged his talent, however, and Eddie eventually became one of *The Times*'s most respected photographers.

Over the years, whenever I recalled the special relationship between Hausner, the neophyte photographer, and Sulzberger, the eminent publisher, I found myself chuckling over a particular postwar episode. Eddie was assigned to cover the arrival of the SS *France,* one of the great ocean liners of the day. Madeleine Carroll happened to be aboard, and when she debarked, all the photographers except Eddie took pictures of her sitting on the ship's railing with her legs crossed, her skirt provocatively pulled up above her knees.

"Why didn't you take a picture of me?" she asked Eddie.

"I work for *The Times,* and my paper won't print pictures showing legs." They compromised on a glamorous head shot.

That night when leaving *The Times* at 11:30, Eddie ran into Sulzberger in the lobby. The publisher, smoking a pipe, dressed in a loosely belted camel's-hair coat and sporting a green Tyrolean hat adorned with a feather, was arm in arm with Madeleine Carroll.

"Sergeant," said Sulzberger, using his usual salutation for Eddie, "I'd like you to meet Miss Carroll."

"We've already met," she said, smiling. "He photographed me on the ship."

Sulzberger asked Eddie whether it was a good picture. "Very good," said Eddie, explaining it had been crowded out of the first edition.

"Well, we'll have to do something about that," the publisher said.

Eddie, with much the same flutter I had felt on first encountering Madeleine Carroll at *The Times,* watched her as she entered Sulzberger's new blue Chrysler convertible. Like me, Eddie couldn't help but take pride in our publisher's good taste.

The photo of her appeared in the late edition of the paper. Eddie found out the next day that the publisher had called the bullpen to suggest room be made for it.

TEN

THE EXPANSION OF THE POSTWAR *TIMES*, now that structural steel had become available again, included plans to annex the property behind our building. I assigned myself to collaborate with one of the young women on my staff, Lee McCabe—who was less prickly about my editing than Barbara—on a series for *Timesweek* about the new addition.

We published blueprints of the building's design, which would extend *The Times* from Forty-third to Forty-fourth Street. An entrance on Forty-fourth would make *The Times* a neighbor of Sardi's restaurant, which sat adjacent to the construction site. At a time when Broadway was reinventing itself—propelled by the smash success of *Oklahoma!*—Sardi's was a refuge for actors, directors and producers, a place whose patrons knew better than to approach a celebrity for an autograph. The food, always presented with a flourish, featured such dishes as roast beef in a silver tureen carved at the table, and spaghetti with clam sauce, assembled under the diner's eye by a punctilious waiter, and turned out from gleaming copper pans.

Lee McCabe and I couldn't afford to eat there, but we patronized the bar, discussing our planned coverage—and flirting. We soon got to know Vincent Sardi, Sr., who seemed to live at the restaurant, greeting guests and checking on the service. He told us he was not looking forward to the construction of *The Times*'s annex, to be preceded by the demolition of the Forty-fourth Street Theater. He feared he might be forced to close temporarily because of noise and debris.

With his crop of white hair, erect carriage and impeccable manners, Mr. Sardi epitomized the patrician host. No patron ever addressed him by his first name. A few years after arriving in America in 1907 from a village in northern Italy, he met and married a pretty woman from the same province. Eugenia was a good cook and together they opened a trattoria in a brownstone on Forty-fourth Street east of Eighth Avenue, the site later occupied by the St. James Theater. Broadway's leading theater owners, Lee and J. J. Shubert, offered to build the Sardis a new restaurant on property they owned a little east of the trattoria.

The establishment prospered, despite gangland harassment during Prohibition. Mr. Sardi's son, Vincent Jr., who began training to take over the restaurant upon his return from the Marines after the war, once told me that rival mobsters demanded his father pay "protection" money. When Owney Madden, the gangster about whom Jack Tell had given me an earful, heard that Mr. Sardi was being threatened, he assured him he need never worry again. Madden, who was genuinely fond of the Sardis, appointed himself their protector—without charge.

While the demolition of the Forty-fourth Street Theater in December of 1945 was bothersome, it was as nothing compared with the ensuing excavation into the bedrock. The drilling and dynamiting threw Sardi's kitchen into an uproar. Soufflés fell, sauces spilled, dishes rattled. Jimmy, the captain, shrugged off the ruckus. "Just like my four years in a war plant—everybody shouting themselves hoarse," he said. Ushers at the Paramount Theater a block away had to duck when plaster was jarred from their locker-room ceiling. It became part of their new routine to reassure the audience during the blasting.

One night when Lee McCabe and I were at the bar, I fell into conversation with Irving Hoffman, the press agent I had occasionally run into on my way to Eddie Jaffe's flat. He asked if I'd heard the story Turner Catledge was telling friends about a recent incident he described as "Mr. Sardi's revenge." Catledge had brought Iphigene Sulzberger to lunch during the excavation. Mr. Sardi showed them to a banquette along the wall, smack up against the construction site. As they were served their main course, a dynamite explosion set their dishes and silverware bouncing around the table. Mrs. Sulzberger stared at Catledge in shock, but quickly recovered her equilibrium. She was determined, she told Catledge, not to move their table. They deserved what they were getting, she said. One explosion followed another. When they rose to leave, poker-faced, Mr. Sardi smilingly bade them a good afternoon.

A FEW DAYS AFTER CHRISTMAS, *Timesweek* threw a party for its staff at a Ukrainian beer hall on lower Second Avenue. I escorted Lee McCabe as well as my other *Timesweek* recruit, Sally McKay, and secretly hoped that Barbara Stone would be there. She arrived wearing a slinky black dress that took my breath away.

The Ukrainian band played frenzied gypsy music and the beer flowed. After twirling first Lee and then Sally around the dance floor, I asked Barbara to dance. She declined, but emboldened by beer and the gypsy music, I picked her up and carried her to the floor. She kicked in playful resistance and her shoes flew off, so she danced with me in her stocking feet.

The band at last called it quits, and the lot of us trooped merrily to Café Society. I managed to sit next to Barbara at our cramped table. In an undertone, she questioned me about Lee, creating, to my delight, the clear impression she was jealous. The next day, we bumped into each other in the *Times* morgue. Barbara gave me the warmest smile she had yet vouchsafed—and I began to think that she might, after all, be attainable.

That New Year's Eve, when I reported for work, Wilson Fairbanks, smiling mischievously, asked, "Why don't you have a date with a nice girl tonight?" I pointed out the obvious fact that I was working. "It's so quiet here," he said. "If you have a girl to go out with, I'll give you the rest of the night off."

My mind immediately turned to Barbara, though I suspected she'd made plans for New Year's Eve long since. But I had nothing to lose, so I mustered my courage and dialed the number of her rooming house on Morton Street. She had told me she lived on the second floor of the five-story building, a run-down walk-up brownstone. Her room, for which she paid seven dollars a week, had no stove, nor even a hot plate, and she shared a community bathroom on the floor above. The building, she said, was filled with striving young artists and writers.

The public telephone in the hallway on her floor rang, the landlady answered and hollered down the hall for Barbara. In moments, Barbara was on the line. For a second I was struck mute. But I managed to mumble, "I know this is very last-minute, but if you happen by any chance to be free tonight, I'd love to see you."

"You must be out of your mind! It's New Year's Eve!" But she giggled, which I took as a hopeful sign.

"Don't be angry, please," I begged, explaining that I'd been given the night off on condition I could find a date.

"I guess Lee McCabe must have turned you down," she taunted.

"Don't be mean."

She told me she did have a date—with an old friend, a private on leave from the Army—and that they were going to a party given by an aunt (her father's sister) at her apartment on Central Park West. She said she felt sorry for me and thought her friend wouldn't mind if I joined them. And, she said pointedly, there would probably be unattached girls at the party, among whom I might find a date. She told me to meet her at the apartment at eleven o'clock. It wasn't exactly the arrangement I'd hoped for, but who knew? It didn't sound as though she was romantically interested in her own date.

Reporters from the city room were throwing a party of their own in a suite at the Hotel Pennsylvania, across from Penn Station. The hotel housed

one of the liveliest cabarets in the city, where Fred Waring and his Pennsyl-
vanians presided nightly. Before heading uptown to meet Barbara, I gave
Pat Spiegel, one of the organizers of the reporters' bash, the two-dollar cover
for myself and a date—craftily planning to lure Barbara there later on.

The apartment of Barbara's aunt was filled with revelers of all ages, some
having dropped in on their way to other parties. Barbara and her date
greeted me like an old friend, and I was introduced all around. At midnight,
a somewhat emotional toast was made by an elderly friend of Barbara's aunt:
"We emerged victorious from a life-or-death struggle in which all we cher-
ish most was threatened with annihilation. Many heroes now lie buried, including our dauntless commander, Franklin Roosevelt. Let us embark on
the new year with vigor and gratitude, and revel in the bounties of peace."

Champagne glasses were raised, tears welled in many eyes, and "Auld
Lang Syne" was sung. I couldn't help but be moved, but I must admit that
my thoughts quickly turned to the matter of winning the girl of my dreams.
Why shouldn't I, too, participate in this new era of optimism?

I told Barbara about the party downtown, suggesting it would be a good
idea for us to be in the company of reporters, since she aimed to be a reporter
herself. She looked over at her date and saw he was engaged with an attractive young woman. If we could take both of them with us to the party, she
would come with me, she said. I agreed to fork over the extra two dollars it
would cost me, and the four of us hailed a cab and headed for the Hotel
Pennsylvania.

I remember that night as a kind of dream. We danced a lot. We stepped
onto the terrace of the rented suite, and were greeted by a dust of lightly
falling snow. I kissed her, for the first time. Soon after, we slipped away,
clinging to each other as we walked down Seventh Avenue. We talked about
our aspirations to become reporters and confided in each other about our
widely disparate childhoods and family lives.

Still impressed with Barbara's relationship to S. N. Behrman, I asked her
how her mother had happened to meet him. It was then that she casually disclosed yet another item of her family history—that her mother was the
younger sister of the violin virtuoso Jascha Heifetz. Because of Heifetz's
celebrity, Barbara said, her mother grew up among the cream of musicians,
artists and writers, including George Gershwin, Harpo Marx, Somerset
Maugham, Robert Sherwood, Dorothy Parker and Behrman. Heifetz, who
had been born in Russia, was revered by everyone in my Bronx neighborhood, and I told Barbara that my parents would be thrilled to learn that my
New Year's Eve date was Heifetz's niece.

Barbara and I stopped at Louie's, the saloon in Sheridan Square, and I asked the bartender, with whom I'd become friends, if he'd sell me a bottle of champagne to take home—even though I knew such a sale was illegal.

"How much have you got?" he asked.

"Three bucks," I said.

He slyly handed me a bottle.

Barbara was touched. On my meager salary, three dollars—not to mention the four I'd already spent to get us all into the Hotel Pennsylvania—was extravagant indeed.

We walked to her rooming house. She lit a couple of candles and put on a Billie Holiday record. On a table lay Erich Maria Remarque's recently published *Arch of Triumph,* a lush Parisian romance about young lovers who subsist on passion and Calvados. I had just read the book myself, and we shared our enthusiasm for its bittersweet romance; in the days to come we happily consumed our own share of Calvados.

I uncorked the warmish champagne as I'd seen Cary Grant do it, and it erupted like Old Faithful. By the time we finished drinking what was left, we knew we were in love. For Barbara and me, there was no more romantic place than Greenwich Village, with its easygoing writers and painters, jazz musicians and actors. No one had much money or cared, and no one seemed to need much sleep.

Barbara proposed we rent an apartment together, but I was not the free spirit she was, and I hesitated. We were still in an era of conventional social standards and, hard as I tried, I couldn't quite shake loose from my Bronx background. Hollywood reflected and reinforced a prudish code of morality by way of the Hays Office, created by the industry in 1934 to forestall government censorship. Among its rulings was that couples on the screen, even if married, must sleep in separate beds. If a man and a woman were merely sitting together on the same bed, the man was obliged to keep one foot on the floor.

In my own culture, which wouldn't have dreamed of faulting Hollywood, unmarried couples did not live openly together, and I was uncomfortable about transgressing this ingrained taboo. So, for a time, I became a subway-riding nomad, spending several nights a week in Barbara's room, but for the sake of appearances returning some nights to my parents' Bronx apartment.

I found it incongruous that a woman of Barbara's background should be living in such a mouse hole. I thought she should ask her parents for some money, so she could move to better quarters. But she seemed quite content to scrape along on her own. She told me cheerfully that she often subsisted on a banana or an apple until evening, when she could usually count on an uptown boyfriend to take her to dinner. Besides, she said, she really enjoyed the atmosphere of her rooming house.

The muted sound of wind instruments drifted down the staircase from the rooms above, occupied by jazz musicians. A warmhearted black prostitute in her early thirties lived on Barbara's floor. During pauses in the march of sailors to her door, she sometimes chatted with Barbara about her plans to retire and marry a rich man, who would love and protect her. But Barbara had only a nodding acquaintance with most of the other tenants. Like true New Yorkers, they minded their own business.

One of our favorite Village haunts was a smoky jazz club on Seventh Avenue and Tenth Street. A thick sirloin steak with french fries cost a dollar, but the real attraction was the New Orleans–style jazz of Miff Mole and his Dixieland Quartet, which also boasted the talents of Mugsy Spanier and Pee Wee Russell. In the 1920s Mole had been a ground-breaking trombone player on New York's jazz circuit. To me, his playing was still among the freshest around.

We were regulars, and we became friends with the band, which often serenaded Barbara. They introduced us to other jazzmen who lived in the Village, bringing us into a new and exotic fold. Once while we were all hanging out between sets, Mugsy produced a joint, lit it and offered it around. I had never seen marijuana—or weed, as Mugsy called it. I didn't know anyone who smoked it, and something told me that it wasn't for me. Barbara, ever the more daring, tried it and said it didn't do much for her. We stayed with beer and an occasional Scotch and water.

Now I can see how much Barbara and I had come to depend on each other. When we were apart for even a few hours, we would send each other notes at *The Times*. For her birthday, I had planned to take her to dinner at Café Society. I was off that day, and she was to meet me right after she finished work. Her boss, Charles Merz, the chief editorial writer, handed her his lead piece to take to the composing room to be set in type. She put it into her desk drawer and went to the rest room to freshen her makeup, planning to drop off the editorial on her way out of the building. But in her haste to meet me on time, she forgot to retrieve it.

By the time the composing room noticed the absence of the editorial, Merz was on a train to Boston. His space was filled with an improvised piece for the first edition. He called to check in before the second edition went to press, and dictated his editorial over the phone. When Barbara opened her desk the next morning, the sight of the undelivered copy sent her into a panic. Merz returned from Boston later that morning, and she went to his office to apologize, but—although he was a kind and gentle man—he fired her.

Barbara wrote him a note explaining how distracted she had been by her birthday celebration, and pleading to be reinstated. Since she already had started writing a profile of Merz for *Timesweek,* she suggested he might allow her to stay on the job at least until it was finished. He assented, and liked her profile so much that he allowed her to keep her job. Not long after, however, Barbara did lose her post, when George Barrett, whom she'd replaced, received his Army discharge. George was soon promoted to reporter, and Barbara began writing freelance, at which she eventually became very successful.

When Barbara was at last convinced that I was the man for her, she decided—with considerable trepidation—to introduce me to her mother. Relations between them had always been edgy, and were particularly strained since a misunderstanding of some sort at Christmas. A small family dinner was scheduled at the Behrman apartment, but I was far from sanguine about the meeting.

ELEVEN

THE BEHRMAN PENTHOUSE at Eighty-eighth Street and Madison Avenue was subleased from Diana Barrymore, whose life had been blighted by her brilliant but erratic actor father, John. Anyone familiar with the tabloids, as I confess I was, knew she had been named "Personality Debutante of 1938," had gone to Hollywood after a stint on Broadway and had begun her decline into alcoholism.

The apartment was very Hollywood with its jade-green walls, love seats set into carved gilt frames, floor-to-ceiling smoked mirrors, pale carpeting that felt a foot thick and French doors opening onto a narrow terrace.

Behrman took this ambiance in stride, accustomed as he was to Hollywood settings, but Barbara's mother, Elza—whose taste in furnishings was understated—always felt compelled to apologize for the apartment's showiness, explaining that it was temporary housing. The Behrmans had spent the war years at their summer home in Connecticut, and were now looking for permanent quarters in Manhattan.

Elza was an attractive woman of forty, with manners that were at once charming and reserved. Her short-cut, curly, dark brown hair contrasted strikingly with the intense blue of her eyes. Barbara had inherited her slight figure, small hands and feet and delicate features. I was surprised at the trace of Russian accent in Elza's speech, which Barbara had never thought to mention.

I guess I must have expected Behrman to look something like the debonair Noël Coward, and it was a bit of a shock to be greeted instead by a short, rotund, owlish-looking man, with wispy graying hair surrounding an almost bald pate, and thick spectacles. He wore a well-cut tweed jacket over a tan silk shirt and a cashmere cardigan but, in spite of his expensive tailoring, he looked rumpled. He gripped my hand firmly and, with a broad smile, said that he'd been looking forward to meeting Barbara's new conquest. His geniality put me instantly at ease.

The dining room, its walls painted cocoa brown, held a gleaming, black oblong table set with crystal and heavy silver. The floor was inlaid with polished black-and-white diamond-shaped tiles. When we went in to dinner, Elza sat at the head of the table, Behrman at the foot, and Barbara and I faced each other between them.

Behrman, a chain-smoker (though he never inhaled), immediately lit a cigarette. He always forgot he was smoking, and allowed his ash to drop where it would—frequently burning holes in his custom-tailored shirts and his Sulka ties. (I noticed that Elza winced when the ashes fell, but she said nothing.)

I tried with some effort to hide my anxiety as I came under Elza's scrutiny. Barbara had warned me of her mother's critical attitude toward her friends, along with her hypersensitivity about good table manners, an area in which I knew I lacked polish. But Behrman, I believed, saw me as a younger version of himself, struggling to transcend the birthright of an immigrant's son. He seemed aware of the spot I found myself in, and I could sense his compassion.

To my great relief, Behrman immediately began telling stories. He was, as Barbara had described him, the wittiest of conversationalists. He had an even rarer quality; somehow, he made the rest of us feel witty, too.

His sophistication and eloquence were all the more remarkable given his background. He had been raised on Providence Street in Worcester, Massachusetts, in a neighborhood of immigrant Eastern European Jews. His father frequently read aloud from the Talmud and Scriptures. His mother never learned to speak English. When she attended a traveling production of one of her son's plays in Worcester with a relative, her only reaction (in Yiddish) was, "Tell me, why doesn't my son get married?"

After attending Clark College in Worcester for two years, Behrman went to Harvard on a scholarship and was accepted into George Pierce Baker's playwriting course. In New York, unable to break into the theater, he entered Columbia in 1918, where he earned an M.A. in English.

Trying to survive as a writer, Behrman described the next phase of his life as "cadaverous days." While *The New Yorker* and a few other magazines accepted an occasional article from him, it was not until 1927, with the Broadway production of his first play, *The Second Man,* that he found success. Until then he had kept himself alive first as a theatrical press agent and then as a member of *The New York Times Book Review,* where he was in charge of the "Letters to the Editor" department—a job he found so tedious he began writing letters to himself under various assumed names. They were good letters, but when the subterfuge was discovered, he was fired.

While his plays were characterized by the critics as "comedies of manners" and "drawing room comedies," Behrman refuted these labels, saying, "There are no drawing rooms in America, and very few manners either." There was little action in his plays, but—when he was in top form—the twists in conversations between his characters, and the insights into society's elite, provided theatergoers with an evening's ample entertainment. His were works about the refined rich, whom he kept satirizing. Fanny Brice, commenting on his elegance of expression coupled with his lower-class Jewish roots, referred to him as the "Silk Herring."

His plays starred actors like the Lunts, Katharine Cornell, Laurence Olivier and Ina Claire. And he worked on screenplays for, most notably, Greta Garbo, including *Ninotchka,* one of her biggest hits. (He was called in as a script doctor, but received no screen credit.) Then he effectually killed her career with the ill-conceived *Two-Faced Woman*—the last movie she ever made.

UNTUTORED AS I WAS in fancy dinner-table etiquette, I knew enough to be startled when the soup course was served; Behrman ignored his spoon and slurped directly from his soup bowl. Though amazed at his manners, I must say they made me feel more comfortable. If I used the wrong fork, which I was sure to do, he, at least, wouldn't notice.

He asked a lot of questions about *The Times,* which he read cover to cover every day. I was describing the morgue to him when the dessert course was about to be served, and I hadn't noticed the arrival of the fingerbowls. The maid offered a platter containing a delectable-looking fluffy chocolate concoction, and, as I reached for the serving spoon, I glanced down and saw the small glass bowl of colorless liquid sitting atop a white lace doily in the center of my dessert plate.

I didn't know if I was meant to put the dessert into it, or pour its contents over the dessert, or what. I was too rattled to look around and see how others at the table had dealt with it. (Barbara later told me she had frantically tried to catch my eye and show me what to do.) As I hesitated, flushed of face and with pounding heart, Elza reached over and deftly removed bowl and doily, trying to suppress a look of pity for my ill-breeding.

My discomfort redoubled when Elza took advantage of a lull in the conversation to question me about my prospects as Barbara's future husband. From what Barbara had told me, Elza seemed to take only a minimal interest in her daughter's welfare, and I was surprised that she should express any concern at all. Indeed, Barbara had given me the impression that Elza would be only too glad to have her daughter off her hands.

As I was soon to realize, however, Elza could be capricious—even at times treacherous—when it came to her dealings with Barbara. Tonight, probably foreseeing the uncomfortable day when she would have to introduce me—unformed young man that I was—to her family and friends as her son-in-law, she began to assume a proprietary attitude.

"Where do you two plan to live when you're married?" she asked, after the coffee was served. "Will you be able to afford a decent apartment?"

I couldn't resist responding with a question of my own. "Has Barbara ever told you how she's been living since she left college?" Unperturbed by my implied rebuke, Elza coolly replied, "When she chose to throw away her college education, I thought it was time to let her sink or swim."

Behrman tactfully interposed with another anecdote—so smoothly recounted I wondered if all his stories were rehearsed. (Indeed, he later recorded this anecdote in his memoir *People in a Diary.*) He told of Ina Claire reading a long and complex scene during rehearsals of his 1932 play *Biography.* "When I praised Ina on her impressive delivery, she replied, 'Honest to God, Sam, I didn't understand one word of it!'" ("Sam" was short for the Samuel of "S. N." His middle name was Nathaniel.) He invited me now to call him by the family nickname, Berrie.

During cordials in the living room, Behrman encouraged me to talk more about my recent life, and somehow I drifted onto the subject of Eddie Jaffe and the wild nights at Duffy's Tavern. A bit hesitantly, and with Barbara chiming in, I told him that she and I had tentatively outlined a play—a comedy (we hoped) about Duffy's milieu that we wanted to call *Elbow Room*. We explained we were currently struggling to get our first-act curtain down.

Behrman laughed. "I've had that problem." To our surprise, he said he would give us a $500 reward if we did get the curtain down. "I'm sure you know that George Kaufman started writing plays while he was working at your paper," he said by way of encouragement, and sailed into one of his favorite Kaufman stories. It was actually about Kaufman's wife, Beatrice, a fiercely egocentric woman.

It seems Beatrice took a young lover off to a country inn for a tryst, having carefully made reservations under an assumed name. When the lovers arrived, they discovered there had been some sort of mix-up. The desk clerk had no record of the reservation and the inn had no rooms left. Beatrice, accustomed to the kind of deferential service proffered whenever she traveled with her famous husband, confronted the inn's manager, demanding he produce a room at once. "Do you realize," she said, "that you are turning away Mrs. George S. Kaufman?"

Barbara had told me that Behrman kept a diary—in virtually indecipherable longhand—in which he wrote every night before he went to sleep. As we were leaving, she opened the door to a hall closet, where he stored the scores of neatly piled notebooks, distinguished by their black-and-white cardboard covers, the kind I used as a schoolboy. It was from these notebooks that he eventually extracted the entries for his memoir.

When Barbara and I said good night, I was so intoxicated by Behrman's conversation that my discomfort at Elza's obvious disapproval of me had all but vanished. And I couldn't help mentioning to Barbara, as we walked to the subway station, what I thought was at least a small vindication of my honor.

"You were so concerned that my table manners wouldn't measure up to your mother's sense of refinement," I said, "yet your stepfather didn't bother to use his soup spoon!"

Barbara shrugged. "I guess you could say he's earned the right to be eccentric. I wouldn't be surprised if someday you'll be able to drink your soup that way, too."

Exhilarated by Behrman's apparent interest in our play, Barbara and I stayed up until dawn polishing the plot. But, although we tried on and off during the next several weeks to get that curtain down, we never succeeded.

I concluded I was no Kaufman, and concentrated harder on achieving the realistic goal of becoming a *Times* reporter.

Two weeks after the family dinner, Elza invited Barbara and me to a Jascha Heifetz concert at Carnegie Hall, where I sat in the family box and was introduced to Barbara's grandmother Anna, her aunt Pauline (Elza's sister), Pauline's husband, Samuel Chotzinoff, and a couple of cousins. Following the encores, we all proceeded backstage.

As we milled about in an anteroom awaiting our turn to greet the famous man, Barbara introduced me to Grandpa Heifetz, Elza and Jascha's father. He was a roly-poly, gnomelike man who carried a cane. Dressed in a dark suit, his bald pate covered by a homburg, he was the first member of Barbara's family who, it seemed to me, was utterly without pretensions. During the concert, I was told, he had sat in the orchestra, which he preferred. When we approached Heifetz, Grandpa introduced me to him, very sweetly, I thought, as "Barbara's gentleman." Heifetz smiled stiffly; it was the same remote, masklike smile with which he greeted everyone, including his mother.

We all repaired to the apartment of Barbara's aunt Pauline, across the street from Carnegie Hall. Grandpa, whose name was Ruven, sat quietly in a corner, evidently accustomed to being ignored. But, good reporter that I was learning to be—and feeling less intimidated by him than anyone else in the room except Barbara—I pulled up a chair and talked to him. He was delighted to have a fresh audience for his oft-told story of how he discovered his son's genius.

Jascha was born, according to his own account, in the Russian city of Vilna on February 2, 1901 (or possibly, as Barbara's mother believed, in 1900; if this date is true, Grandma Heifetz must have snipped off a year to make her prodigy even more of a wonder). His father played first violin in the symphony orchestra, and his mother played the trumpet. When Jascha was in his crib, Ruven noticed that the baby's mood varied with the tempo and harmonies of whatever piece of music was being practiced. If the melody was lively, Jascha kicked and gurgled. If it was mournful, Jascha wailed. Ruven suspected he had a musical prodigy for a son.

Jascha was given his first violin when he was three. At five, he was enrolled in the Royal School of Music. Leopold Auer, acknowledged as the world's foremost violin teacher, heard the boy play, and invited Jascha to study at the conservatory in St. Petersburg. He made his debut there at seven.

At ten, Jascha toured Europe to great acclaim and, by twelve, he was one of the most-talked-about musicians on the continent. In 1917, Ruven, Anna and their three children fled Russia to escape the revolution, crossing through Siberia, China and Japan, en route to the United States.

On October 27 of that year, Heifetz made his American debut at Carnegie Hall, and a story entered the annals of musical lore. For those who haven't heard it, here it is: The audience was filled with musicians eager to hear this fifteen-year-old prodigy whose reputation had glowingly preceded him. As Heifetz played with unmatched brilliance, the violinist Mischa Elman, who was in the audience, leaned over to his companion, the pianist Leopold Godowsky, and whispered, "It's getting hot in here, isn't it?" "Not for pianists," Godowsky replied.

Heifetz became, arguably, the greatest violin virtuoso of all time. When the great conductor Arturo Toscanini first heard Heifetz, he was awestruck by his dazzling technique, later commenting, "I nearly lost my mind." George Bernard Shaw, when he was a music critic, heard the nineteen-year-old Heifetz play, and wrote him a letter:

> My dear Heifetz:
> Your recital has filled me and my wife with anxiety. If you pro-voke a jealous God by playing with such superhuman perfection, you will die young. I earnestly advise you to play something badly every night before going to bed, instead of saying your prayers. No mortal should presume to play so faultlessly.

When Barbara's and my first son, Michael, was born, Grandpa Heifetz was among our early visitors. He arrived with a tuning fork. None of his grandchildren—though some had perfect pitch and all received musical training—turned out to be prodigies. But he was hoping, he said, that his first great-grandchild would be "another Jascha." Sadly for poor Grandpa, when he held the humming fork to our infant Michael's ear, there was no re-action at all.

Grandpa Heifetz was a kind, well-meaning man, but his family had no patience for his literal-mindedness. He was apt to corner you and pepper you with comments and questions about such household items as Scotch tape (wasn't it remarkable, he ruminated, how the little reel was enclosed in its own housing, and could be bitten off by those cunning little teeth?). He had a vague notion that members of his family deliberately withheld or misrep-resented vital information about the objects of his perplexity, and he could be relentless in his cross-examinations, hoping to trap a daughter or son-in-law or grandchild into an inadvertent contradiction. All of them had learned to duck, but Grandpa could see I was a pushover.

Once he cornered me into explaining the shmoo, a whimsical character invented by Al Capp for his cartoon strip *L'il Abner*. The shmoo was a species of animal that L'il Abner found in a valley. More than just friendly critters, shmoos were a good source of food, because they produced eggs on demand, gave bottled milk, butter wrapped in waxed paper and, in loving moments, cheesecakes. If looked at hungrily they would die from the rapturous idea of providing a service to humanity. If you broiled their meat, it tasted like the best steak; fried, it was like chicken—and it had no bones.

A poll revealed that while only six percent of Americans knew the name of the vice president of the United States, thirty-three percent knew all about the shmoo. But explaining the concept to Grandpa was like trying to build a house out of butter. I couldn't simply describe the shmoo—I had to explain the concept of the comic strip, which led to the topic of syndicated comics, then to the meaning, origin and practices of syndicates and, finally, freedom of the press, which landed us on one of Grandpa's favorite subjects—the lack of freedom in Russia. I finally got him back to New York by quoting some circulation figures of New York newspapers. Grandpa loved statistics.

Returning to the shmoo, Grandpa wanted to know if the word was in the dictionary. I explained it hadn't been included yet. This gave Grandpa an opportunity to hold forth on the miracle of the dictionary. "One man, to take together all those words in one book! How does he find all those words?"

TWELVE

M Y WILLINGNESS TO LISTEN patiently to Grandpa ensured my welcome with at least part of the Heifetz family. Elza's older sister, Pauline, the family beauty and live wire, was, if anything, haughtier than Elza—but it wasn't her daughter I was planning to marry, and so she tolerated me.

Pauline's Russian accent was more pronounced than Elza's, and Elza maintained that Pauline deliberately exaggerated the accent because she thought it was cute. Her pronunciation had overtones of French, a language both sisters spoke fluently. Elza, who had always resented living in Pauline's shadow, enjoyed telling a mocking story about her sister's fractured English. She was driving with Pauline somewhere on a country road, when Pauline nearly scared her out of her wits by shouting, *"Cochon! Cochon!"* Elza slammed on the brakes to avoid hitting the pig that Pauline evidently saw in the road. It turned out Pauline was merely mispronouncing a road sign that read, "Caution."

To my mind, neither Pauline nor Elza took at all after their mother, and Barbara agreed with me. Anna Heifetz was a tall, stout, maternal-looking woman with a humorous sparkle in her eyes, a spontaneous smile, and a chain-smoker's cough. Her children's friends adored her and called her "Mother," and I quickly saw why. She was gracious to me and told Barbara I was *simpatico*. Barbara's few truly fond childhood memories were of summer afternoons spent playing casino with Grandma.

Although it had been Ruven Heifetz who discovered Jascha's talent, it was Anna who astutely managed his boyhood career. It was she who had organized the family's escape from Russia and their subsequent establishment in the United States.

Anna made some canny real estate investments, including the purchase of a brownstone off Central Park West and a country house in Narragansett Pier, Rhode Island, and together with Jascha's ever-increasing concert fees, the Heifetz family had managed to live very well. No one in the family ever heard Jascha express any gratitude to his mother for her labors on his behalf. He was the least sentimental of men. But when he was old enough to manage his own career, he provided her with a comfortable income.

Pauline was married to Samuel Chotzinoff, who had been the music critic for the *New York World* and later for the *Post* (before it went tabloid). An accomplished musician himself, he had once served as Heifetz's accompanist, which was how he and Pauline had met. His talent was revealed to the world through an accident. He'd been engaged to perform piano solos from behind the curtain for the play *The Concert,* in which the star, Leo Dietrichstein, mimed playing a piano onstage.

The act was so precisely timed that even the critics were hoodwinked, and Dietrichstein's piano virtuosity received rave reviews. The truth emerged one night when Chotzinoff was ill and another pianist sat in. Insufficiently rehearsed, he began to play before Dietrichstein touched the keys, thus revealing Chotzinoff as the real virtuoso. His career as an upfront accompanist was launched when he was engaged by the violinist Efrem Zimbalist.

Chotzinoff was a scholarly man with a biting wit, and he did not scruple to turn it on his brother-in-law. While Pauline and Elza were in awe of

Jascha, "Chotzie," as he was known, could not resist mocking Jascha's often ill-suppressed pomposity and the literal-mindedness he had inherited from his father. To Elza's displeasure, Berrie, too, sometimes satirized Jascha. He referred to his brother-in-law as "the fiddle player," and affected to believe he was an idiot savant. Berrie once told me about a visit to Jascha in California, during which Jascha entertained him by demonstrating the efficiency of his most recent purchase, the newly invented electric pencil sharpener.

"It was such a relief not having to make conversation with him," Berrie said, "that I happily ran all over the house, up and down stairs, finding pencils for him to sharpen. Then we sent out for more pencils. We kept at it for the better part of an hour. Jascha was enchanted by how well we'd hit it off."

Chotzinoff was best known for his coup in convincing Arturo Toscanini, soon after his retirement as conductor of the New York Philharmonic Symphony Orchestra, to create the NBC Symphony of the Air. The Chotzinoff apartment was a musical salon, and after a while I grew accustomed to finding guests like Toscanini, Heifetz, Vladimir Horowitz or Gregor Piatigorsky exchanging shop talk and sometimes tinkering playfully with the living room Steinway.

Barbara and I were invited to celebrate New Year's 1947 at Toscanini's Riverdale estate overlooking the Hudson. Elza, Pauline and their friends put on a show satirizing various musicians, much of which eluded me as I was as yet unfamiliar with their idiosyncrasies. Afterward, a jazz record was played and guests began dancing. Toscanini, with couples spinning around him, stood in the middle of the floor, his hand cupped to his ear, so intent on the music that he seemed lost in a world of his own.

I DECIDED THE TIME had come for Barbara to meet my parents, and I cautioned them that she wasn't like any of my other girlfriends. When we arrived at their shop, we waited outside for it to empty of customers. Noticing Barbara and me through the store window, my mother smiled sweetly at Barbara and waved to us.

My parents took Barbara to their hearts at once. My mother told me later that Barbara was a "girl of quality"—but didn't I think we were both too young to get married? I reminded her that she was only nineteen when she married my father. After this mild demurral, she assured me that both she and my father were prepared to welcome Barbara as a daughter. My brother, Harold, who had himself married young, was equally accepting—although he and his wife, Sylvia, were bemused by the bohemian life Barbara and

I were living in Greenwich Village. They themselves lived in Brooklyn, and Harold, who had just landed a job with an esteemed CPA firm, was on his way to achieving the solid financial security for which he had always yearned.

Barbara insisted I graduate from NYU before we marry. But between my wooing and my working, I had little time for writing term papers or studying for exams. By semester's end, although I had managed to turn in most of my reports, I still had not completed a major paper—on the New England Transcendentalists—for an American literature class taught by the widely respected Professor Oscar Cargill.

Barbara had kept pace with me on my required reading, since she was as interested in Thoreau and Emerson as I was. The day before my paper was due—the same morning as my final exam—Barbara urged me to come to her room right after work and finish the report. She said she was prepared to ply me with coffee throughout the night, if need be.

I was exhausted when I arrived at midnight and, instead of coffee, took a swig of Calvados, hoping it would perk me up. I promptly passed out. When I opened my eyes, it was eight-fifteen and the sun was shining. The exam was scheduled for nine. Terror seized me.

"Why didn't you wake me?" I cried, seeing Barbara sitting calmly at the table. Her expression was both serene and mischievous as she handed me a sheaf of neatly typed pages headed "The Emersonian Influence on Whitman." "It's a digest of the talks we've had over the past few months," she said. "It's my wedding present to you."

Professor Cargill gave Barbara's paper an A+, and my exam a C.

We were married on June 2, 1946, in the Behrman apartment, with only immediate family present: my parents; my brother and his wife; Barbara's mother and stepfather; her father, Harold Stone; her fifteen-year-old brother, Harold Jr.; and her nine-year-old half brother, David Behrman.

Barbara, at nineteen, looked ethereally lovely in a street-length white silk dress and a white lace Juliet cap. But I felt ill at ease in my new light gray-blue suit, which I thought inappropriate attire for a groom. My utilitarian wardrobe up to then had consisted of two Wallachs suits: a gray plaid flannel and a tan tweed, plus a pair of navy blue slacks. I had hoped to please my new mother-in-law by wearing a proper dark blue suit for my wedding, but I couldn't find one.

Accompanied by my father, I had gone from one men's store to the next—East Side, West Side, uptown and down—and eventually discovered that male civilian clothes had not been a manufacturer's priority during the war. Stores were still awaiting the delivery of their peacetime orders and my size, "extra-long," seemed to be nonexistent. I finally had to settle for the only suit that fit me—that inappropriate light gray-blue.

And that same afternoon, I paid a somewhat timid first visit to Tiffany's to buy a plain gold wedding band (Barbara's choice), which I ordered engraved with a favorite line from Goethe: "Linger awhile, so fair thou art."

Although a rabbi performed the ceremony (at my parents' insistence), Barbara's family seemed to regard the wedding as a youthful lark. Elza—with a cynicism that I found hard to forgive—made it clear she didn't expect the marriage to last. She took Barbara aside to tell her, "I'm not going to give you my wedding present just yet. You may need the money for an abortion."

Behrman, in a jovial mood, playfully told Barbara it still wasn't too late to change her mind; if she decided to throw me over, he would be glad to take her away at once—on a logging expedition. And Harold Stone, clearly uncomfortable with the whole situation, asked us why on earth we hadn't just opted for a justice of the peace. "Don't you know it's much harder to get divorced when you've been married by a rabbi?" (Himself about to marry his third wife, he knew whereof he spoke.)

Harold, then in his early forties, still looked like the dashingly handsome playboy he had been twenty years earlier when he'd married Elza Heifetz. Born on the Lower East Side, he was the third child and first son of Romanian immigrants. His father, Adolph Finklestein, had changed his name and founded F. & W. Grand, the chain of five-and-ten-cent stores that for a time competed successfully with Woolworth's.

Harold had always compensated with flair for what he lacked in substance. He dropped out of college after his second year to concentrate on having a good time. Wiry and athletic, he was a skier and polo player. He looked a lot like the film star Brian Donlevy before there was a Brian Donlevy. In fact, as a young man he'd been urged to test for the movies, but declined, preferring instead a token job in his father's business, and living on the substantial income from a trust fund his father had set up for him. He was openhanded, charming and thoroughly likable, but he was fated to remain an eternal adolescent. At twenty, he was one of the country's youngest millionaires and was known to the maître d' of every smart speakeasy and supper club in Manhattan.

When he met Elza, she was appearing with her sister, Pauline, in the chorus of a Broadway musical called *Dream Girls*. Neither of them had had any stage experience, but were hired for the publicity value of their status as "the beautiful Heifetz sisters" and, as such, they were fleetingly the toast of the town.

Elza was then still living at home with her mother. She felt diminished by her genius brother and her vivacious sister, who by now was married to Chotzinoff. When Harold Stone came along, she was entranced not only by the prospect of marriage to a handsome, rich man-about-town but also by the promise of escape from her overwhelming family. Elza and Harold became a much-photographed celebrity couple and, when they eloped, Elza told the press, "It was a case of love at first sight. We're married, and oh, so happy! I'm through with the stage forever—I'm Mrs. Harold Stone now, first, last and always."

Barbara had told me about touring in Europe as a child. Her parents gambled on the Riviera, and later she learned about one night there, which happened to coincide with the day of the American stock market crash. That night, Harold won $50,000 at the roulette table. He was so enchanted with the tidy little pile of $10,000 chips placed before him that, with Elza's amused encouragement, he decided not to cash them in, but to take them back to New York to show off to his friends. When he proudly displayed his winnings, he was told bluntly, "It's lucky you have these chips because it's all you've got left in the world. You've been wiped out." In fact, Harold's father managed to hang on for a while longer, but there was no more trust fund income.

Although Harold pursued various business ventures, it was years before he once again began to prosper. Elza was unwilling to wait. The glamour had worn off and with the nudging of her mother as well as Pauline and Chotzie, who had always regarded Harold as a lightweight, she asked for a divorce.

At the time of Barbara's and my wedding, Harold was the co-proprietor of yet another five-and-ten-cent chain, M. H. Lamston, founded with a friend, Mortimer Lahm. The business was successful enough, but because Harold had to pay alimony and had become a racetrack addict, he was perpetually in debt. He never stopped blaming his problems on the breakup of his first marriage. Elza, he told me more than once, had been the love of his life and, despite his subsequent marriages, he'd never gotten over her.

Wilson Fairbanks had needled the bullpen into giving Barbara and me a three-paragraph wedding announcement—highly unusual in that day when such listings were normally reserved for members of the Social Register. Mr. Fairbanks countered any accusations of nepotism by citing Barbara's ties to Heifetz and Behrman.

It was one of his last acts as telegraph editor, before he retired on June 1. He moved to his Vermont farm, where he grew a variety of crops and began translating the works of Homer into English. He was succeeded by Frederick Austin, and Grover Loud became assistant telegraph editor.

Trying to live up to *The Times*'s reputation as a "paper of record," *Timesweek* published in its entirety Mr. Fairbanks's long farewell address to his fellow editors. It's hard to imagine a *Times* editor delivering so hortatory a speech today—or to picture a group of fellow editors meekly listening to it:

"We stand at the crossroads of the world's news," declaimed Mr. Fairbanks. "If we but lift the eyes of imagination, we catch all the vast panorama of the world's life—history in the making—mankind on the march. Pieces of paper weave the fascinating picture—a never ceasing and ever changing fabric of events. . . . In the mass here are nations upset, peoples slaughtered, dictators overthrown.

"As newspapermen we have a great task laid upon us. We have to assemble and present the record to the waiting throng outside. Thus we are peculiar people, standing between the actors in life's dramas, little and big, and the spectators (who are our readers) and revealing the former to the latter—without prejudice, without passion, accurately and completely."

AFTER BARBARA AND I exchanged vows and I stamped on the nuptial wineglass, we boarded the State of Maine Express at Grand Central Terminal. In our compartment, we held our own champagne celebration. We were heading for Sebasticook Lake, outside Newport, Maine, a wooded resort that Grover Loud had recommended as unrivaled anywhere in the world for romantic beauty—"the perfect spot for a honeymoon."

We had rented a primitive cabin for a month, the vast lake at our front door. We fetched our water from a hand-pumped well and had to walk a mile or so into Newport to use a telephone. But Loud had not misled us. It was beautiful, and it was certainly remote. It was even downright spooky at times. One night, we walked into town and saw a horror movie. While talking about it on the deserted country road that led back to the cabin, we so frightened ourselves that we ran all the way home.

We spent our days lying in the sun, reading, swimming and canoeing. One evening we walked into Newport to have dinner at Jones's Inn, where Barbara wanted to introduce me to lobster. My parents had always avoided shellfish, and I'd never had the courage to try lobster on my own. We had remembered to pack our wartime ration books, which, as still required, we turned over to the waiter to entitle us to servings of melted butter.

Face to face with the lobster, I hesitated to attack it. Barbara mocked me: "You're a newspaperman, you live in the Village, you play the horses, you hobnob with the likes of Eddie Jaffe, you're a jazz buff, and you're afraid to eat lobster?" Oh, well, I thought. I ate it—and loved it. Actually, I wasn't a total stranger to exotic food. When I was twelve, there was a so-called Appetizing store in my Bronx neighborhood, where the window displayed a row of small, beguiling, red-cellophane-wrapped glass jars of pressed caviar, priced at fifty cents. I had never seen caviar before, but saved my weekly allowance and daringly bought a jar. I was hooked for life.

When we returned to New York, Barbara and I moved in temporarily with my parents in their four-room Bronx flat. We had thought we'd quickly find a small apartment, but discovered that the postwar housing shortage had not abated. With the great influx of returning soldiers, affordable apartments were still hard to find.

So great was the need that a government housing order had been issued, blocking nearly all new construction except housing for veterans. Warren Moscow's apartment search upon his return from Guam was so fruitless that he posted a notice on the bulletin board at *The Times:* "Please do not disturb the quiet of the city room with unseemly laughter . . . but if anyone knows anyone who has a friend who knows about an apartment, the information would be greatly appreciated." When Moscow's strategy proved successful, a copy editor, Sam Sharkey, adopted it. He had been on the hunt for over seven months, during which time he commuted to work from Philadelphia.

Even Lee Cooper, the real estate editor, bemoaned the housing situation in a *Timesweek* piece: "The hard fact is, you cannot get blood out of a turnip. There is simply nothing available in the way of a desirable apartment in the city—at a newspaperman's rent level. There is a thirty-two-room apartment vacant on the Upper East Side at about $20,000 a year in case anyone is interested. . . . Just to let you know that the housing crisis really has hit home (no pun intended), I want it known that the real estate editor himself is in the market for new living quarters."

Barbara and I were marooned for six months in the Bronx. She explored it as she would have toured a small foreign country, taking leisurely strolls on the Grand Concourse and visiting the monuments of my childhood, from the abandoned lots where I had played to Loew's Paradise and the Ascot, the Bronx's first art cinema, where I'd seen my first foreign-language films.

Barbara became my mother's apprentice in the kitchen, where she learned to prepare gefilte fish and chicken soup. My mother also made dresses for Barbara, a real boon during those early days of our marriage when we were on a strict budget. In some ways, my mother became the indulgent mother Barbara never had. At last, a customer at my parents' store brought word of an apartment available at eighty dollars a month. It was only one room on the top floor of a four-floor walk-up. But the address was tony—39 East Sixty-fifth Street, between Madison and Park Avenues, only three doors west of the house once occupied by Sara Delano Roosevelt, FDR's mother. There was a tiny, but well-equipped, kitchenette and a bathroom with a tub and shower.

We had to buy the furniture that came with the apartment (a common practice in those days), but luckily it was both tasteful and comfortable. Elza somewhat grudgingly released the wedding gift she had withheld so that we could pay for the furniture. The apartment had only one exposure, and it was stifling in the summer; but it was our own.

Barbara began submitting freelance ideas to magazines, but for the time being I was the sole breadwinner, eagerly awaiting promotion to reporter. Starting reporters earned seventy-five dollars a week, which would enable Barbara and me to get by. For the first time, I was concerned about money, and glad I'd joined the Newspaper Guild—in those days a voluntary union that had won minimum salary scales and a forty-hour workweek. I worked harder than ever writing in-depth *Timesweek* articles, hoping to be recognized by the city editor as a prospect for the reportorial staff.

I continued to earn extra money writing "CGO" filler copy on weekends; and I broke into a rewarding new income source—freelance articles for the Sunday arts section. Jack Gould, red-haired and feisty, was the critic and editor for radio and television (still in its infancy). He was likable and approachable and we had established a friendly give-and-take. He liked to rib me about why it was taking me so long to make it to reporter. "How did you manage to persuade such a pretty girl to marry you," he would ask, "when you can't persuade the city editor to promote you?"

I worked up the nerve to ask Jack for an assignment—although I well knew that clerks and news assistants rarely, if ever, had their story ideas accepted. Stories in Section 2 of the Sunday paper, also known as the Sunday Drama Section and years later rechristened Arts & Leisure, were usually assigned to prominent staff reporters or experienced outside writers. The average fee was fifty dollars, and, moreover, the stories were bylined.

I told Jack about what I thought would make a really good radio piece—the actor J. Scott Smart, who was playing the title role in *The Fat Man*, Dashiell Hammett's new private-eye series that was a kind of sequel to *The Thin Man*. Barbara and I had become fans of the series, and I'd read that Smart weighed 265 pounds—an instance of typecasting rare for radio. Jack chuckled. "Not a bad angle," he said, and gave me the assignment. "And be sure you point out high in the story that if *The Fat Man* is ever tagged for TV, Smart will be a natural for the role."

I interviewed Smart, and my column-length article ran July 24, 1947, in Section 2 under my very first *New York Times* byline. My parents read it, my friends read it. Barbara alerted her mother and Berrie to be sure they read it, and they invited us to dinner to celebrate. I thought I detected a slight thaw in Elza's attitude. Berrie said he found the article amusing, and was certain it augured good things for me at *The Times*. But I was disappointed to find that at the paper itself the byline went basically unnoticed. As far as the city room was concerned, the only byline that counted was the one in the daily paper. And that, for the time being, eluded me.

THIRTEEN

"THE MOST USEFUL MAN on a newspaper is one who can edit," decreed Adolph Ochs in a speech at the Columbia School of Journalism in 1925. He described the copy editor as "a news digester" who had a duty "to go through the process of elimination, saving the newspaper space and the reader time."

Reporters naturally took umbrage, and Ochs's paean to copy editors still could stir debate in the city room two decades later. I often heard complaints from reporters that *The Times* regarded itself as essentially an editor's—rather than a reporter's—newspaper.

"Writers there are galore," Ochs had continued, but good copy editors—men who could put a story "in printable form with its values disclosed and brought within the understanding of the reader"—were in short supply.

One day Roe Eastman, a city desk copy editor (and a devout adherent of Ochs's dictum) told me about some especially sloppy copy he had handled in recent days—much of it, he implied, written under the influence of alcohol.

I suggested he articulate his ire in an article for *Timesweek*, not anticipating the controversy it would provoke.

Eastman wrote that if not for the skills of copy editors, who were often "slandered" by reporters for altering their stories, newspapers could not be published at all. And he cited some examples of "egregious" passages deleted or changed by copy editors. His first example: "The casket was opened so that the followers of the church could gaze upon their priest. The bishop was in a fine state of preservation owing to the special embalming fluid used." Another example: "The roommate could advance no motive for the suicide other than Anderson had been a morbid youth given over to reading deep, classical literature."

In a rebuttal submitted to *Timesweek*, Herman Dinsmore, himself a copy editor (on the cable desk), surprisingly came to the defense of "good reporters." While conceding there were stories requiring stern editing, he said copy editors could be overzealous at times. Their function, he held, was to fine-tune the reporter's grammar, not to make arbitrary changes or rewrite a story; many a good story had been weakened by autocratic copy editors. He said foreign correspondents conveyed their strange milieus by "colors and nuances" and copy editors must not be "bent on unreasonable rearrangement or idle word changing."

The debate persisted in issue after issue of *Timesweek*. Wilson Fairbanks, who remained abreast of the goings-on at *The Times*, mailed his salute to copy editors from Vermont, citing Carr Van Anda's maxim: "A newspaper is made on the desk." Mr. Fairbanks went on to defend the copy editor's mandate to ascertain a story was "decisively aligned with the principles" of *The Times*: "And if he feels that elimination, in small or large part, or even rewriting is needed to accomplish this end, then by all means, let him do that."

Dinsmore parried, explaining he wasn't defending bad reporting, but good reporting. He hoped his article would serve as a caution to copy editors with a penchant for "word managing" to let good copy stand on its own.

The reporters at first remained on the sidelines, savoring the spectacle of editors battling among themselves. But then Harold Callender, the Paris bureau chief, chimed in—supporting Dinsmore's pro-reporter view, of course: "Surely Mr. Fairbanks must have known a couple of good reporters who did not require such heroics from the copy desk; reporters whom the desk trusted to be, if not 'absolutely right' (a quality hardly short of divinity) yet fairly right—as right, let us say, as the copy editor could be who was not on the spot whence the story came and could not possibly know who was 'absolutely right.' Perhaps Mr. Dinsmore has known more reporters who knew how to write a story or at any rate whose judgment of facts was almost equal to that of the copy editor."

The continuing debate helped me understand, for the first time, the innate power that can be wielded by a publication's managing editor, even in the case of a miniature paper like *Timesweek*. I was pleased to have brought a smoldering issue to wide attention. While I tried to empathize with each side, my private sympathy was with the reporters; after all, I hoped soon to be one of them. (It never occurred to me I might someday be an editor.)

I had seen editors save the reputations of reporters who turned in sloppy copy, but I had also witnessed bungling editors ruin good writing. Stories were sometimes cut in half, with imaginative phrases, transitional sentences and perceptive insights amputated. And sometimes leads were arbitrarily altered—not always for the better. Once, a few years after I became a reporter, I was briefly hospitalized with the flu. An article I had written a week earlier, recommending plays to see during the Christmas season, was published just as I was recuperating. The copy editor rewrote my lead, giving it what he must have believed was an elegant seasonal flourish: "Now that the turkey repasts have been properly digested and the calorie-counters are resolutely counting again, a number of citizens will begin thinking about Christmas, New Year's Eve and theater tickets." Reading that sentence under my byline brought my symptoms raging back.

With the success of the copyediting debate, I was emboldened to take *Timesweek* into the field of investigative journalism. My first target was the cafeteria, often maligned by the staff for its practice of serving reheated leftovers—especially knockwurst with sauerkraut—and day-old bread. I thought such an exposé would bring both plaudits for *Timesweek* and culinary improvements; but I miscalculated.

I assigned the investigation to Richard F. Shepard, a newly arrived copyboy. Fresh from the Merchant Marine, Dick found the city room more tumultuous than life at sea. Like me, he aspired to be a reporter, but his assignment for *Timesweek*, it turned out, was not any help to him. One day, after he had begun interviewing reporters about their experiences with the cafeteria's food, I found a long blue envelope in my mailbox. I knew it could mean only one thing: a summons from A. H. Sulzberger. I wondered what I'd done wrong.

In the outer office of the publisher's hallowed fourteenth-floor sanctuary, his secretary told me he was on the phone and I'd have to wait a few minutes. I paced down the hallway and peered into the boardroom of dark wood walls and brass chandeliers. It was grander than I'd imagined, more so than any boardroom portrayed in the movies. Inside was the longest table I'd ever seen, made of solid mahogany and surrounded by twenty armchairs. At the far end of the room was a cavernous marble fireplace, over which hung a portrait of Adolph Ochs. The walls were decorated with framed photos of world figures who had visited *The Times*, among them Roosevelt, Churchill, Einstein, Lindbergh and a smattering of European heads of state.

The secretary beckoned, and I entered the publisher's private office, as stately as the boardroom, if considerably smaller. Mr. Sulzberger wore a stern expression.

"Well, young man," he began. "I hear you've assigned a story on complaints about the food served in the cafeteria." There was a long pause, and my heart pounded. "Do you think it's wise for a house organ to publicly embarrass a loyal employee of *The Times*? Mr. Blitz, our cafeteria manager, makes every human effort to please the staff. *Timesweek*, up to now, seemed to have been guided by the same principles as *The Times*, and you should have learned that we are not a crusading newspaper. *Timesweek* doesn't need a Lincoln Steffens off on a muckraking expedition, especially within our own company. Don't you agree?"

What choice did I have? I apologized, and left more than slightly shaken. I had to admit he had a point. Somewhat shamefaced, I returned to the city room to tell Dick, "I'm afraid our investigative reporting days are over."

Even though the story never ran, John Blitz responded to the unpublished complaints almost overnight. More variety was added to the menu, quality and freshness were improved and greater care was given to presentation.

Dick went on to become one of the best reporters at *The Times*. His stories, reflecting his gentle nature and warm heart, were laced with the kind of wry humor that made readers laugh out loud. I once sat next to a woman on a crowded Broadway bus when she broke into a spontaneous chuckle while reading one of Dick's articles.

If Dick had a mistress, it was the city. He loved roaming its motley neighborhoods, talking to strangers. Conversant in nine languages, he could speak to immigrant New Yorkers in their native tongues, stepping behind cultural doors closed to most reporters. I'll always remember my astonishment the first time we went to Chinatown together, where Dick was greeted like family by the restaurateur and the two conversed in Chinese.

When he was covering the beat known as "ship news," Dick befriended a Greek hot dog vendor at the Battery named John Spheris. One afternoon as he was about to return to the city room after interviewing the president of

Cunard White Star, Dick was spotted by Spheris. The vendor begged Dick to delay his return and man his cart for an hour while he made a court appearance.

Ever willing to do a favor, Dick donned Spheris's mustard-stained apron. A few minutes later, the Cunard president he had interviewed strolled by, and Dick imagined he must have thought that Dick had to moonlight selling hot dogs because *The Times* didn't pay its staff well enough. By the time Dick finally got back to the city room, his arms were so tired from spreading condiments he could hardly type.

When Dick eventually rose to become culture editor, he pleaded to be demoted back to reporter. He hated the confrontations that were inherently part of an editor's world. The deciding event was a loud argument between the television reporter and the television critic over the handling of a story. The reporter—a homicidal glint in his eye—chased the critic around the desks of the culture department. Dick managed to get between them in an attempt to stave off their blows, taking a hard punch or two himself. I was then assistant managing editor and Dick came to my office.

"You must understand," he said, "I really like being at the bottom of the ladder. Please let me go back there and please never move me up again." Dick returned to what he loved most—writing about people and giving no one orders.

Striving harder than ever to win the recognition I hoped would get my promotion, I asked Bill Laurence if I might publish his secret letter of 1945 in which he tried to alert Edwin James to the imminent dropping of the atom bomb. The letter had been written from Oak Ridge, Tennessee, the day before Laurence left for New Mexico to witness the first atomic explosion, and he had forgotten about it until just recently, when James came across it while cleaning out his desk. If I wanted the letter for *Timesweek*, Laurence said, I was welcome to it.

Laurence told me his reasons for sending the letter: "I felt the urge to tip off James that the Zero Hour for the Big Secret was approaching. One of my worries was that the story might come around deadline time, with all bedlam breaking loose around poor Ted Bernstein's head. Ted does not know to this day how solicitous I was of his nervous system. So without violating security, I typed a letter to James."

As I knew I was handling a historic document, as well as *Timesweek*'s biggest scoop, I took the precaution of having the story copyrighted. After it appeared on June 11, 1947, the *Reader's Digest* asked to republish it, and it was the talk of the city room. When I handed the $1,000 check to Bill, he invited Barbara and me to a celebratory dinner at the Hotel Astor.

Over dessert, I asked his opinion about a rather unorthodox stratagem Gene Davis and I had devised that might accelerate our promotions. We were becoming restless, especially since John Meixner, who had joined the paper a year or so before we did, had just moved up to reporter (and quit *Timesweek*).

When Laurence heard our idea, he roared with laughter. "Nobody's ever tried that before," he said. "I think it's worth a shot. If nothing else, you'll crack a few smiles among the editors."

Thus encouraged, Davis and I went to the composing room the next day, and asked a foreman we knew to assign a Linotype operator to set an article we had written under the headline:

WANTED: TWO JOBS
Timesweek Editors Ask Advancement
on Basis of Good Work Done

The article, which was set in type to look like a story in proof form, began:

Gene Davis and Arthur Gelb, editors of *Timesweek*, today requested promotions in a letter to Edwin L. James, Managing Editor.

Outlining the reasons prompting their desire to advance, Mr. Davis and Mr. Gelb explained that they had gained enough experience as editors of the house organ and as assistants to Wilson L. Fairbanks, former Telegraph Editor, and his successor, Frederick A. Austin, to more than warrant *The Times* taking a chance on giving them better positions.

Davis and I reminded James of the accolades we had received from reporters, editors and the publisher, and noted that several universities had asked to use *Timesweek* in their journalism courses. "We are grateful for this acclaim," we wrote, "but would like a few new suits to wear with our laurels."

We delivered our handiwork to James's mailbox, and didn't have to wait long for a reply. The next day, city editor David Joseph called me to his desk. Without fanfare, he told me that—although Davis would have to wait a little longer—I was assigned to the reportorial staff as of next week. At last!

Joseph shook my hand. "Your hand is cold now," he said gently, "but it'll warm up. Try not to be so anxious." So, I thought, Joseph might have a heart after all. His manner had been generally distant. Though a reporter for nine years before becoming assistant city editor in 1917, he was a breed apart from his convivial staff. A fastidious dresser and pipe smoker, he displayed the Phi Beta Kappa key he'd earned at Columbia on a gold chain across his vest.

Nobody questioned Joseph's dedication. But his colorless personality made him less than a favorite with reporters who had worked under Bruce Rae, the flamboyant former night city editor now directing a new publication called *The Times Overseas Weekly*. Mike Berger, Murray Schumach, Pat Spiegel and others deplored the languor at the helm, recalling Rae with retrospective reverence.

William Bruce Rae, the son of Scottish immigrants, was born in New Jersey and grew up in Greenwich Village and Washington Heights. He started at *The Times* in 1909 as a sixteen-year-old office boy in the business department. With his dream of becoming a reporter, he would linger in the city room after his shift ended, praying for news to break after most of the staff had gone home for the night.

Rae's persistence finally earned him an eight-line story involving city birds, but he had to wait months more, until March 1916, for his real chance. The night city editor rushed over to Rae, still an office boy but the only person available to do legwork. "A guide at Bay Shore has gone nuts and shot some Wall Street duck hunters in Great South Bay," he told Rae. "He's holed up in a cabin with a rifle right now. Get out there fast and call me collect as soon as you get the facts." When Rae arrived in Bay Shore, a town on the south fork of Long Island, he joined a cadre of top reporters sent by the other papers. After shooting at the police for hours, the guide shot himself. Rae phoned in a rich array of facts to Elmer Davis, the legendary rewrite man, who praised his achievement to the city editor. Rae was promoted to reporter the next day.

He covered some of New York's most sensational murders and disasters, using an evocative journalistic style salted with colorful detail. It was Rae's crisp lead describing Lindbergh's triumphant welcome by New Yorkers in 1927 that earned him his first byline: "Charles A. Lindbergh descended modestly on New York yesterday on the wave of the greatest reception the city had ever accorded a private citizen. He came as he went, out of the clouds, on the wings of a swooping plane. Millions beheld his blond boyish head as he rode through six miles of streets and cheered from the depths of their hearts. There was never anything like it."

In 1930, Rae, who had been a reporter's reporter, became a reporter's editor. In contrast to David Joseph, Rae had never attended college. He was known for his rigorous standards, loyalty to his staff, uncanny nose for news and scathing sense of humor. When a report came in about twenty-four policemen from Port Jervis, New York, being injured in a football game played against convicts from Sing Sing, Rae told his reporter, "Before you begin to write, find out how many cops there are in Port Jervis." It turned out there were only four; the injured players had been "ringers." *The Times* was the only paper to disclose this angle.

"He not only disliked a careless or sloppy story, he hated it," one reporter said of Rae. "He did not merely like a good story, well handled, he loved it." Another reporter said, "My idea of a journalism school is that dour little Scotsman slumped in his chair, glaring over his ulcers at a reporter and daring him not to write the best damn story of which he was capable."

I regretted that I was working for Joseph, who never inspired that kind of fealty, rather than for Rae. When I confided in Grover Loud my dashed hopes of reporting to an imaginative city editor like Rae, he assured me things could be worse. At least, he said, grinning, Joseph was no Charles Chapin. Loud was referring to the infamous city editor of the old *Evening World* who had a sadistic streak; he once ordered a reporter back to a criminal's roost although he had been threatened with death if he turned up there again. Chapin fatally shot his wife and died in Sing Sing of natural causes before his scheduled execution in the electric chair.

Joseph, I gradually discovered, was quite human. With a smile, he handed me my long coveted "working press card." Shaped like a shield, with my photo at the top and my name printed in the middle, the yellow card allowed me to pass police and fire lines wherever formed. It was signed by the police and fire commissioners.

Joseph then led me to the ancient wooden desk assigned to me at the rear of the city room, and introduced me to my Underwood. I asked about the fate of *Timesweek*, and he told me that Ruth Adler, of the marketing-promotion department, would take over as editor and that my offspring's name would be changed to *Times Talk*. It became a glossy publication, more magazine than newspaper. Although it flourished under Adler's stewardship, its slick new design seemed almost too perfect—out of step with the city room, which was anything but slick. When the initial issue appeared a few weeks later, its polished prose unsettled me, since much of it surpassed the high standards I had tried so hard to set for *Timesweek*. Mike Berger requested my candid opinion of *Timesweek*'s successor, and I said I had found it surprisingly well written, especially for a first issue.

"I don't know much about Ruth Adler but she sure can write," I added, trying to mask my discomfort. But I was soon relieved to discover through city-room gossip that Ruth's inaugural feat was due to Mike himself. He was having an affair with her and it was he who was writing those sparkling, unsigned stories to help launch her in her post.

I often found myself overcome with nostalgia for *Timesweek*, the little paper that had given me a basic foundation in the philosophy and production of *The Times* such as no copyboy before me had been privileged to acquire. But what soon was to sadden me more were the departures of John Meixner and Gene Davis, each deciding to leave *The Times* for personal reasons not long after they became reporters.

Murray Schumach and Pat Spiegel were the first to congratulate me on my promotion. Like Mike Berger, Murray was a gentle adviser to young reporters. Seeing me seated in a glow of joy at my newly acquired desk, he told me to take it easy and not be in too much of a hurry to become a star.

"Remember, reporters move up slowly here and for good reason," he once said. "When you get discouraged, keep in mind that it took me seven years to get my first byline. It took Bruce Rae eleven." Murray approved of the policy: "When the credit goes to the paper rather than the reporter, you get more teamwork among the staff. Personal vanities are curtailed. You are important not as an individual but because you represent *The New York Times*."

Everyone was aware, according to Murray, that when Van Anda was engaged by Ochs as managing editor in 1904, he committed himself to his publisher's policy of keeping reporters from getting between the reader and the story. Van Anda insisted that bylines be limited to very special achievement and, during his first six years at *The Times*, no bylines were awarded.

He finally relented in 1910 and signed the page-one story on the Jim Jeffries–Jack Johnson championship bout. He had hired the world-renowned fighter John L. Sullivan to cover the spectacle, convinced that his byline would boost circulation—and it did. Staff writers who filed accompanying stories did not receive bylines and, a decade later, when the sports department organized a delegation to complain about the policy, Van Anda declared: "Gentlemen, *The Times* is not running a reporters' directory."

Among Murray's other gems of advice to cub reporters like me: "You must start gathering consequential sources and get them to trust you, so when you call them and say, 'I'm with *The Times*,' they'll answer your questions without hesitation." I began recording the names and phone numbers of my key contacts, one by one, as I encountered them. Murray, even-tempered and wise, had grown up in a working-class family, in Brooklyn's Brownsville section, and made his mark as a probing neighborhood reporter. He was Mike Berger's acolyte, revering his master and emulating his style, to the point of adopting Mike's tic of vigorously rubbing his hands together before starting to type.

Although I was only twenty-three and Murray was almost ten years older, he never patronized me and, in fact, always treated me as an equal. We became fast friends. When he needed a new apartment, the one next to Barbara's and mine on Sixty-fifth Street happened to be available, and he moved in.

Murray had one of the most inquiring and analytical minds of any city reporter. A wiry man poised to grapple with the implications of a breaking story, always with an original point of view, he could also assume a contemplative stance. We often reminisced about our backgrounds in the outer boroughs.

Murray, whose parents were Eastern European Jews, was the eldest of three sons raised by an indomitable mother, Minnie, after she and her husband separated. She struggled as a dressmaker to make ends meet during the Depression. In 1930, Murray found work as a copyboy at *The Times* to help support his family. He took courses at CCNY, but his basic education came from books he borrowed, starting as a teenager, from the Brooklyn Public Library.

On our time off, Barbara and I occasionally accompanied Murray on strolls around the city, into the neighborhoods he knew so well and which today, for the most part, no longer exist as neighborhoods. "Before the war, *The Times* had intensive coverage in Brooklyn," he later recorded in his oral history. "For example, we had one man covering Flatbush, and a man each in Coney Island and Williamsburg—in addition to our reporter at Brooklyn Police Headquarters. We had men in Queens and the Bronx. And neighborhood news is still essential because the city isn't just one big map—it's lots of little maps, and unless you know what's going on within those little maps, you'll never really know what's going on in the city."

"Where do you begin if you have to go into an unfamiliar neighborhood to get a story?" we cub reporters would ask him.

"The church or synagogue is a good place to start, because priests and rabbis usually know what's happening in their communities," he'd say. "And you can talk to members of the congregation. Visit stores in the main shopping areas—the people who live nearby frequent local markets, so you can get a good cross-section of the neighborhood. Be observant. Notice if there are bars on the windows near the fire escapes and how many storefronts have iron gates. See if people tend their lawns.

"A good approach is to ask a householder about his garbage collection. The important thing is to make the person you're interviewing feel as important as any statesman or celebrity. Once you convince them that you really do want to know what they're thinking, they'll relax and talk about almost anything."

DURING MY FIRST WEEK as a reporter, Joseph handed me a short AP story that came in over the wires. He told me to confirm the dispatch and write a few paragraphs based on it. *The Times* never published local AP stories verbatim, always recrafting them into *Times* style, and improving on them with additional information, if possible.

The AP copy concerned a two-year-old boy who had fallen to his death from a window in a Yorkville apartment building. A seasoned reporter would have phoned the police station to confirm the accuracy of the AP details, then started typing. But I, with the misplaced zeal of a cub, took off for the scene of the accident.

On my way, I stopped by the police station in the precinct where the child had fallen to check the "aided card"—a pink index card on which the bare facts of a police action were recorded and made available to reporters. Minor stories were often written solely from the information on these cards but, if necessary, a reporter could try to reach the police officer of record, whose name was provided. In this instance, everything on the card was also in the AP story, so I continued on my mission.

The apartment was a third-floor walk-up in a middle-class neighborhood. Both parents had been at work when their child, left in the care of a neighbor, clambered atop a toy chest, whose lid was level with the sill of an open window.

By the time I arrived, the police and neighbors had long since dispersed. I found the apartment door ajar and unthinkingly walked into the living room—to stumble upon the grief-stricken young couple, seated on a couch, silently clinging to each other.

"I'm from *The Times*," I murmured. Suddenly, I was struck by the enormity of my mistake. They stared at me in numb disbelief, and before I could even utter an apology for my intrusion, they walked to another room, shutting the door. Flushed with shame, I called out, "I'm sorry," and left. I was so embarrassed that I lost interest in interviewing the superintendent and neighboring tenants, whom I probably should have talked to in the first place.

Back at the office I rewrote the AP copy as a three-paragraph story, and I sought out Grover Loud to help me overcome my distress. "It's a common mistake," he said consolingly, while letting me know he didn't condone my approach to this particular story. "We often walk a hazardous balance between going after facts and potentially hurting people through our invasiveness. Important stories, of course, demand inquiry, but others, like yours, really don't. You must aim to do as little damage to people as possible in the proper course of gathering the news."

As with all new reporters, I was first assigned to a series of "shorts" such as the Yorkville piece. These were essentially routine stories of a few paragraphs each about local events, sometimes of a quirky nature, but of enough interest to compete for space in each edition.

In assigning shorts, an editor would use the headline designation, ordering, for example, a "D-head"—a three- or four-paragraph story. "K-heads" were one-paragraph mentions; "M-heads" could take up to one-third of a column. Bylines were never given for shorts, but *The Times* later offered a twenty-five-dollar publisher's prize for "Best Short of the Month," ensuring that even these filler pieces were written with care. The longer stories I aspired to were called "spreads," but it was more than two weeks before I wrote one. For the time being I was content to write shorts, and was even happier when chosen to cover a story as a legman for the city room's top spot-news reporters.

When the American Legion held its national convention in New York during the last days of August 1947, I was assigned to do legwork for Frank Adams, one of the best-rounded men on the paper, who was versed in science, politics, history and the game of bridge. The speed and accuracy of his writing on breaking stories was matched only by two or three reporters on the staff, his memory was nearly photographic, his tenacity in digging for facts was unsurpassed.

There were times when his pursuit of a story led him into trouble, as in the case of a double kidnap-murder in 1926. Adams went to the police station in an attempt to interview the accused, insane killer. Two policemen barred his way. "I'm from *The Times*," he said. "We're holding our presses for this guy. We'd like his confession." The officers said nothing and, when Adams persisted, they flung him down a flight of stairs. (With aching bones and sans confession, he nonetheless managed to gather enough facts to file a fine story.)

The American Legion, recently strengthened by new recruits from World War II, invaded Manhattan like an occupying army. From morning to night,

I covered their midtown antics, compiling reports for Adams, and was pleased he chose some of my facts to enrich his stories. The fifty thousand Legionnaires brought along their boozy clowning, and hotels removed furniture from lobbies, lamps from bedrooms and even phone books, fearing they'd be hurled from windows as lethal confetti. After some debate, it was decided not to remove the Gideon Bibles, in hopes they would deter "the wickedly intentioned."

I witnessed one group of Legionnaires carry some of their compatriots through Times Square on a bed commandeered from their hotel. At the end of the convention, one manager said his hotel sustained twenty thousand dollars in damages due to the "rowdyism, vulgarity and vandalism." Furnishings had been destroyed, towels shredded and carpeting scarred by cigarette burns. Another hotel reported that two thousand empty liquor bottles had been tossed from windows into an interior courtyard.

Armed with "jump boxes," contraptions that delivered electric shocks through a walking stick, Legionnaires declared open season on pedestrians, whose shrill cries signaled their distress. Well-dressed men and women were targeted by one Legionnaire, who swiped at them with a gooey-looking paintbrush. I saw one victim strike the mad artist with his umbrella before discovering the brush was dry. Snakes and baby alligators terrorized some passersby, while others were assaulted with water pistols.

As midtown began to resemble a madhouse, I watched New Yorkers finally retaliate with water guns purchased from street vendors. And all New Yorkers cheered when Legionnaire snipers stationed outside the Hotel Pennsylvania were forced to withdraw as a city sanitation truck opened fire with its water hose. Later, a gang of mischief-makers froze Times Square traffic. Overtaking the cop on duty, they waved cars on in four directions at once. When the intersection became hopelessly snarled, they retreated with shouts of glee.

There was actually a serious side to the convention, which took place in Madison Square Garden. As a powerful policy-making lobby, the Legion strove to improve housing and employment conditions for veterans, and its platform was debated and voted upon. The hottest issue was universal military training for all men when they reached eighteen. As the possibility loomed of confrontation with the Soviet Union, the Legion urged legislation for mandatory conscription as the only means to prepare American troops; Russia, the Legion argued, would be reluctant to challenge a ready army.

President Truman expressed support for this stance in a message read at the Garden. New York governor Thomas E. Dewey, Generals Dwight D.

Eisenhower and Carl Spaatz, and Admiral Chester W. Nimitz, all of whom addressed the convention, gave their support to the Legion as well. Truman and Dewey were already the anticipated rivals for the presidency in 1948, and both sought the Legion's endorsement.

The convention closed with a parade that drew two million spectators and lasted twelve hours. Manhattan was collectively relieved when the Legionnaires finally packed their bags, and sanitation crews began their cleanup, which took several days.

I had walked miles recording the Legionnaires' disruptive behavior and sat for hours listening to their speeches at the Garden during the long weekend. While I wrote a few short pieces myself, most of the information I gathered was incorporated into Adams's columns. He was pleased enough with my work to commend me to Joseph as "diligent, motivated and willing to do nearly anything to get a story."

As a result, I was assigned to fill in for vacationing *Times* men at Police Headquarters. Mike Berger assured me it was an ideal place for basic training, and reminded me he himself had once covered the police. The few policemen with whom I'd had contact were those who patrolled the Bronx neighborhood of my youth, and they had left me with a positive impression.

Most had Irish working-class backgrounds. Their salaries were low, they were on duty six or seven days a week and often worked overtime without extra pay. But the jobs offered security, required little formal education and commanded respect in the neighborhoods where they were familiar beacons. They patrolled the sidewalks day and night, swinging their billy clubs, which they now and then threatened to use to keep order.

A cop on my Bronx block, whom everyone called Frank, knew all the children by name. He would pat me on the head, ask how school was, and guide me safely across the street to the candy store. He and the other cops on their beats knew all the shop owners, and it was customary to give them gifts at Christmastime. My parents, for example, offered dresses to those who had young daughters. On days of bitter cold, my father invited patrolmen into the back of the shop for a shot of schnapps.

The sergeant in our precinct, known for his incorruptibility, was a habitual visitor to the shop. When he was off duty, he joined my father and a neighbor for pinochle in the back room. Once, when a greedy cop persistently asked my parents for dresses, my father mentioned the fact to the sergeant. That cop was reassigned to Staten Island and, shortly afterward, resigned from the force.

The only trouble I ever had with the police was when I was seventeen and fancied myself a young Thomas Wolfe. After reading *The Web and the Rock* and *Of Time and the River*, I strolled for miles composing verses about the city's pervasive beauty. One sunny day I hiked across the George Washington Bridge into New Jersey and didn't stop walking until I found myself in Englewood.

As I approached the end of the quiet main street, a police cruiser pulled alongside. Through his rolled-down window, the cop asked, "What are you doing here?"

"Walking," I said.

"Where do you live?"

"The Bronx."

"You walked here from the Bronx?"

"Yes, sir."

"Get in the back of the car."

I was driven to the station and led down to a basement room by two policemen. I was confused and nervous. I didn't know what they thought I had done. The policeman asked for my identification but, since I didn't carry a wallet, I had none.

"How much money do you have on you?" one of the policemen asked.

"Fifty cents."

"We could charge you with vagrancy," he said menacingly.

I was frightened. It was getting late and I was sure I would be jailed unless I could reach my parents by phone.

"I've never done anything wrong," I insisted. "Please let me call my mother."

After more questioning, the cops acquiesced. I phoned my mother at the shop.

"I'm at a police station in New Jersey," I told her.

"What are you doing there? Are you hurt?"

"They want to charge me with vagrancy."

"Let me talk to the policeman," she said.

The officer got on the line, and I could gauge my mother's anger by the pitch of her voice coming through the phone. "How dare you! Arresting an innocent boy for walking in your town! He enjoys walking. What's wrong with that? Since when is walking a crime! So he doesn't have any money on him—he's a student! What kind of country do you think this is? Do you think we're in Russia? For God's sake, let my son come home!"

The policeman apologized to my mother. He then apologized to me, offering to drive me back over the bridge to a subway stop. On the way, he explained that the town had been wary of outsiders ever since the kidnapping of the Lindbergh baby in 1932. The town police were on perpetual guard against strangers because Lindbergh's in-laws, the Morrows, lived in Englewood, and Lindbergh, his wife and their children often visited.

FOURTEEN

P AT SPIEGEL VOLUNTEERED to accompany me on my first night as a police reporter—for the 7:00 P.M. to 3:20 A.M. shift. My station was "the shack," the reporters' hangout in a small, drab structure across the street from the rear entrance of Police Headquarters in the heart of Little Italy.

Completed in 1909, Headquarters did not have a press room, as does today's more spacious building. As we arrived at the shack, Pat and I watched a group of men in handcuffs being led from a police van. They were taken down a flight of stairs where, Pat explained, they would be booked for arraignment in court.

The shack was situated at 4 Centre Market Place on a block of dingy shops and narrow three-story tenements. Next door was a gunsmith from whom cops bought their weapons at a discount. A renovated tenement itself, the shack consisted of three floors of offices rented jointly by all the city's newspapers and wire services.

Fire bells were affixed to the shack's façade and, said Pat, when the bells rang at least three times the reporters knew it was a fire that might be worth chasing. Pat pointed out a row of colored lightbulbs that were also mounted on the front of the shack—a different color for each of the major papers. When a phone rang inside, a corresponding light flashed, summoning a reporter on the street.

As Pat and I entered the shack, police-band radios were crackling. Pat led me to the *Times* office on the second floor, roomier than I had anticipated, and furnished with two old desks, two upright phones and two typewriters, mainly for use by reporters from the city room assigned to major breaking stories at Headquarters; they sometimes typed up their notes at the shack before returning to the office.

In 1940, the decrepit building had been purchased as an investment by an entrepreneurial police reporter, Teddy Prager of the *Daily News*, who added such amenities as fluorescent lighting, decent bathroom facilities and steel casement windows as the inducement for newspapers to rent office space.

Although spare, the quarters for my generation of police reporter were deemed luxurious. Before 1940, reporters had worked out of a warren of ill-ventilated, often unheated, vermin-infested rooms, scattered among the few crumbling tenements on the block. During winter months, they often had to work in their overcoats.

The shack, I soon discovered, never closed. Seven days a week, the day shift was replaced by the night shift, followed by the early-morning shift known as the "lobster trick," for no paper could afford to overlook a good police story whenever it broke. My new colleagues seemed somewhat removed from the reporters of the city room. Most of them, like Mike Berger, had never finished grammar school, but unlike Berger, they were bereft of writing skills. Newspapers hired them for their street smarts and their ability to ferret out facts swiftly.

The majority were sons of immigrants—Italians living in the area of the shack itself; Irish, mainly from Hell's Kitchen; Jews out of the Lower East Side, the Bronx or Brooklyn. Their families were the working class that had struggled to survive the Depression. Their fathers had toiled mostly as construction laborers, truck drivers or garment workers, and they spoke in the patois of their blue-collar neighborhoods, a speech glamorized in the movies by such natives of Hell's Kitchen as James Cagney and Alice Faye. Many of the reporters were, as Jack Tell might have said, "dese, dem and dose kind of guys." They came from the same backgrounds as did a legion of cops and gangsters, and where you ended up often seemed to be a matter of luck.

Occasionally, when a shack legman phoned into rewrite, his speech presented a problem. *The Times* once published an erroneous story because a rewrite man was confused by the reporter's dialect. Though this was a kidnap-murder case in which the victim had been brutally slaughtered, the headline read: "Funeral Follows Inquest with Verdict of Death by Poison." The legman had said over the phone, "The deceased came to her death at the hands of a poisson or poissons unknown, acting with homicidal intent."

Because I didn't speak their language and was the only one among them with a college degree, the shack reporters were initially suspicious of me. Would I follow the unwritten rules of pack reporting?

When a report came over the police radio, I did indeed follow the pack as they ran from the shack with homemade notepads of folded copy paper stuffed into their back pockets and thick soft-lead pencils enabling them to scribble fast. By foot, cab, bus or subway, we converged on a scene in a haphazard frenzy. Though we rushed to meet edition deadlines, we didn't compete against one another. Before anyone called his office, we came together and shared every scrap of information we each had gathered.

This inviolable tenet provided us with a sense of security. We knew we couldn't be reprimanded for missing an important fact since everyone had access to the same information. If a reporter withheld anything, he was shunned by his fellows. Since every paper's rewrite battery received the same set of facts, the resulting articles were distinguished from one another by each rewrite man's particular sensibility, his wit, his skill under pressure.

Even though rewrite men rarely received bylines, the nuances of their style were often recognized by their fellow reporters. On *The Times*, the style of a police story tended toward a tone of lofty detachment, while its chief rival, the *Herald Tribune*, was apt to be a bit earthier. At the other extreme were the Hearst papers, the *Daily Mirror* and the *Journal-American*, which, along with the *Daily News*, were blithely strident.

In one instance, I covered a murder in a Little Italy tenement. The dead man had been butchered in his sleep by his wife, after she caught him cheating. The corpse had been removed by the time we were allowed into the apartment, but I called in a graphic description of the blood that soaked the bed and pooled on the floor, and repeated what the police told the pack about the manner in which his throat had been slashed and his body stabbed. "Hold on," the rewrite man rebuked me. "This is *The Times*, not the *Mirror*. We don't serve gore at the breakfast table."

At *The Times*, general-assignment reporters would sometimes be asked to fill in on the rewrite bank. Star reporters such as Berger and Adams usually remained in the office in reserve, in case a big story broke that demanded expert coverage. While waiting, they read the paper or played cards until taking their turns crafting stories based on facts phoned in by legmen. Most of the younger reporters like myself felt that Joseph, in his need for security, was overly concerned about missing a big story, and we thought his reserve policy was a pitiful waste of first-rate talent.

Some police reporters were good with their fists and, in the early decades of the century, there was almost as much action in the shack as on the streets. Once, John J. Gordon, the night police reporter for *The Times*, punched Teddy Prager in the nose, knocking him to the head of a stone stairway. Another reporter caught Prager, saving him from a probable broken neck. In those days, a nightlong poker game was played in a back room, referred to as the "den of the forty thieves." Reporters there feasted on clams steamed open atop gas heaters, and washed down with bottles of Madeira.

If there was a lull in criminal activity, reporters were not above "piping" a story. During World War I, a reporter once defaced a park statue of the poet Heine, and then wrote a story condemning the "vandalism of ignorant, unthinking groups." Ethical standards had risen considerably by the time Pat Spiegel escorted me to the shack on my first night, but there were lapses, notably with regard to expense accounts.

If I used a public phone or took a taxi or subway to get to a story, I paid out of pocket, noted what I spent, and was reimbursed at the end of the week. But, Pat told me, I could slip a few extra charges into my account, in cases where I could have legitimately taken a subway or cab, but walked instead. I felt uneasy about doing it, but Pat explained it was an accepted practice.

Not only were salaries low, but police reporters never claimed overtime for the long hours they worked—and those few extra dollars a week were significant. Moreover, if one reporter didn't pad his account, he'd make all the other reporters look bad and would be ostracized. The editors, Pat said, were aware of the padding and looked the other way. Of course, you couldn't be glaringly obvious about it, or the editors would be forced to say something. There was a fine balance between padding too much and too little—two to four dollars a week was the acceptable range.

What I was to hear over and over again at the shack was that a reporter was only as good as his contacts, and each man jealously nurtured friendships with street cops and police officials. They also took advantage of a policeman's desire for promotion. Once, when a man was fatally shot, two reporters discovered the murder weapon behind a bedroom door. Keeping their find from the lieutenant in charge, they gave it to a patrolman they knew, who was later promoted for "uncovering" the evidence. He never forgot his debt, and became a valuable informant as he rose through the ranks.

Upon returning to the shack from a story, reporters often walked down the block to the Headquarters Tavern, where they mingled with the cops. I didn't speak much at the shack or in the tavern until I felt accepted by the pack. I knew I was truly accepted the day Johnny Weisberger of the *Journal-American* showed me his revolver. Sid Livingston and Tommy Weber of the same paper also packed revolvers, and the three were known as the *Journal-American* "gun squad." They patrolled lower Manhattan in company cars painted bright orange, their ears glued to the police radio. When they heard a "Signal 30," which meant "stick-up in progress," they sped to the scene to aid in the arrest.

Walter Winchell, in the role of police buff, also chased Signal 30s late at night in his private black car and occasionally in the light-yellow radio car owned by the *Daily Mirror* (the New York outlet for his syndicated column);

the grandson of William Randolph Hearst, also a police buff and known to police reporters as Bunky, liked acting as Winchell's chauffeur. Winchell usually arrived at the same time as the police, who routinely gave him the facts as they uncovered them. For a patrolman to have his name in a Winchell column was more than an ego boost—it could lead to a promotion. When the pack arrived at the scene, Winchell would hold court like the commissioner himself, as he magnanimously shared the facts with us.

Now and then an intrepid reporter tried to capture a "perp" himself, but the police frowned on such audacity. A classic case involved a *Daily News* photographer, Alan Aaronson. He was in the vicinity of a liquor store robbery that was announced over his car radio, and he arrived at the scene ahead of the police.

He saw a man, revolver in hand, run from the store and down the subway entrance on the corner. Aaronson gave chase and managed to strike the man with his Speed Graphic, knocking him down the subway stairs as the cops arrived. Aaronson felt like a hero for foiling the bandit's escape. But he was quickly brought to earth when the cop told him, "You better get out of here. The man you clobbered was the liquor store owner. He was chasing the robber down the stairs."

One of the first reporters I came to know at the shack was Arthur Rosenfeld of the *Post*. Slim and dark-complected, he was somewhat better educated than the rest of the pack, and was a kind of Jewish *consigliere* to the entire neighborhood. He had a reputation for altruism and common sense, and was known to have powerful connections.

He intervened with Con Edison on behalf of his neighbors' unpaid electric bills. He filled out job applications for semi-literate residents. He fixed tickets through functionaries in the traffic department. He put in a good word with top police brass for detectives who did him favors. Called Artie by everyone, he knew the best places on the Lower East Side for corned beef and pastrami. A regular at the Crown Deli on Delancey Street, he'd pick up sandwiches for his fellow reporters. The merchants on Grand Street knew him, and often gave him complimentary sausages to take back to the shack.

Particularly attached to Artie was Mike Finnegan, a police reporter for the *World-Telegram*. Finnegan was an anomaly: his reporting was inept and he couldn't write a coherent sentence. Nevertheless, he was a valuable contributor to the pack because cops loved him for his natural Irish wit, and fed him information they withheld from other reporters. The pack, in turn, helped him organize the information he called in to his paper; he could not have functioned without that assistance.

Finnegan would eavesdrop when Rosenfeld phoned in his facts to the *Post* and he'd copy down what Artie said. He'd then call in his story from these notes. One day Artie phoned about the theft of an antique volume of *Julius Caesar.* When Artie finished, Finnegan gave his rewrite man the same facts, verbatim. The rewrite man asked Finnegan, with suppressed glee, "Who was Julius Caesar?" Finnegan put his hand over the mouthpiece and bellowed the inquiry to Artie in the next office. Without missing a beat, Artie yelled back, "Second baseman for the Washington Senators." Finnegan, of course, repeated the line to his rewrite man, and the story became shack legend.

A man I enjoyed getting to know was an ex–police reporter for City News, the local wire service that predated the AP local. Known as the Baron, he was a short, paunchy man who wore a beret over his long hair. His real name was De Hirsh Margules, and he had become a recognized Greenwich Village abstract artist but he dropped by to visit his old comrades from time to time.

Unlike the men at the shack, the Baron believed he possessed the soul of a poet and yearned to write his own articles. One day City News was short-staffed and he was summoned from the shack to the office to assist on rewrite. He'd never before written a story, but he believed there was nothing to it. He was given a report about a building that had collapsed, and he proceeded to write his lead: "Bricks, bricks, bricks, bricks—a veritable deluge of bricks—cascaded tonight into West Twenty-fourth Street." He was sent back to the shack forthwith.

After a couple of months at Headquarters, I was transferred to the East Fifty-first Street police shack to fill in on nights, covering all police activity from Twenty-third to 104th Street on Manhattan's East Side. It was a territory of dramatic contrasts—on one hand, a grubby side of New York; on the other, the "Silk Stocking District," where even crimes such as petty burglaries made the paper because of its wealthy and prominent residents. Similar offenses wouldn't have been mentioned had they occurred in the poor or ethnic neighborhoods.

The "East Side shack," unlike the one at Headquarters, consisted of one room on the ground floor of an old brownstone, two doors west of the Seventeenth Precinct's station house. Only a few papers sent reporters to that beat, and they shared the confined space with its two public phone booths.

Although I made rounds on foot, I never left the shack for too long. If a story broke, I needed to be by the phones to receive my assignment from my editors—who kept on top of all important reported crimes in the city through wire-service bulletins. Since I used the phones all night to check with my office and with the station houses on my beat, I arrived at work at seven o'clock with my pockets bulging with nickels.

No paper could have survived without "AP local." Their reporters covered the city like a net, twenty-four hours a day. *The Times* would have had to hire a score of extra reporters to perform the function of the wire services—the United Press local as well as the AP (which had by now absorbed City News). In addition to pointing our own reporters in the direction of a story, the AP provided the unadorned facts against which a rewrite man could check his own legman's information to assure accuracy and completeness.

Moe Berman was the night AP man at the East Side shack. Unlike most of the men I'd worked with at Headquarters, he was uncommonly polite and mild-spoken, had a smooth, innocent face and appeared scholarly in his rimless glasses. I discovered to my pleasant surprise that he was an inveterate reader of classical novels. If another reporter misspoke or said something crass, he'd throw me a knowing smile, shaking his head.

Moe was respected by the police because he never missed an angle. A general assignment beat was his for the asking, but he chose to stay in the shack, where he had established a routine and had ample opportunity to read on slow nights while the rest of the reporters played cards. They asked Moe and me to pipe down when we started discussing Huxley, Dreiser or Dostoevsky, who were among his literary gods.

Though there were many long hours when nothing happened, we were sporadically alerted to felons brought in handcuffs to the second-floor detectives' squad room of the neighboring station house. Once, just before two A.M., a nineteen-year-old named Ralph Barrows was fingerprinted and charged with the brutal murder of a textile executive in a suite at the Waldorf-Astoria. The story kept me busy for several days.

The victim, Cameron MacKellar, had been discovered by a maid early the previous morning. Among items scattered on the rug, the police found a matchbook with the imprint "West Forty-fifth Street Café." They kept this information from the press, thinking the killer might show up there. Detectives had a description of him from members of the hotel staff, who had seen him with MacKellar in the lobby. Their instinct was right.

Moe got a tip from a cop at the station house that the café was being watched. He suggested we walk over there and, just as we arrived, Barrows was being handcuffed. Moe and I phoned in simultaneously to our offices, and my desk was impressed that my report got there before the AP bulletin arrived. The motive for the murder was unclear, but the police believed Barrows had become enraged when he tried to rob MacKellar and discovered he had only a few dollars. Barrows, however, asserted he had struck MacKellar to repulse "improper advances."

Barrows's credibility was thin, because his police record included a number of assault convictions. His story was further undermined when his mother issued a statement saying he was "never a normal boy" and that she had taken him to psychiatrists "in an effort to learn the cause of his often peculiar behavior." I tried to organize my facts in story form before phoning in to rewrite and was pleased that my dictated sentences reached print basically unchanged.

Since the investigation took the detectives to the block where Barrows lived, on West Fifty-sixth street, I sought the help of Philly Meagher, *The Times*'s most storied police reporter, who covered all precincts on Manhattan's West Side at night. I phoned him at the West Side shack, situated in a brownstone across the street from the West Fifty-fourth Street station house, then part of the busiest police precinct in the country.

At five-foot-four, weighing 120 pounds, Philly looked like a leprechaun with his long chin and pointed ears. He was familiar not only to the police, but also to many of the residents of the West Side. Priding himself on his sources in Hell's Kitchen, where he had grown up, he was quickly able to assemble key details about Barrows's life that helped me fill in my stories.

Philly had been on the beat since 1926, and his reputation soared one November night in 1928, when a man was shot at the Park Central Hotel (later renamed the Park Sheraton) on Seventh Avenue and Fifty-sixth Street. Picking up the report at the station house, Philly ran to the hotel. A cop he knew whispered to him, "That guy on the ambulance stretcher is Arnold Rothstein." He was bleeding from a hole in his abdomen.

Rothstein was the gambler reputed to be the architect behind the 1919 World Series fix—the "Black Sox" scandal—and the model for the character Meyer Wolfsheim in *The Great Gatsby.* He ran nightclubs and betting parlors and served as a middleman in payoffs between bootleggers and the police. Gunned down only a few minutes after he had left Lindy's for the Park Central, he died at the hospital, refusing to identify his assassin. Philly told me he had quickly called Bruce Rae, and *The Times* boasted a one-edition beat—a scoop that was the envy of all competitors.

When there was no action at the East Side shack, reporters sometimes jumped ship, leaving me to cover for them. My pride in being a *Times* man wouldn't permit any dereliction of duty. Every so often, Barbara came to the shack after midnight and stayed until I received my "Good night" at 3:20. We then walked the quiet city hand in hand, home to Sixty-fifth Street. At such times, I felt like the king of these deserted streets. "Imagine," I'd tell Barbara, "this is mine, all mine! I'm responsible to the readers of *The Times* for anything that happens here."

We strolled by mansions on side streets, and I fantasized about living in one someday, with Barbara (and our future children). When we reached the all-night newsstand on Fifty-ninth Street and Madison Avenue, we'd buy the updated editions of *The Times* and the *Herald Tribune*. Finally at home, I'd check on my stories as Barbara prepared a snack of scrambled eggs.

My assignment to the East Side shack, I soon learned, was a test to gauge how well I would perform in the most sophisticated area of the city, yielding the sort of upper-crust crime news savored by *Times* readers. One day I was asked to report to David Joseph before going to the shack. He shook my hand, reminded me how cold it had been on the day he promoted me to reporter, and noted it had warmed up. He offered me a newly created beat and a small raise. Because I had demonstrated motivation and responsibility, he said, he thought I could handle the assignment, which he called "East Side Days."

My new beat would include not only police matters in the district I had been covering at night, but cases brought before the Mid-Manhattan Magistrates Court on East Fifty-seventh Street. In addition, I would be expected to report on stories involving police action at such landmarks as Central Park, Bellevue Hospital and Grand Central Terminal. What's more, Joseph said, I could return to the office to write my stories, if there was sufficient time to do so, rather than calling in my gathered facts to rewrite from the press room in Magistrates Court.

No police assignment on the paper offered more opportunity than my new beat, and I headed to Mike Berger's desk to share my jubilation. He was quick to give me stern instructions: "Don't make a move on that beat without checking in with Dick Feehan of the AP, or your job will be at risk." He warned me not to expect the comradely collaboration I had found in working with the pack at various police reporter shacks.

I'd already heard of Feehan's prowess as a reporter from his younger brother, Syl, whom I had met at the Headquarters shack when he occasionally filled in on the AP night shift. "Remember," continued Mike, "Dick is the godfather of the beat you'll be covering and, if he doesn't accept you, you're in lots of trouble. Don't do anything to cross him."

When I arrived, tense and concerned, at Mid-Manhattan Court the next day, Dick was seated at a table in a back room near the judge's chambers. His lips were frozen in a snarl, he spoke in a growl and looked like a match for James Cagney at his hardboiled worst. He wore a fedora, navy blue double-breasted suit, white shirt and a striped red-and-blue tie. He had grown up in one of those rough blue-collar neighborhoods where some kids became gangsters and some cops, and Dick appeared to possess aspects of both.

During Prohibition, like other teenagers from his neighborhood, he had delivered barrels of booze for a rumrunner. Boats bearing the cargo, anchored six miles off the East End of Long Island, between Montauk and Amagansett, were met by smaller, faster craft that ferried the barrels to shore. They were then loaded onto trains (the rail men having been paid off) and routed to Manhattan, where they were transferred onto trucks. Cops were bribed to protect the operation from rival bootleggers. Dick carried the barrels to warehouses, stores and restaurants, and came to know a mob chieftain or two.

In those times, no gangster could enter Harlem or the Bronx without Dutch Schultz's permission. Nor could an outsider go to the West Side without the approval of Vincent "Mad Dog" Coll, or to the Brooklyn waterfront without Albert Anastasia's okay. The notion of a territorial boss was superimposed by Feehan on the East Side reportorial district he controlled. He took command of police news flowing from his district and, if a reporter failed to gain his support, all police sources evaporated.

Feehan had built his contacts in every echelon of the police force. He had made it his business to befriend patrolmen over the years, drinking with them and putting their names in his stories. He came to know their families, and was invited to their weddings. He had grown up with many of them and, even though he didn't wear their uniform, they considered him one of them.

When they were eventually promoted to brass ranks, they knew Dick's discretion could be relied on, and they had no qualms about revealing details of a crime before they were made public. At a crime scene, a detective would signal him with a nod, and meet him around a corner. There, Dick would get his scoop.

Dick achieved an additional advantage when his brother Syl married the sister of Ed Feeley, assistant chief inspector of detectives on the East Side. In fact, all police officials, including the commissioner, liked him. Once, when a cop interposed himself between Dick and a story he was pursuing, Dick knocked the cop to the ground. The precinct captain apologized to Dick for the subordinate's rudeness.

Dick shared his information with only a few favored reporters, and was ruthless when competing with other wire services. One of his triumphs had come on the morning of July 26, 1938, when a twenty-six-year-old man named John Warde crawled through the window of his room at the Hotel Gotham onto an eighteen-inch-wide ledge one hundred sixty feet above Fifty-fifth Street near Fifth Avenue. Warde, who had held jobs as a bank clerk and chauffeur in Southampton, Long Island, had been plagued by depression.

Once on the ledge, he hesitated, seemingly torn between jumping and returning to his room. The police, inside the room, attempted for hours to talk him in from his perch, just out of their reach from the window. One officer disguised himself as a bellboy and tried to sway him with the argument that if he jumped, the hotel would get a bad reputation, visitors would stop coming and he, the bellboy, would lose his job, forcing him, his wife and three (invented) children to go on relief. Though Warde apparently believed him, it wasn't enough to lure him back.

The exasperated cops discussed various far-fetched strategies, such as grabbing him by the leg with a pair of outsized tongs. But their best bet, they concluded, was to keep offering him ice water, in the hope he'd need to use the bathroom. Warde did drink glass after glass—demanding that the "bellboy" sample the water first to make sure it wasn't drugged. And he astonished everyone by holding his water like a sponge. As the hours slid by, the police ordered up a gigantic cargo net, planning to attach it to the building a few floors below Warde's ledge, then raise it to the roof, thereby trapping Warde inside it.

Down below, scores of spectators filled the street by late afternoon. Sidewalk psychologists exchanged theories about the man's dilemma and wagers were placed on whether he would jump. Peddlers hawked bargain-priced opera glasses. Sixty policemen tried to keep order, a hook-and-ladder fire truck stood by, and a legion of reporters were calling in their stories for updated editions.

The only phone booth on the block that afforded a view of the ledge was just inside the front window of a United Cigar store. Reporters took turns throughout the afternoon and evening, reaching their offices from this booth to relay developments. Around 10:30 P.M., a policeman tipped off Feehan that the detectives upstairs were convinced Warde was at his wit's end and appeared set to jump. Dick made a dash for the phone booth, grabbed its occupant by his jacket and yanked him out. He then dialed the AP desk, instructing his rewrite man to keep the line open. The minutes passed, and Dick gruffly waved off reporters clamoring for their turn.

The hotel ledge was brightly lit by police searchlights. At 10:38, when Warde finally stepped off the ledge and plunged through the glass marquee over the hotel entrance, Feehan had a clear view from the cigar store window. "He jumped!" Feehan shouted into the phone. That was all the rewrite man needed to top the running story with a quick bulletin. It went out on the wire to newspapers all over the country, which published it as page-one news. Feehan then unscrewed the mouthpiece of the phone, put it in his pocket and walked away. While the other reporters scurried for functioning phones, Dick knew he had scored a five-minute beat on the story for the AP, quite a triumph in an era when newspapers kept postscripting their editions to keep important events up to date.

I INTRODUCED MYSELF to Feehan in Mid-Manhattan Court and to the only other reporter assigned to the beat, Wally Yerks of the New York *Sun.* An amiable man about to retire, Yerks—never much of a reporter to begin with—was now enjoying what was essentially a sinecure, since the *Sun,* like the other papers, relied on Feehan's AP reports for all breaking news. Yerks functioned mainly as a kind of errand boy for Feehan and was visibly in awe of him. When Yerks judged a story to be really worth filing, he'd snap to attention and recite by rote the old truism attributed to the *Sun's* onetime city editor, John Bogart: "When a dog bites a man, that's not news, but when a man bites a dog, that's news."

I explained to Feehan that *The Times* had decided to try me out on its newly established East Side day beat. Muttering a grumpy hello, he assessed me suspiciously, and I had a feeling he would be unhelpful; after all, he had heretofore been the sole source for *The Times* on breaking East Side police stories.

I tried to ingratiate myself by asking permission to accompany him every time he went on a story. At first, he rebuffed me. I kept trying to track down leads on my own and followed a number of stories that Dick didn't pursue. And I made sure to share all my information with him before calling in or writing my own stories. My tactics finally paid off. Dick actually went so far as to acknowledge that he liked my reporting and, one afternoon, he invited me along to check on a hotel jewelry heist. After my story was published, he said, "You did a good job. Let's get a drink."

We went to Flannery's, on Third Avenue between Sixty-seventh and Sixty-eighth Streets. Only a block or so from FBI headquarters, it was a haunt for FBI men as well as cops from the Sixty-seventh Street station house, despite their well-known rivalry, and Dick had close ties to both.

Every once in a while a patrolman would arrive at the bar, sent by his desk sergeant to apprise Dick of ongoing police activities in the precinct.

Following Dick's lead, I ordered Irish whiskey—Jameson's. Dick told me he never drank Bushmills because it was from Belfast and violated his Catholic sensibilities. He'd often order his whiskey with milk, as a concession to a chronic ulcer.

FIFTEEN

ALONG WITH DICK FEEHAN, I spent several hours of each day listening to court testimony. Magistrates Court was the lowest level in the city's judicial system. The judges, most of them Democratic Party hacks, were appointed by the mayor. Frequently baffled by one or another aspect of the bizarre cases that came before them, they occasionally turned to Feehan and me for advice on sentencing.

Disputes between neighbors, husbands and wives, tenants and landlords, shopkeepers and customers were the daily fare, with most defendants given suspended sentences so as not to overcrowd the jails. One story I covered concerned a fifty-year-old woman brought to court by her landlord. She had packed her four-room apartment, the adjoining hallways, the cellar and the backyard with trash she collected on nighttime forays through midtown.

The housing inspector testified that more than one truck would be required to haul away the tons of garbage the woman had amassed, which—despite her sixteen cats—had drawn rats. The judge initially set her bail at $2,500 because she had threatened to torch the building if brought into court. But she was feeble and essentially helpless, and Feehan and I voiced our sympathy for her, suggesting a reduction to $500. The judge compromised, resetting her bail at $1,000.

Other cases revealed the sleaziest side of New York. It was surprisingly common for a man to be arrested for rubbing against a woman at the Central Park Zoo or for pinching her bottom—a misdemeanor for which Enrico Caruso had been arrested in 1906 (and bailed out by the Metropolitan Opera Club). For some reason, most of these incidents took place in the Primate House, earning for this class of offenders the epithet "monkey-housers."

Then there were homosexuals entrapped by undercover cops in subway station toilets. The detectives positioned themselves at urinals with their pants unzipped, waiting for their prey. Observing these arrested men, I learned a lesson about stereotyping. Some of them were powerfully built and looked like football players or truck drivers. I had previously subscribed to the general misconception that homosexuals were effeminate.

Some cases were purely entertaining, such as the arraignment of the passenger on a city bus who paid his five-cent fare with a five-dollar bill. The driver gave him back $4.95, all in nickels. Infuriated by having to pocket ninety-nine nickels, the passenger began pelting the driver with them as the bus pulled away. The court proceedings made a good story. Dick hadn't filed anything and, when he read my story, he said he had made a mistake. From Dick, that was a compliment, indeed.

Feehan welcomed me along on every story and introduced me to the men on the force, instructing them to give me any information I requested. I became his apprentice on the beat and his crony in the barroom. He regularly partook of small luxuries, such as the barbershop at the Waldorf-Astoria, and prodded me to do the same, saying, "You've got to treat yourself right once in a while."

Compared with my neighborhood barbershop, the one at the Waldorf was a tonsorial palace. It seemed to be a block long, with two rows of twenty chairs each and mirrors stretching the length of the immaculate room. It catered to the city's power culture—clipping and shaving business magnates, politicians, entertainers and philanthropists. Dick and I took chairs next to each other. "Give the kid the deluxe," he instructed the barber. It included haircut, shampoo, shave, facial massage, tanning lamp, and shoeshine. I declined the manicure, something for which I never acquired a liking.

While the barber was cutting my hair, Frank Costello entered, accompanied by a pair of subordinates. Faultlessly tailored, he swaggered toward us and shook hands warmly with Dick, who had known him since their bootlegging days. He took the chair next to mine, and I secretly tried to study the man I knew to be New York's key Mafia boss, once dubbed by law enforcement officials "Prime Minister of the Underworld."

A partner of Meyer Lansky and Lucky Luciano, Costello specialized in buying politicians, and was said to "own" city commissioners as well as justices on the New York State Supreme Court. Though I had heard stories about gangsters from my colleagues at the paper, Costello was the first ranking mobster I personally met. His henchmen periodically interrupted the barber's work to whisper in Costello's ear and receive terse instructions. I decided against asking him for an interview, fearing such a request might upset Costello and embarrass Dick. With our faces and shoes freshly shined, Dick and I bade Costello farewell and returned to the court pressroom.

I've never known a reporter who, in addition to his underworld connections, had more clout with the top police brass than Dick, and he did not hesitate to use it. He got promotions for cops who cooperated with him on stories and who, of course, never forgot his favor. It was rumored that a cop who wanted to become a plainclothesman in Harlem, a job that guaranteed lush graft, had offered Dick $1,500 to put in a good word with the brass. I never mustered the nerve to ask Dick whether that rumor was true.

But I found it hard to believe, since Dick never hesitated to provide ample news coverage when rogue cops were transferred out of Harlem under suspicion of taking payoffs to protect the area's oldest organized gambling operation. This betting racket was known to everyone as "policy" or "numbers" and, despite periodic raids, both city and federal, it continued to flourish. In 1948, during my time on the police beat, arrests of policy operators reached a peak of 8,097. (Finally, a decade later, the police commissioner, under public pressure, transferred the entire Harlem plainclothes division to other parts of the city. But even then, the betting continued under the protection of replacement cops.)

Dick educated me about why he believed it was impossible to eradicate the racket. Harlem's economic stability, he explained, depended largely on the spoils of policy, which involved an estimated 500,000 daily players with their bets believed to reach a total of $10 million or more annually. Profits from this gargantuan illicit operation often financed the start-up of legitimate Harlem stores and even larger businesses, and helped established enterprises forestall bankruptcy.

When an important policy figure was arrested from time to time, Dick and I headed to Harlem's East 104th Street station house for the booking. "The Feds must be about to pounce," he said. He meant, of course, that the police were trying to keep ahead of a possible federal inquiry. Some of *The Times*'s top reporters occasionally tried to penetrate the endemic police corruption surrounding policy, but a code of silence prevailed. Even the honest cops looked the other way, for no cop in those days, fearing for his life, would have dreamed of talking to a reporter.

Policy players might bet as low as a nickel or a dime on a combination of any three numbers. To win, the numbers had to correspond to the three "numbers of the day"—those designated by the men who ran the racket, and based on, say, the first three numbers of the published daily total of stock market sales. The return on a winning bet was phenomenal, a dime bet sometimes paying up to a hundred dollars.

An army of thousands of "runners" collected the bets, which were recorded on slips of paper by regular customers—in their homes, on the street or in their workplaces. The betting slips found their way up the line to the central policy banker. Dick told me the racket had been under the jurisdiction of black entrepreneurs in Harlem until the early 1930s, when Dutch Schultz's gang seized control. Schultz's most powerful rival, whom he tried unsuccessfully to have murdered, was a millionaire black woman, Madame Stephanie St. Clair, who called herself the Queen of Policy. In 1935, when Schultz, after being shot, lay mortally wounded in a Newark hospital, she sent him a telegram: "As ye sow, so shall ye reap."

ONE DAY DICK SAID, "Why don't you bring your wife around? I'd like to take you both to dinner." Barbara met us at Cristo's, an unpretentious tavern on Lexington Avenue, around the corner from the Fifty-first Street station house. Dick warmed to her immediately, and told me, "She's much too pretty for you." Smiling appreciatively, Barbara asked Dick what he thought of me as a reporter. "Every good police reporter has his own tricks," was the reply, "and Arthur's going to have to learn them all. Once he masters them, he'll give us old guys tough competition."

"What are some of your tricks?" Barbara asked. Feehan laughed, and zestfully described his scoop of the man on the ledge. "I didn't know you could remove the mouthpiece from a phone," Barbara said. "Does it unscrew easily?"

"Follow me and I'll show you," said Dick, and led us to the phone booth near the tavern's entrance. It was occupied by a talkative middle-aged man. After impatiently waiting a minute, Dick knocked on the glass, indicating he'd like to use the phone. When the man ignored him, Dick opened the door and pulled him out. The man took one look at the snarling Feehan and hastily retreated. Dick then unscrewed the phone's mouthpiece and tossed it to Barbara. "Keep it as a souvenir," he said. Barbara insisted he screw it back on.

The following day, Dick and I checked on a cop's report of two men found dead in their apartment on Second Avenue. The men, who were brothers in their fifties, had died of carbon monoxide fumes from a faulty heater in their living room, their partly clad bodies ruddy from the effects of the poison.

I had never seen death before, and was unprepared for the fetid scene that greeted us. The men were bachelors, unemployed and without friends, and their bodies had lain undiscovered for some days. In eerie fascination, I stared at the bodies, suddenly aware that their flesh seemed to be moving, alive with creeping vermin.

"What is that?" I asked Dick, trying to suppress my horror.

"You've never seen maggots before?" asked Dick.

On my way to the city room by taxi, I started writing my story on folded copy paper. At my desk, I finished in longhand the half-column story Joseph had ordered and then typed it. It was a lengthy process, but I wanted to send the cleanest possible work to the copy desk, feeling somewhat insecure about typing the story from scratch.

The story ran the next day with only minor changes, but it soon became clear that I had to abandon this method because I had almost missed the deadline a couple of times. I now acquired new respect for the city room's clocks, which were synchronized to the second. Like all reporters, I became a clock watcher; as the deadline drew near, I turned from my typewriter to one of the sixteen wall clocks spaced around the city room.

It had also become my habit, while writing a story, to consult *The Times*'s Style Book. Compiled by Robert Garst and bound in a maroon hard cover, it was the bible of the city room, and was supplied to all the paper's reporters and editors. Listing a myriad do's and don'ts of prescribed usage, the book covered the fine points of punctuation, capitalization and abbreviation and featured a particularly piquant section on current rules regarding names and titles.

It required, for example, that "except in the case of preeminent individuals the full name of the official or other person must be given the first time the name is mentioned." When a public official had several titles, it further insisted, "he should be referred to by his ranking title, then identified by the subsidiary title which is pertinent to the immediate story, and in subsequent references to him the ranking title is again employed. One reason for the more meticulous recording of full names is that many of the figures in the current news will pass from the pages of newspapers in a few years, but *The New York Times* remains as a permanent record which will be searched for its accounts of events long after the principals of those events have gone from memory."

The Style Book also cited rules for the correct use of honorifics. Throughout a court trial, for example, a defendant was referred to as "Mr.," but the moment he was found guilty or confessed, he was referred to by his last name only. Somewhat frivolously, it was deemed proper to refer to "the Smith girl," though use of the phrase "the Smith woman" was avoided because it "sounded offensive." Juvenile criminals remained anonymous.

In 1973, the "Mr." policy was changed, after Spiro Agnew stepped down as vice president under a cloud and pleaded no contest to a charge of evading income tax. It was decided to let him keep "Mr." out of respect for the office he had once held, but there followed much discussion among reporters and editors over which crimes constituted "non-Mr. offenses."

The policy about who deserves an honorific has never been consistent. Sports figures, for example, are never called "Mr."—probably because the title sounds overrefined in a sports context. (And Meat Loaf is never referred to as Mr. Loaf.) The honorific for prominent dead persons, like Einstein, Roosevelt or Hemingway, is automatically buried with them. Whether the very famous living receive an honorific or not often seems to be up to the arbitrary judgment of the copy desk.

In 1951, Ted Bernstein created a "bulletin of second guessing" that was, in effect, an ongoing supplement to the Style Book. Christened "Winners & Sinners" and distributed to the entire staff every couple of weeks, the printed sheet announced that its purpose was "to make The Times better—better written, better edited, more interesting, easier to understand." When "Winners & Sinners complimented a reporter for using a graceful or witty phrase, it was regarded as a special honor.

Ted never named the sinners but since the grammatical misdeed was excerpted and dated, the culprit readily could be identified. "When an issue of W & S appears on my desk," commented Brooks Atkinson, "I run through it hastily to see whether Ted has caught me dangling a participle on my knee. If not, I go back to the first item to read the whole issue with pleasure and awe. . . . Ted can incinerate a sinner with one flash of lightning. ('English is poor taught, too,' he says, sardonically rebuking a staff illiterate for having used an adjective rather than an adverb.)"

Typical of the mistakes Bernstein plucked from the paper for Winners & Sinners was the one he published under the heading "Spoon-feeding," mocking a sentence that appeared in a cooking advice column: "Now throw in two tablespoons full of chopped parsley and cook ten more minutes. The quail ought to be tender by then . . ." Bernstein's comment: "Never mind the quail; how are we ever going to get those spoons tender? (Make it 'tablespoonfuls.')" In yet another typical rebuke, headed "Insex," Bernstein quoted the headline "Elm Beetle Infestation Ravishing Thousands of Trees in Greenwich." His riposte: "Keep your mind on your work, buster. The word you want is 'ravaging.'"

DICK FEEHAN AND I were joined on our rounds one day by Sidney Kingsley, author of the Broadway hits *Men in White* and *Dead End*. He had dedicated himself to writing a realistic drama about the police and planned to spend months getting to know the cops and detectives behind the scenes in one Manhattan precinct. For his research, with permission from the commissioner, he chose the Seventeenth Precinct—aware it offered the best burglaries and murders in town, and having been forewarned that Dick Feehan's cooperation was even more important than the commissioner's.

It was Kingsley's good luck that Dick had enjoyed the film version of *Dead End,* in which Humphrey Bogart played the gangster. He welcomed Kingsley, inviting him to tag along with us whenever he wished. As it happened, on Kingsley's first day at the station house, there was a jewelry heist at the Ritz-Carlton and Kingsley went with us to the hotel. Dick explained that thieves, lured by the district's wealth, "worked in the East Side but lived mostly on the West Side, which is, therefore, a safer residential area." I had recently reported on burglaries amounting to tens of thousands of dollars at the Hotel Madison and the Waldorf-Astoria. In one instance, jewelry valued at $20,000 was stolen from a suite occupied by Henry Luce (of *Time*) and his wife, Clare Boothe, while they were sleeping. The hotels were beginning to suffer from the bad publicity.

When we arrived at the Ritz-Carlton, we discovered that jewelry worth $30,000 had been lifted from a suite. The manager, when he learned I was from *The Times*, took me aside and tucked a ten-dollar bill into my jacket breast pocket. "Keep this under your hat, newsman," he whispered. I was genuinely shocked, and tried to hand him back his bribe. When he wouldn't take it, I threw it on the carpet and went to a phone to call in the story. Dick shrugged off the manager's gesture, but Kingsley seemed as shocked as I was at this brazen attempt to silence me.

Kingsley was at heart an investigative reporter. Before beginning to write a new play, he would collect background details to authenticate his characters and dialogue. When he wrote *Men in White*, which won the Pulitzer Prize in 1933, he spent weeks in a hospital, observing the efforts of doctors and nurses to save lives under often unbearable pressure.

Detective Story evolved as essentially a morality play about the uses and abuses of force by the police and, by implication, in the world outside. His basic theme was the effect of police power on society, and he set the play in a fictitious station house he called the Twenty-first Precinct.

"Three days before the Red coup in Czechoslovakia," he later explained in an interview in *The Times*, "the headlines said: 'Reds Take Over Police.' At the same time, the story from France was that something like a coup had been prevented because the Reds had failed in taking over the police. In Berlin today, the basic issue is who will control the chief of police."

Obviously concerned with the Soviet reach for power in Europe, Kingsley added: "The police power is a symbol, or you might say one of the measuring rods of freedom in a society. When the police power answers to a democratic code of human rights, you have a free society."

Kingsley was interested to learn of instances of police brutality. On the basis of Dick's guarded descriptions of what he said were "occasional" acts of physical abuse "behind closed doors," Kingsley invented a detective with an obsessive hatred for any and all lawbreakers, who believes democracy is inefficient and decides he is the law. The cop beats up an arrested abortionist at the station house. "He has a medieval attitude—just as the Communists have—that he has a mission to make people abide by the right as he sees it," said Kingsley, "or personally bring them to account if they don't."

When Kingsley invited Dick and me to see the play in March 1949, we were startled by the precise realism of the set: the drab, spare squad room with walls painted olive green to waist height and a paler green from there to the ceiling. We also recognized bits of authentic dialogue and familiar characters. We were sure he had based much of the character of his police reporter on Moe Berman, who in the play became Joe Feinson, a City College graduate who waxes emotional about his love for his job and for the police.

The play is set on the night of a full moon, surely the product of conversations Kingsley and I had had about lunar effects on the city's less stable citizens. One night at the station house, I told him that mental aberrations seemed to surface under the spell of the full moon and we could expect some strange visitors, people claiming they were being followed, had hexes put on them or were receiving subliminal transmissions from the Empire State Building. My paper, I said, received similar visitations at such times.

In those days, access to the *Times* city room was as easy as entering a bookstore. A reporter would be sent to the reception desk to try to get rid of an unwelcome visitor without causing a stir. In the late 1960s, guards were placed on the ground floor—a result of bomb threats—and the lunar loonies stopped coming.

DICK FEEHAN WAS SOMETIMES assigned by his desk to a story in his district without police or courtroom ramifications, and, on at least one such occasion, he became the focus of the news himself. Because AP reports on diplomats and other prominent persons visiting Manhattan's East Side were welcomed by newspapers everywhere, Dick, as the district's AP man, was treated with respect by those he was assigned to cover. Even President Truman, on visits to New York, acknowledged Dick when he spotted him among the press contingent.

There was one dignitary, however, whom Dick failed to impress—Andrei Gromyko, the taciturn Soviet representative to the UN. It was a time when any action of Gromyko's was big news, especially his abrupt protest walkouts from the Security Council. He froze out reporters trying to elicit comment with habitual sullen silence.

Since Gromyko resided in Dick's territory, at the Soviet delegation residence at 680 Park Avenue, Dick had the morning Gromyko watch for several weeks. When Gromyko left the building to enter his limousine, he always ignored Dick, as he did all members of the press. Dick would get no response, even to such an inconsequential question as, "How are you today, Mr. Gromyko?"

One morning Gromyko took Dick aback by finally talking, even though all he said was, "I don't want to speak to you." Dick shot back, "I don't want to speak to you either, but I have to." Several newspapers found even so tame an utterance worth reporting. It didn't take much longer before Dick's persistence apparently won Gromyko's respect, and he became the only street reporter to whom Gromyko would respond.

Although Dick had become my primary mentor outside the office, Mike Berger, who occasionally took my stories by phone, continued to impart smart lessons at every opportunity. My first major running story was about the murder of a thirty-six-year-old businesswoman named Vera Lotito, in her apartment on East Fifty-fifth Street.

Her body was discovered by her husband when he returned home from work. She had been bound with neckties, strangled and stabbed repeatedly, with no known motive. A blouse had been spread over her face. The police said nothing was missing save her wedding and engagement rings. A detective, who knew Dick, allowed us to examine the crime scene before the medical examiner arrived, and I phoned in the notes I had taken to Mike Berger.

"What color were the ties?" he asked.

"I'm not sure. I think one of them was brown."

"You think one of them was brown? I need to know the actual colors."

I said I'd go back and check. One tie was bluish-brown, another was brown and yellow, a third was gray. I called Mike, and apologized for the oversight.

"Okay," he said. "What color was the blouse?"

I didn't know, so I went back again. "It was pink," I told Mike.

"Great. What kind of furniture was in the room?"

I paused. I told him I'd call him back, and returned to the apartment.

"There's a beige couch, a chest of wooden drawers, and a coffee table, and a couple of beige armchairs, one with a fur coat draped over the back."

Mike was relentless. "What kind of fur?" he asked. "Mink, sable, fox?"

I hung up once more and meekly met the gaze of the detective who opened the door for the fifth time. "I hope this is the last time," he said. The coat was mink.

Berger, of course, demanded those details to teach me a lesson (as he did, I later learned, with other young reporters). "I'm just doing to you what someone did to me when I was your age," he explained. The next time I phoned in a story I began rattling off so many minutiae that he interrupted me.

"Whoa! Hold it!" he said. "This is a half-column story. You're giving me enough for a book."

The Lotito case continued for days, and I wrote a number of the follow-up articles myself. The murderer was finally caught when he tried to pawn a raccoon coat that he had taken as part of his haul.

"I thought the only items missing were two rings," I said to Dick.

"Sometimes the detectives don't give us the whole story if they think that withholding information will help them catch a bad guy," he said. "By keeping the loot out of the papers, they hope to lull the killer into a sense of false security, figuring he might slip up. And he did."

The detectives had asked pawnbrokers to keep an eye open for Mrs. Lotito's coat, as well as for her wristwatch and a number of her husband's suits. When one pawnbroker received a phone call asking if he would take a raccoon coat, he said yes, then alerted the police. The police staked out the pawnshop, spotted the killer and, after a prolonged chase, brought him in. I was certain that Dick had known these details all along, but kept them to himself out of loyalty to the police.

AFTER NEARLY A YEAR on the police beat, I covered a story that made international headlines. On August 7, 1948, *The Times* received a tip that Oksana Kasenkina, a Russian teacher who tutored the children of Soviet diplomats, had been kidnapped from a farm near Nyack run by the Tolstoy Foundation, where she was hiding to avoid an impending mandated trip to the Soviet Union. According to *The Times*'s source, Russian officials had forcibly returned her to the consulate in New York, where she was presently locked up.

The Soviets admitted they had brought Mrs. Kasenkina back to the city, but claimed they had rescued her from the clutches of terrorists: "She came willingly. She was not kidnapped. She wrote to us and asked us to get her out. She wants to go to Russia." They said the Tolstoy Foundation had abducted her against her will and that she was voluntarily staying in the consulate for her own protection. Kasenkina, under pressure, endorsed the official statement.

Over the next few days, allegations that she was being held as a hostage in the consulate could not be disregarded, and the Soviet consul general, Jacob Lomakin, was served with a writ of habeas corpus from the State Supreme Court ordering him to produce Kasenkina before a judge. Lomakin ignored it, and the Russians filed a formal protest with the State Department. As suspense grew over the standoff, I was sent to post myself outside the Soviet consulate to await breaking developments along with reporters from all the other papers. Ten photographers were also on the scene, though all except one took up their stations in the bar of the Pierre Hotel across the street.

Fred Sass, a photographer for *The Times*, who didn't drink, stayed in the street and was the only one to hear a concierge, from the social club in the building next door to the consulate, shout: "Hey, fellows! A woman just jumped out of the back window!" Sass followed the concierge into the club's basement and through a door that opened onto a courtyard divided from the consulate by a concrete wall and an iron fence. By standing on a box, Sass could see all the action and started shooting with his Speed Graphic.

Kasenkina had leaped from a third-floor window. An insulated wire broke her fall, sparing her from instant death, though she suffered broken bones, internal bleeding and a concussion. Sass told me, in a statement he later amplified for publication in *The Times*, that he saw a woman lying on her back, rocking from side to side. A police sergeant and a patrolman came through the building adjoining the consulate followed by more photographers and reporters, me included.

A man and a woman emerged from the consulate and, when they started to move Kasenkina, she moaned something that a woman reporter who knew Russian said meant "Leave me alone." The Russians, heedless of the policemen's warning not to touch her, carried her inside. But they finally relented, allowing her to be taken by ambulance to Roosevelt Hospital.

One of the pictures that Sass took prior to the arrival of other photographers showed Kasenkina crumpled on the ground, entwined in wire, before anyone had moved her. It perfectly captured the agony of the moment and was unanimously proclaimed by his colleagues as a shoo-in for the Pulitzer

Prize but, to everyone's dismay, the photo wasn't published. The bullpen killed it because Kasenkina's garter belt was exposed.

The paper, of course, had not yet emerged from a period of blue-nosed censorship of photos, no better than when the kissing Monroe–DiMaggio photo had so outraged the publisher. The rules were unfathomable to everyone in the city room, especially since the bullpen had agreed years before to run the grisly photo of the upside-down-hanging corpses of Mussolini and his mistress.

The questionable rules were still in effect many years later, and, in 1959, a photo by Eddie Hausner of four teary-eyed pallbearers carrying a casket of a murdered boy into a Bronx church was ordered killed by the bullpen editors. The sight of a child's casket, they explained, might disturb the sensibilities of our readers at the breakfast table.

DURING KASENKINA'S STAY at Roosevelt Hospital, Soviet officials maintained that she had been happy in the consulate and free to come and go as she pleased. They suggested that perhaps she was mentally unstable, a typical Soviet ploy in such situations.

Kasenkina, however, after gaining consciousness, told a different story to the press. She said she had been kept prisoner in the consulate and had tried to escape because she feared for her life. She wanted to stay in America, she said, because, in 1937, the Soviet government had seized her husband and he had "disappeared." Later, they drafted her son into an army division without training him, and he was killed in Leningrad in 1942. Kasenkina believed the Russians were planning to exile her to Siberia. She said she loved her country and her people, but could not agree with the Communist regime.

The State Department condemned the kidnapping and offered Kasenkina asylum. Consul General Lomakin was expelled on the grounds that he had "abused his position and grossly violated the proper standards of official conduct." The Soviet government denied all allegations, shut down its consulates in New York and San Francisco, asked for immediate closure of the American consulate in Vladivostok, and withdrew from discussions regarding a new American consulate in Leningrad.

As this was my district, I was the primary legman for *The Times* on the story. The paper ruled it was too big for me to handle, and asked me to call in my facts to one of the star reporters, Charles Grutzner. Dick Feehan furnished me with bits of detail that the cops had shared with him but that he didn't file to his desk. The details were just what *The Times* wanted, and it gave me an edge over other reporters, especially those of the *Herald Tribune.*

Grutzner was pleased with my legwork and was generous enough to commend me in a note to Robert Garst, who had recently succeeded Joseph as city editor. Joseph had held the position with decreasing effectiveness for two decades and Catledge had finally found a way to remove him: he persuaded James to "promote" Joseph to a token job as Catledge's assistant.

Not long after, to my surprise and delight, Garst offered me a promotion. I was given the choice of taking over the Health, Hospitals and Sanitation beat, plus coverage of the State Office Building across the street, or becoming a labor reporter under the venerated chief labor writer, A. H. Raskin.

Both jobs were tempting, so I placed my dilemma before my mentors— Berger, Schumach and Spiegel. They were all of the same mind: Take Health, Hospitals and Sanitation, they counseled, pointing out that I'd have my own beat, my own territory in both city and state governments.

"You'll get to demonstrate what you can do by yourself," said Mike. "It's the best way to earn a byline and gain further recognition."

Regretfully, in late September 1948, I parted from Dick Feehan, to begin my new assignment downtown.

SIXTEEN

R OBERT GARST TOLD ME that my new beat, varied as it was, would allow me to develop as a "self-starter." Absent any breaking news, I would be expected to dream up my own ideas for stories, the more the better.

While no other newspapers posted reporters to this beat, Garst explained, *The Times* was convinced it could be mined for the kind of stories that illustrated how well the city was carrying out its health, hospitals and sanitation policies—stories that would appeal to our discriminating readers.

"I think the other papers are making a mistake and I'm sure you'll be able to demonstrate that," Garst said. He had long campaigned for more space in the paper for in-depth city coverage, and for front-page positioning of such stories.

Garst's city editorship fell somewhere between the lively Bruce Rae's and the languid David Joseph's. A spindly Virginian, Garst was in his late forties. Except for a year when he worked as a reporter for the United Press, he had devoted his entire twenty-three years as a newspaperman to editing. He had been hired by *The Times* in 1925 as a copy editor on the city desk.

Most reporters thought Garst uncaring, even icy. But, having come to know him during my days at *Timesweek*, I found his coolness somewhat Gary Cooperesque; he was, in my view, patient and courtly, if laconic.

I agreed with A. H. Raskin, who viewed Garst's persona with humor. "Holding down a job that usually pays off in ulcers, insomnia or nervous breakdowns," Raskin wrote in *Times Talk*, "Bob Garst manages to keep so cool they turn the air-conditioning off when he comes in on a summer day."

Only in rare moments of crisis did Garst display any emotion, indicated by a flush that slowly rose from his neck to his forehead. "He took the Lindbergh kidnapping in his stride when he was just a pinch hitter on the city desk," recalled Raskin. "He had Bruce Rae breathing down his neck. Bruce was in the bullpen, then serving as assistant night managing editor, but he could not resist the itch to take over. When Bob stayed serene under the double pressure of the story and the supervision, most *Times* men were ready to bet nothing in the news could ever ruffle him."

When I nervously began suggesting story ideas to Garst, he would smile reassuringly, ask a precise question or two and then usually give me the space I requested. My beat was situated in the downtown complex that included City Hall as well as the federal and state courts and the city's criminal courts. My principal responsibilities were the state attorney general, the motor vehicle bureau (both in the State Office Building at 80 Centre Street) and the city's commissioners of health, hospitals and sanitation (at 125 Worth Street).

Karl Pretshold greeted me at the Health Department, where he served as the commissioner's public information officer. Like Raymond McCaw, he had been a tramp reporter, roaming from city to city, picking up newspaper jobs. Pretshold was obliged to settle down when he married and began having children. But he was still a newspaperman at heart and seemed to derive vicarious satisfaction from providing me with sources and tips.

One morning, a week after our first meeting, I found Pretshold in his office, his long legs propped on his desk, his glasses pushed up on his forehead, a pencil wedged behind his ear and a cigarette between nicotine-stained fingers. "I see you haven't had a good story yet," he said. "I swear it's not always this quiet around here. A year ago I didn't even have time for a smoke."

His office, he explained, had then been the epicenter of information about one of the worst health scares in the city's history. I immediately knew he was referring to a frightening three weeks that still haunted New Yorkers. According to Pretshold, it was he who had kept the press alerted with hourly bulletins, beginning on April 4, 1947, only moments after the health commissioner received word from the United States Army Medical School Laboratory in Washington that specimens taken from three patients at Bellevue Hospital, one of whom had already died, had been identified as smallpox. The city's last major smallpox epidemic had been in 1901, and had claimed 720 lives.

Familiar with the nightmarish episode, I found myself reliving the horror as Pretshold recounted the role he'd played. On March 5, a portly man, his face flushed and his eyes glassy, appeared at Bellevue complaining of headaches, lassitude and lack of appetite. When he was examined, his temperature was 102. Several doctors studied the large red patches on his chest and arms. But the rash completely baffled them because few doctors in the country had ever seen a case of smallpox.

The victim, a businessman who had arrived at a hotel in New York on his way from Mexico to Maine for a holiday, died five days later, but not before infecting three more people, who themselves infected eight others. Just before he died, his fever had reached 105 and his body was completely covered by the red boil-like patches. By moving quickly, the city forestalled a catastrophe.

Six million New Yorkers, including Barbara and me and everyone at *The Times*, were vaccinated. We had all waited at emergency clinics for hours, on lines often several blocks long. My parents, who had not been vaccinated since they were children in Europe, suffered from feverishly red and swollen areas on their vaccinated arms.

From the dead businessman's wife, Pretshold had obtained a list of all the towns where their bus had stopped on their way to New York, so that people in those towns could also be vaccinated. By May 2, the danger of an epidemic was declared over. On the basis of statistics of recent epidemics in other cities, said Pretshold, more than 28,000 New Yorkers could have contracted smallpox and more than 1,000 could have died, had the Health Department not been on its toes.

"And now for present matters—helping get you a good story to file," Pretshold said. "We have to do something about that right away."

He made a phone call, apparently to someone in the building. Within a couple of minutes, a chubby, balding man entered the office. "I'd like you to meet Samuel Plotkin," said Pretshold. "He commands two hundred inspectors in our food poisoning division. No one in the city is more feared by food code violators."

I said I had no inkling that food poisoning was a hot issue in New York. "Why don't you join me on my rounds this afternoon, and see for yourself?" Plotkin urged, eyes twinkling in anticipation of what he had in store for me.

On our way to a butcher shop uptown, he said it was not uncommon for a proprietor to make stale meat appear fresh by injecting it with sulfur dioxide. There were three ways, he explained, to test the wholesomeness of a particular food: chemical analysis, bacteriological analysis and tasting. Lab testing was time-consuming and complicated, and Plotkin's method of choice was tasting.

As we entered the butcher shop, he flashed his ID and demanded to be shown the chopped meat. The husky butcher, scowling and protesting, led us to a walk-in refrigerator. Plotkin pinched a sample of meat and placed it in his mouth. The effect was literally electrifying. The butcher had injected the meat with sulfur dioxide which, when it made contact with Plotkin's metal fillings, set up a miniature electric cell.

"Zounds!" Plotkin muttered, wrapping a sample of meat in waxed paper for conclusive testing in the lab. He warned the proprietor he faced a severe fine and cautioned him to mend his ways immediately or confront even harsher penalties.

"That was an easy one," Plotkin said, as we walked out. "Once, when I discovered tainted meat in a large establishment, five butchers blocked my exit, each brandishing a bloody cleaver. For a moment, I saw myself being ground into sausage, and I dashed for the door." The suddenness of his move took the butchers by surprise, and he escaped. On another occasion, a butcher locked him in the walk-in refrigerator and left him there for what seemed like several hours.

As the city's official taster, Plotkin told me he felt like the poison testers for ancient kings. When he tasted a morsel of suspect food, his heart was in his mouth as well. Once, he was asked by the police to sample some sugar-coated almonds, which had been sent as a gift to a woman by her son-in-law. The woman had recently persuaded her daughter to leave her husband and, leery of the gift, she called the police, who forwarded the almonds to Plotkin. He tasted a grain of the "sugar" coating, which he suspected was strychnine. It was.

One day I joined Plotkin in his search for wild, poisonous mushrooms. New York stores in those days often bought baskets of mushrooms from amateur pickers. Several people had recently died after eating a poisonous variety, while dozens more became ill.

Plotkin started a crusade to ban amateur mushroom gatherers from New

York's marketplace. "While only two percent of mushroom species are toxic, they grow in abundance," he warned. "The poisonous and nonpoisonous types can look so much alike that it takes an expert to distinguish them."

He told me mushroom gatherers often used tests based on superstition to distinguish between the species. They included picking mushrooms under a full moon and away from rusty nails and snake holes; cooking them with a coin (if the coin blackened, the fungus was harmful)—or simply assuming that pretty mushrooms were safe. "Unfortunately," Plotkin said, "the 'death cup' is but one example of a fungus as breathtakingly beautiful and delicious as it is deadly."

Shellfish also found their way into markets through dubious sources. "Bootleggers," as they were known, harvested clams, mussels and oysters from the polluted waters of Jamaica Bay, Little Neck, Eastchester and other areas, sometimes leading to cases of typhoid, dysentery and other intestinal diseases. The Health Department's bureau of food and drugs had begun cracking down on offenders in an effort dubbed "Operation Shellfish," which employed a fleet of rowboat agents. Six hundred bootleggers were apprehended in the course of the operation and more than nine thousand pounds of mollusks were condemned before reaching the stores.

Plotkin surprised me one day by announcing that his targets for the next several weeks would be the city's finest restaurants. Noting there were twenty-two thousand restaurants in New York, he said that some of the best gave him the worst headaches. I had assumed the better establishments would not stoop to serve tainted food, but Plotkin assured me otherwise. "Hollandaise sauce is one of the bureau's worst problems," he said, explaining that forty serious cases of food poisoning, and hundreds of minor cases, were attributed every year to what he called the "aristocrat" of French sauces.

If improperly handled, Plotkin explained, hollandaise was an explosive breeding ground for pathogen-producing salmonella. Slight aberrations in cooking temperature and introduction of impurities into the concoction of egg yolks, butter and lemon juice could incubate the bacteria and encourage it to multiply quickly.

Notices were sent to every restaurant advising chefs to "follow strictly the principles suggested by the bureau of food and drugs or to discontinue the preparation of hollandaise." These rules required that chefs have clean hands with no open cuts, that ingredients be wholesome, that utensils be scrupulously scrubbed and egg shells cleaned before breaking. Excessive handling when separating the white from the yolk was discouraged and a sauce older than two hours had to be discarded.

Chefs were touchy about anyone looking over their shoulders, and Plotkin's inspections were met with resistance. One irate chef was impeded by his manager as he lunged at Plotkin with a knife. Plotkin was unruffled. Another chef bluntly refused to reveal the "secret technique" he had learned in France, but Plotkin insisted. Sullenly, the chef demonstrated how he strained the sauce through a cheesecloth bag that was squeezed with bare hands. It was the last sauce the chef made that way.

Garst agreed the Plotkin chronicles were good copy, and before long other papers sent reporters to cover this rich terrain. Barbara, however, was less than enthusiastic about my beat, with good cause. I stopped eating mushrooms and shellfish, and wouldn't touch hollandaise sauce, mayonnaise, custard or any concoction containing egg yolks, butter or cream.

Ever leery of the produce Barbara brought home, I occasionally called Plotkin to ask him about the reliability of a particular store, and would sometimes interrupt Barbara's preparations to consult him on the safest way to cook certain dishes. In exasperation, Barbara said, "Why don't you marry Plotkin and let him cook for you?"

I also tried to alert Barbara to Plotkin's investigations into how food shops cheated naive customers of $40 million a year. At his suggestion, I accompanied a female agent from the bureau of weights and measures to a suspect market. Pretending to be a customer, she ordered a chicken and, as it was about to be placed on the scale, she clutched it and plunged her fingers into the cavity containing the gizzard. To my amazement—and to that of the market's other customers—she pulled out a lead weight. The butcher received a summons that led to a $100 fine (for a first offense).

In other shops, the agent caught butchers sneakily pressing down on scales while orders were being weighed. In one case, the agent found a culprit who had attached one end of a string to the bottom of his scale and the other to a floor pedal; by stepping on the pedal, he could add as much weight as he pleased.

There came a time when Garst understandably began to tire of Plotkin stories. Casting about, I found a fruitful new source—the metropolitan infrastructure. It wasn't long before Robert Moses, the city construction coordinator and commissioner of parks, as well as the chairman of the Long Island State Park Commission and the Triborough Bridge and Tunnel Authority (to mention only a few of his numerous titles), invited me to his office. "I've got something interesting to tell you," he said.

Moses was New York's development czar, the man most responsible for the sweeping physical changes in the city after the war. Educated at Yale,

Oxford and Columbia, he had been a close advisor to Governor Al Smith and was given an unprecedented free hand by Mayor La Guardia and his City Hall successors.

A good friend of the Sulzberger family, Moses often found a sympathetic ally in the editorial pages of *The Times*. On his sixty-fifth birthday, a few years after I met him, the paper wrote that Moses had "always been the strongman" under all mayors, "looking far ahead of the current visible objectives, impatient with those who disagree with him but free of bitterness when the battle is over, a master of the ridicule that leaves an opponent hanging in tatters, but back again the next week, with the past forgotten, appealing in the public interest for support to bring some fine new dream to reality."

By now, Moses was credited with the creation of the Henry Hudson Parkway, the Belt Parkway and the Marine Parkway—among many other massive public works. Often wielding more power than the mayors he served, he exercised all manner of influence in the name of progress. It clearly didn't bother him that his proposed construction of a mammoth highway system—thirteen north-south arteries that would accommodate ever-faster-moving vehicles to the suburbs—would dispossess thousands of city tenants and destroy their neighborhoods. He argued that his strategies would, in the long run, actually improve daily life for the majority of New Yorkers: land values would soar, he promised, and all New Yorkers would eventually benefit from a thriving economy.

On October 27, 1948, when I went to meet Moses in his office under the toll plaza of the Triborough Bridge, I found a man of tall, powerful build, every bit as imposing as his reputation, and I was disarmed when he offered me roasted peanuts from a large bowl. But then, with no further pleasantries, he unrolled a huge map on his outsize desk. Proudly, he disclosed details of his current working plan—the blueprint for a six-lane, $40 million highway through a part of the Bronx and along the banks of the Harlem River to the Westchester County line.

The highway was to be called the Major Deegan Expressway, in honor of a former major in the Army Corps of Engineers and a founding member of the American Legion. Assuring me he would not give the story to any other paper, Moses said he trusted I would handle the details accurately (knowing, I'm sure, that a blue envelope from my publisher would await me if I didn't).

He said he was not yet able to supply specific information about how the highway would be built and was vague about what would happen to property along the route. With hindsight, I realized I should have pressed him for more details. I might then, for instance, have discovered his plan to run the highway through a marshy area of Van Cortlandt Park, which—as he was well aware—was prized by bird-watchers (and was to cause cries of outrage when his strategy came to light).

At the time, though, I was too inexperienced to realize that I was, in effect, being conned by a master con artist. Aware that Moses was admired in particular by Iphigene Sulzberger and always treated with respect, if not downright awe, by the hierarchy of *The Times*, I believed I had lucked into the best story of my career so far.

I had no inkling then of the devastation that would accompany Moses' grandiose dream, no concept of the arrogance with which he would disregard the pleas of the poor and lower-middle-class families threatened with eviction. This was especially true of two later plans: the Cross-Bronx Expressway, which would cause incalculable destruction to a large section of the Bronx, and the Lower Manhattan Expressway, which was stopped in its tracks by a populist rebellion in Greenwich Village.

I gradually became aware of the ruthlessness that was to undo him. As his power unraveled, I began to see him—as, at last, did my peers in the city room—as a figure of pathos. Our paths continued to cross in later years, not always pleasantly.

Back in the city room, innocent of what was to come, I told Garst about my scoop and he was pleased. After half the story had left my typewriter, Murray Schumach whispered to me that he'd heard it was going to be signed. I was so thrilled I could hardly stay in my seat long enough to finish the story. Finally, a byline in the daily paper! I had to feign ignorance, because the city-room code decreed that a reporter learned of his byline only by seeing it when he opened the paper.

As I finished typing, I saw Arthur Altschul, a staff reporter, smiling in front of my desk. "Murray let me in on the news," he said. "I'd like to invite you to '21' for a toast and dinner—with Barbara, of course, and Murray." I had never been to the "21" Club, the former speakeasy that was now a swanky restaurant. Once we were there, Arthur ordered champagne.

All of us in the city room believed the rumor that Arthur was the richest reporter in New York. But he rarely talked about his materially privileged (but emotionally deprived) childhood. His father, Frank Altschul, was a senior partner at Wall Street's Lazard Frères, and his uncle was a former New York governor, Herbert H. Lehman. Arthur was resented by some of his fellow reporters for having been hired despite his lack of newspaper experience. Everyone knew that his father was Arthur Hays Sulzberger's friend and that it was pull that had landed him the job after his discharge as a Marine lieutenant.

He felt like an outsider, until Murray Schumach, with his innate kindness, befriended him. Arthur's life thereupon assumed an upward turn. On Friday nights, Murray took him to Brooklyn by subway for dinner at his mother's apartment. Minnie Schumach lit the Sabbath candles and served a feast including gefilte fish and chicken soup. Arthur once told me it was the first time he had ever witnessed a mother in the kitchen, cooking a meal for her family.

After a few years on the paper, Arthur left for Wall Street. He said that Robert Lehman, senior partner at Lehman Brothers and a distant cousin, had urged him to come to work in his firm. "I finally realized I'd never be a star like Murray," he explained. "I simply don't have a natural talent for reporting; I was wasting my time in journalism." Over the years, I enjoyed watching Arthur blossom on Wall Street, where he clearly belonged.

MY STORY ABOUT ROBERT MOSES and the Major Deegan Expressway, which led the second section of the paper on February 28, 1948, was a clean beat. When the first edition hit the stands, the *Herald Tribune* made frantic attempts to reach Moses, trying to match us for their later editions, but they were unable to find him. It was an era when newspapers still insisted on receiving their facts straight from the source. The *Tribune* would never have led a story with "*The New York Times* reported that . . . ," as many publications later began doing. And it wasn't until the following day that competing papers managed to confirm *The Times*'s exclusive account.

The same day that my Deegan Expressway story was published, President Truman arrived to campaign in New York, in what most people believed was an exercise in futility. Ed Flynn, Democratic political boss of the Bronx, felt obliged to ride in the president's car, but had to be coerced to leave it to stand beside Truman when he made his campaign stops. Flynn feared he would sully his reputation by endorsing a doomed candidate.

Every major poll predicted New York's Governor Dewey would win not just the state but the nation, and all foresaw a landslide. One of Truman's problems was that he was dwarfed by comparison with Roosevelt. As far back as June, *The Times*'s political sage, James Hagerty, had predicted that whoever was nominated at the Republican convention would become the next president. The most recent *Times* poll called it at 345 electoral votes for Dewey, 105 for Truman, and 38 for the States' Rights Party candidate, South Carolina governor Strom Thurmond.

In New York, many liberals I knew opposed Truman's anti-Communist "containment" policies—believing that the Soviet Union was basically peace-loving; for this as well as other reasons, they supported Henry A. Wallace, once Roosevelt's vice president and now running as the candidate for the newly organized left-wing Progressive Party. But Truman happily did not give up. At one whistle-stop after another throughout the country, he hammered away at Dewey and his conservative record.

In the city room, many of us—led by Grover Loud and Bill Laurence—supported Truman for his earthy candor, as opposed to Dewey's tiresome pomposity. (While striving for fairness in the news columns, reporters and editors made no attempt when talking among themselves to contain their personal political passions.) We worried that Dewey would reverse Roosevelt's New Deal achievements, and we appreciated Alice Roosevelt Longworth's much-quoted gibe: "Can you vote for a man that looks like the bridegroom on a wedding cake?"

But Scotty Reston, who led *The Times*'s campaign coverage as national correspondent, was credited with the funniest anti-Dewey line, which Bill Laurence circled in red and posted on the city-room bulletin board. To assess the governor's public appeal, Reston had briefly joined Dewey's whistle-stop tour. Wearied by the banality of his speeches from the rear platform, Reston wrote at the tail end of his story that the train left "with a little jerk."

On Election Day, on my way home from my beat, I stopped at the city room to look in on the night's frenzy, and joined the Dewey disparagers among the staff who were praying for a miracle. *The Times* had prepared articles and editorials in advance, all assuming victory for Dewey. The Sunday *Magazine* was set to roll with a cover portrait of Dewey. Nothing had been readied for a Truman win.

Around eleven P.M., with the race tighter than anyone had predicted, a rewrite man hurriedly composed a brief sketch of Truman's life, and the editorial board began preparing copy congratulating him just in case he squeaked through. Edwin James, with Turner Catledge at his side, commanded the troops. I had never before seen the two top editors in shirt-sleeves, looking so exasperated.

A spokesman for the Dewey camp finally admitted their candidate was not having the forecasted easy time. "We're in there fighting," he said. "The returns are still coming in but it looks like we won't know definitely until midmorning. We are not making any predictions or claims."

Truman went to bed early. "I don't expect final results until morning," he said. The president woke up twice to listen to the radio, and heard the commentator, H. V. Kaltenborn, declare at midnight that he was ahead by a million votes, but nonetheless certain to lose. At four A.M., Truman was up by two million votes, but Kaltenborn still predicted the president's doom.

At last, James reversed the paper's course and proclaimed Truman the winner. Led by Laurence, a group of staffers, including myself, cheered. Truman won by a margin of 2,188,054 in the popular vote, and garnered 303 electoral votes to Dewey's 189 and Thurmond's 39. The strong turnout for Wallace in New York threw the state to Dewey, but the Progressive Party candidate did not fare well in the rest of the country.

Not all newspapers were as cautious as *The Times*. The most grievous error was made by the *Chicago Tribune*, whose early edition announced "Dewey Defeats Truman," a headline that will always stand as a symbol of the press's fallibility. The Alsop brothers, Joseph and Stewart, in their syndicated column, also placed Dewey in the Oval Office. They shamefacedly wrote the next day: "There is only one question on which professional politicians, poll takers, political reporters and other wiseacres and prognosticators can any longer speak with much authority. That is how they want their crow cooked."

Gripped by the spectacle of the paper running at top speed that election night, I pined to be back on the telegraph desk. I missed the nightly action and the role I had played—however minor—in producing the big deadline stories that surprised the world by morning.

I was unaccustomed to sitting on the sidelines, and it was somewhat grudgingly that I kept my appointment the next day with officials of the Health Department. What they told me erased any remnant of nostalgia for the telegraph desk, and I plunged into investigating the background data they gave me: Polio was climbing to epidemic proportions; tuberculosis continued to be the the city's number-one infectious killer, claiming more lives than all other infectious diseases combined, with no cure in sight; and almost 29,000 cases of measles had resulted in twenty-five deaths in1948.

My newly acquired gastronomic and medical knowledge was beginning to weigh on me. Not only was I compulsively suspicious of seafood, hamburgers and egg products, I worried about a headache (which could be the first symptom of a tropical disease) and a cough (which could mean the onset of TB).

And I began fretting about smallpox when Pretshold informed me of a new epidemic in Scotland, which caused New York authorities to quarantine arrivals from the British Isles for up to fourteen days unless they could prove they had been vaccinated in the past six months. And then, God help us, there was psittacosis, a virus carried by pigeons that caused high fevers, headaches, respiratory distress and, in some cases, death.

I was rapidly becoming a confirmed hypochondriac, and the doctors I interviewed played to my neurotic tendencies, recounting case after case of horrifying symptoms. Rabies, they told me, was one hundred percent fatal. An average of 25,000 dog bites was reported yearly, in addition to 1,000 cat bites, 423 rat bites, a handful (or mouthful) from horses and squirrels as well as animals found at the zoo. In those days, anyone suspected of having been bitten by a rabid animal required fourteen painful injections. Moreover, a victim had to receive the treatment even without knowing if he or she had contracted rabies. By the time symptoms appeared it was too late. After writing a story about rabies, I gave dogs on the street a wide berth.

One bizarre episode involving my Health Department watch brought me face to face with a skunk named Blossom. The Madison Square Boys Club applied for a permit to keep her in the city as a mascot. The amiable nine-pound skunk had somehow wandered into their summer playground when it was a baby, and one of the boys had been allowed to take it home. It had been deodorized and housebroken, and enjoyed playing with the club's two dogs. After some debate, the Health Department concluded that Blossom could not be considered a wild animal, and approved the permit.

Sensing an entertaining feature piece, I arranged to visit the Boys Club, and convinced a reluctant Eddie Hausner to take photos. The only source of refreshment at the club was the water fountain but, noticing that some children had pressed their mouths against the spout, I didn't drink from it. Eddie, however, was blind to the risk. I considered warning him but thought he'd mock my hypervigilance against germs, as other friends did.

Not long after, Eddie felt a painful swelling in his groin. He had contracted mumps, and feared he might become sterile (sometimes the result of adult mumps). "You shouldn't have taken a drink from that water fountain," I told him, unable to resist.

"If you're so smart, you should have stopped me," he said. "If I can't have children, it's your fault." He didn't speak to me for weeks (and didn't stop worrying until he married and had a child, the first of four).

NEAR MY DESK at the back of the city room sat a small contingent of staffers collectively known as the radio broadcast desk. They wrote the hourly news bulletins for the *Times*-owned WQXR, whose listeners were mostly devoted readers of the paper itself. From seven A.M. to midnight, WQXR played recorded classical music, save for four minutes of news bulletins at the top of each hour, culled from *Times* stories as well as items from the news services.

If fledgling reporters were plagued by insecurities about how we were measuring up—would Garst ever tell us when he liked our work?—the bulletin writers were even more in limbo. Whereas the reporters, me included, studied one another's published stories, trying to gauge who among us was beginning to soar or starting to slip, the broadcast staffers—all avidly striving to become reporters—lived in a state of frustrating anonymity. I couldn't understand why it was taking so long for one staffer in particular to be promoted to reporter.

He was Bernard Kalb, who at twenty-six had been writing bulletins for two years, when we became friends in the fall of 1948. Bernie's deepest ambition was to go abroad as a foreign correspondent—a goal he finally achieved with great distinction, first for *The Times* and later for CBS. (He went on to serve as NBC State Department correspondent.) During the Vietnam War he was one of the early TV correspondents to grasp and convey to the public the tragedy of Saigon in its death throes.

While still a captive of the *Times* broadcast desk, Bernie frequently demonstrated his talent in witty freelance articles for the paper's Sunday sections, and I was disappointed by Garst's failure to appreciate his flair.

The similarities of our backgrounds gave me the eerie sense that Bernie was almost my mirror image. Like me, he'd grown up in the Bronx, the son of immigrant parents. His good-natured father, Max, was born in Poland and his strong-willed mother, Bella, in the Ukraine. Max was a tailor and, during the Depression, kept his family afloat by working in a garment factory downtown and, for a time, running a dry-cleaning store in the East Bronx. The Kalb family—which also included an older sister, Estelle, and a younger brother, Marvin—would occasionally move, as had mine, because of the lure of a customary three months' free rent.

We enjoyed dissecting our roots, which Bernie labeled "the two-cents plain culture" (referring to a small glass of seltzer served over the counter at the corner candy store). We also reminisced about those snacks of "gribenes" our mothers tossed us from apartment windows when we played in the streets. Bernie recalled those snacks as "our early start into cholesterol." And we compared the quirky Bronx argot we grew up with—and had to unlearn—like "make out the light" (instead of "turn off the lamp").

In outgrowing the culture of the two-cents plain, Bernie began buying his suits at Brooks Brothers, which he characterized as "the quartermaster to the insecure." He had no reason to feel insecure in his Ivy League getup—the three-button suit with unpadded shoulders, the blue or white button-down oxford shirt and the striped rep tie. In his Brooks uniform, with his innocent swagger and virile good looks, he drew admiring female glances both in and out of the city room. Bernie was tall and dark, his features distinguished by bushy black eyebrows and the glint of an anticipatory smile. (After a while, tiring of the traditional Brooks look, he bought a tux a few doors up Madison Avenue at Paul Stuart, fitting himself happily into that establishment's slightly more modish, slimmer-styled suit—and he convinced me to follow his sartorial path.)

In January 1949, Barbara and I exchanged our one-room walk-up for two large rooms in an ancient but sturdy edifice, recently renovated to include an elevator, on Madison Avenue and Thirtieth Street. When Bernie saw our spacious layout, with its high-ceilinged living room and marbled fireplace, he insisted we give a grand party.

We were aware that he celebrated his birthday over two days, February 4 and 5. His birth certificate, he once told us, listed the date as the fifth, but his mother insisted he had been born on the fourth. Since my birthday was February 3, and Barbara's was the sixth, he thought the three of us should throw a four-day birthday party.

Friends came and went to the marathon celebration, beginning at our place, switching to Bernie's Greenwich Village apartment and finally back to ours. Bernie hung salamis from the ceiling of his living room and supplied knives, inviting guests to help themselves. Since most of our mutual friends were writers, I was surprised to find the jazz saxophonist Bud Freeman at Bernie's apartment. He told me he hadn't seen Bernie since 1946, when both were discharged after serving two years in the Army at one of the bleakest places on earth. He said eccentrics like him and Bernie, after being drafted, were dispatched to a far-flung outpost called Adak, in the Aleutian Islands, the frozen archipelago between Alaska and the Soviet Union.

Bernie had spent most of his Army service working on a mimeographed daily newspaper, the *Adakian*, published out of a Quonset hut. The editor was Sergeant Dashiell Hammett, known to his men as Sam (a name he later dropped). Sam by this time had written not only *The Thin Man* but also *The Maltese Falcon*.

As Bernie liked to tell the story: "Sam was famous, rich and almost fifty—achievements beyond our wildest dreams. We were a bunch of enthusiastic semiliterates, mostly in our early twenties, white and black, who had been trained to serve interchangeably as infantrymen or journalists." The

Adakian was distributed to the thousands of GIs on their barren isle of ice. The staff monitored the short-wave broadcasts throughout each night to produce a morning paper with the latest news.

After a year, Bernie said, life on Adak grew unbearable. A number of men in the unit feigned mental instability, hoping for discharge. But since many of them had displayed highly eccentric behavior from the day of arrival, their applications were disregarded by their officers. Every so often, Bud Freeman appeared in his full-dress uniform, his rifle brightly polished, and stood at rigid attention before his commanding officer. "I'm ready to go home," declared Private Freeman. The CO, telling him his timing was premature, suggested he relax and offered him a cup of coffee. Freeman promptly poured the coffee into his ear—a good try, but it didn't get him sprung.

Bernie's eighteen-year-old brother, a student at CCNY, also showed up at our birthday party. Bernie adored Marvin, watching over him more like a father than a brother. Once, when Bernie, Marvin and I were at a luncheonette, a counterman shouted an expletive. Bernie grabbed the man by his tie and warned him, "Don't ever again say that in front of my brother."

Early on, Bernie recognized the Soviet Union as the coming story, and urged Marvin to pursue Russian studies following his graduation in 1950. As a result, Marvin went on to attend the Russian Institute at Harvard, with Bernie contributing to his tuition. His Harvard studies, in addition to his later travels to the Soviet Union, eventually led to a post as diplomatic correspondent for CBS and later NBC.

Bernie was an odd blend of the unconventional and the puritanical. He also combined an unswerving patriotism with a fascination and sympathy for other cultures—particularly Asian. Even when no longer a correspondent, he took irrepressible delight in roaming the world, often accompanied by his wife, Phyllis, reveling in adventures they contrived for themselves.

Shielding his brother from expletives was typical of Bernie's sense of morality—for large issues as well as minor ones. In 1986, when he was assistant secretary of state for public affairs, serving as spokesman for Secretary George P. Shultz, he resigned to protest a secret "disinformation program" by the Reagan administration, as reported by the *Washington Post*. It was described as an overall strategy that included misleading the press by planting false stories aimed at toppling Libyan dictator Muammar el-Qaddafi. A story that led page one of *The Times* quoted Bernie as saying that "faith in the word of America is the pulse beat of our democracy. Anything that hurts America's credibility hurts America."

It was Bernie, a close friend of Abe Rosenthal since 1946, who brought us together. We all three longed to become foreign correspondents, but Abe, by this time, was way ahead of us, for his reputation had soared as a correspondent with *The Times*'s United Nations bureau. The UN was then housed at temporary headquarters at Lake Success on Long Island, awaiting its move on January 9, 1951, to its newly constructed skyscraper overlooking the East River. The UN was a prized assignment, for in that Cold War era it was a daily source of multiple front-page stories.

Before I came to know Bernie, he and Abe had shared a subleased apartment at the Hotel des Artistes on West Sixty-seventh Street. But for Abe, this carefree bachelor life was short-lived. The secretary at *The Times*'s UN bureau was Ann Burke, one of the three pretty Irish women I had recruited for my *Timesweek* staff.

She was in awe of Abe's talent and in a state of constant giggles over his wit. And he was captivated by her golden hair, blue eyes and unfailingly high spirits. Like Abe, she'd had a sickly, underprivileged youth. As a child, she'd been stricken by rickets. Her father was a problem drinker and her mother almost single-handedly raised her, her sister Kathleen (now back at the paper after her service with the WAVES) and a younger brother. But there was no sign of past struggles in Ann's sunny outlook.

It wasn't long before Abe and Ann were in love. Bernie was best man at their wedding, after which they left for Paris, where Abe combined their honeymoon with his coverage of a UN conference. When they returned to New York to an apartment in Greenwich Village, they joined Bernie, Barbara and me in a closely knit quintet. And since Abe and I found marriage to be a blissful state, we urged it on Bernie, who demurred, assuring us he was relishing his bachelorhood.

Abe, Bernie and I regarded ourselves as experts at one-upmanship, but Bernie and I had to admit that Abe usually managed to outdo us. I can recall only two instances when I bested him.

One of those times I had to resort to physical force—an unanswerable argument since I was bigger than Abe. At dinner in Barbara's and my apartment one evening in 1951, we were discussing J. D. Salinger, and the conversation turned to a story of his that had appeared in *The New Yorker*, "A Perfect Day for Bananafish."

On and off for the previous three years, Abe and I had been arguing about the meaning of that enigmatic story, each of us attributing a different motive to the suicide of Seymour Glass on his honeymoon. On this particular evening, the wine we were drinking made us ever more argumentative. As we left the dinner table, I insisted Abe's version was cockeyed, and he retorted that mine was far-fetched. Exasperated, I wrestled him to the floor and sat on his chest until he admitted I was right.

As I now keep reminding myself, we were very young.

The other time I triumphed over Abe (with Barbara's help) became a kind of city-room legend, which I could not resist documenting in *Times Talk* (and which Gay Talese picked up in *The Kingdom and the Power*, his 1969 history of *The Times*).

The story began when Barbara and I left a neighborhood movie house on the Upper East Side and realized we were on the same block Abe and Ann had recently moved to. We impulsively phoned to congratulate them on their anniversary. Although it was rather late, Ann asked us to come for a quick cup of coffee. We bought a pound cake at a neighborhood grocery, and when we presented ourselves at their new apartment, we all decided to forget the coffee and drink Scotch instead.

"Abe said we had to take the pound cake home with us," I wrote in my *Times Talk* article. "We refused. As we were getting into the elevator to leave, Abe thrust the box with the pound cake at us, but, quick as a wink, and just as the door was closing, I hurled the package back at him. The Rosenthals lived on the second floor, and the elevator was pretty slow. When we reached the lobby, the doorman handed us the package, with which Abe had run down the stairs. Did you ever hear of anyone so stubborn?

"We had to take it, of course, but as soon as we got home, we called for a Western Union messenger and had it sent right back to the Rosenthals. (The forty-cent pound cake now had about three dollars invested in it, but it was the moral issue that mattered.) We didn't hear anything for the next day or two, but then slices of it began arriving in the mail, and within the next few weeks, whenever a friend of Abe's and mine, like Bernie Kalb or Hal Faber (a reporter who had recently become a friend), came over to our house, he brought a slice, too, with Abe's greetings.

"Well, it kept going back and forth like that for a while and then one day, when the Rosenthals were at our house for dinner, Barbara sneakily slit open Abe's overcoat lining and sewed in the cake—reduced, by now, to a handful of crumbs. I called him when he got home, and told him he had the cake. He admitted that we had outdone him in ingenuity and he gave up."

WHILE ABE AND I, each in our own way, moved ahead as reporters, Bernie remained stuck on the broadcast desk. His talent was beginning to be recognized outside *The Times*, however. The influential *Saturday Review of Liter-*

ature assigned him to write a cover interview every week with the author whose new book received the featured review. His subjects ranged from Hemingway, upon publication of *The Old Man and the Sea*, to John Steinbeck and *East of Eden*.

One day, when Bernie was at the *Saturday Review* turning in an interview, a lovely brunette with large blue-green eyes emerged from the office of the magazine's editor, Norman Cousins. Bernie thought he was face to face with Ingrid Bergman's younger sister, so marked was the resemblance. As he later said, he was "so discombobulated" he had to sit down—which he did, on his brand-new fedora.

When he recovered his senses, he learned that the young woman's name was Phyllis Bernstein, that she was Cousins's secretary and that she harbored a secret desire to write. Although Phyllis was as shy and reserved as Bernie was gregarious, he managed to persuade her to dine with him at a small French restaurant on East Fifty-sixth Street. She had yet to learn that eating in a restaurant with Bernie could be a traumatic experience; condescending waiters were Bernie's natural enemies, and it was rare for him to get through a meal without a spirited challenge about the service.

Bernie and Phyllis did not get off to a good start, although in this instance waiters were not the problem. They found it difficult to converse, and each felt uneasy and bored. Before giving up, Bernie tried a final—and not very original—gambit. Had Phyllis by any chance read a good book recently? She said she had loved *Cry, the Beloved Country*, Alan Paton's tragic novel about South Africa.

Bernie sprang to life. "Is there anything in the novel that has stuck in your mind?" he inquired.

"Yes," replied Phyllis.

"Wait!" Bernie commanded. "Stop right there!"

He ripped a sheet of paper from a notepad, tore it in two, and gave one half to Phyllis. "Write down the sentence that struck you, and I'll do the same."

They exchanged papers, and found that each had recorded the same sentence: "Nothing is ever quiet, except for fools."

Bernie suddenly saw Phyllis in a new light. No longer bored, he discovered she was witty, had an appealing laugh, was a sensitive observer of life and, most important, appreciated him. They began seeing each other regularly and soon acknowledged they were in love. Both indecisive, however, they could not commit themselves. Phyllis was the only child of an unhappy marriage and Bernie resisted giving up his freedom.

Not long after they'd met, Bernie, on a vacation from *The Times*, had accompanied Phyllis to Europe, where she decided to remain to work and study for a year, in Heidelberg and Paris. Toward the end of that year, Barbara wrote to Phyllis saying her stepfather's longtime secretary was about to quit and asking if she'd be interested in the job. It was a varied and not too taxing assignment, involving research and travel, and Barbara thought Phyllis would enjoy it. Phyllis agreed, and when she returned from abroad, she took it on.

Barbara's stepfather grew fond of Phyllis, as she did of him, and the new connection brought Barbara and me even closer to Phyllis and Bernie. Except for their continued waffling and periodic crises over whether they should marry, the four of us, along with Abe and Ann, spent some of the happiest and most carefree days of our lives together. It took nine years, with considerable backing and forthing, for Bernie and Phyllis to make up their minds to marry—and in short order they produced four daughters.

SEVENTEEN

WITH THE APPROACH OF SUMMER 1950, Elza and Berrie invited Barbara and me to spend two weeks in June in a rambling oceanfront house they'd rented on Fire Island.

Not yet assaulted by celebrity, the island was a tranquil refuge, a long, narrow sand spit that we reached by ferry from Bay Shore on Long Island's southern mainland, only forty-five miles from Manhattan. The small ferryboats were converted rumrunners that made the eight-mile trip in about a half-hour. Automobiles were barred from the island, and luggage, small children and groceries were transported by handcarts, sometimes drawn by bicycles.

Ocean Beach, the small enclave where the Behrmans rented their house, was a community of five hundred cottages occupied during the summer months. The Behrmans paid two thousand dollars for the season, a whopping price for that time, but there were many cottages available for as little as seventy-five dollars a week. A double room at one of the island's very few hotels averaged nine dollars a night.

I marveled at the stretches of pristine beach and dunes, the pure sea air and the abundance of bushes bursting with blackberries. (I was less aware of the abundance of poison ivy.) Ignorant of the unwritten rule among island veterans to keep their haven as much of a secret as possible, I called *The Times*'s Sunday travel editor to suggest an article about Ocean Beach.

He accepted the idea and the long article I wrote, accompanied by five prominent photos, caused an uproar among the old-timers. What I hadn't known was that *The New Yorker*'s celebrated theater critic, Wolcott Gibbs, an Ocean Beach fixture for the past fourteen years, had recently come under attack by his fellow longtime residents for a series of stories in his magazine set on a thinly disguised Fire Island. Gibbs was actually being shunned, for word had spread that he was adapting his stories for a Broadway play to be called *Season in the Sun*. As one veteran islander complained to me: "I hate to think about the crowds we'll have next summer after that play is produced."

My travel piece was vilified by the diehards as the last straw, and Dana Wallace, the island's sole professional photographer, whom I had engaged to illustrate the article, warned that he didn't think prolonging my visit would be healthy. A particularly belligerent barfly at McGuire's saloon, he cautioned, had announced the previous evening that he intended to punch me in the nose. He was a fisherman I had quoted in my article.

The fisherman didn't bother making good his threat. But as I look back on that incident, I profoundly sympathize with his distress. When Barbara and I visited the island not long after, we were surprised to find Ocean Beach overrun with weekend tourists. Many of the newcomers were writers, artists and theater people who either had seen the publicity about Gibbs's forthcoming play or had read my *Times* article. Bernie Kalb, for instance, beguiled by my description of Fire Island, had rented one of the last available hotel rooms the weekend following publication of the story.

That Saturday night in July, Ocean Beach became a bacchanalia. Bernie, Barbara and I attended a party to which a hundred invitations had been issued. Four hundred people showed up. In feverish holiday mode, determined to conform to what had fast become the bohemian dress code, Bernie and I sallied forth in ripped shorts and shirts.

Berrie shook his head in bemusement at the Mardi Gras evolving along a boardwalk close to his house, distressed that his cherished quiet and privacy were evaporating. He took shelter in a remote upstairs bedroom that Elza had converted into a study, and rarely left it. (He never returned to Fire Island after that summer.)

Wolcott Gibbs, who held Berrie in esteem, was a passionate fisherman, and he arrived one Sunday morning at his friend's house to present him with the twenty-pound striped bass he had just caught. Gibbs, then forty-eight, was a thin man with unruly hair bleached blond by the sun, a scrubby blond mustache and a two-day blond stubble. He was dressed in bathing trunks and a crumpled white linen shirt. I told him Behrman had locked himself in his room and might not reappear until summer's end.

Gibbs, crestfallen, left. But he returned with his fish a few hours later, wobbly from the effects of alcohol. Berrie was still in his room, I informed him. "By God," said Gibbs, "he's a hard man to give a fish to."

To cheer Gibbs, I asked if he'd like me to offer an article to the *Times* Sunday Drama Section about his new play. Would he agree to an interview? He invited me to walk home with him, and I joined him and his rejected fish on a zigzag route across the beach to a square, gray house fronting on the ocean. We entered the sun-flooded living room, where a cocktail shaker of martinis sparkled beside a typewriter on a low table.

Gibbs poured martinis for both of us and curled himself into a love seat, idly depressing and releasing the shift lock of his typewriter with his big toe. I pulled up a chair and began asking questions. "The theme of my play," he said, "is how a man thinks he can escape from a world of vacant, used-up people to a retreat like Fire Island. But he is horrified to find that people don't change much from place to place. One of the good things is that I have no telephone. That's mainly so Harold Ross can't call me. And, of course, it's very relaxing to go swimming. I don't take my typewriter down to the beach. Moss Hart, who used to live here, is the only writer I've ever known who could type a play in the sand."

Berrie had once told me that Harold Ross venerated Gibbs not only as one of the ranking stylists of his magazine, but also as an editor. The reason many nonfiction pieces in *The New Yorker* appeared to be written in basically the same style, Berrie explained, was that Gibbs heavily edited them. As the afternoon wore on, and more martinis were consumed, I asked Gibbs about his editing technique.

After initially hesitating, he disclosed his curious method. Each time Ross gave him a long, convoluted article to smooth into *New Yorker* style, he would book a hotel suite in midtown and lay out the manuscript page by page on the floor. Then, with a pair of scissors, he'd cut the article into paragraphs and rearrange them in what he regarded as correct order. Next, he wrote new transitions to join the rearranged paragraphs. After that, he line-edited the manuscript from beginning to end.

I asked Gibbs about some of the writers I most admired, and he said many of them underwent his surgery. Gibbs's adage was well known at *The New Yorker*: "Preserve the writer's style, if he is a writer and if he has a style." Somewhat disillusioned, I thanked Gibbs for the interview and left.

The next day Gibbs called on me at the Behrman house to apologize for having been drunk during our interview. "I hope you're not planning to use what I told you about editing," he said. "I'm sure you'll agree that it's unethical to quote someone in a fog of martinis." He did not specifically retract his statement about the surgery he said he performed, but I came to believe it must have been a drunken exaggeration. He then went on to tell me that he was once faced with a similar dilemma, when he was working on a profile of Lucius Beebe, the outrageous poet and prankster who was a society columnist for the *Herald Tribune* and a contributor to *The New Yorker*.

"Beebe's juicy confessions," continued Gibbs, "were made when he was drunk. I thought I had written a darn good piece, but I finally decided, in fairness, to tear it up. I hope you'll do the same for me." (Apparently Gibbs did not offer similar advice to Lillian Ross, who was widely criticized for quoting at length a drunken Ernest Hemingway in a *New Yorker* profile.)

My conscience obliged me to do as Gibbs asked—for his sake, as well as for the sake of the writers he claimed to have whipped into shape. Whenever I read their flawless prose after that, I always wondered how much of it was actually Gibbs. (Almost all those writers, along with Gibbs, are gone now.)

When *Season in the Sun* opened on Broadway on September 28, 1950, the critics were kind, and Gibbs became perhaps the first major American theater critic to have written a Broadway hit. "I hear you've written a good play," Ross told him. "I suppose you're going to quit the magazine, now you're a millionaire."

When I visited Gibbs in his New York garden apartment for a follow-up interview, he said he'd told Ross he would keep his job at the magazine for the security it provided, but would also try to do more creative writing. In fact, he said, he would have quit *The New Yorker* if his play had flopped: "What right would I have had to write about other people's plays if I wrote a bad one myself?" He had always felt, he said, that drama criticism was "a silly occupation for a grown man." The remark startled me, echoing as it did Brooks Atkinson's earlier disparagement of the job prior to his going off to China as a war correspondent.

"It's so easy to make fun of bad plays," continued Gibbs, "and most plays are bad. Although I don't think I pan more plays than my fellow critics, I will admit that I write more disagreeably than most. But now that I've found it isn't as simple getting a play into production as I had thought, I will probably become a more benign critic."

IN EARLY DECEMBER, Barbara and I decided that between us we were now earning enough to start a family. When Barbara became pregnant, her obstetrician told her of an experiment called "natural childbirth," recently begun by the Lying-In branch of New York Hospital and adapted from the English method of Dr. Grantly Dick-Read. A small group of expectant mothers would be taught how to give birth with a minimum of anesthesia, thereby allowing them to participate fully in the joy of delivering their babies. Barbara eagerly agreed to join the experiment, which meant attending a series of lectures and exercise sessions given by a licensed midwife.

I balked at first when I learned that the training included me; I would be expected to stay with Barbara, rubbing her back and reminding her of how she'd been taught to breathe during her labor phase. What's more, I was then expected to accompany her into the delivery room and witness the actual birth.

It was a somewhat radical idea for its time, and friends to whom we confided our plans to participate in the program—including Abe and Bernie—called us foolhardy. They predicted I'd never be able to perform my role as observer at the delivery. But Barbara persuaded me to at least try, and my mother urged me to relax, and not to think of "natural childbirth" as a new method; she said she and her mother and grandmother had all given birth without anesthesia and that my father had been at her side during my birth.

Barbara herself planned to take notes during the whole process for a possible magazine article. (*Woman's Home Companion* paid her the astounding fee of $3,000. Neither Abe Rosenthal's mother nor mine could get over the fact that Barbara had earned it "just for having a baby." And when she turned the article into a book, they held her in even greater awe.)

In the early morning of August 27, Barbara went into labor. I dutifully stayed with her at Lying-In, rubbed her back and reminded her how to breathe. There were two panicky and very vocal mothers on the labor floor who were not part of the natural childbirth experiment and, I had to admit, I was relieved when the nurses suggested I leave during the actual delivery. Barbara, who was wide awake and insisted that her pains were entirely bearable, said she'd see me very soon.

This was an era when new fathers were not granted time off from work, and I was about to check in with my office at one P.M., when Barbara's doctor found me in the lobby. Beaming, he announced that I was the father of a seven-pound, seven-ounce boy and that Barbara was in fine shape.

Before hurrying to her side, I called my desk. An assistant city editor told me an AP bulletin had just come in about the Health Department's investigation into the past year's accident mortality rates, which showed an alarming growth in carbon monoxide deaths from faulty household gas-burning appliances. With the arrival of cool weather, the Health Department feared that city residents were likely to keep their windows shut, allowing no escape for the hard-to-detect poisonous carbon monoxide fumes. A million leaflets warning of the danger in English, Spanish, Yiddish, Italian, Polish and Chinese were about to be distributed throughout the city.

Because the story broke on my beat, it never crossed my mind to beg off the assignment. I said I'd get on it as soon as I had a chance to see my new son. Then I dashed upstairs to Barbara. Since she'd had only a minimum of anesthesia, she was wide awake (if a little giddy) and proudly showed me our baby, snug in a basket cradle beside her bed. (Part of the natural childbirth experience was "rooming in," whereby Barbara could keep the baby with her and "demand-feed" him.) We had decided to name our son Michael, even though we knew that, according to a 1950 Health Department survey, it was the third most common boy's name. (Robert was first and John was second.)

Barbara felt perky enough to have changed into a frilly nightgown and had applied a touch of makeup. She was disappointed I couldn't stay with her to preen over our achievement, and tried to suppress her resentment toward my unfeeling editors. She told me to hurry back after I'd written my story.

At the Health Department, Karl Pretshold threw his arms around me, opened a bottle of wine, and made some calls to help me gather the facts for my story as quickly as possible. But when I got to the city room, in contrast to my warm reception at the Health Department, I felt deflated by the business-as-usual attitude. A couple of editors congratulated me—somewhat coolly I thought, since they seemed interested only in my story, which they wanted in haste because it was a strong candidate for page one. That's where it found its place, and Barbara and I agreed that celebrating the birth of our first child with a front-page byline made my brief absence forgivable.

Several days after we'd brought Michael home, our euphoria was punctured. He developed a mysterious fever, and our pediatrician ordered him back to the hospital for observation. I had been earnestly trying to overcome my hypochondria, but Michael's illness threw me into a phobic panic.

Although he was pronounced out of danger within three days, and we were allowed to bring him back to our apartment, I was plagued by fear of a relapse. When friends and relatives, including Barbara's parents and my own, arrived for visits, I insisted they wear the gauze masks I had brought home in ample supply from the hospital.

One evening, Karl Pretshold and Sam Plotkin arrived for a surprise visit with baby gifts. When I handed them the masks they asked to talk to me privately in the living room. Pretshold said he knew how much I respected Plotkin as one of the country's foremost microbe hunters and suggested I listen to what he had to say. Plotkin patiently tried to allay my unrealistic fears, urging me not to embarrass Barbara. Feeling reassured, I promised I'd discard the masks. A week later, when I could laugh about my neurotic seizure, Barbara confessed that she had asked Pretshold and Plotkin to come to her aid.

Plotkin constantly kept me on the run, issuing bulletins on his battle against life-threatening diseases. In one scary case, he informed me that the deadly nerve toxin botulin had been detected in a Borden's Liederkranz cheese spread. His inspectors, in a random check, had found fifty-five contaminated jars in eighteen markets. When I spoke with a vice president of the company, he insisted that publicity was unnecessary, as care was being taken to recall every jar of the cheese.

I told Garst about the contaminated cheese, and he asked me to write an M-head (four or five paragraphs) to warn consumers. While I was typing, my phone rang. It was Borden's vice president.

"I hear you're writing that story about our cheese," he said. "You know ninety percent of it has already been taken off the shelves. There's no need for a story now."

"But that means ten percent of it is still out there," I said.

"We'll get it all," he assured me.

"I don't want to argue with you," I said, "but there's still a chance that someone could eat it and die."

"You'll just create unnecessary panic and hurt the name of a good company. Besides, Borden's is a regular advertiser in *The Times*."

"And *The Times* can't be influenced by its advertisers," I said, and hung up.

Ten minutes later, Garst approached my desk. "I understand you received a call from a gentleman at Borden's, as I just have," he said. "What did I ask you to write?"

"Four or five paragraphs," I said, fearing he might kill the story.

"Why don't you expand it to two-thirds of a column?"

That was one of my proudest moments at *The Times*. I wrote an article that was headlined: "New Warning Out on Cheese Spread." (I never again bought a packaged cheese spread.)

SINCE I HAD BY NOW covered the broad scope of health stories, I began longing more than ever for the big scoop with which to astound my editors. That day finally came in February 1952, when Karl Pretshold took me aside in a Health Department hallway to whisper a secret about an amazing new drug being tested at a city tuberculosis hospital that was having dramatic results. Trying to suppress his excitement, he implied that a TB cure might have been discovered.

How, I asked, could such a remarkable development have remained under wraps? He said he had no further information and suggested I check my sources at the Department of Hospitals, situated on the floor above.

Half a million people in the United States had active tuberculosis, and it was the leading cause of death among those aged fifteen to thirty-four. Though large doses of streptomycin were sometimes successful in slowing the progress of TB, the antibiotic was essentially inadequate and often had debilitating side effects, including deafness.

The recommended care for TB was bed rest, wholesome food and fresh air. Those who could afford it went to sanatoriums upstate in Saranac Lake, the Southwest or Switzerland. Even though the therapy was generally ineffectual, tuberculosis treatment had become a giant industry. If Pretshold's tip could be substantiated, the story would be one of the most significant in modern medical history.

I went to see Richard Dougherty, the press agent for the Department of Hospitals (the equivalent post held by Pretshold in the Health Department). Dick had been a general-assignment reporter for the *Herald Tribune*, and I first came to know him when I was on the police beat. When I mentioned the TB experiments, it was clear I had jolted him. "Please don't even ask me about this," he said, shutting me off. I then called several doctors whom I thought might be on the inside track, but all professed to know nothing.

When I told Pretshold I had hit a dead end, he said he'd poke around to see what he could find out. He didn't disappoint me. A few days later, he reported that the experiments had been under way for eight months at Sea View Hospital on Staten Island, one of the city's principal TB facilities for indigent patients.

At Sea View, those of the bedridden believed to be on death's edge had been given the new drug and were now walking around the ward. I went to Sea View, but every doctor I tried to talk to claimed ignorance. I finally phoned the director's office and a man who refused to identify himself said: "The phone is probably tapped. I'd be fired if it was learned I was talking to a reporter." Though he gave me no information, his reaction convinced me of the story's legitimacy.

I went back to Dick Dougherty and urged him to get me an immediate appointment with Dr. Marcus D. Kogel, the hospitals commissioner. Dr. Kogel, an earnest, bespectacled man with a crew cut, was a humanist dedicated to improving medical care for the poor. When I met with him, I came right to the point: "I don't understand why the Sea View experiment is being kept secret. If this drug is as good as I understand it to be, why should it be hidden from the public for even a day? TB patients in hospitals all over the country are dying."

Dr. Kogel was obviously under a strain. "Let me sleep on it," he said. "I'll let you know tomorrow whether I can discuss all this with you."

The next afternoon, Earl Wilson's gossip column in the *New York Post* contained a line mentioning that experiments were being performed at a local hospital with a miracle TB drug. Pretshold told me he had heard the *Post* had assigned three reporters to the story, and he feared they might beat me.

Late that afternoon, Dr. Kogel summoned me to his office. "I've decided you're right," he said. "This drug should become public knowledge." He then disclosed the principal results of the experiment. Two young doctors at Sea View, he said, were working with a drug manufactured by Hoffman–La Roche that was noninvasive and inexpensive. New York Hospital and other top-flight institutions had chosen not to experiment on their wealthy patients but, when the drug was offered to Sea View, the indigent patients there desperately leaped at the chance.

The results in case after case, Dr. Kogel said, were stunning. Symptoms vanished, and those who had been days away from death gained weight and had color in their faces. Some patients felt so revived they danced in the wards.

He explained that the astonishing news had been kept under wraps because the Tuberculosis Association—then the most powerful medical fraternity— had pressured the Sea View doctors to delay publishing any information until association doctors had a chance to catch up with the experiments. They demanded that their own findings be released to the public simultaneously with Sea View's.

It was clear that prominent doctors at prestigious TB institutions, aware of the earthshaking medical advance heralded by the new drug, feared their reputations were at stake. Having failed to obtain the drug in the first place and lagging behind a city facility for the indigent, they dreaded professional embarrassment. (I was to learn later from the doctors at Sea View that they had been threatened with ruin if they divulged the results of their work before the major hospitals caught up. It had also been insinuated, they told me, that they could be drafted into the Army and find themselves on a plane to Korea.)

I knew I had a bombshell of a story. But Dr. Kogel insisted on a condition before he spoke to me. He beseeched me to write only the bare essentials for the time being, so that the revelations could not be traced to his office. He also asked me not to mention Sea View for my first story and refused to be quoted as a source, as he had no wish to be the target of an infuriated Tuberculosis Association. But he promised he would continue cooperating with me after my story broke.

I thanked him, and rushed to the city room. With my heart thumping, I gave Garst the details of my scoop. He appeared calm as always but, as I continued talking, his face reddened and I could tell he was uneasy.

"I don't want you to think I don't trust you," he said, "but this story, if true, is a striking development. I don't think you or I have the medical expertise to weigh the facts you've amassed so far." He then called Bill Laurence to his desk and asked me to repeat what I had told him.

Garst suggested that Laurence check the facts with his own impeccable sources, even if it meant waiting another day. Meanwhile, I called Dr. Kogel and managed to convince him that *The Times* needed to use his name to lend authority to the article.

But while waiting for Bill Laurence's confirmation, I became deeply anxious. On the verge of a journalistic triumph, I was in danger of losing my jump on the story. Hints about the miracle drug were by now percolating in other newsrooms. The *Herald Tribune*, for example, had begun pursuing leads and I worried that Dick Dougherty might have tipped off his old colleagues there. I waited nervously that night at my corner newsstand for the *Trib*'s early edition and was relieved when there was no story.

The next day, Laurence verified my information and recommended that we run the story immediately. Garst suggested that the article might have more credibility if Laurence's byline were attached to it. But Laurence was steadfast in his refusal. "This is Arthur's story," he said, "and it should run under his byline. I'll do the follow-up story tomorrow." The story ran at the top of page one on February 21, 1952, under the headline:

NEW MYSTERY DRUG
RAISES HOPES HERE
OF ERADICATING TB

Chemical Developed with Aid
of Hospitals Department
Is Tested on 150 Patients

Results Amaze Doctors

But It Is Too Soon They Warn
to Label Treatment a "Cure"

Details Kept Secret

As requested, I wrote only the bare details and reminded readers that, though anecdotal evidence was promising, it would be premature to hail the drug as the ultimate cure. The day following publication of my story, its revelations made headlines in papers all over the world. The flurry of attention that the story attracted quickly brought forth new facts. I learned that the drug, isonicotinic acid hydrazide, would cost fifty cents a pill. A month later, the price dropped dramatically—to three cents—bringing treatment within just about anyone's budget.

The medical establishment pounced on *The Times* for publishing the story without its approval. Garst, backed by Catledge, had in fact made an unorthodox decision. *The Times* generally withheld such stories until they appeared in medical journals, to avoid having to backtrack if a disclosure expressed a false optimism betrayed by further testing. Such articles raised the hopes of patients, and were certain to cause greater distress if a treatment did not match its early boasts.

A group of high-ranking tuberculosis specialists met with the publisher. Asserting that the story had been premature, they demanded that it be retracted. Catledge asked me to defend the article in a memo, which he forwarded to Sulzberger. I cited doctors, including Kogel, who believed that the story advanced, rather than hindered, further experimentation with the drug. Many TB victims, who had suspected they had the disease but were reluctant to seek medical attention, voluntarily began to report their symptoms to the Hospitals Department and request the drug; the head start over the planned announcement in a medical journal would expedite the achievement of conclusive results; other pharmaceutical companies were now planning to manufacture another form of the drug.

I reminded Catledge and Sulzberger that even had we not published the story, it would have been broken within days by another paper. I also mentioned that a number of doctors had derided the resentment expressed by some Tuberculosis Association officials, attributing their criticism to the fear that the new drug, if it lived up to its potential, might put them out of business. After receiving my memo, Sulzberger gave me his full support, and awarded me my first publisher's prize. (In 1950, the publisher announced six prizes monthly as an extra incentive for superior reporting and writing.)

In addition to a check for $100, I received a letter from the publisher noting that my article had refrained from "raising futile hopes in present sufferers of tuberculosis, carefully guarding against the story's boomeranging into a beat which we would later wish that we had not published." He added that the story "might serve as a model of medical reporting in the general press."

The medical establishment, however, would not concede its point, and the cover story in the May 1952 issue of *Medical Economics* was devoted to my disclosure of the new drug. It warned of the dangers of premature announcements and urged doctors to stonewall the press until further findings had been confirmed in professional periodicals.

One great satisfaction I derived from the story was being able to help Brooks Atkinson's ailing secretary, Clara Rotter. A tiny woman whom tuberculosis had reduced to skin and bones, she had stopped coming to work, and everyone at *The Times* sensed the inevitable. On the day the TB story appeared, she called to ask me how she could obtain the drug. I put her doctor in touch with the doctors at Sea View, and her symptoms were arrested in a remarkably short time.

The drug turned out to be everything it had been claimed to be. It succeeded in closing down tuberculosis hospitals in this country and abroad as it virtually vanquished the "white plague." The story was the biggest I covered in my career, and it taught me to be wary of the efforts by recognized authorities to connive against the public welfare, for their own benefit. Nearly fifty years later, I am still appalled that the Tuberculosis Association put its own interests before those of the dying.

I KNEW IT WAS UNLIKELY that I'd ever again find a story on my beat as compelling as the TB scoop, and I began to sense it was time to move on to a new challenge. Not that I didn't appreciate what the beat had done for me. It had given me a rich lode of reportorial experience, stimulating me to think up my own ideas for coverage. It also had provided the opportunity to form a relationship with the publisher's son, Punch Sulzberger, who would be publisher himself one day.

In the spring of 1951, Garst had called me to ask if I would arrange for Punch to shadow me on my beat for a couple of weeks. Punch was the youngest—and only boy—among Sulzberger's four children. (Of the three daughters, the last—born three years before Punch—was named Judy, and that accounted for her brother's nickname.) Punch had graduated from Columbia and recently returned from Korea, where he had served as a first lieutenant in the Marines. As a boy, he hadn't expressed much interest in *The Times,* but now his father wanted to expose him to all aspects of newspaper work. Garst informed me that Punch, who would be an intern of sorts in a number of the paper's departments, would be ready to report to me daily beginning Monday.

Putting my best foot forward, as what reporter wouldn't, for the publisher's son, I arrived for work punctually at ten A.M. He was already there, waiting for me. The next day I showed up fifteen minutes earlier; again, Punch was already there. Each day I arrived earlier than the day before, but no matter how early I showed up, Punch was there ahead of me. That was my first glimpse of his obsession with punctuality. I tried my best to emulate it as, ultimately, did the rest of the paper's top executives.

A couple of years younger than I, Punch, though polite and pleasant, seemed a trifle distant in our weeks together, and it wasn't until years later that we formed a lasting friendship. He did, however, take a keen interest in my beat, even though, he told me, he found it rather tame compared with his recent adventures among the reporters at the Bronx police shack. He described one occasion when—along with the rest of the pack—he rushed to the home of a popular soul singer, supposedly on the verge of death. As the reporters were leaving, one of the singer's friends at the death vigil tucked a twenty-dollar bill into the breast pocket of Punch's jacket—presumably in the hope of ensuring a good obituary in *The Times.* Punch, bewildered, said nothing about the bill until everyone arrived back at the shack; he then turned it over to his colleagues, who sent out for beer, admonishing Punch not to mention the incident to "your old man." (As it turned out, there was no obit, for the singer recovered.)

That same year, as Punch's career on *The Times* was being weighed, his father initiated significant managerial changes. Early in 1951, with Edwin James in failing health, Arthur Hays Sulzberger wanted to send a clear signal that Turner Catledge would be the next managing editor. Accordingly, he created a new temporary (and somewhat confusing) title for Catledge as second-in-command under managing editor James: "executive managing editor."

His mandate was to consolidate the paper's various units, at last bringing the day-side and night-side operations together under one jurisdiction, and pointedly placing him over night managing editor Raymond McCaw. With James's death on December 3, 1951, Catledge took over as managing editor (minus the "executive"), with greater power than anyone who had previously held that job.

Catledge at once set out to streamline the paper. Among his priorities was the abolition of what he called "dukedoms"—independent bureaucratic entities led by strong-willed editors who hardly ever talked to one another. In his determination to coordinate coverage, he inaugurated a daily four P.M. conference in his office, at which the heads of all major news desks offered their story recommendations for page one.

Catledge also demanded a better mix of stories. He asked editors to be sure to allot space for the 500-word spot-news stories he called the "meat and potatoes" of the daily report. These half-column pieces, usually filed by beat reporters and crammed with revealing facts, were often killed to allow additional space for the major articles, which, according to Catledge, were in most cases already too long.

In addition, he urged reporters to shorten their sentences, write crisp leads and convey directly the essence of their stories. But in one ill-considered gesture, scoffed at by the staff, he created the post of "writing consultant," instructing a pedantic assistant city editor named Richard Burritt to take us on one at a time. When Burritt got to me, I found his suggestions simpleminded. And when it was Mike Berger's turn to be instructed, Burritt tried to show him how his story in the paper that day could have been improved by trimming. When word of Burritt's meddling in the case of Berger—who had won the Pulitzer the previous year—traveled through the city room, the staff exploded with such derision that the writing consultant's post came to an abrupt end.

Catledge himself kept after us constantly with suggestions on how to improve *The Times*. With the 1952 presidential election approaching, and remembering the press's embarrassment in 1948, he issued a list of "ground rules." Though Eisenhower's victory over Adlai E. Stevenson seemed assured, Catledge ordered that predictions were to be generally avoided: "They are permissible only when the person making the prediction is unquestionably qualified to do so and may be quoted." He further insisted that reporters give equal credence to the opinions of average folks as they did to those of political pundits by quoting "filling station attendants, who are virtually automatic poll-takers; hotel desk clerks; hotel lobby cigar-stand operators; taxi drivers and similar working people who come in contact frequently with the public."

One of Catledge's most startling decisions was to overhaul the city-room hierarchy. He began to overturn Ochs's paternalistic principles, cutting, for a start, some of the dead wood from administrative posts—those staffers who had traditionally been permitted to keep their jobs even if they weren't any longer of practical service.

First on his agenda was a truly bold move—to force David Joseph to retire as his assistant managing editor. He had been with the paper forty-four years and Catledge had grown increasingly critical of his lackluster performance. It became evident that Joseph in his token position as Catledge's assistant had simply become a nuisance; what Catledge needed was a strong assistant managing editor to help him carry out his newly broadened plans.

Years later, when I became metropolitan editor, Catledge told me about Joseph's unorthodox departure. Sensing Catledge had finally run out of patience, Joseph approached him in his office, and asked if he could sit in his place for a moment. "If I were you," he said, after Catledge welcomed him to sit at his desk, "I'd ask for my resignation or retirement." The reverberations of Joseph's "retirement" were felt by all. This was the first time in my tenure that a top editor was pushed out. He was sixty-five, but no retirement age had yet been mandated for top executives.

Catledge then appointed two assistant managing editors—Bob Garst and Ted Bernstein—instructing them to keep in close contact with him on a daily basis. Garst was to assist him on the day side and Bernstein on the night side. In his new post, Bernstein took over command of the bullpen, succeeding Raymond McCaw who, after twenty-nine years on the paper, had retired.

Frank Adams became the city editor and, remembering his earlier enthusiastic support of my work, I anticipated a happy rapport with my new boss. But our relationship soon soured. Toward the end of 1952, not long after Adams's appointment, Barbara called me at the Health Department to tell me my father had suffered a stroke and been admitted to New York Hospital. I said I'd get right over there, and asked Barbara to call the city desk to say that I could be reached at the hospital, if needed.

By late morning the next day, my father appeared to be stable and I left him with my mother and a nurse to go to my beat. I checked in with my office, as I always did upon arrival, and was told that Adams wanted to see me immediately. I had heard about his temper, but had never witnessed it. When I approached his desk, his cheeks swelled and his face got as red as a fire truck.

"How dare you leave your beat without permission!" he shouted. "That is an unforgivable offense, and I've noted it in your permanent record." Shocked, I tried to explain the circumstances, but Adams didn't want to hear excuses.

A couple of weeks later, I found a two-sentence memo from Adams in my city-room mailbox, informing me of a switch in my assignment. I was instructed to report to the rewrite battery the following Friday at 7:00 P.M. for the last shift ending at 3:20 A.M. I was stunned—the more so since such assignments were usually issued in person.

Approaching Adams at his desk, I told him I was puzzled by this move, especially on such short notice. I knew, of course, that reporters were sometimes assigned as a reward to rewrite because of their special ability to turn in smooth copy under deadline pressure, while others were assigned there to speed up and sharpen their own languid prose. In my case, was this a promotion or a demotion? "I don't want to go into it," Adams snapped. "I just want you to do it." Once again, his harshness baffled me, especially since editors had always treated me with courtesy and consideration.

Years later, I found the proof that he was punishing me. When I became deputy metropolitan editor with access to the staff files, I discovered Adams's note severely criticizing me for abandoning my beat. There was no mention of extenuating circumstances. I crumpled the note and tossed it in the wastepaper basket.

EIGHTEEN

ON JANUARY 9, 1953, assaulted by a biting wind and sheets of freezing rain, I left home for *The Times* filled with foreboding about my first night on rewrite. Would I be able to come through night after night under pressure of deadline?

"You've got the ice story," said Frank Adams, upon my arrival, pointing to the aisle desk he'd assigned to me. It was one of nine on the rewrite battery's three rows that faced the night city desk only a few feet distant.

I Ieaped upon my desk in the second row were AP bulletins and memos from staff reporters as well as from stringers in the suburbs, all containing details about the fierce storm that was ravaging the tristate area. Ice-laden trees had fallen across roads and onto power lines, leaving thousands of houses in Connecticut, Westchester and northern New Jersey without electricity or phone service.

I stared at the clock on the post nearby, and continued to do so every few minutes, measuring how much time remained to deadline. It was now 7:15. This, doubtless, would be a front-page story of some length and I figured I had only a little more than an hour to gather and organize the facts before starting to type. I had never before written a major breaking story under deadline pressure, and I plunged into it, working the phones to reach reporters.

There was no time to worry about failure as I began shuffling through the piles of papers on my desk, struggling to put them into some kind of coherent sequence. Billie Barrett, the lone woman on rewrite, whose desk was directly in front of mine, took pity and offered to help put at least the wire-service copy in chronological order, as I jotted down updates from reporters calling in from various boroughs and counties.

After close to an hour, Adams approached. "It's getting late," he said. "It seems you've got enough for a couple of columns. You'd better start writing."

With my heart skipping a beat or two and my eyes darting from the clock to my notes, I began typing. I knew by now how much I could write in a given period of time, and the clock helped me pace myself. But on this night, the second hand seemed to tick off the minutes much faster than usual.

When I had run copy eight years earlier, I vowed never to yell "Boy!" or "Copy!" if I landed on rewrite one day, and that I'd carry my own copy to the desk. But as the deadline neared, with no time to spare, I shamelessly shouted, "Copy!" Sammy Solovitz, now assistant head of the copyboys, made a point of rushing over to take my copy himself, throwing me a patronizing grin, and I sheepishly muttered, "Thanks, Sammy."

Paragraph by paragraph, my story was ripped from my Underwood and whisked to the city desk for editing. I finished with a few moments to spare. The story's lead described the storm as "one of the worst in a generation," and detailed the power outages and perilous road conditions.

The George Washington Bridge was closed because ice had fallen from its overhead cables and smashed through automobile windshields. The blocks between Forty-second and Forty-third Streets bordering on Third and Lexington Avenues were also closed because chunks of ice "as large as a dinner plate" were tumbling from the top of the Chrysler Building. And homeowners in powerless areas were trying, with limited success, to rediscover the primitive skills of cooking in their fireplaces. The story was played high on the front page and, as was normal for rewrite, went unsigned.

After all my misgivings, I began to feel invincible, euphoric; I was suddenly sure I could handle anything that rewrite required. After the last edition went to press, I thanked Billie Barrett for her help. "Rewrite's like a commune," she told me. "We all try to help each other, especially on the big stories."

A few years older than I, Billie, whose given name was Grace, was rosy-cheeked and slightly plump. Her short hair and square, rimless glasses gave her a misleading look of severity. She had been *The Times*'s first female correspondent at Columbia University, where she earned a master's degree in journalism. After graduating, she did a stint on general assignment before becoming the first woman rewrite "man," a position she requested, eager to push past the established gender boundaries of what was still a male domain.

Initially, legmen were confused when they phoned in their facts and the city desk switched them to "Barrett on rewrite." Thinking a new operator had come on the phone when a woman's voice answered, they demanded to be transferred to "Barrett on rewrite." Billie would then have to explain that she was Barrett. She quickly earned the respect of all the rewrite men and, though she maintained a ladylike demeanor and didn't go to the saloons, was accepted as one of them.

It didn't bother Billie to be mistaken for a telephone operator. The paper's twenty-five "phone girls," as they were known, were among the most valued members of the staff, and no one was more aware of their importance than the rewrite bank. They were unfailingly gracious, and when I started on rewrite, Eleanor LaManda, the night telephone supervisor, who had been on the paper since 1926, rang me. "Welcome to rewrite, Arthur. You're going to do just fine," she said sweetly, considerably allaying my first-night jitters.

When we needed help in finding elusive sources, Eleanor and her staff often rescued us. They consulted their books of unlisted phone numbers and cross-references with addresses. If their initial attempts failed to pinpoint the location of a source, they might call a next-door neighbor or a building superintendent. They knew all the tricks for tracking down someone in another part of the country; they had friends among telephone operators who were more than willing to be of service.

An outstanding example of such service occurred one night in 1949 shortly after the final edition went to press. One of the operators, Agnes Reddy, was preparing to go home when a call came in that James V. Forrestal, the secretary of defense, had jumped to his death. She phoned the neighborhood saloons and managed to summon a sufficient number of printers and pressmen back to *The Times* to get out an Extra at six A.M.

The matriarch of the switchboard was Mary Ann Timmons, who had been with *The Times* since 1918. When Mary was on duty, a problem seldom went unsolved. I had heard the story passed down over the years about a Russian plane crash in a remote region of Canada and how Mary, when asked if she could find a telephone in the icebound vicinity, reached an operator in charge of a party line seven miles from the accident and pleaded for assistance. The Canadian operator managed to enlist a French trapper willing to mush the seven snowy, treacherous miles to get to the plane and crew. Employing sign language, he obtained some essential facts that were eventually transmitted to rewrite for a page-one story.

At that time Mary had recently been promoted to chief operator, one of seven women who made up what Ochs affectionately, if somewhat condescendingly, called his "beauty parlor." In 1929, when the first commercial transatlantic phone call came through the switchboard, Ochs forgot the greeting he'd prepared for the occasion, and impulsively asked his chief operator what he should say. "Just ask about the weather over there," Mary advised, and he did just that.

An even more essential resource for rewrite was the morgue, with its twenty-two million clippings about the known and little-known filed in manila folders dating from the 1870s and stacked floor to ceiling in blocklong aisles of metal storage drawers. When I started on rewrite, there were a dozen or so morgue clerks, cutters, indexers and filers, who pored over each day's editions to extract articles and clippings for the folders.

Without the morgue, none of us in that era of pre-electronic data retrieval could have survived a night on rewrite. Reliance on the morgue, as vital a tool of our craft as the telephone, was nothing less than Pavlovian. As soon as a story broke and the name of anyone involved in it became known— or the identity of the place where a murder, a bombing, an accident or a political confrontation was confirmed—there was a race to the morgue. The card catalogue of names was urgently consulted followed by a search in one of the drawers for the designated folder of newspaper "clips" that, we prayed, would provide the background for our story.

Using straightedge and razor, the clerks clipped stories from various editions of *The Times* as well as from other leading publications—perhaps an in-depth analysis from *Harper's*, a profile from *The New Yorker* or a report from a trade paper such as *Variety*. If a story in *The Times* (before copy machines existed) contained twenty names, twenty copies of the same story were clipped, and each copy was filed in a folder bearing the name of the individual listed in the story. Copies of the story were also clipped for file in subject folders arranged alphabetically—as, for example, Bosnia, United Nations, Texas, bats, salamanders or flywheels.

Whenever a person's name or a subject again appeared in the paper, the clipping was added to the designated folder. This was a painstaking process that had been going on for decades, which meant that some major figures commanded as many as fifty folders; in the case of a president, for example, the folders tracked his ascent from small-town politics to the world stage. On the other hand, there were many folders with only a single clip—the one time that a person's name had appeared in the paper, possibly for an arrest for a petty offense, an injury in an auto accident or attendance at a society ball.

I once escorted Barbara's cousin, Susie, through the rows of storage drawers. To demonstrate the definitive nature of the archives, I suggested we look up her father, a doctor named Harold Otto, who had a successful practice but was not at all famous. Susie was surprised that he was even listed in the card catalogue. We found the designated drawer and pulled his folder. It held only one frayed clip, a one-paragraph story datelined Norwalk, Connecticut, that had appeared twenty years earlier, under the heading: "Dr. Otto Arrested for Nude Bathing."

Sorting through the clippings, I sometimes found surprising facts that could enrich my story and, within ten or fifteen minutes, I could become an "authority" on a subject.

Over three thousand advance obituaries were also filed in the morgue. In the event of an important death, I would dig out the prepared obit and merely update it as necessary, saving precious time as the edition was closing. On-the-spot obituaries were often prepared almost entirely from clippings in the morgue.

Never had the morgue been more indispensable than on the night of April 15, 1912, when the SS *Titanic* sank. During the time I was a copyboy fetching clip folders for editors, Tommy Bracken, who had been in charge of the morgue for five decades, enjoyed reminiscing about how he and his single assistant worked until dawn, ferreting from file drawers a treasure of facts about the numerous celebrated passengers known to be aboard the doomed ship. No other paper came close to matching *The Times*'s biographical detail for the morning editions.

Sometimes a simple phone call, a quick trip to the morgue or a report from a district man was all I needed to write a story. Other times, the entire battery teamed up to put a story together, especially when the deadline neared. This was the case on March 4, 1953, shortly after midnight, when an AP bulletin reported that Joseph Stalin had suffered a "serious" stroke.

The hour was late, the presses were stopped. All of us in the city room understood that this was the biggest story since the end of the war. Reporters and editors were summoned from their beds. The switchboard began running at full tilt, connecting us to correspondents, Russian specialists and medical experts around the world.

Relying on my old contacts, I phoned a neurologist at Bellevue Hospital, who, upon hearing of Stalin's condition, assessed the situation. "The odds are terribly against him," he said. "He could die at any moment, if he is not already dead."

Harrison E. Salisbury, our Moscow correspondent, let us know that Stalin was being treated with everything from the newest drugs to leeches. But Salisbury was having great difficulty pinning down facts, since Soviet officials, running more scared than ever, were anything but cooperative. Russian experts, reached by members of the rewrite battery, made it clear there was no known protocol for succession of power in the Soviet government. All of us on rewrite worked up profiles about Stalin's potential heirs—names only vaguely familiar to most of us at that time: Lavrenti P. Beria, Kliment Y. Voroshilov, Georgi M. Malenkov, and Nikita S. Khrushchev.

"Grave danger could arise from reckless action on the part of new Kremlin leadership," said Averell Harriman, former U.S. ambassador to the Soviet Union. "Tensions will continue not just until his successor emerges but until that man proves his ability, if he can, to dominate the Communist Party, the secret police, the army, in fact the whole Soviet apparatus."

Stalin's morgue folders were raided for background information. The entire rewrite team worked on a two-page advance obituary that traced his life from his early days as the son of a poor, alcoholic shoemaker. We distributed the clip folders among us and pored through them. I was surprised to find that, though contemporary Communists hailed Stalin as a genius, Lenin had described him as "crude," "rough," and as a "cook who will prepare only peppery dishes."

Ted Bernstein coordinated the city-room juggernaut. More cigarettes were surely smoked that night than on any other since my arrival at the paper, and more small fires were started by butts tossed carelessly into trash baskets. When the presses started up again for the late edition, we had not yet confirmed that Stalin was dead. We awaited word from Harrison Salisbury, whose efforts to reach us were frustrated by Soviet censors. Finally, at six A.M., Bernstein decided to call it a night, leaving the day side to take over the death watch.

That night on rewrite, with Stalin's fate still up in the air, we worked on polishing the advance obit and sidebars and continued to solicit comments from Russian experts. It wasn't until 8:11 on the following night, March 6, that a bulletin came over the wires, announcing that Stalin had been pronounced dead. Though much of our material was ready to go, we waited for fresh news about the exact circumstances of his last hours, updates on the transfer of power and reactions from international leaders. We on the rewrite bank excerpted editorials about Stalin from papers around the country, providing a varied cross-section of opinion on the life and death of America's arch nemesis.

The Times's own editorial concluded that Stalin "wore the mantle of the high priest of utopian communism, but his rule produced a reality most reminiscent of George Orwell's vision of hell on earth. It would be hypocritical to say that we regret his passing . . . our children's children will still be paying the price for the evil which he brought into the world."

No one was more valuable on the rewrite bank that night than Wayne Phillips, who sat next to me. He hoped someday to be *The Times*'s Moscow correspondent and, in his spare time, he had been compiling an encyclopedia about all things Russian. On slow nights, he spent hours in the morgue collecting facts about Soviet society, geography, history and government.

ALMOST ALL OF US ON REWRITE, in fact, were occupied with personal research projects during evening lulls—freelance articles or books. We were aware that entire books had been written on rewrite before our time (though most were abandoned before completion). The classic completed example was *The Gangs of New York*, written by Herbert Asbury while on rewrite at the *Herald Tribune*. Night after night he studied old clips from the *Tribune* morgue, where he found all his material about the fierce street gangs that menaced the city in earlier decades.

As for myself, I made use of the downtime to think up and write freelance articles for the Sunday Drama Section. During the day, I would meet with various show-business personalities, then write about them at my desk while waiting for news to break. For whatever reason, most of my subjects were young and appealing actresses who had recently made their Broadway debuts.

It was a joy to interview the twenty-four-year-old Julie Harris. I'd been bowled over by her dazzling turn as the twelve-year-old Frankie Addams in Carson McCullers's *The Member of the Wedding*. The slight, blue-eyed actress didn't look much older than twelve offstage. She had recently been shorn of her waist-long auburn hair, because her role called for a crew cut—which had inspired her to buy her first hat.

But it was worth it, she said. "I loved the book and was terribly eager to play Frankie. My father saw the play and told me I wasn't acting. He claims I was like Frankie—headstrong, mulish and never willing to admit being wrong about anything."

While Julie Harris was making a career of playing young girls, Maureen Stapleton, not even a year older, was cast as the forty-year-old Serafina Delle Rose in Tennessee Williams's *The Rose Tattoo*. "I guess I've always looked older than my age," she said when I interviewed her at her apartment. "Even when I was ten, I couldn't get into a movie at half price." She confided that the producers of *The Rose Tattoo* told her they were worried she wouldn't be able to do justice to the role. "I can't promise anything," she replied. "I might really be terrible." But Williams wanted her, and told the producers, "I don't care if she turns into a deaf-mute on opening night."

Her narrative was interrupted by musical gurgles from the next room. "Excuse me," Maureen said, "but there's a man in the nursery to whom attention must be paid." She returned, carrying her seven-month-old son, Daniel, and explaining, "The nurse is off and it's my day with the baby."

Soon, Daniel started screaming. "When in doubt, feed him," she said, and thrust the crying infant into my arms while she prepared his lunch. What great material for my story, I thought, sure that this was a rare occurrence in the history of Broadway interviews. A couple of days later, however, I saw a piece about Maureen in *The New Yorker* in which the writer was "spontaneously" handed the baby.

One of my most memorable early interviews was with Audrey Hepburn, who had just made her debut on Broadway in *Gigi*, an adaptation of Colette's novel. I was sure that Audrey, then twenty-two and playing a gawky French adolescent, would become a glittering star. When I arrived at her suite in the Blackstone Hotel at 11:30 A.M., she told me she had just awakened. Dressed in a flowered green-and-white robe, she settled into an armchair and, in her lilting English accent, confided: "I'm sure there's plenty lacking in my performance and the critics could have said so, but they have given a beginner a break. I would have been happy if they just hadn't given me bad reviews."

She told me about her difficult childhood in Holland during the war. "My mother decided to raise money for the underground, and I gave performances with a pianist friend in our house. I had started training in ballet at twelve. My mother made my costumes and I arranged the dances. The Germans thought people were just coming to tea. After the occupation, I wanted to be a dancer, but I had to give it up. I had lost my stamina because of living on bad food. I was ill after the liberation. We were all thoroughly starved.'"

After a couple of hours, Audrey said she had to meet a friend. "Why don't we continue the interview over dinner at the Plaza?" she suggested. I went to *The Times* to type my notes and called Barbara to explain that I couldn't be home for dinner because I had to work and complete my interview. "You call that work?" Barbara sniffed.

At dinner, Audrey prattled amusingly about her embryonic career. "I watched when my name went up in lights for the first time on the marquee the other day, and I handed up the last letter of the name for good luck. People always ask me if I'm related to Katharine Hepburn. Paramount, which just signed me to a movie contract, advised me to change my name. I felt bad about that. I started my career as Hepburn and they know me as Hepburn in England. If I changed my name it would mean a lot of hard work would be thrown away. After all, there are two Taylors and two Crawfords, aren't there?" She threw me a mischievous glance. By evening's end, I was thoroughly under her spell.

Of course, I enjoyed interviewing glamorous actresses, and the extra income those interviews brought in was welcome. But there was a downside, I discovered. One afternoon Barbara called me to the phone, saying there was a woman on the line who said she had to talk to me urgently. When I said hello, the woman's voice demanded, "Where are you?"

"I'm at home," I said. "Who is this?"

"You don't sound like yourself. Is this Arthur Gelb of *The Times?*"

"Yes."

"Well, you were supposed to meet me half an hour ago."

"There's some mistake," I said. "What is this all about?"

She seemed bewildered. "Are there two Arthur Gelbs at *The Times?* I found your number in the phone book."

I asked her to describe the Arthur Gelb with whom she had a date, and she described a man with a crew cut, a pudgy face, a mustache and rimless glasses. I immediately recognized the description. It was Alden Whitman, the night man on the city copy desk.

The young woman on the phone, who said she was an aspiring actress, had recently met Whitman at Sardi's bar; he told her he was "Arthur Gelb," and she recognized the name as a writer for the Sunday Drama Section. He had promised to introduce her to producers, assuring her he could get her a part in a play. I told her I was terribly sorry, but someone obviously had been using my name, and I would try to get to the bottom of it.

When I arrived at *The Times* that night, I called Alden aside. "How dare you use my name?" I said. "Aside from hurting that girl, don't you understand how you're hurting me?" I stopped just short of threatening his life. He got the message and the incident was never repeated. But it was not easy for me, after that, to accept him as part of the comradely group that formed the night staff.

The rewrite bank now included George Barrett (no relation to Billie), recently returned from his *Times* assignment in Korea; Tad Szulc, who had come to *The Times* from the UP bureau at the United Nations; and Max Frankel, a recent graduate of Columbia. We became a close-knit unit, preparing weekly feasts for the night staff—from editors to copyboys—and calling ourselves "The Night Rewrite Gourmet Society."

Every Wednesday, we took turns splurging on ethnic delicacies. I brought smoked salmon, herring, bagels and cheeses from Zabar's—at that time a small Jewish "appetizing" store with sawdust on the floor and barrels of pickles out front. Tad Szulc brought Italian sausage and antipasto; Wayne Phillips served borscht and pierogi; George Barrett ordered food from Chinatown.

Some nights after the first edition had gone to press a few of us headed for Bleeck's, the Blue Ribbon or Gough's, the most recent of the neighborhood newspaper saloons. A one-story structure built in 1947 diagonally across Forty-third Street from *The Times* and adjacent to the site of the defunct Childs barroom, Gough's was working-class and scruffy. It began as a late-night hangout popular with pressmen and printers, who enjoyed its no-frills atmosphere and reasonable prices. They were followed by the night rewrite battery and night copy editors, some of whom gave up Bleeck's in preference to Gough's ample drinks and sliced-steak sandwiches lathered in garlic gravy.

In common with many Irish saloons, Gough's featured a portrait of John L. Sullivan over its bar, but not in his usual fighting stance; he was posed, after his retirement from the ring, wearing a suit. The smoke in the bar was often so thick you could barely make out the painting. Upon entering Gough's one night, Homer Bigart asked, "Which day of the week do they change the air in here?"

Since Gough's bordered on Times Square, footloose strangers would wander in from time to time. Once Wayne Phillips interrupted his supper at Gough's long enough to fetch Szulc and me from the city room to witness an impromptu performance that he assured us could be marketed to Barnum & Bailey as a sideshow attraction and make us rich. He led us to the back room at Gough's, where a nicely dressed young woman awaited us. On cue, she asked Wayne to place "another half-dollar on the edge of the table." She lifted her skirt, gripped the coin with her privates and removed it from the table. Everyone applauded. After a drink, she left with her well-earned half-dollar, Wayne resumed his supper and Tad and I returned to the rewrite bank.

When we felt flush, we'd treat ourselves to supper at Sardi's. One night Tad, George and I were finishing our meal when a party of four including Marilyn Monroe was directed to a table next to ours in the front room. She was by now the country's reigning love goddess and she radiated even more sensuality in person than she did on screen. A skin-tight, low-cut dress bared her creamy shoulders and back.

As we were drinking, we were seized with the idea of touching her skin. We each contributed a couple of dollars to a kitty, the prize for the one who touched her first. I had the advantage because my seat was closest to Marilyn's table. Brave with drink, I leaned back as if to stretch and grazed her shoulder with my index finger. Before I could gloat, she spun around and shouted, "Who did that?" The restaurant fell silent. I forgot how to breathe.

Knowing my face would betray me, I kept my back to her while my mind conjured up the tabloid headlines: "Marilyn Monroe Molested by Drunken *Times* Reporter." Fortunately, her friends managed to settle her down. We paid our check and slipped out. I did collect the kitty back in the city room, but it had not been worth the price I paid in terror. The rest of the rewrite bank thought it was hilarious.

Each night, unpredictability continued to be the hallmark of rewrite. I never knew what news service bulletins would be awaiting me—a police investigation, a storm, an obituary or a plane crash. Such was the case on Friday, June 19, 1953, when I arrived at my desk at seven P.M.

Frank Adams, who seemed on edge, told me to get the clips on Julius and Ethel Rosenberg and prepare to write the first edition story that would lead page one. The Rosenbergs were scheduled to be electrocuted in Sing Sing that night, after President Eisenhower had denied a request for clemency. They had been appealing their case for two years after being convicted of conspiring to steal atomic secrets (for transfer to the Soviet Union).

Since they were expected to go to the chair shortly after eight P.M., there would be little time to file a complete story before deadline. As a rule, Sing Sing executions took place at eleven P.M., but, amid protests surrounding the couple's capital sentence, the officials decreed the switch had to be thrown before sunset, the start of the Jewish Sabbath.

Times reporter William Conklin had left for Sing Sing earlier in the day. Upon arriving, he had been herded into a room with reporters from the other papers. To his dismay, the warden announced that no one—except for two pool reporters chosen to witness the event—would be let out until the electrocutions had taken place. He believed that was the only way he could assure fairness, since all the reporters would get the account from the pool reporters and have access to the phones at the same time.

Under Adams's instructions, Conklin had prepared background material for his story, but he failed to leave it at the city desk before heading for Sing Sing. He had thought he would have adequate time to file it from the prison press room, not anticipating he'd be held incommunicado.

I tore through the clips and finished the story just before eight o'clock. There was still no word from Conklin. Adams suggested I make a last-gasp attempt to reach him, so I phoned Sing Sing. I pleaded to be put through to the warden's office. An assistant answered, and explained Conklin's situation.

As we were talking, I heard a voice in the background shouting that Ethel Rosenberg's execution had just taken place. "It's done?" I asked. "Yes," said the assistant, "Julius, 8:06, and Ethel a minute ago," and hung up. The city-room clock read 8:17 P.M. I was able to top my background material with a couple of sentences, enough for the paper to go to press with a first-edition headline announcing the executions.

The Times was the first paper on the street with the story, which was comprehensively updated for a special postscript as soon as Conklin was able to call in. It was then that I learned the gory details and, the pressure of dead-line lifted, I began to feel ill: It had taken three jolts to kill Julius, and five to kill Ethel. One witness said that Ethel faced death "with the most composed look you ever saw."

After nights of such intensity, the rewrite crew followed its normal pat-tern of unwinding at Bleeck's or, once in while, at an after-hours place in the Village. I sometimes didn't make it home until dawn, when I would fall into exhausted slumber. It wasn't long before Barbara began to tire of my routine, especially since she was balancing her care of Michael with freelance writing. Finally realizing how much strain I was putting on our marriage, I quit my after-work cavorting, heading for home as soon as the paper closed at 3:20.

The time had come when Barbara and I, determined to earn some real money, decided to collaborate on a major work that might bring us a re-spectable advance on royalties. We settled on a book about Bellevue Hospi-tal, which had fascinated me from my earliest days on the paper—ever since I had helped Pat Spiegel report on the injured at Bellevue's emergency room when the plane crashed into the Empire State Building.

I knew, of course, that Bellevue, the world-renowned teaching hospital, was affiliated with three medical schools and, when I covered the Health and Hospitals Departments, I had followed revolutionary medical proce-dures there. I witnessed one of the first open-heart surgeries and reported on all kinds of emergency cases, as well as experiments with new drugs and procedures for esoteric diseases and mental illnesses. Barbara and I con-vinced our prospective publisher, Doubleday, that there was no hospital any-where like it, and we signed a contract. We believed the story of Bellevue could most effectively be told through the eyes of its longtime deputy med-ical superintendent, Dr. Salvatore R. Cutolo. When we broached the project to him, he agreed to collaborate with us.

This was the first time Barbara and I worked together on a major proj-ect and, we quickly realized, we had to learn how to avoid getting on each other's nerves. I did most of the research and Barbara did most of the writ-ing. Much of the historical information came from files in the *Times* morgue, which I spent hours perusing during slow times on night rewrite. During the day, I made rounds with Dr. Cutolo and other doctors on Bellevue's wards.

Barbara was pregnant again, and our apartment was beginning to feel cramped. We had also concluded that the noisy wholesale-carpet area we called home was no place to raise children. When we took Michael for his morning airing to the park at Madison Square, his carriage blanket became coated with dust. We finally found more spacious quarters uptown—a four-room penthouse at Seventy-ninth Street and Amsterdam Avenue. Because West Side neighborhoods were beginning to show signs of decline, the rents were low, but sunlight poured through the living room windows and the terrace afforded captivating views of the Manhattan skyline.

Penthouse living turned out to be less glamorous than we had anticipated. On windy days, smoke from the surrounding chimneys blotted out our views. Our ceiling leaked when there was a heavy rain. In winter, our pipes froze. We were nervous about our vulnerability to the growing trend of burglaries. We had too many casual visitors, especially in summer, who came to sunbathe on our terrace, and stayed until we fed them.

Nevertheless, we were grateful for the additional space when Peter, our second son, was born on November 10, 1953. This time, I got the day off, and I was with Barbara in the delivery room. In fact, I held Peter before Barbara did.

NINETEEN

SHORT OF BEING POSTED to a foreign country, assignment to the United Nations during the early days of the cold war was as exotic as a newspaper tour could get. Every year the *Times* UN bureau requested additional reporters from the city staff to help cover the General Assembly as well as its various committees, and Abe Rosenthal had made a point of asking Frank Adams for me. I was expected to return to rewrite when the Assembly concluded its business.

In mid-October 1953, I reported to *The Times*'s UN offices, a fourth-floor suite with a river view. I soon found myself amid the turbans and flowing robes of delegates from the original sixty member nations in the gleaming glass skyscraper that had opened two years earlier. Along with some of the other reporters who, like me, were children of immigrants, I was conscious of being, as it were, only a step removed from the shtetels of Europe. Yet here I was at the center (or so we believed at the time) of the international diplomatic playing field, as a reporter recording the global debate for the world's leading newspaper.

Although Abe Rosenthal was generally recognized as the most knowledgeable *Times* man at the UN, he reported to the bureau chief, Thomas Hamilton—an accomplished correspondent himself, but no match for Abe's extraordinary talents. Hamilton, a Rhodes Scholar, had spent time in Chile, London and Spain, where he wrote a book condemning the Franco regime. When he was subsequently expelled, he was transferred by *The Times* to its Washington bureau. With so wide a background, he seemed the perfect choice to lead his paper's UN coverage. But he resented the fact that Abe could write rings around him, and he made Abe's life miserable.

On many days, stormy debates and complex behind-the-scenes negotiations were considered so newsworthy that two or three stories could end up on the front page. Hamilton would deliberately wait until only an hour before deadline to pick what he regarded as the plum page-one stories for himself; then he'd assign the lesser stories to Abe. Thus Abe had to keep abreast of all aspects of every story, never knowing until late in the day which he would have to write.

All of us reporters were aware of Hamilton's insecurities regarding Abe, and it became a UN game to observe the nightly ritual. When Abe at last received his assignment, he lit a cigarette and paced the corridor outside the *Times* office, puffing nonstop while he organized his story in his head, oblivious of the traffic streaming past. Then, typing at his desk, never pausing or crossing anything out, he wrote with such flavor and depth that his stories were often placed above Hamilton's on the front page.

The cable-desk editors appreciated Abe's clean copy, but Abe didn't appreciate their occasional tampering—especially when, to save space, they deleted a smoothly crafted transitional paragraph and substituted their all-purpose transitional word, "Yet" (followed by a comma, of course). Abe called them "The Yetties."

Abe brought *The Times* many plaudits for his scoops, especially those involving the tight-lipped Russian delegation. He scored a beat, for example, by reporting that Jacob Malik was going to replace Andrei Gromyko and, somewhat later, he was able to announce Malik's successor.

Abe had spotted a new member of the Russian delegation seated right behind Malik during a Security Council session, and asked a minor Russian diplomat about him. The diplomat was evasive. But later, in the informal atmosphere of the delegates' lounge, he approached Abe. "You seem interested in our delegation," he said. "You might be interested to know that Malik is leaving, to be replaced by Valerin A. Zorin."

IT WAS TOM HAMILTON who handed me my UN press credentials and assigned me to the Second Committee, which dealt with economic issues, particularly the assistance programs to struggling nations. I knew scarcely anything about economics, and was given the beat because I was the only reporter available in the bureau with no other assignment.

Abe, who tried hard not to treat me like a serf in the land where he was king, reminded me that I had known basically nothing about health when I started on that beat. "You don't need to be an expert," he told me. "You just need to be a good reporter. I'll introduce you to some of the key sources, and you'll quickly get to know most of the delegates. Plunge in with your usual enthusiasm and you'll be writing with authority in a matter of days."

Abe then suggested we visit the delegates' lounge, a vast, populous room with a well-stocked bar that drew delegates and Secretariat officials for gossip and relaxation. Before and after formal UN deliberations, a reporter could buttonhole anyone in the lounge, from foreign ministers and top-ranking Secretariat officials, to delegation chiefs, bright young staffers and an army of public-relations advisors and lobbyists.

"Walk the full length of this room," Abe suggested, "and come back and tell me what you've discovered." I took the block-long stroll and when I returned I told Abe I saw groups of people talking the way they would in any barroom. Abe said to wait for him while he took the same stroll. "What did you discover?" I asked when he returned. "I've got three stories," he smugly replied.

I never did come close to matching Abe's all-around reportorial talent. But my own strolls did from time to time yield an offbeat idea—one of them provided by the new secretary general of the United Nations, Dag Hammarskjöld, who knew of my interest in the theater and happened to be a theater buff himself. He told me that Broadway's grande dame Katharine Cornell had been making frequent visits to the UN under his guidance, to absorb atmosphere for a forthcoming play called *The Prescott Proposals*, in which she was to portray the American delegate to the UN.

When I interviewed her, she told me candidly that if she had "a real honest-to-goodness brain" she would actually like to be a delegate. The story I wrote included a note about the production's one stumbling block: Russel Crouse, the play's coauthor with Howard Lindsay, told me they couldn't find an actor to portray the Pakistani delegate. He had taken to approaching every man who looked as though he hailed from Karachi, and one day he spotted someone walking down First Avenue who seemed perfect for the role.

Crouse told him he was searching for an actor from his part of the world, and suggested he read for the play. A woman accompanying Crouse's target burst out laughing. "You have just asked one of the United Nations' delegates from India to play a delegate from Pakistan," she said. In the end, it was a man of Indian descent who actually was cast. (He just happened to be an Equity actor.)

ON NOVEMBER 28, as the 1953 General Assembly was drawing to a close and I prepared to return to the rewrite battery, the Photo Engravers Union called a strike against New York newspapers. As a member of the Newspaper Guild and a pro-union child of the Depression, I instinctively went along with the other unions in refusing to cross the picket lines. But in truth, I had little sympathy for the photo engravers, who balked at settling for the weekly package raise of $3.75 offered by the publishers. What really upset me was being forced to stay away from the paper for the ten days the strike lasted—only to see the engravers settle for the very package originally offered.

Arthur Hays Sulzberger, in a report to the staff that was remarkable for its candor, expressed his distress, declaring the shutdown had cost *The Times* serious advertising losses and financially weakened his family-owned paper for the first time since its postwar economic blossoming.

"Bear in mind that there is no fortune supporting *The Times*," he warned (in an era when the paper was innocent of executive bonuses and stock options). "We are all salaried employees of a great institution which has to be operated at a profit." He went on to point out—to the genuine surprise of most of us on the paper—that this year, as had been the case for the past twenty-five years, no dividends had been paid on the common stock of *The Times*. "Instead," he said, "every endeavor has been made to plough money back into the plant, the staff, and the company as a whole."

Had it not been for the strike, he added, 1953 might have been the paper's best year. "The loss sustained as a result of that ten-day shutdown accounts for the poor showing that we made for the year. Virtually all, and I mean that literally, of the anticipated profit from 1953 was wiped out." His wry conclusion: "Those who like fruit should not pluck all the blossoms from the tree."

THE STRIKE OVER, I had no regrets about giving up my UN assignment—mainly because my hours on night rewrite allowed me to spend more time with my two sons during the day. I would wake at noon and play with them on our penthouse terrace. After their naps, Barbara and I took them for outings in Central Park, Peter in his carriage and Michael toddling by my side.

I also enjoyed returning to the pace of rewrite's breaking stories. Shortly after I got back, on January 23, 1954, a bulletin reported that a small plane carrying Ernest Hemingway and his wife, Mary, had crashed in the Ugandan jungle near Lake Albert. Later reports said Hemingway had been killed.

His plane had been spotted by air search teams but they saw no sign of life. After our rewrite bank assembled the obit, Frank Adams asked me to call contemporary writers to assess Hemingway's stature. Within two hours, our switchboard operators had helped me track down nine prominent literary figures, among them Archibald MacLeish, Alfred Kazin, John O'Hara, Carlos Baker and Van Wyck Brooks, who noted that Hemingway "was in his way a typical American, and there was something permanently adolescent about him that stood for a certain immaturity in the American mind . . . but he was unquestionably a great writer, a great artist in prose." Marc Connelly, in a remark that seems ironic in view of Hemingway's ultimate fate, said, "His laughter was the deep laughter of the healthy, sane, unafraid inhabitant of a confusing world."

The bullpen sensibly decided to hold the story until Hemingway's death could be verified. But two days later, on January 25, the editors changed their minds and ordered that the story run. Just before the edition went to press, however, an AP bulletin came over the wires stating that Hemingway was alive. He and his wife and their pilot had sustained minor injuries, but climbed out of the wreckage. They spent the night in the bush and were rescued the next day by a boatload of tourists who were sightseeing on the lake. Hemingway took it all in stride, no doubt exaggerating the scenario to suit his daredevil image. "We had emergency goods, but were short on water," he said. "We took turns going to the river, but the elephants were very stuffy about it."

Obviously the obit didn't run, and neither did my story, but I felt my work hadn't been completely in vain. It had been set in proof, and I mailed it to Hemingway, thinking he would be amused to see how he would have been eulogized in *The Times*. He sent back a note thanking me for the care I had put into the article and for "leaving out all of the derogatory opinions of my work that you surely received."

The news clippings from the morgue had been a key component of the Hemingway obit. But the morgue failed us two weeks later, on February 7, when we were alerted to the death of another literary figure, Maxwell Bodenheim, the quintessential Greenwich Village poet, who was found murdered along with his wife in their apartment.

Wayne Phillips was assigned to write the obit and, confronted by a fast-approaching deadline, he raced to the morgue—only to discover there was no Bodenheim folder; it had been either misfiled or stolen. All of us on the rewrite bank pitched in to help him. Wayne called Police Headquarters and reached the officer of record. Billie Barrett tracked down Bodenheim's family and Tad Szulc made calls to literary critics. On a long shot, I phoned the Baron, my old acquaintance from the police reporters' shack. It turned out that he not only had been a good friend of Bodenheim, but had actually been the person who identified the body for the police.

Wayne Phillips was rewarded with the rare rewriteman's byline—proof of the efficacy of our teamwork, on which we continued to build. With journalistic hubris, we affixed a small sign to one of the front desks: "The Most Reliable Bank in the World."

A theft of morgue clips was not common, but I recall one egregious case that occurred in 1972, when I was metropolitan editor and in charge of assigning obituaries. When my desk was notified by the Los Angeles Medical Center that Walter Winchell had died, I sent a copyboy to the morgue to fetch the folder that should have held his advance obit. It wasn't there. As in the case of Bodenheim, a team was assembled to gather as much information as quickly as possible from various sources. Alden Whitman, who by then had been assigned to the obit desk, speedily fashioned a two-column story and we made the first edition. It was later rumored that Winchell, some years before his death, had asked Jack Tell to let him see the advance obit, which, understandably, was a serious violation of *Times* rules. Winchell, it was believed, thought the obit too critical and destroyed it.

There were other occasions when the morgue let us down, as was the case on March 21, a few weeks after the Bodenheim murder, when we received an AP bulletin announcing the death in Boston of Walter Howey, who had been injured in an auto accident. The prototype for Walter Burns, the manipulative managing editor in *The Front Page,* Howey had represented Chicago journalism of the 1920s at its most raucous. But while Howey had masterminded hundreds of stories and his fame was acknowledged in city rooms throughout the country, he had led a guarded private life, rarely allowing himself to be written about. The result of this extreme reticence was that there were only three short clips about him in his morgue folder—scarcely sufficient material on which to base the full-scale obit he deserved.

I eyed the clock. There were forty minutes to deadline. Just then, Bernie Kalb, who had at long last been transferred from the broadcast desk to a reportorial beat—phoned me from the shack at Police Headquarters. He was bored and wanted to chat, but I cut him short, telling him of my dilemma.

"Why don't you call Charles MacArthur?" was his inspired suggestion. "After working as a reporter under Howey in Chicago and writing *The Front Page*, he should be able to give you everything you need."

The switchboard operators tried to find MacArthur's unlisted number, but it was one of the rare times they failed. I knew the drama department kept its own files of phone numbers, and I figured I might track MacArthur through the number of his wife, Helen Hayes. A watchman unlocked the department's door, and there in the files was the actress's private number in the suburb of Nyack. When I called, Helen Hayes answered.

I explained my mission. "Oh, my husband will want to talk to you," she said, and handed the phone to MacArthur. I told him I had to write Howey's obit and his morgue folder was empty.

"How much time have you got?" he asked.

"About half an hour."

"Well, why don't you just interview me, and quote me directly?"

MacArthur had an encyclopedic memory, and he provided facts and anecdotes that surpassed anything I could have hoped for. Howey, at twenty-two, he said, "roared into Chicago like thunder out of China." He got his big break in 1903, when he stumbled onto a tremendous story: "He spotted some elves coming out of a manhole. They turned out to be a group of actors who had escaped by an underground passage from the flaming Iroquois theater." It was the most lethal fire to date in United States history, far more costly even than the Great Chicago Fire of 1871. Some six hundred people were killed, trapped inside the theater after stage curtains were ignited by an arc light.

In 1919, Howey was managing editor of William Randolph Hearst's *Herald and Examiner* when it was the sole Chicago paper to support the winning mayoral candidate, William Hale Thompson, who ran on the platform: "Keep King George out of Chicago!"

"Howey's reward," MacArthur told me, "was a newspaperman's dream. Two city patrolmen and a sergeant were stationed in our city room and were subject to the orders of the paper's reporters. We went out and arrested people whenever we had to. Our private interrogation quarters was at a nearby hotel. Our policemen would keep rival photographers from taking pictures at the scene of a crime, and we got one exclusive story after another. The other papers howled with rage, but what could they do? Walter had the resignations of half a dozen city officials in his desk to be used at his convenience."

Handling obits and breaking news stories against deadline, the rewrite bank reveled in camaraderie. During lulls, when we weren't on meal breaks or playing cards or working on outside writing projects, we analyzed the early edition—the stories deserving praise and those we deemed mediocre. And we griped about the latest petty edicts of the reigning editors.

What most earned our ire were the periodic cost-saving measures, particularly one about economizing on the soft-lead Ebony pencils we relied on for taking notes. This essential tool of our trade, we were informed by memo, was costly and must be rationed. To obtain a new pencil, a staffer had to turn in at least one-third of a used pencil to the city desk clerk. One night, when the clerk who kept all pencils locked in his desk drawer left early, our rewrite staff was confronted with a shortage.

By the time our shift ended, we were so infuriated that we rounded up every used pencil we could find—nineteen of them—grinding them down in the sharpener to stubs one inch long. We put all the stubs into an envelope, and addressed it to Frank Adams with a note signed by each of us: "We need twenty new pencils to replace these nineteen stubs. We regret that we lost the twentieth in the sharpener." The pencil edict was revoked.

IN THE EARLY FALL OF 1954, *The Times* switched me from rewrite back to the UN bureau, in anticipation of the next General Assembly. One day in mid-October, in the delegates' lounge, I ran into Dr. Frank Calderone, the former New York assistant health commissioner, whom I had interviewed for my story about poisonous mushrooms. He was now the director of the UN Health Service Clinic and a leading administrator of the World Health Organization, as well as an authority on global immunization and the spread of communicable diseases.

Dr. Calderone remembered me and, while we were at the bar in the delegates' lounge, he confided that his clinic had been treating many UN staffers for emotional problems. "They are of different national backgrounds and temperaments and frequently find it difficult to adjust to the environment here," he told me, sadly. Their typical symptoms, he said, were loneliness, depression and anxiety, and these sometimes resulted in gastric ulcers and skin rashes—perfectly understandable in young men and women who had left their homelands for a strange country whose language they did not speak and who felt isolated. But in that era, the need for psychiatric therapy was regarded as a character defect, and it was rare for anyone to seek help— or, in the event, to admit it. The fact that Dr. Calderone was willing to discuss the problem represented a kind of breakthrough.

Both Abe Rosenthal and Tom Hamilton were impressed that I had managed to get the story and, when it appeared on the front page of the first edition on October 20, 1954, under the headline "UN Aides Getting Psychiatric Help," the effect was electric. In the vicinity of the UN, *The Times* sold out not long after the edition hit the newsstands, and word of the story spread quickly. There was such an uproar among the delegates that Dr. Calderone was forced to resign. He said he wasn't sorry he gave me the story, though he had not realized it would cause such a tempest.

When the General Assembly concluded its session, I returned to the city room, and was pleased that Bernie Kalb, who like me had been assigned temporarily to the UN bureau, joined me on rewrite. As for Abe, he at last landed a foreign assignment. *The Times* often had gone to absurd extremes to avoid having to publish a Jewish-sounding byline. Abe was one of three popular young reporters whose given name of Abraham had their bylines arbitrarily shortened to include only their first initials: A. M. Rosenthal; A. H. Raskin (who eventually became deputy editor of the editorial page) and A. H. Weiler (who became movie editor).

And when it came to assignments abroad, even that compromise did not seem to be enough. Abe had long fumed over the injustice that allowed Jewish staffers with neutral-sounding names like Milton Bracker, Sydney Gruson and Henry Giniger to be assigned variously to Rome, London and Paris. And he could never understand why the powers who dictated such decisions permitted bylines with full names like those of Meyer Berger and Irving Spiegel. My theory was that *The Times* was reacting to the era's bigots who used "Abe" or "Abie" to stereotype the Jewish immigrant in the same way that "Mickey" or "Mick" was used to denigrate the Irish.

Abe himself longed for Paris, but Cyrus L. Sulzberger, a nephew of the publisher and chief of foreign correspondents, himself stationed in Paris, cautioned the paper's hierarchy that "one Jew in the Paris bureau was enough."

The "one" he referred to was Giniger; Cyrus evidently didn't think of himself as Jewish.

But *The Times* was beginning to see the folly of keeping a highly talented reporter from going abroad because of a Jewish byline and it all turned out for the best. Abe was posted to New Delhi, an assignment tailored to his curiosity and writing skills. India, coping with its new independence, had proclaimed its neutrality under Nehru, trying to sidestep the cold war antagonisms between the U.S. and the USSR. For Abe, there was more than enough to explore.

Now that Barbara's and my book about Bellevue was being readied for publication, I, too, anticipated a foreign assignment, though the fact that Barbara and I had two young sons seemed something of a deterrent to us. Frank Adams, with whom I had long since resumed friendly relations, tried to convince me that having a family shouldn't prevent acceptance of a foreign assignment. But I remembered the case of John Callahan, a debonair *Times* man who every year signaled summer's advent by swaggering into the city room in a straw hat and bow tie.

Callahan wanted so badly to go abroad that he assured Catledge his pregnant wife, Lavina, and their five children would be content to stay behind. In 1953, Callahan was posted to Karachi, whose miserable living conditions made it one of the least desirable of foreign assignments. It was important as a continuing story, however, because Pakistan was still reeling from its 1947 partition from India.

Two months after her husband's departure, Lavina gave birth and, unable to manage without her husband, complained bitterly to Catledge. He felt obliged to send the entire family to Pakistan, which cost the paper a small fortune. The Callahans found a large house with five servants, but sanitary conditions in the city were abysmal; there was only one street equipped with a sewer.

"If Lavina Callahan could go to Karachi with six kids," Adams asked, "why can't you go abroad with two?" The mention of Karachi—as likely an assignment as any—gave me misgivings. But I never did find out where the paper might have sent me.

One night, when I had returned to the rewrite battery and was awaiting my new assignment, Brooks Atkinson came by after writing one of his theater reviews. He said he wanted to congratulate Barbara and me on our good fortune. "Word travels fast in the city room," he said. "I hear you've hit the jackpot."

He was referring to the purchase of our book, which we'd decided to call *Bellevue Is My Home*, by *The Saturday Evening Post*. The weekly planned to run it as a prominently displayed five-part serialization and pay us $30,000, a staggering sum for a magazine to offer in those days.

I was delighted that Brooks had taken the time to chat with me. After his triumphant reporting on General Stilwell in China, he had stayed abroad as a foreign correspondent and won a Pulitzer Prize for his coverage from Moscow. He was now back running the six-member theater department, having resumed his position as the most influential newspaper critic in the country. Off Broadway was beginning to boom, and he knew I took an interest in its experimental productions—and was willing to bear with its cramped, ill-ventilated spaces and backless wooden benches.

"There's an opening in my department," he said. "You seem to enjoy writing about the theater for our Sunday pages. You'd be reviewing plays as well as reporting. This could be a real opportunity for you. There's much to be said for a foreign assignment, but you can always go overseas."

When I told Barbara about Brooks's offer, she pointed out that the job combined my two loves, journalism and the theater. "And," she reminded me, "you couldn't work for anyone you respect more than Brooks."

It was true that Brooks Atkinson, aside from embodying the highest journalistic standards, whether reporting from Moscow or Broadway, was a moral institution. With his deeply felt principles mirroring those of Emerson and Thoreau, he was regarded by the paper's staff as the "conscience of *The Times*" and was often invited to the publisher's office to help resolve ethical questions.

Thus far, I had written theater features and interviews only on a freelance basis and at my own pace. As a second-string critic, I would have to write reviews in the space of an hour or less. In those days of competitive morning newspapers, reviews had to be filed for the second edition, which closed at midnight.

Opening nights were scheduled for 8:30 P.M., and the curtain came down between 10:30 and 11:00. I would have to rush back to the office, scribbling notes in the back of a taxi, and then type my review without looking back. When I voiced my apprehension, Atkinson assured me that fresh first thoughts, quickly expressed, were what constituted a good newspaper review. Second thoughts could be written up for the Sunday Drama Section. I accepted his offer—and could only hope that my experience on rewrite would provide the speed (never mind the analytical ability) to stumble along in his footsteps.

TWENTY

E ARLY IN 1955, when I moved into the Drama Department—a glass-partitioned enclave situated, along with the paper's other culture fiefdoms, slightly west of the city room—I was happy to be in the company of a gallery of glamorous ghosts.

Notable among them were Alexander Woollcott, the acerbic man-about-town who had preceded Brooks Atkinson as chief drama critic and become as much of a celebrity as the playwrights and actors he praised and excoriated; George S. Kaufman, who had written his early Broadway comedies while serving in the drama department; and Herman J. Mankiewicz, who later was the coauthor with Orson Welles of the film masterpiece *Citizen Kane.*

Like me, both Kaufman and Mankiewicz had been second-string critics and feature writers and, together with Woollcott, had belonged to that wittily snobbish congregation known as the Algonquin Round Table. I listened raptly to Brooks's stories about these three dazzling and volatile noncon-formists, all of whom happened to turn up in the *Times* drama department around the same time. Brooks, having worked alongside all three, recalled their holding court at their desks, entertaining city-room reporters with their wicked barbs aimed at Broadway and Hollywood notables—and not infrequently at one another.

Brooks patiently coached me, much as had my city-room mentors, explaining, for example, the drama department's symbiotic relationship with Broadway. Theater, he pointed out, was a homegrown product that flourished in our own backyard with its shimmering stars and suspenseful opening nights. As a result, theater news was allotted more space in the paper by far than any of the other arts.

The drama department also had more floor space. But since our glass-enclosed office was shared by six staff members, we felt like fish colliding in a bowl. Brooks himself commanded a bit more privacy, his space separated by a waist-high metal partition topped by glass panels. He and I fell into a habit of talking there for hours. On the one solid wall—bare of Broadway memorabilia—hung a caricature of Joe Jackson, an early-twentieth-century clown known for his comic bicycle act; a woodcut of Walden Pond; a large color sketch of birds by Roger Tory Peterson; and a portrait of a pipe-smoking Henry Taylor Parker, drama critic of the defunct *Boston Evening Transcript*, Brooks's mentor before he came to *The Times* at twenty-eight, and whom he somewhat resembled.

Brooks, binoculars slung around his neck, regularly went on bird-watching expeditions in Central Park and Van Cortlandt Park and, every so often, invited me to join him. Nature was essential to his peace of mind. On weekends, he retreated to his farmhouse in the Catskills for gardening and walks through the woods. His Manhattan apartment on Riverside Drive afforded him a panoramic view of circling birds and bustling boats.

Seated in his office swivel chair, Brooks could easily have been mistaken for a faculty member of an Ivy League college: lean, with short-cropped graying hair, button-down oxford shirt, striped bow tie. His eyes twinkled behind pale-rimmed glasses, as he drew contemplatively on a pipe.

Born in Melrose, Massachusetts, in 1894, Brooks was captivated by newspapers from childhood. At eight, he bought a small hand-set printing press with rubber type and published a newsy pamphlet called "The Watchout." When he was fourteen, he purchased a lead-type press for thirty-five dollars, began printing "The Puritan" and joined the National Amateur Press Association.

At Harvard, he took the drama course taught by George Pierce Baker (who had earlier instructed Eugene O'Neill, Bill Laurence and S. N. Behrman). Increasingly attracted to the theater, he wrote articles about George Bernard Shaw that he sold to the *Boston Herald*. After graduating in 1917, he worked briefly for the *Springfield Daily News*. While serving in the infantry during World War I, he purchased his first copy of *The Times*. He paid two cents for it outside his barracks at Camp Upton, Long Island, and was immediately struck by its form and content.

At war's end, he joined the *Boston Evening Transcript*, but continued to read *The Times*. On the *Transcript*, he became a police reporter but, he told me, he had no talent for chasing crimes and fires. In his off-hours, he wrote drama articles for H. T. Parker, who soon took Brooks on as his assistant. "We have not had Parker's peer since William Hazlitt," Brooks once said, referring to the early-nineteenth-century English critic and essayist. Brooks described Parker as "a strange little fellow touched by genius."

In 1922, a list of *Times* editors appeared in the paper to mark Adolph Ochs's twenty-fifth anniversary as publisher, and Brooks noted the name of Carr Van Anda as managing editor. He instantly wrote to him asking for a job. Van Anda replied, inviting Brooks to drop by *The Times* when he next came to New York. That very day, Brooks bought a train ticket for New York.

He told me that when he got to Grand Central Terminal he realized he was incorrectly dressed for a business interview. Instead of the de rigueur stiff white collar, he was wearing a shirt with a soft collar. He popped into the nearby Weber and Heilbroner, purchased the required symbol of serious purpose, and then phoned Van Anda to announce he was in New York, just a few blocks from *The Times*.

Van Anda, amused, received Brooks cordially, but told him the paper had no openings in the drama department. He asked if Brooks had ever written book reviews. Brooks had, and Van Anda offered him the editorship of the Sunday *Book Review*, a section especially dear to Ochs. He had inaugurated it as a Saturday tabloid on October 10, 1896, the same year he took over *The Times*, and switched publication to Sunday on January 29, 1911. Although startled, Brooks accepted. Van Anda told him to come back the next day to have a chat with Mr. Ochs.

When the publisher asked Brooks what he thought of *The Times Book Review*, he answered with characteristic candor: "I prefer the *Evening Post Review*."

"Dear me," said Ochs, "maybe you're going to give us some trouble." He hired him nonetheless and Brooks remained editor of the *Book Review* for two and a half years.

During that time, Alexander Woollcott, as chief drama critic, occasionally asked Brooks to help out on nights when several plays opened simultaneously—not unusual in those days when theater dominated the entertainment world. Brooks recalled one particular night when eleven shows opened.

Woollcott, born in 1887 in an experimental commune in Red Bank, New Jersey, had originally been hired as a reporter for *The Times* in 1909, when he was twenty-two. He made his mark with two stories: When the *Titanic* sank in April 1912, Van Anda sent him to Nova Scotia, where he reported with rich detail on the recovery of bodies. He followed that story with lively coverage of the arrest of Charles Becker, the police lieutenant who had hired a hit squad to murder the gangster Herman "Beansy" Rosenthal near Times Square. (Becker was electrocuted at Sing Sing.)

After a turn on rewrite, Woollcott took over the drama department in 1914 when the incumbent critic, Adolph Klauber, married Jane Cowl, the Broadway star, and left *The Times* to produce her shows. When offered the critic's position, Woollcott asked if he could be spared the then routine job of soliciting advertisements from producers, and Ochs agreed.

Brooks told me how surprised he was at Woollcott's rapid ascent to power, despite his often capricious judgment and somewhat untidy writing style. It appeared that his flamboyant, self-promoting public persona was enough to persuade his readers that he was a man of impeccable taste.

Brooks's own style, while not lacking in wit, was reserved and a model of exactitude. He believed Woollcott was often carried away by the sound of his own words. He could be overly effusive when he liked a show, but when he disliked something, he was sometimes unnecessarily cruel and sarcastic— not to mention vulgar. After seeing one play that particularly disappointed him, Woollcott wrote, "If this play lasts overnight it should not only be considered a long run but a revival as well."

After Woollcott wrote a blistering review of *Taking Chances*, a silly French farce that opened at the Shubert Theater in 1915, the Shuberts—J.J., Sam and Lee, a Broadway force to be reckoned with—barred him from all their houses. Ochs, refusing to be cowed, retaliated by forbidding the drama staff to review any Shubert productions and stopped running their ads.

After a lengthy stalemate, the Shuberts conceded. There had been a steady decline in ticket sales at the box office, and they came to realize they needed *The Times* more than *The Times* needed them. Woollcott was allowed back into their theaters, and Ochs had demonstrated he would allow no one to bully his paper. But the Shubert offices—along with various other producers—never did stop complaining about what they considered unfair treatment by *Times* critics.

In 1989, for example, when I was managing editor, the publisher forwarded a complaint from the Shubert organization about our drama critic Frank Rich, and I sent him the following memo:

"I guess I will never understand why, despite our abundant and caring coverage, producers and theater owners complain about us. This has been the case ever since I can remember. Even the cherished Brooks Atkinson during the 1950s was often harshly attacked by a group of producers led by David Merrick. Brooks finally got fed up and told me that was one of the reasons he decided to give up the job. I suppose it's their way of trying to put us on the defensive and it can't be taken too seriously."

GEORGE S. KAUFMAN, then drama editor of the *New York Tribune* and a dynamo of creative energy, soon entered Woollcott's circle of clever friends. At a party, they met Herman Mankiewicz, who was just as quick as they at turning a phrase and whose sardonic humor Woollcott adored. The friendship formed by the three was interrupted by World War I. The rumpled Mankiewicz, who looked nothing like a military man, joined the Marines, and the obese Woollcott, who wore thick lenses, was accepted by the Army, which assigned him to *Stars and Stripes* under its editor, Harold Ross.

Kaufman, who did not enlist, remained at the *Tribune*. A little over six feet—not including his thicket of black hair—he wore a perpetually worried look that belied his mirthful patter. Born in Pittsburgh in 1889, he began working on the *Washington Times* as a humor columnist in 1912.

He later took a job as a ship news reporter at the *Tribune*, where his love of theater was noticed by the young assistant managing editor, a newspaper prodigy named Lester Markel, who had graduated from the Columbia School of Journalism in 1914. Markel, who had hurtled up the ranks of the *Tribune* with unprecedented speed, promoted Kaufman to drama editor. In late 1917, when the critic's job fell open at the *Tribune*, it was awarded to Heywood Broun, then a sportswriter, rather than to Kaufman. Incensed, he offered his services to *The Times*, where he learned that the critic's post was being held open for Woollcott's return from the Army. But he accepted the drama editor's slot at a respectable increase over his weekly *Tribune* salary of thirty-six dollars.

While awaiting Woollcott's return, Kaufman not only edited the section but reviewed plays and founded the column "News and Gossip of the Rialto" (adapted from a line in *The Merchant of Venice*), which featured tidbits of Broadway gossip and endured for decades as a drama-page staple. In another change, Kaufman discontinued the dubious practice of accepting articles written by press agents about their own productions, causing one agent to plead, "How am I expected to get the name of the actress I represent into *The Times*?" "Shoot her," Kaufman suggested.

In 1918, with energy to spare, Kaufman began writing comedies, eventually earning, Brooks guessed, something like three thousand dollars a week on Broadway (as compared with his weekly *Times* salary of eighty dollars). But in an era indifferent to what today would be decried as a conflict of interest, he stayed at the paper, fearing his next play might be a flop. "I also suspected George found his *Times* job a convenient excuse for leaving a boring dinner party," Atkinson once said. "He could always say he was suddenly needed back at the paper." Thus Kaufman worked bizarre hours, racing back and forth between the drama department and the theater.

Woollcott returned to *The Times* as chief critic in August 1919, and, between him and Kaufman, the drama pages crackled with comical wordplay, much like a printed version of the verbal sparring at the Algonquin Round

Table, where the two met for lunch with the likes of Harold Ross, Tallulah Bankhead, Charles MacArthur, Dorothy Parker and Harpo Marx.

In the fall of 1922, Woollcott let it be known that the *Herald* had offered him five times more than the four hundred dollars a month he was earning at *The Times*, and he was considering switching papers. Although Ochs had always supported Woollcott, he was not overly fond of him and didn't try to keep him. Brooks told me he had agreed with Ochs that Woollcott's self-invented celebrity had set him above the paper instead of subordinate to it. Public detachment was what Ochs continued to expect of all *Times* staffers, including himself.

Since Kaufman was no longer interested in the time-consuming job of first-string critic, Woollcott was succeeded by John Corbin, an Oxford-educated Shakespeare scholar, who soon decided he preferred writing editorials, and he was followed by the erudite critic for *The New Republic*, Stark Young. Accustomed to writing at a leisurely pace for his weekly magazine, Young did not perform well under deadline pressure. When Young finally gave up in 1925, Ochs asked Brooks to switch from the *Book Review* to the drama critic's post.

With Woollcott's departure, Kaufman found a worthy new verbal sparring partner in Herman Mankiewicz, who had just returned from Berlin. He had gone there after the war with his new wife on the half-promise of a newspaper job, which fell through. He began sending Kaufman witty articles and reviews, and Kaufman published them periodically in a column called "News of the Berlin Stage."

Kaufman brought Mankiewicz to the *Times* drama department at the start of 1923, when he required extra help to cover the ever-expanding news about New York's more than two hundred seasonal productions. Mankiewicz had a talent for reviewing, but his unbounded thirst got in the way. Once, in 1925, he was so drunk he passed out as he began typing his review of a revival of *The School for Scandal*.

The revival happened to be a vanity production to showcase Gladys Wallis, the wife of Samuel Insull, the Chicago utilities czar who had backed the show. Wallis, then in her fifties, was starring as the youthful Lady Teazle. Mankiewicz started his review by calling Wallis "a hopelessly incompetent amateur" and collapsed. According to Brooks, Kaufman struggled to revive him and finally was able to send him home. The review had to be pushed back a day, but *Times* editors in that era were forgiving. They did not hold reporters or critics to the standards of sobriety later imposed.

Mankiewicz did not waste the episode. In *Citizen Kane,* he scripted a scene in which the critic, portrayed by Joseph Cotten, gets drunk because he feels obliged to pan the performance of his boss's wife. He falls asleep and doesn't finish the review. His boss, Citizen Kane, finishes the pan for him and then fires him.

Mankiewicz was not the only theater critic with a weakness for drink. Brooks told me that Howard Barnes, critic at the *Herald Tribune* in the 1940s, was often drunk on opening nights. Producers repeatedly called Helen Rogers Reid, the chairman and power at the paper, to complain, but she consistently refused to believe them. One wintry night, Barnes was clearly in an alcoholic haze. The next morning, the show's producer called Reid, who again rose to her critic's defense.

"This time we have evidence," the producer claimed.

"What do you mean?" asked Reid.

"We found his shoes under his seat. He left in the snow in his stocking feet."

The incident eventually led to Barnes's dismissal in 1951, when he was succeeded by Walter Kerr, critic of the Catholic weekly *Commonweal* (and who some years later ably succeeded Atkinson at *The Times*).

Herman, according to Brooks, made him laugh more than anyone he had ever worked with, but was "the laziest man in the history of the paper." If he wrote a few paragraphs, Brooks said, Mankiewicz considered it a productive day. In 1926, Mankiewicz left *The Times* to become *The New Yorker*'s first drama critic, a post he held until he was fired a year later—and moved to Hollywood.

Kaufman stayed with the paper until 1930, continuing to write criticism and articles while also turning out a string of Broadway hits with such partners as Marc Connelly, Ring Lardner, Edna Ferber and Moss Hart. Brooks finally gave him an ultimatum: He needed a full-time assistant, and Kaufman had to choose between working on the paper or in the theater. Kaufman later told me he was beginning to feel secure financially for the first time. And so, albeit reluctantly, he gave up the newspaper life that had never bored him.

In 1950, I came to know Kaufman as a result of an article I wrote about his direction of *Guys and Dolls*, the smash Broadway musical based on Damon Runyon's characters. I found him surprisingly subdued at rehearsals and I elicited no witticisms to quote for my article. At times, he seemed even somber, especially when overcome by hypochondriacal terror. Having endured Plotkin's tales of diseases, I sympathized with Kaufman's distress as he turned doorknobs with his hand inside his jacket pocket to keep germs at bay.

But Kaufman was warm and approachable and willingly answered all my questions, as though remembering he was once on my side of the fence.

He said he had been a loyal reader of my Health Department coverage and hoped Plotkin would forever remain on duty protecting New Yorkers against such evils as food poisoning.

Kaufman then sent his regards to the drama department, advising me not to get too chummy with Sam Zolotow, the canny theater columnist. "You'll end up as one of his slaves," he cautioned. Sam, who had been with *The Times* even longer than Brooks, had joined the drama department as a copyboy in 1919. But in no sense did he seem an underling. "From the first," Woollcott wrote in a profile for *The New Yorker*, "there was in his breezy manner of taking possession a not implausible intention to own the newspaper itself at his earliest convenience."

When I told Sam about Kaufman's warning, he asked if I knew what Kaufman was most revered for when he worked in the drama department. I said I assumed it was for his hit plays, but Sam chuckled. In the early 1930s, Sam reminded me, Kaufman had an extramarital liaison with the alluring actress Mary Astor, later famous for her performance in *The Maltese Falcon*. She had kept a diary, recording Kaufman's sexual prowess. Many of these details were published in the tabloids when the diary was presented as evidence by her husband's lawyers in a court battle over custody of the couple's daughters.

But even the tabloids found some of the entries too racy for their readers. Sam, however, had kept an unexpurgated copy in his desk of some of the diary's spicier passages that he had obtained from the reporter assigned to the court, and he showed them to me. In one entry, Mary Astor expressed her admiration of Kaufman's "remarkable staying power" in bed: "I don't see how he does it! He is perfect." And in another passage, she exclaimed: "Was any woman ever happier? It seems that George is just hard all the time."

"Forget about his plays," said Sam. "All of us at *The Times*, from the publisher down, were in awe of his private parts."

It was also Sam who told me that after Kaufman's wife, Beatrice, had a stillborn baby, the couple slept in separate bedrooms and each took lovers. "After the stillbirth, he no longer saw Beatrice as an object of desire," Sam said philosophically.

Raised on the Lower East Side by immigrant parents, Sam had no formal education and was always on the hunt for high-flown locutions that he believed mimicked the speech patterns of Woollcott and Kaufman. He once told a reader who phoned for an opinion of a particular comedy: "I am able to assure you, Madame, that it is as droll a whimsy as these old eyes have seen in a month of first nights." The "old eyes" were an intense blue, and his thick hair had begun to turn gray when I met him.

When he became a drama reporter—thirty years before I joined the department—he quickly dominated the coverage of theater news. His column was littered with misapplied words tendered by press agents trying to curry favor—words like "quidnunc" and "flâneur." Despite these affectations, his ferocious pursuit of items dealing with secret contract negotiations, backstage bickering and production profit margins, along with gossip about rehearsals and out-of-town tryouts, made his column must reading for theater professionals as well as devoted audiences.

Sam had the instincts of an accountant and the soul of a blackmailer. When talking to a producer, playwright or director who seemed not to be coming clean, Sam would growl into the phone, "So, you don't care to cooperate with *The New York Times?*" and hang up abruptly. Invariably, the source would call back within minutes and spill everything. "Only a noodle head tries to hoax Sam," Dick Maney, the preeminent Broadway press agent, told me.

Theater friends of Brooks who wrote letters to keep him confidentially abreast of their work couldn't figure out how the information ended up in Sam's column, even when Brooks was out of town and hadn't opened his mail. Moss Hart told Brooks he thought Sam might be steaming open the letters and resealing the envelopes. After Robert Whitehead, the producer, voiced the same complaint, Brooks decided to test the theory. He suggested both Hart and Whitehead address envelopes to Brooks, enclosing notes reading, "We're on to you, Sam!"—and slip a hair under the flap of each envelope. The envelopes arrived sealed on Brooks's desk, but the hairs were gone.

It was this wily manipulator with whom I unwittingly found myself competing for news in the drama department. The antithesis of the rewrite bank, the drama enclave functioned on an every-man-for-himself principle. Together with a reporter named Louis Calta, Sam and I alternated writing the daily drama column, which consisted of a half-dozen news briefs led by a significant exclusive item. Sam wrote the column three times a week and Lou twice a week. I wrote it once a week, squeezing it in among my feature articles and Off Broadway reviews, as well as substituting now and then for Lewis Funke on his Sunday "News and Gossip of the Rialto" column.

Funke approached his job as drama editor with timidity, while Calta was easygoing and self-assured. The one thing all four of us had in common was a lust for exclusive news items that would win a nod of approval from Brooks. We guarded our items like jewels. Anything one of us carelessly mentioned was apt to be appropriated by one of the others. We worked in such secrecy that we occasionally discovered that all three of us were digging for the same story at the same time.

One way I gathered exclusive items, a method I never revealed to my office rivals, was by visiting my in-laws as often as I could, since they routinely entertained such theater royalty as Laurence Olivier, the Lunts and Mary Martin. But my most valued connection was Dick Maney, who often tipped me off to news about the stars he represented. Press agents like Maney and drama reporters each needed the other in the cutthroat realm of column-item gathering. The press agent's goal was to get as much publicity for a show as possible, and his best outlet was the newspapers. The reporter needed to fill his column with fresh Broadway news, and the press agent often was a prime source. It was up to the reporter to separate the facts from the hype, which press agents rarely did. Dick Maney was an exception; he never misled me.

Since the 1920s, Dick had represented many of the biggest Broadway hits. He was brash and quick-witted, and I respected his attitude toward the theater: Embrace it with all your heart, but never hesitate to encourage critics to "bat the ears off cheap and vulgar plays," even if they happened to be productions he had been hired to tout. When Dick and I eventually became good friends, he confided he had given up the idea of being a newspaperman because he needed to earn more money than reporters were paid in those preunion days. He loved the theater, and as a Broadway press agent he could command an income triple that of most city-room reporters. Because he was an original and could write humorously, the Sunday *Magazine* invited him every so often to submit articles, and, although most press agents were condescended to by the city room, Dick had the respect of everyone from Brooks to Mike Berger.

One of the times Dick enabled me to triumph over Sam Zolotow came on a Sunday when Sam had to attend a wedding and asked me to fill in for him. That afternoon Dick called to tell me that Rex Harrison and Julie Andrews were about to be signed for the starring roles in the as yet untitled musical version of *Pygmalion*. Dick gave me their private numbers, cautioning, "Sam must never know I'm responsible for this, or it will be my demise."

The next morning, my column, with comment from Harrison and Andrews, was the talk of Broadway. The show, of course, became *My Fair Lady*. Sam, furious he had taken the day off, demanded to know my source for the scoop, but I stayed firm. He never again took a Sunday off.

Maney also helped me gain entrée to the Actors Studio, an inner sanctum normally barred to reporters and critics. But Dick convinced three of its founders—Elia Kazan, the director; Cheryl Crawford, the producer; and

Lee Strasberg, the teacher—that the Studio should no longer be kept secret from the press.

The Studio had been created in 1948 to give gifted actors a chance to further develop. There was no tuition, talent being the only prerequisite for admittance. Employing the Stanislavsky method, Strasberg worked with a long list of budding and experienced players—among them Marlon Brando, Eli Wallach, Julie Harris, James Dean, Karl Malden, Eva Marie Saint, Lee J. Cobb and Shelley Winters.

The Method, as it became known, demanded that actors must understand themselves to understand their characters. When I interviewed Viveca Lindfors, who starred in the play *Anastasia* as the czarist princess, in one of the most emotionally evocative performances of the 1955 season, she told me, "What I tried to do was recall the suffering within me, so that I could find the feelings of Anastasia." To portray Anastasia's grief for the death of her family, Lindfors tortured herself endlessly with memories of her own brother's death two years earlier. The Method was not a formula and could not create talent, Strasberg told me, quoting Madame Barbara Bulgakov, a teacher who had studied under Stanislavsky himself: "Talent is intuitive—it's there or it's not. But the Method can help release a talent."

One person I did not expect to see at the Studio was Marilyn Monroe, whose talent Strasberg was trying to release. She was one of the few Hollywood stars allowed access to the Studio and it appeared to me that her fellow actors were uncomfortable in her proximity, aware of her self-consciousness in reading lines. Strasberg, however, treated her like an adopted daughter—coaxing her to probe her innermost emotions and bring them to the surface.

One day he sweet-talked her into performing for the first time before a live audience composed of Studio members. With Maureen Stapleton supporting her in the barroom scene from O'Neill's *"Anna Christie,"* she read the role of the reformed prostitute. Her delivery sounded forced, and I felt sorry for her. Inordinately driven by a Pygmalion complex, Strasberg pushed her in what I thought was a misguided effort to transform her from the screen's undisputed universal love goddess and a gifted comedian into a dramatic actress.

SOMETIMES, to my exasperation, I seemed to be spending as much time competing with Sam Zolotow as learning from Brooks Atkinson. The two men, who genuinely liked each other, were opposites. Where Sam could be coarse, Brooks was ever refined. While Sam entered the fray and sometimes even instigated it, Brooks remained coolly aloof. And while Sam was truly feared, Brooks was universally embraced for his sense of fairness, even though the theater maintained that his reviews too often were responsible for breaking a play—an assertion he heartily refuted.

"There is no joy as great as that of reporting that a good play has come to town," Brooks once told me. He never hesitated to pan a play that deserved it, but he refused to drag it through the mud. "There's no need to kick an author when he's down," he would say. "It's easy to disparage a show in paragraph after paragraph, but it's equally effective to keep a bad review brief, burying the production as quickly as you can."

I tried to absorb everything Brooks could teach me, since my goal by now was to become the first-string critic when Brooks saw fit to retire. It was his straightforward sensibility about the theater and his humanity that I hoped to emulate. I grew familiar with the "Atkinson Method," which had gone unchanged since Brooks first arrived in the drama department. At 4:30 P.M. on opening nights, his wife, Oriana, poured him a rye old-fashioned and they chatted until five o'clock, when they ate their unorthodoxly early dinner. The meal was followed by an hour's nap, and he and Oriana left for the theater soon after seven. More often than not, they were the first arrivals for the eight-o'clock curtain.

Opening nights were great New York Happenings, reverberating with both anticipation and terror. The aisle seats were filled with critics from newspapers and magazines. "First-nighters" could wait up to read the reviews in the late editions of the morning papers, which hit the newsstands a little past midnight. It was traditional for the cast to adjourn to Sardi's after the show, and be applauded by fellow diners who had been in the audience.

By far the most glamorous opening night in my memory was celebrated at Sardi's after the curtain came down on *My Fair Lady*. There were a dozen curtain calls, the audience cheering wildly. When the performers—stars as well as chorus—took their final bows, the curtain stayed up, with most of the cast frozen on the stage, stunned by the fervent reaction. At our table at Sardi's, Barbara and I watched as each performer entered for the cast party; everyone stood and applauded. Even the producer, Herman Levin, received an ovation, the first time I remembered a producer being thus saluted.

Opening-night patrons at Sardi's awaited the arrival of *The Times* and the *Herald Tribune*. As was customary, a copy of each paper would be handed around by the waiters to every table. If the reviews were laudatory, patrons might stay, celebrating, past four A.M., the official closing time. If the reviews were bad, the restaurant grew somber, the cast would slink out and Sardi's emptied at an early hour.

Brooks's personal code forbade him to discuss a play, even with his wife, until after his review was written—though he occasionally exchanged enigmatic glances with her during the performance. He never left his seat during intermission, shunning lounge gossip as unprofessional. When the curtain fell, he raced up the aisle, sometimes allowing Oriana to clear a path. After putting her in a taxi for home, he went to the office. "On the way," he once told me, "I always try to compose the lead sentence in my head."

At his desk, Brooks would light his pipe and begin writing swiftly in longhand, in pencil, on sheets of lined yellow paper. A copyboy sat nearby and took his sheets, a paragraph at a time, to the copy desk and then to the composing room, where it was set in type by Linotype operators familiar with his script. When he finished writing, he ascended to the composing room, to check his proofs. Unlike reporters' stories, critics' copy was never arbitrarily changed by copy editors. Although questions could be raised, even a correction in grammar had to be approved by the critic. All Brooks had to do in the composing room was make sure his review was free of typographical errors.

The only time one of Brooks's reviews was altered was in 1934, when he covered the Broadway opening of Sean O'Casey's *Within the Gates*. One of the characters was called "The Whore," and the copy desk had prudishly replaced "whore" with "woman of ill repute." When Brooks explained to Raymond McCaw that "The Whore" was the actual name of a character and that the play was not the least bit smutty, McCaw asked Brooks if he would be satisfied with just one "whore," since he couldn't allow the word to be splashed all over the paper. Brooks accepted the compromise.

In the name of impartiality, Brooks tried to keep his distance from professional theater people, wanting to be considered, as he put it, a "disinterested" theatergoer. "I know that a bad review can destroy a friendship," he told me, "and sometimes a critic unconsciously may be harder on his friends to avert accusations of favoritism. It's too troublesome and compromising, almost incestuous, to have friends in the business." Among the select few were Boris Aronson, the scenic designer, but he also casually socialized with Moss Hart, Helen Hayes, Lillian Gish and S. N. Behrman.

MOST OF MY REVIEWING was confined to Off Broadway, and I became a loyal patron of its shoestring productions—seldom seen classics and experimental new plays—at converted clubs, lofts, stores or cellars operating under cabaret licenses. The designation "Off Broadway" referred to spaces with a seating capacity of less than three hundred, and they were scattered from Greenwich Village to Times Square to the East Seventies. Quarters were cramped and stuffy and the seats generally uncomfortable. But a sense of intimacy could render a good play more moving than in a Broadway theater.

Although the Off Broadway movement basically began in late 1947 with the production of Sartre's *The Respectful Prostitute* by a company calling itself New Stages, it truly caught fire in 1952. It was then that the Circle in the Square presented its revival of Tennessee Williams's *Summer and Smoke*, which had flopped on Broadway four years earlier. Combining the imaginative staging of José Quintero and the breathtaking acting of Geraldine Page, the play exuded the subtle nuances and raw power it had lacked in its uptown première.

Only one major critic at first deigned to make the trip to Sheridan Square. "Nothing has happened for quite a long time as admirable as the new production at the Circle in the Square," wrote Brooks Atkinson. "*Summer and Smoke* opened there last night in a sensitive, highly personal performance." Other critics and theatergoers followed Brooks downtown, packing the Circle night after night.

By the time it became my beat, Off Broadway was approaching maturity with revivals of Ibsen, Strindberg, Chekhov and Shakespeare. Brecht's *The Threepenny Opera* opened at the Theater de Lys in 1954 and kept going for 2,611 performances, until December 1961—a run unmatched by any musical at that time.

Brooks assigned me to review Off Broadway because he felt I'd be in tune with the producers, directors and actors, who were of my own generation. And my increasing responsibility for Off Broadway gave him a chance to catch his breath. As it was, he felt committed to reviewing every production on Broadway, once even attending an opening when he was ill with a high fever.

Brooks never stopped instructing me, even on issues that might have seemed trivial to a layman. I had noticed, for instance, that he never applauded at an opening and—wondering if I should follow his example—I asked him why. "I am there in a professional capacity," he said, "and I don't make up my mind until the play is over, at which time I have to race up the aisle. If I feel like applauding, I have an excellent opportunity to do so in the paper the next morning."

Following his example, no member of the *Times* drama department applauded or discussed the play publicly until the review came out. But there was one notable exception. When the curtain fell on *Long Day's Journey Into*

Night in 1956, nothing could have kept me from joining the protracted standing ovation for O'Neill and the play's extraordinary cast.

I also asked Brooks if it was ever advisable to do any preparation before seeing a play, such as reading the script. He told me not to: "Go fresh, just like any member of the audience. We are not academics, we are basically reporters and the news we are reporting is whether or not a play is good." He said he had made one exception to this rule. In 1931, when O'Neill asked him to read the script of *Mourning Becomes Electra*, shortly before the play went into rehearsal, he agreed. "How could I say no to O'Neill?" said Brooks.

Mourning Becomes Electra was originally written as a trilogy of full-length plays, each to be performed on a separate night. Brooks told me he loved the first play, found the second weak and the third better than the second but not as good as the first. When Brooks gave his opinion, O'Neill was distressed, and asked Brooks to visit him for the weekend at his rented house on Long Island. After Brooks arrived, O'Neill seemed to sense that he had crossed a sacred boundary by involving him so deeply, and Brooks told me they did not talk much about the play.

During rehearsals, it became apparent that the trilogy was, indeed, unwieldy and that the emotional impact would be diminished if spread over three nights. O'Neill edited it down to be performed in a single night, with a dinner intermission. Brooks gave the play a rave review.

EVERY THURSDAY until seven P.M., I found myself in the composing room making up the Sunday Drama Section, which went to press that night in advance of Sunday distribution. The first page, except for one column allotted to the film critic, Bosley Crowther, was devoted to coverage of the theater.

Atkinson's critique led the page. A caricature by Al Hirschfeld—the section's weekly graphic signature—was at the top and under it was the "News and Gossip of the Rialto" column written by Lewis Funke (or by me when he was ill or on vacation). The other feature on the first page (which jumped to an inside page) was pegged to what we believed would be the most interesting Broadway opening of the week; it was written sometimes by me, sometimes by an outside contributor.

Since the Broadway theater was in its glory with new productions opening three or four times a week during the height of the season, we often had difficulty choosing the show to be caricatured. But Hirschfeld—who was beloved by *Times* readers—was partial to productions with stars whose familiar features and gestures could readily be exaggerated. He couldn't resist trying new ways to satirize the swan neck of which Lynn Fontanne was so vain, Carol Channing's saucer eyes and large mouth, Zero Mostel's wild stare or Ray Bolger's rubbery legs. An actor didn't truly arrive until crowned by a Hirschfeld caricature.

Sitting in an ancient barber's chair in his Upper East Side brownstone, his pen flowing magically over outsize slabs of stiff white cardboard, Al recorded the parade of plays and musicals week after week. One of my dividends was being the first to see Al's incisive, quirky, often hilarious rendering. When he delivered his latest creation to me every Tuesday afternoon, after having made sketches during the show's rehearsals, it was an Occasion. The drawing was always wrapped in brown paper on which he had drawn a self-caricature—long black beard, flowing mustache, bushy eyebrows, his forefinger pointing to a handwritten warning: "Do Not Step On, Set Fire To or Dunk in Hot Chicken Fat!!"

As I unwrapped it, I'd find myself surrounded by Brooks Atkinson and a crew of editors and reporters seeking a private preview. We were proud of Al's genius and gloated that our friends at the *Herald Tribune* would eat their hearts out. Al belonged exclusively to us! The *Herald Tribune* had had Al first, but hadn't had the smarts to sign him to a contract.

Born in 1903, Al had been sketching since the age of fourteen in his hometown of St. Louis. He studied art in Paris and New York, where he began haunting vaudeville comedy acts, and went to work in the art departments of two motion picture studios. In 1926, when he was twenty-three, he accompanied Dick Maney to one of the shows the press agent was touting, in which the French actor Sacha Guitry was starring. Al made sketches of Guitry on his *Playbill* that impressed Maney, who took the doodles to the theater editor at the *Herald Tribune*. The editor ordered a Guitry drawing, and Al was on his way. He started freelancing for the *Herald Tribune* and, later, for any paper that asked him; in the late 1920s, he accepted *The Times*'s offer of exclusivity.

Every so often, a star would complain that Al's caricature had distorted his or her features, but Brooks Atkinson ignored these cavils, even when forwarded to him by the publisher. For Brooks, Al could do no wrong. Al and Brooks became dear friends, and when Oriana was unable to accompany her husband to an opening, Al would take her place. During intermission they always seemed to have a lot to say to each other, and I found it hard to believe, despite Brooks's rule, that they made no comment on the play. I once asked Brooks what he and Al talked about, and he said they mostly appraised the pretty women in the audience.

Al died in 2003, five months shy of his hundredth birthday on June 21. We had been friends and colleagues for more than fifty years. Until his final days, his newest caricatures appeared in the Sunday theater pages. As he had advanced serenely into his senior years, his admirers often queried me about what I thought was the secret of his longevity. Al jokingly attributed it to his love of bourbon, but I believe it was his amazingly calm and joyous nature and his attunement to the comedic side of life.

Just a week before he died, Ric Burns and I interviewed him for a forthcoming PBS documentary about Eugene O'Neill, and he entertained us with stories about having accompanied the often gloomy O'Neill to the hot jazz and ragtime speakeasies of Fifty-second Street and to the six-day relay bicycle races in the old Madison Square Garden.

A few months earlier, when I told Al that Louise (his wife) and I planned to co-chair a centennial celebration in his honor and that Rocco Landesman had agreed to rename his Broadway theater, the Martin Beck, the Al Hirschfeld Theater, I had never seen Al so moved. He was looking forward to a helluva party in June, when his name would light up the new marquee.

Al never stopped drawing. Just hours before he died, he was ill in bed and feverish. He lifted his arm and his hand drew lines in the air as though he were at work in his barber's chair. That's where he was the day before, working on a caricature of the Marx Brothers for a private commission. He hadn't quite finished it—and I like to think that Al, with his irrepressible zest for his art, was completing this work, in his head, during his final moments.

IN THE OLD DAYS, after Al delivered his drawing, I'd measure the length of the stories in proof that were set to run in the coming Sunday Drama Section. Armed with my measurements, along with Al's drawing and the photographs I had collected to illustrate the various articles, I'd head for the art department on the ninth floor—where the Drama Section was laid out page by page. The man working his legerdemain with his soft-lead pencil and a T-square on a raised, slanted drawing board was the jovial, pipe-smoking art director, George Cowan. Week after week, he took all the ingredients I gave him and somehow managed to piece the section together without my having to make drastic cuts in the stories. I was especially comforted when he'd lay out my own story, making certain I'd not have to cut as much as one line.

George was the first person I worked with at *The Times* who cared about the paper's graphic-design standards. Playing a pioneering role in what was to evolve as modern newspaper design, he gave me my basic foundation on the imaginative use of art and graphics in making a newspaper visually inviting to readers. "It was only recently that a few people began to understand that art could not only be decorative in a newspaper but could enrich, enlarge and clarify journalism," Abe Rosenthal, then executive editor, said in his eulogy at George's funeral in 1979. "George was one of those very few people. And in the days before artists and designers and art directors were recognized as being as much a part of the paper as reporters and photographers and editors, George was practically a one-man art underground."

My next step was to take George's make-up pages to the composing room, where Frank Allgeier, a master compositor assigned weekly to the Drama Section, took charge of the newly set galleys of type. Over the next two days, as a first step in the publishing process, he'd meticulously follow George's design to fit the type and the photo engravings into an iron page mold. Frank seemed able to bend the rows of type when I needed to slip in an extra line or two in a story or caption. I used to watch in amazement as he moved the type around to create space where there had been none.

Lewis Funke, living in terror that Lester Markel might find errors in the Sunday drama pages, sometimes double-checked my work in the composing room. Since the daily paper and the Sunday sections were two separate entities, the drama department served two masters; as drama editor, Funke was the contact between our department and Markel, who took sadistic relish in bullying him in front of reporters and critics.

Despite his churlishness, Markel was regarded by the publisher as a newspaper seer. He had been hired away from the *Tribune* by Adolph Ochs in 1923, and was given license to make any changes he felt would distinguish the Sunday paper. He began, with a staff of five, to modernize the Sunday *Magazine,* enlarge the *Book Review* and spruce up the Drama Section. His principal addition was the News of the Week in Review, which became a model for news publications nationwide, as it laced the previous week's top stories with perspective and interpretation.

"I don't believe in Gallup Poll editors who give the reader what they think he wants," Markel once said. "I try to please myself." I admired his philosophy and it seemed to work, but he carried it out like a despot. He was jealous of his superiors and contemptuous of his subordinates. His staff disparaged him behind his back for his Napoleonic arrogance and for belittling them in public. ("Here comes Gloom Talese," he was apt to remark sourly to an assistant as Gay Talese, a valued contributor to his magazine, approached his desk.)

When the News of the Week in Review won a special Pulitzer Prize citation in 1953 for bringing "enlightenment and intelligent commentary to its readers," Markel was traveling abroad, and the Review staff celebrated at Sardi's. The day he returned, he summoned Jane Krieger Rosen, a member of the Review staff since 1949, to his office.

"How is it," he asked petulantly, "that I never heard congratulations from any of you about winning the Pulitzer?" Jane, nonplussed, found herself tartly replying: "Mr. Markel, we were all surprised we never heard from you, to congratulate us!" The framed citation hung in the Sunday department for a short time; then it disappeared. Markel had appropriated it for his apartment.

It amused everyone in the theater that Markel's ego was such that he insisted Broadway producers seat him on the aisle in front of Brooks on opening nights. The producers all capitulated, for no one dared offend him; feature articles in the Sunday sections were deemed essential to the box-office success of a Broadway show.

The Sunday staff prayed daily for Markel's retirement. Praying with them, very likely, was Turner Catledge, who was trying to convince the publisher to consolidate the Sunday and daily papers under one executive editor—himself.

Sy Peck, one of Markel's desk editors responsible for overseeing the Sunday Drama Section, often joined me in the composing room to check proofs and examine layouts. Although he had no control over the section's content—which was determined by Brooks—Peck had to make sure it adhered to Sunday department style.

A former movie reviewer for *PM*, Sy was a film encyclopedia; off the top of his head, he could answer just about any question relating to any movie ever made. Although he always arrived at the composing room grumbling about Markel's unrelieved sarcasm, he would soon regain his good nature.

I didn't have much personal contact with Markel, which was how I preferred it. He impinged on my life only once. The occasion was an Off Broadway review I wrote, which resulted in a schism between him and Brooks that was never to be bridged.

TWENTY-ONE

M Y RUN-IN WITH LESTER MARKEL came on November 4, 1955, after I reviewed a satirical comedy called *Trouble in Mind*, by Alice Childress, an author unfamiliar to me at the time.

As soon as the curtain rose at the Greenwich Mews Theater on West Thirteenth Street—an intimate space that served as the Village Presbyterian Church on Sundays and the Brotherhood Synagogue on Saturdays—I knew I was witnessing an unusual theatrical event. To begin with, the play had an integrated cast—rare for that era.

Alice Childress, who was listed in the program notes as having performed in an all-black Broadway melodrama, *Anna Lucasta*, that I had seen a few years earlier, had set *Trouble in Mind* backstage at a Broadway theater during the first rehearsal of an all-black melodrama dealing with a Negro lynching in the South.

Sprinkling her dialogue with barbed comments about the plight of black actors in a theater world controlled by white producers and directors, Childress depicted the zealous competition for the occasional black parts in "white" plays—minor roles that were usually stereotypes. She also had some pointed things to say about the state of jitters in an entertainment world much investigated by congressional committees over the past decade.

In my review, I described the production as "a fresh, lively and cutting satire . . . an original play full of vitality, and well worth the trip downtown." What I didn't know (and it wouldn't have affected my review in any case) was that Childress had been implicated by one of the many anti-Communist publications that believed it had a mandate to expose existing or potential subversives. As nonsensical as it may now seem, the rave review I gave the play led to my being cited as a "fellow traveler" in a red-hunting news bulletin occasionally produced with the support of an organization calling itself Red Channels.

As it happened, *The Times* at that moment was under suspicion by the Senate Internal Security Subcommittee, headed by James O. Eastland of Mississippi. Eastland, it seemed, was trying to discredit the paper for its outspoken opposition to his segregationist agenda. Not a subtle man, he had warned on the Senate floor against the "mongrelization" of races. He wanted to ban blacks and whites from eating at the same tables in public, and once said, "If it came to fighting, I'd fight for Mississippi against the United States, even if it meant going out into the streets and shooting Negroes."

Eastland found backup for his suspicions of *The Times* when Harvey Matusow, an admitted former Communist, testified before his subcommittee on October 8, 1952, that "*The New York Times* has well over one hundred dues-paying members" in the Communist Party. A few weeks later he amended his statement, declaring that "the Sunday section of *The New York Times* alone has 126 dues-paying Communists" (although, in fact, the paper's Sunday staff totaled only ninety-two).

Matusow also testified he knew ten thousand New York Communist Party members by sight, even though—according to FBI chief J. Edgar Hoover—there were only eleven thousand Communists in the entire city. (A number of them, it was later revealed, were FBI informants.)

The country was gripped by a terror that Communism could destroy America from within, and newspapers worried that they might be tainted as "Red sympathizers." The fear of Communist infiltration was so pervasive that Matusow's irresponsible accusations went virtually undisputed. His numbers quickly became ammunition for governmental inquiries and received prominent play in the media. At first, except for a few courageous commentators, such as the *Post* columnist Murray Kempton, the press in general failed to analyze the allegations or raise doubts about their author's legitimacy.

IT WAS, OF COURSE, Joseph McCarthy, the Republican senator from Wisconsin, who had set the agenda. After General Eisenhower's Republican landslide victory in 1952, which also brought his party to power in the Senate, McCarthy became chairman of the Committee on Government Operations and of its Permanent Subcommittee on Investigations; he was off and running, ready to expose anyone and everyone who, in his eyes, was "soft on Communism." He had previously accused the State Department and now he took on the Army and former President Truman himself.

Jack Gould, in his television columns in *The Times*, was among the early few to lash out at the networks for their "poor judgment" in giving McCarthy so much free airtime. But it wasn't until Edward R. Murrow, in his CBS program *See It Now* on March 9, 1956, raised questions about McCarthy's bullying tactics that the senator's poll ratings began to drop. Even though Murrow acknowledged to friends that he had been late in speaking out, Gould praised his action as heroic, considering how McCarthy had cowed the networks and their sponsors.

Harvey Matusow's shaky credentials had stood basically unchallenged for too long. He was a twenty-eight-year-old Bronx-born former Army sergeant whose parents operated a small cigar counter in a downtown office building. According to a friend, he joined the Communist Party in 1947 to meet girls, and he struggled to support himself by selling ads for the *Daily Worker* and as a salesclerk in a Communist bookstore.

After he left the party in 1951, he was recruited by the FBI as a paid informer and later as a paid witness for McCarthy's Subcommittee on Investigations; his testimony led to the conviction of twelve secondary Communist leaders on charges of conspiring to advocate the overthrow of the United States government by force.

When Matusow's accusations about *The Times* reached Arthur Hays Sulzberger, he sent the paper's general manager, Julius Ochs Adler, to consult with the FBI. Hoover told Adler he had doubts about Matusow and said not to worry. In fact, a year later—in September 1953—Matusow abruptly declared he had "got religion" and phoned *The Times* to retract his charges. In a sworn affidavit, he said he actually knew of only three Communists on the paper—two were in the commercial department and one was a news clerk who had already been fired for laziness. His original figures, he conceded had been "essentially an unverified estimate."

The Eastland subcommittee, however, chose to ignore Matusow's retraction when it began investigating the New York press—specifically *The Times*—in the spring of 1955. Lester Markel felt the pressure more than anyone, since his Sunday department had been explicitly named as a Red harbor.

For the first time anyone could remember, Markel seemed shaken. Thus, when my name appeared in the anti-Communist news bulletin, he was glad to divert attention from his Sunday staff to the daily staff. He asked Turner Catledge to inquire into my associations.

By then the atmosphere in the country was so fraught with witch-hunt paranoia that anyone who had ever publicly espoused progressive causes worried about potential accusations of guilt by association. Anyone who had signed a petition for a cause that had Communist support could be queried by an investigator searching through his past affiliations. Anonymous accusations flew back and forth, and the press—especially the tabloids and the gossip columnists led by Walter Winchell—often reported such accusations, not bothering to seek confirmation.

Scarcely any of my colleagues openly dared to criticize the Senate sub-committee's wild allegations, and that early period of congressional sleuthing was not one of which *The Times* could be proud. After much debate at the highest levels over what to do, Arthur Hays Sulzberger approved a policy directing staff members accused of having had Communist Party affiliations to answer questions about their past.

The publisher argued that since the First Amendment granted the right of freedom of the press, a responsibility was imposed on staffers to be thoroughly candid about themselves and any dubious associations they might be harboring. He and his assistants decided that any staffer called before the subcommittee must not take the Fifth Amendment to protect himself against self-incrimination. In addition, convincing assurances must be given to *The Times* that all past Communist affiliations had been completely severed. *The Times*, to its credit, did not insist—as other organizations did—that an employee reveal names of others he believed to be members of the party.

Catledge warned Atkinson that Markel demanded to know if I now was or had ever been a Communist. Luckily for me, Brooks, with his ingrained New England ethic, told him flatly that it was nobody's business, and he had no intention of asking me.

Brooks then called me into his office and explained the situation, which was the first I had heard about it. "You have a tough time ahead of you," he said. He told me Markel had assigned Sy Peck, who had recently admitted to being an ex-Communist, to see the Childress play and report back if anything in it was subversive.

"Stay strong," counseled Brooks. "I want you to know that if you are forced off the paper, I'm walking out with you."

I found the situation preposterous—though considering the madness of the period, I wasn't really that surprised. Grateful for Brooks's support, I assured him I was not at all reluctant to discuss privately with him my affiliations. Like him, I said, I was a New Deal liberal. I had signed a few of the numerous petitions that circulated around CCNY when I was a student there, had met Paul Robeson (later accused of having Communist ties) and, as a Bronx adolescent, had contributed a dollar to a fund in support of the Abraham Lincoln Brigade's fight against Franco's fascist forces in Spain.

But, as I explained to Brooks, I had never been a Communist, either in spirit or on paper. I said I hadn't even been tempted by campus recruiters promising that girls in the party practiced "free love." Brooks chuckled.

"I didn't ask you that question," he said, "and I never would. But since you've told me, it gives me what I need to refute Markel."

Brooks then wrote Markel one of the nastiest letters I'd ever read, calling him, among other things, a coward. He next informed Catledge that he would not stand for having me investigated. Catledge, who himself had no taste for the purging, said that as long as Eastland left me alone, so would the paper. His decision seemed vindicated when Peck reported he had found no trace of Communist propaganda in *Trouble in Mind.*

Brooks and Markel became sworn adversaries who didn't speak to one another for years, and it's amusing to note that in a roundabout way it was their enmity that brought Marilyn Monroe to *The Times* on a celebrated visit. The complex circumstances of her appearance at the paper took root on March 2, 1958, when Broadway paid tribute to Brooks with a surprise party at Sardi's. It was an unprecedented show of affection for a critic, by those upon whom he had passed judgment during the past thirty-five years.

Since it was all designed as a surprise for Brooks, Paula Strasberg, wife of Lee Strasberg, and one of the organizers of the celebration, asked me to inquire of Oriana Atkinson whether she would cooperate to make sure her husband got to the party without suspecting what was in store for him; they feared he might not show up if he knew.

"Who would be invited?" Oriana asked me. Just about everyone in the theater who matters, I told her, as well as members of the *Times* drama department, the publisher and other *Times* executives. "Okay with me," Oriana acquiesced, "but there is one condition: They can invite anyone they want to—anyone but Lester Markel."

I don't think there ever was a theater party like it. Everyone who was invited showed up: Laurence Olivier, Katharine Cornell, Tennessee Williams, Thornton Wilder, Richard Rodgers, Oscar Hammerstein and Marilyn Monroe, to name just a few of the 130 guests who came to toast Brooks. The entire *Times* drama department was there, along with Turner Catledge and Iphigene Sulzberger (her husband was ill). Hammerstein presided over the entertainment, which included a duet for Brooks, written by Howard Dietz and Arthur Schwartz, and adoringly sung by Helen Hayes and Mary Martin.

Brooks, who had believed he was on his way to an anniversary party for the Strasbergs, was stunned when he entered Sardi's to a standing ovation. I had never before seen him lower his gentlemanly guard and allow himself to be so emotionally moved. His face reddened and for a moment I thought he might become tearful. Later he told me he had "one quick, painful thought." He had said to himself, "There isn't one person in this room I haven't panned, one time or another."

Murray Schumach wrote the story for *The Times*, and the drama department composed a mock front page of the Sunday Drama Section. Each of us wrote a piece about Brooks, and Al Hirschfeld caricatured him smiling mysteriously at his desk, pencil in hand, with a devil and an angel (each with Brooks's features) hovering over him.

When Markel saw Murray's article the next morning, he was enraged. He liked to think he was loved by the theater and couldn't fathom why he had been excluded. He ordered Lewis Funke to his office to explain. I saw that Funke was quaking and ashen when he started for the eighth floor. He didn't want to tell Markel it was Oriana who had excluded him, for fear that would upset Brooks, so he placed the blame on Paula Strasberg. Funke told me that Markel swore, "That woman's daughter will never see print in the Sunday section again if I can help it." Paula's daughter, Susan Strasberg, was a promising actress who had starred on Broadway in *The Diary of Anne Frank* in 1955.

Markel couldn't completely fulfill his threat, in part because of the prominence of Lee Strasberg. But Susan, in the next several years, was in an undeniable slump. She had taken a few ill-chosen roles in Hollywood flops and had returned to Broadway in a play that was poorly received.

Mentions of her in the Sunday *Times* were meager, and Paula, finally realizing that her family had somehow landed on the wrong side of Markel, called Funke to ask if Markel bore Susan ill will. Funke told Paula that Markel believed it was her fault he had not been invited to the Atkinson gala, and had been upset with the Strasbergs ever since. Funke didn't bother mentioning it was he who had given Markel that impression.

Paula at once went about setting things right. She invited Markel to a small dinner at her home for Marilyn Monroe on September 28, 1959. Markel eagerly accepted, and found himself seated next to Monroe, who had been coached to flirt with him. At evening's end, he invited her to come and tour *The Times*.

The next day, I watched as Markel, with the screen goddess on his arm, strolled through the city room, smirking at the startled reporters and editors. She was particularly interested in the morgue, and Markel obligingly had the drawer containing her clippings rolled out.

Markel retired his rancor toward the Strasbergs—but unfortunately it was too late to rehabilitate Susan's career, which never lived up to its early promise.

MURRAY SCHUMACH, who had become our Hollywood correspondent not long after the Atkinson party, boldly challenged the movie studios' hypocritical stance that they did not buy scripts from blacklisted screenwriters suspected of having Communist ties. (In fact, they continued to buy their scripts from "fronts.")

"The producer," wrote Murray, "nearly always knows who the real writer is and often discusses rewrites with him in person." This pretense, Murray suggested, required a special kind of logic. "The studio, since it claims there is no blacklist, cannot admit it is refusing to use certain writers. That would be an admission that there is a blacklist. At the same time it dare not admit it is using writers who are on the 'nonexistent' blacklist."

Murray continued writing articles in that vein. One night he returned from a concert and found the word "Commie" spray-painted on his front door. He called the police who, he later told me, were unsympathetic. They suggested that Murray stop writing pro-Communist stories, and he responded, "Maybe I will. Maybe I'll start writing stories about how money is being paid to people by storekeepers on Sunset Boulevard, and who's doing the collecting." The cops, Murray told me, "kept quiet after that, and I never had another problem."

Murray told me nobody at the paper ever questioned his forthright approach. As for myself, I always appreciated the relative ease with which I eluded investigation at *The Times*. But this was not the case for other staffers when a month later, in December 1955, thirty-eight New York newspaper employees were called before the Eastland subcommittee, thirty of them from *The Times*. Another hearing was held the first week of January 1956, to which eighteen witnesses were summoned; fifteen were connected to *The Times*, only a few of them from the news department.

These numbers reinforced the perception that Senator Eastland and his hatchet man, J. G. Sourwine, the subcommittee's chief counsel and a rabid "Red hunter," had singled out *The Times* for scrutiny. Sulzberger now had to consider how the paper was going to deal with so many subpoenaed employees, especially since letters (often from southern locales) poured into the paper, condemning it as "Communist" for allowing suspected employees to keep their jobs. After wrestling with the issue, he somewhat eased his earlier policy, regarded by many staffers as ambiguous. He decided to judge each case on its own merits, rather than summarily firing those implicated by the subcommittee.

His main concern was whether Communists were in positions where, it might be perceived, their politics affected the impartial delivery of news. It was finally decreed that if a subpoenaed employee cooperated with *The Times*'s internal investigation, often regardless of whether he cooperated with the subcommittee, he would not be fired, though he might be switched to a less sensitive assignment.

Although Brooks and other high-ranking staffers believed an individual's political beliefs were personal, the publisher and his top aides were of the opinion that suspected employees had to come clean with the management "for *The Times*'s own protection."

On January 5, 1956, the paper published an editorial proposed by the publisher and written by Charles Merz that publicly attempted to clarify *The Times*'s revised position. It was still fuzzy in spots but on the whole resounded with more courage than most media companies showed.

"We would not knowingly employ a Communist Party member in the news or editorial departments . . . because we would not trust his ability to report the news objectively or to comment on it honestly," the editorial began. But continuing in a more defiant tone that gave heart not only to our own city room, but also to city rooms all over the country, it said:

"It is our own business to decide whom we shall employ and not employ. We do not propose to turn over that function to the Eastland subcommittee. Nor do we propose to permit the Eastland subcommittee, or any other agency outside this office, to determine in any way the policies of this newspaper. . . . It will continue to condemn discrimination, whether in the South or in the North. It will continue to defend civil liberties. It will continue to challenge the unbridled power of government authority. It will continue to enlist goodwill against prejudice and confidence against fear. . . . Long after segregation has lost its final battle in the South, long after all that was known as McCarthyism is a dim, unwelcome memory. . . . *The New York Times* will still be speaking for the men who make it, and only for the men who make it, and speaking, without fear or favor, the truth as it sees it."

Of the *Times* men subpoenaed, I had worked closely with three: Sy Peck (who checked my make-up of the Sunday drama pages), Alden Whitman (who had edited my copy when I was on rewrite) and Robert Shelton (a copy reader on the culture copy desk who edited some of my drama articles). All three testified on January 6, the day following publication of the *Times* editorial.

Alden told the subcommittee he had been active in the Communist Party from 1935 to 1948, and a member of the cell at the *Herald Tribune*, where he worked from 1943 to 1951. The cell, he said, had "perhaps half a dozen members." He further acknowledged he had run copy for Tass in 1949 and had once belonged to organizations listed by the subcommittee as Communist fronts, such as the National Committee for People's Rights and the New York Peace Committee. He also confessed to having written fifty articles under a pseudonym for the *Daily Worker*.

But Alden, even when threatened with contempt of Congress, refused to name names. "Were I to answer Mr. Sourwine's question," he told the subcommittee, "my feeling is that I would tend to the loss of my own self-respect and feelings of conscience in the matter." He said he had been forthright about his case with the management of *The Times*, and that they had not tried to influence his testimony, though he was reassigned from his post as head of a copy desk to a lower position "until this thing blew over."

Peck testified that he had been in the party from 1937 to 1949, but had never been a Communist while employed with *The Times*, where he started in 1952. He, too, refused to name names, declaring such a demand was beyond the committee's scope of jurisdiction. He did not "take the Fifth," he said, because he handled news copy for the paper, and the management had told him they could not condone such a move. *The Times*, he added, would judge his case "upon its merits as it progressed."

Robert Shelton's case was nothing less than Kafkaesque. When a committee aide delivered the original subpoenas to *The Times* on November 14, 1955, none of them bore Robert's name. One, however, was addressed to "*Willard* Shelton," the name of a columnist on the *Chicago Sun*. When the aide learned there was no Willard Shelton at *The Times*, he asked if there were any other Sheltons on the paper. When he was told there were a few and was given their names, the aide scribbled in ink "or Robert Shelton" on Willard's subpoena, and served it to Robert.

The committee had taken a wild guess, but Robert did, indeed, have a Communist past, which he had kept concealed. I learned several years later that he had confided his past Communist connection to Catledge and Sulzberger, who did not urge him to make it public. Robert told them he had supported Henry Wallace in the 1948 presidential election while a student at Northwestern University; this had led to his joining the Communist Party, which he left after graduation in 1950.

When he came to *The Times* as a copyboy in 1951, he drifted back into the party in a cell at the paper consisting of "three or four people." He told Catledge and Sulzberger that he had made "a final and irrevocable break" in the fall of 1952. His disclosure was good enough for them. They deemed him a "loyal American" and took no action against him for refusing to answer the subcommittee's questions.

He pleaded protection under the First Amendment's guarantees of freedom of speech, freedom of the press and freedom of association: "I would decline similarly if asked whether I was or had ever been a Democrat, Republican, Socialist, Jew, Catholic or Protestant, vegetarian, prohibitionist or sun-worshipper."

Meanwhile, *The Times*'s assertive editorial stand had elicited support from many newspapers across the country. "The whole of the American heritage cries out against this kind of congressional intrusion into the affairs of [the] press," declared the *Washington Post*. And among the smaller papers, the *Hartford Courant* noted: "This is not the first time that senators have tried to push newspapers around through investigations wrapped in the mantle of patriotism."

In light of intensifying public outrage over the subcommittee's smear campaign, I was taken aback—along with many of my *Times* colleagues—when Peck, Whitman and Shelton all were convicted of contempt of Congress. But they stayed in their jobs throughout a tortuous series of appeals.

Despite *The Times*'s forbearance, all three endured considerable personal anguish. Sy Peck's case was the first to be adjudicated. Found guilty of contempt on April 30, 1957, he was fined $500, received a suspended sentence of thirty days and was put on probation for a year.

While his appeal was pending, the Supreme Court announced a decision that directly affected his case; it overturned the conviction of John T. Watkins, a labor leader who—like Peck—had refused to name names before a congressional committee. The Watkins decision held that all questions posed by a committee had to be relevant to its specified purpose, and that—due to the "confusing breadth" and "nebulous" boundaries the committee claimed—it had no legal right to ask such questions. Peck, his case remanded to the lower court, was acquitted of all charges. He continued productively at *The Times* and eventually was promoted to culture editor.

Robert Shelton, less fortunate than Peck, had to battle his charges up to the Supreme Court. In the city room, Robert held forth to me and other colleagues about the reasons he had been unwilling to answer the committee's questions. If the government began to control who worked on newspapers, he said, it would invariably end up controlling newspaper content as well: "Am I a Communist? Am I not a Communist? It doesn't matter and they don't have a right to know. I am a newspaperman. So long as the paper is pleased with my work, that's what counts."

When his case first came up on June 18, 1960, before the Federal Court of Appeals, presided over by Warren E. Burger (the conservative later appointed to the Supreme Court by Nixon), Shelton stated in an affidavit: "This subcommittee is nudging the end of my copy pencil, it is peeking over my shoulder as I work. . . . If as a result of my being called here, I am put under mental pressure to change one word or a sentence in material that I edit, an abridgment of freedom of the press will have taken place."

Robert's plea failed to sway Burger, and that's when the case went to the Supreme Court. But even before his appeal, Robert, with my encouragement, was trying to take his mind off his legal problem with a new professional interest. He began reviewing folk music for the paper, frequenting the blossoming coffeehouses of Greenwich Village, and he later became best known for his landmark review on September 29, 1961, of a twenty-year-old musician he called "one of the most distinctive stylists to play in a Manhattan cabaret in months."

"His clothes may need a bit of tailoring," Robert wrote, "but when he works his guitar, harmonica or piano and composes new songs faster than he can remember them, there is no doubt that he is bursting at the seams with talent. . . . Mr. Dylan's voice is anything but pretty. He is consciously trying to recapture the rude beauty of a southern field hand musing in melody on his back porch. All the 'husk and bark' are left on his notes, and a searing intensity pervades his songs . . . it matters less where he has been than where he is going, and that would seem to be straight up." Robert befriended the young Bob Dylan and, under a pseudonym, wrote the liner notes for Dylan's first album.

Robert's appeal was heard before the Supreme Court on December 7, along with Alden Whitman's. Alden had traveled a similar route of convictions and appeals. His basic stance had been that the Eastland Committee had no right to ask him to inform on others about activities that were legal, such as membership in a political party.

In May 1962, the Supreme Court overturned both Robert Shelton's and Alden Whitman's convictions on grounds that the subcommittee had not specified the "subject under inquiry" during the initial hearings. Robert's other arguments did not go unheeded. Justice William O. Douglas wrote in his opinion that further indictments in these cases should be forbidden because they did, in fact, violate freedom of the press.

THE MCCARTHY ERA was a dark and scary period of my newspaper days. Though it has become, as Charles Merz predicted, a "dim, unwelcome memory," it still haunts those of us who lived through it. At a dinner party I attended nearly half a century later, Betty Comden, who with Adolph Green wrote such screenplays as *Singin' in the Rain*, recalled she had been summoned to the office of Louis B. Mayer's associate when she was working in Hollywood on *The Band Wagon* for Metro-Goldwyn-Mayer. Though she had not been named by any anti-Communist publications, she was asked, "Were you ever a member of the Communist Party?" Comden said, "No."

She told us at the dinner that she still suffered from guilt for answering the question, and said she wished she had had the courage to say it was none of anyone's business. At the time, however, she feared her refusal might result in throwing away a lifetime of accomplishment. She had come out of the Depression and, after working her way onto Broadway, had made it to Hollywood. She had never been a Communist, but it was the principle that had mattered and, she found, mattered still.

When I imagine what I would have done if I had been called before the Eastland Committee, I like to think I would have stood strong. In my heart I know I would not have named anyone. But I wonder if I would have had the strength to insist that the committee had no right to question me about my own political beliefs.

I believe I would have upheld the values of press freedom. If, however, I truly feared for the well-being of my family, would I have buckled? I'm grateful I never had to find out, and I've always felt indebted to Brooks Atkinson for sheltering me from that fate at *The Times*.

TWENTY-TWO

IN 1956, there were as yet no guards on duty in the lobby of the *Times* building and anyone could walk into the drama department. July and August were quiet months on Broadway, and Brooks's secretary Clara Rotter and I were the only ones in the department at noon on August 10.

Clara was treasured by Brooks, who sought her wisdom when he needed down-to-earth advice. Although she weighed no more than ninety pounds even after being cured of tuberculosis, she was a determined barrier to her boss. No one could gain access to Brooks's private cubicle without her approval. Her importance was acknowledged by the entire theater world and, when Broadway press agents took the required exam for acceptance into their union, a key question was, "Who is Clara Rotter?"

Brooks was away on his annual European playgoing pilgrimage, Funke and Zolotow were on vacation, and Calta was out on a story. All was peaceful—until an agitated man in his mid-thirties bounded in.

The day was a scorcher and the visitor's wavy, black hair was damp with perspiration. He looked as harassed as Hamlet, who—I was to discover later—was his literary hero. "Where's Mr. Atkinson?" he barked. "I must see Mr. Atkinson right away." His manner was almost menacing and Clara said, shakily, "He's not here!" I rose to stand between them. "Who are you and what do you want?" I demanded, concerned he might be a crazed actor bent on revenge for a panning by Brooks.

"I'm Joseph Papp, head of the Shakespeare Workshop, and I need help."

I was relieved to recognize his name. The drama pages had run a few minor but positive items about his neophyte workshop and his determination to enlighten all of New York through free performances of Shakespeare. But I knew nothing else about him. I told him who I was and tried to calm him, explaining that Atkinson was in London for another week.

He was crestfallen. It was urgent, he said, that his free production of *The Taming of the Shrew* at the East River Amphitheater be reviewed that very night. "Since Mr. Atkinson isn't available," he said, "you must review us!"

"There's no way I can do that," I said. "The department is operating with a skeleton staff, and I have to get out the Sunday Drama Section. When Mr. Atkinson gets back, I'll try to persuade him to go."

"I can't wait," he countered. "Since my company charges no admission, we've run out of money. Unless we get some publicity in *The Times* that results in public contributions, we'll have to close in two days. I'm not asking you for a good review, I'll take my chances on that. Just please come and see the show. It's a question of life or death for our company."

Papp fervently expounded his goal of bringing the masses into the theater, members of the working class who had never seen Shakespeare performed. He was convinced they'd be entranced by Shakespeare's realistic characters, lusty dialogue, universal themes—and action. His actors were not paid, he said, but he owed money for rental of costumes and equipment and, if he failed to erase his debts immediately, his season would come to an abrupt end. I admired his fervor, but I had a pile of work on my desk and, that evening, I had planned to take Barbara to dinner and a Broadway play.

I didn't know I was dealing with a man who would become legendary for refusing to take "no" for an answer. "Well," said Papp, "I'm going to camp here until you decide to come tonight. You'll have to call the police to remove me." I tried to steer him gently to the door, but he sat down on the floor. "No," he said. "I'm desperate." I agreed to show up that night if he'd leave now and let me finish my work.

After he left, I looked up the few small items about Papp in the morgue: He had founded the Shakespeare Workshop in 1954, and initially based his productions in the Emmanuel Presbyterian Church on the Lower East Side. In a cramped space that had served as a Sunday-school classroom since 1873 and was substandard even for Off Broadway, Papp produced *Much Ado About Nothing, As You Like It, Macbeth, Two Gentlemen of Verona* and *Romeo and Juliet*. Despite free admission, audiences were slim and the productions received little notice in the press.

In 1956, Robert Moses, one of whose many titles was commissioner of parks and who was a lover of Shakespeare, had granted Papp free use of the East River Amphitheater, near the entry to the Manhattan Bridge and at the edge of a working-class housing project, for a summer Shakespeare Festival.

Obsessed with Shakespeare, Papp peppered his conversation with quotations from the plays and sonnets. He refused to allow American actors to feign English accents, which he believed would alienate his unsophisticated audiences. Challenging the purists, he fought to present the Bard as a contemporary writer on universal themes with his speeches delivered in contemporary cadence.

Barbara was a good sport about the change in plans. The sky looked threatening when we arrived at the amphitheater. "I hope it doesn't rain," I muttered, "because I'm not coming back again tomorrow night."

Papp's production of *The Taming of the Shrew* began against the backdrop of the East River—tooting tugboats, cars rumbling over the bridge—and there were flashes of heat lightning. My attention was drawn immediately to the audience. I had never sat among such an ethnically diverse theater crowd, nor one in which so many children were seated side by side with the elderly. Puerto Rican and Italian families of the Lower East Side, not normally patrons of Shakespeare revivals on Broadway, roared with laughter at the antics of Colleen Dewhurst's Katharine and Jack Cannon's Petruchio.

Thoroughly captivated by the performance, the audience responded with the same robust spirit as fans in the pit were known to have reacted in Shakespeare's own time. As I watched the play, I also kept an eye on the crowd, and before the first scene ended I knew Papp had created something to marvel at.

Dewhurst, in her first major role, was a plucky and lovely Kate, already beaming the star quality soon to make her one of America's foremost actresses. At 9:45, as the first act was ending and Petruchio had just finished giving Kate a sound trouncing, it began to thunder. The 1,800 spectators were leaning raptly forward on tiers of wooden benches.

And then it started to pour. Papp announced over the loudspeaker that the show had to be halted, amid exclamations of dismay in a blending of dialects that could be heard only on the Lower East Side. Many of the disappointed shouts came from children.

Barbara and I went up onto the stage to congratulate the cast of forty-five, who gathered around Papp, getting drenched, as were we. "It was terrific," I told Papp. "I guess I'll have to come back another night to review it."

"It'll be too late," he said. "Can't you write something for tomorrow's edition? Did you hear their laughter? Do you realize this is the first time most of them have ever seen live theater? Is this something worth doing or not?"

As Barbara and I headed for a taxi, we agreed it was impossible not to be impressed with this brash, quixotic and all but penniless impresario who insisted that free Shakespeare was the burning social and cultural issue of our time.

Impulsively, I decided to go back to the office and write a review of the first act. Appraising a partial performance was unconventional, to say the least, but I had earlier reserved space in the paper for a review. I now somehow felt obliged to help save the show—not so much for Papp but for the new crop of theatergoers blossoming on the Lower East Side.

Under the headline "Rained Out," I lauded the actors and wrote that if ever an audience was with a play, this one was. Toward the end of the review, I explained that the company needed to raise $750 immediately or it would be forced to close, forgoing its last performances and canceling its next scheduled production, *Twelfth Night*. "It seems a shame," I added, "that a project evidently bringing so much joy to so many people should be permitted to die a-borning."

The next morning I received a phone call from Herman Levin, now the abundantly prosperous producer of *My Fair Lady*. Having grown up on the Lower East Side himself, he said he could visualize the audience and wanted to help. I told him how to reach Papp, whom he had never met, and he sent a check that day for the $750, thereby saving the remainder of the Shakespeare Festival's season.

Moreover, the interest of regular theatergoers, who rarely ventured downtown, was piqued, and they began arriving at the amphitheater, some in chauffeur-driven cars, to queue at the entrance alongside laborers and their children.

When Brooks returned from London, where he had read my review, he asked me if the show was truly as good as I had represented it. I urged him to go downtown to see for himself, and I was relieved when he wrote a two-column Sunday article, in which he described the production as "one of the pleasantest episodes in the outdoor nightlife of New York during the summer." And when he credited my review for having drawn Levin's last-minute reprieve, I was filled with pride.

The unequivocal endorsement of the country's most respected theater critic gave Papp the boost he had craved. First-string critics from other publications who rarely ventured Off Broadway flocked to the hard benches of the amphitheater and contributions from uptowners flowed in.

I saw Papp smile for the first time when he visited the drama department to thank Brooks and me. Brooks, who was occupied with his upcoming Sunday article, suggested I take Joe down to Sardi's for a drink.

Papp gradually became a stimulating and entertaining presence in my life, but our relationship had its ups and downs. Not all his experimental productions clicked and, if I now and then wrote a negative review, I could expect an angry phone call, followed by an extended period of sulky silence.

This was the pitfall, of course, in establishing even casual friendships with people you wrote about, but I was drawn to creative talents. And I was vigilant about not allowing any relationship to influence my reviews. I faced that challenge for the first time in December when I reviewed *Titus Andronicus* in Papp's winter quarters at the downtown church. Noting that the play was produced under the auspices of the same group that had given us the stylish production of *The Taming of the Shrew* the previous summer, I wrote, "It is possible to forgive them their present wastefulness."

The unwritten code at *The Times*, as previously noted, decreed that not a word of a critic's copy could be changed without the critic's approval, since even a slight revision might throw the review off balance. But the copy editor felt my review was worded so strongly that it had to be toned down. The next day, I complained to Brooks, who complained to Turner Catledge. It was the last time a review of mine was altered without my permission.

When Papp called to complain about a poor notice, he invariably told me I had completely misunderstood the production's intent, and I'd ask whether he wanted me to give readers pabulum or the truth as I saw it. The only way I could end his diatribe was to hang up on him. But the rebukes he pelted me with were mild compared with his public disparagement of Walter Kerr of the *Herald Tribune*, who reigned in the same high-powered critical league as Brooks.

Papp not only denounced Kerr for panning one of his productions, but went so far as to bar him from his theater. I told Papp it was the most idiotic move he had ever made, and reminded him of what had happened when the Shuberts barred Alexander Woollcott. I suggested he apologize. He said he didn't regret barring Kerr, nastily adding that Kerr shouldn't be allowed into any theater that presented serious work. But as I expected, Papp's impulsive edict was soon revoked.

Over the next few years, Papp's professional fortunes fluctuated. Almost predictably, he would reach the end of his financial shoestring and threaten to close his season earlier than planned. He would phone me and I would mention his financial needs in my column. A day or two later, just as predictably, I would find myself writing that he had obtained the sought-after funding and could continue the run—sometimes even extending it. His company was always on the edge of collapse and always miraculously rescued at the last minute.

With the success of his first summer festival, Papp became single-minded about planting Shakespearean seeds across the metropolitan area. The Shakespeare Workshop began performing in public schools, and Papp constructed a Mobile Theater that, while unwieldy, could be driven from park to park and set up as a stage.

In 1957, he obtained a permit from the Parks Department to present three plays from his Mobile Theater in Central Park, prior to a tour of the outer boroughs. The tour was canceled due to various logistical obstacles, and Papp's Mobile Theater remained parked near Central Park's Belvedere Lake, where his company continued to perform.

Concurrently, Papp began pressuring Robert Moses to build a permanent theater in Central Park, and lobbied politicians for city funding. Moses, already rankled that Papp had essentially staked a squatter's claim in the park for the summer, denied his request, suggesting he instead move back to the East River Amphitheater, and this time charge admission to offset his mounting costs.

A muted battle—one that I frequently reported on—persisted between

Moses and Papp throughout 1958, with Papp proving as obstinate as Moses. The more he pushed Moses for city money and a home in Central Park, the greater did the commissioner resist, determined to crush Papp once and for all.

Moses tried at first to outfox Papp through what he perceived to be the producer's most exploitable weakness—his unyielding determination to maintain a free admission policy to Shakespeare in the park. Thus, in 1959, Moses proclaimed that if Papp wanted an operating permit he would have to sign a standard Parks Department concession contract setting aside ten percent of his gross receipts to help pay maintenance and landscaping costs incurred by the Festival's damage to the lawn.

But of course, since Papp charged no admission, there were no gross receipts. By trying to force Papp to charge admission under the terms of a contract, Moses believed his adversary would have to abandon Central Park. But Papp loudly protested the arbitrary ruling to City Hall and the press, determined to fight Moses to a standstill. The fencing match became front-page news and dominated my beat that spring.

No one challenging Moses until then had ever had a hope of winning—let alone a struggling producer relatively unknown outside of theater circles. The parks commissioner, still wielding as much power as when he had told me about his plan to build the Major Deegan Expressway in the Bronx, was accustomed to getting his way, whether by force or manipulation.

But Brooks and I agreed Moses was now taking on a young, vigorous, worthy opponent, who was not unlike a formerly young, vigorous Robert Moses. I checked with each of them from time to time so I could alert *Times* readers to what had become a David–Goliath battle. Newspaper editorials universally supported Papp. The *Post*, for example, sarcastically observed, "We assume that as in other great decisions, Mr. Moses reached this one after an extended consultation with himself." And the *Herald Tribune* noted that "Fiorello La Guardia once said: 'When I make a mistake, it's a beaut.' The same thing goes, we think, for Bob Moses."

New Yorkers were outraged that so fresh and imaginative a cultural project might have to be abandoned. Some sent bags of grass seed to Moses's office after he made an issue over the cost of repairing the lawn. As public sentiment continued to surge, Moses unleashed yet another attack that he hoped would finally finish off Papp. He reminded the press that Papp had taken the Fifth Amendment twelve times before the House Un-American Activities Committee a year earlier. Moses sent me an anonymous letter he claimed to have received from a former member of the Shakespeare Festival.

"It is strange," the letter read, "that [Papp] expects even more cooperation with government when it is a matter of record that he was unwilling to cooperate with government when it attempted to investigate Communist subversion and penetration into the theater."

A card-carrying Communist since the early 1940s, Papp told me he had left the party in the early 1950s, when his wife convinced him that his misguided politics placed their family in jeopardy. He did not consider himself a subversive or a radical, but rather an idealist who wanted to make the world a better place to live in.

It was when Papp first became interested in a theater career that he shortened his family name, Papirofsky. His father was a trunk maker and his mother was a garment worker, both Eastern European Jewish immigrants. He had empathized with the downtrodden since his boyhood in Brooklyn when he helped his parents make ends meet by plucking chickens, shining shoes and selling peanuts. During the Depression, his struggling parents were several times dispossessed, forced to scoop up their children and meager belongings and search for new lodgings, sometimes at nightfall. His childhood dream was to live in a house furnished with lamps, rather than naked lightbulbs.

The FBI tracked Papp for a number of years before he was subpoenaed by the House Un-American Activities Committee. He refused to name names, and it was true he pleaded the Fifth a dozen times. He was promptly fired from his new day job as a stage manager at CBS. With the backing of the Radio and Television Directors Guild, however, he appealed and was reinstated. Having proved his point, he quit CBS a few months later to devote himself fully to his Shakespeare Festival.

Moses's resurrection of Papp's Communist past backfired. In a statement Papp sent me for publication, he said he was "amazed that the commissioner would stoop to this kind of tactic," noting that Moses must have felt desperate to "resort to character assassination in order to answer his critics."

Even Mayor Wagner derided Moses for circulating the unsigned letter. Clare Baldwin, assistant superintendent of schools, said he intended to go ahead with plans for Papp to present Shakespeare in the public schools the following fall. "As far as I know," Baldwin said, "Shakespeare was never a Communist. I suppose if he were alive today someone might call him that."

In the end, it seemed the conflict was more about personality than policy. Before the battle, Moses had been, after all, an ardent supporter of art in the parks and had himself paved the way for Papp's first season at the East River

Amphitheater. Recognizing the paradox, Mayor Wagner gathered a group of city administrators and theater notables to discuss options that might resolve the dilemma (while allowing Moses to save face).

Since the fundamental concept of free Shakespeare had now drawn wide support, some city officials offered a bold idea: If Papp were replaced as the head of the Festival, Moses would likely be inclined to compromise. Murmurs of support followed, and it was suggested that the replacement be Robert Whitehead, the highly respected producer of such Broadway hits as *The Member of the Wedding* and *Bus Stop* (and later *The Visit*, *A Man for All Seasons* and *The Prime of Miss Jean Brodie*).

Whitehead promptly quashed the idea. For free Shakespeare to succeed, he said, the producer had to be slightly insane and completely impassioned and Papp was the only man he knew who fit that description. If the city wanted free Shakespeare, it needed Papp. If it rejected Papp, it was rejecting free Shakespeare. Everyone present recognized the validity of Whitehead's statement, and City Hall support for Papp was assured. There was one catch: The all-powerful Moses refused to cooperate.

On May 18, the Shakespeare Workshop sued Moses to compel him to issue a permit. On June 2, the case was heard by the State Supreme Court, which said that it was "most sympathetic to those who feel that the Shakespeare Festival has been a bright constellation in New York City's cultural firmament," but held it was "powerless to substitute [its] own views for those of the commissioner."

When I called Papp for comment, he shrugged off his defeat. He said he would appeal at once and, meanwhile, begin focusing on which plays he might yet have time to produce during a shortened season. He continued to solicit contributions for the Festival, as though victory were a matter of course and the court proceedings nothing more than a temporary nuisance.

On June 17, the Appellate Court returned a unanimous verdict in favor of the Festival. "In no aspect of the case," the court ruled, "do we perceive a rational basis for [Moses'] insistence upon an admission charge contrary to the wishes, policy and purposes of the petitioner. No useful purpose is served by the requirement that petitioner make an admission charge and retain 90 percent thereof when petitioner desires no part of it. Such a requirement incident to the issuance of a park permit is clearly arbitrary, capricious and unreasonable."

Papp, it was further decided, should reimburse the Parks Department for any damage to the lawn, but did not have to obtain the money through ticket sales. At long last, the Festival got under way on August 3 with *Julius*

Caesar. Some fifteen hundred people were already in line for the resumption of Central Park performances.

Rather than gloat over his victory, Papp was clever enough to appease Moses, praising his parks leadership and enabling him to save face. Before long, Moses offered to help Papp obtain $20,000 from the city. Later that summer, Moses pushed through a $250,000 plan to build a permanent home for free Shakespeare in Central Park, a vast amphitheater later named in honor of George T. Delacorte, its principal private donor.

Papp told me weeks later that his battle with Moses had been the best thing that ever happened to him. He said that everyone in New York now knew about the Shakespeare Festival and the name of its creator. Sponsors came to him from all over, and although he was still beset by periodic financial headaches, fund-raising was no longer the overwhelming problem it had once been. Moreover, free Shakespeare had now become a fixture of the city's landscape, and belonged to all New Yorkers.

My friendship with Papp endured. I had watched him evolve as one of the most visionary and controversial personalities in the history of the theater, his obstinacy inseparable from his genius. Reacting against what he called "that old whore Broadway," he helped keep theater on the cutting edge of artistic development and social commentary.

At the renovated Astor Library on lower Manhattan's Lafayette Street, where he later founded the year-round Public Theater, he introduced such landmark offerings as *Hair, That Championship Season* and—most notably and profitably—*A Chorus Line*. Throughout his career, he remained as true to his ideals and as tenacious in pursuit of them as when he first bullied me into reviewing *The Taming of the Shrew* in the glorious theater season of 1956.

Several months after Papp died in October 1991, the New York Shakespeare Festival (as Joe Papp's offspring was by then called) honored his memory in a theaterwide salute, "Wednesday in the Park for Joe." Joe's widow, Gail, asked Barbara to write about him for the program.

"Joe was too honest to court popularity," Barbara wrote. "He always knew when he was taking a risk and he had his share of critical failures. And when a failure was recorded in terms that Joe felt was unfair, he flew into battle yet again. He banned critics from his theater. He wrote blistering letters to their editors. He telephoned the critics themselves to give them a piece of his mind. When he thought he was right and you disagreed with him, he was worse than impossible. That's how visionaries are...."

"Joe's final struggle, of course, was with cancer and it was his bravest. He was distraught with grief over his son's death from AIDS and for a time he lost the heart to fight his own illness. But he found his will, and once again resolved to do battle.

"He compared himself, in a diary entry, with 'a bird that lay stunned on the porch after trying to pass through what it imagined was open space and finding instead a hard-surfaced transparent glass, dropping to the deck, bewildered, almost dead of utter surprise . . .'

"When I visited Joe in the hospital a few weeks before his death, I found him heavily medicated, his speech slurred. His cancer was out of control. But his eyes were alive with spirit and humor.

"His specialist told me that Joe was a phenomenon of mental acuity. Despite all the drugs and pain, Joe had been punning. Punning, the doctor said, required a nimbleness of mind that was simply incompatible with the sort of condition Joe was in. The doctor was awed by a mind that, not withstanding profound medication, could stay so brilliantly alert.

"'Oh, just point to a tree, to a hummingbird fluttering in a mammoth bush,' Joe wrote shortly before his death. 'Gail's joy in the tiny creature . . . and my happiness for the moment is complete. After that I'll take up graver matters.'"

TWENTY-THREE

HAVING PERHAPS CAUGHT FIRE from Joe Papp's passionate embrace of free Shakespeare, the 1955–1956 season went on to break new ground in theater history. Broadway began reviving from McCarthy-era doldrums marked by social conformity. While the flurry of experimentation continued Off Broadway, a number of convention-flouting productions opened on Broadway—most of them originating abroad, and challenging uptown audiences to take their theater seriously:

Jean Giradoux's antiwar satire *Tiger at the Gates*; Jean Anouilh's *The Lark*, his poetic reexamination of Joan of Arc; Enid Bagnold's acerbic comedy of English manners *The Chalk Garden*, and a pair of hit plays by contemporary Americans—*The Diary of Anne Frank*, by Frances Goodrich and Albert Hackett, and *The Matchmaker*, by Thornton Wilder (and all of this followed within two years by one of Broadway's most memorable satirical dramas, starring Alfred Lunt and Lynn Fontanne, Friedrich Dürrenmatt's *The Visit*, the shocking indictment of the greed and corruptibility of a representative society). And in the persevering musical category, *My Fair Lady* acquired almost instantly the status of legend.

Of the season's straight plays were two that I thought stretched the limits of theatrical imagination fathoms beyond anything I had yet encountered: Samuel Beckett's *Waiting for Godot* and Eugene O'Neill's *Long Day's Journey Into Night*.

European audiences had already saluted each of these plays as masterpieces—O'Neill's autobiographical tragedy when it had its première some months earlier in Stockholm, and Beckett's existential tragicomedy already seen in Paris, Rome, Frankfurt, Helsinki and London. O'Neill's deceptively "naturalistic" portrait of a doomed family left theatergoers emotionally drained, while Beckett's haunted and hollow characters aroused hot debate about the play's meaning. "Pity the critic who seeks a chink in its armor, for it is all chink," read a typical review from an English publication. "It has no plot, no denouement, no beginning, no middle and no end." The reviewer then went on to praise it glowingly.

Jean Anouilh proclaimed *Waiting for Godot* as the most significant event in French theater in a quarter-century. Thornton Wilder saw it five times in Europe and spent impassioned hours discussing its nuances with the producer, Michael Myerberg, who brought it to Broadway on April 19. And Tennessee Williams, calling it one of the greatest plays of modern times, invested his own money in the American production.

Myerberg was one of the most daring and intellectual of Broadway producers, and it didn't surprise me that he was willing to gamble on so unconventional a play. But it did surprise me that he decided to preview the play in Miami, where sixty percent of the opening-night audience walked out after the first act. When I interviewed Myerberg, he told me he had mistakenly tried to slant the Florida production toward wide popular appeal—and had learned his lesson. In New York, he would target a purely "thinking audience," and pray there would be seventy thousand "curious minds" in the city—the number necessary to make the production a paying proposition.

"Every line in the play is meaningful. There are wheels within wheels within wheels—meanings within meanings within meanings," said Myerberg, following his discussions with Thornton Wilder, whom he admired and trusted. Myerberg's Broadway production of Wilder's comedy *The Skin of Our Teeth*, which tried to find meaning in humanity's ability to survive calamities and had won a Pulitzer Prize in 1942, had been for its time as un-orthodox as *Waiting for Godot*.

Nobody, however, seemed to agree on the meanings within meanings, and the author declined to offer any clues. "The play means all things to all people," Myerberg said he had concluded. "We're all waiting for Godot, for something to give our own lives meaning and importance. Maybe if you don't spell out the meaning too clearly, you're better off." The reason play-goers in Florida had reacted negatively, Myerberg believed, was because of the emptiness of their own lives as personified on stage by the two tramps. "Their lives have no meaning, no purpose, despite wealth and position, and they, too, are waiting for Godot," concluded Myerberg.

But New York audiences loved the production, and its run was extended twice. The triumph of *Waiting for Godot* fueled my hope that Broadway could thrive economically on yeasty ideas as well as confectionery.

It was seven months later—on November 7—that O'Neill's reputation as America's greatest playwright was finally reestablished with the Broad-way opening of *Long Day's Journey Into Night*. That production, starring Fredric March, Florence Eldridge and Jason Robards, marked the begin-ning of Barbara's and my enduring fascination with O'Neill's life and artis-tic vision.

O'Neill, reclusive during much of his life, had given few interviews, and the family secrets revealed in *Long Day's Journey*—particularly his mother's drug addiction and his father's miserliness—added a shocking realism to the play's tragic outlook. *Long Day's Journey* became the dramatic sensation of the 1956 theater season, and won for O'Neill posthumously his fourth Pulitzer Prize. Barbara and I had never before experienced such an emo-tionally charged opening night. Not since Arthur Miller's *Death of a Sales-man* in 1949 had I left a theater feeling so heartbroken.

To my surprise, Wolcott Gibbs, still reviewing for *The New Yorker* and seated a couple of rows in front of me, was the sole member of the audience who seemed unresponsive to the tragic truths being unraveled on stage. He hadn't been entirely sober when he arrived at the theater and, during the sec-ond of the play's four acts, he twisted in his aisle seat and faced toward the back of the auditorium. The moment the act ended, he left the theater and no review appeared in his magazine that week. When his review, somewhat muddled, did run a week later, I asked him why he had left so abruptly. The play "cut too close," he said.

When the curtain fell after nearly four hours, there was a prolonged, awed silence. With the theater absolutely still for almost a minute, the exhausted actors reappeared for their bows. The playgoers rose to their feet, rocking the theater with thunderous applause. They started to surge down the aisles toward the stage apron, in an instinctive attempt to make contact with the cast that had so emotionally shaken them.

Brooks, in *The Times*, said it for us all: "*Long Day's Journey Into Night* is like a Dostoevsky novel in which Strindberg had written the dialogue. For this saga of the damned is horrifying and devastating in a classical tradition." He concluded that the play "restores the drama to literature and the theater to art."

As America's only dramatist to win the Nobel Prize, O'Neill, during the 1920s and 1930s, had staggered both critics and audiences with his ceaseless flow of experimental dramas. Ill health forced him into seclusion in the late 1930s, when he wrote his final autobiographical masterpieces—*The Iceman Cometh, Long Day's Journey Into Night* and *A Moon for the Misbegotten*. Although suffering from a debilitating neurological disorder, he returned to Broadway in 1946 with a production of *The Iceman Cometh*.

That happened to be the year Barbara and I were married, and shortly after returning from our honeymoon, we welcomed the news about the scheduled première on October 9. Our shared admiration for O'Neill had never flagged and, while we were both too young to have seen an original O'Neill production, we had faithfully read all the published plays. Undaunted upon learning that *The Iceman Cometh* would run five hours (not including an hour's break for dinner), I hurried to the Martin Beck Theater box office and splurged. It was the first time I had ever bought orchestra seats. Barbara and I were overwhelmed by the play, unable to absorb all its tragic layers in one viewing. (I later realized the production did not do the play justice, being seriously flawed in both casting and direction.)

Now, on May 8, 1956, three years after O'Neill's death, *The Iceman Cometh* was being revived Off Broadway, at Circle in the Square, an intimate space in Greenwich Village where the audience was ranged on three sides of the open stage. The director was José Quintero, who had breathed new life into Tennessee Williams's *Summer and Smoke* two years earlier. For Barbara and me, the revival of *The Iceman Cometh* sparked a chain of events that was to dominate the next six years of our lives.

I was unable to attend the afternoon opening, because I was working against deadline to close the Sunday Drama Section. When Brooks finally appeared in the composing room to check the proofs of the review he had just written, I asked him about the production. "There's an actor playing Hickey named Jason Robards, Jr.," he said, "and he's pure gold."

When Barbara and I saw the play several days later, I thought Robards's performance was the best I had witnessed by an American actor—from the moment he sailed jauntily onstage, straw-hatted, flashily dressed, eyes gleaming satanically, croaking the line: "And another little drink won't do us any harm!" For me, his portrayal was even more of a tour de force than Brando's atavistic performance in *A Streetcar Named Desire*, and I felt saddened that O'Neill hadn't lived to see what Robards had so passionately wrought.

A few months later, when Robards made his Broadway debut in *Long Day's Journey Into Night*, he gave a magisterial performance as Jamie Tyrone, the character who stood for O'Neill's older brother—and I thought it even surpassed the magnificence of his Hickey. I wanted to be the first to interview him following his performance, so I called him the next day to suggest we meet at Sardi's for lunch. When he walked in, he appeared shorter than his six feet because of a slouch, which he told me was due to his youthful addiction to baseball and the catcher's stance he had to assume.

He was a spare man with a long, craggily handsome face that ended in a jutting chin. His hazel eyes were deep set and tired and his dark hair, flecked with gray, made him look weathered beyond his thirty-four years. When groping for a phrase during the interview, he snapped his fingers nervously and chuckled self-consciously, mannerisms he had incorporated into Hickey's character and that now were part of Jamie's persona.

Robards dwelt on the remarkable parallels between his own life and the character he was playing. Like Jamie, he was the son of a once famous actor. Also like Jamie, he had had his battles with alcohol (a habit he eventually kicked). O'Neill, of course, knew all about destructive drinking and filled his plays with references to whiskey.

"Jamie is the kind of drunk I understand," Robards told me. "He's a two-purpose drunk—the kind who, when he really wants to say something, says it and then covers up as a drunk. He switches back and forth. That's the way I used to drink ... when living started getting complicated."

Robards was born in Chicago in 1922, and moved to Hollywood with his father when he was five after his parents divorced. Within a few years, his father's career was in a slump, and Robards acquired a distaste for the fickleness and phoniness of Hollywood. Looking to get as far away from it as he could, he joined the Navy in 1940 and served on a ship that was sunk near Guadalcanal. Once discharged, he followed what he called an "inward drive" to be an actor. His father encouraged him to attend the American Academy of Dramatic Art. "Don't hang around Hollywood," his father advised. "Go to New York, because this town will kill you. This is a place where you sit on your duff doing westerns for seven years."

When Robards heard that Quintero was casting for *Iceman*, Robards auditioned and got the part after one reading. I wanted to know why he was so attracted to Hickey. "When Hickey comes on in the fourth act," he explained, "and he starts by saying, 'Well, well, how is everybody doing?' nobody answers and he goes into a long, guilt-ridden speech. I instinctively understood him. Like Hickey, we all want approval, especially as actors. I'm not particularly theoretical or brainy, but this speech struck something. The need for approval. I don't say I'm as guilt ridden as Hickey is, but it started things going inside me."

This was but the first time that Robards helped illuminate for me the complexities of O'Neill's characters. In one interpretation after another, he was spiritually attuned to O'Neill's tragic vision, and uncannily connected with the tormented souls of O'Neill's creative imagination. Over the next forty-five years, Barbara and I spent many hours with Jason, analyzing and reanalyzing the nuances of O'Neill's major characters.

Because of the obvious autobiographical derivation of *Long Day's Journey Into Night*—and because, surprisingly, there had never been a full-scale biography of O'Neill—several publishers thought the time had come to put such a work into production. Cass Canfield, the chairman of the venerable publishing firm of Harper & Brothers, approached his friend Brooks Atkinson about the project. Brooks agreed the book should be done, but he told Canfield, "It's too enormous a job for a man in his sixties." Instead, Brooks proposed Barbara and me, assuring Canfield that O'Neill was "a subject right up their alley."

Brooks then pitched the idea to me, explaining that under *Times* rules I would not be allowed a leave of absence, but with Barbara as my collaborator we could hope to achieve the project. He volunteered to be our behind-the-scenes advisor.

Barbara and I barely thought twice. What an opportunity—to write the original biography of a great artist, exploring primary sources never tapped before. Brooks thought we would be paid the same advance he'd been offered—$15,000, a sizable sum for that day. But Harper, understandably not having the same faith in us, reduced the amount. In our innocence, we signed the contract for $5,000.

We did manage to persuade our editor at Harper, Simon Michael Bessie, to let us limit the scope of the book to O'Neill's first forty years, starting with the early acting career of O'Neill's father, James, and concluding with O'Neill's debut in 1920 as a Broadway playwright with *Beyond the Horizon*. We would thus avoid becoming embroiled with his widow, Carlotta. Brooks warned us she would not welcome being written about. She and O'Neill had married in 1929, and their final years had been stormy. Often overbearing, she was the possessive caretaker of his estate and, although we were sticking to O'Neill's early career, she steadfastly refused to allow access to his letters and other documents in the O'Neill collection at the Yale University Library.

Inexperienced as we were, we blithely estimated it would take only two years to complete our planned first half of O'Neill's life. But gradually, Carlotta began to loosen up—mainly at Brooks's urging—and allowed us partial glimpses into the O'Neill archives and also into her own recollections of her life with O'Neill.

WE REALIZED WE HAD to finish our research through the end of O'Neill's life, if we wanted to understand the first half. Our two years gradually stretched into five and a half, and we found ourselves embarked on a full-scale biography. Our social life ground to a halt. Every surface of our apartment was piled high with research documents, notes and reference books. Most disconcerting of all, we began to run out of money for travel and research. Harper, acknowledging that the project was no longer a mere half a life, advanced us an additional $10,000. But it wasn't enough.

Since we no longer had the time to earn extra money writing freelance articles, we were obliged to borrow. As we began going into serious debt, Berrie felt sorry for us. Although Barbara's pride forbade her from asking her mother for help, he insisted on trying to rescue us—and we gratefully accepted a loan of $15,000. By the time we finished the manuscript, our total debt amounted to $30,000.

Often, after completing my assignments at *The Times*, I would go home, nap for an hour, eat dinner, then work with Barbara on the biography until three A.M. My energy for the project seemed inexhaustible. I'd awake at six A.M. to put in a few hours writing before going to *The Times*.

While I was at the paper, Barbara researched, interviewed and wrote. Since my parents were now retired, they helped look after Michael and Peter, spending almost as much time with the children as Barbara and I did. We never could have written the book without their help, and ultimately dedicated it to them.

By this time, we had moved to an apartment on East Eighty-sixth Street, conveniently situated only a few blocks from P.S. 6, where we registered Michael in kindergarten. Regarded as one of the best public schools in Manhattan, P.S. 6 was a testing ground for innovative educational programs.

We found our apartment through Abe and Ann Rosenthal, who had introduced us to the management of the building, in which they lived, before departing for New Delhi. Barbara and I exchanged frequent letters with Abe and Ann, who had fallen in love with India. We gave them news of Michael and Peter, as well as "Gene O'Neill," as our boys had begun familiarly to call him. And Abe and Ann wrote about their lavish dinner parties for fifty or more, including top government officials and visitors from America.

Since Abe was paid a first-world salary while living in a third-world country, he and Ann were able to rent an enormous house and engage a huge staff of servants, including a gardener, a cook, two bearers, a laundress and a seamstress, two ayahs to care for their children, a club-wielding night watchman hired to scare off robbers and a loyal but nearsighted driver, named Abdul.

Despite their high style of living, sanitation was a fantasy and illness was a constant. A day with a calm stomach, Abe wrote to us, was worth celebrating. When their third son, Andrew, was born in 1956, he contracted a frightening case of dysentery. The pediatrician cautioned Ann to boil even the bathwater from that day on. Andrew stayed healthy in body and mind (sufficiently so as to become assistant managing editor of *The Times* in 2001).

As was apparent from his news reports and magazine articles, Abe instinctively grasped the Indian psyche as it was emerging from the ravages of colonialism following World War II, and the Indians loved him for it. I wrote him how much his stories were appreciated in New York. I also kept in touch with Bernie Kalb, who had left rewrite and was now in Indonesia—alone, as he and Phyllis had still not made up their minds to marry.

"The food here is extraordinarily, giftedly lousy," Bernie wrote, "exactly the sort of arrangement that would make your old Health Department habits reemerge. You'd starve to death. Me, I've only put on thirty pounds, so far, but I'm new out here. I just had a Chinese dinner down the street with the AP guy; now I'm back in my room. 'Down the street' means an alley full of whores (50 rupiahs—or $1.50), past sleeping goats, tired, sick rickshaw drivers, and half a dozen naked kids. 'My room,' I won't even bother describing because you'll feel lousy for three days and have to take a bath and won't let Michael talk to strangers for three years. The AP correspondent comes to Jakarta with his own toilet seat. That's a very big deal. I've forgotten how they feel already."

Bernie said, however, that his assignment was the right thing in his life at this point. "Gelbo, you're too stupid and successful to understand all this, but for the first time in years I feel as though my head is filling up, as though I'm learning, and I love it. What the hell is the business of life all about? I talked it over the other day with Santayana [one of his nicknames for Abe]— I didn't hear him too well, also he was talking in Yiddish, which I can't understand—but we both agreed that life's a pile of learning, and that's what I've been doing."

Bernie invited lizards into his office to eat the insects and found himself craving malted milk shakes. "A man can go berserk in these parts, wanting a malted and not being able to get one," he wrote. "What's more, not even getting a look of recognition, of an inner response, when I step up to a counter here, careful not to kill more than a million roaches, and ask for a big one with three scoops of ice cream. I live only for the day of malteds. It's like an eerie vision in my mind—a tall glass of the stuff running over with a creamy richness into which I can plunge, bare feet, headfirst. Otherwise I'm fine."

He also bought a nuri bird, which could talk. "I'm trying to get it to say 'mazel tov,'" he wrote. "I figure it will be good for my ego. I mean, I walk into the house and 'nuri' says 'mazel tov,' and I say 'thanks,' and I'm sure I must have done something absolutely marvelous during the day. Maybe even filed a story."

Abe wrote to Barbara and me about a visit Bernie paid him in New Delhi: "Firmly clutching his stomach, a roll of toilet paper in one hand and an economy-sized jar of antibiotics in the other, Bernard Kalb, correspondent, lover, explorer and dysentery sufferer, left New Delhi the other day for Calcutta. Now, you ask, and well may you ask, how he can clutch his stomach with both hands occupied. Ah, there, the answer is one of the mysteries of the East. All I can tell you, and I know you find it hard to believe, wrapped as you are in malteds and cellophane, is that if you have dysentery, you clutch.

"Seeing Bernie was magnificent, just wonderful. The minute he stepped out of the plane at Delhi, the minute I saw his ugly, bearded face and that stupid pink shirt he thinks is the height of fashion, it was as if we had seen each other the day before. 'Gladiola,' he shouted happily. 'Borgen!' This had a great effect on the plainclothes detectives who meet every plane—they knew it was some sort of code, but what?"

Bernie wrote us about the same visit: "Abe and Ann are living wonderfully. Their house is a huge palace of sorts, crowded with rooms, and I think Abe has taken the unemployment problem off of Prime Minister Nehru's hands by hiring about 7,650 servants. He hired about another 2,000 for a party he threw.

"Outside, there are dozens of sacred cows (they were not invited to the party) and they come sniffing up to the walls surrounding the house, a squarish three-story affair imaginatively air-conditioned. It's quite something. The kids are fine—Danny waltzes all over the place, trailing Jonnie, who is as boyish and smiling as ever. Little Andy is a sort of carbon copy of Danny, the same wide smile, the same blue eyes, the same tilted tiny nose. Altogether, the Rosenthals add up to a lot of wonderful Rosenthals. Our one regret was that you, Gelbo, were not around. There was a big hole in the night, in the talk, in the barrels of reminiscence, and it was you. Good God, we're all in our thirties. When did that happen—behind my back?"

We all missed each other deeply, our affection often couched in good-natured ribbing. Abe and Bernie never tired of mocking the large payoff Barbara and I had earned for the Bellevue book, as if we had joined ranks with the Rockefellers, leaving our old friends in third-world squalor. (We were too proud to tell them about the debt O'Neill was causing us to sink into.)

We kept an eye out for each other's articles in the paper, and commented about them (often sardonically) in our letters. After my scathing review of Papp's production of *Titus Andronicus*, Abe wrote: "Well, so much for that little fellow, Shakespeare. Mr. Gelb, I adore you and admire you. NEVER will I question the overmastering ego of a man who can wipe out Shakespeare in a three-paragraph review."

Barbara and I were tempted to visit all of them in Asia, especially to see Abe's new son, but the only traveling we could justify was in the service of our biography, and O'Neill had never been to India. Instead, we crisscrossed America, tracking down people who had known our subject. Since many were elderly, Barbara and I felt it was a race against time to find them.

We wrote to all the sailors' institutes and retirement homes, hoping an old salt might remember O'Neill from his seafaring days. One important discovery, for example, was Joseph James "Slim" Martin, a former sailor and ironworker who had been acquainted with O'Neill. When we found him at a hospital for the chronically ill in New York, he was confined to a closed ward because of alcoholism. But to Barbara and me, he appeared rehabilitated, and we managed to have him transferred to a regular ward and arranged to get him a pair of glasses. He spent days recording his memories of O'Neill.

In the summer of 1957, Barbara and I rented a house in New London,

Connecticut, where O'Neill had spent his childhood summers with his family. There, while my parents took our sons for daily outings to the beach bordering Long Island Sound, we sought out locals who remembered the O'Neills. One day, Barbara and I visited O'Neill's ninety-year-old cousin, Lillian Brennan, who was institutionalized with senile dementia. She was completely out of touch with the present, but clearly recalled events from the late 1800s and early 1900s, giving us a unique picture of O'Neill's mother as a young married woman.

We interviewed four hundred people in all and, at last, Carlotta agreed to see us for the book. We had met her only once, when Brooks, to whom she occasionally turned for guidance, had invited her to *The Times* for an interview pegged to the opening of *Long Day's Journey Into Night*. It was decided that Sy Peck should write the story because I had been swamped with other assignments. But Barbara and I suggested we be allowed to record the interview and Brooks obtained Carlotta's permission for us to do so. The ninety-minute tape is the first of three lengthy recordings that I made of Carlotta's revelations of her life with O'Neill.

Carlotta eventually invited Barbara and me to lunch at her favorite restaurant, Quo Vadis, in the quiet, elegant Lowell Hotel where she then lived, and where she ordered her habitual Monterey cocktail, a blend of Cointreau and gin that she claimed to have invented. At sixty-eight, she wore her thick, silky, iron-gray hair brushed straight back. Her face, virtually unlined, was devoid of makeup and her glasses were darkly tinted. In the role she had long since assumed of the widow in perpetual mourning, she was dressed entirely in black, including onyx jewelry.

We had been told that Carlotta was more comfortable in the company of men than women, and weren't surprised that, after our first few meetings, she insisted on seeing me alone. She was touchy about certain subjects—O'Neill's two previous wives; his daughter, Oona, who was married to Charlie Chaplin; his older son, by his first wife, who had killed himself at forty. She also preferred to skirt the details of O'Neill's early, bohemian existence. As far as Carlotta was concerned, O'Neill's life began when she entered it in 1926, when they were both thirty-eight.

She believed she had saved O'Neill from drinking himself to death, and she maintained that if it hadn't been for her gift of peaceful seclusion he would never have been able to write his final masterpieces—and she was probably right. When she later moved from the Lowell to an even more luxurious suite at the nearby Carlton House, she would darken the room by drawing the drapes, and then slip into a stream-of-consciousness reverie about her life with O'Neill. She never allowed me to take notes and I trained myself to memorize her monologues. As soon as I left the suite, I sat in the lobby jotting down everything of importance she had confided.

In the course of writing our biography, José Quintero, like Jason Robards, often astounded Barbara and me with his insights into the forces that had shaped O'Neill's genius. Born in Panama City in 1924, Quintero fled his martinet father and his Catholic roots in the mid-1940s, settling in California. He began studying medicine but, when he took a drama course to help improve his English, he discovered his lifelong passion. He boarded a Greyhound bus for New York, and eventually spent a few seasons directing summer theater in upstate Woodstock. There he met Theodore Mann, with whom he founded Circle in the Square in 1951.

Barbara and I were in awe of Quintero, the director, but it was Quintero, the man, whom we came to love. Carlotta once told us he reminded her of O'Neill. Although he was Panamanian, he did indeed resemble O'Neill: He was slim and handsome, and his dark-brown eyes were both penetrating and melancholy.

Carlotta could not help indulging in romantic fantasies about Quintero, and she presented him with O'Neill's wedding ring. One day, while I was interviewing her after the two Monterey cocktails she sipped at lunch, she told me, "One thing you must realize about O'Neill: The Irish don't know how to make love. Everything is quick with them. There's no romance, just a physical act. The Latins, on the other hand, know how to romance a woman. They can just sit on the edge of a tub watching her bathe and appreciate her beauty."

Carlotta, of course, may have been unaware of José's homosexuality. Even in the theater, a milieu more receptive to gays than probably any other profession, there was sometimes a reluctance to acknowledge their preference. While we assumed José was gay, the subject never came up. But one day he invited us to dinner at his apartment on lower Fifth Avenue, and Barbara turned out to be the only woman guest. There were five urbane male couples at the dinner table, including Quintero and his companion. We assumed he was making a statement for our edification.

Sometime later, Quintero settled down with Nicholas Tsacrios, who played an immensely supportive role in his life, helping José come to terms with the insecurity that had plagued him since childhood. It was Nick who helped him finally give up drinking.

Unlike Jason and José, Barbara and I never felt haunted by O'Neill's specter, but he virtually did become a member of our family for the more than five years we researched his life. He was a household name to Michael and Peter from the time they were five and three. We once took them to the Shakespeare Garden in Central Park and, pointing to his statue, we explained that Shakespeare was the world's greatest playwright. Peter, then five, was indignant. "Oh, yeah?" he said. "And what about Gene O'Neill?"

TWENTY-FOUR

MY FASCINATION WITH O'NEILL inspired me to investigate how other dramatists—whether established or merely hopeful—dealt with the vicissitudes of creating and mounting a play.

No playwright was more candid with me about his works in progress than Tennessee Williams. I first interviewed him in 1957, when *Orpheus Descending* was about to open. And in subsequent meetings he confided at length about the specter of failure that haunted him—and this despite the Pulitzer Prizes he had already won for *A Streetcar Named Desire* and *Cat on a Hot Tin Roof*. His primal fear was that Broadway audiences would reject him because of the growing violence he felt compelled to inject into his plays.

At the conclusion of *Orpheus*, a lynch mob sets the protagonist on fire with a blowtorch and, when Tennessee heard that theatergoers were critical of the play's violent ending, it made him feel he had become "a homicidal maniac, if not worse." Possibly he was exaggerating the reactions, he allowed, but nevertheless he had grown "a little frightened." It was then that he impulsively decided to produce his new experimental work in an atmosphere removed, as he put it (echoing O'Neill), from "the commercial needs of Broadway."

"I've always been startled by people who are antagonized by plays for reasons other than the quality of the work," he said. "Some of my plays, I think, have suffered from a reaction of ethical bias and an imposed and conventional morality."

When I again interviewed him in January 1958, about his surprising decision to present his new play—actually a twin bill with the overall title *Garden District*—Off Broadway, he told me the move was not intended to deprecate Broadway. Disclosing that he had gone into analysis soon after the opening of *Orpheus*, he said he had come to realize he couldn't cope emotionally with doing another controversial play on Broadway. "The financial risk of Off Broadway is not so great," he explained, "and the conditions, therefore, are less of a life-and-death matter."

He also believed Off Broadway's audiences would be more accepting of his lurid theme. The second play of his twin bill, *Suddenly Last Summer*, he told me, was bound to arouse some controversy, containing as it did a shockingly violent occurrence with symbolic significance and—he acknowledged with childlike glee—it also contained murder and cannibalism. But though Off Broadway audiences responded positively (I among them) and *Garden District* had a good run, Tennessee was still unhappy. He found he missed the jittery glamour and high stakes of a Broadway production.

Nothing if not contradictory, Tennessee had a radical change of heart in 1959, when he again sought acceptance on Broadway with *Sweet Bird of Youth*. He characterized this latest play, to be directed by Elia Kazan (who had staged all his plays since *The Glass Menagerie* in 1947), as "an examination of what is really corrupt in life."

Like *Orpheus Descending*, his original script had contained physical violence. But he so much wanted Broadway approval that he was willing to compromise his artistic vision by toning down the violence, going so far as to alter an important aspect of the plot that dealt with emasculation. "I decided it wasn't wise to end another play on such a violent note," he said. "I had to devise a way of getting the same impact without such violence." He got what he wanted, for despite some critical carping, *Sweet Bird* was a commercial success.

Far less successful was his next play, *Period of Adjustment*, produced on Broadway in the fall of 1960. Tennessee called it his most realistic play—"a play with humor . . . an unambitious play." He told me he only wanted "to tell the truth about a little occurrence in life without blowing it up beyond its natural limits." His characters, at the end, still have problems, but "they have found each other, and maybe they can now solve their problems." Most surprising for a Williams play, it had a nontragic ending.

Tennessee was devastated when Kazan withdrew as the director. To my astonishment, Tennessee—aware he was talking for the record—was candid about what had gone awry between him and Kazan. At his East Side brownstone, after pouring himself a triple martini, he disputed Kazan's public statement that he had abandoned the production because it conflicted with his work on a movie. Whatever the real reason, it obviously wasn't an easy decision for Kazan. He had already parted company with Arthur Miller, who had been critical of his decision to name names during the Senate hearings into Communist infiltration of the arts.

"Kazan has suddenly gotten the crazy idea that he is not good for my work," Tennessee blurted out. "We met Monday night for drinks. He showed up looking rather shaky and gray in the face, and told me he definitely couldn't do my new play. I tried my best to make him change his mind, but he was adamant."

Tennessee said he thought Kazan had been "upset by people who accuse him of looking for popular success—people who snipe at his so-called melodramatic interpretation of my plays. I've been so preoccupied with my own work that I wasn't aware of how much sniping was going on.

"The fact is, Kazan has been falsely blamed for my own desire for success. It's quite true that I want to reach a mass audience. I feel it can dig what I have to say, perhaps better than a lot of intellectuals can. I'm not an intellectual. And perhaps, at times, I've exceeded the dignified limits in trying to hold an audience, but it's wrong to blame Kazan for this. My cornpone melodrama is all my own. I want excitement in the theater. Wherever I've been excessive, it's due to a certain hysteria on my part that takes over. By accident of nature, I have a tendency toward romanticism and a taste for the theatrical. Kazan simply tried to interpret, honestly, what I have to say. He has helped me reach a bigger audience, which is my aim in life—the bigger the better. His withdrawal has been shattering for me. I felt at home with him."

Brooks called *Period of Adjustment* (in the end directed by George Roy Hill) "a commonplace comedy," writing that Williams, in his attempt to be less repellent than in the past, "sounded like an avuncular marriage counselor." It was soon after that Tennessee seems to have begun on his destructive downward path.

A curious aspect of my interviews with Tennessee was his intense eagerness to learn about O'Neill, all but exceeding my own wish to understand him. I once mentioned that Clifford Odets had told me he was thinking of writing a play about O'Neill's last turbulent years with Carlotta (which he never did), and Tennessee looked askance. He said he had been turning the very idea over in his own mind (he never wrote it either).

I began to suspect Tennessee was jealous of O'Neill. In his later years, O'Neill became something of an obsession, and Tennessee was so sensitive that when he read any mention of O'Neill in *The Times*, he perceived it as a personal slight—as though his own work were being disparaged. During his last years, dazed with drugs and alcohol, he became increasingly bitter about my lecturing and writing articles about O'Neill's plays. Mutual friends told me he believed my admiration for O'Neill had somehow diminished him. He couldn't seem to grasp that it was his own tragic inability to sustain his poetic talent that did him in.

IT WAS A GIVEN that the playwrights I interviewed for *The Times* were those who had upcoming New York productions. In the spring of 1960, Brendan Behan, the bawdy, iconoclastic ex-revolutionary, arrived from Dublin for the scheduled Broadway opening September 20 of his farcical tragedy, *The Hostage*, in which he satirized the pretentious aspects of religion, politics and nationalism. I arranged to see him at the Algonquin Hotel, where he had checked in with his wife, Beatrice.

Behan was already known in America for his book *Borstal Boy*, about his confinement to a reform school after being accused of attempted sabotage against the British. New Yorkers also knew him for the Off Broadway production of his play *The Quare Fellow*. But much of his notoriety, sadly, was due to his inebriated antics while holding court in Third Avenue saloons.

At brunch in the Algonquin's dining room, I was glad to find him subdued and—for once—unquestionably sober. Sipping ice water, he said it was his grandmother who had started him on whiskey and stout when he was six. But he assured me he hadn't had a drop in several months.

His courtly behavior was in dramatic contrast to press reports I'd read about his recent drunken sprees, at times spinning out of control. In London, where *The Hostage* ran for more than a year, he often slipped into the audience and heckled his cast, which heckled him back with ad-libbed dialogue. Working-class audiences at the unpretentious Theater Royal were delighted, but after the play moved to the West End, upper-crust theatergoers were baffled and annoyed when a drunken Behan turned up.

His wife, dark-haired, slender and self-effacing, tried her best to keep Brendan away from the bottle. Under her watchful eye, he put on a grand show as he talked to me almost nonstop for three hours. Patrons at other tables stared at the odd sight of the stocky, rumpled, ruddy-cheeked, green-eyed Behan with his mop of wildly unkempt hair and his conspicuously toothless grin.

Behan spouted whatever came to his mind, punctuating his remarks with expletives. No subject was off-limits, from sex to religion. On the subject of religion, he elaborated: "I suppose I am inclined to believe in all that the Catholic Church teaches. I am accused of being blasphemous. But blasphemy is the comic verse of belief. Certain things must be restrained in the world for our convenience—but for our convenience only. Why can't we let it go at that? The nearest thing to a horrifying act in a reasonable society is a crime against a child. One thing I respect about Catholic teaching is that one mortal sin is as bad as another."

Behan, then thirty-seven, recounted in his melodic brogue how he had made his stage debut in Dublin when he was ten: "There were three theaters on the north side of the River Liffey, the Rotunda, the Star and the Torch. The Rotunda put on an act featuring a singing newsboy. This was in the area where everyone was either the father, mother, brother or sister of a newsboy, if not a newsboy himself, and the act was a winner. The Star went the Rotunda one better, and put on an act with a *crippled* singing newsboy. The manager of the Torch decided to outdo the Star by putting on an act with a *blind,* crippled singing newsboy. He gave me the job, I went on and got lots of cheers."

Abruptly leaping to his feet, Behan tore into the bathetic lyrics of the poor, crippled, blind newsboy, whose heart overflowed with joy and who could hear sweet voices calling. After a spirited jig, he flung himself back into his chair, seemingly wounded that nobody applauded.

But Mary Bodne, the Algonquin's matronly owner for the past fifteen years who by now was accustomed to the eccentricities of her patrons, came by to compliment him. And with typical chivalry, he said, "Mary, your son will live to be pope." It didn't bother Behan that Mary was Jewish, and did not have a son.

In and out of reform school he had read voraciously—and was influenced mainly by Sean O'Casey and James Joyce. He said he wrote his first play in jail. "It was called *The Landlady* and was about a boy who was going to marry a girl who lived in the kitchen and tried to commit suicide. Anything written in jail is rubbish, and that includes *Pilgrim's Progress.*"

Behan relished mimicking Irish actors and politicians, in a nonstop stream of parody: "Why do I ridicule my country? The first duty of a writer is to let his country down. He knows his own people the best. The best form of politics you can have in an imperfect world is where politicians have to play up to people by giving them such things as better housing. The dangerous politicians are the ones who call for sacrifice and duty to one's country. They are entitled to six ounces of lead between the eyes—not in the brain, because they have no brain."

Beatrice excused herself to go to their room. The minute she was out of sight, Behan grabbed me by the elbow. "Let's go for a walk," he said. Before

I knew it we were entering a seedy saloon called Kilroy's, on Sixth Avenue. Behan promptly ordered a whiskey, and again began discussing religion. "I'm not religious unless I'm ill," he said. "The only time I cross myself is when I pass a funeral."

He then analyzed the redemptive ending of *The Hostage*, which involved a young Irish country girl's love for a Cockney soldier being held as a hostage by the Irish Republican Army. Her beloved is ultimately killed, then resurrected. I asked Behan what influenced the bizarre plot. "If a writer doesn't put in his experiences," he responded, "he puts in his hopes and regrets. I don't say that I had the ambition to be hung, but I did have the ambition of going to bed with the girl."

Actually, *The Hostage* was based on two people, explained Behan. "One was a British soldier who had been held by friends of mine in the IRA. They didn't give him a girl, like in the play, but they did give him Guinness stout and food. The best way to keep him quiet was to give him stout. He said he had never had such a good time. The other fellow was an Englishman I read about who was captured by the Egyptians during the Suez crisis—he was locked in a cupboard, where he smothered."

As we walked back to the Algonquin, Behan elaborated on why the dead hostage comes alive again at the play's end. "Why? Send the audience home happy. Death is vulgarized when looked upon as an end. It may be an end in this world as far as the bloke is concerned, but life goes on. I don't know what life is—whether there is a life force." Behan's voice trailed off. "I'm a very confused man. But I'm all for resurrection. There should be resurrection every week for the dead."

BEHAN'S SENTIMENTS about the dead strongly affected me at the time, for I was still mourning my father, who had suffered a massive stroke a year earlier and died after many months in a coma. Two weeks before he was stricken, a doctor had pronounced him in the best of health following his regular physical exam.

One night, Barbara and I went to the theater, leaving my parents, as we often did, to care for their grandchildren. They were to spend the night at our apartment, since we were planning to join friends for an after-theater supper. When we got home after midnight, my father was awake. He said he had taken aspirin for a headache and mild dizziness. In the morning, he told me his symptoms were worse. I called his doctor, who diagnosed his condition as a minor stroke. The doctor didn't seem at all concerned, prescribed a sedative and bed rest, and said he'd come back the next day. It was too late. When my father told me he could no longer tolerate the dizziness, I called an ambulance, which took him to New York Hospital. The next day, he fell into a coma.

The prognosis was poor, and my mother refused to leave his side. For two weeks, she slept in a chair by his bed. Barbara and I brought her changes of clothing, but could not persuade her to come home with us to rest. Miraculously, he awoke after two weeks and was completely lucid. He remained in the hospital, where we talked about many things, especially his childhood in Europe. I was finally able to convince my mother to spend a night at our home for undisturbed sleep. The night of her absence, my father slipped back into a coma, from which he never emerged.

After some weeks, with no sign of hope for recovery, he was transferred to St. Barnabas, an exemplary chronic disease hospital in the Bronx, where the nuns provided tender care. My mother spent a week at a time by his bed, then came to our apartment to rest for one day before returning to the hospital. The nuns said they had never seen anyone as devoted as my mother. Barbara and I were concerned about her own deteriorating health and we spelled each other to check on her at the hospital.

I was able to spend an hour with my mother and brother at my father's bedside before he died. Harold and I tried to console my mother, who seemed utterly adrift. She was cradling my father in her arms, and for a while I thought she would never let go. (Although she outlived my father by twenty-five years, she never really recovered from losing him.)

When I returned to work, Clara told Brooks I was disconsolate. In his office, he talked to me at some length about the bond he had had with his own father and the difficulty he'd had in coming to grips with the finality of his death. Because Brooks was a stoical New Englander, not always comfortable expressing emotion, I was greatly touched by his attempt to console me.

I began going to the Actors' Temple near *The Times*—on Forty-seventh Street west of Eighth Avenue—to say Kaddish, the ancient prayer for the dead. There I befriended Louis Malamud, the cheery, rotund sexton, who sometimes entertained such members of his congregation as George Jessel, Sophie Tucker, Eddie Fisher and Red Buttons in a small side room, offering them whiskey and theater gossip. In return, they gave him complimentary tickets to Broadway shows. He told me he'd recently seen Paddy Chayefsky's hit comedy *The Tenth Man*. The title referred to the minyan, the ten Jewish men required to conduct a prayer service. It was the sexton's job before each evening's service to make sure a minyan was assembled.

Malamud told me that the play didn't accurately convey the atmosphere of a synagogue like his. "Such a poor-looking congregation I don't think you can find even on Long Island," he said. But he was amused by Chayefsky's final scene, in which a Jewish policeman is pressed into service as the tenth man during a dybbuk exorcism ritual. The sexton knew what it was like to be pushed to extremes to round out his nightly prayer service, since very few Jewish people any longer lived in the area and he himself often had to rely on the police for help.

The West Forty-seventh Street station house was only a few doors from the temple, and was presided over by a sympathetic Irish lieutenant, whom I remembered from my police reporting days. When the hard-pressed Malamud stepped into the police station, the lieutenant quickly sent out a radio call. Within minutes, a Jewish cop would be found and he'd roll up to the door of the temple in a prowl car.

Once, Malamud entered the station house and waited respectfully while the lieutenant listened to a well-dressed man reporting a robbery. The lieutenant caught Malamud's eye and asked the man if he happened to be Jewish. Somewhat startled, the man said he was. "The sexton needs a minyan," said the lieutenant, and Malamud triumphantly bore off his tenth man.

AFTER MY COMMITTED MOURNING PERIOD, I threw myself back into the job of interviewing playwrights. I found James Thurber, whose *Thurber Carnival* had opened on Broadway in February 1960, brooding about the difficulties of theatrical collaboration. At his home in West Cornwall, Connecticut, he complained about the hardships of the six-city pre-Broadway tryout. His play was a hit, but Thurber was grumpy. He was suffering from exhaustion and a serious throat infection, and he derived more pleasure, he said, from polishing his own sentences in his own room than collaborating with fifteen people in a theater.

The theater, he elaborated, was not a place for a careful writer. "I am a perfectionist. I've often spent as much as a year and a half writing something, and then thrown it away. When I get stuck in writing, I draw. I like to take my time."

This attitude had not endeared him to Herman Shumlin, the producer of *The Male Animal*, a play Thurber had written in 1940. He had told Shumlin during the out-of-town tryout that he'd like to spend another year improving the play. "Dammit, we open next Monday in New York," was Shumlin's final word.

Yet Thurber conceded he was considering an idea for still another play—about Harold Ross and *The New Yorker*—but had no plans to start working on it for quite some time. "That's the trouble with this country," he said. "A man has a success on Broadway—or anywhere else for that matter—and he feels he has to follow it up quickly with another success. It's the American disease of jet propulsion.

"Look how they're dying off! Thirty-two men on *The New Yorker* have died since I went to work there in 1927. Two-thirds of the old Algonquin group is gone. Stanley Walker [the retired city editor of the *Herald Tribune*] and I recently counted a hundred thirty men we knew who had died under the age of sixty-four. This is probably the only country in the world that has only two writers—Carl Sandburg and Robert Frost—still working in their eighties."

Among the many other writers I interviewed in the following months was Thornton Wilder. Recalling the plush armchairs, soft lighting and living room–like comfort of the Algonquin from my interview with Brendan Behan, I invited Wilder to meet me there for cocktails on October 5, 1961.

The winner of three Pulitzer Prizes—for *Our Town, The Skin of Our Teeth* and the novel *The Bridge of San Luis Rey*—Wilder was at work on a cycle of fourteen one-act plays, to be his first new stage project in almost twenty years. The one-acters were divided into two series of seven plays each, under the headings *The Seven Ages of Man* and *The Seven Deadly Sins*.

He intended the cycle as his artistic summing up—reflecting, he said, the tendency of the mature artist in all ages to forge a definitive statement of his crystallized philosophy. At sixty-three, balding and gray-mustached, Wilder, though reluctant to dwell on his plays in detail, was in high spirits and happy to expand on his theories of art and history in general.

"I am interested in the drives that operate in every society and in every man," he said. "Pride, avarice and envy are in every home." One of the themes that preoccupied him in *The Seven Ages of Man* was the battle on the part of children for self-improvement, constantly thwarted by adults. "Infancy," the first in this cycle, presented two babies in perambulators, to be played by grown men in pleated caps, airing their grievances on the subject. "The reason why the world is in such a sloppy state," pronounced Wilder, "is that our parents were so stupid."

He said his new works would not abandon the comic interpretation of man's destiny that was Wilder's trademark: "Because we live in the twentieth century, overhung by very real anxiety, we have to use the comic spirit. No statement of gravity can be adequate to the gravity of the age in which we live."

He was contemptuous of what he characterized as the current "scrounging for survival," believing we should concentrate our first effort on acquiring mature self-knowledge. "Survival must have quality," he said, "or it ain't worth a bean. Anyway, it's better to burn up mature than immature."

Wilder was just beginning to gather steam and I was scribbling notes as fast as I could, barely able to keep pace with his stream of aphorisms. "The theater in the great ages," he said, "carried on its shoulders the liveliest realization of public consciousness. The tragic and comic poets of Greece, along with Lope de Vega, Corneille, Racine, Shakespeare, were recognized by their contemporaries as expressing what every citizen felt dimly and rejoiced to hear concretely."

Wilder went on to disparage current audiences for their tepid tastes in drama: "A public of thin blood likes thin plays." Audiences, he maintained, had grown to like the fact that plays were soothing and not disturbing. "We are told that at the first performance of Euripedes' *Medea*, strong men fainted and several children were prematurely born. The theater can still do this. It can be restored to its commanding position as a critic of society and as a factor by which a nation recognizes its mission and its greatness."

He pointed out that while in other ages the theater was the greatest of all the arts, it had by now dwindled into a minor art—rarely comparable to a superior symphony concert or a major exhibition of painting or sculpture. In 1938, having set *Our Town* on a bare stage, he was critical of the current overuse of scenery and pleaded for a return to arena staging, with the audience seated on three sides. "The box-set play encourages the anecdote," he said. "The unencumbered stage encourages the truth operative in everyone. The less seen, the more heard. The eye is the enemy of the ear in real drama. All the masters knew this. Plays of all great ages were performed with a minimum of scenery and with the public on three sides. We have to kick the proscenium down."

Three hours had passed and my writing hand was starting to ache. Stimulated but feeling intellectually overfed, I walked the three blocks back to *The Times*, acutely aware that Wilder's philosophical ramblings would make a lively story. But I didn't expect Ted Bernstein to play it on page one. He let the interview run for two columns under the head "Thornton Wilder, 63, Sums Up Life and Art in New Play Cycle." I found Ted's effort to try something new—placing a theater interview on the front page—heartening. As far as I could remember, he had never allowed a cultural story without a hard-news peg to appear on the front page.

What Ochs had succeeded in imbedding in every top editor's mind was that the front page of *The Times* was sacrosanct. It was the most successful news page in the country, and changes in style or content were to be made, if at all, with extreme caution. This was an uncommonly bold move on Bernstein's part, demonstrating that he, at least, was not a man of "thin blood."

TWENTY-FIVE

IN MY DRIVE TO UNDERSTAND the creative process, I didn't focus exclusively on the established writers. I hastened to search out the younger, untried playwrights who were breaking new ground Off Broadway, boldly challenging the righteous assumptions of what they saw as a stagnant society. Within months of each other, two previously unproduced young authors rocked the downtown scene with a pair of avant-garde plays, both featuring suicidal protagonists.

The first of these, which opened in July 1959 at the Living Theatre—perhaps Off Broadway's most maverick ensemble—was *The Connection*, by Jack Gelber, a twenty-seven-year-old rebel from a slum on Chicago's West Side. His play was an appallingly realistic depiction of the spreading drug culture that was still unfamiliar to most New Yorkers.

The second, which had its première at the Provincetown Playhouse in January 1960, was *The Zoo Story* by Edward Albee, who had been abandoned by his parents at his birth thirty-one years earlier and adopted by a wealthy New York family against whom he was obviously in rebellion. His short two-character play anticipated the widening breach in middle-class family communication that was to form an endlessly popular subject of drama in the decade to follow.

In *The Connection*, the stage set depicted, with startling authenticity, a squalid apartment jammed with dazed dope addicts. Entering the theater, I joined an audience confronted by a curtainless stage, and found myself at once engaged with the anguish of addicts awaiting the arrival of the pusher who would alleviate their craving.

The Zoo Story, which shared a double bill with Beckett's new one-act play, *Krapp's Last Tape*, was a dialogue between two strangers in Central Park—one a middle-aged successful publisher, the other a drifter in his late thirties. Their acerbic give-and-take revealed the publisher as a man deeply dissatisfied with his life, despite his possession of everything that conventional society deemed essential to contentment—a wife, an Upper East Side residence and two each of daughters, cats, parakeets and television sets. The drifter, profoundly disaffected and hungering for truth in a hypocritical world, taunted and prodded the publisher into acknowledging his own craven acceptance of a life he actually deplored. In the end it was the angry drifter who emerged as the play's hero, albeit a hero so beset by rage that no one, myself included, would choose to encounter him in our own lives.

I agreed with the critical acclaim accorded both plays, and was eager to talk with their authors. Barbara, equally impressed, suggested we invite them to our apartment for dinner. A couple of months earlier, I had interviewed Gelber by phone for my column, but Albee had never been interviewed. They were both surprisingly forthcoming, following dinner and wine.

Albee, who was dark and lean and chose his words carefully, told us he had been adopted when he was two weeks old, soon after his abandonment. His adoptive grandfather was the Albee who cofounded the Keith–Albee vaudeville circuit, and he saw his first show, *Jumbo*, when he was five. He was sent to Choate, and was later expelled from Trinity College for cutting classes and failing to attend chapel. He said he had been estranged from his foster parents since 1950, when at twenty-one he left home against their wishes to pursue a writing career.

We discussed the "nihilism" imputed by some critics to the plays of both Albee and Gelber. Both writers refuted that characterization. Albee, in fact, insisted his play was not even pessimistic: The drifter, "though he dies, passes on an awareness of life to the other character in the play and the play, therefore, is obviously not a denial of life."

Albee became slightly flustered when I pried further into the play's meaning. "What does it mean?" he said. "I can only answer that by reading the play to you." But he quickly collected himself. "There are truly some things in it that I don't really understand. An awful lot of the play comes from my subconscious."

His favorite author, he said, was Jean Genet, and, like Genet, he was interested in digging so deep under the skin that it became practically intolerable. He said he wanted the audience to run out of the theater, but to come back and see the play again. His interest in Genet had "something to do with the conscious and the unconscious both being on the surface at the same time, and with levels of reality and the whole question of identity."

I think I was the first to learn about the work in progress that was to make Albee's Broadway reputation two years later. He told me that he was calling it *Exorcism* and that it dealt with "two couples in the course of a degrading, drunken two A.M. party. The older couple have created a fantasy child of nineteen, whom they drag out to advance their divergent viewpoints. The father eventually decides the child must be exorcised." With a wan smile, he added, "I have a subtitle for it. It is *Who's Afraid of Virginia Woolf?*"

Gelber, fair-haired with a candid, boyish face, told me he was married and the father of an eight-month-old son. His father was a sheet-metal worker addicted to gambling, and his earliest influences were the movies, the circus and jazz. "I liked to read and I felt superior to the other kids in the neighborhood. I was a scholar and they were juvenile delinquents."

Gelber tried drugs for the first time at the University of Illinois, where he majored in journalism, and learned about every type of narcotic by studying medical journals. Then he moved to San Francisco's North Beach and found work in a shipyard, but was fired after he grew a beard, which his boss saw as a fire hazard. The characters in *The Connection* were based on people he knew. He said he recognized their despair and, before sinking too deeply himself into drugs, he left for New York. He maintained his play illustrated his faith in life—"not in terms of a hero that finds salvation, but in terms of continuity of life." It was long after midnight before the two writers departed. By then, they had agreed that Broadway must be shocked out of its lethargy. Their dream was to make the commercial theater accept them on their own innovative terms.

I was disappointed that Gelber, although he gave playwrights who followed him considerable food for thought, never achieved his goal—but Albee surely did, becoming a three-time Pulitzer Prize winner.

After the combined interviews appeared in *The Times*, Albee wrote to thank me. "I was relieved to discover that—in print, at least—I hadn't made a complete jackass of myself shooting my mouth off about something I actually know relatively little about: the theater. I shudder whenever beginners like myself end up pontificating.

"Couple of people asked me if Genet really was my favorite playwright and I had to admit that no, truthfully, my favorite playwright was me. But I did think that Mr. Genet was the most important man writing right now. And it's funny; I hadn't thought that I'd hit so viciously at my mother as your reporting made it seem. I suspect I'd best shut up about that particular area of my life; my attitude emerges as unbecoming."

I HAD LEARNED, by now, that most serious playwrights tended to bridle— some more combatively than others—when pressed to expound on the deeper meaning of a particular work. Nonetheless, I continued to probe and, since most of the writers I interviewed were eager for the cachet conveyed by an article in *The Times*, they usually made an effort—if not wholeheartedly, at least politely—to satisfy my curiosity.

Not so, Eugene Ionesco.

An icon of the French avant-garde, he appeared indifferent to the mixed reception accorded his play *The Killers* when it opened Off Broadway in March 1960. Atkinson, who had begun his review, "There must be an easier way for Eugene Ionesco to say what he has in mind," suggested I interview the playwright to see whether I could penetrate at least some small part of his meaning. I wrote to Ionesco in Paris, asking him to what he attributed the nihilistic trend in his own writing and that of his contemporaries. I received a condescending reply that I possibly deserved:

"Don't you believe one asks too many questions of authors? One discusses too much the works that are played, and that is normal. But one goes on to demand of the author what he thinks of his works. One comments on the comments and one explains the explanations. The work itself is lost from view; it is lost under a mountain of discussions; one cannot see more than the mountain."

To my next question, "What is the theme of *The Killers*?" he answered, "Do you yourself know the work? If not, go to see it. If yes, you know the theme, then tell it to me yourself."

Ionesco then continued to amuse himself by "explaining" the play in terms that obscured its meaning even further:

"Berenger, the principal character is an anti-killer. He implores the killer not to kill anymore. What is the Killer? He is not the one who goes on killing or supposedly doing evil. The one who has done evil in the past may not want to do it anymore. That is the case with Chessman. If the social machinery wishes to kill those who have ceased to do evil, it is the Society that becomes the killer, that becomes unforgivable; because in doing that it provokes the apparition of enemies of society, and it prepares new killers." I reported to Atkinson that evidently there was no easier way for Ionesco to say what he had in mind. The interview never ran.

PRODDED BY HIS Yankee conscience and work ethic, Brooks felt compelled to cover not only every Broadway première of consequence but also many of the Off Broadway openings for the daily paper, in addition to composing a weekly essay expressing his second thoughts for the Sunday Drama Section.

Even when there was an opening every night of the week, Brooks would be in his aisle seat taking notes. I was stunned, therefore, when on February 22, 1960, he asked me to review a Broadway play called *The Cool World* in his place. Telephoning me at the office from his apartment an hour before the curtain, he said he was in bed, dizzy and feverish. He was sure I could handle it.

I was concerned he might be seriously ill. On the other hand, I was elated at the chance to review my first Broadway play. I suspected that he was, in fact, offering me a chance to prove myself as his possible successor when he retired. He had recently hinted that he was anticipating a less stressful life that would allow him some leisure time on his farm in the Catskills.

Written by a former English instructor, Warren Miller, and staged by the film director Robert Rossen, *The Cool World* starred Billy Dee Williams as a small-time marijuana dealer in East Harlem. In what I fear was a rather lengthy review, I praised the play for its authenticity, saying it was "enough to scare hell out of all northern armchair liberals who wax indignant over the integration issue in the South but who are blind and deaf to what goes on at home." But I felt obliged to point out (perhaps a bit ponderously) that the play was less "a work of art" than "an illustrated social sermon."

When Brooks appeared the next morning in the office, apparently recovered, he said he liked my review and admitted he had wanted to demonstrate to Catledge et al. that I was ready to function as chief theater critic. Confirming that he planned to retire soon, he said it was his strong wish that I succeed him. In about six months, he would begin writing a Tuesday and Friday column, to be called "Critic at Large," on any subject striking his fancy. I couldn't imagine *The Times* without Brooks as drama critic, and I was startled—and flattered—to learn I was his choice to follow him.

It turned out, however, that Brooks did not have the final say, and the next months saw some heated upper-echelon wrangling, accompanied by rumors galore, a not-uncommon situation when members of the hierarchy were confronted with a need to make major staff changes. The first of many letters I received during this nerve-wracking period was Murray Schumach's assessment of possible in-house candidates:

"Lewis Funke's main advantage is that he is next in line. His age is right. If Brooks speaks up for him, he might get it. Seymour Peck's qualifications are obvious. In addition, it would give Markel a chance to have his man in an important third-floor spot. But I think he will be ruled out by his Communist background. Gilbert Millstein [an editor and writer on the Sunday *Magazine*] has style and enthusiasm for the theater. Though not as knowledgeable as Peck, he is capable of considerable wit and untainted by radical politics.

"That leaves only Arthur Gelb. He has only one drawback. He would have to be stepped over his present editor, Funke. *The Times* is very unlikely to do this. But if Funke becomes critic, then Gelb certainly becomes drama editor."

Next, Barbara heard from Abe Rosenthal. "The suspense is killing you? Christ, think what it is doing to us here, out of touch with the gossip, but knowing the only important thing is whether Gelb is going to get the job or *The Times* will revert to unspeakable fascism. We have even been afraid to write and ask about it because we knew that Arthur must be walking the wire that separates his present state, whatever the official psychiatric term for it is, from complete, certifiable lunacy, as a result of the B. Atkinson business. And we didn't want to push him over. But I gather, from the sly references in your letter, that the Pick Gelb movement has had some success. Anyway, it would be almost impossible to conceive of them not picking Arthur. I mean it, and so, I am sure, does everyone else."

Several weeks went by without a decision while Abe—as well as Bernie Kalb—sent encouraging letters from abroad. Meanwhile, in New York, Brooks was lobbying Catledge and the publisher, Orvil Dryfoos, on my behalf. Dryfoos had succeeded his ailing father-in-law (who remained as chairman of the *Times* board).

When I still hadn't heard anything from Catledge by midsummer, I began to lose hope, but Brooks evidently thought there was still a chance for me, and contrived to give me one more showcase. From London, where he went every summer after the end of the New York season, he phoned, asking me to fill his usual Sunday Drama spot with a salute to Oscar Hammerstein II, who had died of cancer at sixty-five on August 23. Brooks's Sunday column was read with near reverence by the theater community.

He said he believed the tribute should be written from New York, the city of which Hammerstein was so much a part. The section's deadline was the next day, and I began writing a bit desperately. My first thought was to call Berrie, who had been Hammerstein's close friend, and asked his help in explaining the lyricist's special gift. "He was content to say what he thought simply and clearly and sympathetically, without the spurious adornment of what passes for sophistication," said Berrie. "He was, to quote his own lyrics, 'as corny as Kansas in August,' by which I mean that he was genuine where others were clever, understanding where others were superior, kind when kindness was needed. He was strong and balanced and sensitive. He had the basic virtues."

From there I went on to describe how Hammerstein's guileless vision had transformed the razzle-dazzle musical into widely accepted folk art—

with the sunny lyrics of *Oklahoma!*, the bittersweet *Carousel*, the poignant if sentimental *South Pacific* and the romantic *The King and I*. His was the voice that seemed to embody the escapist yearnings of the period.

Brooks called to say he loved my article but, alas, it was too late. He sadly confided that the final decision was that I was too young—at thirty-five!— and not yet sufficiently seasoned to succeed him. The youth revolution in America was yet to arrive and *The Times* was not about to ruffle its own stodgy traditions. That afternoon Catledge told me, "You have many years ahead of you. Bide your time, and your day will come."

Howard Taubman, the *Times* music critic, who hadn't even made Murray's list of prospects, won the job. He had joined the music department as a reporter in 1930, a year after his graduation from Cornell University, and eventually became one of the most authoritative music critics in the country.

I was, of course, bitterly disappointed and I vowed that if I ever became a top editor, I'd give assignments and promotions regardless of age. After the announcement, Brooks invited me to his Riverside Drive apartment, where he apologized for having raised my hopes. He had generously commented about Taubman in *Times Talk* that anyone who could write about a technical subject like music could write about the more accessible topic of drama. But in truth he was incensed at Taubman's appointment. He told me a theater critic must be immersed in the subtleties and complexities of the stage. He must know its past as well as its current history and must have credibility in theater circles as a trustworthy voice. Brooks said he would not be surprised if I decided to leave the paper.

The O'Neill biography was certain to be a success, he assured me, and he cited Kaufman and Mankiewicz as examples of drama staffers who had gone on to write books and plays. I told Brooks I'd been thinking along those lines, but that Barbara and I had to count on my *Times* income while completing our O'Neill book. I'd have to wait until publication before considering so radical a change.

ABE AND BERNIE both commiserated with me from afar, which helped a little. Abe, who had been transferred from India to Poland in 1958, was now in Geneva awaiting his next assignment. He had been expelled by the Polish government in November 1959, for "exposing too deeply the internal situation in Poland." He inquired whether the government thought his reports were baseless, and received this reply: "The question of falseness or otherwise does not enter the question. You have written very deeply and in detail about the internal situation, party matters and leadership matters, and the Polish government cannot tolerate such probing reporting."

The Pulitzer committee agreed with the Communist regime about Abe's persistent probing and awarded him their prize for foreign reporting. "I wanted it a lot," Abe wrote to Barbara and me, "but I didn't know that when it came it would fill me with such happiness. So many nice things happened with it; couple of hundred letters, some from people I hadn't heard from in twenty years—high school teachers, relatives, Jews. I showed Jonnie the ad *The Times* ran. A little small, but the thought was there. Jonnie looked at it a minute and asked for the *Tribune* funnies . . . I am off to Paris for a big conference. The whole gay, mad whirl of us international journalists will be there and I am practicing lowering my sweet little eyes and mumbling, 'Oh, I didn't really deserve the prize.' My ass, I didn't deserve it; maybe not for the Polish stuff, but I wrote a beauty of an advance obit on Miriam Hopkins once and it went totally unrecognized, so I figure I had it coming."

I wrote a long profile of Abe for *Times Talk*, pegged to his winning the Pulitzer, describing our tradition of one-upmanship, in the bantering tone that often characterized our letters. Abe never minded our lampooning when it was kept between us, but was upset that I didn't treat his achievement with the respect it deserved in public. Ann, however, loved it. "You gave me ten minutes of uninterrupted hysterical laughter," she wrote. "Also, being the sentimental slob that I am, I felt a bit weepy over some of the anecdotes."

Abe and Ann found Geneva bland after India and Poland. But they knew it was a temporary post and hoped that Abe's Pulitzer might give him the clout to land the Paris bureau. After a few weeks, Abe grew fidgety and called the foreign desk to volunteer his assistance in covering the civil war in the Congo. It was a four-week assignment, but a scary one. "I was constantly being shot at," he said. "Every time I approached a soldier, he'd aim his rifle. The soldiers all seemed terrified and so was I." Not long after his return to Geneva, Abe was informed of his new assignment. It wasn't Paris but a city he came to love even more—Tokyo.

Bernie was still in Jakarta, though no longer on his own. He had telephoned me on Saturday evening, July 31, 1958, while on home leave in New York, to announce that he and Phyllis were to be married the next day and would sail on the *Île de France* for a honeymoon in Paris before he resumed his post in Jakarta. He asked me to be his best man at the wedding, attended by only a few friends and family members. The end of this nine-year roller-coaster courtship was an event greeted with deep sighs of relief. "Now we can all get some sleep," Abe cabled us.

Mailing us her first impressions of Jakarta, Phyllis said, "No sooner does one turn the corner but that one is confronted by a new vista—a new nook— each more miserable than the last. The architecture, laid out by the Dutch, has the lightness and taste of somebody else's mother's gefilte fish. But it's home, and we love it." They named their first daughter Tanah—Indonesian for "land," symbolizing "the beauty of Indonesia's mountains, valleys, rivers, islands, sunsets."

On September 7, 1960, the new Broadway season began with a ceremony renaming the Mansfield Theater in honor of Brooks Atkinson, who had launched his "Critic at Large" column the previous day. A week earlier, Howard Taubman had taken over as drama critic and, as was his prerogative, started reviewing the important shows. Although a gem would at times come my way, sitting through one second-rate Off Broadway production after another was becoming tedious.

The approaching presidential conventions were a welcome distraction for the city room, with the staff not so exhilarated since Truman beat Dewey in 1948. Most of us hoped fervently that John Kennedy would squash Richard Nixon and rid the country of the doldrums of the Eisenhower–Nixon administration. Even Turner Catledge had trouble maintaining his nonpartisan public stance.

Earlier in the year, I had learned that ex-President Truman would be attending Gore Vidal's Broadway comedy hit *The Best Man*. On April 25, I arranged to get the seat directly behind Truman and took notes of his reactions. Studded with lines about political chicanery, the play was set in two hotel rooms during the upcoming presidential convention of 1960 (the summer when Kennedy and Nixon were to be nominated). The dialogue referred to Nixon's hypocritical TV speech assuring viewers he hadn't benefited from a secret fund raised on his behalf. He then won over many viewers by famously pleading there was one gift he had received but would never give up—a cocker spaniel sent by a Texan, which his six-year-old daughter had named Checkers. At the line in the play, "You may have to pull a Nixon— go on TV and cry on the nation's shoulder—and take two cocker spaniels if necessary," Truman roared with laughter.

Not even Truman was more devoted to the Democratic Party than Tallulah Bankhead, Broadway's most flamboyant leading lady. Her father, William B. Bankhead of Alabama, had served as Speaker of the House and had been a stalwart supporter of Roosevelt. Every so often, when the news flow slowed, I'd call her for her personal and eccentric updates on the campaign. That August, after a three-year absence from Broadway, Tallulah was about to begin rehearsing for a play called *Midgie Purvis*. In her throaty voice, she prefaced her comments to me with the plea, "Please, dahling, make me sound witty, chahming, adorable, brilliant and only use one goddamn." She then launched into a witty, charming soliloquy that touched only briefly on politics:

"Dahling, I'm in bed watching *Edge of Night* and I wouldn't interrupt this for anyone but *The Times*, Adlai, Kennedy, Johnson or Truman. I think Kennedy is going to make a great president. I do what I can to sell the Democratic ticket to train porters and cabdrivers, but they're all Democrats anyway. All artists, intellectuals and minorities are Democrats. I hope the Republicans won't hold this against me. They have all the money, and they're the ones who can afford to buy tickets to my play.

"I don't get out much anymore, dahling. And I never leave the East Side. I haven't been to a nightclub in ten years, and the theater bores me—and besides, I haven't got any clothes. I have two sick dogs on the bed with me—one has eczema and the other just had a heart attack. They'll recover. I'm drinking un-spiked tomato juice and I've just been reading a vicious magazine—*Time*. I've also been reading a great deal on the porpoise. You know, *porpoise,* dahling! It's my first love these days. It has a larger brain than man. It came out of the sea years ago, and went back. Man didn't have the brains to do that. I'm going to get one soon—the five-foot variety. I'll have a pool built for it in the country, and I'll talk to it—they can talk, you know. I've already owned a lion, a monkey and a myna bird.

"Midgie Purvis is my second love. She's a baby-sitter, you know. We have to cast three children in the show, and I don't much like to work with children. They're terrible scene stealers. I worked with one child I liked in *The Skin of Our Teeth*, but he was an exception. He was a ten-year-old who read the *Racing Form* and gave me tips on horses."

TWENTY-SIX

WHILE I WATCHED the theater continue to blossom with new dramatists expressing their discontent with the world around them, I also
grew aware that the city's intimate nightclubs and cabarets were enjoying a
renaissance after a decade of decline. They, too, were providing a platform
for the kind of dissenting voices that always had appealed to me.

The Times generally ignored the satirical cabaret performers on the theory that such entertainment was not sufficiently highbrow. I believed I could
change the editors' minds—and, incidentally, create a beat all my own. I
would discover truly gifted newcomers before they were showcased on television by such as Jack Paar for his late-night talk show or Ed Sullivan for his
variety hour.

The young stand-up comics I set out to review aimed their irony at government and social institutions, and the best among them were well versed
in literature, the Bible, psychology and current events. At times, I saw them
as our new evangelists, using the cabaret stage as a pulpit to shock audiences
into an awareness of the hypocritical, repressive aspects of our culture.

They happily mined the smug, conservative Eisenhower era in which
racial prejudice, civic apathy, economic unrest and McCarthyism flourished.
The movement proliferated across the country: in Chicago, Mister Kelly's,
the Compass and later Second City; in San Francisco, the hungry i and the
Purple Onion; in St. Louis, the Crystal Palace; and in Minneapolis, Fred-
die's. They spawned the improvisers Mike Nichols and Elaine May and
stand-up comics like Mort Sahl, Shelley Berman, Bob Newhart, Milt Kamen
and a host of others who sooner or later landed in the clubs of New York and
went on to enrich the early days of television and sometimes the Broadway
stage and Hollywood. One of the highlights of the 1960–1961 Broadway season was An Evening with Mike Nichols and Elaine May, based on skits they
had honed at the Compass.

Howard Taubman gave me free rein to explore the field, and I asked
Manhattan club owners to alert me to anyone especially fresh and daring
whom they were planning to showcase. The uptown clubs were generally

classier, but often talented young performers broke in their acts downtown, moving them uptown once their reputations were established.

Max Gordon, a pioneer in cabaret entertainment, generally had the pick of the crop for his two clubs. His uptown club, the Blue Angel, had flourished on East Fifty-fifth Street since 1943, and his downtown club, the Village Vanguard, on Seventh Avenue, had achieved fame during the 1930s for presenting a revue featuring Adolph Green, Betty Comden and Judy Holliday, all barely out of their teens.

By 1960, the Blue Angel had become a mecca for the bold new comics, and it was there that I reviewed Dick Gregory when he made his New York debut in March 1961. At the time he was the only black comic who could challenge cosmopolitan white audiences. "They call me the Negro Mort Sahl," he said the night I first saw him. "In the Congo they call Sahl the white Dick Gregory." His act consisted largely of reducing racial clichés to absurdity, piercing the foibles of both blacks and whites with genial wit and no evident trace of rancor. At his best he was a brilliant caricaturist.

"I sat in a restaurant for nine months," he said, "and when they finally integrated, they didn't have what I wanted." Then he referred to the time a waitress told him, "We don't serve colored people here," to which he replied, "That's okay. I don't eat colored people. Bring me a whole fried chicken." Another quip: "When I get drunk, I think I'm Polish. One night I got so drunk I moved out of my own neighborhood." Gregory also enjoyed targeting the city's growing crime problem: "I'm glad they've cut the police working week down to forty hours; now if they can just get the hoodlums to keep the same hours."

Max Gordon never seemed to get around to repainting the Blue Angel's peeling façade or refurbishing its shabby-elegant interior. Barbara and I dined in the outer room on the best filet mignon in town, before watching the ten-thirty show in the dark, narrow inner room. Its banquettes were upholstered in quilted gray velvet and its proscenium was adorned with a plump angel, the club's namesake. An entertainer once aptly described the room as "a large coffin."

As rare a phenomenon as the successful black comic was the female comic. Kaye Ballard, Dorothy Loudon and Jane Connell were among the women who performed "special bits"—humorous songs, skits and satirical takeoffs— but few women were invited into the demanding arena of cabaret stand-ups.

One of the first was Phyllis Diller, whom I reviewed in 1961 at the Bon Soir, a tiny space on West Eighth Street in Greenwich Village, so dimly lighted that the waiters carried flashlights. Diller's humor was pointedly personal rather than political. She used her husband as a comic scapegoat in the same way that many male comics used their wives. She had a genius for building rapid-fire joke upon joke and, just when you thought she'd exhausted the subject, she'd toss out the funniest line of all.

After the show, I asked her why she thought women comics were so rare. She said stand-up was intimidating to women, because it required tremendous stamina, a thick skin, the courage to buck stiff competition in a predominantly male field and a speed that discouraged hecklers. "I don't have hecklers," she said. "My timing is so precise, a heckler would have to make an appointment to put a word in."

The Bon Soir had been a proving ground not only for her but also for a number of other young stars-to-be. The first time I visited the club in late 1960, the emcee announced that the comic I'd come to see would not appear due to illness, and a neophyte singer would take his place.

Well, this neophyte slithered onto the stage, wearing a vintage beaded dress and looking no more than eighteen. She was not alluring in any conventional way, but I was immediately aware of a presence. And when she began to sing, it was clear that here was a unique talent. I didn't have the expertise to analyze a singer in depth, so I wrote a short review, signed only with initials, that began, "A startlingly young, stylish and vibrant-voiced gamine named Barbra Streisand is one of the pleasures of a club called the Bon Soir." *Variety* had given her a routine two-paragraph review a month earlier, but mine was her first really positive notice. Returning for a second look, *Variety* predicted her career would take off if only she'd have a "nose bob."

WHEN I WENT to see Mort Sahl, among the first of the irreverent comics, he was perched on his trademark tall stool, wearing a collegiate sweater over a shirt with an open collar, looking young and innocent. He had been performing since 1953 and I knew of his reputation, but still, I was unprepared for his often hilarious skewering of establishment figures.

Sahl zestfully chided the Eisenhower administration and courageously ridiculed McCarthy at the height of his power. He would arrive onstage carrying a rolled-up newspaper, to which he had taped words to cue himself. One of his cracks dealt with a suggested answer to an investigative committee: "I didn't mean to be subversive, but I was new in the community and wanted to meet girls."

When I had coffee with him after one of his later performances during the Kennedy years, Sahl, who had volunteered jokes for the Kennedy election campaign, denied the criticism that the humorous sting had largely gone out of his routine. Dismissing my comment that he was becoming soft on Kennedy, Sahl said, "Of course, I attack President Kennedy. I resent the idolatry." But his heart did not seem to be in it. The sort of political dismemberment he had pioneered was now being more vigorously pursued by others, including Dick Gregory.

I had a hard time convincing my editors that Lenny Bruce was an appropriate subject for review. The most audacious and iconoclastic of the new stand-ups, Bruce was pushing satire to its outermost limits and Howard Taubman cautioned me that Frank Adams and the bullpen considered him "too scatological" for the daily paper. Adams said I could try a review—but he wouldn't promise it would see print.

In early December 1960, I went to see Bruce at a cavernous uptown club called Basin Street East. A slightly built, dark-haired, tired-looking man of thirty-five, he made his appearance carrying a hand-held microphone and pacing the stage like a caged and hungry panther. He billed his act "for adults only."

In my review, I did think it necessary to warn the easily shocked that Bruce regarded the nightclub stage as the last frontier of uninhibited entertainment, and that no holds were barred at Basin Street. I pointed out that there were probably a good many adults who would find him offensive—less for his Anglo-Saxon phrases than for his attacks on such institutions as the medical profession and the law—and for his mockery of pseudo-liberalism and religious piety. He declared himself pleased, for example, by a new trend toward "people leaving the church and going back to God."

Although Bruce seemed bent on antagonizing his audience, there was a fierce morality beneath his brashness. He excoriated what he called "sanctimonious liberals" who preached but could not practice integration, illustrating his point with examples of the early Romans who thought there was "something dirty" about the Christians and were apt to ask, "Would you want your sister to marry one?"

After the show, I asked Bruce a few questions to incorporate as background in my review, and he told me he was genuinely pleased that *The Times* had finally gotten around to noticing him. Despite the epithets of "sick" and "way out" that were hurled at him, Bruce said, he regarded himself as a spokesman for religious, moral and ethical ideas. He quoted the remark made to him by the jazz musician Stan Kenton: "You're really a preacher, and the nightclubs are becoming churches because of your moralizing." Kenton was right.

The day after my review appeared, Bruce called me at the paper, saying he'd added some new material and wondered if I could find time to see his show again that night. The place was jammed and Bruce had already begun his routine when Barbara and I arrived at Basin Street. He broke off and, pointing at me, said—to my embarrassment and amusement—"Put the spotlight on that man. That's Arthur Gelb. He introduced sex to *The New York Times*."

Proof of Bruce's success in shredding propriety lay in the interruptions of his act in various cities by the police, who arrested him on obscenity charges. During the next couple of years, he often sent me postcard bulletins from cities where he had run afoul of the law. The cards were illustrated with rude self-caricatures. But toward the end of his short life, the cards became rambling and often incoherent, as did his stage appearances. One night, Barbara and I caught Bruce's act at Max Gordon's Village Vanguard. Bruce wasn't funny, and he looked emaciated and ill. Clearly strung-out, he barely acknowledged our greeting after his performance.

In April 1964, Bruce was again arrested on obscenity charges, this time by the police in New York. I was asked to appear at his trial in Criminal Court as an expert witness, along with others who had written about him, to testify that his performances had important "social value." But Catledge told me not to do so, on the ground it would hurt the paper's reputation for impartiality. I suggested to Bruce's lawyer that he use my review instead—and he submitted it, asking the court how a man could be guilty of obscenity if a family newspaper like *The Times* had published a laudatory review of him.

Although one hundred prominent persons, including Lionel Trilling, James Jones, Robert Lowell and Dr. Reinhold Niebuhr, signed a statement defending Bruce as a social satirist in the tradition of Swift, Rabelais and Twain, two of the three Criminal Court judges found his work "patently offensive to the average person in the community, as judged by present standards." Bruce was convicted, but—eighteen months after his death at forty in 1966 from a heroin overdose—the decision was overturned by the Appellate Term of the State Supreme Court. Its ruling quoted a U.S. Supreme Court opinion that the prosecution in obscenity cases must show that the material under attack was "utterly without redeeming social value," and said the city had failed to prove its case. But sadly, the Bruce decision was reversed two years later by the New York Court of Appeals, the state's highest court.

Bruce was mourned by acolytes everywhere, and a tribute to his strange genius that particularly affected me was offered by Nelson Algren, the novelist whose style was once likened to Bruce's: "You're wrong if you think I'd take offense in being compared with Lenny Bruce. I don't consider him to be sick, dirty, or a nut. He's simply a man who finds the sickness, dirtiness, and nuttiness that pass for good health, morality, and sanity among us, intolerable . . . There is not a novelist, poet, short-story writer or essayist working in the U.S. today, for my money, that is saying anything as true as Bruce."

THE CLUB OWNERS, eager to show their appreciation for the attention being paid them by *The Times* after years of being ignored, sent over complimentary drinks to my table and offered gratis food as well. Many reporters in those more relaxed times had no qualms about accepting freebies, but I insisted on paying my bill—and I put the charges on my expense account.

Concerned about these expenses, Frank Adams consulted Turner Catledge. "If they want to give you a drink or two," Catledge told me, "where's the harm? Just make sure it doesn't influence you in what you write."

Later in the year, however, a national scandal erupted involving "payola," the payments made by record companies to disk jockeys at radio stations in return for airing their records. *The Times* initiated a stricter policy, forbidding staffers to accept free meals and, before the Christmas holidays, the publisher sent a memo reminding the staff not to accept any gift with a value greater than ten dollars (later, with inflation, raised to twenty-five). From then on, my cabaret expense accounts went unquestioned.

In October 1960, after several months of cabaret reviewing, I began hearing rumors about the police demanding graft from club owners. Recalling the stories I'd heard while on the police beat, I can't say I was surprised. When I asked Max Gordon about the rumors, he said they were true.

Since cabarets were licensed by the Police Department, rather than the Department of Licenses, the cops had absolute power over them. They demanded payoffs, threatening to close the clubs for minor violations. Moreover, Max told me, performers with minor offenses on their records paid bribes to obtain their licenses.

As I took out a notepad, Max said, "Are you crazy? You can't print what I told you." I tried to persuade him that a story would expose the culprits and free him and his colleagues from their grip. "I won't be around to appreciate your good deed," he said. "I've got a family and a business to protect. If word gets out that I've been squealing about bribes, I'm finished, maybe terminally." He suggested I talk to Art D'Lugoff who, he said, was braver.

The Brooklyn-born D'Lugoff, with his trademark black beard and heavy black-framed glasses, had a reputation for spunk and vision, having established himself as the premier impresario of Greenwich Village. He had been operating the Village Gate on Bleecker Street since 1957. It was a huge barn of a club with black walls and long tables arranged around support poles that ran from floor to ceiling. Like Max Gordon, he was always on the lookout for new talent, and he featured the best folk musicians and singers, among them Mahalia Jackson, Odetta, Nina Simone, Pete Seeger and Theodore Bikel, as well as jazz greats like Miles Davis, Dizzy Gillespie and John Coltrane.

When I asked D'Lugoff about police payoffs, he conceded they were a fact of cabaret life. But unlike Max, he was planning to do something about it. Itemizing a list of grievances against the Police Department's cabaret bureau, he said I could quote him. He told me, for example, that the bureau harassed "noncooperative" club owners by ferreting out petty "violations," such as insufficient soap in the rest rooms and dimming of the lights during a show (prohibited under the law in "bars and grills"). He also accused the bureau of an "outrageous, humiliating violation" of civil liberties, citing its practice of licensing all cabaret employees, including star entertainers. To obtain cabaret work permits, they had to be photographed and fingerprinted. If an entertainer had a minor infraction on his or her record, the required cabaret card might not be issued without a payoff.

D'Lugoff invited me to a small, private meeting in early November of the newly organized Citizens Emergency Committee, which was about to launch a campaign to protest corrupt police practices and free the 1,200 licensed clubs from questionable oversight. The meeting was held at the East Seventy-second Street apartment of George Plimpton, editor of *The Paris Review*. Among the others present, in addition to D'Lugoff, were Jason Epstein, an editor and vice president at Random House; Robert Silvers, then an editor of *Harper's* magazine (and later co-editor of *The New York Review of Books*); Harold Humes, Jr., a novelist; Norman Podhoretz, editor of *Commentary*; Barney Rosset, publisher of Grove Press; Donald Ogden Stewart, staff writer for *The New Yorker*; and Norman Mailer.

I gathered enough facts to write a story about the committee's plans to petition Governor Nelson Rockefeller for a state inquiry into accusations of police corruption in the cabarets. After the article appeared on page one, Mayor Wagner ordered a "sweeping" investigation of the charges. Most damning was the case of the humorist known as Lord Buckley, who died of a stroke a few days before the committee publicized its cause. His cabaret license had been revoked a month earlier on the ground that he had failed in his application to list arrests almost two decades earlier for being drunk and possessing marijuana. Buckley had claimed the questions on the application had confused him.

Harold Humes testified under oath at a preliminary Police Department hearing that Buckley had been offered an opportunity to "buy" back his cabaret card during a Police Honor Legion dinner, to which Buckley had been prodded into donating his services. During the dinner, Humes said, a man told Buckley that his card would be restored if he brought "not less than $100" to a deputy police commissioner. The man then pointed out the deputy commissioner and gave Buckley a telephone number to call and make arrangements for the drop. Another witness verified Humes's story.

Police Commissioner Stephen P. Kennedy denied all the allegations, but said his department was looking into the charges. He asked club owners and performers who had any information about license bribery to come forward and offered "immunity to any entertainer who has . . . given a gratuity to this department."

At one point, a lawyer for the committee called Kennedy "a disgrace to the City of New York" and asked for his resignation, whereupon the commissioner angrily demanded the lawyer's expulsion from the state bar. At a press conference after the hearing, Kennedy said, "I was annoyed by the insulting remarks [and] should have ignored them. But there's no sense in being Irish unless you show it from time to time."

The following spring, I shared D'Lugoff's satisfaction when cabaret supervision was transferred by City Hall from the Police Department to the Department of Licenses. Actually, the police preferred this decision to a thorough investigation of their practices, which would have revealed much worse corruption. Eventually, the law requiring photographs and fingerprints was revoked.

It was a relief to get back to reviewing comics again when a new batch began flowing into the clubs. Max Gordon urged me to see the stand-up he was introducing at the Blue Angel, who, he said, had recently traded the rabbinical pulpit for the stage. Jackie Mason's material was neither religious nor political, and he seemed less of a preacher than Bruce, Gregory or Sahl. With a deadpan delivery, jabbing the air with his right hand for emphasis, he mostly poked fun at himself.

"I used to be so self-conscious," he confided to his audience, "that when I attended a football game, every time the players went into a huddle, I thought they were talking about me." To overcome his problem, he confided, he went to a psychoanalyst, who charged twenty-five dollars per visit. He rolled his eyes in disbelief. "For twenty-five dollars, I don't visit, I move in." The analyst then asked him to tell him the first thing that came to his mind. "I want twenty-four dollars change," replied Mason.

Although it was somewhat far afield, I couldn't resist attending the improvisational comedy show by the Compass Players, when my family and I vacationed on Cape Cod in 1962. The group featured Alan Alda, son of Robert Alda, who had starred as Sky Masterson in the original *Guys and Dolls*. I'd never heard of Alan, the son, and I was curious. He was very young but, even then, it seemed to me he had talent to spare. The Compass specialized in political satire, and Alan's impersonation of President Kennedy was all the more topical since Kennedy, at that moment, was vacationing at the nearby family compound. I filed a rave review, and a few days later I received a letter from Alan's mother, ecstatic over her son's first notice: "God bless you, dear, for giving my son, Alan Alda, such an extensive and wonderful write-up." Alda, who went into television not long after I saw him, was one of the few comedians of that time who managed to avoid serving a long apprenticeship in cabarets.

A step below the cabarets was the coffeehouse scene in Greenwich Village, where folk musicians regularly made their debuts. Patrons, mostly young, paid a one-dollar cover charge to sit as long as they liked, drinking in the entertainment with their nonalcoholic beverages. A *Times* colleague whose taste I trusted told me, "You have to go see this kid who has just opened at a coffeehouse called the Bitter End."

When Barbara and I went to the Bitter End, we were among 140 people seated in old church pews. There was no curtain, just a bare brick wall behind the stage, onto which fidgeted a wisp of a man who looked browbeaten before he even began to talk. His name was Woody Allen. Then twenty-six, Allen had been writing for Sid Caesar, Art Carney and Garry Moore since 1958. Intrinsically shy, he slowly warmed to the notion of delivering his own jokes and spent two years honing his material at the coffeehouses. By the time I saw him on November 20, 1962, he had come into his own.

Allen approached the microphone on the unadorned platform as though he were afraid it would bite him. As he went on to make clear, he *was* afraid it would bite him. In his monologue, grotesque hazards—now, of course, a staple of his movies—stalked him twenty-four hours a day. He launched into a zany distortion of the facts of his life—starting with a girl he met at NYU shortly before he flunked out. This girl, whose favorite form of recreation was "listening to Marcel Marceau LPs," introduced him to a group that included a pseudo-postimpressionist artist who unsuccessfully attempted to cut off his ear with an electric razor.

After his set, Barbara and I visited Allen backstage so I could ask him a few questions. He seemed more interested in Barbara than in me, and asked why I was philandering with someone so young. He turned to her in wonder: "You look like a college girl." She told him she had flunked out of college. Allen, who had himself been bounced out of NYU at the end of his first semester, said he had no regrets, and hoped she didn't either. A few days later, I received a letter from him: "That you grouped me with Sahl, Perelman and Chaplin showed extreme perception and good taste on your part and has made me thoroughly unbearable to my friends. Business at the Bitter End took a turn for the booming since the review appeared.

"I hope you and your wife will sometime get the opportunity (if you are so inclined) to come down again, this time just to enjoy and perhaps have coffee (or a drink—you newspaper men are all alike) with me. Please tell Mrs. Gelb that I am sorry she was thrown out of college."

TWENTY-SEVEN

A s I watched the inauguration of President Kennedy on television on that frigid and blustery January 20, 1961, I was gratified to see the arts represented by Robert Frost. Following the invocation and the swearing-in, I found it an auspicious sign that the revered poet was the one person Kennedy chose to address the nation. Frost began to recite from the poem he had written to extol the day.

Many will recall that after struggling to read the first three lines, the glare of the sun reflecting off the snow prevented him from going on and, thinking quickly, he launched into a recitation from memory of an earlier poem, "The Gift Outright," which saluted the arts.

It made for stirring theater. Frost's emotional embrace, with the entire country tuned in, augured a prominent role for the arts under the new administration. Brooks, Berrie and my other friends in the cultural world had already been impressed with the many portents. Arthur Schlesinger, Jr., not only a historian and biographer but also the film critic for a magazine called *Show*, was set to become one of the president's closest assistants. We also liked the idea that the Kennedys attended the theater. I had occasionally spotted them at opening nights when Kennedy was a senator.

Unlike any White House couple in recent decades, they began infusing the capital with culture and, to my delight, they maintained that exposure to the arts was good for everyone. We soon learned that it was Jackie—lifelong balletomane, concert patron and devotee of the classics—who actually set the cultural tone. The president's taste, as I discovered somewhat later when I wrote an article with Barbara for *The Times Sunday Magazine*, was not as lofty as the First Lady's, running mostly to Broadway musicals and films like *La Dolce Vita* and *Spartacus*. He was known to sit placidly through a familiar Tchaikovsky symphony but was apt to fidget when exposed to anything more esoteric. He was a dogged reader of history and political biography, while his taste in fiction more or less began and ended with Ian Fleming.

But the fact that the president was known for his dedication to touch football and sailing, and had won a Purple Heart, made his embrace of the arts all the more potent. "When Kennedy endorses ballet, painting and theater, the average man is bound to change his mind about such things being effete," Dore Schary, the former head of MGM, and author of *Sunrise at Campobello*, once told me. Arthur Schlesinger said Kennedy was doing for culture "what Teddy Roosevelt did for tennis when he rescued it from being considered a sissy sport."

At the time, Washington was a cultural backwater, lagging far behind London and Paris—not to mention New York. It did have its share of splendid museums and art galleries, but the performing arts were restricted to a single experimental theater, the Arena Stage, and one commercial playhouse, the National (home to pre-Broadway tryouts and road companies); its National Symphony Orchestra was not in the first rank; its Opera Society was limited in resources; and its homegrown ballet company performed only sporadically. Congress generally considered the arts frivolous, and one representative from Virginia, resisting support for the arts, observed that poker was "an artful occupation" and it was therefore logical to subsidize poker players.

As part of their initiative to promote the arts in the capital, the Kennedys began hosting white-tie command performances at the White House. One of the earliest of these events featured an evening of Shakespeare, inspired by

Queen Victoria's drawing room performances at Windsor Castle in the 1880s. It seemed I was the only reporter invited to document the occasion. I was advised by the White House that following the state dinner honoring El-Ferik Ibrahim Abboud, ruler of Sudan—who had established a national theater in his country during a phase of enlightenment the previous year— the murder scene from *Macbeth* and four other Shakespearean excerpts would be performed in the East Ballroom.

I arrived in Washington on October 4, 1961, picked up my rented white tie and tails—the first time I'd ever worn them—and checked into the Willard Hotel near the White House. Pamela Turnure, Jackie Kennedy's press secretary, phoned to ask if I would like to come over early to check out the evening's preparations.

She led me to the East Room, where the finishing touches were being put on a new stage designed for special performances—an ingeniously constructed platform, with three tiers ranging in height from eighteen inches to two and a half feet, and with an oval forestage. Situated at the north end of the ballroom directly underneath a huge crystal chandelier, the open stage was backed by dark-red velour flats.

Later that evening, feeling more than a bit awkward in my unaccustomed tails, I was instantly put at ease by Jackie's graciousness. She said she felt it was important for a *Times* critic to be present "the first time that Shakespeare is being played in the White House." She also told me she and the president had particularly requested excerpts from *Macbeth* and *Henry V* because they wanted some "red meat," not just scenes from Shakespeare's comedies.

Jack Landau, the thirty-five-year-old American director, had carefully selected the scenes with the tensions of current world affairs in mind. In recognition of the fact that the guest of honor was the head of an unaligned nation, the program was designed to form an artistic unity and show that Shakespeare's wisdom and universality could foster understanding for all mankind.

The program ended with Prospero's speech from *The Tempest*, starting "Our revels now have ended," into which, Landau believed, might be read a warning about megaton bombs: "The solemn temples, the great globe itself, / Yea, all which it inherit, shall dissolve, / And, like this insubstantial pageant faded, / Leave not a rack behind."

With the performance over, the president congratulated the repertory troupe, composed mainly of young unknowns, then asked a guest, the eminent actor Sir Ralph Richardson, to stand. "Go back to England," the president wisecracked, "and tell them that an American writer named Shakespeare would be worth playing in your country."

The performance ended at eleven, and I was eager to get back to my hotel to file my story, but I was told that protocol forbade my departure until after the president took his. Mingling with his guests, Kennedy was in no hurry. He beamed when Lincoln Kirstein, an administrator of the Shakespeare Festival of Connecticut (and a co-founder of the New York City Ballet), told him that the evening marked "the beginning of a cultural renaissance in the White House." When Kennedy at last made his exit, I raced back up Pennsylvania Avenue to the Willard, my tails flapping. I phoned the city room and dictated a two-column story that was played across the bottom of page one, accompanied by two three-column pictures under a four-column head.

I was shortly to learn, however, that I had inadvertently made a serious gaffe with regard to *Times* protocol, having failed to notify the Washington bureau that I was working on a story involving the White House. Nor had I taken the time to check in at the bureau when I arrived. The story came as a surprise to the proprietary Scotty Reston, now in command of the bureau, and he was furious. Reston, who had succeeded Arthur Krock in 1953 as the chief Washington correspondent, ran his domain like an independent publication, fiercely protecting his handpicked, largely Ivy League staff who were known as "Scotty's boys." Even though he was nominally under Turner Catledge's authority, Reston reported directly to the publisher, who was profoundly respectful of his inside-Washington editorial-page columns.

When I arrived at *The Times* the following day, Catledge congratulated me on my scoop but, with the trace of a sly smile, said Scotty was justified in being upset that I had not filed my story from the bureau. "I told him that in the future that's what you'll do," said Catledge. "So don't let it worry you, and enjoy your triumph."

Actually, this had not been the first time I neglected to check in with the bureau on a working trip to Washington, but I assumed that Scotty did not pay close attention to the theater pages since he had failed to acknowledge my occasional reports from the capital. Some months earlier, I had interviewed John V. Lindsay, the Republican representative who was running for reelection in New York's gerrymandered Seventeenth Congressional District, which encompassed Broadway and most of Off Broadway, as well as the so-called Silk Stocking District of Manhattan's Upper East Side. In Congress, Lindsay was working to abolish the ten-percent federal tax on theater tickets and, more important, as a member of the Judiciary Committee, had recently helped hammer out the Civil Rights Act of 1960. In one of my articles from Washington, I wrote that he was "likely to have a bright future in both politics and theater."

On his frequent trips back to New York, the thirty-eight-year-old Lindsay—tall, lean, blond and distinctively Ivy League—enjoyed moonlighting as the narrator in an Off Broadway revival of *John Brown's Body*, a staged reading of the Stephen Vincent Benét epic. "I admit I've gotten as much charge out of playing the role as I did out of the Civil Rights Act debate," Lindsay later confided over lunch at Sardi's. "If the voters throw me out in November, I know where I'm going—onstage." With disarming candor, he once told me he had a trait that qualified him for both acting and politics.

"I am the greatest ham in the world," he confessed. "What impels a man to become a trial lawyer, which is what I was before I went into politics? The ham in him. There is also some ham in politics. You have to do some acting when you're debating or lecturing in front of an audience."

My interview with Lindsay prompted his rival in the congressional campaign, William vanden Heuvel, to demand "equal time." Vanden Heuvel said he was disappointed that *John Brown's Body* had abruptly closed. He had wanted to attend to see whether Lindsay's acting merited support. "I had a thousand leaflets mimeographed," he added, "which I planned to distribute at the theater during his next appearance. They read: 'Keep Lindsay onstage. Vote for vanden Heuvel.'" But vanden Heuvel privately acknowledged that his chances of beating Lindsay were slim, and he was right.

IT WAS FORTUNATE for me that Clifton Daniel, who had become assistant managing editor in 1957, was an advocate of arts coverage. A silver-haired, superbly tailored man-about-town, he and his wife, Margaret Truman, the former president's only child, hobnobbed with social and political figures at the swankiest Manhattan dinner parties, when not at the theater or the opera.

Though Daniel's determination to strengthen *The Times*'s cultural pages was certainly a product of his personal interests, he made the sensible argument that the arts were a major industry in New York, and that any newspaper that did not extensively cover them "should be judged derelict."

His image as a city-room dandy concealed his humble roots as the son of a pharmacist from Zebulon, North Carolina, then a town of five hundred.

While in high school, he became a reporter for the *Record*, the local paper, and helped out in the drugstore. "It was a lucky coincidence," he once said, "because there was no better place in town to gather news. The chief of police and the deputy sheriff used to hang around there all the time. We took calls for the doctors. Visiting politicians dropped in to shake hands. Farmers talked about the price of tobacco and cotton. I can still remember one night when a fellow walked in, apparently holding his head on with his hands. His throat was cut from ear to ear. I got a doctor for him—and a story for the *Record*."

After graduating from the University of North Carolina in 1933, where he was editor of the literary magazine, Daniel covered politics for the *Raleigh Observer* in his home state and then worked for the AP in New York, Washington, Bern and London, where he was hired by *The Times* in 1944 and assigned to cover the Supreme Headquarters of the Allied Expeditionary Force. His lucid style, reminiscent of Edwin L. James's European reporting, brought him fans both in and outside the paper.

At war's end, Daniel was reassigned to the Middle East, where he reported on the Israeli war for independence in 1948. Recalled to the London bureau, he had his suits made in Savile Row, earned the nickname "Sheik of Fleet Street" and blended in perfectly when he covered the coronation of Elizabeth II.

I later learned he was an authority on the arcana of men's attire. In 1967, responding to an article in our paper about a formal dinner, at which the male guests were described as wearing medals on their tuxedos, he sent me a memo questioning whether the guests indeed wore tuxedos, or if the dinner was "a white tie affair." In the single-spaced three-page memo, he listed the various kinds of costume—color, fabric and cut—correctly worn to banquets, weddings, funerals, opening nights at the opera, garden parties and racecourses. He included, as well, minute details of the accessories—shirt, tie, shoes, hat, gloves, jewelry—that were properly worn with, respectively, a cutaway, tailcoat, frock coat, dinner jacket (or tuxedo). His problem with our story, as he explained, was that decorations were correctly worn only with a tailcoat.

After a tour in Germany, Daniel took over the Moscow bureau in 1954 and tried his best to bring a human element to his stories. He escorted his readers from the bleak Russian countryside, where "factories seen across the field and mines with towering slag heaps are giving off steam and smoke," to the Bolshoi Theater's "burnished gilt balconies and vivid red draperies." He returned to New York some thirty pounds thinner in late 1955, and the following year married Margaret Truman. His appreciation of the arts brought us into frequent contact. Unlike some reporters, who thought him snobbish, I found him unpretentious, friendly and supportive.

When, a few months after the White House Shakespeare evening, I told Daniel I wanted to go back to Washington to write an article about the Kennedys and culture, he asked Reston's permission and Reston, by now sufficiently appeased, replied, "We look forward to seeing Arthur Gelb, though frankly we have no political cabarets and not much culture."

I discovered that, for the most part, Reston was right. It would take much more than the occasional presidential command performance to change Washington's image as a cultural wasteland. There were, however, a few cabaret comedy troupes beginning to take root, their material given an additional edge because they dared to spoof the nation's leadership right under its collective nose.

Then Lester Markel, who had taken note of Barbara's and my collaboration on our O'Neill biography, assigned us to a Sunday *Magazine* article that would exhaustively assess plans for change in the Washington cultural climate pegged to the arrival of the Kennedys. We talked to just about everyone in the capital who had an interest in the arts—from the editor of the *Shakespeare Quarterly* to members of the Folger Shakespeare Library to the staff of the Arena Stage, that lone outpost of the avant-garde.

Our article ultimately focused on the Kennedys themselves, who had continued inviting artists, from Pablo Casals to Carl Sandburg, to perform on the new White House stage. (Jackie told us they were planning to host bimonthly events on the lawn for young people, including ballet, jazz, theater, poetry and concerts.)

The Kennedys made a point of attending the opening performances of the opera and the symphony, and Jackie went to the Library of Congress for a reading from the works of Oscar Wilde. Their continuing efforts to spread the cultural word in the capital did not always proceed smoothly. A wag from the London *Times* explained that the performing arts suffered "because Washington society prefers talking to listening."

But even in the face of entrenched anti-aestheticism, the president began speaking out for a national cultural center comparable in scope to New York's Lincoln Center for the Performing Arts. (When it finally opened in Washington in 1971, it was named the John F. Kennedy Center for the Performing Arts.)

LINCOLN CENTER, constructed on a fourteen-acre site between Broadway and Tenth Avenue in the blocks of the mid-sixties, was conceived in 1957 as a national incubator and showcase for the best talents in music, dance and theater. This vastly ambitious plan, of course, required massive sums of money to be raised from individual contributors and foundations, as well as city, state and federal governments. There was much initial opposition from those who felt the project was too costly and grandiose and would create paralyzing traffic jams. As the Center suffered delay after delay, its original budget of $142 million rose to $160 million. In the end, however, it led to the revitalization of Manhattan's Upper West Side.

Together with others at *The Times*, I tracked the progress of the Center's development for several years, from both the economic and artistic points of view, and it seemed a miracle when the first building, Philharmonic Hall (later renamed Avery Fisher Hall), opened on September 23, 1962. Only a month earlier, the lobby had been a jungle of raw plastered walls, pitted ceilings, gaping door frames and railless staircases. The auditorium itself was a tangle of cable, canvas, scrap and scaffolding.

The invited guests had to step gingerly to avoid the mud from the surrounding construction site, much of which had been artfully concealed by canvas draping. But despite the mess, Barbara and I found the première even more dazzling than an opening at the opera. As Leonard Bernstein stepped onto the podium to lead the Philharmonic Symphony Orchestra, the audience, including Jackie Kennedy, broke into cheers. (The critics, while also generally exuberant, had some misgivings. *The Times*'s Harold C. Schonberg deplored the hall's acoustics and persisted in his campaign for improvement until major renovations helped correct the problem.)

Another of the Center's nonprofit constituents, the Vivian Beaumont Theater, fared less well than Philharmonic Hall, and its stormy inception bespoke an embattled future over how the theater should be run and who should run it. The Beaumont was to be the first playhouse built in New York since Broadway's Ethel Barrymore Theater in 1928.

The architects, in collaboration with the project's artistic directors, Robert Whitehead and Elia Kazan, had designed a state-of-the-art auditorium believed to be more versatile than any previously constructed. It had a capacity of 1,100 seats, spaced for comfort and set at a sharp rake to ensure the best possible sight lines. "Each member of the audience," Whitehead told me, "must be able to see the expression in the eyes of a face as small as Julie Harris's."

The first seven rows could, when needed, be hydraulically sunk into the basement, permitting the addition of a thrust stage. The stage walls could slide, narrowing or widening the performance space as required, or the proscenium could be entirely closed, confining all the action to the thrust stage, with the audience wrapped around on three sides. The opening was set for the fall of 1963, and Whitehead and Kazan went to work creating a national repertory company, with Harold Clurman, the director and critic, serving as their advisor. "There's nothing we won't be able to do in this theater," Whitehead assured me. "We'll be able to put on plays in any style— from the Greeks to Beckett."

In the theater world, Whitehead was revered as a producer and Kazan had been grudgingly forgiven by some of his critics for his cooperation with the House Un-American Activities Committee. Both believed that the repertory company would lead to greater artistic experimentation. Kazan, in fact, planned to sever his relationship with Broadway completely, to focus on Lincoln Center and occasional films.

"I've had Broadway and I'm not even reading scripts anymore for Broadway production," he told me. "The whole Broadway setup is inimical to the theater. It's almost impossible to do artistically daring work because of the current economy. Costs have become so absurd, producers are actually abandoning plays they know to be worthwhile, because of the high cost of running them. I was disgusted with the short rehearsal periods I had foisted on me."

Whitehead, on the other hand, was convinced that good drama more often than not equaled big box-office receipts. He believed it was artistically unhealthy not to make money in the theater and he was not concerned with the growing economic strain of production. Ironically, both men found themselves confronting more problems than they'd ever faced on Broadway. After signing several major actors for their repertory company and convincing two prominent Broadway playwrights to give them their new scripts— *After the Fall*, Arthur Miller's first play since 1956, and *But for Whom Charlie*, by S. N. Behrman—they were informed that the Beaumont Theater would not be completed on schedule.

Fearing that a year's postponement would result in the loss to Broadway of both plays, as well as some of their actors, Whitehead and Kazan came up with the idea of an interim structure—a temporary tent-theater to be erected on Lincoln Center's grounds. But the theater's board rejected the proposal as too cumbersome an installation in the midst of the construction site.

One board member, however, Dr. George D. Stoddard, chancellor of New York University, was sufficiently imaginative not only to endorse the idea of the tent but also to offer a site on his campus for a temporary metal structure that would seat 1,170. Whitehead leaped at the opportunity, and at once embarked on a battle to win majority board approval. When the board turned him down, the American National Theater and Academy came through with the $400,000 required for the tent's construction.

Jason Robards was the lead in the first offering, *After the Fall*, a psychological drama loosely based on Arthur Miller's marriage to Marilyn Monroe. Whitehead told me it was he who had encouraged Miller to write the play after the marriage broke up. Aside from his screenplay for *The Misfits*, Miller, consumed by his stormy relationship with Monroe, had not written a producible work in six years.

The play also included obvious references to Kazan's testimony before the anti-Communist investigating committee, which had caused the scandalous rupture between Miller and Kazan. It was Whitehead who had succeeded in at last reuniting the two titans. Whitehead believed that Kazan was the best possible director for *After the Fall*, but was certain Miller would never approach him on his own. Whitehead thought that if Miller were willing to collaborate again, Kazan would be professionally accepted even by some who could not forgive him for his House committee testimony. Whitehead told me Miller and Kazan had actually greeted his suggestion for a renewed partnership "with relief."

The play, which Whitehead regarded as Miller's most mature work save for *Death of a Salesman*, was a success. But Behrman's play (which seemed somehow dated) was a flop, as was the revival of an elaborately conceived but artistically minor O'Neill play, *Marco Millions*. Despite these two failures, Whitehead and Kazan felt they deserved credit for their willingness to gamble on serious, if flawed, works—for expending the highest level of production on them, and for getting a complex theatrical experiment off the ground in record time.

The company, still operating out of its temporary tent and still assuming the privilege to experiment and possibly fail, began its second season with Kazan's brave but uneven direction of the Jacobean classic *The Changeling,* followed by Miller's *Incident at Vichy*, which was not well received. Most board members, annoyed from the start by what they viewed as the condescending attitude of Whitehead and Kazan, decided the time had arrived to have their own way. And before the season was over, word reached Whitehead and Kazan that Herman Krawitz, a top executive at the Metropolitan Opera, was being courted as their replacement. I had a good story when they called to let me know they had promptly quit.

The board's impatience in not allowing the newborn repertory its share of experimental failures seemed to support the often advanced argument that the United States, unlike England, could never muster support for a national repertory theater with sufficient time and funds to develop risky new ideas. Like everything else in the cultural world, though, the failure involved egos and politics. Whitehead had made his first enemies over the issue of the tent, and the board had resented his victory. Neither was the board pleased that Whitehead always held it to its word, demanding that promised funding be delivered on time. Virtually all the money, he later told me, had been spent by the board on the building itself (designed by Eero Saarinen), causing financial neglect of the artistic development of the repertory company.

With most board members seeming less concerned about art than money, they came to view Whitehead as a persistent nuisance. They welcomed his resignation—and the Beaumont went on to make a series of mistakes in the years to come.

When Jules Irving and Herbert Blau, who operated the San Francisco Actors' Workshop, were engaged to run the theater, they were generally derided by the press as small-time. In 1973, Joe Papp took over, but after a few years he found the job an uncomfortable fit. He returned to full-time management of his Public Theater, where his production of *A Chorus Line* exploded into a great hit. When he departed the Beaumont, he sourly predicted it could never succeed, no matter who was in charge. His grim forecast held true until 1985, when a new partnership took over—Gregory Mosher, as artistic director, and Bernard Gersten, Joe Papp's former second-in-command, as managing director. Mosher was succeeded six years later by André Bishop. The team of Gersten and Bishop became happy survivors.

WHILE CULTURAL CHANGES were taking root nationally during the early 1960s, *The Times* was undergoing its own major shifts. On the night of March 15, 1961, the revolving electric bulletin sign in Times Square announced that the company would sell its venerable building that housed the sign. Arthur Hays Sulzberger explained it did not fit into the paper's plans for expansion. All of us in the city room found it hard to believe that the Times Tower with its magnificent gothic façade (later tastelessly modernized by its new owners) would no longer represent the glory of the paper at the world's crossroads.

As though that were not enough of a change for us veterans in the city room, on April 24, 1961, Sulzberger announced his retirement as publisher.

Since his son, Punch, was considered not yet seasoned enough, he passed the title to his son-in-law Orvil Dryfoos, who had long served as his right-hand man. Although Sulzberger's announcement had been expected for some time, we who had worked for him were saddened by the end of an era that had taken *The Times* from the Depression and World War II to the United Nations and the cold war.

In November 1957, Sulzberger had suffered a stroke while traveling in Burma with Iphigene, his nephew Cyrus, and Bernie Kalb. Taking command, Bernie enlisted the best doctors in Rangoon and arranged a special flight home for the publisher and his wife. Following his recovery, Sulzberger began giving Dryfoos more directorial responsibilities. He had added the title of chairman of the board to his own title of publisher, and offered Dryfoos the title of president. But after a second stroke, in 1959, Sulzberger began to falter seriously. He needed to rely more and more on medication, and his retirement appeared imminent.

He had been grooming his son-in-law since 1942, shortly after Dryfoos married the oldest of his three daughters, Marian. A Dartmouth graduate and a former securities trader on Wall Street, Dryfoos was trained much in the same fashion as Sulzberger himself. He had served as a reporter on the city staff, worked in the composing room, and gradually acquired firsthand familiarity with the paper's many aspects. Even after being named president, he continued to attend Catledge's daily page-one news conferences. Reflecting on his own rise at *The Times*, Sulzberger once wrote to Dryfoos: "Remember that none of it would have happened . . . except for the fact that I was sensible enough to marry the boss's daughter, and you were, too."

The transfer of power was seamless. Sulzberger remained chairman of the board as well as a director of the paper, and Dryfoos, as publisher, kept *The Times* dedicated to its traditions. Big changes were in store, however, for the drama department, as well as all the other cultural departments. Catledge and Daniel believed our arts coverage could be vastly enriched by a thorough reorganization—the first such overhaul since Adolph Ochs had planted the seeds of sophisticated cultural coverage at *The Times* in 1896.

In early February 1962, a memo by Catledge took all the critics and arts reporters by surprise. Work stopped while we chewed over the announcement, analyzing how it might affect each of us. The critics were alarmed because up to now they had called their own shots, leisurely overseeing their separate fiefdoms in what evidently struck Catledge and Daniel as unsupervised management chaos, even anarchy.

The memo informed us that Joseph G. Herzberg, an assistant city editor, would become the paper's first cultural news editor—and the first editor on a daily newspaper to direct overall cultural coverage on a day-to-day basis. Since he had arrived on the paper two years after I left the city room for the drama department, I barely knew him.

Catledge said he had asked Herzberg to bring order by consolidating the various arts departments into a single, enlarged cultural news department, which would now have equal status with all the major news desks. In addition, the new department would be represented by Herzberg at the daily page-one news conference, the first time cultural news was given such recognition.

With Catledge's mandate to reinvent the cultural coverage, Herzberg was asked to assess the staff's weaknesses. Since Herzberg's reputation as a stickler for perfection was legendary, most of our critics, whose newspaper roots had not been planted in the city room, were uneasy over the plans he might have for them.

For myself, I welcomed the idea of a strong hand, believing a tougher approach was bound to eliminate internal competition for space and positioning of stories, normally decided haphazardly by the copy desk and the make-up desk, neither of which had much background in weighing the relative importance of cultural news.

In another memo, this one to the entire news staff (and which I felt was a vindication of my decision to join the drama department in 1954), Catledge cited, as a major reason for the change, the upsurge of interest in the arts that had been sweeping the country in recent years: "Evidences of this cultural boom are right here in Manhattan—in Lincoln Center, which is to be a focus of American culture—and in Washington, where the White House, for the first time in half a century, is lending encouragement in the arts. Statistics show that more people are going to museums than ever before—art galleries are drawing bigger crowds than baseball games. All these things have increased the volume, variety and importance of cultural news in the daily paper."

From the day Herzberg took over the cultural department, his actions matched his reputation. His authority was unquestioned, his manner serene. He did not wait long to make his stunning initial move. He ordered the tearing down of glass partitions separating the various independent enclaves, and consolidated them all under his command. The department now resembled a smaller version of the open city room, and the staff began calling it "Culture Gulch." He had his own desk placed at one end of the gulch, from which he could view all the other desks—now lined up in rows facing him.

During his long service as city editor on the *Herald Tribune*, Herzberg had kept his staff on the move, and his wisdom and fairness were universally respected. Like Mike Berger and Bruce Rae and other natural writers of his newspaper generation, he was self-taught. He never attended college but it would have been hard to find anyone in any city room more learned, sophisticated or well traveled. He never uttered an ill-considered phrase, and frequently made arcane literary, historical and biblical references. He once described the modern newspaper as "Thucydides sweating to make a deadline."

Though Herzberg was fifty-five, eighteen years older than I, we found we had shared similar roots. Born in Harlem in 1907, he was raised in the Bronx. In 1925, soon after he graduated from Townsend Harris High School, he joined the *Herald Tribune* as a copyboy. He went from there to reporter and rewrite and then, in 1946, to city editor.

When Herzberg entered my life, he had a thatch of wavy gray hair and was my height, but would have been taller if not for a slight stoop. He walked slowly and talked slowly, a cigarette ever wedged in the corner of his mouth.

I had no inkling at the time of his appointment that he had a secret plan involving me. He knew that Barbara and I had recently completed our O'Neill biography, because Brooks, who had read the proofs, had championed it during their lunch a couple of days earlier. Herzberg told me he, too, would like to read the proofs, and I gave him a set, telling him the book would be published at the end of March.

Although publication was weeks off, Brooks heralded it in his "Critic at Large" column. "As currently constituted," he began, tongue in cheek, "the manuscript measures thirteen and a half inches when piled on the desk. It weighs twenty-six and a half pounds on the bathroom scale. It contains 1,414 pages and is longer than *Strange Interlude, Mourning Becomes Electra* and *The Iceman Cometh* combined."

A few days after Herzberg asked for the proofs, Barbara and I were called into the offices of Harper & Brothers. We were led to a wood-paneled boardroom with a large oval table around which a dozen or so editors sat. To our shock when we entered, they all rose and applauded. Our editors told us they had the highest hopes for our book, and were eager for us to commit to another biography—this time for a sizable advance. They put forward Henry Luce as a subject. Too weary to commit ourselves, Barbara and I asked them to give us a few months to think about it.

Eventually, they accepted our alternative proposal—a biography of John Reed, the radical American journalist who had been a friend and contemporary of O'Neill and who for us epitomized the political side of avant-garde America between the two world wars. His landmark book about the Russian Revolution, *Ten Days That Shook the World*, so impressed Lenin that when Reed died of typhus in Moscow in 1920, Lenin allowed his body to be buried in the Kremlin wall.

TWENTY-EIGHT

WHEN JOE HERZBERG finished reading the proofs of our biography, he invited me to join him for coffee in the cafeteria. The book impressed him, he said, and he wondered if I had plans to write another. I told him about the John Reed project, explaining it would probably take Barbara and me three years to complete.

"How are you going to do it?" he asked. I told him Barbara and I had agreed I should resign from *The Times* so that I could devote full time to collaborating with her on writing books.

Herzberg saw I was wavering, and urged me to reconsider. "You love the paper," he said. "You've spent your entire adult life here. I'd like you to help me shape the new cultural department. You'll be my deputy. We'll reorganize the coverage together."

He offered me two positions I could hold concurrently: deputy cultural editor and chief cultural correspondent. In addition to coming up with fresh ideas for coverage, I'd have the freedom to create my own assignments in all areas of culture. He explained he needed someone with my background at the paper as well as my cultural contacts. As an inducement, he offered me a significant raise.

That evening I went over every aspect of the offer with Barbara. The position, which was being tailored for me, would compensate somewhat for my not having been named drama critic. Not only would I be able to influence *The Times*'s cultural coverage on all fronts, but also—with what I allowed myself to think of as poetic justice—I would be the boss of Howard Taubman and Lewis Funke.

Barbara said she could do the bulk of the work on the Reed book if I helped with its organization and editing. In that way, I could both be her coauthor and carry out my new duties at the paper. When I accepted Herzberg's offer, he said he would make the announcement late in May to give him time to work out various staff shifts.

O'Neill, meanwhile, had become the sole book featured on the cover of Harper's spring catalogue and advance orders from stores around the country were coming in strong. When it was published in late March, Herzberg seemed as joyous about its reception as Barbara and I were. It was featured on the cover of *The Times*'s Sunday *Book Review* as well the covers of the *Herald Tribune* and the *Saturday Review of Literature*, and it was prominently reviewed in *The New Yorker*, among many other publications across the country. Although it was one of the earliest books of general interest to be priced at ten dollars, it landed on *The Times*'s best-seller list. We were at last able to pay off all our debts.

Because leaves of absence were not granted in those days, not many reporters wrote major books, and our biography was cheered by the city room. The staff celebrated us at a luncheon in a private room at Sardi's—where we were toasted by the top brass, including Catledge, Daniel, Adams, Herzberg and Atkinson. There was an eerie moment when I sensed Wilson Fairbanks's presence on the dais, and I imagined him benignly urging me to *keep checking the facts.*

When Herzberg announced my appointment on May 23, 1962, assigning me to a desk adjoining his, I at last became an editor. I began giving assignments, suggesting ideas, reading copy, tightening, cutting and even killing stories. I tried to wield my new power with care but I soon learned that authority, no matter how judiciously exercised, can breed animosity—and not just internally.

Once, for example, I was approached by a committee of playwrights, led by Paddy Chayefsky, who complained that our critics had too much influence and were responsible for closing down too many plays. They suggested *The Times* send two critics to each opening night and twin their reviews the next day, so that critical power would not reside with a single reviewer.

"What if both critics pan the play?" I asked. They admitted they hadn't considered that possibility. I then told them what Adolph Ochs had once said: "It took decades to build *The Times*'s prestige and influence. Why would we want to dilute it?"

Less easy to dismiss were complaints made by Murray Schumach about our film coverage. Murray, with his long experience as a probing reporter in New York, was setting Hollywood on its ear with his penetrating disclosures and his refusal to accept at face value the often phony releases sent by press agents. Delighted that he now had my editor's ear, he wrote to me of his concerns.

"What really gets under my skin," he said, "is seeing, day after day, how the paper is played for a sucker by the movie industry in New York. Earlier today, for instance, when I was talking to Joe Herzberg, I asked him if the financial department had discussed with him the story it had recently run about the boom in movie stocks. No one, he said, had mentioned the story to him before it was written. This is the sort of story planted periodically by the brokerage houses that tinker with entertainment stocks. The truth is that movie stocks are highly speculative. Any *Times* reader who was encouraged to buy movie stocks because of our story is probably cursing the paper by now."

More troubling were Murray's assertions that our chief film critic, Bosley Crowther, was willing to "play the game" with Hollywood studios. "I knew before I left New York that Bos was determined to force me into writing only routine items about casting announcements," Murray told me. "I figured I'd let my detailed stories speak for themselves. Then Bos began carrying gripes about me to Clifton Daniel."

I had always liked Bosley, but my deep respect for Murray kept me attuned to his complaints. Bosley, one of the most listened-to film critics in the country, had been with *The Times* since 1928, and wrote about half of the four hundred film reviews that ran in the paper each year. He had always appeared to be a man of good faith. He deplored Hollywood blacklisting and censorship and often, in his critiques, gave rein to his social conscience. In his review of *The Blackboard Jungle* in 1955, he noted that if the film's portrayal of American schools was accurate, it was a "time for drastic social action." It was true, however, that he had been on the beat for years, had acquired good friends in the industry and at times seemed overly sympathetic to its woes. I assured Murray I'd keep a close watch on news about Hollywood.

In my dual capacity of editor and reporter, I sometimes regretted having to assign a good story instead of tackling it myself. Eventually, though, I began to derive great pleasure from seeing my ideas evolve under various bylines. For example, acting on a tip from Dick Gregory's agent, who had never steered me wrong, I assigned a young staffer named Paul Gardner to review a new stand-up comic—a black student at Temple University appearing weekends at a Greenwich Village coffeehouse called the Gaslight Café. I would love to have reviewed the act myself, but I was proud to read the well-written rave Gardner gave the new comic—Bill Cosby.

Joe Herzberg and I became warm friends. He knew and loved New

York as much as I did, roving its streets uptown and down. In his younger days, he drank and chatted in newspaper haunts, but he no longer attended all manner of theater, concerts and sporting events as he once had. He always had been equally at home in a box at Carnegie Hall as in the bleachers at Yankee Stadium (although, like me, despite his Bronx background, he had rooted for the Giants as a youth). But now he looked forward to his quiet evenings at home in New Canaan, Connecticut, with his wife, Marion, and teenaged son, Paul.

We often lunched together at the Hotel Astor, Sardi's or the Gaiety, which served the world's thickest corned-beef sandwiches. (Joe quipped that Sam Zolotow was the only man he knew who could get his mouth around one.) Over lunch, Joe and I would exchange reminiscences about city-room characters who had brought smiles to our lives in bygone days. He liked to recall the greats he worked with on the *Herald Tribune*—Grantland Rice, the sportswriter; Herbert Asbury, of rewrite; John O'Hara and Paul Bowles, who both left to become major novelists; and Nunnally Johnson, a film reporter who forsook the paper to become one of Hollywood's top writers and directors.

While strolling with Joe in Times Square after lunch, I'd update him on the morning's cultural developments and we'd organize the daily report on our way back to the paper. Our jobs evolved into an ideal partnership. Joe encouraged critics and reporters during the day to strive for their best work and then slaved over their copy. I spent most evenings attending theater, opera or ballet with Barbara, becoming Joe's eyes and ears on the town.

In early October of 1962, Harrison E. Salisbury, recently appointed director of national correspondents, persuaded Joe to let me go to California to write a report assessing the state's cultural trends for *The Times*'s Western Edition, which had begun publishing on the West Coast on October 1. (A forerunner of *The Times*'s national edition, it was doomed to last a mere fifteen months.) Salisbury planned to accompany my page-one article with one of his own for a special twenty-eight-page "California Supplement" on January 3, 1963.

I interviewed dozens of writers, poets and painters from Los Angeles to San Francisco, virtually all of whom told me how much they enjoyed their environment. It was nearly a hundred years since Mark Twain had discovered the joys of being an unemployed writer in San Francisco, and I wrote that he was not the first artist, employed or otherwise, to delight in the benevolent climate and spectacular scenery of California.

Since Twain's day, creative people such as Robinson Jeffers, John Steinbeck, Arnold Schoenberg and Eugene O'Neill had done some of their best work in California, but for the most part West Coast artists did not colonize as they were apt to do in places like Greenwich Village. As an artists' haven, I found California was essentially (in Archibald MacLeish's phrase) "a country in the mind."

Barbara met me in San Francisco because we had received an invitation from Professor Travis Bogard, a distinguished O'Neill scholar at the University of California at Berkeley, to lecture on the new findings in our research. The campus at that time was tranquil. But at a dinner party Bogard and his wife hosted for us at his home, I was surprised by the barrage of invective directed by members of the English Department against the chancellor. Openly influenced by San Francisco's Beat movement, they decried the university's restrictive control over freedom of political expression by both faculty and students.

Little did I suspect, when I visited the apparently calm Berkeley campus on that morning in 1962, that only a year later it would give birth to the Free Speech Movement and see a protest ending in the arrest of 732 students for sitting in at the administration building. Bogard later told me, with undisguised pride, that it was the Berkeley faculty members I had met at his home who inspired their students to challenge the administration, an act of rebellion that eventually led to the birth of student activism on campuses all over the country—the start of a national student movement that ultimately exploded into the anti–Vietnam War campus protests.

OUR NEWLY EXPANDED cultural coverage, which was beginning to have an influence on other papers in the country, was abruptly suspended on December 8, 1962. The day marked the start of the longest newspaper strike in New York history, called by the Big Six printers.

The newspaper unions traditionally joined ranks to present a united front. Hence when the printers walked out, so did reporters, deliverymen, photoengravers, pressmen and all other union members—nineteen thousand employees in all. Many of the reporters represented by the Newspaper Guild were reluctant participants in the strike, but knew they had to rely on solidarity with the printers to maintain their own clout in future negotiations. Except for top editors and executives and their confidential assistants who were exempt from union membership, and a scattering of employees willing to cross the picket lines, everyone else went out on strike.

The greatest fear of the printers' leader, Bertram Powers, was that technology would render his union members obsolete, and he sought to limit mechanization. He insisted, for example, that a share of the savings gained by introduction of new machines be funneled into a fund for retraining, early retirement and unemployment benefits. Among his other major demands was a package increase of $84 a week per employee, in addition to a workweek reduction from thirty-six and a half hours to thirty-five.

The members of the Publishers Association were taken aback by the demands, particularly the $84 a week increase in pay and benefits—especially because only two New York papers, *The Times* and the *News*, were moneymakers. The others survived on subsidies provided by their individual publishers or the large chains that owned them, and they were up against a financial ceiling above which they said they would be forced out of business. Additionally, no paper wanted to limit its right to introduce the best available new technology.

On the evening of December 7, refusing to believe the printers would strike, the Publishers Association, through its spokesman, Amory H. Bradford, vice president and general manager of *The Times*, made the unions a counteroffer: a package increase of $9.20 a week in return for union concessions on mechanization.

At 1:45 A.M., fifteen minutes before the threatened strike deadline, Powers reduced his demands to $38 per week, which the publishers rejected. The strike was called selectively against *The Times*, the *News*, the *Journal-American* and the *World-Telegram & Sun*. Powers said he did not want to sink the other five "marginal" papers (the *Herald Tribune*, the *Post*, the *Mirror*, the *Long Island Star-Journal* and the *Long Island Press*). In accordance with the rules of the Publishers Association, however, the other papers voluntarily shut down their presses.

The strike caught me in a dilemma that differed somewhat from that of most of my colleagues. In my new position, I straddled the fence between editor and reporter. As deputy culture editor, I shared decision-making policy with Joe Herzberg, whose elevated executive role clearly entitled him to an exemption from the union. But *The Times* did not regard deputy editors high enough in the power echelon to request union exemption for them. Thus, as chief cultural correspondent, I kept my union membership and paid my union dues, as I had done since becoming a copyboy in 1944.

When the strike began, I didn't show up for work and Joe called me at home. He argued against my striking, but his heart wasn't in it. Explaining that my personal loyalty lay with the reporters, I also said I could not in good conscience cross a picket line unless I was formally exempted.

The strike began to seem endless, and we all scurried to pick up what jobs we could. Barbara and I had delayed signing a contract for the John Reed book because I had been occupied with my *Times* job and Barbara was busy lecturing on O'Neill to help promote sales. With the onset of the strike, however, we once again became concerned we would be thrust into debt. I juggled a number of freelance assignments that provided a modest temporary income. I reviewed theater for the new public television station, Channel Thirteen (then called WNDT), and I took the job Barbara's father offered me during Christmas week as a floor manager at a branch of his store, Lamston's. I also took on an assignment from the Ford Foundation to write a report on the economic condition of the performing arts.

In early March of 1963, three months into the strike, we thought it expedient to sign a relatively lucrative contract for the John Reed biography. At a strike rally, I told Dick Witkin—*The Times*'s aviation editor, whom I'd got to know when he covered the UN for United Press—about our good fortune, and he urged me to invest the money in a house in the suburbs. He sang the praises of the serene, wooded Westchester town of Harrison, where, he said, the air was pure, neighborhoods were clean and safe and the public schools ranked high. He had recently settled there with his wife, Kate Friedlich, a dancer who had been featured in the original Broadway *Oklahoma!*

I conceded that the secluded suburbs were Dick's natural habitat, but I wasn't sure about myself. He was the son of the Cocoa Exchange founder and a Harvard graduate. Tall and slender, he looked the typical Air Force captain he had been in World War II. The following Saturday he and Kate took Barbara and me on a tour of Harrison and we found an old colonial-style house of red brick, surrounded by oaks and maples, that we thought we could afford. But I still felt torn about leaving the city that had nurtured me.

Barbara and my mother, however, assured me that Harrison was the place to bring up our children, reminding me that Michael would graduate in June from P.S. 6, whose classes went only as far as the sixth grade. If we stayed in the city, he would have to enter the nearby junior high school, which was showing signs of deterioration. Since Barbara and I were at the time philosophically opposed to private school, I finally concluded that a move to the suburbs was the solution. And we also liked the idea of living close to Dick and Kate, whose sons, Tom and Gordon, were roughly the same ages as our boys.

"As long as we were on strike, and things looked desperate, we decided to buy a house," Barbara wrote facetiously to Bernie and Phyllis. "We are going to become suburbanites, God help us. Since making this horrendous decision, we have acquired two lawyers, a tax expert, an architect, a new insurance broker, an appraiser for our papers and manuscripts, miscellaneous plumbers, electricians, carpenters, a kitchen engineer, a furnace contractor and two goldfish. We have not yet engaged a psychiatrist, but we expect we'll need one any minute.

"I keep telling Arthur that we must be terribly rich, or we couldn't afford all this. He agrees, but says he thinks we had more money when we were poor. I am selling all my beaded hats to raise money to pay the moving men. And I have no time to write the new book, because I'm on the phone all day negotiating with lawyers, tax experts, etc.

"P.S. Do you know what Abraham Neanderthal Rosenthal is up to? Rumors, as they say on West Forty-third Street, are rife."

Bernie had left *The Times* a year earlier to create a CBS bureau in Hong Kong, where he was now living with Phyllis, their Indonesian-born Tanah, and Marina, who had been born in New York while Bernie was on a year's fellowship with the Council on Foreign Relations. (Claudia and Sarinah came later, both born in Hong Kong.) Abe, now stationed in Tokyo, often ran into Bernie while covering major Far East stories.

We had written to Bernie, thinking he might have the inside track on the simmering, though vague, gossip heard at union strike meetings about Abe's next assignment, possibly as an editor in New York. But Bernie didn't have a clue, and Abe himself was closemouthed. When I wrote to him about the gossip, he responded: "You sure have great news sources. Frank Adams is city editor, Max Frankel is writing for *The Times*, *Newsweek* never wrote to me, Kitty Teltsch [on the staff of the UN bureau] married Tom Hamilton, and you're fired. Don't bother me. I am too busy sticking pins in voodoo dolls of Leon Edel."

Abe's reference to Edel was to the second of his projected three-volume biography of Henry James, which people were saying was our competitor for the Pulitzer Prize. (Abe's pins didn't work. Bill Laurence, who had been on the three-member jury but recused himself because of our friendship, later confided that the remaining two panelists, after an initial stalemate, eventually decided to vote for Edel. They reasoned that, since we were just beginning biographers, there would be ample opportunity for us to be considered in future years.)

Abe's evasiveness bothered me, but it was difficult for the moment to focus on anything except the strike. The long-drawn-out talks were being attributed to the clashing personalities of the two chief negotiators, Bert Powers and Amory Bradford.

Powers, believing that the Newspaper Guild held more than its share of clout in determining the fate of all newspaper employees, saw his opportunity to strengthen the power of his printers' union. The Publishers Association was infuriated by his negotiating style because he made concessions, then retracted them. Most outside observers thought his demands were unrealistic. One government official said, "He's honest, democratic, clean—and impossible." Bradford, on the other hand, was aloof, conceited and—as one mediator described him—possessed of "a short fuse." His attitude toward Powers was condescending and his manner so icy that another mediator said he wanted to ask the hotel to turn up the heat whenever Bradford walked into the conference room.

When Powers reduced his demands to $16.42 a week, Bradford snidely replied, "How do we fit that into a ten-dollar bill?" He had little patience for the negotiating process and often walked haughtily away from the bargaining table. Once, when he declined to attend a meeting called by Mayor Wagner, Orvil Dryfoos personally intervened, ordering Bradford to reverse his course.

On March 14, 1963, one of the strike mediators commented that "this whole thing" ought to be settled in a psychiatric ward. Within days, however, it appeared that a compromise had been reached based on solutions suggested by Mayor Wagner. The unions would receive an increase in wages and benefits of $12.63 per week and would get their thirty-five-hour workweek in exchange for giving up fifteen minutes a day of "wash-up" time; and a common contract expiration date was established—two years from the signing of new contracts. Teletypesetter tape, one of the new technologies, would be used only for AP and UP tables of stock-market figures, and a panel would be established to determine how much of the savings should go into a workers' fund.

Only the engravers balked at the terms. They demanded paid vacation time over and above the $12.63 in concessions. Powers used all his influence to sway the holdouts, and the strike ended on March 31—114 days after it began—with tragic results for the New York press. Not long after, the *Mirror* shut down, eventually followed by the *Herald Tribune*, the *World-Telegram & Sun* and the *Journal-American*.

I was among the first to return to work that afternoon, and Joe Herzberg greeted me with a fatherly hug. As a token of my return, I presented him with an exclusive story I had written at home the night before, when I learned the end of the strike was imminent. The story, which disclosed President Kennedy's plan to create the country's first Federal Advisory Council on the Arts within two weeks, was played on page one.

Joe told me the strike's end made him happier than he'd been since receiving his first byline. Blithely ignoring the 114-day interruption, Joe and I handed staffers their assignments as they unlocked their desks and began clacking away at their typewriters.

Dryfoos announced that the price of the paper would be raised from a nickel to a dime, and issued a message to the staff:

"It's good to see you back at work! I know you are as glad as I am that *The New York Times* is to resume publication. I trust that there will not be any bitterness about the strike. Nothing should impede us from putting out the best newspaper we know how. . . . Those of you who are returning to work—and those of you who have been working—are the people who make this newspaper the institution it is. Because of you, I have the greatest confidence for the future."

Orvil Dryfoos was fated not to share in that future. He had been afflicted with an enlarged heart since boyhood, and the strain of the strike had proved too great. Less than three months after the settlement, he was hospitalized for heart failure. His death, on May 25, created yet another crisis for the Sulzberger family.

Both Dryfoos and Amory Bradford, *The Times*'s highest-ranking non-family member, had reinforced Arthur Hays Sulzberger's apprehensions about what they all perceived as Punch's immaturity. In 1954, after brief reporting stints in New York and a year with the *Milwaukee Journal*, he worked for a short time in *The Times*'s London, Paris and Rome bureaus.

His formal training, however, had been less than comprehensive and, when he returned to New York in 1955 as assistant to the publisher and then as assistant treasurer, he was often shunted off to run side projects, such as revamping the cafeteria. "I several times told Dryfoos this was a degrading way to treat a future owner of the paper," Catledge once wrote, "but Dryfoos would throw up his hands and say he didn't know what to do with Punch."

Fortunately, Punch's real newspaper education had taken place not at the side of his dominating father or that of his complaisant brother-in-law, but at Turner Catledge's. He called Catledge "the professor," and nearly every evening joined him and his cronies from such departments as circulation and promotion for drinks and shoptalk. Punch felt far more comfortable with Catledge than with his father, and Catledge, who found Punch "witty and good-natured," always encouraged him to ask questions.

With his brother-in-law's death, Punch expected his father to name him both publisher of the newspaper and president of the company, the titles that had given Dryfoos complete control. Bradford, with the same arrogance he had displayed during the strike, believed the ailing Arthur Hays Sulzberger would now have to rely on his experience more than ever. In his mind, with *The Times* still reeling financially from the strike, Sulzberger would have grave concerns about giving Punch control. He suggested that Reston be named publisher, running the news side, and that he be named president, in charge of the business side.

But Sulzberger devised a compromise: Punch as publisher and Bradford as president. Punch adamantly opposed having to share control, especially with a man he disliked as much as he did Bradford. His overbearance during the strike had also undermined him with Iphigene Sulzberger.

When Iphigene went to Punch's office to inform him of his father's compromise, he was furious. He marched into his father's office and declared he would not accept his decision. He demanded he be granted both titles or neither, insisting the power-sharing arrangement with Bradford could not succeed. Swayed by his son's resolve, Sulzberger gave him his blessing. "I don't blame you," he said, in a now famous reply. "I can't stand the son of a bitch either."

On June 20, 1963, Punch became, at thirty-seven, the youngest chief executive in the paper's history. "It is our intention to maintain this family operation and ensure continuance of the newspaper that *The Times* has come to be under those who by sentiment and training are particularly tied to its principles and traditions," said Arthur Hays Sulzberger in his announcement. "My son, Arthur Ochs Sulzberger, has more than proved himself over the many years that he has been here as well as during the difficult period of the recent long strike."

Bradford left the paper soon after. Years later, in Aspen, Colorado, I happened to meet his daughter, and I asked what had become of her father. I was staggered to learn he had grown his hair long, sold most of his possessions and was traveling across the country in a van, accompanied by various hippies he met along the way.

CONCURRENTLY WITH THE CHANGES in the *Times* hierarchy, reports about Abe's new post began to heat up, and Ann, in a letter from Tokyo, finally confirmed them. She wrote us that Abe would return to New York in the fall to replace Frank Adams as city editor.

"I look forward to getting back to my own culture," she told us. "The boys don't know quite what that means, but I know they will enjoy life in the U.S. It will be a blow to Jonnie, who is very firmly established here with his friends and his school, which he loves passionately. Andrew and Danny, like their mother, are wanderers at heart. They are delighted by the news. . . . After nine years, we come back to you and what do you do? Desert us for the suburbs!! I'm just disappointed that you will be so far away from us. I am determined to be in the city at least for a couple of years. This is terribly important to Abe. . . . We have no departure date as yet. It's entirely up to us. It is hard to pry Abe loose from his beloved Tokyo."

A few weeks later, with little advance notice, Abe arrived in New York, leaving Ann and the children temporarily behind in Tokyo, and invited himself to spend a weekend with Barbara and me in Harrison. At our house, after delivering the expected jibes about our grandiose attitude as landowners, Abe disclosed that it was Catledge, during a visit to Tokyo, who had lured him back to New York to be city editor.

Concluding that Frank Adams had passed his prime and that local coverage was unacceptably short of fresh, lively ideas, Catledge told Abe he had analyzed the problem with Ted Bernstein, who had nominated Abe for the job. Adams would be transferred to the editorial page, where he would write commentary about city affairs.

Catledge said he needed Abe to reinvigorate the city staff and raise its standards to the level of the national and foreign reports. Abe's youthful imagination and energy would instill new approaches in city reporting and editing, said Catledge. He promised Abe a free hand to make whatever improvements he found necessary.

Impressed by the esteem in which Abe was held by the city staff—including senior reporters like Homer Bigart, Peter Kihss, Murray Schumach, Edith Evans Asbury, George Barrett and Charles Grutzner, as well as younger ones like McCandlish Phillips, J. Anthony Lukas, Gay Talese and Martin Arnold—Catledge believed they would gladly follow his lead. Emulating a recent change in titles at the *Herald Tribune*, Catledge told Abe his title would be metropolitan editor, and his desk's jurisdiction would be broadened beyond the city and suburbs to include all of New York State, New Jersey and Connecticut.

Abe told me he did not leap at the offer. He longed to remain in Japan—a country he had come to love even more than India. What he really wanted, he told Catledge, was to write an editorial page column headed "Asia." But Catledge hinted strongly that, dream as he might, Abe was not going to get a column. After some weeks of deliberating, Abe told Catledge he would take the job. And, although he had not consulted me, he also said he wanted me to be his deputy. Catledge's response was that both he and Clifton Daniel had expected Abe to ask for me, and he consented.

Abe's trip to New York, it appeared, was made in part to convince me to join him when he took command of the new metropolitan desk. I had mixed feelings about his offer. I was already a deputy editor and, now that the strike was over, Herzberg and I were finally implementing our plans to revolutionize the cultural coverage.

On May 21, 1963, he had sent a memo to the staff that I had helped him draft, asking all department editors to be in the office every day by eleven A.M. "I would like to see ideas flow from each department," he told the editors. "The space allotted must be used for superior copy. Space-filling is ended. The bullpen has been liberal in providing space and we should repay that generosity with good stories, crisply written."

With Clifton Daniel suggesting the names of critics to hire, we had by then engaged Clive Barnes, who covered dance for newspapers in London, to report on dance abroad, and Ada Louise Huxtable, who lived in Manhattan, to be the first full-time staff architecture critic on any American newspaper. Our proudest cultural acquisition, Huxtable had served as assistant curator of architecture and design at the Museum of Modern Art and had contributed notable articles to *Progressive Architecture* and *Art in America*, as well as to *The Times Magazine*.

Huxtable promptly set about condemning the planned demolition of what had been, in 1910, the epitome of modernity—McKim, Mead and White's Pennsylvania Station. Picketing and demonstrations, which began in 1962 to prevent amputating the station's soaring, classical columns in order to construct a new motel-like Madison Square Garden, had left Mayor Wagner and other city fathers unmoved. On May 5, 1963, in an article entitled "How to Kill a City," Huxtable lashed out at the failure of zoning laws to protect historic landmarks:

"If a giant pizza stand were proposed in an area zoned for such usage, and if studies showed acceptable traffic patterns and building densities, the pizza stand would be 'in the public interest,' even if the Parthenon itself stood on the chosen site. Not that Penn Station is the Parthenon, but it might just as well be because we can never again afford a nine-acre structure of superbly detailed solid travertine, any more than we could build one of solid gold. It is a monument to the lost art of magnificent construction, other values aside."

The tragic destruction of Pennsylvania Station proceeded as planned, over clamorous protests by Huxtable, who was to win, among her numerous honorary degrees and other awards, the first Pulitzer Prize for "distinguished criticism." But neither she nor other forward-thinking New Yorkers could prevent the station's Doric columns from being smashed and dumped in Secaucus Meadows, New Jersey.

As part of our toughening up of the coverage, Herzberg and I also encouraged a former city-room reporter, Milton Esterow, to create a new beat—investigations of chicanery in the international art market. No newspaper had paid consistent attention to the behind-the-scenes maneuverings in the art world. Poking around, Esterow discovered the FBI had recently assigned a special agent, Joseph Chapman, to track down the brazen art thieves bedeviling museums, galleries and homes of private collectors. Aware that FBI agents rarely answered reporters' questions, Esterow wrote to J. Edgar Hoover about interviewing Chapman and, to his surprise, was granted permission. With Chapman's cooperation, Esterow filed story after story about thefts from the Riviera to New York. When he left the paper in 1968 to publish books on American art, the beat was continued by another hard-nosed reporter, Grace Glueck. (In 1972, Esterow bought the failing magazine *ARTnews* from *Newsweek*, and turned it into the art magazine with the largest circulation.)

I TOLD ABE I wasn't interested in being deputy metropolitan editor, since I was reluctant to abandon the fledgling culture department and the arts themselves, which had become so intrinsically a part my life. I had the most enjoyable job on the paper, I said—writing about and editing subjects I loved.

But, Abe argued, there was a larger world out there. "Together we can make New York coverage better than it's ever been," he said, "and there's no reason why the coverage can't at times include the arts. We'd have fun working as a team."

He said he was counting on my help since, having been abroad for almost nine years, he wasn't familiar with the dramatic changes taking place in the city, colored by the Vietnam War and the civil rights protests in the South. He added that my familiarity with City Hall, Wagner, Moses, Lindsay, the police and the municipal departments would be invaluable. Most tempting of all, he said he was sure I would succeed him one day as metropolitan editor, as he had set his own sights on higher goals.

While I reweighed my decision, Catledge summoned me to his inner office and, as in the past, invited me to join him in a drink. These days, he drank only moderately, having overcome an earlier problem with alcohol. In 1957, he had fallen in love with and married a vivacious, nurturing woman from New Orleans, Abby Ray Izard, and she had restored the self-confidence that had been eroded by his unhappy previous marriage.

Catledge told me bluntly that it would be a great disappointment to him if I refused Abe's offer. He said Punch, who had been publisher only three months, strongly favored Abe, and that Abe would herald the new wave at *The Times*, assisting Catledge and his team to transform the paper. To help lead the paper into the future, he said, a younger generation of editors had to be groomed now.

"The job we're asking you to do won't be too difficult," he assured me. "You just have to come up with one or two good story ideas a day." Then he said he planned to transfer me to the executive monthly payroll with a $10,000 annual raise that would bring my salary to $25,000. I gulped and said yes.

Contrary to my expectations, Joe Herzberg was genuinely pleased for me. He said he hoped my new job on the city desk, a post similar to the one he had held at the *Herald Tribune* and at *The Times* itself, would prove as exciting for me as it had once been for him. Conceding my love for the theater world, he pointed out that "the hardboiled reporter" in me was sometimes less than fulfilled in the cultural arena—even though culture now belonged to the mainstream of the newspaper's coverage.

To some extent, Joe was right. During the previous few years, I had at times envied Abe's and Bernie's involvement in major world news events, while I was writing about Off Broadway and cabaret comics. Joe suggested I now take the editorial skills I had been practicing on the culture desk and apply them to breaking city news. If I needed guidance, he said, I could always go to him.

Barbara, on the other hand, was of two minds about my promotion. She was happy about my new challenge but she knew that my widening responsibilities meant longer hours and sometimes work on weekends, and this ended any possibility of my collaborating on the Reed biography. We dropped the project and Barbara concentrated on writing for magazines, but a decade later she decided to do the book alone. She scaled back its scope to focus primarily on the period of Reed's liaison with the daring journalist Louise Bryant, who was simultaneously conducting an affair with Eugene O'Neill. The book became *So Short a Time*.

Warren Beatty approached Barbara about the possibility of her being a consultant on a movie about Reed, a role he had long wanted to play. They met to discuss, among other aspects of the story, the love triangle, and Beatty asked Barbara's opinion as to whether Louise would be best portrayed by Jane Fonda, Julie Christie or Diane Keaton. Barbara, in good faith, spent hours with him and—at his suggestion—had her agent draw up a contract. But Beatty suddenly changed his mind about doing the movie.

Sometime later, when Barbara read in *Variety* that Beatty was planning to make a film (without her participation) called *Reds*, about the Reed–Bryant–O'Neill triangle, she consulted her lawyer and sued Paramount Pictures and Beatty. An out-of-court settlement was reached (stipulating that Barbara could not reveal the monetary amount).

Barbara bought an expensive stone-marten coat and wore it to a glamorous Broadway opening night. During intermission, when Jean Kerr and other friends of Barbara's complimented her on her purchase, she blithely informed them, "Warren Beatty bought it for me."

As a kind of introduction to our taking over the metropolitan coverage on September 17, 1963, I suggested Abe join me on a tour of topical cabarets to get a feel of what satirical comics were saying about our government. After watching Dick Gregory's act at Basin Street East, Abe said he'd like to meet him.

Backstage, when I introduced Abe as *The Times*'s newly appointed editor in charge of city coverage, Gregory dropped his comic mask. I couldn't believe the change that suddenly overcame him. He glared at Abe with narrowed eyes and, in a deadly serious tone, he warned him to expect a lot of trouble in his new job. There was a long, uncomfortable pause. I could read Abe's mind: Why on earth had I brought him here?

"Negroes are fed up and there's going to be a revolution," Gregory finally said. "The top of the keg is going to blow off here in New York." Abe and I looked at Gregory as if he were crazed. Then he quoted from Dr. Martin Luther King, Jr.'s speech to two hundred thousand civil rights marchers in Washington on August 28: "There will be neither rest nor tranquillity in America until the Negro is granted his citizenship rights."

Abe and I talked long and earnestly about how to assess Gregory's prophecy, which had certainly unnerved us. In less than a year, his prediction came true, with the explosion of the riots in Harlem. As the 1960s progressed, Gregory's humor gradually took a backseat to his political activism. He eventually left the cabaret scene to participate in demonstrations around the country, gave speeches and lectures and tried to calm the Watts riots in California.

Gregory started down this path after learning of the incarceration of an elderly Negro man during a voter registration drive in Mississippi. The man's wife had died while he was in jail. Gregory began to question whether he could consider himself a success while his people were struggling for their lives. Never affiliated with a single organization, he was always the maverick activist.

He did not advocate the use of force, but once remarked, "There is nothing in the rules which says the Negro must be nonviolent. Nonviolence is a favor, not an obligation." In describing his tactics, he often said, "I will not hit you. I will not kill you. But I will bug you to death." His preferred method of protest was boycotting, not rioting, because afterward "buildings will still be standing, firemen won't be getting shot and Negroes won't be dead." For his various efforts, he was jailed numerous times, and, as he continued to pass up comedy bookings, he sank from a comfortable lifestyle into debt.

TWENTY-NINE

AFTER NEARLY NINE YEARS in "Culture Gulch," I was once again part of the city room I had first entered as a copyboy. Unsurprisingly, there were some notable differences. Metal desks had replaced the splintering wooden ones. Some familiar reportorial faces—among them Mike Berger's, Jim Hagerty's and Lucy Greenbaum's—were gone, replaced by new ones I didn't recognize and who didn't recognize me. There were no more brass spittoons, and gone, too, were the fedoras and green eyeshades once worn by copy editors. I noticed, though, that fast-typing rewrite men still glanced at the wall clocks as I had done when deadline neared.

Other aspects of the city room were as I remembered them. Reporters still sat side by side, no partitions separating them, and impassioned discussions still erupted from time to time in various pockets of the room. The newly renamed "metropolitan" staff was still a white male domain. Only six of the hundred city reporters were women, and we still had only one black reporter—no improvement over the tokenism that George Walker Streator had deplored over our drinks at Childs in 1945.

Sammy Solovitz was still sending copyboys (and a scattering of copy-girls) scurrying on the same missions that had kept me on the run in 1944.

The nonstop card game in the back of the room had only recently been abolished by Catledge. But since all the executives still smoked, no edict had been issued against the tossing of cigarette butts onto the floor.

It soon became apparent that Abe and I were regarded with uneasy puzzlement by the more recently hired reporters. Even the newest recruits knew, of course, of Abe's Pulitzer Prize for his reporting from Poland, and most were aware of his impressive articles from India and Japan. Few, moreover, could have been unaware of his widely acclaimed Sunday *Magazine* essay about his visit to Auschwitz. But since Abe had not worked in New York in nine years, none of the younger reporters had ever met him.

My own situation was somewhat different, for I had kept in touch with a number of city-room staffers during my tenure in the culture department. My desk, after all, was not far from the city room. Many of the hard-nosed reporters, however, paid little heed to cultural reporting and to them I was basically a soft-news feature man.

Consequently, Abe felt compelled—in informing the staff of my appointment as deputy metropolitan editor—to post on the bulletin board, along with the announcement, the *Times Talk* article of 1952, describing my page-one scoop on the new antituberculosis miracle drug. (I removed it, embarrassed that Abe found it necessary to bring me to the city staff's attention in this way, after all my years of writing major stories, magazine pieces and books.)

Abe and I were fully confident we could carry out Turner Catledge's mandate to revitalize local coverage of the news. Each with two decades of experience on the paper, and an ingrained sense of its basic values, we trusted our ability to break the outdated molds and tear down the arbitrary barriers. Our goal was to shape the most comprehensive and imaginative city report ever produced. We were bent on sniffing out every facet of New York's multiple personality: home to eight million diverse New Yorkers, and international capital of the arts, communications and finance.

But it wasn't going to be all coasting. The paper had been very slowly shedding the rigidity of its copyediting, its often stodgy mores and the pinched format that inhibited dramatic display of good stories, with scarcely any space for photographs. It was in many ways still hidebound. We knew we would have to proceed with a measure of caution, since older readers regarded *The Times* as a news bible and did not appreciate any changes at all. (Some even protested when four years later—for the sake of modernity—we dropped the Old English period at the end of the page-one nameplate.)

WE BEGAN BY TURNING the city editor's desk around, in a move both symbolic and practical. Frank Adams had positioned the desk to face Catledge's office, with his back to the city staff. I suppose he considered it both more important and less stressful to keep track of the managing editor's whereabouts than to have unrelieved eye contact with his reporters.

Abe and I chose to face the reporters, not only because we wanted to stay apprised of our staff's goings and comings but to send a signal that the reportorial staff, not the managing editor, was our top priority. I sat directly to Abe's left, a microphone between us on a table, which we used for paging reporters in the distant reaches of the room.

Our next move was to unburden ourselves of the management of reporters' expense accounts and scheduled days off and holidays—the kind of administrative matters with which Adams had occupied much of his time. We preferred to be up to our ears in stories and anything not news related we delegated to assistants.

Looking out across that vast city room, we thought we could discern the reason for the weaknesses in the city report that had led to Adams's transfer. Here at the editor's disposal was the greatest talent pool on any newspaper. But Adams, like David Joseph before him, had a habit of keeping his star reporters sitting idly at their desks, awaiting a major news break.

Abe and I quickly changed all that. In lieu of a significant spot-news story, we didn't hesitate to create a challenging feature idea for one or another of our stars. It's true this could be risky, for sometimes the idea didn't pan out, but often it blossomed into a great page-one story. The main goal was to get the reporters out of the office and, while some of the older ones resented being unglued from their desks to pursue what might turn out to be a chimera, the younger ones appreciated our nontraditional perspective.

Principal among these was Gay Talese, who at thirty was a natural writer with a gift for digging into the offbeat. In the vanguard of our young, talented city reporters, Gay had started his newspaper career at fifteen for a small weekly in his seaside hometown of Ocean City, New Jersey, where he impressed his editor with a lively story about a young, pretty blond summer resident who yearned to become an actress. Her name was Grace Kelly. Gay joined *The Times* as a copyboy in 1953, but a year later, he was drafted into the Army. After submitting articles to military publications and various civilian newspapers, he returned to *The Times* in 1956, and was made a reporter.

In 1959, after Nelson Rockefeller was elected governor, Talese was sent to Albany to assist the four-man bureau and its dour chief, Leo Egan, who had no use for Gay's colorful embellishments of his political stories. Talese complained of being underappreciated and was called back to the city room, where Adams assigned him to minor obituaries. Gay began submitting ideas to the Sunday *Magazine*, which happily accepted twenty of his stylishly written freelance articles.

Talese, who had never met Abe, so admired his dispatches from abroad that he wrote him frequent letters of praise. (In 1980, fifteen years after leaving *The Times* to write books, Talese told a writer for *Women's Wear Daily*: "When I was on *The Times*, I thought there was only one man who could outwrite me—A. M. Rosenthal. As for the rest of them—Reston, Tom Wicker, Tony Lewis—I felt I could outwrite them all. But Rosenthal was better than me as a writer and as a reporter. I read everything he ever wrote, from his days as a correspondent in India and Poland and Japan, until he became metropolitan editor. A few years later I reread his clips to see if he was really as good as I thought he was. He was.")

Near the end of Abe's stay in Japan, Talese had written him that he was fed up with the way Adams was squelching his attempts at original writing. He was going to quit, he said. Abe urged him to wait a few weeks, hinting there might soon be changes at the paper that would result in the writing freedom Talese sought.

WHEN WE TOOK OVER the city staff, Abe and I made it our first priority to free reporters of their perceived writing restrictions, encouraging them to try new approaches, to experiment with their own styles the way we both had tried to do. We pressed them to use similes, imagery, vivid descriptions and lively quotes, assuring them we would protect their stories against the itchy pencils of literal-minded copy editors. For my part, recalling the copy desk's opposition to Murray Schumach's "unfit-to-print" semen-stained handkerchief in his long-ago murder story, I promised we would be considerably more broad-minded. I had no doubt that our new order was long overdue, even though it directly countered the stubbornly held doctrine of my early heroes, Wilson Fairbanks and Grover Loud. As for Adolph Ochs's sanctification of the copy editor as the savior of a newspaper's space and the reader's time—well, different yardsticks apply to different eras.

Determined that his message to reporters also be conveyed to those handling their copy, Abe called a meeting of all the editors under his jurisdiction. He emphasized that he wanted editors to protect good copy and to encourage all reporters to record on-the-scene local color. "This does not mean that we must insert blocks of color in stories simply for the sake of color," he explained. "Rather, we should weave it into the fabric of the story. And we must not cover a story with just our ears—we must also use our eyes." A complete picture, he said, must include what people look like and what they do, as well as what they say.

After a while, in fact, we stopped using the word "color" in urging reporters to brighten their copy because in some cases all they did was to dutifully describe the color of the mayor's tie. Abe put memos on my desk regularly as reminders to keep badgering reporters to make their stories come alive.

"You can write about a legislative session, for instance, without conveying to the reader in any way at all the impression that the reporter was there," he wrote in one such memo. "I am afraid that that is what we usually do. But if a reporter remembers that he is dealing with an actual physical situation and with real live people, he can with a word, phrase, sentence or paragraph give the reader that sense of reality. The problem, of course, is that most reporters don't pay enough attention to it and, when they're jogged, fall into cliché patterns—the high-ceilinged room, the paneled walls or something like that—and then call it a day. We do have quite a number of reporters who can write attractively, but some of them seem to have a kind of schizophrenia. When they're writing a feature story, their typewriters come alive. But when they're handling a straight news story, they seem to forget everything they ever knew about writing. I am not talking about turning news stories into feature stories but simply about giving news events some writing attention and the sense of immediacy that really is part of the story."

Abe himself had been widely acknowledged as a model for this style of writing. Clifton Daniel, soon after Abe became metropolitan editor, wrote to a foreign correspondent urging him to include flashes of color, explicit description and background detail in his stories. "The best hand I ever saw at this was Abe Rosenthal," said Daniel. "Abe never wrote a story from abroad that didn't include some piece of personal observation. And he never complained about lack of space because he seemed to be able to tell any story in six hundred words."

Privately, Abe and I categorized the various reporters' strengths: Some had a natural grace and style, some could sweep up facts under deadline pressure, some were investigative diggers with impeccable sources, others had the ability to analyze a complex situation behind the news, some were experts in fields like law or politics. Above all, we relished the fact that our staff was composed of individualists who did not agree with one another on much of anything—let alone with us. Both Abe and I viewed this as a strength rather than a weakness, and a city editor would have been poorly advised to wish it otherwise. It took a staff of vastly differing outlooks to record the kaleidoscope of the New York day.

Small tragedies and great acts of heroism took place daily in New York. There were enormously complicated facts involving business and legislation, sly bits of chicanery, and causes for both joy and despair. It was vital that our reporters understood how to share with our readers what they saw and heard. I tried to explain that we weren't asking reporters for trivia, but for bits of information they found of sufficient interest to mention to their friends or their spouses at dinner, yet were leaving out of their articles. A story about a celebration at Lincoln Center got a special lift when I asked the reporter to insert a paragraph high up in his account about the ushers, overcome by the spirit of the stage event, bursting into applause. He had mentioned it to me when he returned from his assignment but failed to include it in his copy. Similarly, a reporter covering a tenement fire in an impoverished area had not included in his original story that neighbors shared their own meager food and shelter with the victims.

We soon set about expanding the narrow beat system we had inherited. We urged housing and welfare reporters, for example, to look beyond Manhattan to the other boroughs. We also demanded that our "specialists" devise new ways to apply their expertise. In the field of religion we set our sights on stories about theology rather than sermons. We decided to abolish the columns allotted week after week to the coverage of routine homilies in churches and synagogues, and made every effort to substitute original stories about trends and debates in religious doctrine. George Dugan, the church reporter who had succeeded Rachel McDowell, and Pat Spiegel, still on the "Jewish beat," tried their best to comply with our wishes, but they lacked the theological background we were seeking, and we began a search for a learned religious editor to work with them.

Not all beat reporting demanded writing that sang. Sometimes a clearly organized story brimming with detail was enough to gladden our editors' hearts. But when a story was stylishly written as well, we felt like hugging its author. To let the talented young reporters know how much we valued them, Abe and I began inviting them, one at a time, to lunch with us at Sardi's. We realized that every minute of time either of us gave to a gifted staffer was time well spent, for such discussions almost invariably resulted in a visible enhancement of their work. Devoting the same amount of time to a reporter whose writing was consistently routine yielded no discernible results. So we naturally spent more time with the talented writers, thus inadvertently drawing charges of favoritism.

However much Abe gave the talented reporters their heads, they still complained they felt like poor relations compared to their counterparts on the foreign and national staffs. Many of them looked upon the city staff as simply a stepping-stone to a foreign or national assignment. Their stories were infrequently signed, while reporters in Washington and abroad (with the uppity title of "correspondent") were bylined on everything they wrote. When correspondents visited the home office, Catledge or Daniel entertained them at fashionable restaurants or in their homes. And most hurtful of all, the pay of city reporters was meager compared to the salaries of correspondents.

The first reporter Abe invited to Sardi's was Gay Talese. Although happy to be working under Abe, Gay was chronically restless and was considering well-paying offers to write long articles for such magazines as *Esquire*. Complaining that Adams had refused to raise his weekly salary above $225, he insisted he was entitled to $300. A $75 raise was an unheard-of increase for a general-assignment reporter at a time when the accepted weekly raise was $10 or $15.

The following morning, Abe, unable to disguise his unease, went to see Catledge.

"I can see there's a problem. What is it, Abe?"

"You're asking me to lift the level of the city staff to the level of the foreign and national staffs. It's all a mockery. Do you realize how poorly the good young reporters on the city staff are treated? Their salaries are ridiculously low. They pray for bylines. In the eyes of Clif Daniel and yourself, they don't have social status. When was the last time you invited a city reporter to your home? They're unhappy."

"What do you want me to do?"

"As a start, I need raises for half a dozen of the most talented and underpaid right away. And I don't mean ten dollars. I need fifty-dollar raises, and in Talese's case seventy-five."

"*What?*"

"If I can't get them, I can't do the job you're asking. I can't work with an unhappy staff."

Though far from sanguine, Catledge acquiesced, and the rewarded reporters were exultant.

Abe almost at once had to focus on a new problem—the grumpiness of
some of the senior reporters, who resented being forced into daily assignments not always to their liking. They began by complaining to me.

Homer Bigart, unarguably the paper's top reporter, was particularly bitter
about the changes we were initiating. Bigart, who at fifty-six had the energy
of someone half his age, was in effect the city staff's roving correspondent,
which meant he could occasionally be tapped for special national as well as
foreign assignments. The rest of the time, he covered stories about the city.
The Times had been so gratified when he arrived in 1955 from the *Herald Tribune*, it took out a full-page ad in *The New Yorker* heralding the event. Since
then, he had reported from the Congo, Vietnam and Israel and had covered
the civil rights battles in the South.

With age, Bigart had grown somewhat cranky, and the biting wit for
which he was famous was often delivered these days without a smile. Smoking incessantly, he sat in the front row, directly facing Abe's desk and mine,
glowering at us from behind his spectacles. He was contemptuous of anyone
who presumed to give him orders, and, of course, that included us.

Before our ascension to the metropolitan desk, Bigart had always been
friendly and gracious to both Abe and me. He had invited Barbara and me
to his home for drinks on several occasions and, even though he was chary
with his praise, he had mumbled something nice about our O'Neill book. He
also had mumbled something nice to Abe about his Pulitzer Prize.

Bigart, himself the recipient of two Pulitzers, was the greatest war correspondent of our time. His first Pulitzer was awarded for his coverage in the
Pacific during World War II and the second for his dispatches from Korea.
His daring when covering battles was legendary. "Stay away from Homer,"
a veteran combat colleague once warned rookie correspondents. "He's always trying to build his reputation at the cannon's mouth."

Born in a small town in Pennsylvania, Bigart, unlike Mike Berger and
Bruce Rae, did not scoff at journalism school. In fact, it was at New York
University, where he had majored in English and journalism, that he dis-
covered his vocation. After graduation in 1927, he was hired by the *Herald
Tribune*, and spent five years there as a copyboy. He gradually advanced
from the obituary desk to general assignment to the police beat. But he had
to wait until 1943 for his first big break—as a war correspondent with the
Fifth Army in Italy.

To the dismay of the military, Bigart's reports were devoid of patriotic fervor. Pinned down with Allied troops on the Italian beachhead at Anzio for sixty-two days, he recorded the slaughter as he saw it:

"On the far side of the field sprawled some dead. One boy lay crumpled in a shallow slit trench beneath a rock. Another, still grasping his rifle, peered from behind a tree, staring with sightless eyes toward the Liri plain. A third lay prone where he had fallen. He had heard the warning scream of the German shell. He had dropped flat on his stomach but on level ground affording no cover. Evidently some fragment had killed him instantly, for there had been no struggle."

Bigart's style of unsentimental, incisive war reporting, his imagery unmatched by camera or recording, became his trademark. While in the Pacific, he was among the first contingent of reporters allowed into Hiroshima after the bomb and he witnessed the signing of the Japanese surrender on the USS *Missouri*. "Japan, paying for her desperate throw of the dice at Pearl Harbor," he wrote, "passed from the ranks of the major powers at 9:05 A.M. today when Foreign Minister Mamoru Shigemitsu signed the document of unconditional surrender."

What provided great amusement for his colleagues was his pose of playing dumb when on assignment, an act reinforced by his stutter. Looking angelically innocent behind his spectacles, he seemed to find no question too simple to ask. He made no assumptions, even about seemingly self-evident facts. Other reporters sometimes grew impatient with his endless queries, but Bigart as often as not ended up with details and an overall perspective that his competitors had missed.

After World War II, he went on to cover the Zionist struggle for independence in Palestine and, in 1947, was the first reporter to record a swearing-in ceremony of the underground Haganah, allowing himself to be blindfolded before being led to the group's secret headquarters. The next year found Bigart in Greece, reporting on the Communist revolt.

When George Polk, a CBS correspondent, was killed trying to find the rebel commander, General Markos Vafiades, Bigart adopted the mission as his own. He made contact with rebel agents and traveled for eleven days, initially disguised as a crippled man to avert police questioning. He climbed mountains and rode wooden-saddled mules over rugged goat trails to obtain an interview with the guerrilla leader. "The brown hair under his Partisan cap was long and bushy," wrote Bigart. "His mouth is broad and expressive. He has the gift of a quick and charming smile that can alter instantly a face which, in repose, seems hard, impatient, pitiless."

A similar description (except for the long hair) could have been applied to Bigart, who was tough by any measure. Unlike the other old-timers who had nurtured me, he made little effort to mentor young reporters. Any word of praise from him, however curt, was treasured. But he could be derisive. Bigart was drinking at Bleeck's one evening in the 1950s, and, as the story goes, he was told that Marguerite Higgins, a star correspondent to whom he took a dislike while covering the war in Korea, was going to have a baby. "Who's the m-m-m-mother?" Bigart stuttered. His dislike stemmed from a tour that the veteran Bigart and the younger Higgins had done in Korea for the *Herald Tribune*, and he was still smarting from her flat-footed refusal to accept his suggestions. Months later, upon learning Higgins had given birth, Bigart sneered, "Did she eat it?" (In 1951, Bigart and Higgins were among six correspondents awarded the Pulitzer Prize for their coverage of the Korean War.)

If someone irritated him, there was no escape from his caustic tongue. One night in 1965, he happened to enter Sardi's bar while some of us from the city room were toasting R. W. "Johnny" Apple, a metropolitan reporter about to leave for Vietnam. Apple, in awe of Bigart's early Vietnam coverage, greeted him effusively, saying he needed his advice. "Nobody knows Vietnam better than you do, Homer," he continued, unaware that Bigart had long resented Apple's habit of asking worshipful questions while carelessly flicking cigarette ashes into Bigart's typewriter. Silence fell when Bigart growled his reply: "Kid, I couldn't give less of a shit where you go and what you do." He walked out, leaving Apple visibly crushed. When Apple, after three years of outstanding reporting in Vietnam, visited the city room, Bigart muttered, "Where have you been?"

Apple had been a correspondent for NBC on *The Huntley–Brinkley Report* before becoming Abe's first hire only a month after he took command. A twenty-nine-year-old bachelor with a boyish crew cut, Apple was born in Akron, Ohio, and attended Princeton and Columbia. Before arriving at the paper, he had already made a reputation as a knowledgeable reporter with the determination of a mountain climber. There was no assignment I gave him that he didn't fulfill expertly, but his braggadocio annoyed his fellow reporters.

Abe offered him $300 a week, the same salary he had recently given Talese. But Apple bragged he was being paid $50 more than he actually was, which would have made him the highest-salaried reporter in the city room, except for Homer Bigart. Abe smilingly refused to reveal Apple's salary, not wanting to upset the rest of the reporters, and tried to convince the staff that raising the salary ceiling for any reporter would ultimately benefit all reporters. Nevertheless, many of the veterans felt slighted.

In spite of his swagger, Apple delivered sturdily and often brilliantly. After starting on general assignment, he headed the Albany bureau in 1964. On my visits to the state capital, I enjoyed spending time with him at Keeler's and Jack's, two of the hangouts for politicians and reporters, where he lived it up on lobster and the best wines and cognacs.

He once told me he planned to write a biography of Governor Al Smith. He had begun his research and worked on the project whenever he managed to spare the time. But although he had abundant talent and drive, and distinguished himself in a long career for his coverage in Vietnam, Africa, Moscow, London and Washington, as well as New York, I didn't think he'd ever dedicate himself to writing a major book. Between his devotion to the paper and his appetite for the good life, there never seemed to be time.

DECIDING TO MAKE our point about keeping the star reporters busy, Abe and I assigned Bigart to a local story that we believed would land on the front page.

The biggest New York story of the day was the unsolved double homicide of Janice Wylie and Emily Hoffert, two young professional women slain inside their East Eighty-eighth Street apartment on August 28, 1963. Janice was the daughter of Max Wylie, the writer, and the niece of Philip Wylie, whose books included *Generation of Vipers*. She was a twenty-one-year-old copygirl at *Newsweek*, and Hoffert was a twenty-three-year-old Smith College graduate about to begin a career as a teacher. They shared an apartment with a third woman, Patricia Tolles, who was at work at Time-Life when her roommates were killed.

When she returned home that evening, Tolles found the living room in disarray and the doorway to the service stairs, which she had locked that morning, ajar. She immediately phoned Max Wylie, who lived a few blocks away. He advised her to stay put, touch nothing and wait for him to arrive. He discovered the two bodies, bloodied from multiple knife wounds and bound at the wrists and ankles by strips of bed sheets. Hoffert's jugular vein had been slashed, and her roommate had been stabbed in the heart.

The murderer, after apparently breaking three kitchen knives with the violence of his thrusts, turned to a steak knife. Hoffert was fully dressed. Wylie was nude, the way she usually slept in hot weather. "It was a mass of gore," Max Wylie later said.

The middle-class city, particularly the growing population of independent single young women, tumbled into a panic. East Eighty-eighth Street was a relatively safe neighborhood, the building seemed secure enough, there was no known motive for the crime and the police had no leads. Women complained they no longer felt safe in their own apartments.

It was only three weeks into our tenure on the metropolitan desk when Abe and I asked Bigart to spend a few days investigating all the angles and put together a "take-out"—a comprehensive overview of the case, with as many new details as he could gather by talking to detectives, family members, neighbors, colleagues at work, boyfriends and anyone else who had known the two young women. Bigart shot us a withering look when we told him what we wanted. He couldn't believe he was being assigned to a three-week-old, dead-end story. We urged him to at least give it try. If he couldn't find anything new to write about in the next day or two, he could drop it.

Grudgingly, Bigart called on Kermit Lansner, *Newsweek*'s executive editor (and Janice Wylie's boss), who was a Bigart admirer, and who later told me about it. In a sarcastic stutter, Bigart said, "The ch-ch-ch-chief wants me to b-b-b-break the case."

We hadn't heard from Homer for four days, when on September 28, he lackadaisically reported he had something to write. "One month after the slaying of Janice Wylie and Emily Hoffert, the police have questioned more than 500 persons in one of the most intensive investigations of murder in this city, but the case remains wide open," read his lead. "'There is a complete lack of physical evidence, no description of the murderer, not one substantial clue, not one tangible motive,' a high police official said."

But the details he had accumulated fascinated our readers, and the story was picked up by other papers. In place of hard leads, detectives invented fanciful theories. "The symbolism of the tied bodies suggested that the killer might have been a homosexual," Bigart reported. "Also, the bindings were not torn, as a man might tear them from the bed sheet, but seemed to have been cut with scissors." Any possibility of a female murderer, however, had been ruled out. "No woman was involved," said one detective, citing the force of the blows.

The greatest mystery was how the killer, who "must have been drenched in blood . . . could have left the neighborhood in the bright light of noon without attracting attention." The story was given a good play on page one, and Abe and I had made our point to the staff that we were willing to devote time and space to stories that were intrinsically important even if they didn't necessarily have a hard-news lead.

When we left the city room that night, Abe said, "How about getting a hot dog to celebrate? A hot dog and a front-page story. For me, this is

America." But even while relishing the triumph of Bigart's story, there was that nagging unease—the awareness that in journalism our proudest moments often were achieved at the expense of other people's pain.

The fact that Bigart's story landed on the front page did not appease our ace, who continued to glare at Abe and me whenever he looked up from his typewriter. Finally, one night, Abe said, "I think Homer hates me."

"Homer hates all editors," I replied. "Don't take it personally."

"No," Abe insisted, "I think he really hates me."

"Well, have you tried to talk to him?"

Abe said he hadn't, so we decided then and there to invite Bigart for a drink. It was five o'clock and Homer still had a story to finish. But we knew he could never turn down a free drink. "How about taking a short break and joining Abe and me at Sardi's?" I said. The three of us left the city room by way of the back stairs leading to *The Times*'s exit on Forty-fourth Street, next door to Sardi's. We intended to return the same way in no longer than half an hour, so Bigart could complete his story, and Abe and I could check the stories handed in by the staff before turning them over to the night desk for editing.

At Sardi's bar, Bigart ordered a double Scotch, neat, and Abe and I asked for the same. Bigart downed his drink in a couple of gulps. Abe and I, our honor at stake, followed suit. Bigart promptly ordered another double, and we did, too, again emptying our glasses. Bigart called for a third round, which he and Abe threw back as before. Already a bit woozy, I stealthily poured mine onto the floor under my chair.

By this time, Abe required the support of the bar to remain erect and was exerting a superhuman effort to stay clear-minded. Bigart, to whom we had not even had a chance to speak, sized up the situation. "Take the little man home," he told me.

Bigart left as I paid the check. Abe insisted he could get home without my assistance. I hailed a cab, helped him into the backseat, and gave the driver his address. Back at *The Times*, I found Bigart in the men's room, dunking his head in a washbasin he'd filled with cold water. Calmly, he combed his hair, returned to his desk, finished typing his story and left for home.

Sometime afterward, Homer told me why he was scornful of editors— especially those who had risen from the reportorial ranks as had Abe and I. He felt they had deserted their true calling to take on a destructive mission—that of tinkering with a good reporter's copy. Only rarely in the months to come did Homer drop his guard and soften his attitude toward

Abe and me. One such occasion was his wife's funeral at his home in Connecticut. With tears in his eyes, he allowed us to embrace him. But always, in the office, he remained aloof.

I continued to rack my brain for assignments that might appeal to him. If I came up with one that involved social, racial or political unrest, his face would flush as, snatching up a few sheets of copy paper, he'd dash out of the city room with the bounce of a cub reporter. But if the assignment didn't appeal to him, he'd leave the office, grumbling under his breath.

SITTING TO THE RIGHT of Homer Bigart in the front row was our other star reporter, Peter Kihss. I knew they respected each other, but I never saw them in conversation. I always suspected Peter was too busy to talk. Like Homer, he had made his reputation at the *Herald Tribune* and he shared Homer's antipathy toward editors. "An editor is someone who separates the wheat from the chaff—and sees to it the chaff gets in the paper," Peter would remind me every so often.

I had never known a reporter better able to grasp complex facts, or more skilled in pulling them together into a tight, comprehensible story under deadline pressure. Murray Schumach, soon to return from Hollywood to join Kihss and Bigart in the front row of the room, once commented, "Peter reads columns of figures as others do mystery novels." He was a master of a kind of nuts-and-bolts reporting that is disappearing nowadays. He seldom wrote a personality piece or tried to couch his report in dramatic language. He was interested in welfare statistics, budget dilemmas and health concerns, and reported them in plain, unvarnished paragraphs. Younger reporters respected him but they were relieved it was he, not they, writing on these matters.

Accuracy was sacred to him. Once, when a question arose as to the specific length of a runway at La Guardia Airport, Kihss went out to the field with a tape measure. To settle disputes between the police and the sponsors of civil rights rallies over how many demonstrators were in a crowd, Kihss developed a mathematical formula based on the number of people who could physically occupy one square foot. When applied to photographs of the event, his figures turned out to be much closer to the actual numbers than those given out by either side. Because of his undisputed credibility, no one ever questioned his estimates.

Before coming to *The Times* in 1952 when he was forty, Kihss—Brooklyn-born and a graduate of Columbia—had worked for the AP, the *Washington*

Post, the *World-Telegram* and the *Herald Tribune*, where he started in 1943. Each time he switched papers it was due to ethical conflicts, never over pay. He quit the *Washington Post*, for example, because he thought its business department was influencing news coverage. He left the *Herald Tribune* because he felt his stories were being amputated and adulterated by copy editors.

When he was at the *World-Telegram*, he was the butt of complaints by Mayor La Guardia, who once became particularly incensed when Kihss queried him about helping a former city official get back on the payroll to qualify for a pension. La Guardia grabbed his arm and threatened to throw him down the City Hall steps. "Mr. Mayor," said Kihss, "I don't care what you say. Four hundred thousand readers of the *World-Telegram* want to know, and that's why I'm asking." Kihss recalled there was a sudden silence. "I realized I had seized the stocky little mayor and lifted him right up into the air. I put him down gently—and went quietly into room nine [the press room]." Neither the mayor nor Kihss spoke of the incident again.

During his years with *The Times*, Kihss routinely refused pay raises, maintaining he was overpaid and others deserved them more. In truth, he was worth more than the paper could ever pay him. The first time Abe offered him a raise, Peter turned it down, saying, "Aw, shucks, I haven't earned it."

"Why don't you talk to your wife about this and let me know what she says," Abe suggested. The next day, Peter reluctantly accepted the raise. "You're binding me with chains of gold," he said.

Once, when I visited him in a hospital near his home in Queens, where he was being treated for a heart attack, he demanded that his time out of the office be deducted from his vacation. With the help of his wife, Alice, I was able to talk him out of that. Peter never cared much about vacations. But one summer when Alice insisted he take her on a trip, he sensed that the story he had just completed about city finances—and scheduled to run the following week—might be altered by the desk while he was away. He wrote letters to twenty sources pointing out he could no longer be held responsible for the accuracy of the facts in the story.

It was always a reassuring antidote to Homer Bigart's scowling visage to look up and see Peter's face, bespectacled like Homer's, but with a gaze of gentle abstraction. Telephone receiver cradled against his ear, he would be diligently typing pages of single-spaced notes, preliminary to writing a story. Unlike Homer, he willingly accepted any assignment. His temperament flared only when he felt an editor had mishandled a story, and several times he "quit" when he believed his editors were crowding him. On one such notable occasion, in April 1962, he was assigned to cover the annual convention in New York of the Publishers Association. The event was attended by newspaper executives from all over the country—including the hierarchy of *The Times*—and, of course, the stories were microscopically scrutinized by the bullpen.

The assignment had been traditionally given to Russell Porter, a reporter famous, like Kihss, for his thoroughness and accuracy. But on the first day of the convention, Porter, clad in pajamas, jumped to his death from the window of his tenth-floor apartment. (Callous gossip in the city room had it that the strain of once again having to write the Publishers Association story was simply too much for even a pro like Porter, and he had ended his life as the only way to get out of covering it.) Frank Adams, then still city editor, gave the assignment to Kihss.

All went smoothly until Peter began writing the final convention story, dealing with the formal banquet that closed the event. Arthur Hays Sulzberger was a member of the banquet's host committee and Clif Daniel, who was also at the dinner, kept phoning in the titles of important guests, including some members of British royalty. Those of the top editors who did not attend the dinner hovered around Kihss while he was typing.

Writing with his usual concentration, Peter tried to shrug off the various editors' queries, but Bernstein and Catledge persisted with suggestions for improving his copy. It was finally too much for Peter. He tore the copy out of his typewriter, slammed his desk shut, leaped from his swivel chair and roared, "I quit!" He stayed away for three weeks before Alice, ever the voice of reason, persuaded him to return.

When people talked about *The Times* as a paper of record, it was Peter Kihss they had in mind, and when they talked about a paper without fear or favor, that was Peter again. *The Times* nominated him three times for a Pulitzer Prize. All of us in the city room were dismayed that Peter—one of the greatest practitioners of accurate, balanced, thorough reporting under pressure—failed, year after year, to win.

When Peter retired in 1982 after fifty years as a reporter, Murray Schumach lamented that his friend, whose "rapid speech can spew statistics, names, details of background information like a computer, will not be around anymore to bring perspectives to press conferences and anguish to officials with questions only he can think of."

THIRTY

OFTEN, while working on the Metropolitan Desk, I felt as though Abe and I were two halves of the same person. Though I was formally Abe's deputy, ours was a true partnership—and never did I feel subordinate. We made basically all decisions together and knew each other so well that Abe rarely had to speak a complete sentence before I understood exactly what he was saying, and vice versa.

After having spent the day seated side by side, we often adjourned to Sardi's for dinner, where we planned strategies, discussed news philosophies, developed story ideas and debated which correspondents we might lure back from abroad to join our metropolitan staff. We'd usually consult again on the phone around eleven P.M. after reading the first edition, to see whether any changes should be made for the next edition.

The paper was delivered to Abe's apartment on the Upper East Side as soon as it came off the press. Getting it to my home in Westchester took considerably longer and was not a simple feat, but it was accomplished nightly with the cooperation of the New Haven Railroad. A copyboy picked up the paper from the pressroom and rushed it by taxi to the conductor of the train about to pull out of Grand Central. At the Harrison station, the conductor handed the paper to a waiting taxi driver, who delivered it to my front door.

One difference between Abe's role and mine resulted from our agreement that I "deal below" and Abe "deal above," meaning that I was often responsible for matters involving the staff, while Abe alone took up policy issues with the upper management. This suited me, for I felt at home in the company of reporters and wasn't entirely comfortable with the top brass. Abe, on the other hand, moved with ease in the stratosphere, and was admired and well liked by Punch, Catledge and Daniel. At the time, I kept such a low profile vis-à-vis those three that I doubted I would ever move beyond my current status. I also shied away from official appearances and never made speeches at banquets or awards ceremonies. I was happy to let Abe speak for both of us.

Barbara encouraged me to make myself more visible, but she sympathized with what she believed was a deeply implanted psychological block. I had told her the story of how, when I was in second grade, I had enjoyed cutting up in the back of the room with a few classmates. The teacher kept warning us to behave and finally, one day, she kept us after school. She marched us to the basement, where she sealed our mouths with adhesive tape and forced us to stand with our arms held straight out for half an hour. If our arms began to drop, she smacked our backs with a wooden ruler. I was so scared and humiliated I wouldn't even tell my worried mother why I was late coming home from school. I had nightmares about the episode for months and I never again spoke out of turn in class.

Barbara thought therapy might help me overcome my unease at being the center of attention. I didn't take her advice but, gradually with her encouragement, and Abe's, I managed at last to shrug off my strangling shyness—to the point where Barbara now accuses me of taking too much delight in what she mockingly calls my "holding forth."

Every day, both Abe and I tried to enliven the city coverage. I took pains to tell the younger reporters to be wary of the word "objectivity," frequently trotted out by editors. If it meant "fairness" and "balance" and kept the reporter's personal opinions out of a story, that was fine, but it must not deter a reporter from characterizing a person or scene with an original or pointed phrase. I liked quoting city editor Stanley Walker: "Objectivity produces something like a symmetrical pile of clam shells with all the succulent goodness carefully removed."

The fact that reporters felt intimidated about writing with color, except for what were clearly feature stories, was illustrated one day by McCandlish Phillips. Every bit as talented a writer as Mike Berger, he could almost always be relied upon to convey the essential flavor of an event. But on this day he turned in a story that was uncharacteristically bland. Abe called him to the desk and told him so.

"Isn't this going on page one?" Phillips asked. When Abe confirmed that it was, Phillips said, "Well, I was writing for page one." Abe sent him back to his desk to try it again in his own original style.

At thirty-five, Phillips, the tallest reporter in the city room—six feet, five inches, and almost as lean as a Giacometti—had once been called "the man of the awkward gait and the graceful phrase." His career began as editor of the *Sagamore*, his high school paper in Brookline, Massachusetts. When running the paper began to consume his adolescent life, his father cautioned him to "stop trying to make *The New York Times* out of the *Sagamore*."

But Phillips won a scholarship from the *Boston Globe* for publishing the best high school newspaper in New England. After working for a few

Boston-area papers and serving two years in the Army, he came to *The Times* in November 1952 as a copyboy. He was promoted to reporter in 1955, covered the Brooklyn police shack, then moved to general assignment, where he had been ever since. Phillips was one of the few talented local reporters whose ambition was to remain on the city staff, where in 1960 he became the first *Times* reporter to win the award named in memory of his idol, Meyer Berger.

A Christian fundamentalist, known to his colleagues as Johnny, Phillips had a life outside the paper devoted to prayer and religious study. He kept a Bible on his desk, and gently placed his hand on its cover as if to derive inspiration, whenever I approached him with an assignment. Abe and I marveled at his ability to suppress all traces of his strongly held religious beliefs in the stories he wrote.

There was no reporter on the staff more willing to pursue the ideas I gave him and, if a lead didn't quite pan out, he invariably came back to the city room with a different angle that resulted in an even better story than the original assignment. Phillips was gifted enough to spin almost any ordinary encounter into journalistic gold.

Phillips, who lived in a religious commune near Columbia University, knew the city as well as I did. He once wrote lovingly of the sound of a subway train as it stopped near his apartment overlooking Broadway: "The screech of metal brakes comes up through my windows and into my ears. In vacations in more than twenty years, I can recall having strayed out of the city twice. When people ask me, 'Where did you go on your vacation?' I tell them I went where I would have wanted to go if I lived anywhere else in the world."

I thought of Phillips as Broadway's poet laureate, paying homage to its singular denizens and eccentric institutions. There was no one but Phillips I would have trusted to write the obituary of Lindy's restaurant, which closed on September 21, 1969, the day after Barbara and I had our final meal there.

"What kind of a day is today? It's the kind of a day that if you wanted a slice of cheesecake at Lindy's you couldn't get it," wrote Phillips.

"There hasn't been a day like it since before August 20, 1921, when Leo (Lindy) Lindemann opened the original Lindy's at 1626 Broadway, an all-night deli destined to occupy a special niche in American folklore.

"You would have thought it would last forever, but Lindy's is dead. For some people the world changed a little bit at 1:30 A.M. yesterday, when the big neon sign out front on Broadway at Fifty-first Street was turned off and the revolving door was locked.

"The last dish could have been, but wasn't, a heaping portion of sentiment laced with treacle. There were some who came in and left unaware that it was not an ordinary day. As far as they knew, there would be other days for fist-sized strawberries smothered in thick, whipped cream. . . .

"The locusts stripped the place of menus and ashtrays and other mementos. There were conflicting claimants to possession of the last bagel. As a souvenir, a bagel is not much good. It is perishable and it also lacks proof. Anyone can hold up a bagel and say, 'This is the last bagel from Lindy's.'

"Who knows?"

UNDER FRANK ADAMS, the city report had been solid, but not probing enough for Abe or me. We stressed investigative reporting, getting the story behind the story. We expanded the profiles of people in the news and began assigning "news analysis" articles, known as "Q-heads"—previously the monopoly of the foreign and national desks—to accompany lead stories on major local developments. (News stories answered the question "What?" Q-heads answered the question "Why?")

The challenge was to get reporters to give us comprehensive, lively writing about politics and such specialized areas as religion and architecture, but without inserting their own opinions. Abe and I kept a vigilant watch for any phrase that might cross that sacrosanct line into editorializing. Preserving this sort of detachment meant everything to Abe. More than once, he remarked that he wanted the epitaph on his tombstone to read, "He kept the paper straight."

Only in the case of one staffer did we make an exception. Ada Louise Huxtable wrote news stories for our metropolitan report in addition to writing critiques for Herzberg's culture report. She was entitled, we believed, to express a strong point of view when, for instance, she reported on plans for some new structure. We ultimately solved the problem by creating a special rubric for her news articles: "An Appraisal." The rubric was often essential to characterize the sort of hybrid reporting she did—especially effective when, for example, she caustically declared in a front-page appraisal in 1971 about the opening of Washington's "superscale" Kennedy Center for the Performing Arts that "Albert Speer would have approved."

Among other problems Abe and I confronted was trying to keep the advertising department at a distance from the city room. Abe was vehemently opposed to allowing the business department any influence over news, no matter how subtle. He forbade the advertising department to have any contact with anyone on the staff except for him.

One day, I spotted Warren Wolfe, director of the retail advertising department, talking to an assistant metropolitan editor. It was the first time I had ever seen him in the city room. Knowing he was well aware of our policy, I asked what he was doing there. Abe happened to walk in at that moment, and we discovered that Wolfe was lobbying for space for a story to benefit a particular advertiser. "Get your ass out of here!" shouted Abe, and practically dragged him to the elevator. Wolfe left the paper soon after.

Fundamentally, we wanted local reporters to cover New York with the curiosity of a foreign correspondent in an unfamiliar city. Abe and I ourselves explored neighborhoods throughout the boroughs, where Abe, having been so long away, saw potential stories on every block. On one of our strolls, he asked me whether I had noticed that the homosexual presence in the city seemed to have increased over the past decade. I said the only change I'd noticed was that a number of my own homosexual acquaintances in the arts were coming out of the closet. However, if Abe's view of the general population turned out to be correct, the reasons for the increase would undoubtedly make an interesting story. Why not assign a recently returned foreign correspondent, now on the city staff, to look at the situation with a fresh eye?

Robert Doty, then in his late forties, had been the debonair Paris bureau chief since 1958, previously having covered the Middle East and North Africa. His reporting had always been sensitive and evenhanded. He had been back in New York only a few weeks when Abe and I called him to the desk to explain what we wanted from him. We said, take a month—much longer than normally devoted in those days to a single story.

Doty blanched. Stroking his gray-streaked brush of a mustache with thumb and forefinger, he asked if there was a reason why we were assigning this particular story to him. Clearly he was probing to find if Abe and I suspected he was homosexual. I was amused that he thought it necessary to remind us he was married and the father of two children.

We assured him we weren't challenging his heterosexuality, but he expressed his concern that, following publication of the story, people might question his sexual orientation. (It would be a rare reporter who today, whatever his orientation, would have given the assignment a second thought. Ideally, we probably should have teamed Doty with a gay reporter. But if there were then any gay reporters on *The Times*, they had not as yet declared themselves.)

Doty, being as fair-minded a reporter as existed on any mainstream newspaper, went about the assignment conscientiously, spending the next several weeks frequenting homosexual haunts and talking to psychiatrists, policemen and religious leaders. On December 17, 1963, his six-column story began on page one. Some of its conclusions sound pitifully naive today, but at the time the article was deemed an earnest effort to explain that homosexuality was "the city's most sensitive open secret—the presence of what is probably the greatest homosexual population in the world."

New York's homosexual population, according to Doty, was a solidly established community of "sexual inverts" that acted "as a lodestar, attracting others from all over the country." He identified their neighborhoods as Greenwich Village, the West Seventies and the East Side from the upper Forties through the Seventies. A small area around Eighth Avenue and Forty-second Street was the territory of "those who are universally regarded as the dregs of the invert world—the male prostitutes—the painted, grossly effeminate 'queens' and those who prey on them."

Doty, in his innocence, was surprised to discover that there were homosexual clothing stores, bars, vacation spots (notably Fire Island) and magazines. He reported that homosexuals "arrive to find escape from the legal and social harassment in their smaller home communities, where their deviancy can be hidden only at the price of self-denial." At that time, any sexual act between members of the same sex was punishable by law, and every year more than one thousand men were arrested for "overt homosexual activity," about two-thirds of them entrapped by plainclothes cops in subway toilets.

The overwhelming psychological opinion of the day, Doty revealed, was that homosexuality could be "both prevented and cured . . . that homosexuals are created—generally by ill-adjusted parents—not born." According to the experts quoted, the combination of a cold, hostile father with a "close-binding, intimate" mother was often the recipe for a homosexual son. In that unenlightened era, the therapeutic profession, by and large, was opposed to normalizing homosexuality and treating homosexuals like a legitimate minority. Doctors believed that such an approach would only deter homosexuals from seeking the treatment they required to heal themselves.

There was, however, a homophile movement, which—while nonconfrontational—advocated the "removal of legal, social and cultural discrimination." It is interesting to note that adherents of this group, though convinced homosexuality was inborn rather than learned, nonetheless considered it an illness. A study of three hundred homosexuals by the New York League of Homosexuals, recently merged with the Mattachine Society, had found that though 83 percent would not choose for a son the life that they lived, 97 percent said they themselves would not change their own orientation, even if it were easy to do so.

The *Times* article provoked varied responses. Plaudits came from the psychoanalytic community, criticism from those who felt that Doty's research was essentially one-sided. One letter from a minister praised *The Times* for giving attention to the issue, but noted that Doty had ignored a number of authoritative organizations, individuals and publications. "Perhaps at some future date," the letter added, "[Doty] will do further research and discover that there is much to be said in favor of the homosexual."

We were also alerted to the fact that Doty had missed at least one prominent study—conducted by Dr. Evelyn Hooker in 1956—which concluded "gay men can be as well adjusted as straight men and some are even better adjusted than some straight men." But despite its deficiencies, the story was a bold attempt to bring a complicated issue to center stage and part the curtains a bit for open debate.

Four years later, Doty was back in Europe as chief of the Rome bureau, and when Barbara and I visited him, he told us that trying to probe the homosexual psyche had been one of the most difficult assignments he had undertaken. "I've learned a lot in the last few years," he said. "For a man living the sophisticated life as a traveler in Europe, I'm embarrassed to admit how naive I was."

Intrepid sociological sleuths as we strove to be, Abe and I elected to examine another controversial issue of the day—the shifting pattern of drug use in New York. Once the province of artists and jazz musicians, marijuana and even heroin were just beginning to gain popularity among middle-class teenagers and college students, some of whom came to the city to get high.

I assigned various stories but didn't manage to penetrate the core of the problem until a year later. Since the heart of the action was Greenwich Village, I asked Martin Arnold to rent a room near Sheridan Square for a week and determine how difficult—or easy—it was to buy a "nickel bag" of "grass." I suggested he also go to parties, interview drug users and talk to cops. Although Arnold was in his mid-thirties, he appeared boyish enough to pass as a young hippie. In the city room, he was part of a brash and sometimes mischievous group of Lotharios who competed for the favors of the most appealing woman reporters, secretaries and clerks.

Unorthodox to the core, Arnold told me that when he was seventeen he stood up one day in the middle of his high school history class and made for the door. The teacher asked where he was going, and he replied, "I quit." He never returned to high school, but after a tour in the Army, he enrolled at Adelphi College, where he earned a history degree in three years. He joined *The Times* as a copyboy in 1952, but soon left for a reporting job at *Newsday*. He then spent nearly five years on the rewrite bank at the *Herald Tribune* and later served as assistant city editor there before returning to *The Times* in 1959. Despite his eccentricity, he was a rock-solid reporter. I thought his skills and personality made him the perfect choice for the assignment in the Village.

I sent John Kifner, whom Abe hired as his news clerk in November 1963, after he graduated from Williams College, to assist Arnold, and Kifner fit the part even better. He was the first person to break the city room's unspoken dress code. Casual in the extreme, he wore his shirt collar unbuttoned and didn't wear socks.

Kifner was eager, and reporters had written memos praising his legwork. While Abe approved of his Village assignment, he swore he wouldn't promote Kifner to reporter until he learned how to dress appropriately. A *Times* reporter, Abe held, never knew what assignment he might draw, and it would be insulting to an interviewee and embarrassing to *The Times* if a reporter turned up with an improperly buttoned shirt and no socks. I told Kifner how Abe felt and he sulkily began to button his shirt and wear socks. (After Kifner had distinguished himself on city, national and foreign assignments, I bumped into him one day on Madison Avenue and remarked on how stylishly he was dressed, reminding him of the no-socks episode thirty-five years earlier. Grinning, he lifted his trousers to show me he still wasn't wearing socks.)

Arnold gleefully made the most of his Village assignment, bar-hopping and partying. Marijuana, as he reported in *The Times*, was plentiful: "The availability is such that on a recent visit to the Village, an observer [Arnold], who had never seen marijuana before, was able, for $5, to purchase a 'nickel bag' from a stranger within two hours. It came in an envelope marked 'Graduate School of Journalism, Columbia University.'"

A number of people compared marijuana favorably with alcohol. Arnold quoted a nineteen-year-old at the Juilliard School of Music: "There comes a point where I can channel my thoughts more clearly. I can separate that which is really bothering me from the trivial." And a Hunter College honors graduate said, "I have control with pot. If I drink I might go to a party and go home and go to bed with someone. It's happened. But never with pot."

Arnold also described a darker aspect of drug use through interviews with several heroin addicts. One was a twenty-five-year-old secretary-bookkeeper, who had just emerged from treatment. Arnold reported that "over the course of her addiction she has lived with several men, has married addicts twice and has had two children, has stolen money and property, cashed bad checks and turned to prostitution, for which she was arrested once. When she got to the point where she had to buy about $35 worth of drugs a day, she entered the hospital to withdraw."

Arnold talked to members of the police narcotics bureau—a force of two hundred men and women, the largest such operation in the world. Cops relied on a network of junkie stool pigeons, who informed rather than go to jail themselves. And Arnold learned from his interviews that the bureau, immersed in the temptations of vice and money, was apparently itself corrupt. Cops were said to be on the take, extorting money from dealers in exchange for ignoring them, and at times confiscating and reselling contraband themselves. We were unable, however, to print the accusations because those who made them would not stand behind them.

The article caused a stir when it appeared on the paper's front page on January 4, 1965, particularly among suburban families alerted to a new threat to their adolescent children who enjoyed visiting New York on weekends. My only problem with Arnold's investigation was his expense account, brought to my attention by my news assistant. "Marty," I said, "you can't charge a nickel bag of marijuana to *The Times*. You better make that 'miscellaneous expenses.'"

Like the homosexual survey, the drug story was, for its day, a novel attempt at sociological reporting. If we sometimes stumbled, we were sincerely groping for ways to give our readers an awareness of the complexities and contradictions of the changing city we lived in.

Among the most successful of our desk's innovations was a fresh approach to obituary writing, a challenge Clifton Daniel had urged us to meet, suggesting Alden Whitman as chief obituary writer. Up until then, most obits of well-known persons had been bland factual digests of their lives, routinely assigned to rewrite men or reporters, who tossed them off between breaking stories. Accuracy and brevity were about all that was demanded.

Since the obit page was one of the most-read in any newspaper, we now endeavored to enrich it with in-depth profiles of lives lived—stories, as Daniel liked to say, with the touch of an artist rather than a bookkeeper, so that rays of the subject's personality would shine through. Whitman's chief task was to prepare advance obits of major public figures, and we hit upon the somewhat unorthodox notion of actually interviewing the elderly personalities whose deaths we would eventually chronicle. Daniel enthusiastically endorsed the idea and, in fact, helped arrange Whitman's first interview—with Daniel's father-in-law, Harry Truman. Whitman, nervous about being greeted as a vulture, was relieved when the former president told him, "I know why you're here, and I want to help you all I can."

As our new obituary policy began to take hold, Whitman's interview subjects became ever more tractable. Even Samuel Beckett, who never spoke publicly about himself or his work, agreed to see Whitman on one of his working jaunts abroad. The conversation, Whitman told me, did not get off to a good start, and he was about to give up when Beckett sighed deeply and said, "All right. I am here, you are here, ask me anything you want."

Whitman soon discovered that many of his subjects talked candidly because they knew their revelations would see print only after they were dead. An uncanny number of his subjects died shortly after he interviewed them, and he became known as the angel of death.

THIRTY-ONE

A BE AND I THOUGHT it was time to showcase the wittily written vignettes of city life being produced by such of our stylists as McCandlish Phillips and Gay Talese. And the place to do it—to create our own version of *The New Yorker*'s "Talk of the Town"—was the Second Front, the first page of the second section of the then two-section paper. The layout of that display page, along with page one, was determined by Ted Bernstein's bullpen, and it wasn't long before Abe and Ted were in a confrontation.

On most days the Second Front consisted of one or two newsworthy articles, plus a hodgepodge of short (and sometimes trivial) pieces selected by the bullpen from the daily flow of city or suburban stories. One of Bernstein's arbitrary rules was that no more than one story could "jump" (or continue) from the Second Front to an inside page. All other stories had to begin and end on the Second Front and, if any were too long to fit the space assigned by the bullpen, they were cut.

One day I suggested an idea to Robert Doty about life in a firehouse, pegged to a recent spate of wanton fires in the city. Replete with detail, yet written with a gossamer touch, it was just the sort of thing that would have enlivened the pages of "Talk of the Town." Although aware the story measured a little more than a column in length, Abe took the piece to Bernstein, who agreed the article belonged on the Second Front but, when he later made up the page, he decided to jump a different story.

When Abe saw Bernstein's Second Front layout, he was appalled. Since the firehouse story was not designated to jump, it would have to be cut by half to fit on the page. Abe confronted Bernstein. "In no way can the story be butchered like this," Abe said. "If it isn't allowed to jump, its flavor will be lost. It will be completely ruined." Moreover, argued Abe, if he, as metropolitan editor, believed a story deserved a full column, that was what it should get. Bernstein, never before so boldly challenged, refused to budge. He told Abe if he wouldn't ask his own desk to trim the Doty story, he would do it himself.

Abe stamped back to his desk, stuffed some notes into his pocket and grabbed his coat from the rack. "Where are you going?" I asked. He was in a barely articulate fury. "I'm getting out of here," he sputtered. "I can't take this."

Doty's story was duly trimmed by the bullpen.

Word of the incident traveled around the city room. The next morning Turner Catledge phoned Abe at home and asked to see him. Reminding Catledge that he had given him a mandate to change the city report, Abe told him he couldn't function unless his desk had control over how city stories were written and how long they should run. "I didn't come back from Tokyo to be an assistant to the bullpen. If I give a reporter space for a story, it must appear in the paper that way."

It was a watershed moment. Catledge instructed Bernstein never to contravene Abe's decisions over such matters as story length, and told him to drop his rule permitting only one story to jump from the Second Front. Abe had secured his autonomy over the metropolitan report, and the staff was elated by his victory. Bernstein, who had been instrumental in Abe's elevation to metropolitan editor, resented the rebuff. He commented to colleagues and, later, to Abe himself, "I've created a Frankenstein monster."

But Abe's stand did more than lift the quality of the city report by signaling to reporters that we could and would protect their work. We created the so-called backfield, a new method of handling copy. Under this system, before a story made its way to the copy desk, it was read first by one of two

editors handpicked by Abe and me to work alongside the assistant metropolitan editor in charge at night, Sheldon Binn—an ethical and all-around
solid newspaperman known to everyone as Shelly. After World War II,
when, as a machine gunner in Holland, he nearly died of his wounds, Shelly
worked six years as assistant city editor at the *World-Telegram and Sun* before
joining *The Times* in 1957. Reporters were grateful for his efforts to get them
extra space when a special story required it, and they appreciated his self-
description as "a desk man whose heart lies with the reporters."

For one of the two backfield spots we chose George Barrett, the top man
on the rewrite battery. I had sat next to him there after his return from covering the Korean War and knew his work well. For the second spot, we selected Bill Luce, himself a copy-desk editing wizard. Every day, Abe and I
briefed Binn, Barrett and Luce on the assigned stories to be edited. Once
Binn, Barrett or Luce approved the shape of a story, the copy desk was not
permitted to make any changes except for grammatical errors or incorrect
Times style. Abe and I stopped whatever we were doing every evening at six
o'clock to scan the edited articles before we left the office.

So that the night side would be completely familiar with our day-side assignments, we inaugurated the daily "turnaround" at three P.M., the hour at
which Binn, Barrett and Luce arrived at work. It was the first time that the
day side and night side on any news desk truly communicated with one another, and the stories benefited from this new approach. Whenever we had
more copy than space, Binn would consult with Abe or me to decide what
should be cut or, alternatively, held over for a day.

One of our rules was that the editor with whom an idea originated had
to stay with the story as it developed, questioning the reporter if necessary
and, without being overbearing, helping him maintain focus. We were ever
mindful that the good editor guides with as light a touch as possible but
firmly holds the reins of a story until it is in print. I thought Abe at times
tended to overindulge some of the young reporters whom he particularly
prized. He wanted them to feel the same sense of autonomy he had felt while
reporting from abroad. But the coddling occasionally resulted in unacceptable imperiousness on the part of the reporter toward editors on the desk, including me.

Once, for example, I found myself in a ludicrous confrontation with
David Halberstam, then a thirty-year-old reporter who had recently won
the Pulitzer Prize for his coverage of Vietnam. As one of the journalists who
early on cut through the lies conveying optimism about U.S. involvement, he
wrote, "The official line was that we were winning the war, but in my trips

around the country, I just couldn't accept this as true." American reporters, he continued, were "under constant criticism from officials" for writing the truth. And, indeed, in October 1963, President Kennedy leaned on Punch Sulzberger to take Halberstam out of Vietnam. In one of his first real tests as publisher, Punch stood firm. But in early 1964, Halberstam was finally transferred to the metropolitan desk as part of the strategy of Catledge and Abe to encourage foreign correspondents to spend a year or so familiarizing themselves with the home office.

Soon after, I was tipped off to an imminent showdown within the state's Democratic Party that supposedly would take place the next day at a meeting in upstate Buffalo. Checking the assignment list, I saw that all our political reporters were otherwise occupied and, seeking a sophisticated general-assignment reporter, I spotted Halberstam casually chatting with a couple of colleagues.

A rugged-looking native New Yorker, six feet, two inches tall, Halberstam was cocky about his accomplishments and, when I handed him the instructions for the overnight Buffalo assignment that I had scribbled on a sheet of paper, he crumpled it and thrust it back. "I've just won the Pulitzer and you're sending me to Buffalo?" he demanded. Rather than argue, I went back to the metropolitan desk to tell Abe I was fed up.

Abe had always been lavish in his admiration of Halberstam, and Halberstam, who idolized Abe, believed himself to be among the specially anointed. I had witnessed Halberstam's frequent visits to Abe's desk, kneeling to chat beside his swivel chair, and I had once overheard him say, "You and I, Abe, are the best of our newspaper generations."

I told Abe I'd have to quit, since my authority would be undermined in the eyes of the staff, if Halberstam had his way about the Buffalo assignment. "It's really your fault," I admonished, "because you've been giving him the impression he can get away with being a prima donna. Everyone will soon know he's turned down my assignment. How can I stay and do my job?"

"Give me that piece of paper," Abe said.

He approached Halberstam, who was still talking to his colleagues, and asked to see him privately, steering him to the back of the room. "If I have to make a choice between you and Gelb," Abe told him, "you've lost. I think you should go to Buffalo." Halberstam did go, and apologized to me the next day.

I bore no grudge and I don't believe he did either, and everything was smoothed over quickly. Abe's own relationship with Halberstam eventually soured, however. Halberstam returned overseas to take over the Warsaw bureau and eventually left *The Times* to write best-selling books. One evening, he invited Abe to a party at his home. Gossip about the paper and drink flowed freely, as they normally did at gatherings of writers, and Halberstam at one point, as Abe later told me, voiced some criticism of *The Times*. Abe, as always defensive about the paper to which he was devoting his life, felt betrayed and abruptly headed for the front door. Halberstam followed him out, trying to coax him back, but to no avail. It was the last time they spoke to each other.

Long before their falling-out, Halberstam, originally brought to the paper by Scotty Reston, persuaded Abe to add another Reston disciple, Neil Sheehan, to the metropolitan staff. For the past two years, the twenty-seven-year-old Sheehan had learned the ropes as a United Press International reporter in Vietnam—first by keeping a close eye on Homer Bigart and then by working side by side with Halberstam. Like Halberstam, Sheehan had grown skeptical about the veracity of military briefings.

But whereas Halberstam was brash, Sheehan was diffident. I could sense his nervousness when, on his first day at work, I led him to his desk about midway in the city room, past desks occupied by a group of young, gifted, fiercely competitive reporters—among them Joseph Lelyveld, Sydney H. Schanberg, Francis X. Clines, Bernard Weinraub, Martin Tolchin and William E. Farrell. Sheehan glanced at them apprehensively. For the UPI in Vietnam, he had filed brief dispatches and updated them as the news broke. As a rule he was not required to write a complete story—as he would now be obliged to do for *The Times*. Moreover, he had scant knowledge of New York, never having lived in the city. The tall, lanky Sheehan was born in Holyoke, Massachusetts, of Irish immigrant parents and had attended Harvard on a scholarship.

He asked me to be patient, while he learned to adjust to the rhythm of New York. But on a daily newspaper there was no time for adjustment, and N i didn't really expect there to be. I gave him a crash course in city reporting and suggested he read books by E. B. White and Mike Berger. Then I handed him his first assignment. It wasn't anything earthshaking, but it was a feature that required ingenuity to pin down and, if he succeeded, I was sure it would go a long way toward curing his insecurity.

For that night's edition, I asked him to obtain an interview with Richard Burton, who had just opened on Broadway in *Hamlet*. Burton was one of the world's most sought-after celebrities, and had been ducking interviewers. With the persistence that was to become his trademark, Neil somehow managed to inveigle his way backstage after the matinee, where he cornered Burton. He so charmed him that Burton invited Neil to join him in his limo—to wherever he was going—so that he could be interviewed en route.

Neil entered the limo and found Burton's wife, Elizabeth Taylor, with whom Burton exchanged some caustic comments during the ride. Back in the city room, Neil plunged into his story, punctuating it with humorous touches involving the interplay between Burton and Taylor and gaining confidence with every paragraph. Readers loved it.

Six months later, just as he was acquiring a true feeling for New York, the foreign editor said that Neil was needed in Indonesia, and soon after, he went back to Vietnam. Once again he rode in helicopters to the battlefields and courageously defied military officials.

AS A REPORTER, I had written one or two stories a day. Now I was dealing daily with twenty or more, assigning and editing, arranging for space, helping reporters develop angles, and anticipating that big news break. I believed all of my twenty years' experience at the paper had come together in this one job. Even the lessons learned in my earliest days—creating *Timesweek* and working on the night side when the paper was put together under Wilson Fairbanks, Ted Bernstein and Raymond McCaw—were part of the background I relied upon daily. The spirit of *The Times* flowed like blood through my veins, and my sense of the paper's methods and standards had become instinctual.

I saw stories everywhere. At dinner parties, I would leave with two or three story ideas. Every phone conversation, every movie or play, every walk down the street or trip on the subway brimmed with possibilities. I wrote down every idea that occurred to me, on scraps of paper that I stuffed into my jacket pockets. When I arrived at the office, I would empty my overflowing pockets and sort through the scraps.

To me, there was nothing as stimulating as a good story. I was well aware that not every reporter was eager to chase down the countless (if sometimes dubious) leads I proposed—and some eyed me as though I were some kind of madman. Although many grabbed at my assignments, others would hide in the bathroom or feign activity when they saw me scouting the rows of desks, wearing that "I've got a story for you" look.

For years, I went along with this cat-and-mouse game, and once I had my playful revenge. Just before noon one day, I walked around the city room asking one reporter after another if he happened to be free. The first four I approached claimed they were tied up on assignments I'd given them earlier. The fifth, Peter Millones, allowed that he was available. "Here's a ticket to the World Series," I said. It was a box seat in Shea Stadium, the spectacular year (1969) when the Mets won the series.

Of course, not all of my ideas panned out, nor did I expect them to. Once in a while a reporter spent days chasing down leads that went nowhere. But often those little scraps of paper yielded a gem. Maureen Dowd, the *Times* Op-Ed columnist, once teasingly summed up what it felt like to be a reporter on my staff (and I can see why some reporters were ambivalent about me. I'm not at all sure I'd have wanted to work for me when I was an editor): "It was as though he had some special 3-D glasses that allowed him to see stories where the rest of us just saw jawboning. And when he'd get all excited, eyes going like a slot machine and arms like airplane propellers, the world suddenly seemed charged with A-1 possibilities."

For the first time, under Abe's and my guidance, local news was more than holding its own in the daily competition with national and foreign news for front-page display. Turner Catledge was so pleased with the transformation of the metropolitan report after the first five months that he gave both Abe and me generous raises.

Taking reporters like Neil Sheehan to lunch was one of the most productive, as well as enjoyable, parts of my day. When not lunching with reporters, Abe and I—sometimes separately, sometimes together—might lunch with a prominent politician, an educator, an entertainer or a business tycoon. We would occasionally be the recipients of significant news, which we passed along to our reporters, who at times were chagrined at our being tipped off to information they had missed.

One of the first city officials whom we invited to lunch was New York's police commissioner Michael J. Murphy. We met him several times at Emil's, a restaurant near City Hall popular with politicians. He seemed flattered that we wanted to meet with him. He had never before been approached by an editor from *The Times*.

It was later, at Abe's suggestion, that the publisher invited Murphy to be his guest at a luncheon at *The Times*, a ritual held daily at one o'clock in the publisher's private dining room on the eleventh floor. The "publisher's luncheon," originated by Adolph Ochs, had been graced by presidents, prime ministers and kings, who answered the questions of top *Times* editors off the record. The room was handsomely furnished with prints of old New York and held a table that could seat as many as eighteen. Usually the guest found himself fielding so many questions he barely had a chance to taste his food. I was invited to participate when the guest was someone connected to city affairs. The first time, I was a little nervous and knocked over a glass of water that spilled into Punch Sulzberger's lap. (I can hear Punch saying, That wasn't the *last* time.)

We hosted Commissioner Murphy on November 22, 1963. He spoke about the difficulties of protecting President Kennedy on his visits to New York. The president, he said, liked to stop his motorcade to shake hands with admirers, who lined his route from the airport to Manhattan. It was a tremendous headache for the Police Department, and Murphy said he had personally warned Kennedy to change his habits, for he made an easy target for the unhinged.

At that moment, the phone in the anteroom rang and a waitress summoned Clifton Daniel. He returned to the dining room looking stunned and ashen. "President Kennedy has just been shot in Dallas," he announced. Everyone froze. "Anybody who has work to do had better go downstairs," Daniel said. The chairs were pushed back in a chorus and we all rushed to our desks. I began jotting down assignments in the elevator.

In the city room, the silence was ghostly. Reporters hovered around the wire-service teletype machines waiting to learn the president's fate. When the bulletin arrived announcing he was dead, several reporters wept. The fifty-five-year-old Harrison Salisbury, now head of the national desk, took charge of coordinating the assassination coverage. In 1949, he had transferred to the paper from the United Press in Moscow when *The Times*'s correspondent, Drew Middleton, had left Russia on a vacation and was refused permission to reenter. Salisbury replaced Middleton and, six years later, won a Pulitzer Prize for his Soviet coverage.

I lent Salisbury a number of our metropolitan reporters and assigned others to local angles and to background stories to supplement the national coverage. Following up on what Commissioner Murphy had told us at lunch, I assigned Marty Arnold and Pat Spiegel to a story about the difficulties that Kennedy's gregarious style had created for the police and the warnings the president had received from the commissioner. I sent a copyboy to the morgue to get the advance obit. There was an uncompleted obit by Tom Wicker, the White House correspondent. Since Kennedy was so young, there had been no urgency to finish it quickly. Memories of the frenzy on rewrite surrounding Stalin's death rose to my mind. I summoned Homer Bigart and Seymour Topping, our correspondent on home leave from the

Moscow bureau. I simply said, "We need an updated obit." They got to work, wading through dunes of clippings and, just under deadline, they produced an obit worthy of both a popular president and *The Times*.

Tom Wicker, who was on the press bus in Dallas when Kennedy was shot, performed heroically, piecing together the running story during that afternoon's surrealistic confusion. Wicker raced from the Trade Mart, where the president had been scheduled to speak, to Parkland Hospital, just as the body was being brought out in a bronze coffin. "Mrs. Kennedy walked by the coffin, her hand on it, her head down, her hat gone, her dress and stockings spattered," Tom wrote later in *Times Talk*. "She got into the hearse with the coffin. The staff men crowded into cars and followed. This was just about the only eyewitness matter I got with my own eyes that entire afternoon."

Tom then dashed to the airport for the swearing-in of Vice President Johnson, but he was moments too late. *Air Force One* was just taking off for Washington. But reporters who had witnessed the swearing-in gave Tom the details. "Throughout the day," Tom recalled, "every reporter on the scene seemed to me to do his best to help everyone else. Information came only in bits and pieces. Each man who picked up a bit or a piece passed it on. I know no one who held anything out. Nobody thought about an exclusive. It didn't seem important."

FOUR MONTHS LATER, Commissioner Murphy gave Abe and me a break on a gripping local story. He took his usual seat at his usual table at Emil's, his back to the wall and facing the door, the preference of many police officers as well as mobsters. Abe questioned him about the case of Winston Moseley, who had reportedly confessed to two recent murders in Queens. Murphy said that in all his years on the force, he had never encountered a case quite like the second murder. Thirty-eight neighbors, he explained, had witnessed the protracted attack and slaying of twenty-eight-year-old Catherine Genovese outside her Kew Gardens apartment. All had heard her screams. None had called the police until after she was dead.

Abe and I knew that every once in a while, the story of a single individual came along that symbolized a deep, sometimes disturbing truth about human nature and life in New York. We knew we had such a story in the case of Kitty Genovese. What had been reported in *The Times* initially as a routine account of a murder grew into a story that rocked the city to its core, its impact even greater than that of the still-unsolved Wylie–Hoffert crime.

Abe assigned the story about the unresponsive thirty-eight witnesses to Marty Gansberg, a copy editor who had recently joined the reportorial staff. He went to the precinct house in Queens, where he met with detectives who took him to Kew Gardens, a quiet, residential neighborhood with a number of private homes and faux-Tudor apartment buildings. Gansberg knocked on doors, interviewing neighbors about the murder, and pieced the facts together.

Abe personally edited the story, embellishing it as he saw fit, and it made page one on March 27, 1964, introducing the phrase "public apathy" into the popular lexicon. "For more than half an hour thirty-eight respectable citizens in Queens watched a killer stalk and stab a woman in three separate attacks in Kew Gardens," the article began. "Twice the sound of their voices and the sudden glow of their bedroom lights interrupted him and frightened him off. Each time he returned, sought her out and stabbed her again. Not one person telephoned the police during the assault; one witness called after the woman was dead."

At 3:20 A.M., on March 13, Kitty Genovese had returned from her job as a bar manager and parked her car in the lot at the Long Island Rail Road station one hundred feet from the entrance to her apartment, just as she did every night. But this night, a man lurked in the shadows on the fringes of the parking lot. Genovese apparently saw him, and started for a nearby police call box. She never reached it. The man grabbed her beneath a streetlight in front of a bookstore. "Oh my God, he stabbed me!" Genovese shrieked. "Please help me! Please help me!" Apartment lights went on and a man yelled from his window, "Let that girl alone." The assailant walked away and the apartment lights went out.

Genovese managed to stumble toward her apartment. But the murderer returned, and attacked her again. "I'm dying!" she screamed. "I'm dying!" Again lights went on and windows opened. This time the assailant was seen getting into his car and driving away. It was now 3:35 A.M., and Genovese was still alive. She crawled to the stairs at the entrance of her building and there she collapsed. The murderer then came back one final time to finish the job he had begun more than half an hour earlier.

The first call was made to the police at 3:50 A.M., and they arrived on the scene two minutes later. "The assailant had three chances to kill this woman during a thirty-five-minute period," Assistant Chief Inspector Frederick M. Lussen said. "If we had been called when he first attacked, the woman might not be dead now."

Witnesses gave various excuses for not calling the police. "We thought it was a lover's quarrel," said one housewife. "I didn't want my husband to get involved," said another. "I don't know," said a third. A number of people said they had been afraid to call, but couldn't say what exactly they feared. One man who gave a detailed account of the second attack said, "I was tired. I went back to bed." The man who finally phoned did so after prolonged deliberation. First he called a friend, seeking advice as to whether he should make a report; then he went to a neighbor's apartment to ask her to make the call. "I didn't want to get involved," he admitted.

The city reacted with confusion and shock and outrage. The headline over a *Times* editorial published a day after Gansberg's article summed it up: "What Kind of People Are We?" and asserted: "Seldom has *The Times* published a more horrifying story." Citizens seemed split into two categories: those who righteously condemned the witnesses as if they themselves would have surely phoned the police, and those who shook their heads in sadness and bafflement at the collective moral state of the city.

Psychologists and sociologists weighed in on the seemingly inexplicable behavior. Some blamed it on the emotional demands of city dwelling: "I would assign this to the effect of the megalopolis in which we live which makes closeness very difficult and leads to the alienation of the individual to the group," one said. He was sure it never would have happened in a small community. "The response," he said, " would have been immediate and very human." Others believed that television violence, often blurring the line between fantasy and reality, was a factor.

Abe, particularly mystified by the case, wrote an article for the Sunday *Magazine* entitled "A Study of the Sickness Called Apathy," in which he posited that the witnesses to the murder were no different than other people, that anyone in their place might have failed to act. Thus he encouraged readers to recognize that they must fear the witness in themselves "who whispers to close the window." He adapted his article, telling the story of covering the murder in an eighty-seven-page volume, *Thirty-eight Witnesses*. Inscribing a copy to Barbara and me, he wrote: "Not a whole cake, not even a slice. A crumb from the pound cake. But note—whereas your names are only printed on the cover and frontispiece in that whole ostentatious [O'Neill] book, this slim, elegant volume contains mine 87 times. With mahabat, Abe."

On June 11, Moseley was found guilty of the senseless murder. At the trial, he had admitted killing Genovese, saying he heard one of the neighbors open his window during the assault. "I had a feeling this man would close his window and go back to sleep, and sure enough he did," he added.

A few of the witnesses were called to testify. After they took the stand they spoke to a reporter. "I could cry. Now it's too late," said one. Another said, "Oh, for another chance, though I guess we'd do the same thing again." Moseley was sentenced to death.

THIRTY-TWO

T HE WORLD'S FAIR was preparing for its opening on April 22, and Abe asked me to set up a satellite bureau on the Flushing Meadows site in Queens to report on the extravaganza that its promoters hoped would evolve into a two-year international Coney Island. Along with various states, dozens of foreign countries were constructing gleaming pavilions, in which they were promising to present their proudest wares and liveliest events.

Thinking back to my visits to the 1939 World's Fair as a high school student, I visualized the assignment as a holiday. Instead of commuting to the city room every morning, I began driving to Flushing Meadows. Setting up the bureau was a more daunting job than I'd anticipated, but it turned out to be an editor's dream. I was free to draw on reporters from all parts of *The Times* to write on a variety of topics: business, the arts, religion, civil rights, fashion, food, sports, politics and visiting heads of state. It was like running my own newspaper.

The office assigned to our paper was a miniature city room—twenty-two feet by fifteen. From the fair's administrators, I managed to wangle eight desks with typewriters and telephones, plus a teletype machine. I chose Robert Alden as my deputy, confident I could hand over control of the bureau to him after a couple of months, once a routine was established. He was a crack reporter my age and I trusted his news judgment, his coolheadedness under stress. He had been a correspondent during the Korean War, had manned the Southeast Asia bureau and had reported from Australia. I believed his foreign experience would be a boon to our coverage of the international pavilions and compensate for my own unfamiliarity with life abroad.

The fair had been conceived in 1958 by Robert Kopple, a lawyer who represented major real estate and industrial groups. But when Robert Moses was named president of the World's Fair Corporation in 1959, he insisted on Kopple's ouster. It was Moses' act of revenge against the power-connected lawyer who had fought him on his proposed elevated Manhattan Expressway that would have transected the borough along Thirtieth Street. Moses was still relentlessly maneuvering, much as he had done in his stormy battles with Joe Papp over free Shakespeare in Central Park.

When I visited Moses in his lavishly decorated Flushing Meadows office, he once again offered me peanuts from a large bowl. I detected no softening in his manner. Age, it seemed, had mellowed him not at all. His arrogance in dealing with the European Bureau of International Exhibitions had prompted the withdrawal from the fair of a number of European nations.

Moses apparently had his own private agenda. He saw the fair as the means to realize a lifelong dream—the creation of a great urban park system in Queens that would bear his name. He also sought to resurrect his reputation, recently sullied by the disclosure that Frank Costello and other underworld bosses—unknown to Moses—had been among those behind the huge city housing program that Moses had managed.

Audacious as always, he predicted his World's Fair would turn a rich profit, despite earlier examples to the contrary. The 1939 fair, for one, had returned only thirty-two cents on the dollar to its investors. His optimism was based on advance ticket sales nearing $36 million, and his projected attendance of seventy million during the next two years, which, he claimed, would generate a stunning surplus of as much as $99 million.

As the fair's opening day approached, my bureau braced for civil rights demonstrations. Though I didn't fully comprehend the situation then, threats of mass protests—conveyed to our reporters by black groups—were a harbinger of the riots that were to plague New York that coming summer, making race relations the biggest issue in metropolitan as well as national news.

Even before we learned of the threats, I had been keeping track of the racial tremors in the South. Although I had as yet seen no overt signs that the conflicts were spreading north, I often thought of Dick Gregory's ominous prediction for New York. Shortly before and during my early months on the metropolitan desk in 1963, a succession of racial jolts had rocked the national conscience. On August 28, two hundred thousand blacks and whites had marched in Washington, inspired by Dr. Martin Luther King, Jr.'s speech from the steps of the Lincoln Memorial: "Now is the time to rise from the dark and desolate valley of segregation to the sunlit path of racial justice." A couple of weeks later, President Kennedy called on the National Guard to force Governor George C. Wallace's Alabama troopers to allow the newly desegregated schools to stay open and, on September 15, four girls were killed in the bombing of a black church in the state capital of Birmingham. And with the college student movement exploding in various parts of the country, white students in increasing numbers continued to join black students organizing the voter-rights project for blacks in the South.

It seemed perfectly plausible in this climate of racial unrest that protests on the fair's opening day would materialize, as promised by the Congress of Racial Equality (CORE). Their leaders informed our black reporters they had commitments from two thousand sympathizers to paralyze traffic by abandoning their cars on fair-bound highways.

"The stall-in is on," Junius Griffin, our newly recruited reporter wrote the day before the opening. "That statement by militant integration leaders yesterday ended hopes of averting a massive traffic tie-up on all major routes when the World's Fair opens. Cars from Philadelphia and cities in New Jersey have already arrived in the city to participate. . . . [It] is planned to dramatize the Negroes' dissatisfaction with the pace of civil rights progress."

Abe and I had hired Griffin soon after his nomination for the Pulitzer as one of eight AP reporters responsible for a series about the civil rights movement, "The Deepening Crisis." In the 1950s, Griffin, who was raised in South Carolina, joined the Marines. He became the only black correspondent in the corps to file articles from Korea for Pacific *Stars and Stripes* and later ranked as bureau chief for *Stars and Stripes* in Japan. Griffin became the third black reporter on our staff. Up to now, the small contingent consisted only of Layhmond Robinson, Jr., and Theodore (Ted) Jones, both holdovers from Frank Adams's day.

Robinson, a Navy photographer in World War II, had graduated from Syracuse University. In 1949, he began as a copyboy for *The Times* and, while working nights, enrolled at the Columbia School of Journalism. After earning his degree, he was promoted to reporter and took the path traveled by so many young white staffers—the police beat followed by night rewrite. He eventually became our first black reporter to cover city and state politics. Ted Jones was raised in Harlem and had worked for the *Amsterdam News* while attending City College. After earning a B.A. degree in 1955, he was hired as a copyboy and he, too, added a master's degree from the Columbia School of Journalism. In 1960, he was promoted to reporter and soon became the paper's authority on Harlem. But there weren't many stories about Harlem that *The Times*—or, for that matter, any other white newspaper—deemed newsworthy.

In his story about the impending stall-in, Griffin quoted a CORE leader who proclaimed, "No power on earth can stop it now." The police dispatched 1,100 men to the highways, and the Transit Authority placed one agent on every car of the Flushing-bound subway. As it turned out, the announcement deterred many thousands from attending the opening. President Johnson himself, rather than risk traffic tie-ups, flew directly to the fairgrounds in a helicopter from the recently renamed John F. Kennedy Airport.

But the stall-in never materialized, since only twelve vehicles were abandoned. With all the rhetoric, none of the protest organizers had taken into account the improbability of drivers' abandoning their cars—often their most prized possession—in the middle of a highway. There were, however, disturbances on the subways and demonstrations at the fairground itself. At 7:15 in the morning, a train bound for the fair pulled into a subway station, where some fifty youths waiting on the platform rushed the train doors, jamming them open and chanting "Freedom now!" and "Jim Crow must go!"

When the protesters lay down, twenty transit cops, half of them black, dragged them away by their legs. The demonstrators taunted the black cops, asking if they were called "boy" back at the station house. Physical resistance was met by billy clubs, and four protesters were hospitalized. At the fair, demonstrators targeted the United States Pavilion, where Johnson was to speak. I left my desk for a few minutes to get a sense of what was going on. It was the first time I'd witnessed such brazen organized defiance of the police, and I couldn't help thinking back to the days when an innocent black bystander in Times Square would meekly submit to a cop's gruff command to keep moving. As Johnson stepped to the podium after the last note of "Hail to the Chief," the black demonstrators shouted in unison, "Jim Crow must go!"

James Farmer, CORE's national director, was among those arrested in front of the New York City Pavilion, blocking the entrance to symbolize how blacks had been blocked from good city jobs, houses and schools. He said he wanted to emphasize the contrast between the glittering world of fantasy and the real world of brutality, bigotry and poverty that his people had faced in the hundred years since slavery.

I found visitors to the fair by turns supportive of and angered by the picketers. As I joined our reporters in walking through the crowds, I heard one middle-aged white woman say, "There's a part of me that feels like joining them." But another told her six-year-old daughter as they waded through demonstrators lying down in front of the New York State Pavilion: "When I say step on them, step on them." One man said, "I'm surprised to see so many whites picketing, but of course they're beatniks." White demonstrators, in fact, outnumbered blacks, in some instances by four to one. In all, 299 people were arrested, most charged with disorderly conduct.

Our bureau was pandemonium that night. I had assigned so many stories that some thirty reporters were crammed together inside our one little room and in the corridor outside, vying for the telephones and typewriters. Many reporters, deskless, wrote their stories in longhand while standing, then called them in from public phone booths. Though the weather was damp and nippy, inside the office it was steaming.

When the last lights were turned off in the fair's amusement area at two A.M., I shut down the bureau. Bob Alden and I, as well as several desk assistants, had been at work nonstop for eighteen hours. When we arrived at the nearby motel where we had booked rooms for the several days prior to and following the fair's opening, Bob collapsed on the floor. We were all somewhat dizzy but after ascertaining that every one of the twenty-five stories we'd assigned had made it into the paper, we managed to summon enough strength to toast our triumph with a nightcap. Our staff had filled five pages with spot coverage, sans advertisements. (There had been seven pages of pre-opening features the day before.)

The story possibilities seemed endless. Our reporters compiled yards of facts, from the fair's size (646 acres), to its cost (nearly $1 billion). Some of the popular displays we reported on were a robotic statue of Abraham Lincoln and a "kitchen of tomorrow" complete with a machine that pressed disposable dishes out of thermoplastic film. Fairgoers, our stories noted, could walk through a giant replica of a Chevy V-8 engine, ride a monorail, view Chinese antiquities and marvel over Michelangelo's Pietà, flown in from Rome.

Gay Talese and McCandlish Phillips took turns writing a slice-of-life column, "About the Fair." For one column, Talese asked senior citizens what were the most startling technological advances they had witnessed during their lifetimes. "Zippers," said one man. "I remember the time I went for a suit of clothes and they wanted to sell me a zipper, and I said, 'No sir, I want no part of it.'" Frank Clines and Phil Benjamin filled in for Talese and Phillips on their days off and, with other staffers, they hammered away at problems the fair was experiencing, including financial difficulties. One day, Moses called an impromptu press conference during which he denounced Clines and his colleagues as "jackals working in the underbrush."

The reporters achieved such harmony that Phillips felt privileged to try (unsuccessfully) to lure Clines—who had been drifting away from his Catholic roots—"back to Jesus." The twenty-six-year-old Clines had been raised by poor New York Irish parents in Brooklyn. His mother had grown up in Hell's Kitchen and his father in Jersey City, and Frank had attended parochial school—in the tough district of Red Hook, where many students were believed to be children of Mafia soldiers. He was blessed with teachers who gave him a love of language that inspired him to become a writer.

Both Clines and Benjamin wrote a series of human-interest stories heralded by readers. One such story by Benjamin concerned a resourceful twelve-year-old runaway, Dominic Tucci, a parochial school student who had been living at the fair for over a week. "I slept in the Gas Pavilion for three nights, four nights in the Continental Insurance Pavilion, one night at Coca-Cola and one night in the Johnson's Wax Theater," Dominic boasted. "Every night I'd sneak out and get coins from the fountain at the Bell exhibit, the Unisphere and the what-do-you-call-it, the Astral Fountain." Dominic survived on hamburgers—except on Friday, when he ate chow mein. His mother said she had suspected he was at the fair, but had not looked for him because, "If that's what he wanted, let him have his fling."

Phil Benjamin was a mild-mannered man with a humorous outlook and the potential for a literary career that was tragically cut short. He was married to an emerging writer named Lois Regensburg, who, although among the first of the "women's libbers" in our circle, changed her byline to Lois Benjamin. His friends thought Phil was dominated by Lois, who at times spoke somewhat didactically of her responsibility as a representative of her sex. But despite their clashing personalities, Lois and Phil seemed to enjoy a stable marriage with their two children—until Phil began to stray.

Toward the end of his daily shift at the paper, he often sidled up to a fellow reporter to ask, "Do you have an assignment tonight?" When the reporter disclosed what he was working on, Phil would say, "I'm going to call my wife and tell her I've been asked by Gelb to do legwork for you tonight." For some unfathomable reason, Phil recorded all his infidelities in code in a diary he kept in a safe-deposit box. In 1966, after he died suddenly of a freak reaction to an anesthetic administered during minor surgery, Lois discovered the diary and cracked the code, which proved to be about as complex as something you'd find on the back of a cereal box. Lois, who had never suspected Phil of infidelity, was in a state of shock for some time. She entered intensive therapy, and her psychiatrist, Robert E. Gould, suggested she purge her sense of betrayal through a fictionalized account of her husband's philandering. She married Gould a year later and, in 1970, as Lois Gould, wrote the best-selling novel *Such Good Friends*, in which, after all, she had the last word—and went on to a successful career as a novelist and journalist.

IN ADDITION TO city-room reporters, our critics received my summonses to the fair. Ada Louise Huxtable assessed the architecture: "disconnected, grotesque, lacking in any unity of concept or style." Howard Taubman found none of the entertainment worth his attention. John Canaday raved about the art at the Japanese Pavilion but gave the sculpture at the New York State Pavilion low marks.

The staffer whose visits I most eagerly awaited was our food critic, Craig Claiborne, who always invited me to accompany him on his rounds of the scores of Fair restaurants and concession stands. Claiborne, a graduate of the Swiss Hotel Keepers Association course in cuisine, possessed a palate as educated as those of the finest French chefs. At a single taste, he could deconstruct a complex morsel of food into its components. When I went restaurant-hopping with Craig at the fair, he'd instruct me to only nibble a bit of everything on my plate. Were I to finish an entire meal, he said, I'd be too satiated to move on to the next restaurant. It was not unusual for Claiborne himself to eat (or rather nibble at) three lunches and two dinners in the same day.

We dined at the Indian Pavilion, "a place of genuine elegance and grace," and the Spanish Pavilion, which had "all the elements to make it the most talked-about restaurant at the Fair." But nothing at this fair, Craig told me, offered anything comparable to the exquisite food served at the French Pavilion during the 1939 Fair. Henri Soulé, manager and chief of staff of France's Café de Paris, had been sent to the fair by his government to create a gastronomic paradise intended to settle once and for all any question of which nation ruled the culinary world.

When France fell to the Nazis after the fair opened, Soulé and his staff found themselves stranded in America and, following the fair's closing, Soulé re-created his restaurant at 5 East Fifty-fifth Street in Manhattan, calling it Le Pavillon. It quickly became recognized as the best restaurant in New York. Some time later, Claiborne wrote: "The like of Le Pavillon has not been equaled in Manhattan and I don't think there's a restaurant owner in town who would dispute that."

The respect was mutual, and Soulé once gave the critic a gold pocket watch, engraved "In Gratitude." While Claiborne had misgivings about accepting it, neither did he wish to offend Soulé by returning it. He brought his dilemma to Clifton Daniel, who agreed that, for the sake of Claiborne's impeccable reputation, he should not keep the watch. Daniel and Claiborne each wrote notes to Soulé, delicately explaining why the watch was being regretfully returned. Soulé understood. He stored it in a safe, with instructions that Claiborne was to receive it after retiring from *The Times*. He got it sooner—when Soulé died in 1966.

THE FAIR ULTIMATELY DREW twenty million people fewer than expected. Moses had to borrow funds to open the second season, and the fair corporation defaulted on its bonds after paying twenty-five cents on the dollar. The city received no reimbursement for improvements to the fairgrounds or the surrounding roadways. Moses' last hurrah, while it did provide entertainment for some fifty million visitors, ended as an embarrassing failure.

When Bob Alden, in a front-page story citing the fair's inability to finance the Queens park, asked Moses about reports that the City Council had called for an investigation of the fair's finances, he replied: "Well, that's characteristic of Council members. They're trying to get their names in the paper." And when Alden and other reporters asked why bankers had defected from his finance committee, he said they had resigned because they had been misinformed.

"Was it you who misinformed them?"

"What the hell is the use of asking such a provocative question?" snapped Moses, advising the reporters to settle down and "have a drink."

THIRTY-THREE

ON MY RETURN TO THE CITY ROOM from the fair, I realized it was more than ever imperative to hire additional well-trained black reporters. But the pool of experienced applicants was still small, and Abe and I had been unable to find anyone since Junius Griffin. Had *The Times* earlier on been more aggressive in its recruiting efforts, we might by now have had the black staff we needed. As it was, when race got to be the city's top story, during what shortly came to be known as "the long hot summer," the paper paid the price for its passivity.

On Thursday, July 16, 1964, James Powell, a black fifteen-year-old, was shot and killed by an off-duty police lieutenant, Thomas Gilligan, in front of an apartment building on East Seventy-sixth Street, near the public school the boy attended. The police claimed Powell had charged at Gilligan with a pocket knife and ignored warnings to stop. The incident began when the building superintendent sprayed water on Powell and a few other teenagers.

"They were standing near the stoop," the super said in his Irish brogue. "I wanted to spray the flower boxes. I asked them ten times to move." When he sprayed them accidentally, he said, the boys threw objects at him and chased him inside the building. When they emerged, they encountered Lieutenant Gilligan.

Eyewitnesses disputed the account, maintaining the super intentionally aimed his hose at the youths, saying, "I'm going to wash all the black off you." They also said Gilligan fired without warning and that Powell was not carrying a knife. When police reinforcements showed up at the scene of the shooting, some black teenagers greeted them with a barrage of bottles.

A peaceful student march the next day protested police brutality. On Saturday evening, however, the situation exploded. A CORE rally was held in Harlem to condemn the killing. One of the speakers, the Reverend Nelson C. Dukes of the Fountain Spring Baptist Church, mounted a kitchen chair that served as podium and called on the crowd to march on the 123rd Street police station to demand Gilligan's arrest for murder. When the protesters tried to push their way into the station house they were stopped by a line of cops with locked arms.

The World's Fair protests of just a few months earlier had been but a bland foretaste of the violent Harlem scene, which appeared to take the cops by surprise. The crowd, continuing to swell, shouted for the removal of Police Commissioner Murphy. "Killers, murderers, Murphy's rats!" they taunted. From surrounding rooftops, bottles and trash-can covers rained down on the cops, and a scuffle broke out as the police hastily erected barricades between the station house and the crowd. A busload of police reinforcements finally arrived—a shock unit of handpicked men, all over six feet tall, under thirty years old and trained in judo. By now the entire neighborhood was engulfed in battle. "If I knew this was going to happen, I wouldn't have said anything," a reporter overheard the Reverend Dukes comment.

Shop windows were smashed and stores looted. Trash bins were set aflame, Molotov cocktails burst on the sidewalks and bricks flew at the helmeted cops. Cars driven by unsuspecting whites were pounded. The police fired thousands of live rounds into the air in an attempt to scatter the mob, and those who refused to disperse were clubbed. "Go home, go home," a captain shouted through a megaphone. "We are home, baby!" shouted a rioter.

Rumors of police brutality traveled quickly, inspiring ever-greater fury within the area. One intoxicated woman lay on the sidewalk. She just felt like lying down, she said. "They walk all over me in Greenville, South Carolina. They might as well run over me here." But word spread that the woman had been gunned down "in cold blood" by the cops.

By 3:20 A.M. Sunday, July 19, when we put *The Times* to bed, Harlem was a war zone. The younger cops had never witnessed anything like it. Dodging improvised missiles, they occupied rooftops in full riot gear and patrolled the streets with pistols drawn. Only as dawn broke did Harlem quiet down. Local hospitals treated more than one hundred people for injuries. One man had been killed. And this was only the beginning.

Our reporters—three black and three white—did a good job on what was a new kind of story for New York. But anticipating more violence, Abe and I made elaborate plans for coverage starting at daybreak. When I arrived at the office at seven A.M. on Sunday, I was obliged to call on five additional white reporters to cover the rapidly escalating events, even though I was concerned they might encounter lethal hostility in Harlem.

There was, however, one white reporter whose color I felt would not impede his ability to communicate with factions of the black population. He was M. S. (Meyer) Handler, back on the city staff after having spent thirty years in various European countries as a correspondent. During the past months, to my surprise and admiration, he managed to gain the friendship and trust of Malcolm X, the black militant who pronounced all whites to be "devils" and shuddered at the thought of shaking a white man's hand. Handler, a scholarly man in his late fifties who was fluent in seven languages, including Yiddish and Serbo-Croatian, had honed his gift of communication abroad in encounters with myriad races, religions and social classes.

It had been Handler's own idea to seek out Malcolm X, who later told the biographer Alex Haley that Handler was "the most genuinely unprejudiced white man I ever met." Some months prior to the Harlem riots, Malcolm X had withdrawn from the Black Muslim movement to make a holy pilgrimage to Mecca. Handler excitedly showed me the amazingly candid letter Malcolm X sent him from Saudi Arabia. For the first time, he wrote, he felt "no racial antagonisms toward whites" and sensed no "antagonisms on their part" toward him. Not long after, he amended the statement to Handler: "In the past, yes, I have made sweeping indictments of all white people. I will never be guilty of that again—as I know that some white people are truly sincere, that some are capable of being brotherly toward a black man." Malcolm X's confessed metamorphosis made a dramatic page-one story. (After his assassination in Harlem the following year, Handler was asked by Alex Haley to write the introduction to his *Autobiography of Malcolm X*.)

FORESEEING THE CONTINUANCE of the Harlem rebellion on that Sunday of July 19, I asked Handler to determine what he could learn from his black friends about how they sized up the muddled situation. I also called my old friend photographer Eddie Hausner to let him know that the memorial service for the slain fifteen-year-old James Powell was set for that evening at a funeral home on Seventh Avenue and 132nd Street. "God only knows what's going to happen," I told Eddie. Would the rioters breach the frontiers of their own neighborhood and head downtown?

I suggested Eddie go to the Hotel Theresa at Seventh Avenue and 125th Street, the epicenter of the riot zone, and book a room with windows facing north—toward the funeral parlor. The Theresa was a Harlem landmark and, though its great days had passed, its renown had been temporarily enhanced when Fidel Castro chose to stay there, rather than in a midtown luxury hotel, when he addressed the United Nations in 1960. When Eddie entered the Theresa, he saw no white faces. The desk manager, dubious about renting him a room, finally gave him a key. The room, which cost thirty-five dollars a night, was sparse and a bit grungy, but afforded a clear view of the critical intersections below.

Junius Griffin, noticeably more relaxed than his white colleagues, arrived dressed in a Hawaiian shirt, a Panama hat and brown loafers with tassels. He had always worn a suit and tie in the office, but apparently believed he'd be less conspicuous on the street in his casual outfit. Griffin and Hausner went together to the Mount Morris Presbyterian Church to cover a meeting whose theme was "Is Harlem Mississippi?" There, Jesse Gray, a militant black whose face was bandaged and swollen from a beating he said he had received from the cops the previous night, called for "a hundred skilled black revolutionaries who are ready to die."

"There is only one thing that can correct the situation," declared Gray, "and that's guerrilla warfare. . . . This city can be changed by fifty thousand well-organized Negroes." Edward Mills Davis, a Black Nationalist street speaker, took the podium and requested that "all you black people that have been in the armed services and know anything about guerrilla warfare should come to the aid of our people. . . . If we must die, let us die scientifically."

Hausner, the only white among some five hundred blacks, took the opportune time to slip away to the Theresa, where he was joined by another photographer, John Orris, and a city staff reporter, Joe Lelyveld. From their sixth-floor window, they saw a crowd of over one thousand gathered outside the funeral parlor, but the situation seemed calm and they decided to walk there together up Seventh Avenue. By the time they reached the middle of the block between 126th and 127th Streets, all order had disintegrated. Bottles were thrown near the funeral home and the cops, brandishing nightsticks, rushed at the crowd. Shots were fired into the air and some people began running down Seventh Avenue—on a collision course with our three white *Times* men.

A group of angry teenagers threw them against the side of a stalled mail truck. Somehow, Lelyveld managed to twist himself loose. Hausner blocked a blow aimed at his head, but the sleeve of his suit jacket was ripped open and his elbow was bloodied. Orris got by far the worst of it. Pummeled in the face, blood gushing from his right eye, which was nearly dislodged from its socket, he fell to the ground. Hausner crouched to shield Orris's body with his own and was dealt a few solid kicks before four black Housing Authority cops came running from a nearby project, firing guns at the sidewalk to disperse the teenagers.

Hausner applied a handkerchief to Orris's wound, but it became quickly soaked with blood. The housing cops provided a towel and hustled both men into a basement, where they called Harlem Hospital to send an ambulance for Orris. Somehow Junius Griffin heard what had happened and appeared in the basement before the ambulance arrived. He told Hausner to leave Orris and go back on the street with him. A photographer was needed and, with Orris out of commission, Hausner was the only one left.

"Like hell!" Hausner replied. "I'm going to the hospital with Orris. I don't care if I'm fired. I'm not going to leave him." Hausner later told me he had felt more vulnerable as a white man that evening in Harlem than he had as an eighteen-year-old rifleman during World War II, when he crossed the Rhine under heavy enemy fire. (When Punch Sulzberger learned that Orris was in danger of losing his eye, he phoned Dr. Howard Rusk at New York University's rehabilitation center. Rusk reached the best specialist he knew, an Italian doctor in Rome, and *The Times* arranged for him to fly to New York immediately. He reattached Orris's retina, an advanced surgical procedure for that time, and saved his sight.)

The street situation continued to worsen after Hausner and Orris left the scene. Again, the police were battered with bricks, bottles and gasoline bombs. "The idea is to make a lot of noise—run right at them yelling. That usually breaks a crowd," explained one officer, who had just led such a charge while shooting above the mob. By three A.M., the cops had run out of ammunition and called for more.

Paul Montgomery, a twenty-seven-year-old *Times* reporter who had contributed articles about the history of India to the *Columbia Encyclopedia*, written a commentary on Goethe's *Faust* and taught himself Sanskrit, described in *Times Talk* the strategy he and Frank Clines (with whom he had collaborated on Sunday's page-one story) had worked out for covering the riot: "In essence it was simple—run with the mobs when they attacked the police, then run away from them when it looked like they wanted to attack you. . . . The advantage was that we definitely did not feel left out. Just about everyone we saw wanted to have a talk. 'Hey, whitey, we gonna get you' was the second most popular conversational opening. I cannot repeat the most popular because the Style Book Committee has not yet determined whether it should be hyphenated."

Quiet once again came with the dawn. But on Monday night the rioting reignited, spreading to the Bedford-Stuyvesant section of Brooklyn, and I found myself having to spread our reporters very thin. By the end of the week, as Brooklyn finally simmered down, I had to send reporters upstate to Rochester, which erupted during the early hours of July 25. Rumors spread through the city's black neighborhoods that the police had brutally beaten a black man. Six police cars were overturned, and the police chief's vehicle was set on fire. Within three days, a thousand National Guardsmen had been called in, four hundred persons arrested, and a civil defense helicopter had crashed in the riot area, killing three. The looting was much worse than in Harlem, with entire stores gutted. Tear gas and fire hoses finally broke up the throng.

Civil rights leaders pleaded for calm and a ban on demonstrations until after November's presidential election. They feared that "white backlash" would help Senator Barry Goldwater of Arizona defeat President Johnson. But on August 2, in spite of the pleas, yet another riot gathered steam, this one in Jersey City. Again, the spark was a report of police brutality against a black person. For three nights, with the days between generally calm, police battled the rioters.

By this time, our metropolitan desk had, in effect, become a war bureau, and I dispatched reporters with trepidation. Joe Lelyveld, despite his earlier roughing-up in Harlem, was one of the most eager to return to the battle-field, and I sent him to Jersey City. Joe, who had joined the paper as a copy-boy two years earlier, after graduating with a master's degree in journalism from Columbia, had spunk, smarts and a snappy writing style, but one article he filed from Jersey City caused a brief contretemps between us. He ended the piece with a parable told him by a black high school teacher: One man saw another man beating a donkey. The first approached the second and asked him why he was hitting the animal. "I want him to move, but he won't move," said the donkey owner. "You just have to reason with him," said the other. "May I try?" The donkey owner said, "Sure," so the man picked up a brick and hit the donkey on the head with it. "I thought you were going to reason with him," the owner said. "I am, but first I had to get his attention."

I asked Joe to delete the paragraph, not wanting to invite accusations that *The Times* was indirectly expressing an editorial opinion in a news story. Joe, enamored of his "kicker," refused to make the change and walked out of the city room, and I saw to it that the article ran without the kicker. I intended to bench him the following day, but there was too much news breaking to keep a good reporter unassigned.

WITH HINDSIGHT, I realized there had been scattered warning signs in the spring of 1964 that New York's black neighborhoods were powder kegs waiting for sparks. Indeed, we had recently commissioned a survey of attitudes in the black communities. Admittedly unscientific, it was our first such survey and was conducted mainly by our three black reporters. A total of 190 residents from all boroughs except Staten Island were questioned at length. But by the time we received the results, the riots were already in full flood. Layhmond Robinson, the most experienced of the black reporters, drafted the story in which the respondents voiced complaints about "bad schools, indifferent teachers, the presence of hoodlums or narcotic addicts on their blocks, payoffs to policemen by racketeers or addicts, conniving landlords and rats in homes."

What most interested us was that while most of the blacks interviewed supported demonstrating as a means toward achieving equality, the majority rejected violence—although many did believe that some violence was in-evitable. While the survey indicated the majority of blacks passionately wanted a higher quality of life and equality of opportunity with whites, they felt trapped, as one Harlem schoolteacher phrased it, "between the viciousness of the white man and the viciousness and apathy of a lot of our own people."

A primary reason for conducting our survey was the startling discovery reported to Abe and me by Junius Griffin early in 1964 of the existence of a small group of militant young blacks in Harlem calling themselves "Blood Brothers." Griffin filed several stories about the gang, whose members, he averred, were roaming the streets of Harlem with the avowed intention of attacking whites who worked there. "They are trained to maim and kill," Griffin wrote after being admitted into one of their practice sessions.

Soon after the story appeared, the police attributed four recent murders to the Blood Brothers, who reputedly carried makeshift weapons as well as guns. New initiates, according to Griffin, were taught martial arts on tenement rooftops, and were required to prove their loyalty to the gang by mugging white people. Members of the gang, wrote Griffin, spent half an hour nightly thrusting their hands into pails of raw rice to toughen them. One boy switched to gravel after his sister cooked his equipment for dinner.

Malcolm X—as yet untransformed—was said to be the idol of the Blood Brothers, who in emulation referred to whites as "blue-eyed devils" and "white dogs." The membership had increased slightly that April, Griffin reported, after some youths accidentally overturned a couple of tables at Joe's Fruit Stand while trying to steal produce. A police chase ensued, during which a few youths were injured, including one who lost an eye. Residents brought charges of brutality, declaring they needed protection *from* the police. One Blood Brother, in fact, as quoted by Griffin, declared his gang's main mission was its defense against overzealous cops.

To explain Harlem's inflammation to our readers, Griffin wrote of families crammed into rat-infested one-room flats, sometimes four or five sharing a bed. Heat and plumbing were erratic at best. Those who couldn't even afford a room rented beds by the hour, called "hot beds" because the turnover was so rapid the sheets had no time to cool between customers.

Once Griffin interviewed some teenagers about their aspirations. Most felt it was a white man's world with no room for them. "Whitey ain't going to give me a break nohow, so, man, why should I go to school?" said a fifteen-year-old. Another said, "Why should I learn about Columbus discovering America? They ain't going to ask me that when I try to get a job downtown. They don't teach me nothing about my people and Africa." And they had good grounds for their disillusionment, since twenty-five percent of men in Harlem were unemployed.

As a boy in the Bronx, I went to Woolworth's off the Grand Concourse, where black women from Harlem gathered in the morning, hoping to be chosen for the day as house cleaners. At the "shape-up," as it was called, white housewives inspected the women. A tap on the shoulder meant they were hired, and they went to work for pitiful wages. Not much had improved since then.

In high schools across the country now, they teach rap as literature. But at that time ghetto life was so far removed from mainstream white New York that, when we started running stories about Harlem, we had to include simplistic "translations" of quotes by blacks in the community. We asked the reporters to explain that "whitey" was a "term of contempt," that black people called each other "brother," and that "jiving" meant "to deceive." In describing police prejudice, one teenager in a story said, "He might go up beside your head before you have a chance to say anything." We noted that "go up beside" meant "to hit." When asked if black patrolmen were more compassionate than white, the boy said, "Hell no, them member cops will go up beside your head in a minute." "Member," the reporter explained, was "slang for Negro."

Griffins's Blood Brothers stories provoked a certain amount of controversy, since reporters on other publications found they were unable to make contact with the organization. Accusations of hype, usually leveled against the tabloids, were directed at Griffin and *The Times*. Abe and I questioned him repeatedly, but he never wavered from his claim that his reporting was accurate. He maintained that the public attention he had given the incipient movement scared off and dispersed their members, who were few to begin with. When I happened to talk to him some twenty years later (long after he had quit the paper, first to join Martin Luther King, Jr.'s staff and then to work for Motown Records in Los Angeles), he insisted that every fact in his stories had been the truth. Even though at times I had harbored some doubts, overall I found Griffin's sincerity convincing.

WHILE THE IMPACT of the long hot summer continued spreading to other northern cities, the Democratic Party was readying its convention, scheduled to open August 24 in Atlantic City. Since it was expected to be the scene of mass demonstrations, Abe and I decided to attend (New Jersey being part of our tristate jurisdiction). Harrison Salisbury, in charge of national correspondents and in command of convention coverage, was responsible for booking hotel rooms, which were hard to come by.

It seemed to me that Salisbury was jealous of the esteem in which Abe was held by Punch Sulzberger and Turner Catledge, and saw himself as Abe's rival for future promotion to the top. I couldn't help being amused at the pettiness that motivated the patrician Harrison to obtain rooms for us at a kosher boardinghouse some distance from the principal hotels near the convention center, where he himself was staying along with Punch, Catledge, Reston and other members of the *Times* hierarchy. When Catledge chided him, Salisbury lamely blamed the arrangement on his assistant, who, he said, had failed to inform him that Abe and I had requested accommodations while good hotel rooms were still available.

Although none of the expected demonstrations occurred, I thought the convention presented a shameful display of bias. I watched as separate white and black delegations arrived in Atlantic City from Mississippi, each insisting it represented the state. The black delegates, newly radicalized, argued they were the only lawful group, since the white delegates had forfeited their status by excluding blacks from voting polls. The credentials committee suggested the state's delegation be composed of both blacks and whites, but the blacks refused. I understood their anger and pride as they left Atlantic City for home, not waiting for the nomination of President Johnson and his running mate, Hubert Humphrey.

When I returned to *The Times*, I read Punch's announcement of sweeping changes in the paper's top command—changes that I saw as good omens for Abe and me. Catledge was appointed to the newly created position of executive editor, with, at long last, both the daily and the Sunday staffs united under one command. Both the managing editor and the Sunday editor would report to him, and he in turn would report to the publisher.

Lester Markel, who had been Sunday editor for forty-one years and couldn't bear the idea of reporting to Catledge, huffily accepted the nebulous, face-saving title of "associate editor," and was moved a distance away from the news operation to a new office not far from the publisher's on the fourteenth floor. Markel, in turn, was replaced by Daniel Schwarz, assistant Sunday editor for the past fourteen years—but he'd have nothing like the power once wielded by Markel.

Clifton Daniel, who had served as assistant managing editor for five years, was Catledge's natural successor as managing editor. He took over Catledge's office, and Catledge moved into newly constructed quarters off the city room. Harrison Salisbury was promoted to assistant managing editor. Catledge told Abe, who had hoped for that position, that he wanted him to stay a while longer on the metropolitan desk to make absolutely sure it was running at top speed before I succeeded him.

At Scotty Reston's request, there was also a realignment of responsibilities in the Washington bureau. Believing he needed more time to devote to his editorial-page column, Reston happily yielded his administrative duties to Tom Wicker, whose beat up to now had been the White House. In his new post, Wicker took over as chief Washington correspondent and head of the bureau, while Reston assumed the title of "associate editor," but in his case, unlike Markel's, the honorific implied no diminished power. He retained his behind-the-scenes authority as éminence grise of the Washington bureau, something that had taken him years to establish, and stemmed not only from his influential writings but from his continuing warm ties to the Sulzberger family.

As THE NEW MANAGING EDITOR, Daniel met with Abe and me to discuss the race-related events of 1964, and figure out how to add black reporters to our staff. We also discussed the increasing problems being confronted by the police. We had come to realize that their use of excessive force was only one of the querulous issues on the minds of black residents. Other police tactics, particularly the coercive manner in which confessions were obtained, had come under intense scrutiny, following the long-awaited arrest on April 25 of a confused black suspect, George Whitmore, Jr., in the murders of Janice Wylie and Emily Hoffert. The police said that the nineteen-year-old Whitmore had confessed to the double homicide.

Whitmore had actually gone to the Seventy-third Street station house in Brooklyn as a voluntary witness to the mugging of a woman named Elba Borrero. He claimed to have seen a man fleeing after attacking the woman at knifepoint on April 23 in the borough's Brownsville section. The attack was similar in style to that on Minnie Edmonds, who had been raped and murdered ten days earlier in the same neighborhood. Detectives had no leads in the Edmonds case, but believed there was a good chance the two crimes were connected.

The police at the precinct were suspicious of Whitmore's statement and asked Elba Borrero to come in and take a look at Whitmore. After assessing him through a peephole, she identified him as her attacker. But, to be sure, she said she wanted to hear his voice. The cops told Whitmore to say: "Shut up or I'll kill you. I think I'll kill you first, then I'll rape you." Whitmore complied and Borrero confirmed that he was her attacker.

Then the "questioning" began. By morning, Whitmore had agreed to confess not only to the Borrero attack and the Minnie Edmonds rape-murder, but the still-unsolved Wylie–Hoffert crimes as well. All this occurred two years before the Supreme Court's Miranda decision, prohibiting the questioning of a suspect in custody unless he was informed he could request a lawyer to be present. Whitmore had not requested a lawyer when taken into custody.

Residents of the neighborhood in which the Wylie–Hoffert homicides were committed were grateful to know the killer was finally behind bars. Max Wylie, Janice's father, said he was confident the police had nabbed the right man. But her uncle Philip Wylie said, "It sounds to me like a guy who got scared into making a confession."

That's what it sounded like to Sidney Zion, too. A nonpracticing lawyer who had been a reporter at the *Post* for less than a year, Zion joined our staff a few months before the Whitmore arrest. He initially was interviewed by Harrison Salisbury, in the hope he might fill the opening on the paper's Supreme Court beat recently vacated by Anthony Lewis, who had left Washington to head the London bureau. Casual in both dress and attitude, Zion said later that the very proper Salisbury made him feel as if his fly was open. Salisbury didn't give him the job.

Abe and I, however, thought he'd do well on the metropolitan staff as our local legal expert. Zion was a graduate of Yale Law School, had spent three years as a lawyer and two as an assistant United States attorney in New Jersey. "How would you like to be the Anthony Lewis of New York?" Abe asked him. The Whitmore case was Zion's first major assignment. As a former prosecutor, he knew all about extracting confessions. "This stinks from top to bottom," he told us. "They just fed Whitmore this stuff." I agreed it was quite possible, aware—like most reporters who had covered the police beat—of what often transpired behind the closed doors of a precinct interrogation room.

Zion's instincts were sound. It soon evolved that Whitmore had recanted his confessions to all three crimes with which he was charged, claiming the confessions had been coerced. The police were finally forced to admit that the all-too-tenuous link connecting Whitmore to Wylie–Hoffert was a photograph he carried in his wallet of a blond young woman. Inscribed on the back of the photo was "To George from Louise," in addition to a phone number. Whitmore said he had found the photo at the dump where he worked in his hometown of Wildwood, New Jersey. He said he wrote the note on the photo himself, to impress his friends.

One of the detectives thought the woman looked like Janice Wylie and he and his colleagues, who played good cop–bad cop, hammered away at the bewildered Whitmore, who had an IQ of somewhere between 60 and 90. They finally bullied him into conceding that he had stolen the photo from an apartment on East Eighty-eighth Street in Manhattan (the same street where Wylie and Hoffert were murdered). At that point, Whitmore didn't know there was any crime connected to that address.

The detectives continued to maneuver him, step by step, through the details of the morning of the murders, questioning him over and over on any points he got "wrong," until his answers matched the facts. Then they helped him draw a diagram of the girls' apartment. They went so far as to lie to him when he asked, "What happened to those girls? The girls in the apartment. Are they all right, or what?" A detective told Whitmore he'd just spoken to the girls on the phone, that they'd been in the hospital for a few days, but were okay, and they weren't upset with Whitmore at all.

The Brooklyn police had the confession basically wrapped up by the time detectives from Manhattan arrived. The Manhattan crew was skeptical about its authenticity from the start, but didn't want to step on any toes. Two of their detectives, however, got to work and determined, after extensive digging, that the girl in the photo was not Janice Wylie.

Whitmore was never brought to trial for the Wylie–Hoffert murders. On January 27, 1965, the district attorney discharged him "on his own recognizance" as the confession fell apart under irrefutable charges of coercion. Three days earlier, a new suspect, Richard Robles, had been arrested. A twenty-two-year-old drug addict, Robles had been fingered as the murderer by a fellow junkie. Police installed a bugging device in the junkie's apartment and recorded Robles bragging about the killing. He was convicted on December 1, 1965, and sentenced to life. Though he initially professed his innocence, he later confessed, saying he had broken into the apartment to steal money for his drug habit, and was surprised to find Wylie at home. According to his story, he raped her at knifepoint and was tying her up when Hoffert walked in. "I'm going to remember you for the police," he recalled Hoffert saying. Then he "went bananas."

As for the other two criminal allegations against Whitmore, charges were ultimately dropped in the Edmonds murder case, but he was convicted in the Borrero rape case. He went through a series of appeals, reversals and reconvictions until, finally in 1973, after he had spent four years in prison, the conviction was vacated and the indictment dismissed.

The unraveled Whitmore case stunned the legal system. "Call it what you want—brainwashing, hypnosis, fright. They made him give an untrue confession," said one Manhattan assistant district attorney. Another said,

"This was what we so-called professionals call a run-of-the-mill. Whitmore might well have been slipped into the electric chair and been killed for something he didn't do."

Confessions, which were already being viewed by the courts with skepticism, were now even more suspect, and my staff and I could no longer accept them without raising our own questions. The New York State Court of Appeals had recently established a procedure by which a trial judge was required to certify every confession as voluntary before it could be admitted as evidence. And a few months before Whitmore was arrested, the United States Supreme Court in *Escobedo v. Illinois* established the right of a suspect to have a lawyer present during questioning (though it did not require the police to offer or provide one). Law enforcement officials were in turmoil. Confessions, they said, were essential to winning convictions, and it was unlikely, they argued, that anyone would confess if a lawyer sat at a defendant's side.

In 1966, when the Supreme Court was weighing its Miranda decision—which limited police powers in questioning suspects—the Whitmore case was cited as an example of the abuses within the system. As the court deliberated, one of the major factors under consideration was law enforcement's insistence that it would be emasculated if its ability to obtain confessions was further weakened.

I assigned Zion to write several articles pegged to the debate. For one story, he obtained statistics from various cities proving that less than ten percent of convictions nationwide were based upon confessions. I was convinced the stories we had published helped sway the Supreme Court in favor of Miranda. The court ruled five to four that suspects must be advised of their rights before being interrogated and offered pro bono counsel if needed. In New York, the Whitmore case sparked a review of other convictions based solely on confessions and influenced the state legislature to end capital punishment in 1965.

Zion's legal antennae picked up another questionable arrest in the summer of 1966. Again, the accused was a young black male. Again racial tensions in the city were high. On July 28, Ernest Gallashaw, seventeen, was arrested for fatally shooting an eleven-year-old black named Eric Dean, on a night of violent racial clashes between black and white residents of Brooklyn's East New York section. One thousand cops were assigned to the neighborhood that weekend to restore order. According to the police, Gallashaw had aimed a .25 caliber pistol at a white officer and the bullet accidentally struck Dean.

On September 6, after Gallashaw had been indicted by a grand jury for murder one, I asked Richard Reeves to take on the coverage, because Zion was now busy on another assignment. The thirty-year-old Reeves was a born muckraker whom we had recently brought over from the *Herald Tribune*, where he had probed the ills of city pollution in a multipart series. "I hate to see people get kicked around," he told me while working on an investigation of questionable management practices in city hospitals. Raised in New Jersey, he seemed to have inherited his crusading spirit from his father, a rigidly honest Criminal Court judge, as well as from his grandfather, great-grandfather and several uncles, all Protestant ministers.

Reeves learned that the prosecution was building its case on statements by three witnesses who said they saw Gallashaw shoot Dean. But other people in the neighborhood, ignored by the D.A., contended that Gallashaw was at home when Dean was killed.

After several days of digging, Reeves discovered a tape-recorded interview at the FM radio station WBAI with two boys who said they saw a white man shoot Dean. Reeves found Nathaniel Breaker, one of the boys, and talked to him for four hours. The police, who knew about Breaker's story, had never informed the district attorney, maintaining that Breaker's testimony was unreliable. A few days later, Reeves learned the identity of the key witness for the prosecution—thirteen-year-old James Windley, who said he saw Gallashaw fire as Dean fell at the corner of Dumont Avenue and Ashford Street.

Reeves brought Thomas A. Johnson with him to question young Windley. The thirty-eight-year-old Johnson, who had joined our staff in February 1966, was at that time our only black reporter. Rather than increasing the number of blacks on our staff, we had steadily been losing them. Griffin had by then joined Dr. Martin Luther King's staff, Layhmond Robinson had gone to ABC television, and Ted Jones had left to work for Washington's Office of Economic Opportunity. I couldn't blame them, since newspaper salaries were comparatively low and they saw better opportunities beyond *The Times*.

Indeed, we were lucky to have attracted Johnson to the paper. He brought with him his experience covering protests in Washington, Selma, Harlem and Watts. He had studied journalism at Long Island University on the GI Bill, but, for several years after graduation, he had trouble finding work as a reporter. He became a social investigator for the city's Welfare Department and, with the rise of the civil rights movement and the scarcity of black reporters to cover it, had finally been hired by *Newsday* in 1963, where he quickly established a reputation as unflappable on difficult assignments.

Reeves and Johnson drove to East New York in Johnson's Volkswagen and parked outside James Windley's building. Johnson went up alone to speak to the boy, whose mother was also present in the tidy railroad flat.

Windley told Johnson, "I didn't see nobody shoot nobody. I told the cops the same thing I'm telling you."

"When you signed that paper, did you read it?" Johnson asked.

"Yes."

"What did it say?"

"It said I didn't see nobody shoot nobody!" Windley declared.

When Johnson came back down, he was shaking his head. "This kid says he never saw the shooting," he told Reeves.

Reeves and Johnson knew the name of a second witness—ten-year-old Billy Johnson—but had no idea where he lived. After finding his address at a local playground, where Johnson befriended some of the children, they interviewed young Billy in the kitchen of his mother's cheerless apartment below the elevated IRT tracks, while his seven brothers and sisters lingered in the other rooms. Billy said he had witnessed Dean fall, but had not seen who shot him. He said he never saw Gallashaw at the intersection of Dumont and Ashford.

"Were the police mean to you?" Johnson asked.

"Nope. They shouted some. But it was all right."

The third witness, a young woman, could not be found.

The discoveries by Johnson and Reeves were published in *The Times* on September 15, and kindled protests by civil rights groups who accused the police of framing Gallashaw. As a result of our story, Gallashaw's trial was moved ahead of thirty-one previously pending murder cases. Among the jurors selected, two were black.

The trial was a contradictory hodgepodge. Windley and Billy Johnson both testified that they had seen Gallashaw shoot Dean, adding that they had lied to our reporters. But their testimony kept changing on the stand, and each boy's account of the events contradicted the other's. The only testimony that was consistent was that of Nathaniel Breaker, who insisted he saw a white teenager, known as "Little Joe," shoot Dean. The jury, after deliberating for six and a half hours, returned a verdict of not guilty. The police did not pursue "Little Joe."

It was a stirring moment for our staff. Paul O'Dwyer, Gallashaw's defense attorney, said, "We're blessed by freedom of the press. It wasn't until *The New York Times* sent reporters onto the streets and byways of East New York that the truth came out in this case."

It was such stories that led to Reeves and Johnson moving ahead on the staff. Reeves, with his grasp of the intricacies of government, was soon promoted to City Hall bureau chief and became an instrumental investigator of governmental wrongdoing. Johnson some time later was posted to Africa as a correspondent.

Were Abe and I heading in a direction that Adolph S. Ochs and Arthur Hays Sulzberger had always cautioned against? Were we turning *The Times* into a crusading newspaper? Clifton Daniel once halfheartedly warned me to keep my crusading spirit under control, but I pretended not to hear him. It was *The Times*, after all—in 1870, long before Ochs's era—that had exposed and toppled the corrupt Tammany machine of "Boss" William Marcy Tweed.

THIRTY-FOUR

Dick Witkin and I often commuted to and from work together, sometimes by the New Haven Railroad but often in his station wagon. We talked about everything from our children to our wives to what we'd had for dinner the night before, but mostly we talked about *The Times*.

Dick's car was my incubator. At nine A.M. I slid into the passenger seat eager to share with him an evolving story idea or a touchy personnel issue. By the time we arrived at the office forty-five minutes later, my adrenaline was in full flow.

Dick was a treasured member of the *Times* staff, always on top of breaking aviation news and invariably ahead of everyone else in the field of space exploration. Among his journalistic records of sorts was the extraordinary extent of his coverage in the one month of October 1958, when the United States was taking the lead in aeronautical experimentation following the pioneering Russian launch of *Sputnik* a year earlier. On October 5, Dick was aboard the first commercial jet flight from New York to London on British Overseas Airways. While in flight, he interviewed the passengers and crew, and he finished typing his story by the time the plane landed. On October 11, he was in Cape Canaveral to cover the launch of the unmanned rocket aimed at circling the moon. Though it didn't succeed in its objective, it soared to a record altitude of 80,000 miles. Soon after, Dick reported from Los Angeles

Airport on the unveiling of the experimental X-15, the so-called rocket plane that in August 1960 would reach a record 2,196 miles an hour—around three times the speed of sound. Also that month, on October 26, he reported on the first daily transatlantic jet service from New York to London on Pan American World Airways.

Beyond that, Dick was sure to be on hand for the February 20, 1962, launch of Lieutenant Colonel John H. Glenn into orbit from Cape Canaveral, and wrote the lead article. When word leaked out about heat shield problems encountered by the space capsule during reentry, Dick drew on his special sources within NASA to pin down the details, giving *The Times* its usual vanguard coverage.

One morning, a year or so after we had begun our daily commutes, I told Dick that Abe and I had been discussing the possibility of his switching from aviation to political reporting. We needed a fresh eye, I said, to probe behind the scenes in that tricky, insulated world, and we believed Dick could bring to political reporting the same incisiveness he had brought to his coverage of the UN and the aviation beat.

I saw Dick's jaw tense. After a long silence, he said he thought the beat was too much of a departure from what he was doing. He enjoyed writing about space and aviation, and was looking forward to covering NASA's planned landing of a man on the moon. Moreover, he wasn't sure he had it in him to grasp the ins and outs of city and state politics. "It's a world I really know little about," he said.

"Nonsense," I countered. "Like all good reporters, you can learn quickly to cover just about any subject." I reminded him how, in a short time, he had mastered global politics when he covered the UN for the United Press. Dick argued there were certain specialties that couldn't be learned without years of experience, citing two examples: Ada Louise Huxtable's architectural beat and Bill Laurence's science beat. I didn't think politics was in a class with that kind of specialty. But I wanted to keep Dick happy, so I offered a compromise: He could choose to go back to aviation once the NASA story began shaping up. Dick asked for time to think about it.

That night, as we were driving back to Harrison, it began pouring and the car in front of us stopped abruptly. By all rights, we should have crashed into it. But Dick, with the reflexes of the battle-tested pilot he once was, hit his foot brake while also yanking the emergency brake. We stopped just short of the other car's bumper. Smugly, he turned to me and said, "Just like that, it takes some instinct and experience to cover a particular beat well."

Having made his point, Dick then agreed to take over the political beat.

Even without experience, he soon proved he had the instinct. And he had an invaluable source to start him off—his friend Tim Cooney, who was Mayor Robert Wagner's deputy press agent. Like me, Dick had worked at Channel Thirteen during the long newspaper strike, where he'd met Cooney's wife, Joan Ganz Cooney, the producer who later created *Sesame Street*. The Cooneys occasionally had dinner with the Witkins and, when Dick accepted the political post, Tim decided to help him make his reputation by leaking a hot tip.

Dick came to my desk in the early evening of May 28, 1965, to say he'd just learned that Mayor Wagner was leaning away from running for a fourth term on the Democratic ticket in November. Congressman John V. Lindsay had announced two weeks earlier that he planned to run for mayor on the Republican ticket. He also hoped to obtain Liberal Party support, which he believed would advance his chances of becoming the first Republican mayor of overwhelmingly Democratic New York since Fiorello H. La Guardia left office twenty years earlier. Despite his Episcopalian roots in a city dominated by Roman Catholics and Jews, Lindsay's popularity was soaring.

Dick and I agreed we couldn't go to press with such an important development without direct confirmation from Wagner. He finally tracked Wagner down by phone to his bedroom at Gracie Mansion, and told him what he had heard about his decision "on good authority." Then, gambling, Dick said *The Times* planned to run the story, whether or not the mayor verified it. Though not ready to announce his decision, Wagner evidently reasoned that he'd prefer *The Times* to publish his own account rather than one based on conjecture. The fifty-five-year-old Mayor confided he was giving serious weight to personal considerations. "I find I can't spend as much time as a father should with his boys," he said, a concern of growing importance to him since his wife's death the previous year. "I feel that I must be both a father and a mother."

Dick's sources close to Wagner's team, however, attributed the mayor's reluctance about running to fear of losing to Lindsay. As for Lindsay, he now was saying he felt compelled to run as a matter of conscience.

"I, for one, cannot stand by while the decline and fall of New York continues headlong," he declared, casting himself as the reform candidate. "Cities are for people and for living, and yet under its present tired management, New York City has become a place that is no longer for people or for living. We have seen its strength diminish, its preeminent place in the world of cities lost and its people beset with hopelessness and despair. . . .

"Our streets are dirty and unsafe. The air we breathe increasingly and dangerously is polluted. Crime, brutality and narcotics are rampant. Housing daily becomes less available while our rent increases. Hospitals are neglected. Our schools are run-down and shortchanged, while the children, their teachers and their parents are crowded and harassed. Our parks and playgrounds are eroded, dirty, dangerous and uninhabitable in the darkness, and increasingly dangerous in the light. There is no planning, and the vicious cycle of slum living continues. . . . New York is indeed a city in crisis."

All very true and well said (for neither the first nor the last time). But it was equally true that with Nelson Rockefeller entrenched in the governor's mansion and Senators Jacob Javits and Robert Kennedy with years left to their terms, Lindsay saw the mayoralty as the only way to advance his own political career.

Soon after Lindsay had made up his mind to run, he phoned to remind me we hadn't lunched together since I'd left the culture department. Now that I was involved in the coverage of city affairs, he wanted to fill me in on his political plans. As he had not yet met Abe Rosenthal, did I think he might want to join us? The three of us lunched at Sardi's. It was difficult not to be dazzled by his star quality. The coat-check woman and the waiters fussed over him and Vincent Sardi led us to the best table, as Broadway celebrities smiled up at Lindsay. He impressed Abe and me with his vision of reorganizing the mayor's office, explaining he planned to add new cabinet posts and eliminate others, and generally reinvigorate municipal departments. We were convinced that Lindsay, youthful and energetic at forty-three, posed a serious challenge to the weary Wagner. In Harrison that evening, I told Barbara I believed Lindsay really had it in him to revitalize New York. She said she was tiring of suburban life, and this might be the time to think seriously about getting back to the city where we belonged.

A maverick in his own party, Lindsay was profiting from his condemnation of Senator Barry Goldwater the year before, reinforcing his liberal Republican image. Were Lindsay to form a fusion ticket, inviting running mates from the Democratic and Liberal parties and including various racial minorities that composed swing voting blocks, he was certain to make a formidable candidate. With his charisma, enthusiasm and idealism, he was beginning to remind voters of John F. Kennedy.

Dick beat all other reporters with his Wagner story, which ran under a four-column headline leading page one. Two weeks later, Dick covered Wagner's public announcement that he would not run again. Wiping away tears, he said he had promised his dying wife that his current term would be his last. "The fact is," he said, "that the mayor's office demands the total and constant priority on one's time and mental concentration. . . . I want to give a priority to other needs—the needs of one son on the very threshold of manhood and the needs of another soon approaching that state."

Now it had become a three-way race. City Controller Abraham Beame defeated City Council President Paul Screvane in the Democratic mayoral primary. And William F. Buckley, Jr., editor of *The National Review*, was set to run as the Conservative Party candidate. A Goldwater Republican, he believed Lindsay was as liberal as any Democrat.

Lindsay broke the tradition of waiting until after the Democratic primary to begin campaigning. He spent the summer crisscrossing the neighborhoods of all five boroughs, warming up voters, preaching reform for a city in crisis. Although he looked like (and was) an aristocratic Yalie from Manhattan's Silk Stocking District, he walked the ghetto streets, projecting an image as a man of the people, in a rumpled white shirt. He showed up at the beaches, sometimes in a bathing suit, presenting himself as a man who knew how to have fun. He took swings through the Catskills and the Poconos in appeals to the city's vacationing Jewish voters.

After a while, however, Lindsay's supporters became concerned that their candidate might be suffering from overexposure. New Yorkers appeared to be tiring of his repeated message. Although Beame struck many voters as a walking math textbook, he was, after all, a solid, dependable Democrat. Thus, in the early polls, Beame held a narrow lead over Lindsay, who tried hard to paint Beame as simply another part of the city's creaky Democratic machine.

The campaign went into disarray, on September 17, 1965, when another newspaper strike was called, this one by the Newspaper Guild against *The Times*. Other member papers of the Publishers Association closed their presses in solidarity, making the *Post*—which had left the association during the 114-day strike of 1962–1963—the only daily on the newsstands. The major disputes were over automation, pensions and mandatory union membership of employees. "While it might have been possible to get out a paper if the other unions had also not stopped work, their support of the Guild has prevented this," Punch declared. The presses were silent for twenty-four days.

As a result, the mayoral campaign moved from the newsstand to the television set, and two debates were held among the three candidates. To the surprise of many, Buckley made the most vivid impression, verbally outdancing the somewhat faltering Lindsay. Though no one gave Buckley a chance of winning, Lindsay's camp feared he might steal enough votes from Republicans to give Beame the edge. This perception galvanized Lindsay's forces, who began directing attacks against Buckley. They made much of the reactionary agenda couched within Buckley's waggish jabs and elevated vocabulary, and cast Lindsay as the only true reformer.

Having received an honorable discharge from the Newspaper Guild after two decades of membership, I found myself among the few "exempted" editors in the barren city room. Day after day, Abe and I sat staring out at a sea of empty desks. Even Homer Bigart's glares would have been welcome. We felt miserable and frustrated over missing story after story in the mayoral campaign. In vain, we wished Dick Witkin would abandon the picket line and resume his coverage of the Lindsay, Beame and Buckley camps.

Causing us even greater concern was the imminent approach of an unprecedented local event, so far-reaching that we figured the story would require the services of most of our staff. Set for October 4, the event was Pope Paul VI's arrival in New York to address the United Nations, the first time a pontiff would be setting foot in the New World.

A few days before the planned visit, once Abe and I had analyzed every aspect of the coverage, I drew up the assignment list. We naively believed that the Newspaper Guild, particularly its many Catholic members, would find a way of settling the strike in time to cover one of the most challenging stories in the city's history.

John Cogley, our new religious-news editor, was in place in Rome, ready to make the round-trip flight with the Pope. Cogley was the expert writer and profound scholar for whom Abe and I had been searching to elevate our religion coverage. Formerly the executive editor at *Commonweal*, Cogley wrote with extraordinary clarity about complex religious theory and praxis. He was able to explain theological intricacies in language even an avowed atheist could grasp. What Bill Laurence was to science news, Cogley was to religious news.

But on October 2, only two days before the pope's scheduled arrival, the publishers and the Guild seemed more dug in than ever, and Abe and I began losing hope that a miracle would end the strike in time. We cabled Cogley to join the papal entourage from Rome, strike or no strike. And then Abe received a phone call that turned out to be a miracle of sorts.

Bantam Books proposed that we create a city room at their midtown offices and that we enlist our striking staff to cover the pope's visit—not for *The Times*, but as contract writers for a record-breaking "instant book" that would come off the presses on October 7, only three days after the pope's visit. The stories would be written and edited exactly the way we would have done it all for *The Times*.

I felt schizophrenically glad and sad. After getting clearance from the guild and *The Times*, I phoned fifty-one reporters, photographers and editors who had already been listed on my assignment sheet and asked if they would work the day for Bantam. All eagerly agreed, Homer Bigart the most enthusiastic among them.

At dawn on October 4, the nineteenth day of the strike, Abe and I took over part of the second floor of Bantam's offices on Madison Avenue at Fortieth Street, setting up an impromptu city room with rented tables and chairs. Bantam's stock room was converted into a makeshift bullpen, and we ousted Bantam's vice president in charge of production from his carpeted office.

As "Operation Instant Book" commenced, reporters we hadn't seen in three weeks ambled in for their assignments. Mounds of copy paper were heaped among typewriters, telephones and ashtrays. A coffee bar was set up with containers perpetually replenished. Rented television sets glowed in the background. Some reporters, including Bigart, who was to write the lead story, served as rewrite men. Never leaving the office, they drew their facts principally from legmen phoning in from the scene and from the television monitors.

The street reporters—among them Peter Kihss, Murray Schumach, Martin Arnold, Sydney Schanberg, Dick Witkin and Paul Montgomery— braved the chilly, windy day to move among the four million spectators along the twenty-four-mile route of the papal motorcade from Kennedy Airport to St. Patrick's Cathedral. Only minutes after pulling out of the airport, with a stiff breeze snapping the folds of his cape and threatening to dislodge his hat, the pope changed cars—from an open convertible to a clear plastic bubble-topped Ford limousine, originally designed for President Kennedy.

The seventeen-car entourage drove between the surging walls of cheering onlookers along Queens Boulevard, crossed the Queensboro Bridge and turned up Third Avenue to 125th Street. The pope then went down Fifth Avenue to St. Patrick's, where he rested at Francis Cardinal Spellman's residence. The city was in a holiday mood. Many children from the tristate area, who had been given the day off from school, waved flags and banners. It seemed that everyone, not just Catholics, sought a glimpse of the pope.

The crowd was uncommonly well behaved. Marty Arnold noticed a businessman who put his briefcase down, while another man immediately stepped on it for a better view. "Get off it, you—" the owner started to say. But he caught himself before finishing the phrase, settling for, "Anyway, get off it." A policeman nearby smiled and said, "You see, it's almost as if they were all in church."

Fifteen thousand policemen were on duty—the greatest turnout, wrote Peter Kihss, in the history of the force. Since sixty percent of the Police Department was Catholic, specific orders had been issued forbidding patrolmen from removing their hats, taking part in any religious exercise (including kneeling) and turning from the crowd to see the pope. But officers outside St. Patrick's cleared the way for two small nuns, whom they led by the hand past the wooden barricades for an unobstructed view of His Holiness. The nuns jumped up and down, clapping and giggling like schoolgirls when he drove by.

After visiting with President Johnson at the Waldorf-Astoria, the pope went to the UN, where he appealed for world peace. "War never again!" he declared in French before the General Assembly, with all members present—minus the delegation from Communist Albania. "Let the arms fall from your hands, for one cannot love while holding offensive arms." The pope met individually with dignitaries. Jackie Kennedy knelt, kissed his ring and spoke with him in French. Later, he celebrated mass before an audience of ninety thousand at Yankee Stadium. As the time neared for his entrance, hawkers stopped in silence, cigarettes were extinguished, snack bars closed.

Back at the Bantam office, agitated reporters stood in line waiting for typewriters. No one could quite adjust to the five A.M. deadline set by Bantam. Some rushed unnecessarily, others kept rewriting their stories. Reminiscent of late-night city-room operations during the height of World War II and election nights, trays of sandwiches were ordered in from a nearby deli and consumed at an astonishing rate.

Abe and I backfielded the stories ourselves, then sent them to the copy editors in the stock room. They turned them over to Bantam's production staff, which prepared them for the printers. Homer Bigart handed his lead article to Abe at 4:15 A.M. Abe assessed it self-consciously, under Bigart's watchful eye, then passed it to Shelly Binn at the copy desk. It was the final piece to be turned in. Abe poured Bigart and me the last of the whiskey that had helped sustain the staff through the night, and clicked his own paper cup against ours.

"Well, what did you think of the pope?" Abe asked Bigart.

"I didn't see him," was Bigart's laconic answer.

Bantam editors, art and production staff flew the final manuscript and photographs to Chicago at 7:30 A.M. *The Pope's Journey to the United States* came off the presses two days later. From start to finish, the 160-page book had taken sixty-six and a half hours to produce, a feat listed in the *Guinness Book of World Records* under the heading "Fastest Publishing." By the end of the week, half a million copies were in bookstores worldwide and our man Cogley personally presented a copy to the pontiff at the Vatican.

"We all would have been so much happier if we had been working in our own 229 West Forty-third Street," Abe wrote in the introduction. "But we all have a feeling of satisfaction that on that moment in history we were able to do what we live to do—cover a story."

Abe and I owed much of the project's success to Cogley, whose early guidance and advice on the papal visit validated our uncompromising search for a highly qualified religious editor. A recipient of the St. Francis de Sales Prize of the Catholic Press Association for his coverage of the third session of the Vatican Council in 1964, Cogley regarded himself as a liberal Roman Catholic.

In the mid-1950s, he wrote the *Report on Blacklisting* for the Fund for the Republic, concluding that the practice had become "institutionalized" in film, television and radio. He condemned businesses for taking it upon themselves to judge private citizens. In 1960, he served as a special aide to John F. Kennedy during his presidential campaign and orchestrated the critical meeting between Kennedy and Protestant clergymen in Houston—which helped deflate the controversy over Kennedy's Catholicism. The meeting was later viewed as an essential maneuver in Kennedy's election victory.

Abe and I took great pride in Cogley's stewardship, beginning with his analytical articles on current theological debate and burgeoning religious movements. Was celibacy essential to the nature of the priesthood? Should the Church endorse the use of contraception? Is sexual intercourse outside of marriage a sin? Is evangelism a truly "Christian" practice?

THE NEWSPAPER STRIKE ended at 3:20 P.M. on October 10, 1965, six days after the Pope's visit. Reporters, eager to get back to work, streamed into the city room. I passed out assignments, and, in less than half an hour, it seemed as if the city room had never been deserted.

In the settlement, *The Times* refused to cave in on its right to introduce new technology, but guaranteed that no workers would lose their jobs as a result of automation. Among other stipulations, a new pension program was established, with *The Times* agreeing to pay overtime on out-of-town assignments and compensate for travel time on the job.

The Publishers Association emerged weaker than when the strike began. On day nine of the strike, the *Herald Tribune*, a chief proponent of the managerial alliance, had dropped out and resumed publication in a battle for its very survival. Most of the other papers were also wounded by petty squabbling over the smallest of issues. In one instance, they argued over whether to amend the wording of their requirement for hiring "competent" workers to read "competent and qualified." The issue was finally laid to rest when reference to a dictionary made it clear that there was no substantial difference between the terms. Unfortunately, the troublesome conclusion reached by publishers and unions alike was that striking was an effective way for unions to get what they wanted.

With the end of the strike, Abe and I refocused on coverage of the mayoral race, which was barreling ahead with less than four weeks to go before the election. But one morning, our attention was distracted by a story as perplexing as the Genovese apathy case. Again a tale of a single life, evoking a scalding psychological phenomenon, it stunned our readers. It began with a letter Abe received from a friend in the American Jewish Congress, calling our attention to a *Times* article two days earlier about the testimony of Robert M. Shelton, Imperial Wizard of the United Klans of America, before the House Un-American Activities Committee. The article noted at the end that one Daniel Burros, a resident of Queens, had been identified during the Shelton hearing as a "K.K.K. leader and Nazi."

According to the letter, Burros was the son of Jewish parents. Abe handed me the letter. We looked at each other and simultaneously said, "Phillips!" This evidently perverse character seemed to beg for McCandlish Phillips to investigate his strange world. We told Phillips what little we knew. "Let's take a look at it," Abe said. "Get hold of this guy and see if you can find out what makes a Jewish kid from Queens grow up to be a Nazi."

Phillips got on the phone and managed to gather a few pertinent facts about Burros's life. He told us that if he continued to get lucky, he might be able to pull together some kind of story for that very night. We assigned two reporters to do leg work for him in Queens, checking with schools, ringing doorbells of neighbors and talking to nearby shopkeepers. By late afternoon, a picture of the oxymoronic Jewish Nazi began to come into focus. But we needed to interview him before we could go to press, and as yet there was no sign of his whereabouts.

What Phillips had learned was that Burros was born March 5, 1937, at Lebanon Hospital in the Bronx, the son of George and Esther Burros. George, the son of Russian immigrants, was a World War I veteran, in his mid-forties when Daniel was born. He had suffered a severe throat wound on a French battlefield, which damaged his vocal cords and permanently impaired his speech, and thus exacerbated an innate introversion. Ill health prevented his holding a steady job, so he relied on his government pension. Esther, who had come to New York from Russia when she was four, was a saleswoman in her mid-thirties when she gave birth to her only child.

Daniel grew up in a dreary second-floor tenement in the Richmond Hill section of Queens, a neighborhood with a smattering of Jews. His parents gave him the sole bedroom and slept in the living room. Daniel was enrolled in public schools, and attended a Hebrew school a few afternoons a week. Though his father was a nonpracticing Jew, his mother wanted her son to receive a Jewish education.

Daniel was an odd boy with few friends. He displayed an early devotion to his academic and his religious studies, yet he loved to fight and would provoke boys both bigger and smaller than he, not caring whether he won or lost. He was always striving for admiration and respect, not for his intellectual gifts (his IQ was 154) but for a strength and toughness he wished to embody. He dreamed of attending West Point and joining the Army.

Around the time he entered high school, he abruptly rejected Judaism, and purposely failed his Hebrew course. A talented artist, he began sketching Nazi insignias and German soldiers in his notebooks. A draconian hall monitor, he "took care" of unruly students himself rather than reporting them to school administrators. By his junior year, he was obsessed with his version of "the truth" about World War II and had a sizable collection of Nazi memorabilia.

Burros graduated from high school in 1955 with a grade average of 92 and several stars for excellence in scholarship. He joined the Army that summer. The keenest spit-and-polish soldier in his outfit, he kept his uniform immaculately pressed and his boots glistened. His mind was filled with military lore, and he knew by heart stories of generals who had risen through the ranks by virtue of their strong determination. Everything he yearned for—authority, respect, command—was within reach. But all too quickly his fantasy of being recognized as a born leader was shattered by the mockery of his barracks sidekicks, who saw him as a misfit.

His salutes were a little too snappy, and he was ridiculed for striving to be the officers' pet. He didn't distinguish himself on the obstacle course, the shooting range, in hand-to-hand combat or in the classroom. His peers could strut and talk in a voice of command and no one would laugh, but when Burros affected a swagger or spoke with a bark, he broke people up. In a frantic attempt to gain respect, he began showing off the Nazi medals and German army photos he kept in his trunk. His sergeant warned him if he ever displayed the souvenirs again, he would face a loyalty check.

Burros was sent to Little Rock, Arkansas, of all places, to help maintain the peace as the schools were being desegregated. The experience pushed him yet further to the ultra-right. "I could see that America was becoming a left-wing police state," he later said, admitting that he was ashamed of having played a cooperative role. As humiliations multiplied, Burros wanted out. He staged suicide attempts, once swallowing twenty aspirin. A psychologist concluded that he was "essentially an immature, emotionally unstable person . . . engaged in much childlike fantasy." He was discharged in early 1958 "under honorable conditions by reason of unsuitability, character and behavior disorder."

Back in his parents' apartment, Burros found a job at the Queens Borough Public Library, where he worked until January 1960. He brought a tuna-fish sandwich for lunch every day. "If I ever brought anything else I would have to make up my mind every day what to bring," he explained to the library staff. During this time, his Nazi collection grew, and he began corresponding with anti-Semites around the world. He subscribed to British and German racist periodicals and joined a fascist organization. His rhetoric, which had so far focused on Holocaust revisionism, was becoming more virulent.

In 1960, Burros began making weekend trips to Washington to march with the American Nazi Party, a small but vocal group whose headquarters was a frame house in Arlington, Virginia. He earned the equivalent of Nazi battle stars—a police record consisting of four arrests, a few small fines, and a $100 fine paired with a six-month suspended sentence for defacing the Anti-Defamation League building with swastika stickers.

In June of that year, he moved to Washington and applied for formal membership in the American Nazi Party. Among his reasons for joining: "I wish to preserve the white race and combat the forces of Jewish Bolshevism which seek to destroy our race and nation."

The activities of the American Nazi Party, founded and led by George Lincoln Rockwell, were amateurish efforts to gain publicity by a tiny fringe group with a scary name. Major victories included picketing a local pizza restaurant owned by a Jew, getting into a minor street fight and pasting swastikas on a wall. But the hopes they held for a Jewless future in their self-created fantasy of power and the life they led in their pseudo-military "barracks" were exactly what Burros craved. Finally, he could participate in organized action and talk openly about his ideas, which included innovative ways to torture Jews.

One of his twisted designs was a piano with wires connected to the nerves of Jews, causing victims to twitch and jump as the piano was being played. He drew diagrams of gas chambers and carried a bar of soap whose wrapper read in German, "Made from the finest Jewish fat."

After a year or so, Burros began to sense the impotence of the party and doubted Rockwell's ability to lead. Though his notoriety had grown among fringe factions, he told his comrades he felt mired in futility. Then, in 1965, he saw a rerun of the silent film *The Birth of a Nation*, based on the book *The Klansman*. He mentioned his discovery to Roy Frankhouser, an old acquaintance, who was a leader of the Klan. Frankhouser admired Burros's brand of racism, and brought him to a Klan meeting in Bear, Delaware. Burros was overwhelmed. Until this time, his idea of a meeting had been a handful of men gathered in a small apartment or picketing on a street corner. Now he was amid some 13,000 like-minded people who despised blacks and Jews.

Frankhouser brought Burros before Imperial Wizard Robert Shelton and vouched for his character. "I'll swear by Dan Burros as I would my own life. This man is a hundred percent."

Burros soon became Grand Dragon of New York and King Kleagle (chief organizer) of the state. He gloated over the scarlet robe that signified his rank. He gave speeches about the unity between the North and the South in the fight against "mongrelization" and helped smooth tensions between Manhattan's uptown and downtown Klaverns, which were traditionally at odds because of socioeconomic class differences. Burros had finally attained the prestige and respect for which he had yearned his entire life.

Just as he began to savor it, everything crumbled.

Various government agencies, including the New York City Police Department, that tracked right-wing extremists had files on the twenty-eight-year-old Burros. In the fall of 1965, a government agent doing a cursory investigation of radical right-wing elements stumbled across the marriage certificate of George and Esther, and noticed that the ceremony had been performed by a rabbi. When confronted with this fact, Esther begged the investigator, "Please tell my son I didn't tell you this!" It seems clear that Esther knew something of her son's secret life, though not its full extent. She and her husband evidently lived in a state of denial.

The agent told Daniel Burros what he had discovered, but Burros was able to maintain his charade because the information was not released. When Robert Shelton was called before the House Un-American Activities Committee, however, the agent tipped off Abe Rosenthal's friend at the American Jewish Congress.

After gathering as much information as he could by telephone, Phillips told me he was going to Queens himself—in the late afternoon of Monday, October 25, 1965—to see if he could find and speak with Burros. He was accompanied by Carl Gossett, a tall, husky photographer. They first checked out one address over a pizzeria on Lefferts Boulevard. The manager said no one named Burros lived upstairs, but two neighborhood kids knew of the family, and showed Phillips their building. Beneath a burned-out globe light, the vestibule door was open. They rang the buzzer marked "Burros," but received no answer.

Phillips waited outside. A traffic cop said he had seen George Burros leave a little while earlier, and predicted he'd be home soon. The evening was turning cold and drizzly and, since it was too late to make the first edition, Gossett gave his raincoat to Phillips and went home. Phillips stayed and interviewed neighbors, most of whom said they knew Dan Burros as a quiet young man. "He's a very good boy, never destructive or anything," said one. They clearly had no idea they were living a few doors away from New York's Grand Dragon. But Phillips obtained a good description of Burros— blond, short, stocky, with glasses.

Around seven-thirty, an elderly man got off a bus and headed for the entrance of the building. Taking a chance, Phillips approached him: "Mr. Burros?" he asked. "I'm with *The New York Times*. We have a story about Dan and I need to talk to him." "I got nothing to say," said George Burros, hurrying inside.

Phillips began feeling uneasy about confronting Burros alone at night. He called the office, and Shelly Binn told him to come in. After slipping a note under the Burros's apartment door, he took the subway back to *The Times*. From the city room, he called Abe at home, who told him to hold off writing the story until he was able to talk to Burros.

The next day, Phillips was still unable to make contact with Burros, who, we later learned, had fled to Frankhouser's house in Reading, Pennsylvania, to evade a summons by the House committee. Phillips continued to interview Burros's neighborhood acquaintances and consolidated his information. By Thursday, the only major piece still missing from the story was the personal interview.

Phillips wrote a five-page memo, suggesting he pay an early-morning visit to the Burros apartment. Since Abe was out of town at a conference, I gave Phillips the go-ahead. The next morning (Friday), Phillips, now armed with a photo of Burros, emerged from the elevated station and turned onto Lefferts Boulevard. At that very instant, he caught a glimpse of Burros as he entered a barbershop. Phillips waited outside. It was 8:02 A.M. When Burros emerged, Phillips introduced himself and asked if he had received any of his messages. Burros said he had, relieved that Phillips wasn't a federal marshal.

Phillips suggested they go somewhere to talk, and Burros agreed, obviously having no idea where the conversation would ultimately lead. Burros, Phillips later wrote, was "a round, short, sallow young man who looked a little like a small heap of misery. . . . It seemed to me that he was profoundly embarrassed about himself."

With his practiced technique, Phillips opened him up. Flattered by the attention of a newspaperman, Burros readily produced his Klan identification for Phillips's inspection. Phillips decided the time had come to close in on his story. "There's one thing about you that just does not fit into the picture, and I can't figure it out," he said. "Your parents were married by the Reverend Bernard Kallenberg in a Jewish ceremony in the Bronx."

"Are you going to print that?" snapped Burros. Phillips said he did not have the authority to withhold it. Burros said he was going to have to kill Phillips unless he promised not to publish the story. He threatened to use the vial of acid he claimed he had in his pocket. Phillips didn't believe him, but rather than risk a physical confrontation, he offered a compromise: he would not run the article until he had spoken with Burros again. He gave him his home phone number and told him to call that night. "If you publish that, I'll come and get you and I'll kill you," reiterated Burros. "I don't care what happens to me. I'll be ruined. This is all I've got to live for."

Unable to resist the spirit of Christian charity, Phillips told Burros, "I want to talk to you as one human being to another—not as reporter to subject." Then Phillips quoted the Bible: "It is appointed unto men once to die, but after this the judgment."

Burros said, "I'll take my chances on that when it comes," adding he felt trapped by what Phillips had on him. "No, you're trapped by who you are, by everything you've got mixed into." Phillips again quoted the Bible: "If any man be in Christ, he is a new creature. Old things are passed away; behold all things are become new."

"You're trying to con me," was Burros's response. Phillips insisted he wasn't. "What you have to do, to break the grip fascism has on you, is to call upon the name of Jesus Christ. If you do that, He will take care of the rest." They shook hands and went their separate ways.

Burros called the office four times that day trying to persuade Phillips to kill his story. At last, he said, "I know I can't stop that story, but I'm going to go out in a blaze of glory." He gave no specifics, but said his final bow would be taken at the *Times* building, and that he expected to "catch some lead."

I came down from a publisher's luncheon and found a six-page memo from Phillips on my desk. "I met our man Burros this morning. He told me repeatedly he will kill me," it began. Greatly concerned, I called a deputy police commissioner at headquarters, who offered a bodyguard to take Phillips to and from the office. Clifton Daniel notified *The Times*'s security force as well. Pictures of Burros were given to every guard.

Phillips, who did not think he was in danger as long as the story was unpublished, urged me to run it that night, essentially to end the suspense. I thought we should hold it for at least another day. I asked Phillips what proof we had that Burros was actually Jewish. "Was he bar mitzvahed?" When Phillips said he didn't know, I told him we should try to nail it down, and I assigned Pat Spiegel and Ralph Blumenthal to canvas the Richmond Hill synagogues the next morning during Saturday services.

When Phillips, with his detective escort, was about to depart the city room at midnight Friday after writing a draft of a five-column story, a colleague cautioned him, "Don't go home without leaving your advance obit and a glossy photo. We may need it."

The next morning, Spiegel and Blumenthal started for the synagogues. During the twenty-five years Pat had been covering Jewish affairs, he had never failed to respond resourcefully to a call for help on a story that would carry another reporter's byline. He and other old-timers on the staff believed this was the true test of a thoroughbred reporter—being able to submerge his own ego and be part of an anonymous team.

Pat and Ralph, of course, knew that you don't just walk into a synagogue on a Saturday and start cross-examining the rabbi and members of the congregation. They entered the first synagogue at the start of the morning service, put on prayer shawls and blended with the worshippers. In Yiddish, Pat murmured to a man beside him: "Do you know a young man named Daniel Burros?"

The man turned out to be the president of the shul. He did, as it happened, know Daniel. He said his grandfather had been a founding member of the congregation, but he would say nothing more. After the service, Pat coaxed, charmed and persuaded the rabbi until both the rabbi and the president directed him to another synagogue where, they said, Daniel's bar mitz-vah had taken place.

At that synagogue, Pat, still accompanied by Ralph, was heartily wel-comed because, as it happened, they completed the minyan quorum. But the rabbi proved recalcitrant and Pat, in Yiddish, sternly lectured him. "The Germans had a Hitler, and the Jews have a Hitler, too," he said. At last, he learned that Burros had had his bar mitzvah on March 4, 1950. He was given the details: Burros's Torah portion was Genesis 30, verses 8–10, and his haf-torah was from Ezekiel, and dealt with the destruction of the First Temple.

Moreover, the elders of the synagogue remembered Burros as the kind of boy they could "just lick our fingers about." He loved studying Torah, learned Hebrew quickly and attended morning prayers nearly every day, even after completing his bar mitzvah. For Yom Kippur, the young Burros was given a free admission ticket and came dressed all in white, the tradi-tional color of purification. He regularly participated in a Saturday after-noon Talmud course, and seemed the most interested of all the children.

It was getting close to the early Saturday afternoon deadline for Sunday's paper when Pat phoned in the details. Phillips, who took the call, was im-mensely gratified—and so was I. I gave the order to run the story and tried to convince Phillips to leave town for a while, but he wanted to stay close to his church group.

Meanwhile, Burros had retreated to Frankhouser's headquarters in Reading, a two-story saltbox whose entry was through a barbershop. Burros (according to what Frankhouser told me when I later began working on a book about the case) was near hysteria, ranting about blowing up the House Un-American Activities Committee and *The Times*. He told Frankhouser that a reporter had uncovered a secret about him which was sure to defame the KKK. When Frankhouser asked him what the secret was, Burros said he was an anti-Christian Odinist, part of a Nordic cult. He added that he was going to assassinate the president and offered to kill anyone Frank-houser named. "Just give me their address and I'll go stick up a cab driver and make him take me there and get the job done."

Frankhouser made Burros hand over his pistol and locked it in a cabinet.

When the story failed to appear in Saturday's *Times*, Burros relaxed un-til evening, when he once again turned gloomy, anticipating the next day's paper. Sunday morning, October 31, he rose early to read *The Times* that had been delivered to the house. He scanned page one, muttered, "Oh, my God," then ran up the stairs and demanded his gun back from Frankhouser. "I've got to kill myself," he shouted. "Where in the hell have you taken all the guns?"

Frankhouser wouldn't tell him, but Burros spotted the locked gun cabinet. He attacked it with his hands and feet, trying to break it open with karate chops. He twisted the lock so badly that the door wouldn't open. Then, spying a revolver atop a bureau, he lunged past Frankhouser, grabbed it, and held it to his chest.

"Long live the white race, God bless you, so long," Burros said, backing through a doorway into the living room. "Long live the white race. I've got nothing left to live for." He shot himself once in the chest and again in the right temple.

On Sunday, a metropolitan-desk clerk phoned me at home shortly before one P.M., and I immediately dialed Phillips at his apartment, wanting to break the news before he heard it on the radio. A friend answered the phone and said Phillips was in the shower. I told him it was urgent that I talk to him right away and I'd wait until he could come to the phone. He was there in less than a minute. I tried to tell him what had happened as gently as possible, concerned he might feel some responsibility for Burros's suicide. Phillips seemed more interested in soothing me. "What I think we've seen here, Arthur," he said, "is the God of Israel acting in judgment."

Our story was picked up by newspapers and magazines throughout the world, but the weird episode was not over for Abe and me. Various publishers tried to persuade Phillips to write a book about the case, either by himself or in collaboration with Abe and me, but he refused. Fascinated by the puzzle of Jewish anti-Semitism as personified so frighteningly by Burros, Abe and I decided to write the book ourselves, and it was published in 1967 under the title *One More Victim: The Life and Death of an American Jewish Nazi*.

Delving as deeply as we could, we spent a year reconstructing Burros's life and searching for the clues to his self-hatred—and extrapolating from there the reasons why certain Jews become brainwashed into believing the vile things said about them, condemning themselves to self-loathing. Psychiatrists we interviewed told us it appeared that Burros associated being Jewish with weakness, which he despised in himself. The German soldier represented for him the unattainable power, the ideal nonvictim. It seemed that a significant factor in Burros's denial of his roots had occurred less than a year after his bar mitzvah, when the rabbi to whom he was close—a positive father figure in many ways—left for a larger congregation on Long Island. Burros considered this a betrayal, and it wasn't long before he was doodling swastikas in his notebooks at school.

As part of our research, I drove to Reading to interview Frankhouser. I left Barbara in our hotel room, and she said if she didn't hear from me in an hour she would call the police. As I entered Klan headquarters and spotted the case with the guns, I felt distinctly nervous. Frankhouser, who immediately marked me as a Jew, said, "It's okay. Some of my best friends are Jews. I don't have a problem with them like I do with the niggers."

In one of the more bizarre experiences of my newspaper career, Frankhouser suddenly interrupted our interview and said, "You look like a man of good taste—you have a nice suit, you're from the city." He asked me to wait a minute while he left the room. When he returned, he was decked out in a ruby red Klansman's robe. He strutted around the room, ludicrously aping a runway model. "What do you think?" he asked. "It's brand-new." He seemed honestly to want my opinion, and I told him I thought the robe was very becoming.

THIRTY-FIVE

ON NOVEMBER 1, 1965, the day after Daniel Burros killed himself, Abe and I, with no chance to catch our breath, plunged into preparations for the next day's mayoral election.

On our drive in from Harrison on Election Day, Dick Witkin said he was certain it would be a tight race. He had been covering the tumultuous campaign since its beginning and was to write the lead story that would undoubtedly run under a banner headline across the top of page one. Many Democrats were expected to swing to the Republican or Liberal lines in support of Lindsay's promised reforms. As it turned out, it was, indeed, a very tight race—the closest in a quarter century. Beame did not concede the election until two A.M., when it finally appeared Lindsay had won.

The first Republican to hold the office since Fiorello La Guardia, Lindsay compiled a plurality of 100,000 votes. He was also the first Republican for whom I had personally rooted, even though, as a nonresident of the city, I couldn't vote for him. Concerned as I was about New York's steady decline into decay, I wanted to believe in Lindsay's sincerity and in his fresh ideas that could possibly ease the cumulative economic, racial and social problems. I also thought he had the grit and imagination to do something about calming the unyielding wrath in the minority neighborhoods. "If we join together in the rigorous, exacting struggles ahead," he said in his victory statement, "we assure the eventual conquest of the pending, recurrent and unforeseen crises affecting our city."

Thrust into the national spotlight even before taking office, Lindsay was already being mentioned as a presidential or vice-presidential candidate. Moderate Republicans took heart, seeing his victory as another boost for their alliance against the right wing of their party, still reeling from Goldwater's defeat the previous year. And Lindsay's victory threw both city and state Democrats into a panic, with Senator Robert Kennedy, who had campaigned hard for Beame, failing to solidify his power in New York. As for the third candidate, Buckley, he went back to his writing, never really having taken the race seriously. (During the campaign, he had quipped that if he did win he would demand a recount.)

JUST A WEEK after the election, on November 9, the city room was gearing for its nine-o'clock deadline when, suddenly, at 5:27 P.M., the lights began to flicker. In less than a minute, they went out, plunging the room into blackness. All machinery went dead. As reporters stopped typing, the silence was eerie. It was like a scene out of the sci-fi movie *The Day the Earth Stood Still.*

Along with other staffers I groped my way to a window and looked out on the black void of the streets. A few reporters started making phone calls and discovered not only Manhattan but also much of the Northeast was without electrical power.

Abe phoned from the eleventh-floor cafeteria, to say he was making his way down the stairs to the third floor, and I and other editors pooled our cash and sent clerks and copyboys out to buy flashlights and candles. Then, grabbing a box of wooden matches from my desk, I lighted my way, stumbling about the city room, searching for my staff. "Peter! Peter!" I called, heading toward Kihss's desk. He held out his hand and we made contact. I assigned him to the overall lead, and then felt my way along the desks, assembling a list of other assignments in my head.

Striking matches, I hunted for the reporters on my mental list and, within twenty minutes, I dispatched fifteen of them—to Con Edison to determine the cause of the blackout, to Police Headquarters, to hospitals, and to check whether people were trapped in elevators and subways.

At one point, having run out of matches, I ran headlong into the glass partition that enclosed the real estate department and was knocked down.

Someone helped me to my feet just as clerks and copy boys began returning with boxes of candles and flashlights purchased at various hardware stores. Others carried votive candles generously supplied by churches, and tall tapers donated by restaurants and hotels. The candles were distributed around the city room and soon the faces of reporters and editors began to glow in pools of yellow-orange light. It flashed through my mind that this was how the city room must have looked when *The Times*'s first editor, Henry J. Raymond, put out the inaugural issue on September 18, 1851, by candlelight.

Abe and I coordinated our coverage and, at six o'clock, Ted Bernstein held an editors' conference. If the power returned by midnight, we would be able to run the presses in time to put out the paper. If it didn't, we would have to print elsewhere. Calls were made to New Jersey, which happened to be unaffected by the blackout, and arrangements were concluded to utilize the plant at the *Newark Evening News* if necessary.

Gradually, we learned that this was the largest power outage in history, affecting not only the city but also nine states and two Canadian provinces. The cause was a failure along the Northeast power grid, which connected local networks to the hydroelectric generator at Niagara Falls. Within minutes, communities along the grid had fallen dark, one after another, like a set of dominoes. Thirty million people, spread over 80,000 square miles, were without electricity.

Our reporters began calling in their facts: 800,000 riders were on New York subways when the power went out, and some trains were able to coast into stations as the power drained from their engines. Transit authorities labored to extract passengers from underground tunnels but, at midnight, 10,000 still remained imprisoned. On the Williamsburg Bridge, 1,700 subway riders were stranded for hours before being led to safety.

The blackout had begun during rush hour, and thousands of office workers and apartment-house dwellers were caught in elevators. Fortunately, many elevators were built with devices that, in such cases, took the cars down to the nearest floor where the doors could be opened manually. In some instances, passengers were trapped for hours. In the Pan Am Building and in other skyscrapers, huge holes had to be cut through walls to allow access to the elevator cars.

Some people, such as the tourists atop the Empire State Building, chose to stay where they were rather than undertake the descent by stairs. A group of tourists from France tried to teach the "Marseillaise" to Americans. A group of southerners led a chorus of "Dixie." All admired the view of the full moon over the East River.

A lawyer who had an office on the thirty-second story of a building on Third Avenue said by phone to a reporter, "Thank God we've got some whiskey. First we just sat around having drinks. Now we're having a séance, to communicate with the spirit that caused this bliss. We could have walked down, but it's about six hundred steps, so we're staying and we're all getting to know each other." (Nine months later *The Times* reported a dramatic increase in the birth rate.)

Doctors at Bellevue treated patients by candlelight. In operating and emergency rooms, the Fire Department set up battery-operated generators and lights. In one hospital, a surgical procedure was completed just as the electricity failed. In another, an innovative employee removed the battery from his car and wired up some lights in one of the wards. Doctors were most concerned about the potential for mixing up medicines in the dark, and nurses focused their efforts on reassuring mentally disturbed patients.

Transportation in the city became a nightmare. Taxis were impossible to find, buses bulged with passengers, and traffic lights were out. Thousands trekked home by foot across the Brooklyn and Queensboro Bridges. The eastbound tunnels, whose ventilation systems were down, were closed. The FDR Drive and the West Side Highway—unlit, of course—were still jammed hours after the outage began.

Broadway curtains did not rise, disappointing theatergoers and producers alike, and 30,000 tickets were refunded or exchanged. At Carnegie Hall, Vladimir Horowitz had just begun playing a Chopin Polonaise-Fantaisie before an invited audience when everything went dark. He paused for only a moment when an assistant came out with a flashlight to explain that the power would not be coming back on. Then he started over from the beginning.

New Yorkers were unusually patient and helpful toward one another, as always in the toughest moments. Bystanders assisted people coming out of subway exits and volunteered to take up posts outside of businesses to deter looting—and none was reported. Some went to intersections armed with flashlights to help direct traffic.

For Peter Kihss, who wrapped up the trials of the amazing night in his lead story, it was a shining hour. I thought the staff—having observed him all night as he accomplished his extraordinary feat by the light of two candles—was about to break into applause when he finished. I went over to his desk and, as he stood up, I hugged him. With a bashful smile, he offered a Gary Cooperish "Aw, shucks."

By now, we had received word it was unlikely the blackout would be over by midnight. At nine o'clock, Ted Bernstein, accompanied by a staff of twenty, gathered the edited stories, and was driven by truck to the offices of the *Newark News*. The plan was to produce an eight-page paper without advertisements. "What do you have in the way of forty-eight- or sixty-point type?" Bernstein asked the *Newark News* editor, figuring to top page one with a bold banner headline. "Coming from *The New York Times*, that sounds funny," the editor replied, "but I suppose even *The Times* isn't going to be conservative tonight." The headline was set in 48 point.

The Newark paper had already made up its pages of the day's stock market tables and generously allowed *The Times* to use them. Since they ran over a page, Bernstein, with Clifton Daniel's approval, decided to expand our edition to ten pages. *Times* editors and reporters worked side by side with *Newark News* reporters as copy from both papers went to the composing room at the same time, in a confusion that somehow sorted itself out.

In the meantime, at the *Times* building, we proceeded with plans for a press run if electricity was restored earlier than expected. The paper was remade time and again, shrinking in size with each passing hour. Off-duty employees stranded in the city stayed and performed various jobs to help the staff, such as keeping candles lighted. Also pressed into performing odd jobs were Barbara and Katie Witkin, who had earlier driven into the city to keep a dinner date with Dick and me at Sardi's. Instead, they arranged to have Sardi's send up sandwiches to supplement those prepared by our cafeteria, and they waited in the city room until the edition went to bed, when Dick and I were ready to drive back to Harrison.

At about midnight, Clifton Daniel clambered atop the metropolitan desk and congratulated everyone for an admirable performance under extreme circumstances. Abe and I continued to send men out to the streets, asking them to type up their notes and leave them for Homer Bigart, who would write an overview of the blackout for Thursday's paper. The official "Good night" was given at 12:50 A.M.

The power came on at 4:11 A.M., but by then the presses in Newark were ready to roll. The bizarre ten-page edition, in *Times* style and *Newark News* type, was limited to 480,000 copies, which were delivered to newsstands, airports and bus depots with as much haste as could be mustered. *The Times* was the only morning paper in Manhattan that managed to publish.

Today, when I look at the photographs that were taken in that candlelit city room, I vividly remember the magical—if frantic—atmosphere of the night. In one photo, I'm seated at my desk staring at sheaves of paper, with one hand clasped to my forehead. Abe stands to my right, a glint of light reflected off his glasses, the ember of his cigarette prominent against his shadowy face. Peter Kihss and Shelly Binn lean over my shoulder, their balding heads shining like half-moons. Dick Witkin stands in shadow to my left, a head and a torso minus arms and legs, his dark jacket absorbed by the surrounding blackness. We are huddled intently around a single candle.

AFTER THE BLACKOUT, Abe and I returned our concentration to John Lindsay. He was to be sworn into office at six P.M. on December 31, 1965, in a private ceremony. The mayor's office at the time was in tense contract negotiations with the Transport Workers. Headed by the mercurial Michael J. Quill, the union was threatening a strike against the Transit Authority that would still the city's subway and bus systems starting at five A.M. on New Year's Day. Lindsay had asked Quill for a few days of reprieve to "pull the show together" as the new mayor. Quill, resentful of Lindsay's patronizing manner, refused, calling him a "pipsqueak" and a "juvenile" and deliberately mispronouncing his name as "Linsley."

In the past, each time the TWU contract had come up for renewal the ritual had been the same. Quill would present exorbitant demands and threaten a strike. Then, in a series of cliffhanger talks, the incumbent mayor would cut a deal with Quill for a fraction of what he had asked. But with Lindsay the pattern changed. This time, Quill decided he wanted a strike.

Quill knew full well his demands amounted to extortion, designed to make Lindsay squirm: a thirty-percent pay raise over two years for its 33,000 members; a four-day, thirty-two-hour work week; and six weeks of vacation time after one year of service. With various other demands, the package came to an estimated total cost of $680 million.

The Transit Authority, however, was already operating in the red, $43 million annually. Though required to be a financially self-sustaining enterprise, the Authority depended on subsidies from City Hall to maintain the fifteen-cent subway fare, at that time a political sacred cow. One of the major stumbling blocks during the early negotiations was that neither outgoing Mayor Wagner nor incoming Mayor Lindsay would specify the amount of the subsidy. Hence the Transit Authority, not knowing how much money it would have to bargain with, never made a counteroffer. Finally, in the first minutes of the New Year, a $25 million proposal was put on the table by the Authority. Quill called it a "peanut package" and stalked out of the talks at the Hotel Americana. The strike was on, and New York was without public transportation.

January 1 was a Saturday, leaving two days before the full impact of the walkout would be felt. Lindsay announced that for the time being he would stay out of negotiations and let the mediators do their work. Quill was caustic. The mayor's presence was unnecessary, he said. "We explored his mind yesterday, and we found nothing."

In preparation for Monday, Lindsay urged people to stay out of Manhattan unless they were providing essential services. Only one quarter of the commuters were expected to make it into the city. Those who drove were asked to fill their cars with as many fellow suburbanites as possible. Grueling rush-hour traffic was anticipated, but the greatest fear was a gridlock that could block fire and other emergency crews. Quill, however, protested, "I don't think a strike for a couple of weeks would be a catastrophe. London withstood the Blitz."

To help our own employees get to the office, *The Times* rented nine private buses, and four *Times* delivery trucks were outfitted with wooden benches for twenty-five passengers each. Special routes were established for the shuttle buses but, a week into the strike, the drivers quit, claiming shots had been fired at them. A police ballistics crew reported that the marks on the rear windows of two of the buses might have been made by a slingshot but were definitely not left by bullets. The drivers, however, were scared off, so nine more delivery trucks were pressed into passenger service. *The Times* rented pie trucks to help deliver the papers. For those who couldn't make it home, the eleventh-floor club room at *The Times*, as well as parts of the seventh floor, were transformed into men's dormitories with forty beds. Some 225 rooms were also reserved across the street at the Dixie Hotel for women and additional male staff members.

After twelve days, a deal was finally announced by Douglas L. Mac-Mahon, who took over negotiations for the union when Quill and eight of his aides were jailed for having called the walkout, flouting an enjoinder issued by the State Supreme Court. Minutes after he was locked up on January 4, Quill collapsed from a heart attack and was taken to Bellevue Hospital, where he remained under guard for the duration of the strike.

MacMahon tried to take up where Quill had left off, declaring verbal open season on the mayor. On Monday, January 10, Lindsay was burned in effigy outside City Hall. "I've never met such amateurs in all my life," declared MacMahon, addressing a crowd of 10,000. "It was a sad day when Bob Wagner left this town. [Lindsay] doesn't know what the hell he's doing."

Efforts to free the jailed labor leaders, however, were opposed not by Lindsay but by MacMahon himself, who believed the best way to maintain sympathetic support was to prolong their incarceration. "Our working conditions are hazardous," complained one motorman. "You go home and you stay half an hour in the bathroom blowing the steel dust [from the tracks] out of your nose."

Ultimately, the workmen won a wage increase of fifteen percent over two years, plus a rise in health and welfare benefits. The Transit Authority agreed to spend $3 million to improve working conditions, and took on the cost of supplying employees with uniforms. The total package was estimated at $52 million. Although the settlement fell far short of Quill's unrealistic demands, it was a stunning victory for the union and a financial disaster for the city. Other municipal unions were encouraged to make similar demands, heralding New York's eventual fiscal crisis. Lindsay, combining inexperience and high-handedness, had attempted to bully a proud labor leader and had found himself outmaneuvered.

But most New Yorkers, like myself, didn't quite grasp the dire consequences of the settlement, and continued to be charmed by the new mayor. Our paper's editorial writers, who had warmly embraced Lindsay's vision from the start, went so far as to salute his efforts. A January 13, 1966, editorial stated: "The price is high, but not so high that it violates Mayor Lindsay's pledge never to 'capitulate before the lawless demands of a single power group.' To the extent that the price exceeds that of past agreements, the difference is represented primarily by the need for correcting a vast hangover of inequities and other bona fide grievances left unresolved by twenty years of backdoor contract deals at City Hall. . . . Mr. Lindsay has conducted himself throughout with courage, dignity and good sense."

But the fact remained that commerce during the strike was the slowest it had been since the Depression, costing New York businesses upward of half a billion dollars. Ten percent of garment manufacturers were closed because employees could not get to work. Most others operated far below normal. *The Times* itself lost half a million dollars in advertising.

It was apparent to all that Michael Quill had relished keeping "Linsley" off balance in battle, but it was his last victory. Quill died soon after the deal was struck.

AT A STAFF MEETING, Abe spelled out his plans for future coverage of the Lindsay administration, which he described as "a great opportunity for *The Times* because the entire country will be watching New York, where a presidential candidate may be hatching." Abe pointed out that Lindsay's new programs would be carried out in the spotlight of national "urban development," recognized by governmental leaders, starting with President Johnson himself, as the country's major domestic issue. Thus, Lindsay's attempts to solve these problems needed an entirely fresh reportorial eye.

A dozen reporters were assigned to cover various aspects of the new administration. Lindsay had named Robert Price, his smart and wily campaign manager, as deputy mayor, and enlisted a number of precocious assistants—among them Jeff Greenfield, Steven Brill, Leon Panetta, Jeffrey Katzenberg, Lesley Stahl—all of whom eventually found City Hall a stepping-stone to prominent careers. For the first time, we assigned a full-time reporter to follow the economics of city government—how the city paid for its operations, where the money came from and how the controller, the budget director and other officials coped with fiscal problems. Abe expected the reporter to go beyond the five boroughs, making contact with Washington officials and probing relationships between City Hall and the state capital as well as the business community.

We also assigned reporters to several new beats: social services, neighborhoods and community action, antipoverty and race relations, the environment, landmarks and traffic. And we decided to broaden our coverage of police news to include transit police, the corrections department and the fire department, and to investigate the latest developments in police science and criminology.

Now that the transit strike was behind him, Lindsay took on heroic stature. With his patrician good looks, combined with his apparent humanitarianism, he brought a jauntiness to city life. He urged New Yorkers to have fun. Almost overnight, he turned Central Park into a people's playground, ordering the removal of "Keep off the Grass" signs and scheduling sports and social events on the lawns. As the weather warmed, he walked and bicycled in shirtsleeves, as he had during the campaign, through various neighborhoods, including Harlem and Bedford-Stuyvesant, where black residents felt he demonstrated authentic concern for their living conditions. He rode the subways, chatting with passengers, and was applauded by audiences when he attended Broadway plays, concerts, the ballet and the opera.

Since he was an avowed ham, as he had once confided in his interview with me, he decided to break precedent at the annual Inner Circle dinner show in 1966, produced by New York's present and former City Hall reporters. Political, business and media organizations bought tables at the New York Hilton, and a number of *Times* reporters and editors, including Abe and me, were among the 1,300 formally attired guests. It was a tradition that, after their musical lampoon of City Hall officials, the reporters in the cast turned over the stage to the mayor for his rebuttal speech.

But this time the mayor did the reporters one better. Instead of a speech, Lindsay satirized them in music and lyrics written especially for him by the hit Broadway team of Jerry Bock and Sheldon Harnick. He had rehearsed secretly for days with a supporting cast he himself enlisted—Florence Henderson, the star of the Broadway musical *Fanny,* as well as members of the show's chorus in their sexy costumes.

When Lindsay made his entrance wearing straw hat and white gloves and twirling a cane, for his five-minute soft-shoe routine, the guests, including Governor Rockefeller, Senator Javits and former Mayor Wagner, rose in wild applause. The mayor had himself written two of the most popular lines in the act. In the midst of his soft-shoe with Henderson, he asked, "Florence, are you sure LBJ started this way?" And then Henderson inquired, "Mr. Mayor, when will this be a fun city?" Lindsay replied, while still in step: "When the power brokers get off my battery. What a charge!"

Possibly even more effervescent than Jimmy Walker, Lindsay was sometimes referred to by the press as Mr. New York of Fun City. But he displayed a strong social conscience. Above all, he allied himself with Johnson's Great Society and the civil rights movement. An event that raised the consciousness of the country and affected Lindsay deeply was what became known as "Bloody Sunday," which occurred on March 7, only two months after his election. *The Times*, along with other major papers, sent reporters to Selma, Alabama, one of the most racist cities in the South, to cover the story.

On that Sunday, a fifty-four-mile march, demanding voting rights for blacks, had been scheduled from Selma to the state capitol steps in Montgomery. At one point, the sheriff's posse and state troopers lobbed tear-gas canisters at the three hundred marchers. Gay Talese witnessed what followed: the brutal beating of the marchers with billy clubs, cattle prods and the butts of rifles. Also witnessing the terror was an NBC camera crew. "The film was shown on television and America woke up," Talese recalled years later. "The next day people started pouring into Selma, both whites and blacks, from everywhere and, of course, when the five-day march was rescheduled, 25,000 people showed up at the final protest at the state capitol, to be addressed on its steps by Martin Luther King." The story kept growing and Talese stayed with it for three weeks. For Lindsay and all liberal New Yorkers, Selma became a great rallying cry of the civil rights movement.

But a year or so into his mayoralty, Lindsay found himself all but overwhelmed by his own urban problems. Life in New York was unquestionably deteriorating in 1966, a decline reflected in our daily metropolitan news report. In February, for example, I decided to follow up on a complaint in the "Letters to the Editor" column by one George Ellis, a Puerto Rican immigrant who had owned a clothing store on West 145th Street for twenty-two years:

"Day and night we are at the mercy of the hoodlums that infest our streets. The shops and offices have to operate with doors locked, and are opened only to known customers. Old men and women are robbed almost every week coming from the check cashing place, especially when they receive their Social Security, pension or welfare checks. The women are afraid to go to their churches after dark because the hallways and stoops are so infested with winos and dope addicts. . . . HELP! HELP! HELP!"

Ellis had been mugged twice and burglarized. Between the time he wrote the letter and mailed it, he again became a victim. As reported in the story I assigned, every store on West 145th Street between Seventh and Eighth Avenues was a target; any merchandise that could be lifted, pried or ripped from a table or wall was stolen.

Alerted to the strife on this block by *The Times*, Lindsay traveled to the neighborhood to hear the complaints firsthand, a practice that was to become his trademark. His visit was unannounced. "I wanted to see if patrolmen are coming around," he said.

Shop owners spoke candidly: "I've been held up two times in the last three weeks, and it's driving me out of my mind," said a dry cleaner. "You can't walk the streets around here," a barber told the mayor. Many people, Lindsay learned, were considering closing their businesses and leaving the area. But, although he pledged to increase police protection, there weren't the funds to do so, and nothing changed.

Unemployment in Harlem was still two and a half times higher than in the rest of the city. The ghetto remained cursed with narcotics and a sense of futility. Antipoverty programs were under attack from all quarters for their impotence. "We have had studies and more studies on what should be done in Harlem," said the president of the Consolidated Tenants League. "There are many, many programs 'on paper' but nothing is being done."

New York's problems—and the mayor's—were not limited to the streets. Sydney Schanberg (who later gained fame for his daring reports from Cambodia upon which *The Killing Fields* was based) wrote an article about the squalid state of many of the city's nursing homes. Inspectors, who had been alerted to the deplorable conditions by a number of letters, found many facilities filthy, overcrowded and infested with flies and rats.

One of the worst offenders was a city-run Staten Island home. "The living quarters . . . look like stables," Schanberg wrote. "Unshaven male patients shuffle about the grounds all day in soiled institutional bathrobes and pajamas. . . . Paint is peeling everywhere and the smell of urine is potent." One city official said some nursing homes reminded him of what he had read about "seventeenth-century London lunatic asylums."

The city's schools were also showing signs of trouble. One-fifth of elementary and junior high school students were two or more years behind in reading. As expected, schools in poor ethnic neighborhoods were the worst off. But the degree of the inequity was shocking. At P.S. 6, which my sons had attended before we moved to Harrison, half of the fifth-graders were at least two years above grade level in reading. Other schools in the same district, which included parts of East Harlem, showed the same percentage of fifth-graders to be a year and a half below grade level. This disparity reflected a growing problem. With the white exodus to the suburbs increasing, more than half of the city's elementary pupils were now black and Puerto Rican.

THE ONLY OTHER New York paper that excelled in the coverage of the city's crisis was the *Herald Tribune*. But on September 12, 1966, the *Herald Tribune*, which had been struggling to survive for years, tried to save itself by publishing as a merged paper with the *Journal-American* and the *World-Telegram & Sun*. The venture collapsed after only eight months.

The *Herald Tribune* itself had been created by a merger in 1924 of two venerated papers: the *Herald*, founded in 1835 by James Gordon Bennett, and the *Tribune*, founded in 1841 by Horace Greeley. Although the *Trib*—as we all called it—was *The Times*'s main competition, its demise was not a cause for celebration in our city room. We knew its reporters. We had shared trade gossip with them at Bleeck's, had run into them covering assignments all over town and matched their stories in the paper with ours.

I had never forgotten my first weeks at *The Times* as a copyboy when Sammy Solovitz and I went out nightly to buy the *Trib* at the Times Square newsstand hot off the press so that the bullpen editors could make sure *The Times* wasn't beaten on any major stories. Indeed, from the first day Abe started as metropolitan editor, we had continued that tradition. Every night we read the *Trib* to make sure it didn't have a metropolitan story we had somehow missed.

"It was a competitor of ours, but a competitor that sought survival on the basis of quality, originality and integrity, rather than sensationalism or doctrinaire partisanship," mourned *The Times*'s editorial. "Its strength was sapped by long-term financial ailments that afflict all metropolitan news-papers—rising costs of every kind, population shifts away from the five boroughs, fiercer competition from television, radio and newsmagazines and suburban dailies. Yet the *Herald Tribune* would still be alive without the suffocating impact of strikes."

A number of the *Trib*'s top reporters, sensing its destiny, had already departed for *The Times* or other publications. Many more came to Forty-third Street after the *Trib* shut down its presses for good. Abe and I were concerned at no longer having the *Trib* to compete against. There remained the *Post* and the *News*, of course, but it was the *Trib* whose standards we admired and tried to match (as it had tried to match ours).

We had all but forgotten by now that New York had once prided itself on being a great newspaper town, boasting fifteen dailies of general circulation in 1900. We pledged ourselves to be warier than ever of maintaining our own high standards and assuring they never slipped.

THIRTY-SIX

To my perplexity, when Abe was promoted to assistant managing editor toward the end of 1966, Turner Catledge asked me somewhat sheepishly to serve as *acting* metropolitan editor until further notice. Abe and I had both always taken it for granted that I was the natural choice to succeed him.

I soon discovered that Scotty Reston, still the preeminent columnist writing out of Washington and as ever a confidant of the Sulzberger family, was maneuvering behind the scenes to prevent me from becoming metropolitan editor. I had always admired Scotty's column and taken pride in being his colleague on *The Times*. Previously clueless about upper-echelon politicking at the paper, I was shocked to learn of his opposition. Among the several candidates he suggested was Max Frankel—my old friend on rewrite, now White House correspondent and one of Scotty's protégés. Scotty had long been uncomfortable with the up-front, spontaneous style Abe and I had initiated, so inimical to the reserved, sedate mode practiced by members of the Washington bureau. And he was doubly uneasy with our close, forceful partnership that had contributed toward moving the paper in new directions, earning the enthusiastic support of Catledge and Daniel.

Scotty feared that since Abe and I were poised to keep rising, his traditionally independent Washington bureau might someday be taking orders from us as a team. He had expressed concern to the publisher about our growing influence—and the danger of allowing the Abe–Arthur partnership to flourish. He dared not challenge Abe but thought it expedient to remove me from the succession before it was too late.

Abe urged me to plead my case personally with Punch Sulzberger but I demurred, believing my qualifications should speak for themselves. In any case, Abe as well as Daniel were vigorously lobbying on my behalf. I didn't get much sleep during the next few weeks, but eventually Punch—declaring he was pleased with the changes Abe and I had made—told me he planned to announce my promotion effective January 1. Now that the innovations on the metropolitan desk had taken root, he said, he expected me to make them bloom.

Abe's promotion to assistant managing editor signaled a dramatic change in the paper's operation. Although his title was the same as the two principal assistant managing editors, in practice he had not only been jumped over Daniel's closest assistant, Harrison Salisbury, but he also had been assigned new duties that impinged on the powers of the assistant managing editor in charge of the bullpen, Ted Bernstein.

"Mr. Rosenthal will be responsible for news development," announced Daniel in his memo to all desk editors. "In my absence, he will preside over the news conference, and will be in charge of the managing editor's office. . . . Duplicates of the news summaries [a reporter's brief outline of his story, relied upon by the bullpen in making up page one and the Second Front] should be supplied to him, and he will sit with the bullpen editors as they lay out the paper."

Bernstein could barely mask his distress over Abe's new authority to second-guess him so comprehensively. As for Salisbury, he may have been offended by the move but tried not to show it. Shortly after Daniel confided his plan, he took off for Hanoi and filed a story that dominated the news out of Vietnam for weeks, and which to some extent alleviated the impact of Abe's ascendancy over him.

Salisbury had for some time been seeking permission to enter North Vietnam, and the Hanoi government, to prove that U.S. planes were killing civilians in their bombing missions, at last gave him a much-sought-after visa. In late December, his stories reported that "contrary to the impression given by United States communiqués, on-the-spot inspection indicates that American bombing has been inflicting considerable civilian casualties in Hanoi and its environs for some time past." The reaction was thunderous, with Salisbury hailed by antiwar protesters and defiled in hawkish quarters for not properly attributing his sources and giving comfort to the enemy. *The Times* submitted his stories in 1967 for the Pulitzer, but, while the jury of reporters and editors voted for the entry, the Pulitzer advisory board, dominated by newspaper executives who were hawks on the war, turned it down.

Salisbury kept thinking up traveling assignments and seemed displaced only when he found himself in New York for too many weeks at a stretch. With evidently too little to do in the newsroom, he fell into the habit of looking over my shoulder and questioning my coverage of breaking local stories. Finally, I told him he had to quit his backseat editing and, if he had any complaints, to take them to Abe. He stopped intruding.

ON JANUARY 2, 1967, a day after I had taken over my new post, Abe and I went to Sardi's to celebrate. Abe lifted his glass in a toast. "Your new job is made for you," he said. "You love this city with all your heart, even more than I do. The job will be more yours than it was mine."

In my early days at the paper, when I edited *Timesweek* and then became a cub reporter, I thought there was no more exciting job anywhere than city editor of a New York newspaper, and city editor of *The Times* was of course best of all. Now I was entering the world of legendary editors—Stanley Walker, Bruce Rae, Walter Howey.

"The city editor, if he knows his job, is the real captain of the ship," wrote Charles Edward Russell, who was the first city editor of the *New York World*, from 1894 to 1897. I believed him. Just as I had once, as a police reporter, felt possessively responsible for coverage of the Upper East Side, I now felt possessive about the entire city. (Mine, all mine!)

I wanted a deputy with whom I could communicate in the same sort of·shorthand I'd had with Abe. My first choice was Bernie Kalb, and I tried to persuade him to leave his correspondent's job at CBS, telling him he truly belonged back at *The Times*. But Bernie, while tempted, decided he liked talking even more than writing or editing, and that television was his natural element. He was quizzical about the editor's loss of personal authorship

"Don't you miss having a byline?" he asked.

"It may sound crazy," I said, "but I assigned and edited five stories that made page one today and I feel that almost the entire front page is my byline."

My alternative choice was Robert Alden, who had done well as my deputy at the World's Fair bureau, and I thought reporters would respond to his easy manner. Although my chemistry with Bob was less exhilarating than it was with Abe, we managed to create a rapport that kept the metropolitan report racing. Much of our attention in the first few weeks was devoted to an ongoing story assiduously being tracked by Edith Evans Asbury, an ace investigative reporter. It involved a decision in an upstate court case holding that an Italian-American couple name Liuni could not legally adopt Elizabeth, the four-year-old orphan girl they had fostered since she was five days old. Asbury had been the first reporter to bring the matter to public attention in a page-one story two months earlier.

The Ulster County Welfare commissioner, Joseph Fitzsimmons, a political appointee, had ruled that the Liunis' olive complexion and ethnic background rendered them "unsuitable" as adoptive parents of a blond child with fair skin and blue eyes. He wanted the child put up for adoption by a "more appropriate couple." Neighbors of Michael Liuni, a technician for International Business Machines, were up in arms.

Asbury's initial article brought a cascade of protesting phone calls and letters to the president, the governor and members of Congress, and she followed up with a series of stories that did much to unmask the racism of the legal system. Maintaining that he was following the law in rejecting the adoption, Fitzsimmons cited the Liunis' age (both were forty-eight), their modest income and the fact they had three other children as contributing factors in his decision. But it was their Italian ethnicity that appeared to be the decisive factor.

Following the reaction to Edith's first story, the Liunis were emboldened to take their case to court, which ordered a thorough investigation. But the commissioner refused to budge, and Edith kept filing stories of protest—by psychiatrists, social caseworkers, the American Jewish Congress, the Humane Society, the faculty of Cornell Law School, the students of Yale Divinity School.

On January 6, the court investigator's report was released in favor of the adoption by the Liunis. Written by former Judge William E. O'Connor, who was assigned to represent the true interests of the child, it said in part, "Any rule that would risk the ruination of a child's life should not be followed, regardless of the dignity of the authority promulgating it." Separating Elizabeth from her foster parents would amount to "a governmental sin." He cited the opinions of noted developmental psychologists and pointed out the absurdity of the law by declaring: "Under the rules and guidelines suggested in the instant case, the mother of Jesus would have been unacceptable for motherhood by reason of her age, his foster father would have been rejected for financial reasons."

The mounting storm forced the commissioner "reluctantly" to approve the adoption, allowing Elizabeth to keep her family. In saluting the decision, *The Times*'s editorial page declared that the "glaring weaknesses in present law" needed immediate remedy—and the laws were, indeed, overhauled to prevent damage to children on the basis of such arbitrary rulings.

I'll always be indebted to Edith's stubborn curiosity for getting me started on the right foot in my new post. She understood *The Times*'s Ochsian standards of fairness, integrity and good taste—traditions she absorbed into her bones. She also knew the importance of passing them on to younger reporters who, in turn, passed them on to younger reporters. In my view, that was at the heart of the paper's vigorous survival.

I clearly remember Edith's arrival at *The Times* in 1952, when I was a young reporter. She came from the *World Telegram*, where she had been a women's news editor. But when she started in the city room, she insisted that she not be assigned to stories with "a woman's angle." She was intrepid and relentless in her search for facts and, because she was talented, she was able to demand—and get—the same type of hard-news assignments given to her male peers.

Amidst a sea of mostly scruffy-looking men, Edith—a petite woman with blue eyes and porcelain skin who always wore a chic hat atop her curly, platinum-blond hair—looked daintily feminine. But when working under deadline pressure, she could let loose a booming cry of "Copy!" that always rattled me in my seat three rows behind her.

Edith once told me about the difficulties she had endured as a woman reporter before winning the chance to cover major news stories. And when she did get her chance, her salary was less than that paid to men doing basically the same work. But that's the way it was in most companies, not only in the news business. The biased mindset was that, since women did not have families to support as men did, they should not expect to earn as much as men.

After beginning her career in 1929 as a women's news reporter for the *Cincinnati Times,* Edith moved to Knoxville, Tennessee, to be near an Army officer whom she married (and later divorced). There she worked for the *News-Sentinel*, where she was again ghettoized in the women's department. Four years later, the city editor decided to take a chance and move her to general assignment. She flourished among the all-male city staff, covering everything from police news to President Roosevelt and, before long, she became the paper's star.

Believing she had gone as far as she could in Knoxville, Asbury came to New York, and was hired by the *Post*. One day, she was covering the story about the man on the ledge at the Gotham Hotel who was threatening to jump, the same story that Dick Feehan had once told me about. The man was still on the ledge when Edith was summoned back to the office. Edith thought she was going to be praised for her detailed telephone reports from the scene that day, but the editor didn't even look up when she approached his desk. He told her she was dismissed, citing no reason. It was four days before her six-month anniversary—which would have entitled her to severance pay. Later that day, she learned the *Post* was facing financial trouble.

Asbury borrowed two dollars from a photographer, planning to get drunk. When she realized that two dollars wasn't enough to achieve inebriation, she perched herself on a stool at a United Cigar Store counter and ordered one five-cent cup of coffee after another. She then went home and stayed in bed for a couple of days, until she was again able to face life.

Unemployed and with no savings, she submitted a few articles to a movie magazine and finally found steady work with the city's Housing Authority, where she felt like an outcast—the only WASP (and from the Midwest, to boot) in an office of Jewish and Catholic native New Yorkers. But she familiarized herself with the city's housing problems, acquiring background expertise that later proved useful in assignments at *The Times*.

One day she ran into an AP reporter she had known when both were on the *Post*. The reporter spoke to his editors, who were short of rewrite men due to the war. Edith said she didn't think she had the ability to work on rewrite but, once established at her desk, she performed skillfully. I knew what she meant when she told me, "Rewrite taught me speed."

Occasionally, she was sent out on assignments, and became friendly with some *Times* reporters, including Frank Adams. At a war bond rally she was covering, she met Herbert Asbury, author of *The Gangs of New York* and, at the time, associate editor of *Collier's*. The two fell for each other instantly— she was thirty-five, he was fifty-three—and were married a couple of weeks later. She stopped working for a time, but as the royalties from her husband's book dried up, she took the job as a women's news editor at the *World-Telegram*.

Frustrated with the limitations of women's news, Asbury phoned Frank Adams and asked if he could help her get to *The Times*. He arranged an interview with Robert Garst, at that time the city editor. Garst was impressed with Asbury's résumé, which she jotted down on an index card while riding the subway to Times Square. Since Laurie Johnston, a seasoned writer on the city staff, was going on maternity leave, Garst hired Edith to maintain the skimpy total of four female reporters in the city room. She was both annoyed and amused that he thought it appropriate to bunch all four women together along a single row of desks.

Sometime after her husband died, Edith and Garst kindled an office romance, which they mistakenly thought they were keeping secret. But whenever Edith's phone rang, all eyes flashed toward the bullpen, where, more often than not, Garst was holding his receiver to his ear. I think it's safe to say, though, that Edith didn't receive preferential treatment as a result of the relationship, and the two eventually married.

I never considered Edith's gender when drawing up the assignment sheet, and once I confronted a young assistant editor who had handed her a story with a domestic angle. "I don't know why you assigned Edith to a story about energy-saving in the kitchen," I wrote in a memo. "She told me she hasn't been in the kitchen in years and has no interest in the story at all."

Edith was the first woman voted into the Inner Circle and appeared in its annual political lampoons until she was in her nineties. Until she retired in her seventies, she felt at home when assigned to breaking stories on the street as well as intricate deliberations in the courtroom, where she covered such stories as the tumultuous Black Panther trials. She was often my choice for covering such trials, since she would always probe far beyond the testimony.

POSSIBLY THE MOST offbeat story that occupied me in early January 1967 was one that turned out quite differently from how I had envisioned it. Some weeks earlier, while Abe was still metropolitan editor, rumors began circulating that the Columbia Broadcasting System or some other media conglomerate was trying to buy *The New Yorker*, the iconoclastic weekly all of us read and often envied for its style and verve. We decided to assign a penetrating study of the magazine's inner workings. How was *The New Yorker*'s enigmatic editor, William Shawn, faring? What was the prognosis for the magazine's economic stability? Were any changes in staff and content being contemplated?

Renowned for his personal reticence and his public reluctance to discuss *The New Yorker*'s mystique, Shawn had habitually refused requests for interviews. He had become particularly guarded since the appearance somewhat earlier in the *Tribune* of Tom Wolfe's acerbic analysis of the magazine's weaknesses. My first impulse was to ask Berrie if he'd be willing to talk to a reporter about Shawn and *The New Yorker*, but he said he couldn't do that without Shawn's permission.

Berrie explained that Shawn was not only his editor but his friend. He cautioned that *The New Yorker* staff was absolutely loyal to him and so close-mouthed about what went on in the hushed Shawn sanctum that we would get nowhere fast. Abe and I nonetheless had decided to take a stab at it, agreeing that the best reporter for the assignment was Murray Schumach, who had just returned from Hollywood and was now occupying the front-row seat to Bigart's left. In his long years on the paper, Murray had come to know a legion of writers, including some on *The New Yorker*. He himself had written about stage and film writers, and there was hardly a story involving writers that he was not able to tackle knowledgeably. He wrote many of them for the Sunday *Magazine* and the Sunday Drama Section, as well as the daily paper.

But Murray himself realized that without Shawn's cooperation, it would be impossible to write the kind of intimate story we hoped for. We needed Shawn to free his staff to talk to Murray and we needed Shawn's own assent to be interviewed. An inveterate reader of *The Times,* Shawn was familiar with Murray's balanced and accurate reporting, and he eventually agreed to Murray's written pleas. But there was a catch: Shawn requested that Murray allow him to look over the copy before it went to press, so that he might trap any factual errors, as his reporters sometimes did with subjects. He said it would embarrass him greatly if a story about *The New Yorker* in *The New York Times* contained any mistakes.

It was *Times* policy that the subject of an article never be shown it in advance of publication. But after much discussion Abe and I decided to make an exception. The story was to be about a man acknowledged as one of the few Olympian American editors and a magazine that since the 1920s had maintained the most sophisticated standards in journalism, fiction, cartoons, criticism and poetry. If acceding to Shawn's terms was the only way to get what we thought was an exceptional story, we'd go along this one time. Shawn, after all, had agreed to ask for no changes whatever except in the case of factual errors—and Murray didn't make factual errors.

After gathering his facts over several weeks, Murray wrote a draft of his story that came to 5,500 words (and would have filled an entire page of the paper). It was replete with arcane, shrewd, sprightly observations—exactly what Abe and I had had in mind. Murray called *The New Yorker* "a creature of wondrous paradox," and the piece was by turns laudatory and irreverent.

He described Shawn as a "small, shy, pink-faced man" who "skitters in and out of his office like a mouse pursued by a cat." Because of his dedication to his work and his perfectionism as an editor, he was, in fact, known by his staff as "the Iron Mouse."

Murray found that, in common with the entire *New Yorker* staff, Shawn had no name on his office door. And, like the rest of the offices, Shawn's was dusty and dingy—"about the size of a living room in a low-cost housing project" and "furnished with an old sofa, drab wall-to-wall carpeting, piles of magazines on the floor and on the windowsills, and the usual grimy windows." "We are very thrifty," Murray was informed by R. Hawley Truax, chairman of the magazine's board of directors, and one of its founders. "This place grew up on very economical instincts and philosophy."

Murray wrote about the unusual arrangement between staff writers and the magazine. Instead of being paid salaries, writers drew advances on work in progress. Sometimes they ran into four-figure debt to the magazine, creating a system that one writer described as "a kind of sharecropping." Although Shawn assured Murray that "rejections of pieces by staff writers are so rare as to be regarded practically as calamities," he conceded there was no guarantee that any completed article would be published. Infrequently, a writer was obliged to pay back his advance. This system had been worked out by Harold Ross, the magazine's founder, who maintained that *The New Yorker* bought material, not effort and time. According to one veteran editor, Ross believed "writers were children and couldn't be trusted with money."

But the writers had their compensations. They were not hounded by deadlines, and their space—often divided into multipart articles—was, by journalistic standards, essentially unlimited. Truman Capote's "In Cold Blood" ran 127,026 words; John Bainbridge's profile of Texas, 121,294; S. N. Behrman's profile of Max Beerbohm, 98,653; John Hersey's study of Hiroshima, which was given an entire issue, 31,347; and Rachel Carson's "Silent Spring," 57,406.

Murray explored the social life of the staff, the process of editing and making up each issue, as well as the magazine's business practices. Shawn told Murray that, as was true at *The Times,* the editorial department insisted on absolute independence of pressure from advertisers and from its own advertising and business departments. The editorial department, Murray discovered, had vetoed ads it thought contained editorial material, even overruling the top officers of the company. As an example, he cited the magazine's refusal to run ads featuring women in bikinis. When advertisers protested, pointing out that bikinis could be seen in profusion on any public beach and in displays in many national publications, *The New Yorker* priggishly retorted that they were not yet being worn on Fifth Avenue.

"We do not go beyond consulting our own judgment and tastes and what pleases us and interests us," Shawn told Murray. "The word 'reader' does not come up and, in a way, in the profoundest sense, we are being most respectful toward the reader who is assumed to be not different from oneself. We are exactly like a man writing a book. If he starts thinking about the reader, it is not going to be much of a book."

The magazine in recent years had undergone a number of changes that some critics believed had weakened its content, including a noticeable decrease of precision-crafted humor. The "Talk of the Town" section, which had previously been penned by the likes of Wolcott Gibbs, E. B. White and James Thurber, was now left in the hands of young writers who rarely presumed to spoof their subjects. Similarly, the *New Yorker* "Profiles," which, Murray wrote, once "set an American pattern with detail, wit and acerbic tone, are now lacking in irreverence. Its fiction has been criticized as favoring 'fragile stylists.'"

Shawn, according to Murray's conversations with him, did not share Ross's zest for poking fun at important people: "He also has strict ideas about invasion of privacy. Thus, he will not encourage a piece on someone who does not wish to be publicized unless that person is an important public official." "The real change," Shawn told Murray, "came in the war, with the advent of Nazis, when we found out there really were evil people. It no longer seemed the same to write harshly about somebody who was fairly harmless."

Murray acknowledged that *The New Yorker,* in spite of some carping, had forced even the most influential organs of American journalism to raise their standards, particularly with its unhurried, penetrating, well-written "Reporter at Large" pieces. The trend toward in-depth reporting in both print and television news was directly traceable to *The New Yorker.*

Murray also stressed the lengths to which Shawn had gone to protect the integrity of his magazine. "One of the secrets of the success of *The New Yorker* has been its almost instinctive distrust of giantism with a stress on ever-greater profits. The attitude was demonstrated at the annual stockholders meeting in 1966 when a stockholder urged stock splitting."

"You're in business to make a profit," the stockholder said.

Mr. Truax replied: "We're not in business for profit in the sense that profit comes before the magazine."

We submitted the article to Shawn, as agreed, anticipating quibbles about a minor factual error or two. To our horror, he responded in the form of an eleven-page double-spaced document that went well beyond matters of fact. It appeared that he was hypersensitive to any criticism, implied or explicit, of the magazine, and thought the piece was "written by someone who had the conventional nostalgic view of the 'old days' of *The New Yorker* but had not been reading it in recent years."

"You have described some of the mechanics, some of the surface workings, of the magazine," Shawn wrote. "You have described parts of its body (an arm and a leg, perhaps), but you have left out the mind and the soul. What one gets from your piece is a picture of a lot of dreary, whining writers shut up in their dusty cubicles or pacing the dusty corridors, fretting over money and over whether their pieces will ever appear; and a lot of dreary, whining editors plodding away unimaginatively in somewhat larger dusty offices; and, apparently by accident, the emergence from all this each week of a conceivably admirable magazine. If *The New Yorker* is what you say it is, I don't think it's worth writing about at length in *The Times*."

Shawn took exception (as "factual errors") to the characterization of him as "the Iron Mouse," maintaining with amazing naiveté, "This is the first time I have ever heard the term. I have asked a number of my colleagues whether they have ever heard it and have found none who has." And among his thirty-seven other complaints was his refusal to believe Ross had ever said writers were children who couldn't be trusted with money. If he did say it, protested Shawn, "he was merely being funny."

Utterly superseding his original agreement, Shawn asked that Murray replace one of his quotes about the philosophy of *The New Yorker* with another that he was herewith enclosing. He insisted that the quote be used "exactly as I've written it here, and in its entirety, and in one unbroken quote." It read:

"As for *The New Yorker*'s editorial philosophy, I'd say, to begin with, that 'philosophy' is too formal a word. Moreover, since whatever we have that might pass for a philosophy is never defined intramurally, I don't think it should be defined publicly; as soon as we, or I, said precisely what it was, it would congeal or turn into something else. In a general way, what we have is a constantly developing set of journalistic, literary, and ethical principles and convictions and standards and intuitions and impulses that lead us to write or draw or publish this rather than that. We prefer not to talk about what we are doing and simply do it. If a writer here turns in a manuscript, he needn't explain it; whatever is there in the manuscript is already there, and no amount of explanation can change it. Much the same can be said about the magazine as a whole. It's all there, week by week, right in the magazine; my talking about it can't alter or improve it. Let the explanations and explications, the analyses and appraisals come from others. I can talk a bit about our intentions. We try to produce a climate here in which the people who create the magazine—the writers, the artists, the editors—have the greatest possible freedom to do their own best work and to act upon and shape the magazine. Essentially, our objective is the self-realization of the artists and writers who contribute to the magazine, and everything flows from that; if these people realize themselves, the magazine realizes itself. We try to print short stories, poetry, comic art, criticism, and factual reporting that engage our interest or stir us or afford us some particular delight. We try to be truthful, fair, humane, responsible, rational, and clear. We try to keep the magazine in motion, holding on to whatever from the past we feel is still vital and relevant but maintaining a mood of experiment and letting the magazine change when changes seem to us to be in order and have value. I have moments when I think that what we are trying to do, on a modest scale, is nourish the spirit and help preserve the sanity of our society. If, each week, *The New Yorker* could be what it wishes to be, it would be informative, useful, funny, and beautiful."

Using Shawn's principled, unaltered statement was not in any sense a problem. But with him in such obvious distress and refusing to abide by the original agreement, the article shuttled back and forth among Shawn, Murray and myself. Exasperated, Murray and I realized there would be no pleasing Shawn unless he was given carte blanche to edit the article, and, obviously, we couldn't agree to that. We decided, at last, to put the piece away for the time being and await a strong news peg—at which time we might resume the battle; but after a few years, the article was outdated. It taught me a lesson, though, and I vowed I'd never again make that kind of agreement with an interview subject, no matter who. (The news peg we had been waiting for about *The New Yorker*'s sale—to Condé Nast Publications—arrived eighteen years too late, and Shawn by then had lost his power; he was forced out two years later, in 1987, and replaced by Robert Gottlieb, editor-in-chief of Alfred A. Knopf—over the very vocal protests of 154 *New Yorker* writers, who asked Gottlieb to turn down the appointment.)

DURING THE SUMMER OF 1967, as race riots spread throughout the country, President Johnson formed a commission to study ways of calming the incendiary mood. Chaired by Otto Kerner, governor of Illinois, with Mayor Lindsay as vice chairman, the commission in a report the following year found that "the scarcity of Negroes in responsible news jobs" intensified "the difficulty of communicating the reality of the contemporary American city to white newspaper and television audiences." To me, there was nothing surprising about that, but it did seem to come as a bolt to certain *Times* editors.

Ted Bernstein, for example, sat down to compose a two-page, single-spaced memo labeled "urgent," which he sent on April 29, 1968, to Sulzberger, Catledge, Daniel, Rosenthal, Salisbury and me. After all those sleepy years, it was as though Ted had suddenly been awakened and needed to share his enlightenment with us. It was quite a turnaround, considering he had been among the top editors who used to tell staffers "Forget it" when they reported on police stories involving black perpetrators or victims.

Solemnly he wrote: "Imagine yourself to be a Negro living in a segregated section of the city. You pick up a copy of *The New York Times*. You find that by far the largest number of news items concerning Negroes relate to antagonisms and clashes with whites . . . to items in general that are concerned with the black-white confrontation. . . . Would you feel, as a Negro, that you were being excluded from the community in general in the reporting of the news, and that your segregation was being accentuated? What I propose to overcome this feeling is an intensified effort to find and cover Negro news. There must be countless stories about the Negro middle class—the entrepreneurs, the entertainers, the teachers, the scientists, the clubs, the trade organizations—that we are not reporting."

He went on to propose a singular idea: If *Times* reporters couldn't dig up such stories that were journalistically meaningful, then the paper ought to initiate "a modification of the currently accepted news standards to produce items of interest to the Negro community." Aware, as he hastened to add, "that such a proposal may arouse an instant reflex of resistance," he nevertheless argued that "just as business is relaxing its standards to hire what have hitherto been regarded as unemployables, a newspaper like *The Times* should relax its standards to put to work news items that hitherto have been regarded as unemployable."

I continued to read Ted's memo with mounting astonishment at his uncharacteristic sophistry. "I think there are many activities that we normally would not cover that would interest Negroes and whites as well," he wrote, "and would make the Negroes feel they are part of the community in general and that we are paying attention to them. I do not propose that we should strive to print items that are of merely local interest for the sake of getting in names in the way a suburban newspaper might do, but rather that we should cover news that might otherwise be regarded as not important enough for normal *Times* coverage.

"I don't mean any of this to imply criticism of what our editors are now doing; they are following news standards that have persisted since the beginning of American journalism. What I am suggesting is a variation of these standards as a public obligation, and as necessary to bring about some degree of reconciliation between the races and to draw the blacks into the mainstream of American life."

Abe Rosenthal, with more restraint than I would have expected, answered, in part, that while "a newspaper may relax its hiring standards in order to give certain underprivileged people a chance at a better life" and that "this affects in a positive way the people involved," lowering news standards "would affect in a negative way the whole newspaper and its readership." He added that he believed there was "considerable news within the Negro community fit for us to print by accepted news standards" and "we do not have to lower our accepted news standards in order to print stories that we really do not consider news." What we are all after, he concluded, "is to cover the Negro community, as we do other communities, in the most meaningful and energetic way possible."

The memos and discussions did prompt us to search harder for those meaningful stories. Tom Johnson helped us focus on life in the black middle class—and we came up with a variety of news and features involving politics, society, health and hospitals, education and housing. And the word went out once again that we were looking for qualified staffers to cover black affairs.

In fact, we already had made some real progress. With Johnson still the only black reporter when I began as metropolitan editor, I urged him to conduct a far-reaching search. And to my great satisfaction, in short order he recommended four able black reporters. All four, not surprisingly, had had to struggle longer and harder than their white counterparts to achieve their journalistic credentials. They were all college-educated and already seasoned on other papers.

Earl Caldwell, at twenty-seven, made a dapper entrance into the city room. Wearing a gray flannel Brooks Brothers suit purchased for his inaugural day, he told me he wanted to write like Gay Talese, whom he saw as "larger than life." Caldwell had grown up in the tiny Pennsylvania mountain town of Clearfield, where as a youth he had worked on the local paper under the guidance of an avuncular white editor. After graduating from the University of Buffalo, he wrote for some small papers and then landed at the *Herald Tribune*. When the *Trib* folded, he went briefly to the *Post*.

Gerald Fraser came to us from the *Daily News*. Born in Boston in 1925, he attended the University of Wisconsin, where he had taken journalism courses, and eventually landed on the *Amsterdam News*. In 1963, when black reporters were in demand by white papers to cover the protests in the South, he was hired by the *News*.

Nancy Hicks's clearly written education stories in the *Post* about a complex, volatile situation had impressed me. She had majored in journalism at Long Island University and, at twenty-three, became the youngest reporter— and the first black woman—on our metropolitan staff. (She left *The Times* after her marriage to Robert Maynard, the well-respected *Washington Post* writer, and later publisher of the *Oakland Tribune*.)

The least experienced of the four was Rudy Johnson (no relation to Tom), who had graduated from Temple University with a major in journalism and left the *Newark Star-Ledger* to come to work for us. Tom Johnson assured me he was "sincere and eager," and was certain to grow in the job.

While there were to be additional black reporters on *The Times* in the next few years, the number would always be far from adequate. More blacks were graduating from journalism schools, but some of the most accomplished of them were drifting off to television.

Punch Sulzberger, in the years to come, never stopped putting pressure on every department of *The Times* to employ "more nonwhites." On April 8, 1968, he called a meeting of all company department heads. "The plain fact of the matter," he told us, "is that we have [been neither] as successful nor as active as we should have been in meeting even our minimum requirements . . . we have made too many excuses to ourselves for not doing enough. We now have to put excuses aside, even where there is a touch of validity to them, and work out a meaningful, effective plan of action. Each department head will be held responsible for the future record of his department and will be asked to come up with a practical timetable for his department's program."

And a year later, Punch offered specific guides to meet the goal of enabling "people who have been held back by prejuduce and poverty to earn and enjoy a decent life": develop our internal training programs and initiate new ones to assure equal opportunity and advancement; make sure when employees are hired they receive whatever help is needed to make the grade and that help be continued so that advancement to the top managerial and executive levels is open to all on an absolutely equal basis. "I want to ask all of you to accept a share of the responsibility," Punch said, "for making *The Times* the leader in providing equal opportunity for all."

APART FROM HIRING more black reporters, one of my goals was to rebuild the night rewrite battery. Specifically, I wanted to re-create the nine-member bank on which I'd once proudly served—nine reporters I could absolutely depend on, all of whom could turn out smooth copy under frenzied deadline pressure. I wanted experts who could not only write up stories from facts gathered by phone or morgue research, but also spruce up or even completely rewrite stories poorly assembled by our own reporters in the city room or filed from the field.

As a first move, in early February 1967, I transferred Michael Sterne to rewrite from the reportorial staff. He was an unflappable, quick-thinking former *World-Telegram* reporter whom I had gotten to know when we both appeared on the Channel Thirteen newscasts in 1963, during the 114-day strike. At Sterne's recommendation, I hired his former colleague on the *Telegram*, Sylvan Fox, at that time the only newspaper rewrite man to have ever been awarded a Pulitzer Prize.

He had won it for his story about the crash of a jetliner into Jamaica Bay on takeoff from Idlewild on March 1, 1962. All ninety-five people aboard were killed. From 10:00 A.M. to 5:15 P.M., when the afternoon paper closed for the day, Fox sifted through the avalanche of facts phoned into him from the crash site and wrote and rewrote the dramatic lead story for seven separate editions. Fox was promoted to city editor and, when the *World-Telegram* merged with the *Journal-American* and the *Herald Tribune* as the *World Journal Tribune* in 1966, he was asked to remain in his job—but without an increase in pay for additional duties. Believing that the new conglomerate, which anticipated a circulation of more than one million, was treating him badly, he walked out.

When I engaged him for rewrite, Fox had been working as deputy police commissioner in charge of press relations for several months. As was my custom with new recruits, I invited him to join me at the metropolitan desk for his first week, to get a sense of how the paper operated. But while he was seated next to me on his first day, February 14, a story broke with a most unusual twist.

A man who had robbed a bank was being chased by the police, when he got out of his car and ran into the tall grass of a vast Brooklyn marsh. It seemed he had made a successful getaway, until a police helicopter arrived. Using its rotor blades as a giant fan, the helicopter—in a scene straight out of

Hitchcock—swept the eight-foot-high grass apart, revealing the fugitive, who did not surrender until he'd been struck by four bullets. I told Fox to forget about orientation and get to work on the story, which was tailor-made for him. He scored a page-one byline on his very first day.

Empathizing with my goals, Fox suggested I hire Lawrence Van Gelder, a thirty-four-year-old star rewrite man on the *World Journal Tribune* during its brief life span. The Brooklyn-born Van Gelder had received degrees from Columbia College and Columbia Law School. He had always been interested in journalism, however. At fifteen, he tried to get a job as a *Times* copyboy but was told he was too young.

I gave the lion's share of fast-breaking stories to Fox, Van Gelder and a third ace rewrite man, Alben Krebs, who had earlier come over from the *Herald Tribune*, and each found himself on page one once or twice a week. One night, the three of them privately decided to show me how great they really were. When an AP bulletin announced that a crazed sniper was shooting at people in a Bronx neighborhood, I dispatched two general-assignment reporters to the scene. In the meantime, Fox, Van Gelder and Krebs set out to demonstrate they could construct a solid story about the sniper just by making phone calls from their desks; their aim was to complete the story before the two reporters had a chance to phone in their eyewitness accounts. Racing against time, the three called the police, storekeepers and residents of buildings in the neighborhood. By the time our two reporters in the Bronx called in, Fox, Van Gelder and Krebs had finished their collaboration on a lengthy story, jam-packed with colorful details that the reporters on the scene had been unable to gather.

The youngest member of the rewrite battery was Michael T. Kaufman, who had started on the paper as a gawky, chain-smoking copyboy, while still attending City College. He'd been promoted to reporter at twenty-two, a couple of weeks before Abe had replaced Frank Adams, and Abe, breaking the tradition of making a cub reporter sweat out months without a byline, signed his very first story. Mike began the story—about an imminent drought—with flair: "If more New Yorkers took showers instead of baths, shaved in still water and drank their whiskey neat, the prospects for the city's water supply would improve."

Kaufman often drew assignments in black neighborhoods, and once told me he had begun thinking of himself as a black reporter. Because of his own turbulent background, he understood what it felt like to be an outsider. Before the start of World War II, his parents, Polish Jews, fled to Paris, where

Michael was born in 1938; all of them managed to escape to New York two years later. In 1966, we transferred him from general reporter to the rewrite bank, where he sat in the last row, often deep in thought. Galvanized when Fox and Van Gelder joined the battery, he seized his share of good late-breaking stories, writing sensitively about people in all walks of life.

Always trying to enrich the battery still further, I eventually acquired Robert D. McFadden, an unrivaled Brooklyn police reporter, whom I brought to rewrite after Fox and Van Gelder kept leaving me notes extolling his leg-work. McFadden, who was born in Milwaukee, had started as a reporter with the *Cincinnati Enquirer* after graduating from the University of Wisconsin in 1960, but, a year later, he decided to take a copyboy's job at *The Times*. Within a year, he was promoted to reporter. Some years later, he became the second rewrite man on a New York paper to win a Pulitzer. Soon, with other such experienced additions as Linda Charlton from *Newsday*, rewrite had gained as much prestige as in the days when we called it "the most reliable bank in the world"—and at times even more.

I had plenty of time to plot stories and strategy with the rewrite staff since I often worked late to stay close to a breaking story. Sometimes, I stayed overnight at Bob Alden's elegant duplex apartment overlooking the East River, and I finally realized I could no longer live the life of a suburbanite. Barbara was eager to move back to Manhattan, and we began apartment hunting.

We found a spacious apartment on Broadway in the seventies that was inexpensive and in need of repair. There were many such apartments available on the Upper West Side because of the continuing middle-class flight to the suburbs. Much of the area was in decline, increasingly populated by SROs—single-room-occupancy buildings—and besieged by crime, litter, graffiti, addicts and panhandlers sleeping in doorways or on the sidewalks. It wasn't as bad as in Edith Wharton's New York, when hansom drivers refused to go to the West Side, but to some of my affluent friends, the West Side still represented risky, uncharted territory, and even trips to Zabar's at night were undertaken apprehensively.

A year or so after we moved in, we invited Mollie Parnis, the dress designer, who lived in a Park Avenue co-op, to a dinner party, and she asked Barbara to assure her it was safe to travel to the West Side after dark. Several of my neighbors had been mugged and I myself was once a target, confronted by a shady, nervous character demanding my money or my life. I snarled, "I'm an undercover cop!" and he fled.

Since life in the (relatively) raw was now right outside my door, I began assigning articles on West Side murders, assaults and robberies. Some reporters believed I was on a mission to prod the police into making my own neighborhood more secure. Sid Zion, in fact, announced to the staff that he planned moving near me, since he was certain the mayor would make my new neighborhood the safest in the city by stepping up police presence there. I didn't really mind that reporters felt at ease about twitting me, for I wanted, above all, not to be feared, as city editors often were. I realized, of course, that I wasn't going to be universally loved. What boss ever is?

John Kifner, while he was still a clerk, executed a bit of impudence that became office legend. One day, with news breaking and a stack of staff problems demanding quick solutions, I ordered my lunch sent in. Just as I took the first bite of my corned-beef sandwich, my secretary said I was urgently needed on the phone. I put the sandwich on top of the file cabinet that stood between her and me, and began a long phone conversation. While my secretary also got tied up on the phone, Kifner, thinking the sandwich was hers and aware of her good nature, ate it. When she noticed what he had done, she told him he had eaten the boss's sandwich. Kifner blanched. Had he jeopardized his pending promotion to reporter? When I finished talking on the phone, I reached for my lunch.

"Where's my sandwich?" I demanded of no one in particular.

"You ate it!" Kifner blurted out. Everyone liked Kifner and no one disputed him. I had been so preoccupied, I wasn't really sure whether I had eaten it or not. There was nothing to do but shrug and carry on.

MY FIRST SERIOUS STAFF PROBLEM as metropolitan editor involved a news clerk who was a magna cum laude Harvard graduate. He demonstrated reportorial potential whenever he assisted reporters in the field, and was soon ready for promotion. But within months of becoming a reporter, he began calling in sick, and one day I detected alcohol on his breath.

A few days later, when I again sensed alcohol, he said he'd had just one drink at lunch with fellow reporters. I kept a concerned eye on him and, two weeks later when I returned from an overnight trip, I found a memo from Bob Alden: "Jim was ill again last night. He was due in tonight at 4:00 P.M. It is now 5:15 and we haven't heard from him. There is no answer at his home. On Friday night, Pat Wallace [my news assistant] saw Jim walking in a heavy rain on his way to work, coatless and with his sleeves rolled up. 'He looked like he was on a trip,' Wallace said."

When Jim turned up in the city room a couple of days later, he admitted for the first time that he might have been drinking too much. I suggested he join Alcoholics Anonymous, but he insisted he wasn't an alcoholic and pleaded for another chance. A week later, after again calling in sick, he appeared in the city room with a welt under his eye and a bandage on his jaw. He claimed he had slipped and fallen, but he wasn't a good liar. I sought guidance from our visiting staff psychiatrist.

The psychiatrist, after interviewing Jim, told me: "By giving him chance after chance, you are playing the role of forgiving father and enabling his addiction. Alcoholics need to be dealt with firmly. In some cases, it's just sink or swim."

"What are you actually saying?" I asked.

"You need to fire him. You need to wake him up, make him see what he's doing to himself. He won't get well without treatment, and right now he doesn't think he needs any."

I had never fired anyone and, after some painful soul searching, I decided to follow his advice. I called Jim into my private office and cited the psychiatrist's reasoning. I was enormously relieved when Jim said he understood. Without a murmur of protest, he shook my hand and said good-bye.

The psychiatrist, it turned out, had been on target. Ten months later, Jim phoned. "I'm calling to thank you," he said. "I went home to my parents' in Texas and put myself into therapy. I haven't had a drink in seven months, and don't plan on ever having another." Six months later, he arrived in New York looking healthy and focused. He applied for a job at a publishing firm, and I gave him the recommendation he requested.

Although Jim failed as a reporter, the majority of my other clerks did me proud. Indeed, one of them, Russell Lewis, rose to be president of The New York Times Company. Russ started clerking for me at twenty, as part of a work-period program at his college. By the time he graduated from the State University at Stony Brook and Brooklyn Law School, he had determined where his future lay. Highly motivated but diffident, he was the only one of my clerks who dismissed the chance to be a reporter. But he was fond of newspapers and, after passing his bar exam, he stayed with *The Times*, joining its legal department and participating in cases involving freedom of the press. He kept moving up, and in 1996, Punch Sulzberger appointed him president of the company, overseeing a corporation big enough to be listed among Fortune's 500 leading businesses in the country.

Before becoming my clerk, Lesley Oelsner, like Russ Lewis, had studied law. She had grown up in the privileged Long Island community of Oyster

Bay, and her father expected a debutante's life for her. A graduate of Smith College, she decided to attend New York University Law School and then defied her father by becoming a newspaperwoman.

When Lesley proved herself smart enough to earn a three-week tryout as a reporter, I assigned her to follow Norman Mailer and Jimmy Breslin, who had entered the Democratic primary in 1969—Mailer seeking the mayoral candidacy and Breslin the presidency of the City Council. She wrote about Mailer's platform with tongue in cheek, as he held forth about statehood for New York City, a monorail around Manhattan, surrounding housing projects with giant sequoias, and supplying heroin to addicts who didn't volunteer for methadone treatment. She told me Mailer didn't pay much attention to her but Breslin was friendly. Lesley eventually earned one of the Washington bureau's top assignments—coverage of the Supreme Court.

Then there was Lacey Fosburgh, who, like Lesley, came from a well-to-do background. A graduate of Sarah Lawrence, she had spent two years in India on a Fulbright grant and spoke Hindi. From the moment she became a clerk on the metropolitan desk, she never stopped learning. Murray Schumach, in a salute to the meticulous way she researched her stories, called her "a female Peter Kihss." No one asked me more questions about reporting techniques than Lacey, and at times I felt I was running a journalism school just for her.

She was tall, with long blond hair and a flirtatious smile. The male reporters teased me for keeping her at my elbow for two full years. When I promoted her to reporter, she covered the police and the courts, and a few years later she went to San Francisco, where she married the writer David Harris, and where she reported on the bank robbery trial of Patricia Hearst after her kidnapping by the Symbionese Liberation Army.

My other female clerks who were eventually promoted to reporter included Barbara Campbell and Sandra Blakeslee. Born in St. Louis and a graduate of UCLA, Barbara enriched our growing contingent of black reporters. Sandra, a New Yorker, was a graduate of Berkeley and had spent a year with the Peace Corps in Borneo before coming to *The Times*. She was the daughter of Alton Blakeslee and granddaughter of Howard Blakeslee, both science writers for the AP. In the early 1970s, she became the third generation of Blakeslees to write about science.

Three of my male clerks ultimately distinguished themselves as foreign correspondents. Before going abroad, they covered a variety of beats on the metropolitan staff, including City Hall during the municipal financial crisis in 1975. Steve Weisman, raised in Los Angeles, was our college correspondent at Yale before becoming my clerk. Several years later, he made his mark covering politics, became chief of the Albany bureau and then headed the City Hall bureau. In 1982, he was appointed senior White House correspondent, and later reported from India and Japan. After returning to New York as deputy foreign editor, he joined the editorial board.

John Darnton was the son of Barney Darnton (who had lost his life as a *Times* correspondent in World War II). Darnton had acquired his quiet humor from his father, who, in a *Harper's* magazine article in 1937, coined the remark "Any man who hates dogs and babies can't be all bad"—a quotation wrongly attributed to W. C. Fields. Following stints on the metropolitan staff, he became a correspondent in Nigeria and Kenya and was then assigned to Poland, where his coverage won him the Pulitzer Prize in 1982. He went on to become metropolitan editor, London bureau chief and culture editor.

The clerk who reminded me somewhat of my enthusiastic younger self when I held that post under Wilson Fairbanks was David Shipler. Like Sandra Blakeslee, he was a third-generation journalist, his grandfather having worked for the *Boston Traveler* and his father for Time, Inc. A Dartmouth alumnus, he worked briefly as a clerk for Reston in Washington. I chose him to try a new step in our clerical training program, and promoted him to the newly created category of "reporter on trial," to write the daily News Summary. He quickly measured up under deadline pressure and I soon promoted him again, this time to reporter.

I put him on the housing beat, where his life was threatened when he began looking into a pattern of bribes paid by builders to city inspectors and the police. He was later assigned to the Saigon bureau and then to Moscow, where he and the bureau chief, Christopher Wren, became my guides when I visited them in 1976. We successfully eluded KGB agents and, aware that Shipler's and Wren's apartments were bugged, we never mentioned aloud the names of any nonovert dissidents. Every night, when we made plans to meet the dissidents the next day, we communicated by means of a "magic slate," the children's toy on which written messages could be quickly made to vanish.

In 1987, after heading the Jerusalem bureau, David won the Pulitzer for his book *Arab and Jew: Wounded Spirits in a Promised Land.* (Abe Rosenthal prided himself on having lifted a barrier when he assigned David to Israel. He told Joe Lelyveld, then deputy foreign editor, how delighted he was finally to be sending a Jew to cover Israel. "But I thought we were sending Shipler," said a puzzled Lelyveld. It was only then that Abe learned Shipler was, in fact, a Protestant.)

I have saved Deirdre Carmody for last. Not a clerk on my desk, she was the secretary I inherited from Abe Rosenthal. But she, too, eventually proved herself as a reporter. Deirdre was born in New Haven, Connecticut. Her Irish Catholic father, a successful lawyer, was delighted when she told him she wanted to be a journalist. But when she applied at the *Times* personnel department, she was told the only job available was in the pool of women secretaries. And she was warned: "If you think this will lead to a reporter's job, don't dream of it."

"Women were so stigmatized," Deirdre later told me, "that even the bottom rung of the ladder was above our heads." After she had spent several months as my secretary, I promoted her to reporter. She turned out to be a natural writer, whose stories sparkled with adroit phrases. I gave her an aisle desk in the city room and, in June of 1968, she married a reporter who sat nearby—Peter Millones (who later rose to metropolitan editor and assistant managing editor).

While tensions often ran high around the metropolitan desk, there was always time for levity. Israel Shenker, whom I had hired from *Time* magazine, was, without doubt, the funniest man in the city room, a hilarious match for his friend Zero Mostel, whom he liked to write about. Shenker's specialty was interviewing literary figures, and getting to be one of his subjects was considered a great achievement in the publishing world. He sat in the last row of the room, and whenever he was summoned by microphone to my desk for his assignment, he entertained me with a sly smile and piercing, on-target jibes at entrenched *Times* bureaucracy and red tape. During a periodical austerity kick, the assistant managing editor in charge of budgets warned me that Shenker's expense accounts were becoming exorbitant, and that Abe thought I should remind him that *The Times* wasn't *Time*, where even emergency visits to shrinks were sometimes put on expense accounts.

I asked my new secretary, Linda Feinfeld, to summon Shenker to the desk, and, despite her later denials, I knew she must have tipped him off earlier in the day as to what to expect. I pointed to one entry in his expense account, listing a dinner with the novelist Bernard Malamud at La Grenouille.

"Why did you have to interview Malamud at one of the city's most expensive restaurants?" I asked.

Shenker held a number of hand-printed flash cards. Without saying a word, he shuffled through the cards and thrust up his answer: "Mrs. Malamud chose the restaurant."

"Why did you have to take Mrs. Malamud on the interview?" I continued, by now aware I was acting as his straight man.

Shenker chose another card: "Mrs. Malamud likes to eat."

"And what led you to order such a pricey bottle of wine?"

Shenker's card: "It seemed like a good idea at the time."

And so it went. "You win," I finally said, and sent him and his flash cards back to his desk. Abe heard about my interrogation and decided to ask me a few questions of his own:

The management has decided to conduct a test to determine the precise degree of ignorance about foreign affairs among senior editors of the metropolitan desk. Would you, therefore, please answer the following examination:

1. Name three Cambodian generals whose last names begin with G.
2. In what year did the governor of North Bengal say to the governor of South Bengal: "It is a long time between Chappatis"?
3. Who are Chappatis?
4. Who was the greatest foreign correspondent in India for The New York Times between Robert Trumbull and Elie Abel?
5. Write a 4,000-word essay justifying your answer to Question 4.
6. Expand on Question 5 for another 3,000 words.
7. Hong Kong is the son of King Kong. True or false.
8. What is the capital of France?
9. Put the answer to Question 8 in dollars.
10. In what year did the First Secretary of the North Ukraine say to the First Secretary of the South Ukraine: "It is a long time between pirojki"?
11. Why do you move your lips when you read?

I answered:

1. Min Ho Ghelb, Ursa Gelba, Chu V'an Gleb.
2. The same year that Lee J. Shubert said to David Belasco: "If they can do the Passion Play in Oberammergau, we can do it on Rivington Street."
3. Thought you'd catch me on that one, didn't you? It's not "who." It's "what"; Chappatis are Mexican house slippers.
4. That's a toughie. I think it was A. M. Weiler, but it might have been A. M. Raskin. Anyway, I know it wasn't an Irishman.

5. I'm working on it. You'll have it no later than a year from today.
6. O.K.
7. False. King Kong is the grandson. Viet Kong is the son.
8. De Gaulle.
9. $$$$$$$.
10. The same year that Lee J. Shubert said to David Belasco: "Why didn't you tell me Rivington Street was a Jewish neighborhood?"
11. Because I'm hungry.

In the early summer of 1967, with my staff basically in place six months into my tenure as metropolitan editor, *The Times* began a grand experiment to which I was asked to devote part of my time—the production of an afternoon newspaper. When the *World Journal Tribune* ceased to exist in 1966 (after its brief merger following the collapse of the *Herald Tribune*), the only remaining afternoon newspaper was the *Post*. Punch Sulzberger was interested in marketing a competing afternoon paper, one with the same standards as *The Times* but with a more relaxed personality. While the business side conducted market analyses and reckoned costs, Abe was entrusted with the creation of a prototype.

It was Abe's first major undertaking as assistant managing editor and, in addition to me, he called upon several *Times* editors to help him, including Larry Hauck, one of the stalwart bullpen editors; George Cowan, the veteran art director; John Morris, the newly hired picture editor; Henry Lieberman, the science editor; Mitchel Levitas, a young editor on the Sunday *Magazine*; and James Greenfield, an old friend of Abe's who had recently joined my desk as an assistant metropolitan editor.

Punch had suggested that Abe recruit Lou Silverstein, the promotion art director whose cherubic features alternately expressed worry and joy, and who turned out to be a crucial element in our efforts to produce the prototype. Since Silverstein's regular job was in the promotional rather than the news area of *The Times*, Abe saw him as a dilettante. He chose to ignore Silverstein's brilliant series of ads about *Times* personalities in *The New Yorker*, and dismissed the fact that Punch occasionally assigned him to special tasks for the newspaper itself. Earlier that year, for example, Silverstein had suggested changing the paper's body type from eight point ideal to eight and a half point imperial, which made the type not only bigger but more legible. At the same time, he had also spruced up the top of page one, recommending more forceful lettering for the Old English nameplate, the dropping of the period after the logo and the elimination of rules around the page-one weather box.

Born in Brooklyn in 1919, Silverstein was nine when he earned his first plaudits for his art—portraits of neighbors drawn in chalk on the sidewalk outside his father's grocery store. After graduating from Pratt Institute, he worked for a milk company in Jersey City, where he designed a series of surrealistic bottle caps that became collectors' items. He later worked as art director for a book advertising agency in Manhattan, but gave up the well-paying job to study modern design. In 1949 and 1950, he enrolled at the New Bauhaus in Chicago under László Moholy-Nagy, one of the most influential figures in the modern art movement. With his newly acquired knowledge, Silverstein joined *The Times* in 1952.

Punch asked him to come up with a design for page one of the afternoon paper. Bauhaus on his mind, Silverstein concocted a page that was revolutionary—made up of different-sized headlines stacked in stepladder formation across six columns. Punch told him he liked the general approach, but Abe scorned it as "unrealistic" and lacking "the feel of a newspaper."

Abe warned me to be wary of taking cues from "an ivory-tower artist like Silverstein." What did an artist know about making up a newspaper under deadline pressure? What did he know about the technique, acquired by years of city-room experience, of balancing space for stories and headlines? Why would a newspaper need the makeup frills being suggested by an artist? Silverstein kept proposing ideas and Abe kept rejecting them. At one point, Abe became so fed up with his suggestions that, in mock fright, he crouched under his desk to hide from him.

Silverstein had designed *The New Yorker* ad about Abe when he won the Pulitzer, but had not met him at the time. Silverstein had kept his distance from the city room; although he was justifiably confident as an artist, he was, at first, tentative in dealing with the powers on the third floor. But after a while Abe and Silverstein began listening to and learning from one another. I also saw Silverstein in a new light, becoming gradually aware that his innovative designs had the touch of genius, even though they required modification at times. In the end, Abe often let Silverstein have his way—and Abe, Lou and I were to become partners in numerous design projects in the years to come.

All of us on the afternoon project, which we first christened *New York Today* and, finally, *The New York Forum*, worked together in the eleventh-floor club room with the doors locked and hallway windows covered, keeping all operations confidential. I moved back and forth between our newspaper laboratory and the metropolitan desk. One day Abe told me that if the afternoon paper became a reality with him as editor, he'd like me to be his next-in-command. I wasn't quite sure about that idea, since I loved being metropolitan editor of *The Times* and felt I was just getting warmed up.

The look of the forty-page prototype, under Silverstein's artistic guidance, was a considerable departure from the traditions of *The Times*. To begin with, we used six columns instead of eight, and eliminated the rules between them. The first two inside pages were advertisement-free. More air was provided around the headlines. Teaser heads were introduced. The type itself was not as dense. In fact, the entire layout was lighter, leading to freer, less crowded pages. Stories tended to be shorter and pictures were big and prominently displayed.

We produced two pilot issues. For the first press run in mid-July, Abe, Silverstein and I stayed up until 4:00 A.M. to await the first copies of *New York Today*, which we proudly fondled, still warm off the press. Except for Abe's and mine all twenty copies were destroyed after being shown the next day to members of the top brass. For a second run on September 1, forty-five copies of the retitled *The New York Forum* were printed at 5:30 A.M., in what I believe was the most clandestine press operation in *Times* history. Each copy was numbered and carefully tracked while being examined by Punch and his chief aides. Abe had stated the paper's philosophy on the editorial page:

"The essence of metropolitan New York, its tastes and texture, is the stimulation of variety—variety of peoples, enterprise and talent, and variety of information, opinion and thought. And yet the daily press in New York, the mirror that should reflect and the voice that should express that variety, has itself lost much of the richness that goes with the mixture, has been thinned out to the point where only two morning newspapers exist and only one in the afternoon.

"We believe, on *The New York Times,* that this has lessened the vitality of our city, weakened it economically and intellectually. And we believe therefore that it is bad, too, for *The Times*, for we are an organization that draws its sustenance and spirit from the health of the community in which we publish. Beginning today, *The Times* will publish an afternoon newspaper, in an attempt to fill what we take to be an important gap in our metropolitan life."

Abe continued to work on improving his offspring until early fall, when we received the disappointing news that there would, after all, be no *New*

York Forum. Punch had decided the costs and logistics of producing two newspapers would be prohibitive.

My own belief was that Punch had grown concerned over the probability of losing Abe and other important members of *The Times* to the *Forum*, and leaching talent from the parental paper. But we didn't waste the innovations in style and content that we tested; they were later incorporated into *The Times* itself, and can be found throughout the paper today.

THIRTY-SEVEN

IN JULY OF 1967, shortly before the *Forum* was laid to rest, Clif Daniel invited me to lunch at Sardi's to give me the disconcerting news that Joe Herzberg would soon be leaving his job as culture editor. Clif said that Joe, not feeling well and wanting to take life easier, had proposed a new assignment for himself. From time to time, he would write about academic trends, visiting campuses from coast to coast.

My first unhappy thought was that Clif would ask me to give up the metropolitan desk and go back to culture. Instead, to my pleased astonishment, he offered me command of the culture department—in *addition* to running the metropolitan desk.

"I think it'll work out well for the paper and that you'll find it more a joy than a burden," he assured me. He suggested I move an assistant metropolitan editor to the culture department as my deputy to carry out my ideas for coverage, and asked me to be prepared to take over the culture desk within the week. On July 11, he sent a memo informing the culture department that it would henceforth be under the jurisdiction of the metropolitan desk, adding, "The metropolitan editor, Arthur Gelb, is, of course, a former member of the cultural news department and is fully familiar with its affairs."

Clif and I had a long-established rapport about cultural coverage, and we often discussed ongoing developments in the arts. In 1965, while I was as yet Abe's deputy on the metropolitan desk, Clif expressed his distress about the slippage of our drama reviews since Brooks Atkinson's departure as critic. Toward the end of that year, Daniel, Catledge and Herzberg had grown dissatisfied with Howard Taubman and found an opportune way to replace him. Since Brooks had just reached mandatory retirement at sixty-five, Taub-man was transferred to his "Critic at Large" column. On January 1, 1966, Stanley Kauffmann, film critic and contributing editor at *The New Republic* since 1958, was hired to succeed Taubman as drama critic. That, as it happened, turned out to be a less felicitous choice for *The Times* than Taubman.

Accustomed to the pace of a weekly magazine, Kauffmann faced difficulties in meeting the traditional first-night deadline. As edition times had been gradually pushed ahead to meet the paper's growing circulation and production needs, the critic's last paragraph had to clear the copy desk by 11:30—which meant he sometimes had less than an hour to write his review.

"The European practice of the critic going to the last dress rehearsal has never changed," argued Kauffmann. "It is better for the play because the review gets much fuller consideration. It is better for the public. Who loses? Nobody." After much interoffice wrangling and to the chagrin of Broadway producers and critics from competing publications and from television, he obtained permission from Daniel to review a show's final preview and withhold publication for a day, which would give him twenty-four additional hours for "fuller consideration."

Many producers, directors and actors complained, since they believed the glamour of opening nights would be seriously impaired without the *Times* critic in an aisle seat and without competing critics, who were bound to follow our lead. But only David Merrick, the most contentious of Broadway producers, did anything about it.

Nothing Merrick did could really surprise us any longer, but in this case he was truly inventive. Six weeks after Kauffmann's appointment, Merrick's office sent him tickets to the final preview of his production of Brian Friel's *Philadelphia, Here I Come!* In the envelope was a note that read, "At your peril." Kauffmann found out what that meant when he arrived for the eight-o'clock performance.

Moments before the curtain was to rise, all the lights in the house went dark. Merrick announced from the stage that a rat had become stuck in the generator, knocking out the electrical system and canceling the performance. All the papers, including *The Times*, gave the story prominent display, and Kauffmann had no choice but to return the following night to review the opening performance with all the other critics, who had a satisfying laugh at his expense.

This sour beginning alone was not enough to turn Daniel, Catledge and Herzberg against Kauffmann. Catledge eventually concluded, however, that Kauffmann was overly academic for a daily newspaper. Questioning whether he really had his heart in reviewing Broadway theater, Catledge told Daniel and Herzberg that as far as he was concerned, an adequate replacement for Atkinson had yet to be found. In late spring, Daniel asked me if I was still interested in being drama critic. But by this time, I told him, I was finding my job as deputy metropolitan editor more rewarding than anything I had ever done. I still loved the theater, but what I really looked forward to was succeeding Abe as metropolitan editor. He said he understood.

An ideal drama critic was found when the *Herald Tribune* folded that summer. Catledge, with Punch's hearty approval, wasted no time in going after Walter Kerr. The esteemed fifty-three-year-old critic, who had worked at the *Trib* for fifteen years, accepted Catledge's offer—and Kauffmann was welcomed back to *The New Republic*. I called Brooks to share the happy news, and we agreed it was a momentous move for both *The Times* and the theater. When Walter began reviewing at the start of the new season, it was universally acknowledged that the paper had at last engaged a worthy successor to Brooks.

Kerr, at thirteen, had demonstrated his affinity for criticism when he wrote a weekly column about the movies, "Junior Film Fans," for the Evanston, Illinois, *Review*. A few years later, for other publications, he added theater criticism. After graduating from Northwestern University in 1937, he joined the newly organized drama department at Catholic University in Washington. As a professor, he wrote and staged shows there and then wrote and staged Broadway productions, at times in collaboration with his clever wife, Jean, who had been his student.

Kerr had accepted *The Times*'s offer on the condition that after a year of reviewing for the daily paper he'd be allowed to write exclusively for the Sunday Drama Section and would hand over the daily stint to another critic. Over dinner one night, he told me he was growing weary of the first-night ritual and wanted more leisure time. He also argued that since there was no longer a competing *Tribune* critic, an additional voice on *The Times* would be a salutary move. In a note to Catledge, he wrote, "It might be very valuable for *The Times* to become the vital center of debate through having at least two separate opinions, one daily, one Sunday." I found myself agreeing with Walter, even though his point was essentially the same as that expressed by Paddy Chayefsky's group when they had come to see me several years earlier. Chayefsky, however, had suggested two daily critics side by side.

Like Brooks, Walter was the heart, soul and brain of what newspaper theater criticism should be (and, in later years, I felt the same way about Frank Rich, whom I had lured away from *Time* magazine). He was a critic of such integrity, literary style and far-reaching theater knowledge that he was incapable of writing a review that wasn't worth reading—whether you agreed with him or not.

Acting on Clif Daniel's advice after our lunch at Sardi's, I began thinking of possible candidates for my deputy in the culture department. I decided on Don Forst, whom I had recently recruited to work along with George Barrett and Bill Luce on previewing incoming copy. Now in his early thirties, he had been national editor and executive news editor of the *Herald Tribune* and I had found him likable, responsive and quickly able to assess the merits of a story. Reporters appreciated his good-humored candor and his astute suggestions for improving their copy.

Forst was understandably surprised by the impending changes. I told him I was going to break the news to the culture staff that afternoon to avoid rumors in the city room. I also wanted to put a lid on gossip that was sure to appear in *The Village Voice*, which kept a watchful—and often nasty—eye on behind-the-scenes Kremlinology of *The Times*.

At my request, all the critics left their typewriters for my announcement, and I introduced Forst and assured them that he and I would see to it that their copy received careful handling and good display in the paper. Among those present was Clive Barnes, who in addition to serving as chief dance critic had been sharing the drama beat with Walter Kerr for the past few months. Kerr, after writing daily drama criticism for about a year (as originally agreed), was now the Sunday drama critic. As part of the new arrangement, Barnes became both drama and dance critic for the daily paper.

Barnes, short and somewhat paunchy, was funny and good-natured. Born in London, he attended Oxford and liked playing rugby and cricket. His speech was rapid, and he wrote at high speed as well. He managed to see two Off Broadway performances on Saturdays and two Off Broadway or ballet performances on Sundays, as well as two on Wednesdays (one of them usually a long-running Broadway show for re-review) and one every other night of the week. Soon, Barnes's opinions began to dominate, overshadowing even those of Walter Kerr, since the daily review, rather than Sunday's, seemed to wield a unique power in theater circles. To ease Barnes's workload, I assigned Paul Gardner, the young critic who had "discovered" Bill Cosby, to help with theater reviewing. I hired Mel Gussow from *Newsweek* for the same purpose, and Anna Kisselgoff, a freelance critic in Paris and New York, to assist in reviewing dance.

Barnes's physical opposite in the culture department was John Canaday, the tall, slim, patrician art critic, who once affectionately wrote of Barnes,

"His hair tosses around with a life of its own, his eyes roll and he heaves and surges all over like the Universe." *Times* readers were—rightly—highly respectful of the authoritative Canaday, who with a laudatory review could lure crowds to exhibits, especially at the Metropolitan Museum of Art and the Museum of Modern Art.

Canaday stirred up controversy from his very first review as a *Times* critic. On September 6, 1959, he bravely took on the abstract expressionists. "In the most wonderful and terrible time of history," he wrote, "the abstract expressionists have responded with the narrowest and most lopsided art on record. Never have painters found so little in so much." And never had *The Times* been inundated with so many irate letters from abstract expressionists. Canaday and the paper's second-string art critic, Hilton Kramer, were an unmatchable pair. Kramer possessed one of the most intellectually gifted minds at *The Times*, and was equally at home in the literary world.

Harold C. Schonberg, the music critic, and his later deputy, Donal Henahan, who both were to win Pulitzer Prizes, were a powerhouse combination. And also influential was the later daily book-reviewing team of Christopher Lehmann-Haupt and John Leonard, who moved downstairs from the Sunday *Book Review*. Along with Ada Louise Huxtable and Jack Gould (and his aide, Dick Shepard, who had transferred to television from ship news), they formed a crack cultural assemblage.

Even Bosley Crowther, nearing retirement age as film critic, had had enormous influence on moviemaking during his twenty-seven years on the job—as to some extent had my old friend, the movie editor Abe Weiler, now being assisted by Vincent Canby, a recent hire from *Variety*.

Since I was no stranger to the staff, having worked alongside nearly all the critics during my years in the culture department, the change didn't seem to faze them. Because of my cultural contacts I sometimes came across news developments and story ideas in the arts, and I shared with my staff the leads I picked up at the theater and at concerts, gallery openings, movie previews and dinner parties.

One particular story idea I came up with backfired embarrassingly, however. At a small dinner party, I had been seated next to Wanda Horowitz, who was not only married to Vladimir Horowitz but also happened to be Arturo Toscanini's daughter. Wanda was an irascible woman with a stinging tongue, feared by all of Horowitz's friends. She and I, however, seemed to get on quite well—mainly, I figured, because she respected *The Times* and Harold Schonberg.

I encouraged her to talk about her father and husband, which she never did publicly. Toward the end of the evening, she began complaining about the difficulties she'd endured in catering to two of the music world's most demanding geniuses. I urged her to allow *The Times* to interview her, and she finally agreed—but only if Schonberg would do the story.

The next day, when I told Harold of my coup, he was thrilled. He invited Wanda to lunch at the Algonquin. A couple of hours later, Harold appeared at my desk, looking shaken. "You've just put me through a horrible experience," he said. It appeared that during the interview, Wanda suddenly had a fit. "Why am I talking to you about the miserable life I've been through with those two men!" she shrieked. "They ruined my life and they should roast in hell!" Harold felt like crawling under the table. Pulling himself together, he ushered her into a taxi. He never did get the rest of the interview.

When I introduced Don Forst to the culture department, his welcome seemed assured. Everyone appreciated his irreverent humor and editing skills. Don and I kept in close touch daily and together came up with solutions to knotty problems, such as one presented by Clive Barnes.

Barnes, who clearly enjoyed all aspects of the theater, approved of the nudity in *Hair*, maintaining pornography had redeeming social value. Upon returning from one unabashedly carnal Off Broadway play, he told Don Forst that the male character offered the female character oral sex and, since the act was important to the plot's dénouement, he was searching for an appropriate way to describe it. (It must be recalled that language in those days was much more restricted than in later years.)

"How about the word 'cunnilingus'?" Forst suggested.

"I don't even know how to spell it," replied Barnes. Neither did Forst.

They called *The Times*'s medical department, which gave them the proper spelling. Then they called me to ask whether I thought there would be a problem with the bullpen. Abe happened to be at my desk and I laughingly posed the question, knowing he was always willing to engage in a provocative conversation about sex. We strolled over to where Forst and Barnes were as yet weighing the situation, and Abe offered an alternative: "How about calling it 'an act of affection'?"

Forst said he didn't think that was quite accurate.

"Why don't you call it 'an unnatural act'?" I proposed, somewhat naively, I fear.

"Maybe it is in your set," Forst shot back, "but it isn't in mine."

He urged us to go with "cunnilingus," and Abe said, "No one will know what it means."

"Then it will do them no harm," countered Forst, "and if they look it up, then we've educated somebody." We couldn't argue with that logic, and gave Barnes the go-ahead, a major breakthrough in *Times* usage.

Very soon after I took charge of the culture department, Turner Catledge invited me to his new executive editor's office. He began the conversation by asking what I thought of the Elizabeth Taylor–Richard Burton movie *Cleopatra*. I had a suspicion of what he was leading up to. I answered that I agreed with most of my intelligent friends that the film, a target of ridicule ever since it had opened four years earlier, was a travesty of Hollywood excess and that Bosley's extravagant praise must have been an aberration. I told Turner I remembered counting all the glowing adjectives in Bosley's review: three "brilliant," three "exciting," one "tremendous," one "extraordinary" and one "memorable."

Turner smiled in agreement. "Now, what did you think of *Bonnie and Clyde*?" he asked. I said I thought the film, which had opened only a few weeks before with Warren Beatty and Faye Dunaway, was a clever and quite riveting departure from the typical Hollywood gangland movie.

"Then," said Turner, who had clips of both reviews on his desk, "how do we account to readers for our critic's rave about *Cleopatra*, and his pan of *Bonnie and Clyde* as 'a cheap piece of bald-faced slapstick comedy' and as 'pointless and lacking in taste'?"

Turner said he didn't believe the rumors that Bosley tried to protect the big studios like 20th Century–Fox. "I think he's just simply tired after doing the same thing all these years," he went on. "He's sixty-three, you know. Times are changing and we have to change, too."

When I said I would find it painful to have to urge a veteran like Bosley to step aside, Turner said he would deliver the news himself. He would offer Bosley a delightful new job—traveling to international film festivals and reporting on happenings in the industry all over the world. "But there's something I expect you to do right away," he said. "Find us a young critic with a keen and witty mind who will change our static way of doing movie criticism."

I had been following Renata Adler's writing in *The New Yorker* ever since Berrie had introduced her to William Shawn in 1962. Berrie had met her through his son, David. Barbara and I both were enchanted with Renata when David brought her to our old Eighty-sixth Street apartment and she asked to borrow our ten-year-old Michael to accompany them on a visit to the Central Park Zoo so Renata could quote him for a "Talk of the Town" piece.

With her tall, slender figure, her pale oval face and her dark brown hair wound around her head in a thick braid, Renata reminded me of a Modigliani. She seemed to flit breathlessly in and out of our lives and there was always a sense of mystery about her, like a character in a Muriel Spark novel. At twenty-nine, she had become one of Shawn's protégés. She had reviewed books for a time and reported on a wide range of subjects—from Vietnam, Israel's Six-Day War and the Selma march, to the popularity of group therapy and pop music. She was hardly a seasoned film critic, having reviewed only a few movies, but the quality of her literary criticism convinced me she could bring the appraisal of films into a new realm of perceptivity.

Catledge, Daniel, Salisbury and Abe all agreed she was a good prospect and suggested I engage her on a four-month trial basis. When I offered her the job, she expressed concern about being able to meet so many deadlines, so quickly. But I explained that most movies were previewed days in advance. She said she'd like to talk over the offer with Shawn. What clinched her decision was Shawn's assurance that she would always have a place on *The New Yorker* if she decided to return.

Renata's reign as movie critic marked a highly controversial period in *The Times*'s cultural coverage. She did not hesitate to speak out about what she saw as Hollywood's shoddy standards and phoniness, and the industry snapped back. Actually, Hollywood first began worrying when, a few days before her initial review on January 4, she told *Newsweek* she didn't approve of excessive violence in movies, disclosing she had walked out during the bloody shower scene in *Psycho*. "I have a problem about horror movies that I suppose I will have to get over," she said.

What she felt no need to get over was her dislike of gratuitous screen sex. In her first review, of a film called *The Wicked Dreams of Paula Schultz*, about an East German Olympic star (Elke Sommer) who escapes from a lecherous East German propaganda minister (Werner Klemperer), Renata wrote quirkily that it was "unrelievedly awful in such a number of uninteresting ways." It seemed, she added, "to view the cold war as a vast conspiracy to get people undressed as clumsily and joylessly as possible. In various scenes Miss Sommer has her sweatshirt removed by the weight of some medals on her front, her bathrobe drawn off by a vacuum cleaner . . . and so on."

No film critic for a major paper was as relentlessly tough as Renata. On January 7, as I was certain she would, she lashed out at the violence in two box-office hits, *In Cold Blood* and—most particularly—*The Dirty Dozen*, of which she wrote: "I don't think dwelling on pain or damage to the human body in the film's literal terms can ever be morally or artistically valid."

Even when, now and then, she found herself able to praise a film, she husbanded her adjectives. While she had positive things to say about Mel Brooks's *The Producers* and Stanley Kubrick's *2001: A Space Odyssey*, she wasn't exactly lavish with her praise. Of *The Producers* she wrote, "Some of it is shoddy and gross and cruel; the rest is funny in an entirely unexpected way." As for *2001*, she called it "somewhere between hypnotic and immensely boring."

Renata reserved her harshest criticism for Hollywood at its most extravagant. She lambasted *Funny Girl* as a launching pad for Barbra Streisand: "Almost every shot is held too long, every pointless scene is interminable, sometimes shots are held just to let you know the scene has come to an end."

Accusations flew from the coast that *The Times* had hired a critic who hated movies. On March 22, 1968, United Artists ran a full-page ad in our paper: "Renata Adler of *The New York Times* did not like *In Cold Blood*. She had reservations about *The Graduate, Guess Who's Coming to Dinner?* and *Planet of the Apes*. We're not quite sure how she felt about *Bonnie and Clyde*. [She liked it, despite its violence.] The majority of other critics liked them. Most of all, the public likes them. Now she doesn't like *Here We Go Round the Mulberry Bush*. What a recommendation!"

Renata replied by way of *Newsweek*: "I like movies and I like bad movies but that doesn't mean I have to say they're good. I'm not supposed to be drumming up trade for movies that I like or closing down movies that I don't like." And I told *Newsweek* that Renata had been receiving a lot of fan mail and that "now, and for the foreseeable future, she is our movie critic."

But while standing her ground against mounting industry vitriol, Renata began to find the job had drawbacks at *The Times* itself. She complained to me that the copyediting of her reviews was picayune. As much as I tried to protect her copy, I found there were times when questions about a word or phrase had legitimacy. Don Forst argued that she was sometimes obscure, and tended to forget that we were a paper for the general public, not for film scholars. Though I'd patiently try to work out a compromise when the disputed matter was brought to my attention, Renata's determination to ward off what she called "meddling" finally proved too much for Forst.

I turned over responsibility for her copy to Marvin Siegel, the most adept of the culture line editors. Siegel had recently joined the paper from the *World-Telegram & Sun* and was, I knew, a lifelong movie buff. Renata's copy continued to stretch the boundaries. Once, for example, to achieve the proper mood, she smoked pot before watching the Beatles' *Yellow Submarine*. "It is the perfect film, I think, for children," she wrote in one of her analyses of the movie, "never terrifying, often funny, sometimes inspired and yet (or maybe, and so), there is the matter of pot. There is no question that *Yellow Submarine* (and a lot of totally undistinguished movies, like the Monkees' recent *Head*) are to a certain extent informed by marijuana, and that regardless of what its legal implications are, its aesthetic importance is becoming more than marginal. That sense of perception washed clean . . . is certainly accessible to people who are not high, but in an overstimulated urban environment, probably rarely."

Emotionally exhausted after fourteen months and 179 reviews and articles in *The Times*, Renata told me she wanted to return to *The New Yorker*. She left with an urgent plea: "There's someone who can do this job as well as I can, and will enjoy doing it—Vincent Canby." I didn't disagree. Ever since he came to the paper from *Variety*, I thought he could someday be the lead critic. But I regretted Renata's departure, and thanked her for the gift she had given us—paving the way for her successor to write as boldly as he pleased, to feel free to thumb his nose at Hollywood's sacred traditions, assured of having the paper's support.

I phoned Vincent on St. Martin, where he was vacationing. "Vincent, you have the job, you have it!" I said, neglecting, in my enthusiasm, to mention that Renata was leaving. Vincent, a modest, quiet man, didn't respond. "Isn't that wonderful!" I exclaimed. Finally, he murmured a word or two that I took for approval. "When you get back next week," I said, "we'll have lunch and talk about it." About an hour later, Vincent called back. "Arthur," he said, cool and gentlemanly as always. "I've been thinking about your call. Would you kindly tell me, what is the job you say I've got?"

It wasn't long before Vincent's incisiveness, understanding and humor took our movie criticism a giant step ahead, and he soon became the dean of the country's film critics. He was among the first to hail Woody Allen's originality as a filmmaker and to recognize the poetic genius of François Truffaut. Nothing pleased him more than when Truffaut called him *"un être poétique."* He never allowed personal enmity—and certainly not friendship—to sway his judgment. And sometimes people he didn't like came off better in his reviews than those he did. He loved literature—the novelist William Styron, who had been his classmate at a boarding school in Virginia, said that Vincent had introduced him to E. B. White and Hemingway—and he hated to see language used badly. Once, when he was told an author he didn't like was writing a biography of a show-biz bigwig, his comment was, "Wow, one illiterate writing about another."

ON SEPTEMBER 11, 1967, just two months after Clif Daniel had put me in charge of the culture department, I received a letter from him while I was vacationing with my family on Cape Cod. He wanted me, together with John Morris, the picture editor, to take over the planning of Second Front layouts "fairly soon" after my return.

So that I'd be clear about why he was relieving Ted Bernstein of responsibility for the Second Front, Daniel also sent me a copy of a ground-breaking memo he had written to Bernstein on August 31. In it, Daniel reminded Bernstein that three months earlier he had requested that the Second Front become a page "built around picture layouts proposed by the picture editor in collaboration with other editors" and that "preference should be given to city and suburban subjects." National and international subjects, he added, might be used "in special circumstances."

Daniel's memo to Bernstein went on to express bluntly his annoyance: "It seems to me that the intent of this paragraph has not been fully realized. . . . In the future, I want to give responsibilities for laying out the Second Front to the picture editor and the metropolitan editor. They can consult other desks if national or international subjects are to be used. This new procedure should not be inaugurated until Arthur Gelb returns from his vacation."

Not only was I to be in charge of the Second Front, but my authority as metropolitan editor was being extended to permit me to choose stories for that page from the advance assignment menu of other desks—an inviolate prerogative that up to now had belonged solely to Bernstein's bullpen. I was aware, of course, that Bernstein and the bullpen editors who had preceded him did not regard photos as an essential ingredient in making up the paper, but no one, until Daniel, had ever questioned their authority in the selection process. Since Ted had been an important influence in my career, I felt sorry for the humiliation that the change would put him through, especially in view of the fact that Daniel had informed him he was sending me a copy of the August 31 memo.

Instead of returning to work on Monday, September 18, as planned, I called Daniel to say I would be back on the Thursday before, since I was eager to start work on the Second Front right away. That was okay with him, and he suggested we have lunch on Thursday at Sardi's so he could brief me further.

At lunch, he told me his decision was based partly on his approval of the way the metropolitan report was progressing and on what Abe had told him of the new ideas I had proposed for the *Forum*. Urging me to eliminate from the Second Front the mishmash of short, routine, often trivial, stories, he suggested my goal should be to turn the page into a "journalistic showcase." He wanted especially to see well-written stories about "the high life and low life of the city." He wanted subjects on the page that were wrenching, ironic.

What he sought above all was a page on which, when he himself turned to it every morning, he would discover a stylish layout illustrating an unexpected theme. "As a reader, I want you to surprise me," Daniel said. The only obstacle in planning layouts, he cautioned, was that the publisher wanted the News Summary and Index to remain situated at the bottom of the page, running across six of eight columns. "You'll have to find ways of working around that," he said. (More than a decade later, the News Summary was moved to page two.)

I listened raptly as he went on to explain that the new setup would also provide an experiment in harmony between a major news desk and the picture desk in an effort to make the paper more inviting. He asked me to work hand in hand with John Morris, whose background as a visionary picture editor wasn't being used in the way Daniel had hoped when he'd hired him a few months earlier.

Morris had first been captivated by photography when, as a student at the University of Chicago in 1936, he saw Margaret Bourke-White's picture of the Fort Peck Dam on *Life* magazine's inaugural cover. After graduating, he became an office boy at Time, Inc., where he met the greats of his day: Robert Capa, Alfred Eisenstaedt and Bourke-White herself. Morris worked his way up to become *Life*'s Hollywood correspondent, where he acquired an understanding of how words could effectively complement pictures, and vice versa. In 1943, he was sent to London as picture editor for the special staff assigned to shoot the Normandy invasion, and then served as Paris bureau chief after the liberation.

After stints on *Ladies' Home Journal* and at Magnum, he was named assistant managing editor in charge of graphics at the *Washington Post*, but he was fired over a squabble with his editor. He was working for Time-Life Books when Clifton Daniel brought him to *The Times* to transform the unimaginative way photographs were being used by the paper.

Morris was possibly even more elated than I by our new assignment. For him, the change involved not only the Second Front but the entire paper. In his memo to Bernstein, Daniel ordered that the picture editor also be allowed to participate in laying out other pages of the paper, to see how they could be built around pictures. "In the past," declared the memo, "our procedure has often been to find pictures to break up the text. In the future, our emphasis must be on finding space to accommodate good pictures." (And to keep reminding all desk editors about the necessity of suggesting photos to accompany words, Daniel presented each of us with a paperweight inscribed "Is There a Picture in It?")

Morris and I began treating the Second Front somewhat like a daily magazine, never running more than two photo-embellished stories on the page and often using only one. We positioned spot news stories there when the photos accompanying them were extraordinary. For the first time in the paper's history, pictures were given at least as much prominence as text, and stories were told with images as well as words.

To ensure the page layouts had artistic balance, I received permission from Daniel to transfer make-up jurisdiction of the Second Front from the bullpen to my old friend on the ninth floor, George Cowan, the paper's art director. Until now, George had been consigned to making up the Sunday feature parts of the paper, including the magazine and the Drama Section (where I had first become aware of his imaginative talent).

The first of the new Second Fronts appeared on September 18, 1967, only four days after my lunch with Daniel. I had started making assignments for the page at once and asked Sydney Schanberg to ready a story he had been working on. It was about the aftermath of a riot in Buffalo's East Side ghetto three months earlier. Peppered with revealing anecdotes and candid quotes from city officials, business leaders and working people, black and white, the story was subheaded "The Talk of Buffalo," and was the only one on the page. It was accompanied by six artfully arranged photos by Eddie Hausner, and was a startlingly radical innovation.

Even Scotty Reston, from whom I had never up to then received a word of encouragement, sent congratulations, telling me the page had been admired not only by the bureau but by his friends on the *Washington Post*. And Clif Daniel sent me a memo he had received from Harrison Salisbury: "I'm sure you don't need my cheering to convince you that the new deal on the Second Front is great."

Soon we were featuring Dick Shepard writing about the new wave of carnivals in the country; Ada Louise Huxtable presenting the debate over a new plan for Flushing Meadows Park; Richard Reeves analyzing the pecking order of the mayor's brain trust; McCandlish Phillips's account of an all-night vigil in Central Park, pegged to the mayor's efforts to encourage people to use the park after dark in mild weather; Charles Grutzner's survey of crime in the suburbs; Earl Caldwell's view of Harlem's improved night life in the wake of the riots; an article by John Leo, whom I had hired from *Commonweal*, to write about intellectual trends in philosophy, literature and religion, on how ex-priests were supporting themselves in the city; and J. Anthony Lukas's look at the impact on the previously obscure southern New Jersey town of Glassboro, three months after Soviet Premier Alexei Kosygin had attended a White House summit there.

Some readers, I learned from their letters, had adopted the habit of turning to the Second Front before reading page one. Reporters competed for Second Front assignments as did photographers. Realizing I was as much interested in their photos as was the picture editor, the fifteen photographers—among them such stars as Ernie Sisto, Eddie Hausner, Neal Boenzi, Pat Burns, Jack Manning, and the three youngest of the group, Don Hogan Charles, Lee Romero and Bart Silverman—came to see me as an ally.

These Second Front features represented the best writing on the paper, and cried out for fastidious editing. Since Marvin Siegel had demonstrated his deftness with Renata Adler's reviews, I designated him the principal editor of the stories, which because of their unusual length we called "takeouts." One of our Second Front innovations was the periodic publication of a series of articles following a single topic over a span of months. The most successful idea—to focus on one particular public-school class throughout the school year—came from a copy editor, Michael Leahy. I asked Joe Lelyveld to find a public school class in Manhattan that he believed was worth writing about for the entire year of 1970–1971, and he came up with Class 4-4 at P.S. 198 at Third Avenue and Ninety-sixth Street, a neighborhood with a mélange of ethnic, racial and religious backgrounds. Joe, taking ardently to the assignment, came to know not only all the pupils in the class as well as their teacher and principal, but also their parents, siblings, and home lives. Through the microcosm of one classroom, he humanized the major issues confronting the educational bureaucracy, with each installment focusing on a different theme.

Another popular series was John Corry's "City Block," a continuing look at New York through the variety of life in the buildings on one particular block—West Eighty-fifth Street between Central Park West and Columbus Avenue—with its sharp contrast between rich and poor. John and I had chosen the block together, after walking up and down the streets of the Upper West Side for a couple of weeks, in search of one that illustrated diversity. Returning to write about the block time and again during 1971 and 1972, John examined issues on the minds of most New Yorkers through the lives

of the block's denizens—from their complaints about landlords, their preju-
dices, their love lives, their ingenuity in surviving the complexities of city living, to how the block's rich and poor differed in their shopping habits.

The Second Front also became a showcase for stories and photos about
the new, freer lifestyle among the younger generation. Regardless of whether
the aesthetic importance of marijuana was "becoming more than marginal,"
as Renata Adler had asserted in her analysis of *Yellow Submarine*, it seemed
that legions of young people were smoking it in 1967. In the three years since
I had sent Marty Arnold and John Kifner to Greenwich Village to investigate the rise in drug use, marijuana had practically become a religion in the
Village and other city neighborhoods, as well as places like San Francisco's
Haight-Ashbury.

At the same time, antiwar protests were proliferating, sometimes rally-
ing crowds of 100,000 or more. Draft cards and American flags were ritually
burned in Central Park. Demonstrators carried daffodils and chanted
"Flower Power." Many painted their faces. Some held banners that read
"Stop the Bombing," "Ho Chi Minh Is a Virgin," or "No Vietnamese Ever
Called Me Nigger."

I assigned a number of reporters to track the hippie explosion of sex,
drugs and rock and roll. Arnold and Kifner, finally a reporter himself, followed the story, and a news intern, Stephen Golden, a nephew of Punch
Sulzberger, wrote a lively Second Front feature about a hippie who became
one of our most valuable sources—a twenty-one-year-old whose real name
was Ronald Johnson, but who was popularly known as Galahad. He created
the first commune in the East Village, an open apartment where anyone
could crash for any amount of time. Since neither he nor his friends had jobs,
he told our reporter that he wasn't sure how the monthly rent money materialized, but somehow it always reached the landlord just in time.

Galahad enforced a policy forbidding drugs and alcohol on the premises,
so the police, who raided the commune regularly, never found any contraband. Another of Galahad's rules was that no one was permitted to sleep
with girls younger than eighteen. Galahad took in teenage runaways, convincing them to return to their families. He believed his commune was providing a necessary public service in giving safe haven to newcomers who
would otherwise be living on the street. And the streets of the East Village,
which had seemed festive and groovy during the summer of 1967, were becoming gray and sinister by fall. "This scene is not the same anymore," noted
one hippie called Gypsy. "There are some very bad vibrations."

Many of the naive middle-class white youths who had migrated to the

Village from the suburbs and Middle America, not to mention New Yorkers arriving by subway, proved easy marks for poor, street-smart blacks and Puerto Ricans who lived in the slum neighborhood bordering Tompkins Square Park. "This scene is getting increasingly violent," another hippie told *The Times*. "The love thing is dead, the flower thing is dead."

His observation was brutally confirmed on October 8, 1967, by the discovery of two naked, bludgeoned bodies in the boiler room of a squalid East Village tenement. One was that of a twenty-one-year-old man, James Hutchinson, who had a police record showing several arrests. A fixture in the hippie community, he went by the name "Groovy," and had been a close friend of Galahad. The other was identified as Linda Fitzpatrick, an eighteen-year-old from an affluent family in Connecticut.

Because Linda Fitzpatrick typified the many young women who had drifted into the Village from privileged homes, Manny Perlmutter's story of the double murder made page one. But when we tried to delve more deeply into the story the following day, Linda's family understandably kept the press at a distance. Then Abe received a call from a friend in Connecticut who happened to know Linda's father. He said that Mr. Fitzpatrick would be willing to talk to *The Times*.

I was certain that Tony Lukas was the ideal reporter for the assignment. Lukas was an imposing man with black hair and an olive complexion, at times intense and brooding, with demons lurking. At other times, on fire with wonder, he would pore over his notes, trying to comprehend and explain motivations and meanings behind his meticulously assembled facts. A thirty-three-year-old Harvard graduate, he had joined *The Times* in 1962 and soon was off to cover the Congo. He bridged cultural gaps there with ease and, after initially being suspected as a spy, was inducted into the Kiyangala-Nansundi tribe as an "Honorary Nephew of the Chief." He was then transferred to New Delhi, where he spent two years before returning to the metropolitan staff in early 1967.

By his own account, he found that "there were things happening in this country which were infinitely more interesting and compelling than abroad." And for him, the city room had all the color of psychedelic subway graffiti. "In the front row was the pure gold of Homer Bigart and the solid silver of Peter Kihss, our two precious metals," he once said at a party for reporters that I hosted. "In the serried rows that followed for almost a city block there were many others. Joe Lelyveld, the imperial purple of future greatness. John Leo in ecclesiastical crimson. John Kifner in the true blue of courage.

Marty Arnold in vivid scarlet and Edith Evans Asbury, the dazzling white of dignity and style."

One of the first assignments I had given Lukas was a two-part series on prostitutes in New York—what he saw as "a world of complete hopelessness and helplessness that the police, courts and prisons have not pierced, but probably have only reinforced." He noted the ineffectuality of long jail terms, as well as the corruption in the vice squads, many of whose officers accepted payoffs to allow hookers to conduct their business. But the most compelling aspect of his reporting were his profiles of the prostitutes themselves, such as Matilda F., who at forty-four had served thirteen years in prison.

"Like so many of her sisters of the streets," wrote Lukas, "Matilda's arms and legs are blotched with purple and pocked with countless jabs of the heroin needle. Like many, she is also a Lesbian who gets no pleasure from the sexual act with her customers, but finds solace with other women. A talk with Matilda reveals she hates men, but most of all she hates herself. Her profession is so profoundly degrading to her that she has lost all semblance of self-respect."

This was the kind of insight the Linda Fitzpatrick story needed. "The family is concerned over the impression that the press has presented of their daughter and they say they want to give us the true picture," I told Lukas. An hour later, after a call to Mr. Fitzpatrick, Lukas drove to Greenwich, Connecticut, and met with the Fitzpatricks in the library of their thirty-room house.

"The family still appeared somewhat numb from the horror of the murder, which was then scarcely four days old," Lukas recalled later in a piece I suggested he write for *Times Talk*. "Mrs. Fitzpatrick, a good-looking blonde who had been a leading model and cover girl in the thirties, hovered on the edge of tears. But she and the family bore themselves with great dignity and restraint for the next three hours as they told me of the Linda they knew. They said they were holding back nothing."

"We have decided to trust you and *The Times* completely," Mr. Fitzpatrick told Lukas.

The family had no inkling that their pretty, well-groomed daughter, affectionately known as "Fitzpoo," had any contact with the sordid elements of Greenwich Village. They were, in fact, unaware that there were any sordid elements in the Village, a neighborhood Mrs. Fitzpatrick knew only for its "dear little shops." Mrs. Fitzpatrick referred to Linda in the present tense, describing her as "a well-rounded, fine, healthy girl." Lukas was shown the girl's athletic awards and horseback riding ribbons. "I don't believe Linda really had anything to do with the hippies," her father told Lukas.

Her parents and older siblings believed in Linda's artistic abilities and showed Tony samples of her artwork—a Paris street scene and some landscapes. Though distressed at her decision to abandon her academic art studies, the Fitzpatricks gave their "reluctant permission" when she told them she wanted to move to the Village to paint.

Lukas gleaned a few key bits of information that, while not quite accurate, were enough to set him on the trail to the true facts. Linda, her parents said, shared a room at the Village Plaza Hotel with a young career girl named Paula Bush. The hotel, Linda had told them, was "a perfectly nice place with a doorman and a television." Mrs. Fitzpatrick said Linda had found work at two shops—first Poster Bazaar, then Imports, Ltd.—where she claimed to be making eighty and eighty-five dollars a week.

When he left the Fitzpatrick estate, Lukas phoned me to say he was going to the Village to check out what the family had told him. I got Kifner to help with the legwork. Lukas soon discovered Linda's parallel surreal universe—a life that bore no resemblance to the picture she had drawn for her parents. The Village Plaza proved to be a seedy rooming house with no doorman, but with peeling paint and a cluster of grimy signs, one of which read "No Outgoing Calls for Transients." The desk clerk clearly remembered Linda, but there was no Paula Bush. "It was Paul Bush," he told Lukas. "Of course, she had lots of other men up there all the time. Anybody off the street. The dirtiest bearded hippies she could find."

Meanwhile, Kifner was looking for Poster Bazaar and Imports, Ltd. No one he talked to had heard of either business. Lukas and Kifner explored a few East Village haunts, including the Limelight and the Psychedelicatessen, then checked out a forwarding address on East Thirteenth Street that Paul Bush had left with the Village Plaza desk clerk. They knocked on the door of the apartment, upon which hung a sign reading "No Visitors After Midnight Unless by Appointment Please." It belonged to Susan and David Robinson, who ran a "crash pad" somewhat similar to Galahad's. Neither answered, but the building super said that Linda had been a frequent visitor.

Lukas returned the next day and found the Robinsons, who spoke with him for hours about Linda. They described how Linda, while she was still living with her parents, and generously supported by them, came to the Village and bought LSD for herself and anyone else who needed some. After tripping all night, she would board a train for Connecticut at Grand Central. "She must have still been flying when she got home," David said.

Contrary to what she told her parents about supporting herself, Linda had no job. She had been employed for three days at a shop called Fred Leighton's Mexican Imports, Ltd., where she earned two dollars an hour and was fired for tardiness. After that, the Robinsons said, she took to begging in Washington Square. The Robinsons showed Lukas some of Linda's drawings. Unlike the disciplined work with which her parents were familiar, they were wildly psychedelic. Susan said that Linda had visited Haight-Ashbury, and claimed she had been driven back with two male witches. "She said one of the warlocks took her mind apart and scattered it all over the room and then put it together again. She said she felt the warlock owned her."

John Kifner, who doggedly chased clues through the alleys of hippieland, finally found the warlock, who was called "Pepsi." He said he had seen Linda and Groovy only hours before they were killed. Linda told him she was high on speed.

Once Lukas was ready to write about the double life of Linda Fitzpatrick, it seemed to him that the story had to be told in two alternating voices, and he did something that to my knowledge had never been tried before by a *Times* reporter. Usurping the editor's prerogative to achieve his dramatic effect, he marked up his copy thus: bold roman type for the passages about Linda's sheltered life with her parents in Connecticut and italics for the alternating paragraphs about her wayward life in the drug subculture of Greenwich Village. I thought it was an approriately imaginative concept.

At five P.M. on Sunday, October 15, as Lukas was completing his story for that night's edition, I left the city room, confident that next morning's *Times* readers were in for an unusually compelling read. Lukas called me at home at 6:30 to say that the bullpen had instructed the copy desk to set his story without the italics. He sounded desperate. This was magazine stuff, the editors told him, not proper usage for the daily paper.

I hurried back to the office. Lukas's eyes were ablaze. I asked the bullpen editor in charge to take a good look at Lukas, who was standing nearby, glowering. "He has a right to be furious," I said. "You're about to maim his piece so it will conform to *your* idea of proper style." The editor looked at Lukas and knew he had lost his battle. The story ran, italics intact, on page one under the headline "The Two Worlds of Linda Fitzpatrick."

Everyone in the city room had expected Tony's article to have an impact, but the shock waves went far beyond what we'd anticipated. The article sounded a significant alarm about the disaffected children of the sixties, and I can't recall a single story in the daily paper that inspired such an outpouring of letters. They were mostly from parents, concerned about their own children, who deplored Linda's tragic fate and who sympathized with the Fitzpatricks. Why were their children rebelling, turning on and tuning out?

Tony and I were genuinely sorry for Linda's parents, who, we were well aware, now had to confront the painful publicity resulting from the disclosure of their daughter's story. We had not made the decision lightly to publish the tragic facts. But, as with any story involving startling personal revelation, a judgment had to be made as to whether it was in the public interest. We became convinced that, if handled sensitively, our exposure of the facts of Linda's colliding worlds would enlighten our readers about a troubling and dangerous social trend.

A few months later, Lukas was at Yale gathering facts about the black studies program, when I received a call that his story had won the Pulitzer. I phoned him immediately and he told me he had escaped to New Haven because he thought it would have been bad luck to await word of the prize in the city room. He said he did not want to come back to celebrate. He was content to spend the rest of the day finishing the reporting at Yale.

It was not until fifteen years later, when I was deputy managing editor, that another reporter's Pulitzer gave me as much personal pleasure as had Tony's. That prize was awarded to Nan Robertson, who had joined *The Times* in 1955 after having worked as a special correspondent in Paris, Berlin, Frankfurt and London for the *Herald Tribune*'s European Edition and at the *Milwaukee Journal*, among other papers. She was later based in Paris for *The Times* and then became a member of the Washington bureau.

In 1982, all of us on the paper were distressed to learn that Nan had been stricken with something called toxic shock syndrome, about which not much was known at the time, except that it could be fatal. Anxiously following her progress, we learned she would eventually recover, but would lose the tips of some of her fingers. Told she was deeply depressed, I called her at the hospital and, after chatting with her for a few moments, I tried to cheer her up with the suggestion that she might want to start thinking about doing a magazine story about the details of her recovery, once she left the hospital.

"It'll make a great magazine cover piece," I told her.

"Are you crazy?" she said. "I may be dying and you're asking me to write a story?" She hung up.

A few weeks later, when she was finally on the mend, she called me.

"I've been thinking about your idea for a story. Were you serious?"

I assured her I was. She turned in just about the best story of her outstanding career. I saw to it that it went on the cover of the magazine as I had promised, and that was the story for which she won her Pulitzer.

THIRTY-EIGHT

"As IN COVERING ANY STORY, accuracy is paramount. The only difference here is that inaccuracy may lead to more serious repercussions than in other stories. You may not be hit with a lawsuit, but you may cause someone's death if what you write escalates a relatively moderate demonstration."

So read part of a memo I sent to the staff on July 17, 1968, regarding the coverage of civil disturbances. "Be particularly careful," it continued, "when summarizing a situation or when paraphrasing quotes. Think twice before using such words as 'riot' or 'violence' or 'sniper.' Also be careful of describing persons in stories as 'militants,' or 'leaders' or even 'spokesmen.' There are various shades of militants these days and someone who claims to be a spokesman for a group may not be telling the truth; better he be identified by title, or, if that's not possible, as an exponent. As always, be wary of crowd estimates. The best approach is to make your own count and then explain in your story the method you used, which is what we should do in any crowd story anyway."

Such a warning, I believed, was warranted in those ominously troubled days of 1968. Dissension between liberal and conservative, black and white, and young and old often reached such a fevered pitch that sometimes it seemed the country was going to split apart. Tempers were violently erupting in civil rights protests and protests against the Vietnam War—at street rallies, marching demonstrations and on campuses throughout the country. Bomb threats by alienated students were not uncommon.

I had written the memo three months after ghettos across the nation had exploded in paroxysms of rage as a result of Martin Luther King, Jr.'s assassination on April 4 in Memphis. John Lindsay, in perhaps his most glorious moment as mayor, had rushed up to Harlem, where he soothed a roiling mob with spontaneous words of reassurance. His physical presence, the fact that he cared enough to expose himself to the very real danger that lurked in the streets, had the desired effect. The city stayed relatively calm. There was vandalism and looting, but, compared with other urban areas where buildings were razed and millions of dollars of damage occurred, New York emerged largely unscathed.

As it happened, the week that King was assassinated was also the most crowded week of news since World War II. It began with President Johnson's startling announcement on Sunday evening, March 31, that he would not run for a second term. Abe and I, with our wives, had been at a friend's dinner party and the television set was turned on for the president's speech. Johnson opened by revealing his decision to curtail the bombing in Vietnam—in itself, a major policy shift. And then, toward the end of his speech, came the earth-shaker: "I shall not seek and I will not accept the nomination." Abe and I rushed back to the city room, where he took command of the general coverage and I rallied my metropolitan troops to provide background material for the national desk.

The impact of the president's announcement continued to make banner headlines all week, and then came the King assassination. At 7:10 on that Thursday night, Claude Sitton, the national editor whose desk was not far from mine, picked up his ringing phone. "King's been shot," he called over to me. The report came from Earl Caldwell, whom Sitton had borrowed from my staff because he needed a black reporter to cover King's march in Memphis for the city's striking sanitation workers.

Caldwell was in his motel room on the ground floor, directly under the balcony where King was standing, when he heard the rifle blast. When he reached the balcony, an aide of King's, the Reverend Ralph D. Abernathy, was bending over him. Caldwell was the only reporter on the scene, and what he wrote became a historical document. "The blood. The wound was as big as your fist," Caldwell later noted in *Times Talk*. "His eyes. They were open but they had such a strange look. Eyes that were not seeing any-thing. . . . 'Write, write down everything you see,' I thought. I began to jot down on paper who was there, what they were doing, time, what they were saying. 'Get it all down, get it all down,' and then a second thought: phone. 'Call the office, call the office,' I kept thinking."

When Caldwell called Sitton, he was breathless. It was ten minutes be-fore the wire-service bulletins started pouring in. As *Times Talk* later re-ported, "Sitton and Gelb played a complicated chess game with their men, moved them around the country, around the city as events dictated." It had already been a big news day for the metropolitan staff with the investiture of New York's new archbishop, Terence J. Cooke, a ceremony attended by President Johnson. Peter Kihss, Murray Schumach and Tony Lukas had just received their "Good night," but I asked them to stay on. At Sitton's request, I sent Lukas, who had just written the story about the president's day in New York, to Memphis to help out Caldwell. I wanted Schumach, who had completed his story about police security for the president, to update the advance obit on King that he had written the previous year.

Kihss was assigned to take Caldwell's detailed notes dictated from Memphis. The story would lead the paper under an eight-column headline. My thoughts momentarily flashed back to the time when George Streator was the single "token Negro" in the city room. Now here was Caldwell phoning in the lead story from Memphis, and Tom Johnson writing the front-page reaction story for the late editions with facts supplied from Harlem by Gerald Fraser and from Bedford-Stuyvesant by Rudy Johnson. The photographer on the dangerous scene in Harlem was Don Hogan Charles, who also was black.

At three A.M., when I left the paper, the streets were deserted, and I wondered whether the anger in Harlem might find its way down to Times Square. There was scarcely a car on the street, and not a taxi in sight. Jittery, I headed for the subway. When I arrived at my station, a gang of six young black men on the street spotted me coming up the subway stairs. "Get whitey!" one of them yelled, and all six ran in my direction. I raced for my apartment house, luckily right across the street and luckily gated. The doorman assessed the scene, opened the gate, allowed me to slip through and then shut it hard behind me, just as the six were about to grab me.

THE SPOTLIGHT ON HARLEM following King's assassination raised the question of whether we should attempt another survey in the black community. Such polls, we had found, were always a matter of delicate balance. In our 1964 survey and in those that followed over the next four years, respondents often expressed suspicion of our questioners, believing they might be prying social workers, or welfare or credit investigators. As a result, our reporters usually sought out interviewees who showed signs of being cooperative, and that limitation in itself cast doubt on the credibility of our polls.

In an attempt to improve our techniques, we made a grave error in 1968. We enlisted the services of the Gallup organization to conduct a Harlem poll especially for us—and it backfired disastrously. It could have destroyed our credibility, not to mention that of the Gallup organization. The poll had been proposed after Turner Catledge, Clif Daniel, Abe Rosenthal and Harrison Salisbury met with Dr. George Gallup, chairman of the American Institute of Public Opinion—as the Gallup organization was formally known—to discuss the idea of a year's experimental collaborative arrangement. Concerned about rival news companies moving ahead of us in polling on general elections, Catledge had suggested that *The Times* order special Gallup polls of issues in the New York region that would run exclusively in our paper.

Salisbury then proposed that Dr. Gallup undertake the most "scientific poll" ever attempted in Harlem—dealing with, among many other issues, housing, confidence in black leaders, welfare services, police brutality, crime, drugs, dirty neighborhoods, poor street lighting, unemployment, overcrowded schools and parental control. In all, I gave Dr. Gallup ninety-two questions based on suggestions from my staff.

The poll was conducted, between August 24 and October 30, 1968, by twenty-six black questioners, after the Gallup organization had devised a "scientific sample" of 399 black residents of Central Harlem. When I received the results from Dr. Gallup, I chose the redoubtable Peter Kihss to write the story. His four-column article reported that nine out of ten blacks expressed deep dissatisfaction with their living conditions, thought government was "too slow" in helping them and believed racial integration was not proceeding fast enough.

Since I wanted photos of some of the respondents to illustrate the text, I asked Dr. Gallup to supply the names and addresses of twenty respondents. I gave the list to a black photographer and a black reporter, Don Hogan Charles and Gerald Fraser, both of whom were familiar with Harlem. When they began checking the list, they were nonplussed to discover that in a number of cases they could not find the respondents named as living at the addresses on the list. Other residents in those buildings told them they had no knowledge of the respondents.

In disbelief, I phoned Dr. Gallup. The next morning he came to see me, looking distraught. He said his preliminary investigation had confirmed our disturbing findings, and declared that the entire poll must be discarded. A secretary recorded our conversation, in which Gallup confided that one of his aides, who had recruited ten pollsters especially for the survey, was "absolutely in tears." She told Gallup that at least two of these temporary employees, fearing to enter the decrepit buildings, had confessed to creating fictitious interviewees and answers to the questionnaires. In some cases, they admitted, they had conducted their interviews in the street and made up the names and addresses of respondents.

"This is the first time out of our eight thousand polls that a poll had to be discarded," Dr. Gallup asserted. "I can assure you we will not make this mistake again. We'll double-check from now on. We certainly should have done it on this one. The big mistake I made was agreeing to do this without knowing all the problems. I do not have enough personal experience in Harlem to know what the problems are. I was particularly naive to think this presented no particular difficulty." He added that he doubted "one can do a poll of Harlem and call it scientific."

Dr. Gallup pleaded for forgiveness. Our experiment had been a bust. I had to kill Peter Kihss's story and I lost confidence in Gallup polls—or any others, for that matter—and during my editorship I never again attempted a "scientific" poll of Harlem.

THE KING ASSASSINATION was only the beginning of the slide into chaos in 1968. Two months later, on June 5, Senator Robert F. Kennedy was fatally shot in Los Angeles. That August, there was anarchy in the streets of Chicago during the Democratic presidential convention. Student demonstrations began shutting down colleges across the country. Earlier that year, on April 23, the campus at Columbia University had erupted, when three hundred students occupied Hamilton Hall, the ivied headquarters of the undergraduate college where one-third of its classes were held. Barricading Dean Henry Coleman in his office, essentially making him a hostage, they vowed to stay "forever" if their demands weren't met. Their action had been organized by Students for a Democratic Society (SDS), principally to halt construction of a new university gymnasium in nearby Morningside Park, as well as to sever Columbia's involvement with the Institute for Defense Analysis. The gymnasium plans were opposed as "racist" because, the students maintained, the building was a wrongful use of public property and would rob the surrounding black neighborhoods of much-needed recreational facilities. The defense institute was engaged in classified activities suspected by the SDS of furthering the country's involvement in Vietnam.

The student radicals, led by Mark Rudd, the twenty-year-old chairman of Columbia's SDS chapter, accused the university administration of being "totally remote," "rigid" and "unresponsive" to their grievances. An hour after seizing Coleman's office, the SDS—which had been joined in battle by the Society of Afro-American Students—drew up their demands: among them, the lifting of the ban on campus demonstrations and amnesty for students involved in protests, current or past, against the gym. Columbia's unpopular vice president, David B. Truman, refused to consider amnesty, saying he'd rather let the protesters stay in the hall "until they get tired." Sympathizers supplied them with food and they hunkered down for the night.

At five o'clock the next morning, April 24, the black students, who had been joined by some Harlem militants, suggested that the whites vacate Hamilton Hall, questioning their degree of commitment and their stomach for violent action. The whites, led by Mark Rudd, headed for Low Library, where they invaded the office of Dr. Grayson Kirk, the university's aloof president. Kirk was not there at the time, and the students scattered books and papers across the floor, damaged bathroom fixtures, cut phone wires, smoked the president's cigars and defaced his pictures. At one point, they left the president's office for the hallway, giving security officers an opportunity to rush in and rescue a Rembrandt painting valued at $450,000.

Early in the afternoon, Dean Coleman was released from Hamilton Hall without explanation. He claimed he had been well treated. "We ate, drank and played cards. We attempted to do some reading and we talked a lot," he said. The black protesters remained barricaded inside the building and, by nightfall, Avery Hall, home of the architecture school, and Fayerweather Hall, which housed the graduate programs in history, economics, sociology and political science, were in the hands of students as well. War had been declared, the campus was effectively shut down, and the police set up a command post. It was then that the male protesters asked their female recruits to cook a meal for them in a kitchen adjoining a lounge. "Liberated women do not cook," someone shouted. "They are not cooks!"

Just past midnight on Friday, April 26, students moved into the mathematics building. Within hours, a skirmish broke out between police and faculty members, who had stationed themselves outside the occupied buildings as a buffer between the students and the cops. Some professors were shoved, punched and hit with nightsticks as they prevented the police from entering Low Library. The police finally retreated, taking up positions in all the buildings not commandeered by protesters. Before daybreak, the administration agreed to suspend work on the gym, but it refused to grant amnesty, an ever more insistent demand of the demonstrators.

With the story growing increasingly complex, I assigned six reporters to phone in the breaking facts to the rewrite bank each day, in addition to filing their own sidebars. I sent Syl Fox, still our rewrite star, to establish a mini-bureau on the Columbia campus. Observing the constantly shifting mood, he organized the day's report and wrote the lead story. The coverage overall was as delicately balanced as I could make it and, for a time, we heard nothing but praise.

The campus remained tense over the weekend. We estimated that between five and six hundred students were in control of five university buildings. Couriers with red armbands scampered among them, relaying messages from one group to another. Uniformed police guarded campus entrances.

Gradually, the schism widened within the total student body of 27,500, as those opposed to the protests organized counterdemonstrations and tried to prevent food from reaching the insurgents, resulting in occasional fistfights. The faculty was also split, some favoring the protesters, others the administration. A number of professors tried reasoning with the protest leaders, warning of possible bloodshed if the occupations lasted much longer. But the students refused to compromise without an assurance of amnesty.

At a journalism awards banquet at a midtown hotel that Monday night, April 29, I happened to be seated next to Police Commissioner Howard R. Leary, who was the very model of an unsmiling, hard-bitten cop. After a drink or two, however, he loosened up and acknowledged that he remembered me from a publisher's lunch at *The Times* a few months back. Chatting casually for a while, our conversation finally turned to Columbia's unrest. He moved his chair closer to mine, and whispered, "I wasn't going to tell you this, but we're going to take Columbia tonight."

When I asked how he planned to go about it, he said his tactical patrol force would assist the regular units to sweep the campus of protestors in the early morning hours, clearing the five occupied buildings with a show of overwhelming force. "We'll have so many men there, they'll see it's pointless to resist," he said. "It's very hush-hush."

Thanking Leary for the tip, I prepared to excuse myself to return to *The Times*. "Before you go," he said, "follow me for a moment." He led me to a phone booth in the lobby, and put in a call to Chief Inspector Sanford D. Garelik.

"Read me tonight's orders," he told Garelik, then passed the receiver to me. After listening to Garelik's official briefing for the commissioner, I handed the receiver back to Leary and made my hasty departure for *The Times*.

I surprised the late staff by my return, rushing to my desk just as the first edition was going to press. After alerting the backfield about the planned police coup, I called Syl Fox and assigned additional reporters to the Columbia campus. I told the bullpen to reserve space for the last edition and the rewrite bank to prepare background material for sidebars. I also sent a copyboy to ask Abe, who was studying up on the counterculture at a performance of *Hair*, to call me. As I was briefing him over the phone, Abe was seized by the kind of journalistic excitement he hadn't felt since his foreign correspondent days, and decided to rush to the scene in person (an unorthodox move for a high-ranking editor).

"Shortly after midnight," Syl Fox wrote for the penultimate edition of the morning's paper, "the campus was a strange and eerie place. Japanese music drifted from a window of Fayerweather Hall . . . everywhere else there was almost deathly silence." At 2:00 A.M., the police, who had been coalescing their forces outside the campus gates all night, severed telephone service and water supplies to the five occupied buildings. At 2:30, they swiftly fanned out across the campus, taking up positions around each of the five halls.

The students inside had reinforced their barricades, sensing the coming assault but with no inkling about when or how the police planned to invade. Throughout the operation, as Syl wrote, the campus was tightly sealed, with all entrances blocked by the police. In the darkness, it was hard to determine what was really happening. The students and many faculty members were furious that the police had stationed themselves on private university property at the request of university officials. Wearing white helmets and carrying flashlights, policemen and a few policewomen at this point had done nothing more than take positions on the campus and ask the protesters to leave the buildings. Although the students refused to depart, the situation on the surface was still relatively calm.

At 3:20 A.M., the deadline for the last *Times* press run, the campus remained quiet and there was nothing new to report. Reporters on the scene and editors in the office had been updating our coverage minute by minute. When the last edition came off the press, Syl's four-column story, which seemed to leave few questions unanswered, put us far ahead of the pack.

The story led page one under a three-column headline:

1,000 POLICE ACT TO OUST STUDENTS
FROM FIVE BUILDINGS AT COLUMBIA,
MOVE IN AT UNIVERSITY'S REQUEST

But in the end, time worked against us. Before wearily calling it a night and going home, I assigned six reporters to remain with the story until they could be relieved by the morning shift. It was the time between the closing of our last edition and its appearance on the newsstands, that the campus erupted in violence.

At five A.M., the police targeted Hamilton Hall. The commanders made every effort to communicate with the black students inside, who were disciplined and well organized. They agreed to surrender the building, and the police secretly entered through a tunnel, avoiding potential confrontations with demonstrators at the university's main entrance on Broadway. Before anyone outside knew what was happening, the students had left and the police emerged from the building.

After this somewhat unexpected initial success, the police's plans to peacefully gain control of the campus fell apart. The police and university officials had critically underestimated the number of students occupying the four remaining buildings, and it turned out that their strategy of intimidating the demonstrators into submission by a massive uniformed presence was flawed from the start. There seemed to be as many demonstrators as police, and they resisted. The police then resorted to force, dragging the most defiant students from the buildings, beating them, kicking them and, in some cases, cracking their heads with nightsticks.

Swinging their clubs from horseback, a mounted unit herded terrified students—many of whom were simply curious onlookers—across the campus, pinning them against the locked gates with no way to escape. One hundred and thirty-two students, four faculty members and twelve policemen suffered cuts and bruises. One of the worst injuries befell a *Times* reporter, Robert McG. Thomas, Jr., who required twelve stitches in the back of his head after being hit by a policeman who used handcuffs as brass knuckles. Though he held his press card high, Thomas was struck repeatedly, then thrown down a flight of stairs. Fortunately, no one was seriously enough injured to require hospitalization.

None of these details, including the fact that 720 students were arrested before daybreak, made the morning's paper. Many students, who were unaware that the paper had gone to press an hour and forty minutes before the police onslaught, believed that *The Times* had deliberately withheld the details of police violence from the story, attributing the silence to Punch Sulzberger's being on Columbia's board of trustees. As far as I was concerned, the one mistake I made that night was in failing to emphasize in the lead story that when the paper went to press at 3:20 A.M. the campus was quiet. From that day on, whenever a story involved a fluid situation, I always insisted that the time of the final press edition appear high up.

For the next day's paper, I was determined to cover the situation definitively. In one of the many stories I assigned, Marty Arnold was asked to detail the numerous instances of police brutality on campus *after* the paper had gone to press. The bullpen editors placed three of the stories on page one but they designated Marty's to run inside, on page thirty-five, with the rest of the Columbia coverage. The fact that this delayed story did not get prominent display also maddened the students.

To make things worse, among the three page-one stories about the Columbia debacle was Abe Rosenthal's eyewitness account written after his impromptu trip to the campus the night before, where he had been one of the few permitted access by the police to President Kirk's office. Although it was extremely rare for an assistant managing editor to file a local story, he made the controversial decision to assume the assignment. Clif Daniel was of two minds about Abe writing the story but decided to leave the final decision to him—and, in fact, left the office before the story appeared, having been summoned to North Carolina upon learning of his father's death.

Abe had been understandably appalled by the chaos in Kirk's office. He wrote of students leaving ugly mementos over the previous week—smashed furniture, shredded books, garbage strewn across the carpet. In his second paragraph, he quoted Kirk exclaiming, "My God, how could human beings do a thing like this?" Abe, exhausted after having been up most of the night, left the office early, and the bullpen placed his article under a three-column head just below the page-one lead story by Sylvan Fox. When I saw the page-one layout, I urged the bullpen editors to twin Arnold's story with Abe's, thus giving balance to the coverage. They insisted that Arnold's account belonged inside with the rest of the Columbia coverage. They were wrong.

A number of reporters were quick to let me know their disapproval of the bullpen's decision, and I tensed for the reaction from an irate campus. Abe was known by many Columbia students to be a top editor at *The Times* and, finding his story critical of the protesters and sympathetic to the university's administrators, they believed the paper had slanted the coverage to please the publisher and his friends. They saw it as an "establishment" conspiracy—the fix was in. (It was several years before *The Times* got back its luster among Columbia students. Oddly, the rift began to mend in the fall of 1970, when we ran a knowledgeable story about Jimi Hendrix, after his death. I was relieved to read a memo from our college stringer, informing me that "guys at Columbia went out of their way to buy *The Times* to save the Hendrix article as a sort of memorial to him.")

The unquiet mood at Columbia in 1968 did not, of course, end when students relinquished the halls. Many students who became radicalized as a direct result of witnessing harsh police action, struck classes for six weeks. Violence sparked anew at the end of May as protesters again seized Hamilton Hall. Fires were set around campus, rocks were thrown at windows, and fighting broke out among students on different sides of the counterculture chasm. The insurgency was quelled by the police, who again showed little grace. Students were clubbed and, though no shots were fired, pistols were drawn. This time, protesters fought back, throwing bricks at policemen and dropping a potted tree onto a patrol car from a height of nearly a hundred feet, but the resistance was brief; the students were leaving for spring break.

The protests did prod long-needed reforms. Dr. Kirk resigned before the start of the fall semester. Plans to build the university gym on Morningside Park were scrapped. Eventually, the university forbade the funding of classified research. Students and faculty were given a voice in making decisions. Columbia became the model for dealing with student protests, which grew in intensity over the next few years on campuses across the country. Not until 1970, however, did any campus get hit with the violation of human rights that struck at Kent State, when four students were shot and killed by the Ohio National Guard.

IN 1968, educational strife in New York was not limited to Columbia. The public school system became a bitter political and racial arena all through the fall. Day after day, I assigned reporters to cover the emotional battles among teachers, principals, parents, pupils, politicians, agitators and just plain bigots—battles that were creating what Lindsay condemned as "intolerable racial and religious tensions."

During my weekly public affairs meeting, reporters agreed that the tipping point had resulted from years of dashed hopes. Despite repeated promises, schools in black and Hispanic neighborhoods had not improved. Inspired by the Supreme Court's *Brown v. Board of Education* decision in 1954 that deemed the legally segregated schools in the South unconstitutional, New York City developed an ambitious busing plan to desegregate schools whose enrollments were based on segregated housing patterns. But many white parents threatened a sulky exodus if their children were obliged to share classrooms with black and newly arrived Puerto Rican students, and the plan was eventually scrapped.

By 1966, minority parents and civil rights groups were calling for "total community control" of public schools. They believed the nine-member Board of Education, basically under mayoral jurisdiction, was unconcerned about whether their children were being properly taught, noting that eighty-five percent of minority students in the city read far below grade level. A well-intentioned Ford Foundation study supported a decentralization experiment and swayed the mayor's vision. As a result, Lindsay, fearful of rioting by blacks, was now prepared to give up mayoral control and to endorse the breakup of the system. But the experiment, initiated in 1967 in the districts of Harlem, Lower Manhattan and Ocean Hill–Brownsville in Brooklyn, had not been thought through, and the tentative mini-program of decentralization fell apart.

The real trouble started in May 1968, when the black-dominated Ocean Hill–Brownsville governing board flexed its muscles and discharged thirteen white union teachers and six administrators, replacing them with the board's own black choices. Teachers, who had already threatened to strike a year before over the explosive issue of decentralization, now followed through. A majority of public schools in the five boroughs were closed, pending a solution to the question of who would control the school system.

In the underprivileged neighborhoods, black parents, together with combative community leaders, argued it was unfair for the entrenched, predominantly white teachers' union to formulate policy, and the newly assertive Ocean Hill–Brownsville governing board refused to capitulate to the striking teachers. This represented a general shift in attitudes within black neighborhoods. As our new education reporter, Nancy Hicks, informed me, the once-magical word "integration" had lost its sanguine ring. Many blacks were now convinced they had to organize on their own to achieve their goals, since "whitey" was not going to do it for them. The new surge in black pride made the timing ideal. In the words of one group of black college students, they had grown from "Negroes" begging for acceptance in a white world, to "blacks" proudly proclaiming their "beautiful heritage."

Parents and their allies in the community took to the streets and blocked school entrances. The teachers' union was perceived by some in the community as virtually a Jewish institution, and racist as well. Some union teachers were assaulted and others were threatened. I assigned story after story about animosities brewing beneath what had once seemed a cordial relationship between blacks and Jews. One of our education writers witnessed a white teacher being shoved and told that if she tried to enter her school she'd become "soap and lampshades." Another Brooklyn demonstrator shouted to a group of teachers: "You're dead. We know your faces. We'll get you, your families, your children." Liberal New York Jews, who had been among the staunchest supporters of the civil rights movement, were incredulous.

On top of a volcano, I counted on a savvy group of education reporters headed by Fred Hechinger. His first request was that I assign Leonard Buder as the lead spot-news writer, because of his ability to meet deadlines on complex breaking developments. Buder had attended Brooklyn College at night while working days as a *Times* copyboy, but he learned his craft—to write accurately and fast—on the job.

Buder began his working day at 7:30 A.M., as the street demonstrations got under way, and often didn't leave for home until three the next morning. Fearless in the face of mounting hostility directed at him from both sides, he delved into every facet of the strike—battles in the streets, courtroom arguments, political maneuvering, labor politics and racial collisions. The bottom line was that the city's more than one million schoolchildren were not being educated. Finally, in mid-November, a settlement was reached among the teachers' union, the mayor and the state commissioner of education—and with one prominent exception citywide classes resumed on November 19.

The Ocean Hill–Brownsville governing board had not been included in the bargaining, which led to disaster in that district for some time. The governing board declared it wanted the power to "hire and fire all principals, assistant principals and teachers," exercise "total control of our money," and spend "money to rehabilitate and build our schools using black and Puerto Rican contractors and neighborhood workers." If teachers were to be hired, contracts awarded, books and pencils purchased, the city's underprivileged wanted to have a say over the disbursement of funds. Community districts won some of those powers with the passage by the state legislature of the somewhat confusing Decentralization Act on April 30, 1969.

The city's public school system was divided into thirty-two separate districts, each governed by a community-elected school board, which assumed many of the powers previously held by the Board of Education. But the plan fell short of the yearned-for principle of "total community control." A restructured central Board of Education, which chose the chancellor, was made up of seven members—one elected from each of the boroughs, two appointed by the mayor—and retained authority over personnel issues, including the hiring and assigning of teachers. Elementary and middle schools came under the control of the community boards, but the Board of Education retained jurisdiction over high schools.

The thirty-two districts were a crazy salad of diverse approaches to education: They differed in standards, methods, ethnic frictions. And as Buder pointed out in a later investigation of decentralization, a number of the districts were riven with financial mismanagement and improprieties. Not only did community control fail to live up to its hopes at the time, but—more than three decades later—New York's school system was still dysfunctional, despite major efforts to reform it. In 2002, the system was again centralized, this time under complete control of the mayor. But the questions still being posed by parents and educators are essentially the same as those we raised in our city-room public affairs meetings and in the pages of *The Times* during the initial decentralization debate in the late 1960s.

COMMUNITY SCHOOL BOARDS controlled the new pattern of patronage, which pleased black and Hispanic politicians. They were aware that the ghetto residents of New York's past—Irish, Italians and Jews—had achieved better lives through patronage, in which jobs often were provided to both qualified and unqualified people in exchange for loyalty at the voting booth.

At one of our public affairs meetings in the spring of 1968, when I suggested looking into political patronage, the reporters scoffed at the idea, arguing that patronage was a relic of the past. All except Marty Tolchin.

On January 1 of that year, Tolchin had succeeded Richard Reeves as City Hall bureau chief, when Reeves replaced Dick Witkin as chief political reporter. (Witkin wanted to return to his first love, space exploration.) Like so many of us on the metropolitan staff, Tolchin knew and loved the city. He was born in Brooklyn in 1928 to Russian immigrant parents, and attended Bronx High School of Science. To learn more about the West, he had gone to the University of Utah, after which he returned to enroll at New York Law School. Tolchin joined *The Times* as a copyboy in 1954 and became one of two male writers in the women's news department, attracting our attention with his thoughtful coverage of parents and children. But his true passion was investigative reporting.

Tolchin pounced on the idea of scrutinizing the practice of political patronage and—somewhat to his surprise—found it flourishing. Some of the career politicians he interviewed assured him that patronage was essential to the two-party system. Others had the audacity to make a distinction between "dishonest graft" (blackmail and bribery) and "honest graft" (using inside information to make a profit, or awarding lucrative contracts in exchange for influence with a particular electorate). Marty's investigation was published on page one on June 17, 1968, and he later wrote a book on the subject with his wife, Susan.

Though Lindsay had sworn to rid the city of its power brokers, patronage was actually on the rise during his administration, albeit in a different form. Now it was the civil service sector, composed primarily of educated middle-class people, who reaped the bounty. Patronage no longer served its original function of benefiting the underprivileged. Theoretically, the political clubhouse favors of decades past, doled out to the poor, had been replaced by the city's new antipoverty programs, organized by the Lindsay administration under one super-agency, the Human Resources Administration (HRA). Its goal was to support the indigent temporarily with welfare, help them deal with personal issues and then provide useful job training to make them productive new members of the workforce.

But, thanks to a tip from Bronx congressman James Scheuer, I learned that not all the money earmarked for the HRA was arriving at its intended destinations. The word was that corruption within the agency had sluiced millions of dollars from the poor into the bank accounts of agency employees. A quiet probe by city and federal investigators had just begun. I asked Richard Reeves to confirm rumors of these alleged inequities, and gave him a team of three reporters to help investigate—all formerly on the *Trib*: Barney Collier, Richard Phalon and Richard Severo.

Collier came to *The Times* in 1966, after winning a number of awards for his reporting on South America. He fancied himself as a kind of secret agent, relishing hushed phone conversations, confidential memos and mysterious trips out of town. When he was stationed at the *Trib*'s Washington bureau, he kept a packed suitcase under his desk in case he had to board a plane on the spur of the moment. Phalon, who in his youth had been a grave digger, a freight handler and a letter carrier, worked his way through college while serving as a copyboy for the *Daily News*. He had joined *The Times*'s financial department in 1964. Severo, who at one point had been an investigative reporter for the *Washington Post*, arrived at *The Times* in early 1968, and covered criminal courts. He quickly proved himself as one of the most gutsy reporters on my staff.

We all met for lunch in October 1968 to discuss how we wanted to handle the HRA investigation. None of us was overjoyed about tackling the story, because, philosophically, we all supported the city's antipoverty efforts. In the end, it was Tom Johnson who stiffened our resolve. He was at the time working on a different story, but I had asked him to join us for lunch. "The facts are the facts and corruption is corruption, and we're newspapermen," he said.

Over the next few months, the team worked together in a small office off the city room that I had commandeered. The four reporters compiled mountains of statements and documents, but had difficulty pinning down the last key pieces. Exasperated, I ordered them out of the office on January 2, 1969, asking them not to return until they were ready to write. On January 7, they returned with the facts that tied up the story.

For the next five days—until their story was published on January 12— they were inseparable. They spent evenings at Reeves's apartment or at Collier's when not in their *Times* office, where I sometimes sneakily moved ahead the desk clock to speed the flow of copy. The office was strewn with coffee containers, razors, neckties and miscellaneous papers.

What evolved was a picture of corruption, searing in scale even for New York. Lincoln Steffens would have been proud of us. One complex scheme, embarked upon in October 1968, while the organization was under investigation by the district attorney, involved four stolen HRA checks totaling over $1 million and headed for a private Swiss bank account. Chase Manhattan, the bank upon which the checks were drawn, had grown suspicious, stopped payment and notified the D.A.'s office. The result was a number of arrests.

But many other scams flourished. The Neighborhood Youth Corps, a division of the HRA that supplied jobs to underprivileged teenagers, was taken for $2.7 million. A sizable share was pocketed by a group of five black men originally from North Carolina who called themselves the "Durham Mob." Members of the mob included the payroll director of the Youth Corps as well as its onetime chief fiscal officer. One man who knew them told Reeves about a meeting they had held in the fall of 1967, when their embezzlement plans were conceived. At one point, the informant said, a young man mounted a chair and shouted, "What do we want?"

"Money!" the others called back.

"How are we going to get it?"

"Steal!"

By manipulating computers and inventing thousands of nonexistent Youth Corps members, the mob conned the Corps out of $1.73 million. In fact, nearly forty percent of the people on the 1967 payroll did not actually exist. Social Security payments withheld from thousands of Youth Corps paychecks were never forwarded to the federal government. Checks sent from the U.S. Department of Labor to the city controller, totaling over $6 million, were intercepted and deposited directly into the Youth Corps account. Money was then withdrawn by a fiscal officer as cash, which he claimed to have used to pay overtime salaries. Welfare workers in Brooklyn authorized emergency payments to welfare recipients in exchange for kickbacks of up to eighty percent. A bizarre, convoluted plot to bury $52,000 of HRA funds in a California real estate deal was foiled just in time.

Mayor Lindsay was apoplectic. This was the biggest scandal of his administration to date, though it was not the first. One year earlier, in December 1967, I had assigned a major investigation of Lindsay's close personal friend James Marcus, who served as commissioner of water supply, gas and electricity, and who was eventually indicted for taking kickbacks on city contracts. More damaging than the fraud was Marcus's mob connection. It seemed he was under orders from Anthony "Tony Ducks" Corallo, an underboss in the Lucchese crime family, who had loaned Marcus a substantial sum of money.

The case sparked an inquiry into Mafia infiltration in city government. In an outstanding investigative story, Marty Arnold cast light on a man with a Walter Mittyesque mind who convinced others, including the mayor, to accept his inflated, if not wholly fabricated, credentials. Marcus had charmed Lily Lodge, daughter of former Governor John Davis Lodge of Connecticut, into marriage, proposing to her only nine hours after they'd met. Lily Marcus, who had known John Lindsay for years, had introduced her husband to Lindsay during his run for Congress in 1964. Marcus got on famously with the mayor, who soon gave him the job of water commissioner. In that post, Marcus awarded a company an $840,000 reservoir-cleaning contract, from which he took $16,000 of a $40,000 kickback. Corallo, who earned the nickname "Tony Ducks" because of his many dismissed arrests, took the larger piece of the action.

Marcus had been introduced to Corallo by a labor lawyer named Herbert Itkin, a man with a background at least as bizarre as Marcus's, who became our next target. I asked Marty Arnold to investigate Itkin's relationship to City Hall.

Itkin became the chief witness against Marcus and Corallo. He worked with the FBI and the CIA and was ranked by the United States Attorney's office as "the most valuable informer the FBI has ever had outside the espionage field." Itkin seemed at times like a whole cast of characters rather than one man. He related wild tales about facing down Mafia killers, wrote pornographic spy stories and admitted to his wife that he lied even to his own psychiatrist. His father-in-law once telephoned the CIA and said: "Does Herbert Itkin work for you? If he does, don't believe anything he says." Then he hung up.

Itkin kept all the dirty money he made in sting operations and the federal agents knew it, apparently willing to consider it a bonus for his hard work. "I have lived years of deceit and lies and danger for my country," said Itkin, who described himself as a "patriot." Explaining why he introduced Marcus to the Mafia, Itkin said, "Marcus was weak. I just opened avenues for him he wanted to take anyway." Marcus pleaded guilty to accepting a bribe and was sentenced to fifteen months in prison. Corallo was hit with a three-year sentence. Itkin himself walked.

The Marcus–Corallo–Itkin investigations, together with our revelations in the HRA scandal, represented my further commitment to investigative reporting. In the HRA investigation, never before had I switched four top reporters from their daily beats to pursue a single story over a period of months. Our efforts were validated by congressional investigators who, after two weeks, concluded that they did not need—indeed could not find— "more evidence than *The Times* had published."

WHILE THE LINDSAY ADMINISTRATION was enmeshed in problems in 1968, the *Times* hierarchy was confronting some unpleasant internal issues of its own. Having brought the Sunday and daily papers together under Turner Catledge as executive editor in 1964, the last remaining freewheeling fiefdom within the news area was Scotty Reston's Washington bureau. As an old Washington hand himself, Catledge was becoming increasingly dissatisfied with the performance of the Reston-created bureau.

The *Washington Post*, following a feisty push by its new managing editor, Ben Bradlee, was too often ahead of *The Times*, and Catledge—as well as Daniel and Rosenthal—grumbled about Wicker's leisurely pace as chief of the bureau. Wicker, like Reston before him, was finding it difficult to concentrate on his supervisory role while also writing an editorial page column three times a week.

In early January 1968, Catledge, Daniel and Rosenthal decided the time had come to bring the Washington bureau under the tight control of the managing editor's office in New York, which would have not only jurisdiction over the daily Washington report but also responsibility for hiring and firing staffers—traditionally the guarded domain of Reston, as it had been for Arthur Krock before him.

Punch Sulzberger agreed that relieving Wicker of his administrative duties would considerably strengthen the bureau's coverage. Reston, who had retained his unofficial authority as the ranking Washington columnist and as a close friend of the Sulzberger family, at first offered no demurral when informed of the plan. For Wicker's replacement as bureau chief, Abe suggested James Greenfield, the editor who had recently come to the paper as one of my assistants.

Greenfield, universally liked for his easy charm and respected for his news insights, became pals with Abe when he had been stationed in New Delhi for Time-Life in 1955. Greenfield's wife, Margaret, who had met Jimmy when she was an airline stewardess in Asia for Pan Am, bonded with Ann Rosenthal when their husbands roamed the subcontinent.

In 1958, *Time* had named Greenfield deputy London bureau chief and he stayed there until 1961, when he became chief diplomatic correspondent in Washington. The following year he was recruited by the Kennedy administration as deputy assistant secretary of state for public affairs and, later under President Johnson, he was promoted to assistant secretary. Johnson, however, regarded Greenfield as bearing the Kennedy stamp, and kept him out of his inner circle. He resigned in 1966 along with Pierre Salinger (who had remained as White House press secretary after Kennedy's assassination). Both took executive posts with Continental Airlines.

But Greenfield was a newsman at heart and, in June 1967, he had come to New York to be interviewed for a job with CBS News. He called Abe, and the two met for lunch at Sardi's. "Don't commit yourself to CBS," Abe told his friend. "You belong on *The Times*." Abe had just been charged with developing the afternoon paper and wanted Greenfield to join our team. I suggested he come on board as one of my assistants. First, however, he had to be approved by Clifton Daniel.

Daniel and his wife, Margaret Truman, invited Greenfield and his wife to dinner. Greenfield was recounting some of his experiences in the State Department when Margaret abruptly turned frosty. She said her father hated the State Department, believing it had always tried to undercut him. Greenfield was sure he had blundered and that Daniel would turn him down. But the next day, Daniel agreed to hire him.

Since his experience in foreign and domestic affairs ran deep, he was regularly asked by editors from the other desks for his advice. His Rolodex bulged with government sources. And during his tenure at the State Department, he had earned the respect, even the embrace, of the press corps. One correspondent said of him: "The nice thing about Jim is that he went from newsman to bureaucrat without becoming stuffy. He's a square shooter and he doesn't try to play the old cat-and-mouse game."

After pondering the situation, Scotty urged that Greenfield's move to Washington be postponed for a few months. But his advice was ignored and everything was set for Greenfield to take over the bureau toward the beginning of February 1968. Punch was fond of Wicker, but had been persuaded by Catledge that Tom would consent to the new arrangement. Punch then took it upon himself to tell the plan to Wicker, who said he would resign.

The uproar in Washington rocked New York. Though we thought that no one from New York was more qualified than Greenfield to head the bureau, the Washington staff was uniformly opposed to the appointment. Pointing out that Greenfield had been with the paper less than a year, they also argued he would be biased toward Democrats, since he had been part of the Kennedy and Johnson administrations. We suspected that the bureau was reflecting Reston's territorial fears—that the bureau would ultimately have to answer to New York. The Washington staffers were "Scotty's boys," always protected by him from New York's rigorous and arbitrary demands. What made them particularly wary was Greenfield's friendship with Abe, whom they feared was autocratic.

The ensuing power struggle was unequaled in the history of the news department. Max Frankel, too, threatened to resign, for Frankel had expected he would be named to succeed Wicker as bureau chief. Punch found himself in a bind.

Reston, who by this time was lodging strong objections to the Greenfield plan, hinted to Punch that he also might resign. Frankel came to New York to talk to Catledge and make a special plea to Punch at his home. In addition, Wicker's wife, Neva, had herself appealed to Punch's wife, Carol, and Carol made it clear she opposed the move—as did Iphigene Sulzberger. Punch grappled with the dilemma for a couple of days. Then, on February 7, the day before Greenfield was scheduled to take over as bureau chief, Punch reversed course.

Greenfield resigned the moment Abe gave him the bad news. He told me he couldn't even face cleaning out his desk, and asked if I would send him his favorite sweater and a few other items from his drawer. He then walked out.

Reston phoned Greenfield at home that evening and asked what it would take to lure him back to the paper. "I've made my decision," Greenfield told him stonily. When I spoke with him later that night, Greenfield said, "I loved everything about the entire eight months I spent at *The Times*, except the last ten minutes." Catledge and Abe stewed but held their tongues. In public, Catledge appeared stoical while Abe was left dazed and distraught; though he felt betrayed by the paper he loved, he tried to shrug off his pain. "We're only hired hands, after all," he told me, half in anger, half in resignation. Daniel, however, could not contain his anger. He gave the publisher an unrestrained dressing-down, which ultimately derailed his career.

Punch was embarrassed by the Washington fiasco, which was given wide coverage in the press. The staffs in New York and in Washington felt humiliated by gossip over the rift. Punch appeared to have lost some of his confidence in his old mentor, Turner, while his mother argued that only Scotty could restore harmony.

Not long after, Punch turned the news department power structure upside down. In May 1968, he moved Catledge upstairs with the face-saving title of vice president, and made him a member of the Times Company board. Reston came to New York to succeed Catledge as executive editor on June 8 (while retaining his editorial-page column).

On December 1, at Punch's strong urging, Reston promoted Abe to associate managing editor, but he did so halfheartedly, since Abe was not one of Scotty's boys and his striving, emotional persona made Scotty feel uncomfortable. The appointment, however, clearly signaled that Abe was to succeed Daniel—who, for the time being, Punch left in place as managing editor. Wicker was given the honorific of associate editor, and Punch added the names of both Tom and Abe to the masthead. Frankel succeeded Wicker as Washington correspondent and head of the bureau, while Wicker retained his own editorial page column. Rather than New York's absorbing Washington, it seemed that Washington had annexed New York.

While Punch was trying to repair the fractures, it soon became apparent that Scotty was an inadequate replacement for Catledge and that Abe, in effect, was running day-to-day operations. Scotty presided over morning "think tank" meetings with his top desk editors like a pipe-puffing professor leading a seminar. At times he seemed shrouded in Presbyterian rectitude.

Seated at the conference table straight-backed, he'd often stare off into the middle distance, as if pondering the world's destiny, puzzling over the grand scheme of things, talking about "finding America." He would make suggestions for coverage that were vague and abstract, more appropriate for an academic monthly magazine than a daily paper whose lifeblood was hard news for the next day's editions. Bewildered glances were exchanged among the editors, as all waited for Scotty to come to his point. He rarely did. While he had once been an inspired Washington correspondent, it was clear he didn't have the instincts for running a complex daily operation like *The Times*.

Reporters in the city room, ever conscious of Scotty's two Pulitzers and his reputation as a great reporter, puzzled over his hesitancy in biting into a hot story. He truly astonished the staff a year later, when he was vacationing at his summer home on Martha's Vineyard and was among the first to learn about the drowning of Mary Jo Kopechne, who had been in the car that Senator Edward Kennedy drove off the bridge at Chappaquiddick. Scotty volunteered to file the story.

When Abe read Scotty's lead, "Tragedy has again struck the Kennedy family," he couldn't believe it. Abe called Scotty and, as gently as possible, told him he must rewrite the story because it had a completely wrong slant. Abe patiently explained that this was a story about the death of a young woman in a car driven by an influential senator on a deserted beach. Scotty resentfully agreed to make the requested changes. Then, when Abe told him he was sending Joe Lelyveld to Martha's Vineyard to follow the story the next day, he tried to dissuade Abe, insisting it was, as he saw it, "simply a one-day story" about a tragic, accidental death. I told Abe that Scotty should have thanked him for saving him from grave embarrassment.

Despite their conflicting styles, I couldn't help thinking how many characteristics Scotty and Abe shared, although they came from such dissimilar roots—Scotty's Scotch Presbyterian and Abe's Russian Jewish. Both were raised by struggling immigrant parents and, newly arrived in the United States, battled to overcome poverty. Both had a profound love of their adopted country. They also shared a reverence for *The Times* and, indeed, for the Sulzberger family with its high journalistic standards. But while Scotty had aspired to blend in with smooth upper-class Washington, Abe had retained his unvarnished gutsy New York attitude. The two tried hard to mask an ever-growing dislike for one another—and mostly managed to keep peace for the sake of the paper.

Many of us in New York became disillusioned as we realized that Scotty's close association with the powerful in Washington, especially his friendship with Henry Kissinger, Nixon's national security advisor, had skewed his news judgment. John Corry first made me aware of this. After filling in for a vacationing editor in the Washington bureau during the summer of 1963, Corry told me of an embarrassing incident he had to confront there (and which he later related in his memoir *My Times*).

One Saturday afternoon in August, an AP bulletin arrived at the bureau announcing that Philip Graham, publisher of the *Washington Post*, had fatally shot himself in his home. The veteran bureau correspondent, whom Corry asked to confirm the bulletin, was reluctant to take the assignment. At first, he told the startled Corry he didn't know how to confirm the report without intruding on the Graham family's privacy. Corry suggested he call police headquarters, and was astonished to learn that the number wasn't on file in the office. Dealing as they did with matters of lofty governmental significance, bureau staffers, it seemed, never had the occasion to call the cops on a local story. Corry looked up the number.

The correspondent then told Corry that since Scotty and Graham had been such close friends he didn't see how, without getting Scotty's permission, he could write that Graham had committed suicide. But he failed to reach Scotty, who was in Europe, and an exasperated Corry told him he'd write the word "suicide" into the story himself if the correspondent couldn't bring himself to do so. At length, the correspondent complied. When Scotty returned to the bureau a couple of days later, he made a point of snubbing Corry.

Scotty's warm friendships with Washington's power elite had become so evident by 1973 that Tony Lukas reproached him in the gadfly journalism review he had founded, called *[More]*—the word reporters put at the end of a page to indicate their stories were not yet finished. In a lengthy article, "Say It Ain't So, Scotty," Lukas rebuked him for having assumed the mantle of "Journalism Statesman." Lukas, who had once told me how proud he was to be one of "Scotty's boys," recalled when Reston was "the apotheosis of the Washington correspondent: scrappy but eminently respectable . . . irreverent but responsible." He sorrowfully went on to note that these days "some of those who have worked for and with Reston over the years may wish that he were a little less cozy with power, a little less reverential toward the System, a little more outspoken about the evils they detect in American society."

During Scotty's tenure as executive editor, Lukas wrote, his columns showed signs of deterioration. They were "lofty, above the fray, moralistic, and often downright banal." Lukas's harshest blow, however, was directed at Scotty's later columns on the Watergate scandal (after his return to Washington). He accused Scotty of "treating the whole matter as a relatively minor aberration. . . . If he takes a strong position one day, he takes an equally strong position on the other side several days later."

I was gratified to read Lukas's analysis of Scotty's transformation from scrappy journalist to grandiloquent pundit. It explained to some extent why Scotty could not endorse my own editing style. Lukas wrote: "Reston began disparaging 'the old-fashioned scoop artist' who liked to play 'cops and robbers' with government officials (precisely the rough rodeo act in which he won his own golden spurs). He scorned 'police blotter journalism,' the tendency merely to 'transfer the reporting habits of the police court and the county court house to the great capitals of the world.' Indeed, he called for a more 'thoughtful' journalism which would explain 'what it all means.'" What Scotty apparently failed to realize was that reporters like Homer Bigart or Tony Lukas were able to do both—as Scotty himself once had, starting with his Dumbarton Oaks scoop in 1944. It seems clear, with hindsight, that it was Scotty's scorn for old-fashioned police reporting that led to our Washington bureau's dismal performance in covering Watergate.

What most disturbed us on the metropolitan staff was Scotty's friendship with Mayor Lindsay. As we began to bear down on the workings of his administration, the mayor frequently complained to Reston. After our series on the HRA scandal in 1969, Scotty called Dick Reeves into his office, where he was confronted by Lindsay, who—with Scotty's tacit approval—criticized our coverage. "This is just the Jews getting even with the blacks," Lindsay declared, in a tone implying that Reston, as a fellow WASP, would naturally understand and sympathize. When Lindsay left the office, Scotty turned to Reeves, also a WASP, and asked without emotion, "Do people always talk this way in New York?" Reeves himself was furious at Lindsay's remark—not to mention the embarrassing dressing-down to which he had been subjected.

Scotty often summoned me to his office to question the judgment of a reporter whom Lindsay had criticized as inaccurate. I was obliged to assure him that we published nothing but facts and offered to show him the documentation to back them up. When I was told by a friend at City Hall that Lindsay had complained to Scotty about a story by Peter Kihss, the most meticulous reporter on the staff, I decided I'd had enough. On May 19, 1969, I wrote to Scotty:

"I understand that John Lindsay complained to you the other day about Peter Kihss's story of May 9 on a plan to develop a national seashore here. I gather that the mayor said the story was inaccurate. I thought you should know that, far from being inaccurate, the story was a fine example of Kihss's digging out an exclusive story with his usual thoroughness and reliability. Peter took the last line of a two-page release from the Regional Plan Association and developed it into a front-page scoop. Incidentally, Kihss achieved this despite an attempt by the city's Parks Administration to mislead him. . . . Peter was also lied to by Lindsay's Washington aide in a telephone conversation."

The mayoral complaints did not stop there. A month or so after publication of his initial article on patronage, Marty Tolchin wrote a series about the city's casual use of high-priced consultants for surveys that seemed inane. One study that cost the city $250,000 proved that traffic flowed into Manhattan in the morning and out in the evening. The contracts, Tolchin discovered, were awarded to people who had done polling or rendered other services to Lindsay during his mayoral campaign.

Lindsay once again arrived at *The Times* to register a protest. This time he joined Scotty and me in Abe's office, where he maintained Tolchin had no proof of the charges in his story. I insisted we invite Tolchin in to defend his series. Since he had no idea what the mayor was going to dispute, Tolchin brought an armload of files, which we plunked onto Abe's desk.

"Well, Mr. Mayor," asked Abe, "what seems to be the problem?" Lindsay admitted that the facts in the articles were probably accurate, but said the whole thrust of the series was "know-nothingism" and "Beame-ism"—by which he meant that Tolchin was being petty in scrutinizing the numbers with such care. Reston puffed hard on his pipe and Tolchin sighed with relief. Abe said, "Mr. Mayor, if you have no problem with the facts, there is no problem with the articles."

Although outmaneuvered in that instance, Scotty, all during his term as executive editor, never stopped second-guessing the metropolitan staff's investigative reporting. I persistently cautioned the staff to make certain there was confirmation from at least two sources for any article to which the mayor might take exception. Only weeks after the HRA series began, I found myself confronted with just such a dilemma—in the aftermath of the great blizzard that struck New York on Sunday, February 9, 1969.

The city was paralyzed beneath fifteen inches of snow. Sanitation Department forces mobilized to clear the streets, focusing first on Manhattan. By Wednesday, much of Queens was still snowbound. Though the main thoroughfares were passable, side streets remained buried. Residents had trouble getting to work and neighborhood stores could not receive deliveries. There was a great outpouring of anger at the man who, until now, had been viewed by many New Yorkers as the "white knight" of City Hall.

Lindsay tried to soothe the discontent by going to Queens and assuring its residents that he was doing everything possible. He was bombarded by invective. Curses and insults hailed down from open windows along the route taken by his slow-moving three-car motorcade. Marty Tolchin was in one of the cars, but not the one transporting the mayor.

When he got back to the city room after the tour, Tolchin told me what a WNEW radio reporter who was with Lindsay had told him: A woman had approached the mayor's car and said, "You're doing a good job. You're a wonderful man. Don't listen to these people." Lindsay then was said to have turned to a member of his entourage and declared, "Now that's what I like to hear. Not like those fat Jewish broads shouting from their windows."

I asked Tolchin if he himself had heard any part of the mayor's comment; he said no, but the radio reporter told him he had it on tape. I knew we couldn't run such a story based solely on a secondhand report. I asked Tolchin to get a copy of the tape from the reporter, but he said we would have to talk to the station manager. I spoke to the station manager, who refused to let us have the tape, or even listen to it. Without hard evidence to back up the story, we didn't run it. Tolchin, too, felt it was the right decision. I can only guess why the radio station never aired the tape: If, indeed, it contained the questionable remark, the station manager showed mercy toward the mayor, reasoning that Lindsay had not meant to be anti-Semitic but that, if broadcast, the comment might damage him politically, especially in an election year. Had I been in the station manager's shoes, however, I would have aired the tape, not to try to damage Lindsay, but because, as Tom Johnson had reminded us not too long before, "the facts are the facts."

After publishing the HRA story and Marty Tolchin's investigations of City Hall, my earlier warm relationship with Lindsay finally dissolved. We no longer lunched or met for drinks. I'm afraid he interpreted our critical scrutiny of his administration as a personal attack.

At a party hosted by Abe at his apartment not long after the HRA series, Lindsay shook hands with everyone upon his arrival. When it was my turn to be greeted, I extended my hand, but he turned his back on me.

THIRTY-NINE

Few New Yorkers could recall a time when the problems of urban planning, public health, welfare, racial unrest, street crime, housing and school deterioration loomed as large as they did at the beginning of 1969. Civic leaders congratulated my reporters time and again for their penetrating reports of New York's social climate. Indeed, *The Times*'s top brass was moved to nominate the entire metropolitan staff for numerous awards, saluting us for bringing "a new sophistication to the understanding" of the city's multiple concerns.

The centerpiece of our reporting was the "Changing City" series, which ran daily—from June 1 to June 8—on page one. Each of the eight full-page articles focused on a different aspect of life in New York, illustrating how every major problem was bound inextricably to the others: The city-operated hospital system was understaffed because the city was obliged to earmark much of its budget for welfare, which now supported one out of every eight New Yorkers—many of them impoverished, uneducated blacks and Puerto Ricans, arriving in the city by the hundreds of thousands. One of our articles cited the case of a baby born with cerebral palsy who had been seen by a municipal hospital forty-four times in her first nine months, never once receiving appropriate follow-up care.

At the same time, many middle-class whites and a number of corporations fled to Westchester and other suburbs, depriving the city of taxes it had always counted on. Continuing the domino effect, as the city grew poorer, crime rose sharply. And while the remedy for lawlessness in the streets clearly called for enhanced job training and education, the high schools could not provide it, for they were already struggling to educate 40,000 more students than they were designed to accommodate.

Then there was the alarming condition of increased air and water pollution. New York had become one of the dirtiest cities in the nation. In this spiraling cycle of decay, housing for the poor became a disgrace, especially in such areas as the South Bronx, where landlords increasingly abandoned buildings they saw as fruitless investments. And the city couldn't keep up with waiting lists for decent low-income housing. Civic leaders feared that racially defined ghettos would remain intact unless federal funds provided by the Model Cities program were used to build low-income housing throughout the boroughs, particularly in middle-class areas. Predictably, however, middle-class communities vowed to keep such projects out of their neighborhoods.

Aware of the growing tensions in black communities, Mayor Lindsay warned the police to use restraint in keeping order. As Dr. Arthur Niederhoffer, a respected sociology professor at City University and a former police lieutenant, argued, "Crime prevention and peacekeeping often are antithetical; there are many situations where you can make an arrest but start a riot." Hence, the police became less aggressive in making arrests and while the ghettos stayed cool, crime statistics exploded, hurting local businesses, which in turn hastened the course of economic deterioration.

In many ways, the city's hands were tied. Neither Lindsay, the City Council nor the Board of Estimate could raise taxes, determine the hours a policeman might work, or even increase the price of a dog license without approval from Albany. The state also had a say in how most of the city's funds were spent; and the federal government, which collected $15 billion in income taxes and $6 billion in corporate taxes from the city, returned only $1 billion in aid.

With its financial future bleak, the city was warned by some civic experts that it would soon reach the brink of bankruptcy if it failed to cut funding for municipal improvements and antipoverty programs that it could not afford. Lindsay believed it was his nurturing policies, as well as his frequent calming visits to the ghettos, that kept violence from erupting that summer. Always concerned that the poor might tear the city down in outrage over racial and socioeconomic injustice, he thought he had no choice but to overspend.

One of the very few optimistic notes in that 1969 symphony of despair was what Ada Louise Huxtable characterized in *The Times* as "the year for scuttling expressways." She was referring to Lindsay's cheerful announcement, in step with similar actions in other big cities, that Robert Moses' long-held dream for constructing the Lower Manhattan Expressway was being abandoned. Since it was a mayoral election year, Huxtable pointedly called attention to the fact that the inner-city expressway idea had come "as close to political poison as a candidate can get."

There had long been rumblings of dismay over the heedless way that expressways cut through long-established (if almost always poor) neighborhoods, destroying tenements, streets and parks and uprooting the lives of often elderly residents. If the Lower Manhattan Expressway had been built, it would have eliminated much of the area now known as SoHo.

From the day I took charge of the culture department, Huxtable enlisted me in her determination to shake up the inertia of New Yorkers, who had been mostly mute during such abominable acts as the demolition of Pennsylvania Station and the construction of the Cross-Bronx Expressway. Since the end of World War II, the urban planners' goal of constructing everything on a huge scale had rarely been contested. These planners deplored the city's old low-rise buildings with their hodgepodge of architectural styles, dismissing them as substandard housing—dense and dirty. While their grandiose planning had actually originated in the 1930s, it accelerated alarmingly after World War II.

Protests at last began in earnest in the 1960s—the result of a movement by a group of vigilant New Yorkers who loudly began to insist that they liked the city "the way it is" and demanded that their neighborhoods and landmarks not be destroyed by planners claiming, speciously, that they were saving the city. The protesters saw the planners as the enemy—part of an unholy alliance of unstoppable public and private forces committing vast moral and physical damage across the country; they also likened their struggle against the planners to the grassroots battle against the juggernaut "military industrial complex" that had sucked the country into Vietnam.

The debate over urban development versus preservation in New York was led by Jane Jacobs, the maverick architectural writer and Greenwich Village resident who had turned activist, and by the revered Ada Louise Huxtable. For years, the argument had raged in New York: what was to be swept aside, what was to be built, what was to be left untouched—with Huxtable and other members of my staff covering every skirmish in the ongoing battles.

The first major victory achieved in the neighborhoods was the stopping of the Lower Manhattan Expressway. Led by Jacobs, a motley crew consisting of, among others, Chinese businessmen, denizens of Little Italy and grandparents long ensconced in Greenwich Village was rallied to defeat the plan—and did.

Huxtable eloquently supported Jacobs's call for rationality and humanism, defending the idiosyncratic character and simple, homely virtues of the neighborhoods as they had evolved—the small, low-slung four- and five-story structures that had characterized New York communities for two hundred years, hundreds of them already replaced during the redesign of Second and Third Avenues by what Jacobs decried as sterile apartment houses and housing projects that bore no relationship to the city and its neighborhoods.

Jacobs was undeterred by the powerful forces arrayed against her—not only the banks, insurance companies and real estate interests, but also the federal government itself, through legislation like Title I of the 1949 Fair Housing Act, a conglomerate that was pouring millions of dollars into urban renewal projects.

In addition to leading the fight against the expressway, she fought a valiant, vain battle against the colossal towers of the World Trade Center, whose construction destroyed many historic buildings. And she protested—with equal lack of success—the plans for the sprawling Lincoln Center complex, which would demolish nineteenth-century, human-scale tenements. She believed these buildings, although aging, could be rehabilitated to the enrichment of the established community. She also argued that the cultural institutions, instead of being grouped under one huge Lincoln Center umbrella, should be scattered around Manhattan, thus benefiting half a dozen New York areas (and avoiding the inevitable traffic snarls).

Jacobs did, however, contrive to stop a fourteen-block housing project in the West Village that would have destroyed yet another established neighborhood. And a major victory, heartily endorsed by Huxtable, was the Landmarks Preservation Act of 1965, instrumental in saving countless New York buildings.

TRYING TO STAY abreast of the city's problems, I began meeting with representatives of New York's poor neighborhoods. They were seared by the drug epidemic and the ensuing crime that were destroying their communities. At one meeting in June, I was told about eleven-year-old children who were "sticking spikes in their arms," and about city buses being held up by addicts in daylight. Recently three milk delivery trucks had been hijacked at midday.

There was no consensus, however, on what reforms should be given priority. Some representatives wanted more policemen to patrol their areas and others feared that an increased police presence would result in acts of brutality. As it was, the police were viewed as an alien force, not in sympathy with the needs of their ethnic population. Spokesmen for the neighborhoods suggested the Police Department make greater efforts to recruit blacks and Puerto Ricans. As a rule, they said, the patrolmen were not ordered to get rid of drug dealers, but, rather, were warned to "watch the glass," meaning the A&P store, the corner market and other businesses. I learned that some communities established civilian patrols, such as one on Brooklyn's Pitkin Avenue. Merchants paid teenagers fifty cents an hour to keep pushers and addicts away from their stores.

Sensing an engrossing story, I asked the participants if they would cooperate in a *Times* investigation into the narcotics plague, and they agreed to point out dealers and runners. One man offered to lead a reporter on a tour of schoolyards where drugs were sold, and another volunteered to escort a reporter to a dope factory on Forsythe Street.

I was confident that Dick Severo was the man to dig fearlessly into the world of the ghetto drug trade. It might take as long as three or four months, I said, and assigned Barbara Campbell, on her trial period as a reporter, to assist him with legwork.

Severo began hanging out in the Bronx's Hunts Point area, where it was rare for a resident to die of natural causes, where men fought in the street with knives and guns, where pushers flaunted their wares and addicts sold their bodies or attacked passersby for the price of a fix. Landlords paid no taxes. Sanitation men, fearful of entering the neighborhoods, performed their duties sporadically at best. Patrolmen, immersed in corruption, abandoned the streets to the lawless, and hospitals turned away patients. Parents counted themselves lucky if their children preferred marijuana to heroin.

Severo gave me progress reports, and I was filled with admiration for his courage—but I began to worry about his survival. Severo, who had covered ghetto riots, said they were nowhere near as hair-raising as a stroll through Hunts Point. He dared not drive a car into the area and, every day on the subway, he mentally prepared for his day's encounters, reminding himself that it was not, after all, as bad as fighting in Vietnam.

Nevertheless, he camouflaged himself, wearing dark sunglasses like those worn by addicts to conceal their dilated pupils, and shabby clothes, including the requisite long-sleeved shirt to hide his nonexistent track marks. He never wore a watch and, after a friendly junkie warned him that the pen he usually carried in his shirt pocket was a giveaway, he concealed it.

Half a block from the Forty-first Precinct house, at the corners of Simpson and Westchester Avenues, Severo observed prostitutes openly soliciting and pushers selling dope with the nonchalance of hot dog vendors. He once saw two addicts stab a heroin peddler multiple times, then leave him in the street for dead. One onlooker commented, "Damn. If that man lives he's gonna be madder 'n hell at them two. Them two better watch themselves."

Some landlords Severo interviewed said they paid policemen ten dollars each to act as personal bodyguards when they went to deposit their rent money. One inspired landlord hired a convicted murderer as his building superintendent, who monitored the hallways day and night, napping intermittently. On his rounds, accompanied by a 160-pound German shepherd, he wielded a machete and an ax.

Remarkably, some longtime residents who could have afforded to move refused to leave the neighborhood, and I sympathized with Severo's genuine distress as he told me—upon his return each day from his Hunts Point expeditions—about their stories of anguish. A seventy-four-year-old widow, who had lived there for more than forty years, stayed out of stubbornness and nostalgia, remembering the days when there were cows and trees. Severo discovered her in her one-dollar-a-month basement apartment, in a building that had been condemned by the city as unfit for human habitation. She waded around the apartment in two inches of water. "The junkies, they stole all the pipes upstairs and all the water came down here," she explained.

Severo's most nerve-wracking day, which he later described in *Times Talk*, came when he decided to buy some heroin himself. He joined up with an ex-addict, who agreed to introduce him to a dealer. Overanxious, Severo made a social faux pas by asking for "a two-dollar bag" instead of "a deuce." "All we got is tres," the pusher replied. Severo forked over three dollars.

"You ain't gonna go very far on a tres," the pusher said.

"I don't want to go very far," Severo said.

"He ain't been taking dope long," apologized the ex-addict.

"Well then," the pusher said with a grin, "I guess we'll be seeing a lot more of you."

Severo's investigation became a four-part series that ran September 23 through 26, 1969. In addition to one article devoted solely to Hunts Point, he wrote about the inadequate treatment services for addicts as well as about the vigilante groups whose mission was to rid neighborhoods of pushers and junkies.

In several neighborhoods, Severo reported, residents felt compelled to take the law into their own hands, since the police seemed incapable of dealing with the drug trade. On the Lower East Side, for example, organized bands of blacks and Puerto Ricans assaulted pushers and addicts. "We warn the pushers: In this block you do not push," said one seventeen-year-old member of the clique. "We tell the dope fiends: Here you do not steal. If they listen to us, fine. They push their poison somewhere else. If they do not listen, we get them."

Other Lower East Side residents patrolled their apartment buildings armed with clubs, knives and guns. The police were supportive, showing them how to turn table legs into clubs. The police, in fact, were in a quandary about the drug problem. One Bronx precinct commander pointed out that making heroin more difficult to obtain created a rise in residual crime. Since the price was forced higher, addicts had to steal more than they usually did. The department itself had no standard antidrug policy, and policemen disagreed over whether to arrest pushers and users. In some neighborhoods, cops were reluctant to make arrests because they feared accusations of excessive force. "All I have to do is tell one whore to move on," said an officer, "and around here I'd have fifty people yelling police brutality."

It was common knowledge that the Narcotics Division was corrupt. Some patrolmen took bribes, others contraband. But the department protected its own, and had no wish to investigate itself. Moreover, the only witnesses against the cops were addicts and prostitutes, whose credibility in court was nil.

If the city hoped that rehabilitation could succeed where law enforcement had thus far failed, it would have to wait a long time—just like the addicts who wanted help. There were an estimated 100,000 heroin users in New York. Bellevue had no treatment services. Metropolitan Hospital had eighteen beds marked for drug detoxification, for which the waiting period was at least two months. At Interfaith, which had one hundred beds, drugs were almost as easy to obtain inside the hospital as on the street. No city facility offered immediate acceptance for those who wanted to kick their habits. Moreover, the emphasis was largely limited to detoxification. Implementation of methadone programs was just beginning and outpatient psychotherapy was basically unavailable for those who could not afford to pay for it themselves.

I glowed with Severo when his portrait of the contemporary urban crisis reaped praise from all quarters, but no salute was as significant as that offered by the New York State Court of Appeals. On December 3, 1969, the court used our drug series in rendering its guilty judgment in a narcotics case. The district attorney called me to say he could not remember the state's highest court ever before citing a newspaper article in making a decision. Normally, he said, the court relied only on legal precedents. That they singled out the series, he added, meant they accepted it as "fair, factual and beyond dispute."

DURING THE MONTHS Severo was researching the drug series, I kept Scotty and Abe apprised of what I predicted would be the best investigative series any paper had ever run about the destructive free flow of narcotics into the city's poorest areas. One morning in late May of 1969, Scotty invited me to his office for a chat and commented on the growing strength of the metropolitan coverage. He wondered if, at this point, I had given any thought to my future on the paper. What did he mean? I asked. He said that Dan Schwarz, the Sunday editor, was expected to retire in a year or so, and that he had come to believe I might be the right person to succeed him, on the basis of my experience in the cultural area. But he added that while I would have no problem supervising the Sunday Drama Section and the Sunday *Book Review*, the other Sunday sections—the *Magazine* and the Week in Review—required some foreign experience. Since I'd never been a correspondent abroad, he would like to help me fill that gap.

I was of two minds, as I had been about the drama critic slot. There was no job in the newspaper business I could possibly love and enjoy more than the position I now held, and my first impulse was to tell Scotty I didn't want to give up being metropolitan editor. Yet I realized that Sunday editor doubtless had a grander sweep. The editorship was, at that time, regarded as one of the most influential positions in all of journalism. Although there was no specific date for Schwarz's retirement, Scotty made me feel I was the strongest candidate to succeed him as Sunday editor.

And then came the icing. To be better groomed for the job, Scotty proposed I go abroad to visit the European bureaus, meet statesmen and other key figures, and obtain a general view of the political, cultural and economic scenes in a variety of countries. He also suggested I line up knowledgeable writers in those countries to file columns on a regular basis dealing with the changing cultural climate. "Go for six weeks or so," he said. "Take Barbara. Stay at good hotels. Think of it as a kind of grand tour. You've earned it."

A couple of days later, when I asked Scotty if I could book passage on the *France*, the majestic liner Craig Claiborne recommended for its cuisine—as superb as that of any three-star restaurant in France—he said, "By all means, and, of course, you'll go first class."

Barbara and I did, indeed, enjoy the grand tour, beginning in June. After visiting Paris, Madrid, Barcelona, Vienna, Prague, Berlin and Rome, we arrived in Venice in July. Aside from visiting the well-known sites and dining with movers and shakers in government and the arts in the various cities, we had been given intimate glimpses into local culture by our correspondents. In Venice, our room at the Gritti Palace overlooked the Grand Canal.

After dinner at Harry's Bar one night, I strolled with Barbara along the canals, marveling at my good fortune. Back at our hotel, the phone rang. It was Abe. He told me there would be an announcement by Punch in the next day's paper naming him managing editor. Punch, he said, had forced Clifton Daniel upstairs with that essentially meaningless title of associate editor (doubtless the payback for his indiscreet outburst at the time Punch reversed the Jimmy Greenfield decision). I detected Abe's nervous hesitation as he delivered the rest of his news: he was naming Seymour Topping, the foreign editor since 1966, as his assistant managing editor.

My heart dropped. I couldn't believe that Abe, with whom I had worked as closely as a brother since we started together on the metropolitan desk in 1963, would wait until the last possible moment to spring this news—first, that he was moving to the top, and second, that he was not designating me as his deputy. The Sunday job, after all, had been only a tentative offer, and the date for Schwarz's retirement was still up in the air.

"Before you react," Abe said defensively, "I'm sure you'll become Sunday editor when Schwarz retires in a year or so. Just be patient. When that happens, we'll be the same team we've always been, and we'll cooperate in making the entire paper even greater than it now is."

He then went on to tell me that Scotty, increasingly aware he wasn't suited to be executive editor, had decided to relinquish his post and return to Washington to concentrate on his column, which had been faltering during his thirteen-month tenure in New York. He had been elected a vice president of The Times Company with responsibilities to be focused on the paper's news coverage, whatever that was supposed to mean. (Scotty planned to keep an apartment in New York as well as an office at *The Times*, and would make frequent trips between New York and Washington.) The title of executive editor was abolished (at least for the time being) and Abe, as managing editor, would be the news department's top executive, reporting directly to Punch. The Sunday editor, Dan Schwarz, would also report directly to the publisher.

"Remember," Abe said, "Scotty made you a pretty clear promise, and I'm sure he'll stand by it." I tried hard to accept Abe's reassurance and consoled myself with the fact that I did, after all, still have the job I treasured as metropolitan editor. Nevertheless, I felt betrayed that it was Topping, not I, who had been chosen by Abe to be assistant managing editor.

I told Abe I needed a little time to recover my equilibrium and he said he'd meet me in London, where we'd talk some more. When Barbara and I arrived in London, I checked in with the *Times* bureau chief, Anthony Lewis, who was equally upset about the newly announced promotions. He told me Reston had assured him *he* would be Abe's assistant managing editor.

At lunch in London, Abe explained that Scotty had been dead set against my becoming assistant managing editor and was in fact less than thrilled that Abe had become the managing editor. (I later learned Scotty tried without success to convince Punch that Max Frankel should get the job.) Scotty was still determined to break up Abe and me as a newsroom team, fearing we were too aggressive a combination and would try to impose our own over-achieving style on the paper. Separately we could be contained, Scotty evidently believed, but together we would be overwhelming.

As for Tony Lewis's belief that he was to be named assistant managing editor, Abe confirmed that Scotty had, indeed, assured Tony the job was his—but without having bothered to consult Abe. Abe told me he had protested to Scotty: "You can't choose my assistant. Tony is a first-class correspondent but you must understand that the assistant managing editor is the second-highest-ranking post in the newsroom and Tony has no experience as an editor."

Accepting the fact that I wasn't in the running, Abe insisted he would name his own assistant managing editor or else decline the promotion. He had no hesitation in choosing Topping, whom I had to agree was not only a crackerjack editor but was also well respected by the staff.

According to what Abe told me, Scotty ignored his argument. "You've got the M.E. job," he said to Abe. "What more do you want?" Abe answered that if he couldn't name his own assistant, Scotty could take the managing editor's job and "shove it."

Now it was up to Punch to resolve the impasse.

"Abe wants everything," Scotty complained to the publisher in Abe's presence.

"What I want is my own choice," was Abe's riposte.

"You're pretty tough," Punch allowed with a smile, putting his arm around Abe.

Punch told Abe he could have Topping as his assistant managing editor. (And to compensate for Tony Lewis's humiliation at being turned down by Abe, Punch offered him a column on the editorial page.) Topping proved to be a calming influence on Abe's sometimes volatile nature. Known by all as "Top," he had started as a correspondent in Peking after leaving the Army in 1946. It was in China that he met his pretty wife, Audrey Ronning, whose father, Chester, was the Canadian envoy there. Audrey always accompanied Top to his postings, managing to raise five daughters while pursuing a career as a photographer. In 1960, Top headed *The Times*'s Moscow bureau and, three years later, became chief correspondent for Southeast Asia. Later as foreign editor, he smoothly overcame the many obstacles that surfaced during the coverage of the escalating war in Vietnam, and Abe himself believed Top would be an evenhanded, steady influence as assistant managing editor.

Years later, some amusing light was cast on my not getting the job by, of all people, Joseph Papp. Abe and I were dining with Joe at the Algonquin shortly after Joe—in a move much gossiped about in theatrical circles—had dismissed Bernard Gersten, widely acknowledged as his indispensable right-hand man at the Public Theater. Gersten, it seemed, was perceived by Joe to be crowding him and becoming too assertive. The final straw had been Gersten's surprise birthday celebration for Joe, produced at their summer theater in Central Park with the sort of panache Joe considered uniquely his own. The audience cheered Gersten's all-star presentation and saw him in a new creative light.

Joe, Abe and I had drunk a good bit of wine with dinner, and when Abe bluntly questioned Joe about the real reason he had chosen to sever himself from his old and devoted associate, Joe answered just as bluntly: "Aren't you being naive? Isn't that why you've put someone between yourself and Arthur? Smart executives like you and me eventually learn to be careful about keeping anyone nipping at our heels too close to us. I'll never again put someone like Gersten directly in line of command. I should have known to put a 'Dworkin' between myself and him—just what you did in separating yourself from Arthur. That's why I'm now searching for a 'Dworkin'—and don't ask me what 'Dworkin' means."

After a moment of startled silence, during which Abe appeared to assess the validity of the "Dworkin" theory as it applied to him, he joined Joe in a roar of laughter—and I found myself echoing them, unable to resist the absurdity of it all. Nonetheless, the pain of the betrayal lingered.

WITH TOPPING'S PROMOTION, the foreign editor's job was open, and it was Punch's idea to bring back Jimmy Greenfield to succeed him. Punch and Jimmy had met for the first time since Jimmy's abrupt departure from the paper at Arthur Hays Sulzberger's funeral on December 11 the previous year. They had chatted amiably and the result was Jimmy's reinstatement after an absence of only nine months.

Once things had settled down and I'd had time to reflect, I finally understood the Machiavellian reason behind Scotty's generous gift of travel—a first-class ticket to second-class treatment. Clearly he had wanted me out of the way during discussions of the top-level changes in New York. Abe listened to my theory but made no comment, other than to advise patience and assure me that Scotty and Punch had agreed that the Sunday post would eventually be mine. In fact, Abe said, Dan Schwarz was now in London, and wanted to talk to me about the workings of the Sunday department.

Schwarz invited me on a Thames River cruise with our wives, during which he confirmed that I was being considered as his successor. That sounded a little vague to me, as did his promise to invite me to his home in Scarsdale to spend a casual evening getting to know some members of the Sunday staff.

Schwarz's personality was the opposite of Lester Markel's. He was perhaps the most imperturbable of the ranking editors, always wearing a relaxed smile—yet he ran a tight ship. "It takes toughness as well as kindness," he once said, "to walk the line between giving your people a free hand and still getting what you want." When Barbara and I dined at his home a few weeks later, he was a most amiable host, but I sensed a degree of hostility among the invited members of his staff.

I found out later that their own choice for Schwarz's successor was Lewis Bergman, the editor of the Sunday *Magazine*, who, like me, had spent his entire career at *The Times*. One of the smartest, most unassuming and gentlest of men on the paper, he had started in the Sunday department as an eighteen-year-old copyboy in 1936 and learned on the job. Schwarz himself admitted to me many years later that the Sunday crew was terrified of my taking over because they saw Abe and me as one person and believed that Abe, known as a relentless taskmaster, would re-create Markel's dictatorial regime. At the time, though, Schwarz, while acknowledging that his staff was edgy, nevertheless kept insisting I was in line for the job.

It was all beginning to feel like a not-so-merry-go-round. My discomfort increased when Sydney Gruson told me that Punch had promised him, weeks earlier, that *he* would become Abe's assistant managing editor. Sydney was still fuming, and I didn't have the heart to tell him about Tony Lewis.

At the time, Gruson was Punch's closest assistant, but he yearned to return to the newsroom. Two years earlier, at Punch's request, he had played a major role in assembling a merger of *The Times*'s International Edition, of which he was chief executive officer, and the Paris edition of the *Herald Tribune*. (The merged paper, the *International Herald Tribune*, began publishing in the spring of 1967 with the *Washington Post* as a partner, but *The Times* bought the *Post*'s share in 2002.) In April 1968, after Punch had failed to propose Gruson as publisher of the new merger, he quit to become associate publisher of *Newsday* on Long Island. Nine months later he was hired back by Punch, this time as his most trusted advisor (and in 1970 as the company's executive vice president and in 1979 as a vice chairman).

Like Clifton Daniel, Sydney had adopted a British persona after serving in *The Times*'s London bureau during World War II. You never would have guessed he was born in Dublin in 1916 to struggling Jewish parents, his mother a Dubliner and his father an immigrant from Lithuania. The family's poverty was such that he had to leave school at twelve. The Grusons later moved to Toronto, where Sydney, at fifteen, became an office boy for the *Canadian Press*, eventually rising to reporter. He was dispatched to London in 1943 and, a year later, was hired by *The Times*'s London bureau to cover the Allied advances in the aftermath of D-Day.

On his travels as a correspondent, Gruson was often accompanied by his wife, Flora Lewis, who regularly wrote for *The Times Magazine*, as well as other publications, though not for the daily *Times*. In those days, almost all wives were prohibited from working as correspondents alongside their husbands, a condition Flora bitterly resented. In 1972, after the Grusons were separated (and later divorced), Flora was named head of *The Times*'s Paris bureau by Rosenthal, who called her "the world's greatest correspondent." In 1980, she became the editorial page's foreign affairs columnist, the post inaugurated by Anne O'Hare McCormick.

FORTY

I HADN'T BEEN LONG BACK from Europe when, in mid-August, the Woodstock Music and Art Fair erupted in the Catskill Mountain village of Bethel. Imagining it would be just another big music festival like the annual concerts in Newport, I sent only one reporter, Barney Collier, to cover it. When he arrived on Friday, August 15, he found himself amid 300,000 young people surging into the village. Collier reported epic traffic jams stretching for miles on the road to Max Yasgur's six-hundred-acre dairy farm, where the festival was being held.

Cars, he wrote, crept for the last nine miles at an average speed of one mile per hour. Many thousands of drivers simply abandoned their vehicles on the side of the road or in fields, trekking the remaining distance to the fairgrounds and angering Yasgur's neighbors to the point where they threatened reprisals against his property and his herd. But Yasgur, according to Collier, maintained a philosophical perspective: "I never expected this festival to be this big, but if the generation gap is to be closed, we older people have to do more than we have done."

At home on Saturday morning, I received a phone call from Grace Lichtenstein, one of my reporters, who had heard through the hippie grapevine about the droves descending on Woodstock. "There's probably nobody at the paper that cares about rock and roll, but this story is much bigger than *The Times* thinks it is," Lichtenstein said. "I know Barney Collier is there, but you need to assign more than one reporter."

She herself couldn't go, so I phoned William Farrell, one of the most versatile reporters on the staff, suggesting he hire a helicopter to fly him to Woodstock. An hour later, Dick Reeves called me from Grossinger's, the Catskill resort where he had been trailing Mayor Lindsay in his courtship of vacationing Jewish voters. Reeves said he had never seen a traffic jam quite like this one. All the cars were inching toward the Woodstock music festival. I told him to leave the Lindsay entourage and join Collier and Farrell at Yasgur's farm.

Reeves made it to the town of White Lake, where Canned Heat—one of the groups featured at the festival—was staying, and talked his way onto a helicopter shuttle with the performers. From the air, Reeves was amazed to see an endless sea of bodies. The helicopter landed directly behind the stage on Yasgur's farm, where Reeves met up with Collier and Farrell.

Seeking recognition by *The Times*, the festival promoters kept other papers at a distance, while allowing Collier, Reeves and Farrell full access to the musicians and letting them call the city room from the hook-up phones in their trailers. They also fed them champagne and lobster, which were flown in, along with a liberal supply of pot. The promoters believed the majority of newspapers were scornful of the ragtag audience, their drugs and their hedonism.

The Times's coverage of the festival, the promoters thought, was balanced and they were appreciative that Collier had written in his piece the day before how generally well behaved the crowd was. "I can hardly believe that there haven't been even small incidents of misbehavior by the young people, a state police official was quoted in Collier's article. Another policeman said,

"There hasn't been anybody yelling 'pig' at the cops and when they ask directions they are polite and none of them has really given us any trouble yet." Though Collier mentioned the ubiquitous presence of drugs in his stories, his tone was neither condescending nor censorious.

The promoters were also aware that *The Times* was the only mainstream paper with a full-time rock critic, Mike Jahn, who was on the scene as well. I had hired Jahn in 1968, and the promoters were familiar with his reviews of Janis Joplin, Creedence Clearwater Revival, Sly and the Family Stone, and Country Joe and the Fish.

Even though my older son, Michael, drove me batty playing Bob Dylan's records endlessly at full volume, I felt committed to covering the pop and folk music scene. While I was not about to don bell-bottoms and a headband, I came to see that the young rebels, expressing through music their disillusionment with society's hypocrisy and injustice, were correct in their stand against the war in Vietnam and the lack of progress in the fight against racism.

Mike Jahn was decidedly of the counterculture. Abe's distress over John Kifner's refusal to wear socks a few years earlier seemed ludicrous in light of Jahn's defiantly nonconformist appearance, and I sent a memo to Clif Daniel preparing him for the presence of our new rock critic. "Mr. Jahn wears his hair in a somewhat bizarre style," I wrote. "In fact, he looks like a werewolf. But since his work will not require him to be in the office very much, I don't think he'll bite any of us."

After the 300,000 young people at Woodstock had left the field, which had become a mud pit during a weekend of downpours, I had the sense that something of considerable significance had taken place—but what? I asked four reporters to invite a panel of festivalgoers to *The Times* for a wide-ranging, round-table discussion that we could publish. Five men and one woman, whose ages ranged from sixteen to twenty-two, accepted. All came from comfortable middle-class backgrounds and said they wouldn't have missed Woodstock for anything, and that the weekend had been "heavy." The questions, posed by Dick Reeves, Joe Lelyveld, Mike Kaufman and Mike Jahn, as well as myself, centered on drugs, sex and their hopes for the country's future.

Practically everything at Woodstock, they said, was understood to be collective property. There was a sense throughout of belonging and community. Tents, food and drugs were all freely shared. People readily volunteered to perform community services, whether collecting trash or helping talk someone thorough a bad LSD trip. Drugs were everywhere, and were accepted as the norm. However, one panel member, who had considered taking LSD for the first time, had decided against it after peeking into the "bum-trip tent."

Another participant said he had experienced an aura comparable to Woodstock's once before. "I went to the peace march in Chicago," he told us, "and I found the same thing happening. You'd pass someone young or someone with long hair and you'd smile at each other. Or you'd give each other the peace sign, or know that he was thinking the same way you were thinking. And like the blacks go by each other and say 'brother,' it gave you the same type of unity." To my mind, the essence of Woodstock was expressed by the panelist who said, "I just had a feeling that, wow, there are so many of us, we really have power. I'd always felt like such a minority. But I thought, wow, we're a majority—it felt like that. I felt like, here's the answer to anyone who calls us deviates."

The response to *The Times*'s coverage, picked up by papers worldwide, demonstrated that the weekend in the mud had evidently crystallized the sense of solidarity among youths globally, uniting and empowering them beyond anything they had previously envisioned.

Grace Lichtenstein, pleased with the part she had played in awakening me to the significance of Woodstock, congratulated me on the coverage. In her late twenties, she had recently transferred to the metropolitan staff from *The Times*'s WQXR radio station. Lichtenstein, who affected round, dark-tinted glasses and wore her blond hair long and with bangs, looked small and fragile, but when there was something on her mind she could become an editor's nightmare. She was more outspoken than anyone else on the staff about what she considered social biases on the part of "the establishment"— particularly against women.

Well aware of *The Times*'s style rule that banned the honorific "Ms.," Lichtenstein once wrote it into her copy anyway. I said to her, "You know we can't print that. What is she, a Miss or a Mrs.?"

"If you want to know, you call her," she replied.

Other reporters echoed her protests. A memo I received from Laurie Johnston, about to cover a women's rights conference, broached the subject: "I just dread asking, 'Is it Miss or Mrs.?' and hearing for the hundredth time, 'What difference does that make to *The Times*?'

"Personally, I think it makes for one more little piece of information but then it is certainly something we don't automatically report about men. . . . It does lead to speculation, though: Can just any group think up a title and insist on it? From a feminist viewpoint, is it not equally 'sexist' to discriminate between Mr. and Ms.? Should we drop all such titles? Should we, in an impersonal age, add *more* titles to differentiate ourselves even more, for men as well as women (married or unmarried, parent or nonparent, hetero or homo)?"

Woman reporters persisted in their pro-Ms. argument, and debate among *Times* executives went on incessantly. At first Punch and Abe resisted the change but they finally agreed to go along with what had already become common usage in most publications. On June 19, 1986, the change was ordered for those women who preferred Ms. to Miss or Mrs. Not all did. "*The Times* believes now that 'Ms.' has become a part of the language," Abe conceded in a memo to the staff.

Grace Lichtenstein espoused all minority causes. When Channel Thirteen's cameras were in the office shooting some film about the paper, an interviewer asked Lichtenstein how she felt about working in the city room. She responded that there weren't enough blacks, women, Puerto Ricans or American Indians on the staff. When her comments were aired during the broadcast, she earned her first trip to Abe's office, where he gave her what she later told me was "the dressing-down of my life." Abe, she said, had reprimanded her for being disloyal, and using McCarthyite tactics against the paper.

Though Grace and I butted heads on more than one occasion, I liked her for her keen mind, and absorbed what I could from her hip perspective. In 1971, she persuaded me to urge the bullpen to run a photo of Bob Dylan and George Harrison on page one, along with her article on the Concert for Bangladesh. When the photo-plus-story appeared, *The Times* earned plaudits from college students, and Grace became something of a counterculture hero.

On July 25, 1972, I assigned her to cover a Rolling Stones concert at Madison Square Garden, which also made page one. The day her Stones article ran, she decided to test me, to see to what degree I was an establishment stiff. She invited me to accompany her to the second night of the Stones concerts at the Garden. To her surprise, I accepted.

It was a night I will long remember, as much for the crowds as for Mick Jagger's mesmerizing performance. I don't think I had ever seen an audience so enraptured since Joe Papp's *The Taming of the Shrew* at the East River Amphitheater. Of course this was a different scene entirely. Mostly young white people, dancing, screaming, jumping up and down on their seats, smoking pot. Some were neatly dressed. Others wore torn clothing and even loincloths. Lichtenstein and I ran into a young metropolitan reporter in a corridor at the Garden. He looked at me quizzically, dressed as I was in jacket and tie. (I later removed them.)

In that same summer of 1972, Grace, along with Edith Evans Asbury, Grace Glueck and several other women on my staff, together with women from other areas of the news and business sides of the paper, brought a federal antidiscrimination lawsuit against *The Times*. With the women's movement gaining support across the country, the women's caucus of *The Times* searched pension records, and confirmed that the paper paid women less than men. The average salary of female reporters was $59 a week lower than that of male reporters.

They also found the paper lagged in promoting women to vital decision-making jobs outside their traditional coverage of style, family and fashion. Moreover, of the paper's 425 reporters, only forty were women. True, women had made a few striking gains, but there was still, for example, no woman executive on the masthead. And only one woman, Betsy Wade, had made it to a top post in the hard-news area. She was the head of the foreign copy desk, the highest-ranking woman in the news department.

The reaction among some of my male colleagues to the women's legal action was caustic amusement. They were quick to point out the irony of my having aggressively brought strong women onto the metropolitan staff, only to see them treacherously join ranks with the lawsuit's instigators from other departments, among whom were two highly regarded reporters now in the Washington bureau, Eileen Shanahan and Nan Robertson.

Betsy Wade was the principal plaintiff named in the lawsuit, formally entitled *Elizabeth Boylan et al., Plaintiffs v. The New York Times Company* (Boylan being Betsy's married name). When the suit was ultimately settled, *The Times*—while refusing to admit to any discriminatory employment practices "past or present"—promised to abide by an affirmative-action plan that would place women in important jobs in the news and business areas of the newspaper. For many women, progress was slow, but by early 2003, six of the twenty-two top executives listed on the paper's masthead were women. Two of them were in vanguard positions: Gail Collins, the first woman to be editorial-page editor, and Janet L. Robinson, the paper's first woman president and general manager.

Despite the lawsuit, my own relations with the women on my staff was, I believe, mutually respectful and almost invariably affectionate. I base this conclusion on what many of them, after a friendship of years, have themselves told me. In 2001, a delegation from the Newswomen's Club of New York, among them Edith Evans Asbury, who had just celebrated her ninetieth birthday, visited my office to present me with a special award. The inscription on the plaque read, "To Arthur Gelb, for forwarding the role of women in journalism."

IN SEPTEMBER 1969, when Abe became managing editor, the title regained some of the luster it had lost. Abe at once began tightening control of the news operation. The foreign and national editors were instructed to report to Sy Topping in his new post as assistant managing editor, and I was asked by Abe to report directly to him on all metropolitan and cultural matters.

I, too, made some changes. I asked Syl Fox to become my deputy when Bob Alden decided he'd spent enough time in that role and switched to the real estate news department as its director. (He stayed in that post just over two years before becoming United Nations bureau chief in early 1972. One night in October 1973, he was filing a story on a tumultuous session of the Security Council. He finished dictating his final paragraph to the foreign desk, hung up the telephone and toppled from his chair, dying instantly of a heart attack.)

With the city convulsing, 1969 was also a year marked by Mayor Lindsay's battle for his political survival. The mayoral election was set for November 4, and Lindsay, who had lost the Republican primary on June 17 due to a conservative backlash, was running for reelection on the Independent-Liberal ticket. His challengers were State Senator John J. Marchi of Staten Island, the victor in the Republican primary, and City Controller Mario A. Procaccino, the Democratic candidate.

Throughout the summer, while the polls gave Marchi little chance of winning, Lindsay consistently trailed Procaccino. But as the campaign progressed, Procaccino's lead began to shrink and his managers advised him to shun television debates that would pit him against Lindsay's "movie star" image.

On September 5, I met with Syl Fox and my other desk editors to discuss the torpor of the campaign and I suggested we invite the candidates to debate their differences at the paper. There would be no TV cameras and we would run the text of the debate in the next day's editions. It was an innovative newspaper approach for its day, and Abe loved the idea.

I called Martin Steadman, Procaccino's public relations man and a former *Tribune* staffer whom I had known from my days as a reporter. Improvising as we spoke, I told him the debate would last three hours and that excerpts of equal size would run exclusively in *The Times*. Steadman was lukewarm, but I called Lindsay's and Marchi's campaign managers, telling them I was sure Procaccino would agree to debate. Since Marchi had little to lose and Lindsay had everything to gain, they accepted my invitation.

A few days later, Procaccino was still uncommitted. But I proceeded with plans for the debate, which I scheduled at the *Times* auditorium for Friday, October 10, with the story and text to run the following Monday. Since the three candidates had not appeared together anywhere, the debate would be a news and promotional coup for *The Times*.

But by September 17, I still had no definite answer from Procaccino. Richard Aurelio, Lindsay's campaign manager, said he needed confirmation within five days or Lindsay would be forced to free up the date. He said if Procaccino backed out, he assumed *The Times* would run a story about his unwillingness to appear. I told Steadman about Aurelio's challenging remark and, three days later at a press conference, Procaccino announced he had accepted *The Times*'s invitation. It was the first I heard of Procaccino's acceptance, and the first time that the public was made aware that a debate was even being discussed.

Other newspapers, radio stations and television networks were in a tempest. They phoned me personally, accusing the *Times* of keeping a major story in the public interest to ourselves and suppressing its wider distribution. I probably would have argued the same way had another paper tied up the debate, so I told them I was sorry, but the rules had been set and only the candidates could change them. Abe and I met with Marchi, Lindsay and Procaccino on September 24 and they agreed we could invite reporters from other publications but insisted on a ban on cameras and tape recorders. As for those invited, they had to agree to adhere to our embargo against publication of anything about the debate until after ten P.M. Monday, when *The Times*'s first edition reached city newsstands.

At the meeting, Procaccino requested publication of the complete text, not just excerpts. One of Marchi's advisors protested, claiming that Marchi would get less space since he spoke more slowly than the others. I interjected, "How can you possibly object to full text?" And Marchi, realizing the objection was specious, acquiesced. The debate was pared down to ninety minutes, when we realized there was no way a three-hour session could fit into the allotted three pages. It was decided that I would be the moderator.

I asked the staff to submit questions and received hundreds, and many more were mailed in, unsolicited, by readers. I distilled the pile down to six topics, with the help of the three political reporters I had invited to ask the questions—Dick Reeves, Marty Tolchin and Clayton Knowles, a veteran of the City Hall beat.

At the debate, the candidates—who had not received the questions in advance—sat behind a long table. An audience of 125, mostly reporters from other publications, filled the ninth-floor auditorium. Each candidate articulated his position on the issues more clearly than ever before in the campaign, and took the opportunity to fire mild attacks at the others. But there were no significant revelations.

Lindsay defended his record, emphasizing the increased size of the Police Department and accusing his opponents of remaining "consistently silent in the face of really critical issues" over the three previous years. He declared that "the mayor has to be an activist and . . . use the power of the office in order to lead, to innovate, to bring about changes and to try new things."

Procaccino said he thought "the job of a mayor is just like that of a judge. And that is to stand in the middle of an opposing conflict, to act as mediator first." In a jab at Lindsay, he added, "I think that the people of this city will trust me because I can talk to them, I don't talk down to them."

Marchi, the only candidate who spoke without notes, declared his intention to revise the city charter, delegating some mayoral powers to borough presidents and community planning boards. He got the biggest laugh of the morning when, after each candidate had tiptoed around the subject of taxes, he said, "I think by this time you're getting the idea that you're not getting any new taxes from this table—at least between now and November four."

After the candidates left the building, Lindsay challenged Procaccino to continue the debate in the street, before rolling television cameras. Procaccino declined, saying, "I think Lindsay wants to get sixty-second clips to show that he is taller than I and prettier than Marchi." But soon after, the three did meet for a formal televised debate. The debate at *The Times* had broken the logjam of the campaign.

On November 4, Lindsay won by over 150,000 votes. He dominated in Manhattan and held even with Procaccino in Queens. Marchi took twenty percent of the vote, most notably in areas where Lindsay did poorly, thus keeping Procaccino from capitalizing in Lindsay's weakest districts. Abe Beame retook the city controller's seat, which he had held under Mayor Wagner.

For me, it meant four more years of covering a mayor who was already convinced I was out to get him. And, before six months had passed, he would believe it more than ever.

On November 13, as the metropolitan desk was still quieting down nine days after the election, *The Times* received the first in a string of bomb threats. The building was evacuated from 8:30 to 11:00 that morning. Many employees were unable to make it back to their desks for an additional hour or so due to the bottleneck at the front entrance caused by rigorous security measures. For the first time, all bags and packages were subject to search, and even Clif Daniel was stopped by a guard who sheepishly asked him to open his attaché case. Sy Topping, who was not carrying his *Times* ID card, was not allowed to enter the building until someone confirmed he was the assistant managing editor.

Five days later, the next threat came, and then another, and yet another. After the first couple of building evacuations, I realized that any crackpot with a telephone could critically disrupt the process of getting out the paper. I reserved a suite at the Manhattan Hotel on Eighth Avenue, setting up a temporary desk where reporters could get their assignments and copy could flow smoothly while the police searched for explosives. None were ever found. But we concluded there was only one way to avoid repeated evacuations. *The Times*, which had always allowed visitors free access to the city room and other parts of the building, had to install a security checkpoint, which remains in place to this day.

The Times's fears were not unfounded. Bombs were being set off in downtown Manhattan by various disaffected groups. Macy's at Herald Square had been bombed in October. Two days before the first threat at *The Times*, explosions rocked the headquarters of Chase Manhattan Bank and the General Motors Building. Then, on December 9, a bomb exploded in the stacks at the New York Public Library, causing some damage but injuring no one, since it went off after closing time.

On March 7, 1970, a Greenwich Village town house at 18 West Eleventh Street blew up, killing three members of the radical Weather Underground who used the building as a bomb factory. A large cache of dynamite and homemade pipe bombs was discovered in the wreckage, "enough to blow up most of the block," said one police inspector. The blast wrecked the home of our theater reporter, Mel Gussow, who lived next door. When he heard the news in the city room, he flew to Eleventh Street. Fortunately, his wife and son had been out when the explosion occurred. While they stayed with his parents, Mel helped cover the grisly story and wrote subsequent accounts for the paper.

Then, in the predawn hours of March 12, three blasts were reported within half an hour of one another: one at the offices of Mobil, one at IBM, one at General Telephone and Electronics. At the end of March, an explosion at another makeshift bomb factory destroyed an apartment on the Lower East Side, killing one person. Perhaps most shocking of all was the bomb set off at Police Headquarters on June 9, blasting debris across Centre Street and injuring seven.

Such events had become so common that stories of foiled bombing attempts were buried deep in the paper. These included the arrest of a man caught while attempting to detonate two pipe bombs in front of an Armed Forces Recruiting Center in the Bronx; the discovery of an incendiary device taped under a table at a West Side YWCA; and eleven Molotov cocktails found under five police radio cars in Queens.

Sanford Garelik, the former police chief inspector who had been elected president of the City Council, said that three or four urban guerrilla groups, plus a few smaller terrorist groups, were largely responsible for the attacks. Included among them were the Black Panthers, the Weather Underground, and the Young Lords—a band of militant Puerto Ricans. Garelik described the organizations as "small, in the hundreds," but said they were capable of "great destruction." One psychiatrist who specialized in the study of violence predicted that things were only going to get worse, believing that America had entered a period of "neo-anarchism."

In the midst of all this came the party thrown on January 14, 1970, at Leonard Bernstein's Park Avenue duplex to raise funds for the defense of twenty-one Black Panthers awaiting trial on charges of plotting to blow up department stores, police stations, subway switching stations and the New York Botanical Garden. Immortalized by the term "radical chic," coined by Tom Wolfe in an article for the June 8 issue of *New York* magazine, the famed conductor's soiree was representative of a fad among the liberal white elite to commingle with and lionize dangerous elements. The Panthers, the Young Lords and, later, the Mafia gangster Joey Gallo were sought-after party guests.

Charlotte Curtis, *The Times*'s women's news editor (later style editor) and one of Manhattan's most astute observers of the society set, wrote about the Bernstein party for the paper, subtly satirizing the disjunction of the evening: the way those from the white upper class and those from the black ghettos sized each other up over hors d'oeuvres served (by nonblack servants) on silver platters. Donald Cox, the Black Panther field marshal, assured a female guest that she had nothing to fear, "that she would not be killed even if she is a rich member of the middle class with an avowed capitalist for a husband." Minutes before, Cox had told Bernstein, "If business won't give us full employment, then we must take the means of production and put them in the hands of the people."

"I dig absolutely," Bernstein responded.

Curtis was both courted and feared by her interviewees—courted because they were flattered to be singled out, and feared because she knew how to put her finger on their absurdities. Bernstein and his guests, according to Tom Wolfe, were not among those who felt flattered by Curtis's attention. "It wasn't anything she wrote that infuriated them," Wolfe said. "It was that she put down exactly what they said. That's always what seems cruelest of all, to hold up a mirror to people that way."

Curtis, always stylishly dressed, joined *The Times* as a fashion reporter in 1961 and was assigned to the society beat two years later. It was Clifton Daniel, then assistant managing editor, who had first instructed Curtis to move away from gossip, "to write about society as news and to treat it as sociology." Her irreverent reporting on the capering and posturing of the upper crust was something of a revolution for *The Times*, and her dissections of the elite, together with her coverage of topical issues like birth control, abortion and the feminist movement, earned her a promotion to women's editor in 1965. On January 1, 1974, she became the first woman whose name appeared on *The Times*'s masthead, when she was appointed editor of the Op-Ed page, to succeed Harrison Salisbury upon his retirement. (He had initiated the page four years earlier.)

Curtis's piece on the Bernstein Panther reception elicited a comment from our editorial page: "Emergence of the Black Panthers as the romanticized darlings of the politico-cultural jet set is an affront to the majority of black Americans. . . . The group therapy plus fund-raising soiree at the home of Leonard Bernstein . . . represents the sort of elegant slumming that degrades patrons and patronized alike. It might be dismissed as guilt-relieving fun spiked with social consciousness. . . . Responsible black leadership is not likely to cheer as the Beautiful People create a new myth that Black Panther is Beautiful."

My paper did not stint in its coverage of the Black Panthers, which symbolized the sulfurous black rage in the country. Organized in Oakland, California, by Bobby Seale and Huey Newton in October 1966, it was meant to spread the message of armed self-defense to blacks in the ghettos. They viewed American blacks as a colonized people at war with "the racist white power structure," and looked for inspiration to North Vietnam's fierce stand against foreign occupation.

Only a few months before the reception at the Bernsteins', Bobby Seale had grabbed national headlines as a defendant in the circuslike trial of the "Chicago Eight," which was covered by Tony Lukas for the national desk. Charged along with seven others with conspiracy to incite a riot at the 1968 Democratic National Convention, Seale refused to be defended by William Kunstler, the lawyer chosen by the other defendants. He insisted on defending himself, and his case was separated from the others.

Throughout the trial, Seale slung verbal abuse at Judge Julius Hoffman, calling him "pig," "fascist" and "racist." Hoffman finally ordered Seale bound and gagged and chained to a chair. He was ultimately charged with sixteen counts of contempt and sentenced to a four-year prison term. But in the end, the riot charges against him were dropped and his contempt conviction was reversed.

Seale's courtroom outbursts proved mild in comparison with those of the Panthers on trial in New York, for whom several thousand dollars had been raised at the Bernstein party. Because the accusations against the twenty-one defendants involved a possible menace to public safety, and because I expected things to get out of control quickly, as they had in Chicago, I knew I needed a reporter who was regarded by all as completely fair and accurate and who could stay cool no matter how bombastic the proceedings became. I chose Edith Evans Asbury.

Panther supporters hissed every time Edith entered the courtroom, and shouted epithets. She was occasionally approached during recesses, she told me, by radical sympathizers who tried to bully her into writing favorably about the Panthers. When she ignored the pressure, they cursed her. "They felt if you weren't with them, you had to be against them," Asbury told me. "They couldn't comprehend that I was just a reporter doing my job." She said she never felt really threatened, even though Judge John M. Murtagh had told her he kept a loaded revolver under his robes when in the courtroom.

During the trial's first twelve days there were 665 interruptions. One night, Murtagh's home in Inwood was hit with three fire bombs while he and his family slept. No one was hurt, and the damage to the building was minor. The following day, amidst shouts of invective, Murtagh, who Edith told me admiringly never lost his cool, calmly announced, "I've been called a pig once too often." He recessed the hearing indefinitely, sending the defendants back to their cells until such time as they promised in writing to abide by accepted courtroom etiquette. The hearing finally resumed on April 8, 1970, with what Edith called "consistently dignified behavior among defendants and spectators." The trial itself began September 8 and lasted until May, 14, 1971, when the jury, struck by the contradictory nature of the evidence, took two hours to acquit the defendants.

Also in 1970, Bobby Seale came up on charges again, this time for murder and kidnapping. A hung jury resulted in a mistrial and, due to the difficulty of assembling an impartial jury, the case was never tried again. By 1972, Seale disavowed his mission to overthrow the system, opting to work for change within it instead. He ran for mayor of Oakland that year (and lost).

FORTY-ONE

IN AN ENVIRONMENT where social norms were bending and rebellion was common, some borderline mental cases no longer felt compelled to suppress their aberrations. Aside from the bomb scares, death threats poured into the metropolitan desk, and once, before the new security system was put into place, a man waving a pistol made it into the city room, demanding to see "the metropolitan editor." He was disarmed by a couple of maintenance workers, who called the police. Although I never had to use it, a buzzer was affixed to my desk the next day so I could summon help if needed.

The security system was of no avail when I became a specific target, along with Punch Sulzberger and Abe Rosenthal, of a voluble group of men and women calling themselves Aesthetic Realists. Their guru, Eli Siegel, once defined his convoluted philosophy as "the seeing of the world, art and self as explaining each other: Each is the aesthetic oneness of opposites." Devoted to their mission that homosexuality could, and should, be "cured," they presented me with endless examples, day after day, of men who had been converted to "normal," heterosexual, behavior. I finally assigned a story about their organization but they insisted on further coverage, which was denied. They began wearing lapel buttons declaring themselves "Victims of the Press."

One day fifteen of them pushed their way into the city room, sought out the culture department and surrounded the gentle Dick Shepard, who was typing at his desk. Dick, bewildered, thought to escape them by climbing atop his desk. He stood there, helpless, the way a woman wearing a stereotypical skirt might try to flee a circling mouse, and there he stayed, frozen, until I was able to lead the Realists out to the anteroom with the promise I'd listen to their complaints. Still dissatisfied, they regularly picketed my apartment building as well as Punch's and Abe's. Every morning, when I tried to hail a taxi to take me to work, they shouted epithets. At last I found an escape from my building through a basement maze that led to a side exit. But when I arrived at *The Times*, another Realist unit awaited me, yelling oaths from a picket line.

At the same time, militant gays were vocally expressing their dissatisfaction with *The Times* because the paper had refused to substitute the word "gay" for "homosexual." One directive from the copy desk had explicitly stated, "the word 'gay' as a synonym for homosexual should be used only if it is part of an official, capitalized title of an organization, or if it appears in quoted matter." It wasn't until June 15, 1987—when Max Frankel succeeded Abe Rosenthal as executive editor—that the paper allowed "gay" as a designation for homosexual (and we reluctantly gave up the word as a synonym for "joyful").

The gay world cheered *The Times* and Max in particular for the change, and vilified Abe as antigay because it hadn't happened on his watch. And although changes often took forever at *The Times*, I believe that on this issue, of such poignancy to so many, the paper did tarry for too long. Yes, that was a mistake—but it didn't mean Abe was a homophobe.

In the preceding decades, virtually all homosexuals on the paper remained closeted, as was the case in most organizations, because they feared they would be denied promotions or other opportunities if their sexual orientation were disclosed. For that reason, none ventured to complain to me— or any other top editors as far as I knew—about unjust treatment, or to question the paper's style code.

Gay men at *The Times* surely had reason to be wary. I had not known then, nor had other top editors, that the company's medical department, under its eccentric director, Dr. David Goldstein, looked askance at any hint of homosexuality in a new recruit. Once, after interviewing a bright reportorial prospect, I told him he was hired, pending his passing the medical exam. But after the exam, Dr. Goldstein informed me he had rejected my candidate. I was stumped.

"What did you find wrong with him?" I asked, thinking he had discovered the man was dying of heart disease or something worse.

"I asked him whether he had ever had a homosexual experience," said Goldstein, "and he told me he had once participated in a circle jerk at college."

"And why would that prevent his working here?"

"I'd worry about him being in close proximity to others on your staff."

"That's idiocy," I said. I sat at my desk for a moment in disbelief. I called the reporter and asked him why he had found it necessary to reveal this private matter to the medical department. He said he wanted to answer all questions truthfully, and was upset that the doctor had asked him whether he'd seen a film called *The Sergeant*, in which the character played by Rod Steiger refuses to acknowledge his latent homosexuality. Dr. Goldstein apparently tried to imply that the reporter was, like the character in the movie, suffering from feelings of guilt and denial.

I couldn't help but admire my candidate's honesty and, still furious with Goldstein, I headed for Abe's office. He was as angry as I, and persuaded the publisher not only to overrule Goldstein but to instruct him to stop asking the question.

Goldstein stayed on a while longer, and drew me into battle one final time—when I was set to hire Mel Gussow for the culture staff. After Gussow's medical exam, Goldstein informed me gleefully that Gussow had flunked because he was found to be a heroin addict.

Gussow was nothing of the sort, I said. "Well," Goldstein smugly replied, "his urine showed quinine, and surely you know that heroin is cut with quinine. Do you want an addict on your staff?"

Once again, Goldstein had thrown me into a state of fury. When I told Gussow what Goldstein had said, he assured me he had never used drugs. Suddenly it dawned on him. He'd had a couple of gin and tonics the night before the exam.

I called Goldstein, demanding he give Gussow another urine test. Goldstein did so reluctantly, and, of course, this time Gussow passed and was hired, becoming a highly valued member of the culture staff.

IN MORE WAYS THAN ONE, the paper had been infected by the turmoil of the country. Late in 1969, for example, a young rewrite man whom I had always liked, Mark Hawthorne, let his hair grow and developed a passion for making charcoal rubbings of manhole covers, then silk-screening the images onto plywood.

One day, he simply stopped talking. Toward the end of his shift, during which he had been given no work, I tried to evoke some kind of response, but he remained stubbornly mute. At first I cajoled him, then became stern. Nothing. When I asked if there was anything physically wrong with him, he shook his head.

"Are you planning never to speak again?" I asked.

He nodded.

"Don't you think this is kind of silly?"

He shook his head.

"Well," I said, "how do you expect to work on rewrite? What will you say when you pick up the phone?"

He shrugged.

"Why don't you go home, and not come back until you're able to speak."

When he didn't budge, I said I'd have to ask a security guard to escort him out of the building. With that he got up and left, but once outside, he planted himself cross-legged on the sidewalk, where he began drawing the attention of passersby, a number of whom stopped to stare at him. The lobby guards asked me whether they should call the police. Abe and I went down together to urge him to leave. When he ignored us, we summoned his closest friend on the staff, Michael Kaufman, who pleaded with him to go home. He finally did and I never saw him again.

But Hawthorne bore me no hard feelings. A couple of years later, he sent me a small treasure he had found while rummaging through his deceased father's belongings. It was a canceled check signed by Eugene O'Neill, dated April 2, 1920, and paid to *The New York Times* for a three-dollar annual subscription. O'Neill had briefly shared a hotel room in Greenwich Village with Hawthorne's father, and left a few items behind when he moved on. I wrote Hawthorne that I'd had the check framed for my library wall.

Hawthorne never rejoined society as most people know it. He left his wife and child and moved to Berkeley, where he haunts the streets, adopting different names from day to day. The last I heard of him his name was "Sparky." He is also known as the "Hate Man," because of the way he amicably tells everyone he meets, "I hate you." His local fame is such that his picture graces a postcard, featuring him wearing a skirt, a battered hat, two mismatched shoes and a matted beard. He is smoking a cigarette and giving the world the finger.

At the same time that Hawthorne quit, scattered rumblings began reaching me and other editors about an incipient insurrection by members of the staff. No one confronted us directly with any complaints or demands, but we kept hearing that some of the best and most respected reporters were grumbling about being crimped stylistically by the copy desks. Tony Lukas, we learned, was the instigator of a vague scheme to bring "participatory democracy" to the paper. He had just returned to the city room after covering the trial of the Chicago Seven (down from eight, after Seale's case was separated from the others).

The national desk in New York, he complained, had restricted his portrayal of the bizarre courtroom proceedings, refusing to allow him the same kind of personal writing freedom extended to Nicholas von Hoffman by the *Washington Post*. Von Hoffman, who called the trial "a shoddy parody of jurisprudence," had gleefully described Judge Julius Hoffman as "an aged Hobbit who never stops talking," and depicted defendant Jerry Rubin as a "freelance wild man."

It was quite true that such freewheeling phrases were routinely edited out of Lukas's stories. He was unable, for example, to persuade the copy desk not to delete the beginning of a paragraph, "A man-child from the land of hippiedom . . . ," in referring to the clownish defendant Abbie Hoffman. The desk also cut the ending of one story that stated sarcastically: "The trial will continue tomorrow if the hippies don't blow up the courthouse."

Another example: When Chicago's deputy police chief testified that he saw the defendant David Dellinger leading a militant throng from Grant Park, Dellinger protested, from the defendant's table, "Oh, bullshit!" Judge Hoffman scolded Dellinger for using "that kind of language" and revoked his bail. An editor on the national desk told Lukas to refer to the offensive phrase as "an obscenity." But, Lukas said, if he called it an obscenity most readers would imagine a more objectionable term. The editor countered, "Why don't we call it a 'barnyard epithet'?" And that's how it ran in the paper, to Tony's discomfort, but to the amusement of the rest of the staff.

The desk made other deletions as well, and it seemed that an aggrieved Tony had found a sympathetic ear in—among others—Charlotte Curtis, Paul Montgomery, William Farrell, Alden Whitman and Clive Barnes (who was angry that a line had been deleted from his review of a play about Julius and Ethel Rosenberg because he had expressed what the copy desk considered an unallowable political judgment). In the unsettled climate of the era, all of them, like Tony, found themselves responding emotionally to the stories they covered, and sometimes attempted to weave personal commentary into their copy. This group of mini-revolutionaries came to be mocked by the editors as "The Cabal."

It wasn't that reporters were unmindful of *The Times*'s age-old insistence on opinion-free reporting and, most especially, of Abe's hypersensitivity on the subject (in which I happened to concur). They simply seemed to have decided the time had come to challenge the paper's tight control over copy, much as college students nationwide were currently questioning their curriculums and defying their professors.

Because the social rebellion revolving around Vietnam and civil rights, among other issues, had begun to spill over into the city room, Catledge's mandate to Abe five years earlier—enjoining him to take the paper to greater heights—was not easily realized. Some reporters wanted to liberalize *Times* style with rambling, anecdotal leads on hard-news stories. Others wanted a license for personal expression. And that's where Abe uncompromisingly drew the line. Over and over, he alerted editors to watch the daily copy for editorializing and—most particularly—warned about keeping the paper from moving to the left of center. Center, he insisted, was where the paper must always be. Part of his mindset emanated from his firsthand experience of the harsh, communist life that surrounded him in Poland. And having been imbued with the Ochsian heritage of fairness and balance that made the paper great, he saw it as his mission to defend those traditions.

As time went on, Abe became less patient and more irritable in dealing with reporters whom he felt were not on his wavelength, believing they were less loyal in their devotion to the paper than he was. It got to the point where he could not abide any criticism of the paper's philosophy and, when he was challenged, his temper flared. After work, when we'd unwind at Sardi's, he'd begin to mellow, and, usually by the time we said good night, he had shrugged off his work-related headaches and regained his sense of humor. (I gradually came to realize that during this time Abe was under stress at home as well as in the office; his marriage was unraveling and he was gnawed by guilt about Ann.)

To me, Abe's moods were tantamount to the way he'd pound out five exclamation marks on his typewriter at the end of a sentence and then delete them. Often, when he realized he'd overreacted, he'd apologize. The job was emotionally draining, and it wasn't always easy to maintain an unruffled façade. But if anyone could be justified in his temperamental outbursts, it was Abe, whose journalistic integrity was absolute, and who unquestionably did more than anyone to move the paper ahead even in the most difficult of times. It's true he was something of a monomaniac about *The Times*. But he was a *brilliant* monomaniac.

One day, attempting to caution the cabal, Abe sent a ringing memo to the staff: "Time was when objectivity was taken for granted as a newspaper's goal, if not always an attained goal. But we live in a time of commitment and advocacy when 'tell it like it is' really means 'tell it like I say it is' or 'tell it as I want it to be.' For precisely that reason, it is more important than ever that *The Times* keep objectivity in its news columns as its number one, bedrock principle."

But the cabal, it appeared, was already reaching toward an even more fanciful goal than the mere overthrow of reportorial balance. According to one proposal, reporters would decide among themselves which stories merited coverage and who should cover them. They would then vote on which stories to feature on page one. How they would manage to get the paper to press on time was a minor point they had not thought through.

After several meetings attended by small groups of reporters, Charlotte Curtis arranged a presentation by a founding member of the cooperative that published *Le Monde* in Paris to explain how a newspaper could be operated democratically by members of its own staff.

"I can vividly recall our general bewilderment as our French speaker—who was *Le Monde*'s correspondent at the UN—outlined how his newspaper's cooperative worked," Michael Kaufman told me years later. "To begin with, *Le Monde* sought to limit circulation to a highbrow readership and to shape a political elite. The speaker explained that *Le Monde*'s founders had protected their authority by limiting the paper's membership to all but a small handful of new staffers.

"But the most shocking revelation came when he told us how the members of the cooperative had obtained their franchise in the first place. During World War II, some of the top people at the paper *Le Temps* had supported the Pétainist collaborators. The speaker and his fellow *Le Monde* founders had been in the Resistance, and once peace came, they appealed to their 'friends in the government,' who then turned over the confiscated *Le Temps* plant and presses to them, making them indirectly beholden to the government.

"I think all of us were impressed by the speaker's wartime experiences and the cachet of his having been in the Resistance, but we were baffled by how any of that applied to our situation. And the notion of turning to 'friends in the government' seemed very loony indeed."

Bill Farrell rose to address the speaker on that point: "I'm afraid you do not understand the basic traditions of American journalism in regard to members of the government. We may sometimes lift our skirts for them, but we really draw the line at having our garters snapped."

Farrell's comment effectively reduced the meeting to parody. It was the beginning of the end of the cabal. A couple of reporters finally came to me, explaining that what most of the staff really sought was not "participatory democracy" in any shape or form, but simply access to the top editors, who always seemed too busy to talk to them about ideas for improving the paper's coverage. After thinking that over, I invited members of the cabal and any other interested reporters to a buffet supper at my home. Fifty or so showed up. The evening went well, if for no other reason than that the reporters felt someone was listening to them.

The next day, I called Paul Montgomery, who had not attended my supper, to my desk. "This is *The Times*," I told him. "It will never be a cooperative. If you're unhappy with the way things operate here, you'd better leave." (Eventually he went to Europe for the *Wall Street Journal* and I lost touch with him.)

To Tony Lukas, whom I reached by phone out of town, I conveyed a similar message. The initial spirit of mutiny petered out, and soon the cabal was no more. Tony stayed on the staff a while longer and then left to found *[More]*, the journalism magazine that was very much in the spirit of those times, and he also began to do freelance writing. He and I remained good friends, and I cheered when he won his second Pulitzer Prize for his book about the Boston school crisis, *Common Ground.*

ABE BECAME ever more obsessed with keeping the news columns of *The Times* free of personal opinion. In a spirit of mea culpa seldom encountered in journalism, he initiated a policy of rectifying what the publisher and top editors regarded as "serious lapses of fairness, balance or perspective." In 1972, Abe introduced a daily "Corrections" rubric on the Second Front (later moved to page two) to remedy factual errors. But he soon decided the rubric did not go far enough. There was still no emphatic way to explain (and apologize for) the occasional slips in standards.

On March 31, 1971, in a memo to desk editors, Abe cautioned them to make sure that "a denial of a charge gets decently equal treatment with the charge itself" and that "when a man is acquitted of charges against him, the acquittal gets as much attention as the original charges." As just one example, he cited a recent seven-paragraph story about a police lieutenant who had filed charges of dereliction of duty against his commander. Two months later, when the commander was cleared, we dismissed the story with only one paragraph at the bottom of a page.

"I know of no way of automatically insuring that we are as fair as we want to be," Abe wrote. "The only suggestion I can make is that whenever a denial, a correction or an acquittal comes to the attention of the editor, a red flag should pop up in his mind and he should check the clips to find out what kind of treatment we gave the original story."

The problem was so knotty it took eleven more years to try once again to resolve it. In 1983, upon reading in *The Times* a short negative review of a minor artist's work—an artist, as it happened, he had never heard of—Abe said he was fed up with what he considered a critic's vicious personal attack. He told his editors he had finally come to realize that the daily "Corrections" formula was inadequate in cases where the paper's basic standards were punctured, and that we needed to find a way of dealing with such missteps. Soon after, when an article appeared quoting a complaint by a writer that publishers had "always cheated authors" but failed to reflect the publishers' point of view, Abe insisted on immediate action.

He ordered a new apologia, called "Editors' Note," to appear below the space allotted for "Corrections," whenever a story was deemed particularly deficient in upholding *Times* principles. He wrote the first note himself, point-ing out the story's omission and, knowing Punch felt as he did about the im-portance of keeping the paper from straying, Abe phoned him to announce he had "a nice present for him" and to look for it in the morning edition.

Abe later broadened the "Editors' Note" to explain all manner of lapses in taste and standards. "Part of my job," he told me, "is making sure the news columns are never, through editorializing or personal judgments, pulled to the left or the right. It's like riding a horse down a path and trying to keep it in the center. It's not easy."

LIKE TONY LUKAS, other creatively restless *Times* reporters—among them Gay Talese, Richard Reeves, David Halberstam, Neil Sheehan and David Shipler—believed that they needed the freedom to express themselves more vividly and expansively. In each case, the decision to leave the paper, mostly to write books, proved highly rewarding. Other gifted reporters left for var-ious personal reasons—one of the saddest departures, to me, being that of McCandlish Phillips. He was the most original stylist I'd ever edited, and he cared solely about daily journalism. Only once did he produce a book, a memorable collection of his *Times* stories called *City Notebook*. On Septem-ber 25, 1973, he wrote me he was leaving, because he felt he could "not wisely or safely maintain the pace of the last decade for the next." He went on to explain that "a great factor is a need also for a periodic break from the quite relentless, sustained bearing down at high-pressure that is the life of the heavily assigned reporter." He had always seemed to relish every assignment

I gave him, and I wondered if his departure stemmed from a mystical summons.

As good reporters left the paper, others equally capable arrived to succeed them. But now, more than ever before, many of the recruits were women (although even with these new arrivals, we still had far fewer female than male reporters on our staff).

Among the most noteworthy of the new women was Charlayne Hunter, who before arriving in 1968 had been a staff writer for *The New Yorker* and an anchorwoman for the NBC affiliate in Washington. Reporting had been her passion since, at twelve, she discovered the comic strip character Brenda Starr. She edited her high school paper and sought admission to the University of Georgia, the only college in her state with a journalism program.

The problem was that the 175-year-old university was all white—and Hunter was black. Hunter and a black friend, Hamilton Holmes, with the support of civil rights organizations, brought their case to federal court, seeking an integration order. It took over a year for the court to reach a conclusion, so Hunter began her college education at Wayne State University in Detroit. She was a sophomore when, on January 5, 1961, Federal Judge William Bootle ruled that Hunter and Holmes were "fully qualified for immediate admission [to the University of Georgia] and would already have been admitted had it not been for their race and color." In addition to forcing the university to accept Hunter and Holmes, Judge Bootle forbade it to institute any special requirements for black applicants. This was the first attempt to desegregate Georgia's public education system at any level.

Georgia's governor, S. Ernest Vandiver, Jr., threatened to close the school by cutting off funds, citing a state law barring aid to a desegregated university. Judge Bootle, however, enjoined the governor from doing so, calling the clause "patently unconstitutional." In Washington, the Supreme Court unanimously rejected a request by the state to delay the admission of Hunter and Holmes pending an appeal. Students and locals from the town of Athens took to the streets waving Confederate flags and burning crosses.

When Hunter and Holmes presented themselves for enrollment on January 10, 1961, some two thousand students surrounded the Academic Building, where the two black students paid their tuition and registered for classes. There was no violence, but some students shouted racial slurs and segregationist slogans. Hunter was given a private room in a women's dorm, with her own bathroom and kitchenette, though she was officially welcome to eat in the cafeteria with the other students. Holmes took a room in town, because of a housing shortage on campus.

The school remained tense but peaceful until the next night. After her first day of classes, while Hunter was unpacking, a student mob and Ku Klux Klansmen rioted outside her dorm. They chanted, "Two, four, six, eight, we don't want to integrate," shouted, "Nigger, go home," and hurled rocks through windows. Police finally dispersed them with tear gas and fire hoses. Hunter, whose own window had been smashed, was escorted from the dorm in tears, clinging to a statue of the Madonna. She returned to school the following day. True to character, in the midst of the commotion surrounding her admission, she studied how the journalists who had descended on the campus were covering the story, and made mental notes that later were to inform her development as a reporter.

Many of the stories I assigned to Charlayne were based on her own ideas, and there were occasions when she advised me on how to handle black coverage in general. Her guidance and research were crucial in developing an extraordinary article toward the end of 1969, after I had received a phone call from an anonymous woman in Harlem. She said she had been devastated to learn of the recent death of an eleven-year-old neighborhood boy from an overdose of heroin. Finding her report hard to believe, I asked Joe Lelyveld, whose sensitive writing style had become his trademark, to discover whether it was true and, if so, to examine the boy's life and learn how the social agencies had failed him. Over the years since then, many reports of child drug victims have been published nationwide, but ours marked the first time a newspaper probed the subject so deeply, setting a pattern for coverage of preteenage drug abuse.

Joe needed all the help he could get in talking with Harlem residents, so I agreed that Charlayne should assist him. They spent three weeks on the story, and the fruits of their collaboration appeared January 12, 1970, on page one, above a four-column photo taken of the boy by a friend in his Harlem neighborhood. Assembled from scores of interviews, some gathered at considerable risk from street addicts and narcotics pushers, the story ran almost a full page on the inside jump space. It began:

"Walter Vandermeer—the youngest person ever to be reported dead of an overdose of heroin here—had been identified by many of the social agencies as a child in desperate need of care long before his body was discovered in the common bathroom of a Harlem tenement on Dec. 14, two weeks before his twelfth birthday.

"For most of those agencies he never became more than one case among thousands passing through their revolving doors. Others tried to fit him into their programs but lacked the manpower or resources to focus on him effectively. Eventually he would be shunted off to yet another institution. It was not heartlessness or malfeasance that explains why he usually went unnoticed, just overwhelming numbers. As one school official expressed it, 'There are thousands of Walter Vandermeers out there.'"

According to Joe and Charlayne, Walter had been failed by his family as well as city institutions. He was one of eleven children born to the same mother and five different fathers, and his own father had been deported as an illegal immigrant. He knew neither stability nor succor at home. Living an aimless life, he began sniffing glue at six. At eight, he spent his days playing cards on the stoops. He was kicked out of school in third grade for truancy and behavioral problems and placed in a shelter. By ten he was spending most of his time on the streets. "Walter lived to be thirty in twelve years," one of the street junkies said. "There was nothing about the street he didn't know."

While Joe depended a great deal on Charlayne's contribution, she received only italic recognition at the end of the article, which ran under Joe's byline. In accordance with a long-established policy that took many more years to break, only the reporter actually writing the story was signed. I promised Charlayne I'd one day make it up to her.

After the story appeared, a number of readers wrote to ask whether *The Times*'s Charlayne Hunter was the same as the one who had integrated the University of Georgia—a question that she deflected. She did not want to be anybody's symbol.

It was Charlayne who persuaded *The Times* to drop the designation "Negro" in favor of "black." She and I talked for many hours about it, and she persuaded me to support her when she wrote a powerful memo to Abe, which finally brought about the change—and started a trend at other major publications.

I was proud to have a woman of Charlayne's determination and courage on my staff, and my admiration for her grew with the years. In the spring of 1970, I told her I wanted to establish a Harlem bureau under her command, not as a police beat but as a base from which to file feature stories about the everyday life of the community and about ideas for improving the chronically neglected area. She glowed, as I had expected her to, when I said she would be the first *Times* reporter to run such a bureau. She said she cherished the assignment because "in a sense it was coming back home."

"One thing I'm sure you know," she told me, smiling, "I'm not going to write about people living up there as problems." This was a volatile period, when whites feared going to Harlem, even in the daytime, and some of the reporters mischievously suggested to Charlayne that she ask me for combat pay.

Charlayne insisted I accompany her to find bureau space to rent in a building on or near 125th Street. We took a taxi to Harlem and, after walking several blocks, I noticed four tough-looking youths, heading toward us. It flashed through my mind that they might not appreciate a middle-aged white man accompanying a pretty black woman in her twenties, and I tensed, recalling my experience on the night of the King assassination. Charlayne sensed my discomfort, and, when the youths didn't give way as we approached, she stepped in front of me and ordered them to "get lost." To my surprise, they let us pass. She laughed off the incident, saying that such teenagers shouldn't be taken seriously.

I signed a lease for Charlayne's office on 125th Street, and the bureau soon achieved a reputation for must-read coverage among important figures in the black community as well as our readers in general. Many of her stories—"about people, not problems"—made the Second Front. I was so impressed with what she wrote that sometime later I asked her to become an assistant metropolitan editor. She turned me down, saying she was interested only in reporting.

FORTY-TWO

T HE MOST MOMENTOUS STORY of my tenure as metropolitan editor ran in April of 1970, the same newsworthy month we established the Harlem bureau. It was an exposé of the rampant corruption in the New York City Police Department, and revealed an organized system of extortion and graft condoned by the highest-ranking officials on the force. Even the Mayor's Office, which had been supplied with specific information about crooked practices, chose to look the other way.

David Burnham, one of the very best investigative reporters I ever worked with, was on the story for six months before his series burst onto the front page for three successive days starting April 25. Burnham had come to *The Times* by chance in early August of 1967, from the President's Commission on Law Enforcement and Administration of Justice in Washington, where he was assistant director. The deputy director, Henry Ruth, believed the only way to reform the criminal justice system was to create a training unit to teach reporters how to improve their coverage.

Having worked for *Newsweek*, UPI and CBS, Burnham was skeptical of the plan and, after a few meetings, Ruth's proposal was abandoned. Then Ruth came up with a new strategy. If *The Times* could be encouraged to probe the system more deeply, then other papers doubtless would follow. Burnham was assigned to talk to the metropolitan editor about coverage. He phoned me and I invited him to the city room.

Burnham was a wiry man, prematurely balding, with a hypnotic gaze that seemed to be sizing me up, even as he obligingly filled me in about *his* background: he was thirty-four, Boston-born, a Harvard graduate, the founder of the Cambridge Parachute Club, and had served two years with the Army's 82nd Airborne Division.

Burnham then bluntly stated that the commission believed much of *The Times*'s coverage of law enforcement issues was "not very smart." He had expected me to throw him out, but instead I challenged him to come up with some story ideas to illustrate where our coverage was lacking. He wrote up a list, handed it to me, and, as he later told me, assumed that his *Times* affiliation was scuttled.

As I studied the list, I realized what an asset it would be to have someone on the staff with inside knowledge of the labyrinthine law enforcement world, someone who could cover the police with the shrewdness Sidney Zion had brought to our reporting on the courts. A few days later, I phoned Burnham and offered him a job.

He was surprised but said he'd love to give it a try. The beat I created for him included the offices of five district attorneys, scores of judges, over 30,000 cops and more than enough crime to keep them all busy. Burnham devised a formula to help him sift through and select, out of myriad possibilities, the stories he would write. Simply put, his coverage would focus on trying to answer two questions: Is the particular agency achieving its stated goals? And if not, why not? Burnham would be measuring these agencies with their own yardsticks and would present the facts as he found them, without commentary.

I put him on the traditional three-month probationary plan. Since he had never worked for a daily paper, he had trouble adjusting to deadline requirements, and his writing style was somewhat academic. But with faith in his determination to learn, I extended his trial for another three months.

In his eagerness to succeed, Burnham began working seven days a week, ten hours a day, and his style greatly improved. Obtaining the first precinct-by-precinct figures on crime ever disclosed by the police, he was able to show that the residents of Harlem, the South Bronx and Brooklyn's Bedford-

Stuyvesant were the victims of one-third of all reported violent crimes in the city. He demonstrated that police statistics on crime were inaccurate because many crimes went unreported by residents in poorer areas. Having examined records from the past couple of years of 136 persons accused of muggings, he also showed that the average assailant struck many times before he was caught, that he served only a short jail term and that after his release he resumed mugging—an early study of the recidivist theory.

Finally, in December 1968, Burnham landed a story that earned him a permanent place on the metropolitan staff. He had made friends with a patrolman named Jim Curran, of the police community relations unit. One day, in passing, Curran mentioned that a certain officer was "in the coop." Burnham asked what that meant.

"Oh, you know what the coop is," said Curran.

Burnham said he had no idea. "The coop," explained Curran, "is where cops go to sleep at night while they're on duty."

The information astonished Burnham, and Curran volunteered to show him. Burnham agreed to meet Curran at two o'clock that morning, and they drove to out-of-the-way places throughout the city where they witnessed cops napping in their patrol cars.

I was on a week's vacation at the time, and Burnham reported his discovery to one of my assistant editors, who advised him not to bother, since as far as he knew *The Times* was not interested in "crusading" stories. But Burnham thought this was exactly the type of story the paper should run, since it illustrated the way the Police Department was not living up to its own stated goal of patrolling the streets at night, at a time when reports of crime were soaring and residents were clamoring for more police protection. He decided to work on the story on his own time. Since he was not assigned a photographer, he invited Leland Schwartz, a copyboy who knew how to use a camera, to take pictures. Schwartz got off work at two A.M., and for a couple of nights, the two visited cooping grounds like Fort Greene Park in Brooklyn. They had no trouble getting close enough to take pictures because the patrolmen slept soundly in their cars.

Burnham had already talked to a number of cops, and learned that those who lacked the luxury of a car cooped in all-night movie theaters, hospitals and funeral homes. Since cops were required to call in every hour on the hour during their tours, they carried alarm clocks to signal the start of each hour. There was one coop that was equipped with a telephone, to enable the desk sergeant to reach the sleeping officers if they were "really needed." It was understood by precinct commanders that their men routinely spent a few hours sleeping on the midnight-to-eight-A.M. shift. As long as they called to check in at the appointed times, cooping was tolerated.

When I returned from my vacation in mid-December, Burnham showed me his story, which was the first I heard about it. I got it onto page one the next day, and the reaction was dramatic. "I am embarrassed because I think I was deficient," Police Commissioner Howard Leary publicly stated, and he summoned every precinct captain to a lecture on discipline.

The *Daily News* police reporter told Burnham, "That was no story. Everybody knew it." "Everybody" also knew that corruption existed within the Police Department, though few recognized to what extent. The public generally accepted the official line that there were just "a few rotten apples in the barrel," but did not question the soundness of the barrel itself.

I had wanted the police corruption story for a long time—ever since the late 1940s, when I first learned of the practice of "buying" promotions and, later, when I discovered police graft flourishing in the cabarets and also heard about payoffs in the narcotics bureau. But there was no way to get the story without on-the-record confirmation by sources within the Police Department—and the department was a closed, tightly knit organization with a strict "honor" code of self-protection. It was unimaginable that any officer, even an honest one, would voluntarily turn in a fellow cop. And none ever had—until Frank Serpico.

As I was soon to learn, Serpico had been butting his head against corrupt practices in the Police Department since 1959, when he first became a uniformed patrolman and tried again and again, always unsuccessfully, to alert his superior officers to the situation. Now, ten years and a number of interdepartmental transfers later, he was still being thwarted in his efforts to enlist various top commanders in a cleanup effort—and was, moreover, receiving threats on his life from fellow cops.

In mid-1969, frustrated by the complacency of city officials and fearing that his life was increasingly in danger, Serpico—together with his friend David Durk, a police sergeant assigned to special investigations and who shared his misgivings—brought their complaints to David Burnham. By then, Burnham's reputation for straightforward reporting on the police had soared.

Serpico and Durk arranged to meet Burnham in a Greenwich Village restaurant, the Nine Nine Nine, where they talked about corruption without offering specific details. It was the start of a beautiful friendship. Burnham decided not to tell me what he was working on until he believed he had some of Serpico's revelations pinned down. After some weeks, Burnham was confident he could finally tell me he had a grip on a hell of a story. I encouraged him to keep after it, but weeks later he confessed he had hit a block. Serpico and Durk decided they wouldn't cooperate further with him unless they could meet his editor. They wanted to find out for themselves whether *The Times* would commit to run a story based on their information. And they also sought assurances that we would protect them—at least for the time being—by keeping their identities secret. They told Burnham they were wary of the paper's pro-establishment leanings and their key question was, "Can your editor be trusted?" They said they'd make their decision after talking to me.

When Burnham brought Serpico and Durk to my office a couple of days later, I had trouble believing Serpico was a policeman, even though Burnham had warned me that he was a decoy cop. He had long hair and a bushy, unkempt beard, and was dressed in sandals and clothes that looked as though they had come from a thrift store. He was among the first males in the city to flaunt an earring, and I made a small joke about a new police dress code (which failed to break the ice).

Gradually, during our two-hour discussion, I learned that Serpico was unmarried, lived in Greenwich Village and, for the most part, shunned the company of his fellow cops—who in return disparaged him as "that hippie" and "a psycho." Sergeant Durk, on the other hand, had clipped hair and wore a button-down shirt and a striped tie. An Amherst College graduate, he looked as though he belonged on a campus of the 1950s.

What appeared to be most on their minds was whether *The Times* at some point during our investigation might cave in to political pressure. "I promise you we'll never do that," I said. "We'll run the story all right, but there's a lot to do first. You must understand there can be no mistakes, everything has to be checked and rechecked, for your sakes as well as ours. We can't run your story simply as you relate it. And wherever possible we need documentation. It's a great but complicated story and we want it. But don't be surprised if it takes several months to put it together."

"And what about *The Times*'s own relationship with the police?" asked Durk. "It wouldn't surprise me if your paper makes payoffs to provide smooth passage for its trucks so they can get the paper delivered at night."

"I don't know," I said, "but even if true it won't stop the story."

Serpico and Durk finally relaxed, and we shook hands. With Burnham taking occasional notes, they then, at my request, proceeded to tell me much of the same story they had already conveyed to Burnham:

Serpico, after receiving his training as an undercover cop in January

1966, was assigned to the Ninetieth Precinct in Brooklyn. Even in his early days in uniform, he said, he had been aware of a low level of corruption. Now, when he began working undercover, he was suddenly confronted with the enormity of the situation. After some weeks, he learned that collecting graft appeared to be as integral a part of the job as preventing crime. He began to simmer with inner anger as he realized how many of his fellow cops were on the take, and he yearned to find a way to counter this corruption.

In August, a cop handed him an envelope from a well-known gambler. "I've been holding this for you," he said. "It's from Jewish Max."

"What do I do with it?" asked Serpico.

"Anything you want," replied the cop.

Inside was a wad of bills totaling $300.

It was then—aware he was about to be involved in dangerous business, and realizing there was no one he could go to in his own precinct—that Serpico called his friend David Durk. Sharing Serpico's zeal to cleanse the department of corruption, Durk suggested that together they approach Captain Philip Foran, commander of the detective squad assigned to the Department of Investigation. Foran was Durk's immediate boss, and Durk had once characterized him as "the most honest cop I've ever met." When the three got together, Serpico listed his grievances, including the payoff by Jewish Max. He pulled the envelope containing the $300 from his pocket and handed it to Foran, who glanced at it and handed it back.

"Well, we do one of two things," Foran said. "I'll take you to the commissioner and he'll drag you in front of a grand jury and by the time this thing is through you'll be found floating in the East River, facedown. Or you can forget the whole thing."

Serpico and Durk were dumbfounded. Unhappily conceding that there seemed no alternative but to drop the matter, Serpico still needed to know what to do with the money. "It's up to you," Foran said. Serpico decided to give it to his sergeant, and Foran agreed that was a good idea. ("I gave the envelope to my supervisor," Serpico recalled, "and he snapped it out of my hand like he was an elephant and I had a peanut.")

Unable to get over his dismay about the bribe, Serpico was transferred to the Seventh Division in the South Bronx, where a captain who appeared to be sincere, Cornelius Behan, assured him that the division was free of corruption. But Serpico soon found that far from being clean, the division had a well-organized system for collecting graft. The division's "pad" included a list of businesses, both legitimate and illicit, that regularly compensated the cops for protection. Liquor store owners, for example, paid a monthly fee to permit customers and delivery trucks to double-park without being ticketed. The stores also doled out bottles of liquor to cops upon request.

Even more disturbing to Serpico was the financial relationship between the police and the numbers racket, which flourished much in the same way as it had when Dick Feehan first educated me about it. Policy "bankers" paid large sums to participate in an elaborate scheme designed to keep them in business. In general, those making payoffs—called "cousins"—were left alone, police-protected by what in effect was a gambling license. Any officer who arrested a cousin was reprimanded, and sometimes fined by his peers. Occasionally, however, when the practice was brought by do-gooders to public attention, a few arrests had to be made. The precinct cops notified the numbers operators in advance of the coming raids and often allowed them to substitute an underling at the booking. Sometimes, the bankers scheduled the arrests at their convenience—usually after most of the day's receipts had been collected.

The monthly "nut" at the Seventh Division averaged between $800 and $1,000 per man, with lieutenants earning a double share. Serpico's partner on the beat, initially concerned about Serpico's refusal to accept any money, resigned himself to taking the double share that consequently fell to him. Once, unaware that Serpico was not on the pad, a lieutenant offered his attic as a safe place for Serpico to store his cash.

Sickened by the corruption, Serpico described the lurid details of the situation to Captain Behan, who said he would take the matter up with the Police Department's number-two man, First Deputy Commissioner John Walsh. Walsh had held his post under five successive commissioners, and, with Commissioner Howard Leary often out of town on speaking engagements and conferences, he was generally credited with running the department. His supervisory responsibilities included all anticorruption units.

In the weeks that followed, Serpico went to see Behan several more times. Behan gave Serpico the impression that Walsh wanted him to remain in his division and act as a mole. For a time, Serpico said, he believed he was working undercover directly for Walsh, from whom he expected soon to hear personally. But Walsh never made contact, and Serpico, by the end of 1966, realized there was, in fact, no investigation under way.

Four months later, Durk mentioned Serpico's frustrations to Mayor Lindsay's aide Jay Kriegel. Like Durk an Amherst alumnus, Kriegel was somewhat awed that Durk had chosen to pursue a career as a cop. Kriegel himself had gone on to study law at Harvard and become part of Lindsay's campaign team. He regularly consulted Durk on matters regarding law enforcement, and Durk helped the Lindsay organization compose a white paper on crime. By the spring of 1967, Kriegel was one of Lindsay's closest advisors at City Hall, the staff member responsible for managing police issues. Upon hearing Durk's story, Kriegel suggested Durk bring Serpico to his office in the basement of City Hall.

At their meeting, Serpico told Kriegel he was the only undercover cop in his division not on the pad. But the problem, Serpico emphasized, reached at least as far up as the borough commander, if not higher. He told Kriegel an investigation of the department was required to clean things up, and none of the officials to whom he had complained were willing to act.

According to both Serpico and Durk, Kriegel interrupted occasionally with exclamations of shock and disbelief. He assured them he would go directly to the mayor to develop a plan of action, and pledged to introduce Serpico to Lindsay as soon as possible. Durk said that Kriegel, a few days later, told him that the mayor could not meet with Serpico, and that nothing could be done about his concerns for the time being. Kriegel went on to explain, according to Durk, that Lindsay could not afford to upset the police before a potentially long, hot summer. (Later, as incredible as it may sound, a vice president of the Patrolmen's Benevolent Association told Burnham that graft was viewed as an unwritten part of the city's police pay package—hence the administration's lackadaisical attitude toward corruption.)

It was then, on May 30, 1967, that Serpico and Durk took their claims to another Lindsay appointee, Arnold Fraiman, head of the Department of Investigation, who gave them a classic runaround. At first, Fraiman expressed interest in Serpico's allegations. When Serpico told him that cops on a stakeout often discussed the pad, and what they planned to do with their illicit cash, Fraiman agreed to give Serpico a listening device to plant in a surveillance truck. The bug was actually handed to Durk for delivery to Serpico, but almost immediately, Durk was ordered to "bring it back to the office forthwith." Fraiman would give no reason for his reversal. "Ultimately, after months," Durk told me, "the only answer Fraiman would make was that Serpico was a psycho and that they couldn't get involved and that Serpico just wasn't willing to cooperate. And that just absolutely was not the case."

Stonewalled time and again, Serpico went back to Captain Behan and said that since there was no investigation under way, he had approached "outside agencies" and Behan promised an inquiry. Eventually, by the spring of 1968, a grand jury began looking into the matter of corruption and members of the Seventh Division, regarding Serpico as their nemesis, made threats against him. In one instance an undercover cop poked his revolver in Serpico's belly, muttering, "You're a rotten kind of guy, and if you ever involve me, you know what's going to happen."

As a result of the grand jury hearing, ten policemen were indicted for accepting bribes and another eleven were charged with violating departmental rules. But Serpico was bitter that it had taken so long to begin the investigation and angry that the punishment fell on only a few cops. Convinced the problem did not lie with a handful of crooked cops but with the system as a whole, he believed changes in operations at the top were urgently needed.

The majority of policemen, Serpico came to believe, wanted to be honest, but the pressure to get "on the pad" was so great that they found it easier to capitulate. And, some of these wavering cops reasoned, why should they resist the chance to double their salaries, along with the rest of their colleagues? Realizing that corruption was quietly condoned, if not actively encouraged, by the police hierarchy, Serpico sought a fundamental change in departmental policy, and he was determined to see the blame placed where it belonged.

At the conclusion of our meeting at *The Times*, Serpico and Durk told me they felt reassured that we would stick with the investigation. Burnham continued to work on the story day and night for several weeks. Following new leads provided by Serpico and Durk, he talked with building contractors as well as owners of various businesses—restaurants, garages, taxi companies. They all confided they had to keep paying off the cops to stay in business.

Burnham also found a source within the special investigating unit of the narcotics division, who told him it was standard practice for corrupt cops to demand a payoff of $5,000 from an arrested drug dealer, in exchange for skewed police testimony in court to assure acquittal. And it was not unknown for a cop to sell a tape obtained by wiretap to a major heroin dealer for up to $50,000. Cops also traded confiscated contraband to addicts in exchange for information against other addicts.

As the evidence mounted, it became clear that in running the story we would leave the reputation of the Police Department as well as City Hall in shreds. To be absolutely certain that all the allegations we published were accurate, we felt it essential to have them corroborated by an additional Police Department source beyond Serpico and Durk. We arranged a second meeting at *The Times* on February 12, 1970—at nine P.M., when the city room had quieted down—to which Serpico and Durk brought Inspector Paul Delise, commander of Manhattan North. We had previously learned from Serpico of

Delise's unquestioned honesty. He was so high-principled, in fact, that contemptuous cops called him "Saint Paul." At one point, the fifty-year-old inspector had actually left his desk to become Serpico's partner on his beat, when no one else would pair with him. All three had agreed in advance to talk on the record and we awaited them in a conference room off the city room, where we had set up a tape recorder. Seated around a table, along with our three interview subjects, were Burnham and I, as well as Marty Arnold, who was giving Burnham a helping hand, and Serpico's girlfriend, a fetching blond airline stewardess (evidently brought along to provide him moral support).

I asked questions, along with Burnham and Arnold, and after hearing Serpico's story confirmed by Inspector Delise, I was in no doubt whatever about the veracity of all the allegations. At this meeting, Serpico went beyond the details of his earlier narrative, describing death threats he had received after being transferred from the South Bronx to Manhattan North, ostensibly for his own safety. On his first day at the station house, in a room filled with other cops, an undercover policeman brandished a knife, saying he'd like to cut out his tongue. Knocking the knife out of the cop's hand, Serpico pointed his new, nonissue Browning nine-millimeter at the cop's head. After things quieted down, an officer asked Serpico how many rounds his gun held. Fourteen, he said—as many as the number of cops in the room.

Soon after that incident and to his great relief, Serpico said, Inspector Delise assumed command of Manhattan North. Serpico and Delise learned that the system of payoffs in Manhattan North was far more intricate than the one in the Bronx; retired police officers made the collections to protect those on active duty. But Serpico and Delise had trouble piecing their information together because none of the cops trusted them. When Chief Inspector Joseph McGovern, the top official directly charged with uprooting corruption, was apprised of the situation, he suggested Delise use new recruits from the Police Academy to infiltrate the pad. But Serpico and Delise rejected the idea, not wanting to depend on green cops for such precarious work. McGovern had no further suggestions.

Serpico was then invited to meet with McGovern and, wise from previous experience, he wore a wire. McGovern grew angry when Serpico pressed him to defend his office. "What have we accomplished?" he exclaimed. "I think I have done a damn good job of protecting the commissioner against the onslaughts of outside agencies."

It was past midnight when our session ended, and I was crackling with excitement. I thanked Serpico, Durk and Delise for their courage in coming to us. Asking them to be patient a little longer, I explained we needed more time to clarify the scores of facts Burnham had amassed before the article could be published.

"I knew it," growled Serpico, to whom this evidently sounded like the same old runaround he had been getting for years. *The Times*, he declared, would never publish the story. I tried to calm him by pointing out that the exposé we were about to run would burden us with an enormous responsibility. In good conscience, we needed the extra time to further corroborate some of the new charges, and to interview several additional sources.

Together, Durk and Delise helped persuade Serpico to accept our reasoning, and Delise offered to try to dig up further documentation himself. In the weeks that followed, Burnham, guided by Serpico and Durk, painstakingly assembled the additional facts he needed.

Speaking to *The Times* put Serpico's life at risk again. He and Durk took elaborate measures to assure they were not followed to Forty-third Street and, certain that their phones were tapped, began talking in code. A couple of times when Serpico felt most threatened, he slept overnight on a couch in my office. He attracted attention whenever he entered the city room, for he always looked like the drug addict he pretended to be, in his role as decoy cop.

Burnham's own life had been threatened on a few occasions, beginning with his cooping article—presumably by cops who were irate about his disclosures. Once, he called Assistant Chief Inspector Sidney Cooper and said, "Sid, I just got a death threat. What do I do?"

"Hey, listen, kid," Cooper replied in his gravelly voice, "you never worry about the death threats you get"—implying that if someone wanted to kill Burnham, he wasn't going to call first. One evening during his Serpico investigation, Burnham feared his young daughter had been kidnapped. He frantically searched his neighborhood and called me in a panic, thinking it senseless to call the police. She was nowhere to be found. It turned out that the little girl had never been in danger, but had crawled behind a couch in his living room and fallen asleep.

Accepting the risk inherent in provoking thousands of men who carried guns, Burnham set to work writing his three-part series. At this point, I met with Ivan Veit, *The Times*'s executive vice president, to ask whether the paper was paying off the police at any level (as David Durk had implied was likely). Actually, I had heard rumors for years that *The Times* "tipped" cops to look the other way when newspaper delivery trucks tied up traffic along Forty-third and Forty-fourth Streets. I did not want to be taken by surprise after running Burnham's articles. Veit assured me the paper was clean, and I chose to take his word for it.

Burnham, I learned years later, didn't believe Veit and thought that the circulation department had worked out an arrangement with the cops whereby the delivery trucks could take over the streets every night without penalty. Burnham said he became suspicious when, after his cooping article appeared, our circulation manager had come up to his desk in the city room and suggested he steer clear of police payoff stories. And once, he took Burnham to a "racket," a dinner for a retiring, high-ranking police official. Most of the money collected went directly to the retiring official, and was regarded as a kind of delayed "dividend." *The Times*'s circulation department had bought a table, as had other businesses, in addition to groups Burnham suspected of being Mafia-connected.

In mid-April 1970, Mayor Lindsay heard about the extensive report on police graft we were preparing to publish within a few days. Thus prompted, he announced on April 23 the formation of a five-man committee to review "city procedures for investigating police corruption." Concerned that Lindsay might be trying to sell the public the idea that he had all along been aware of police corruption and that it was he who deserved the credit for investigating it, I was determined to start our series the very next day. I asked Marty Arnold to help Burnham organize his introductory article, calculated to be overwhelming in its scope and detail.

With both Arnold and me standing by to offer any assistance needed, Burnham pounded away into the early hours of the morning, and, after stopping for a few hours of sleep, he finished the first article at noon on Friday, April 24. Even though I realized he was exhausted, I asked him to outline briefly the second article in the series, focusing on gambling graft, and the third, dealing with distrust within police ranks and threats made against informants—namely Serpico.

At 3:30 P.M., Burnham and I agreed that since the opening story contained such damning charges about the extent of the corruption problem and the failure of high-level officials to deal with it, Lindsay and his aides should be given a chance to comment. I asked our City Hall bureau chief, Marty Tolchin, to meet Burnham there, and together they handed a copy of the story to Tom Morgan, Lindsay's press secretary. About an hour later, Morgan returned with a statement from the mayor that began: "Reports of police corruption in *The New York Times* are extremely serious and go to the heart of the effectiveness of law enforcement in our city. These allegations must be investigated thoroughly and prompt action must be taken to change any general practices that can lead to misconduct."

Burnham also went to Arnold Fraiman for comment. Fraiman, whom

Serpico had accused of abruptly and inexplicably dropping the investigation into the Seventh Division, called the claims against him "completely untrue." Fraiman was now a State Supreme Court justice.

Meanwhile, Durk had called Kriegel and got him to acknowledge, on tape, that he remembered the meeting with Serpico, and that he had later told Durk that City Hall could not do anything about police corruption. Kriegel then begged Durk to try to keep the article out of the paper and Durk said he was powerless to stop it, even if he wanted to.

Once Burnham's last paragraph was sent to the composing room, we broke open a bottle to celebrate. It was the culmination of a tense six months. We all went down to Sardi's for a final toast before going our separate bone-weary ways.

I arrived home soon after the first edition hit the stands. The two-column head at the top of page one on April 25 read:

GRAFT PAID TO POLICE HERE
SAID TO RUN INTO MILLIONS

Survey Links Payoffs to Gambling and Narcotics—
Some on Force Accuse Officials of Failure to Act

Mayor Lindsay phoned me at home, asking if he could meet with me at Gracie Mansion in the morning. I said I'd get back to him. I called Burnham, asking if he had any problem about my seeing the mayor without him. If he thought I shouldn't see Lindsay alone, I wouldn't. Burnham said he trusted me, and that he had no problem with Lindsay's request. Then I called Abe Rosenthal to let him know I planned to see Lindsay in the morning, and he said he wanted to come along.

Lindsay and Deputy Mayor Richard Aurelio met with us in the mayor's study. Using a forceful—almost threatening—tone, Lindsay declared that *The Times* had made a big mistake in running Burnham's story. He said he had found out who our main anonymous source was, describing Serpico as a disgruntled cop who was mentally unhinged and unreliable. We would be sorry and humiliated that we had trusted him, he said.

I told Lindsay I regretted his decision to challenge our story, and said we had numerous sources and stacks of documents and tape-recorded conversations corroborating what we had published. We would continue to publish the series. *The Times*, I added, had no fear of being embarrassed over this story, which we regarded as a service to the public, and we were not the ones who would be humiliated if challenged.

Since there was nothing more to discuss, Abe and I left. It is worth noting that Lindsay never chose to make his objections public.

There is no doubt that Burnham's series was the impetus for the creation of a municipal probe the following month. But the objectivity of this five-member in-house committee appointed by Lindsay was questionable at best, especially since it included Police Commissioner Leary. Over the protests of Sanford Garelik, now the elected City Council president (and formerly chief inspector of the Police Department), Lindsay was pressured into appointing Whitman Knapp, a Wall Street lawyer, to chair an independent investigating body that came to be known as the Knapp Commission.

Leary resigned as police commissioner in the fall of 1970, followed closely by First Deputy Commissioner Walsh. Leary was replaced by Patrick Murphy, a onetime New York cop who had become the police commissioner of Detroit. His reputation as an honest cop was unassailable, and he promised to enforce a new ethic in the department and to cooperate fully with the Knapp Commission.

Knapp turned out to be a surprisingly zealous inquisitor. We all assumed that Lindsay had chosen Knapp because he thought he would not proceed aggressively. Although Knapp had been an assistant district attorney under Thomas Dewey, he had spent most of his career in a Wall Street firm and was very much part of the New York WASP tradition—hence Lindsay must have counted him a natural ally. Knapp was also saddled with two major drawbacks, a minuscule budget and a limited time to exercise subpoena power.

But Knapp proved to be smart, tough and relentless. When a member of the City Council, Matthew Troy, who had close ties to the Patrolmen's Benevolent Association, managed to get the funding cut for the Knapp Commission after its first six months, Knapp appealed to the Law Enforcement Assistance Administration, part of the federal Justice Department under President Nixon. When he received the money to proceed, Burnham and I believed Nixon was not nearly as concerned about police corruption as he was about Lindsay's anticipated switch to the Democratic party and his run for the presidency in 1972. We thought Nixon would have gladly funded any panel that might have blemished Lindsay's record.

While the Knapp Commission was digging for facts, Frank Serpico was back on the job, working undercover for the narcotics division in Brooklyn. On February 3, 1971, he was shot in the face by a heroin dealer while making a bust in Williamsburg. Miraculously, he survived, but he has carried on ever since with bullet fragments in his head. It is doubtful that what actually happened that night will ever be finally resolved, but suspicions were immediately aroused that Serpico had been set up by his fellow officers. Burnham visited Serpico in the hospital early in the morning after the incident, and the wounded cop told him he had no proof that it had been other than an accident.

The Knapp Commission's study came to a climax with its hearings in the fall of 1971. The commission opened the session by stating that "the [police] department has a serious corruption problem that must be characterized as extensive." Supporting the sweeping lead of Burnham's first story, the commission emphasized that a substantial majority of police officers were taking bribes.

And, validating what Serpico had maintained all along, the commission said: "The main thrust of our findings . . . is that the problem of police corruption cannot be solved merely by focusing on individual acts of wrongdoing. It arises out of an endemic condition which must be attacked on all fronts." Footage from a surveillance film played at the hearing showed a cop haggling with an undercover commission agent disguised as a middleman for Xaviera Hollander, the madam of a luxurious East Side brothel. The cop set the madam's monthly payoff at $1,100. Later, the same cop negotiated a fee for a change in testimony in a court case against Hollander. He initially asked for "ten big ones," but settled for $3,500, since he had a vested interest in her acquittal. Were she to be convicted, he said, "the golden goose is gone. You lose, I lose, we're all out of a lot of [obscenity] business. I don't want to see her go. I hate to see her go."

The cop, William Phillips, was the star witness during the first round of hearings, which lasted for nine days in October. Phillips, who received immunity for his testimony, was unabashedly proud of his crimes and once called himself a "super thief." He stated that every plainclothesman he knew was on the pad, gave names, dates and places, and described specific instances of corrupt acts, such as the time three police officers divided $80,000 of the $137,000 seized in one Harlem drug bust. Or the time a drug addict was ordered by a cop to steal expensive cases of liquor, which he wanted for his daughter's wedding. The cop paid the addict in confiscated heroin.

While the October hearings addressed the rot within the force, it was felt by many that they failed to deal thoroughly with the feigned ignorance of the department's top brass and City Hall. When another round of hearings began, Serpico, although still on sick leave recovering from the gunshot wound, told his story on December 14, 1971.

Over the next few days, the other principals in the case took the stand. Inspector Behan said he thought Serpico had been exaggerating when he first reported corruption at the Seventh Division, but said he had informed former First Deputy Commissioner Walsh of Serpico's allegations. Walsh admitted that he had received a detailed report from Behan about charges of corruption in gambling enforcement but that he had completely forgotten about it, saying, "The incident left my mind." Justice Fraiman also confessed to his own inaction.

Jay Kriegel contradicted his earlier sworn testimony regarding his and Mayor Lindsay's role in the affair. Kriegel had stated in July that he had discussed the meeting between himself, Serpico and Durk with Mayor Lindsay, and had told Lindsay that the two officers had not been able to get any action from within the department. Now, Kriegel said, "I talked to the mayor at some length about that incident, and I am clear now that following the meeting with Frank and David, that I did not report to him that allegation." He said he had mentioned the meeting to Lindsay only in very general terms. It was apparent to Burnham that Kriegel was trying to cover for the mayor.

The Manhattan district attorney, Frank Hogan, studied the transcripts of the hearings to determine whether any officials in the Lindsay administration had committed "perjury, malfeasance and/or misfeasance." He announced in April 1972 that he was ready to file perjury charges against Kriegel because of the conflicts in his testimony. But at the last minute he refrained, saying that "the people would not be able to establish beyond a reasonable doubt that there was a willful, irreconcilable inconsistency" in Kriegel's sworn statements.

The Knapp Commission released its final report in December 1972. It concluded that the Police Department "failed to investigate allegations of serious misconduct," noting that all of the top officials "failed to act when informed of widespread bribery among plainclothes policemen." "The department," it continued, "was given reason to believe that some of its members were extortionists, murderers and heroin entrepreneurs and made no attempt to verify these suspicions or dispute them. . . . The various units charged with searching out misconduct within the department and maintaining internal discipline were widely dispersed, poorly coordinated, undermanned and, in many instances, so misdirected that they were totally ineffective in rooting out corrupt policemen."

The commission pointed out that city law enforcement gave no assistance to federal investigators looking into corruption, and produced a note from Chief McGovern that read, "[Walsh] doesn't want to help the Feds lock up local police. Let them arrest federal people."

No specific judgment was issued as to whether Lindsay himself was culpable for the laxity in pursuing Serpico's allegations, but the commission determined that "the mayor's office did not see to it that the specific charges of corruption were investigated." Further, it said that Lindsay, as the chief executive officer of New York City, "cannot escape responsibility" for the breadth of corruption in the police force.

With the Serpico affair, the last of Lindsay's patrician magic dissolved. Fewer and fewer New Yorkers believed him when he preached urban idealism. Plainly, he was not above the muck of traditional politics, and his pronouncements about his mayoralty seemed all the more hypocritical when measured against the righteous rhetoric.

Serpico retired from the force in June 1972. He had been awarded the Police Department's Medal of Honor. He viewed it with scorn, since he received it for being, as quoted in Peter Maas's *Serpico*, "stupid enough to have been shot in the face," not for reporting corruption. Maas had written the book after David Burnham declined to do so. Burnham, ethical to the bone, did not feel he should profit from having performed a public service.

Burnham was so pious about ethics that his *Times* colleague Dick Severo suggested the appropriate next step for him was archbishop of Canterbury. And Mike Kaufman, who sat next to him in the city room, once remarked that Burnham "has all those wonderful upstanding attributes like decency and self-discipline that normally would make you hate a person. On him they look good."

When the movie *Serpico*, based on Maas's book and starring Al Pacino, was released, Burnham asked that his name be removed from one of the opening scenes. As a result, when the *New York Times* reporter answers the phone in the movie, Burnham's name is garbled and unintelligible. Burnham did this, he told me, because popular films had a way of becoming entrenched as history. He believed that too many liberties with the facts had been taken in the film and he did not want his name to be considered an endorsement.

At one point during the Knapp Commission hearings, I leaned back in my chair and said to Marty Arnold, "You know, all this only came to pass because at the right moment those three crazy guys came together—Durk, Serpico and Burnham."

Arnold decided to write a piece for *Times Talk* and interviewed Burnham the next day. He swore that Burnham told him, "All this came to pass because at the right moment those three crazy guys came together—Durk, Serpico and Gelb."

A few days later, when this story had made the rounds, Abe summed it up for *Times Talk*: "It was four crazy guys, but each one only saw three crazies."

Serpico retired, and the last time I saw him was at Peter Maas's funeral in 2001, when he delivered a touching eulogy. He appeared to be at peace with himself.

FORTY-THREE

A TTACKS ON *THE TIMES* in those years came sporadically from political adherents of every stripe, but mainly from readers and journals on the left. The editors and the publisher vigilantly tried to uphold the granite tradition of fairness and accuracy on which the paper had been founded. In the climate of social upheaval and sour disillusionment over the Vietnam War, however, there were those who persisted in accusing the paper of not being critical enough of governmental agencies.

After all the investigations *The Times* had published, they still chose to believe the paper was a tool of the establishment. While there was a slip now and then, we tried our best not to give credence to baseless conspiracy theories floating around at any one time. Occasionally we were criticized for publishing a particular story, at other times we were targeted for not having published a story. But, at the least, there was always on our part a powerful determination to achieve balance and coherence, all of us aware of the scrutiny we were under by our smart readers.

If any one event exemplified how far *The Times* was from being in the government's pocket, it was the decision in the spring of 1971 to publish the so-called Pentagon Papers—the top-secret history of American involvement in Vietnam. (The decision to publish did not help us much with arch-conservatives, who regarded *The Times* as the exponent of liberal—often Jewish liberal—propaganda.)

Formally entitled *History of U.S. Decision-Making Process on Vietnam Policy*, the forty-seven volumes were commissioned by Secretary of Defense Robert S. McNamara in 1967. He wanted answers as to how and why America had allowed itself to become ensnared in the disastrous conflict in which he himself had played a major role. One of the basic questions was: Should we have gone into Vietnam in the first place? McNamara guaranteed the authors anonymity, and more than seven thousand pages of their report (directed by Leslie H. Gelb, who years later became an editor and a columnist at *The Times*) was composed of a narrative history based on the actual documents written by the decision makers themselves. The documents were appended to related sections of the narrative.

These papers were meant to be read only by the highest government officials. But Daniel Ellsberg, one of the anonymous authors—who had left government service to teach and do private research on Vietnam—was convinced the public had a right to read them. Consequently, at the end of March 1971, he got in touch with Neil Sheehan, then an investigative correspondent in the Washington bureau specializing in subjects involving military and political affairs. Ellsberg described the contents of the papers, and Neil quickly realized it was essential to enlighten the public about these crucial documents. He was confident that *The Times* would provide the staff, space and time to do justice to the data. He also knew he had to proceed without delay, especially since discovering that the Institute for Policy Studies, a left-wing Washington think tank, had access to the papers and planned to publish parts of them in a book.

Neil was invited to read the papers at the apartment of Ellsberg's brother-in-law in Cambridge, Massachusetts. Ellsberg, under increasing strain, finally gave Neil a set of keys so he could come and go as he pleased. Keeping his promise not to reveal Ellsberg as the source, Neil eventually assumed he had tacit permission to have the two million words copied. They revealed in detail the years of government blunders and lies—the extent of the covert war and the costly and tragic stalemate in which the Army had been mired during the late 1960s.

By this time Neil had informed Scotty Reston and Max Frankel of his coup, and Reston, after a few days, told him, "You have clearance, young man. Proceed." Abe then asked Neil to bring the documents to New York. In the meantime, Abe briefed Punch, assuring him that the documents were authentic and that he planned to publish them. Punch, although impressed with the vast significance of the story, was at the same time dismayed. "The more I listened the more certain I became that the entire operation smelled of twenty years to life," Punch recalled years later, speaking at the Committee to Protect Journalists. "I quickly called *The Times*'s longtime outside lawyers." Not untypically for a law firm, Lord, Day and Lord took a conservative position. Their senior partner told Punch that if the paper chose to publish the documents his firm would refuse to defend us.

"With all that cheerful advice," Punch said, "I called Abe Rosenthal and told him that if I were going to go to jail for publishing something, I thought it made sense to read it. 'Do you wish to read it all?' he inquired. 'Yes,' I responded, 'all of it.' From the glee in his voice, I should have smelled a rat. It wasn't too long before there was a knock at the door and in comes Abe pushing a large cart overflowing with papers. With a beatific smile, he announced, 'Here you are. Happy reading.' . . . What became clear after reading was that these were extraordinary documents proving deceit of the American people by their elected officials. I had no doubt the American people had a right to read them and that we at *The Times* had a right to publish them."

The story was to be prepared in absolute secrecy. For the next ten weeks, Neil Sheehan was stationed in the Hilton Hotel on Sixth Avenue, where he lived and worked in a three-room suite with Hedrick Smith, a correspondent about to head our bureau in Moscow and for now dividing the writing task with Neil. A nearby suite was shared by Gerald Gold and Allan Siegal, both of the foreign desk, who selected the texts to be published, and who edited the copy as it was produced by Sheehan and Smith. As more and more staffers were diverted to "Project X," nine rooms ultimately were rented at the Hilton and the order was given that no one show up in the city room, to shield those involved from the queries of co-workers. Only the staff researcher Linda Amster, who needed access to the morgue, was permitted to shuttle back and forth. Over two and a half months, seventy-five reporters, editors, secretaries and production department personnel were involved in Project X.

Jim Greenfield, as foreign editor, was directly in charge of the project, but Abe was in overall command. As always, he demanded "objectivity" from his reporters and editors. "We are not going to tell the *New York Times* story of the war," he told the staff. "We are going to tell the Pentagon story. That's what we have that nobody else has."

Lord, Day and Lord predicted that the government would move to halt publication and might well charge the paper, its publisher and its editors with violating the Espionage Act. Louis Loeb, a key partner of the firm and for many years the personal lawyer to the Sulzberger family, played Cassandra. Warning of imminent jail terms and financial ruin for the paper, he continued to recommend against publishing. But James Goodale, our in-house counsel, believed *The Times* had the First Amendment squarely on its side. The government might take the paper to court, he said, but it would never win a conviction.

For Abe, publishing the story was a matter of sheer principle, consequences be damned. Although he had not initially been a critic of our involvement in the war, he never wavered for a moment. At one point, Sheehan remembers Abe telling him, "As free journalists, we must publish this material. It's our duty. Forget about any legal arguments. Push them out of your mind. And personal opinion doesn't enter into this. It all belongs in the public domain."

In fact, Punch had not yet made a final decision, but the major editors joined Abe in voting for publication. Some thought it would be prudent to run articles summarizing the documents, peppered with a few quotes. Abe argued that publishing the actual documents was journalistically the most responsible course, as well as the best protection against possible government accusations of misinterpretation. Abe told Punch, "No documents, no story." He made up his mind to quit the paper if Punch, in the end, vetoed publication. He told me that no decision he ever made as chief editor had been as troubling.

By early June, he was suffering from exhaustion. It was the first time since I had known him that I was concerned about both his physical and mental well-being. He was so emotionally drained and so sleep-deprived that I finally called Ann to tell her I was bringing him home before he collapsed. Ann and I got him into bed, and he passed out. He slept for hours. Late the next morning, he was back at work, still pale but ready to keep going.

There came a point when the decision whether or not to publish finally had to be made, and Abe, at Punch's request, summed up the pros and cons. It was Punch who was burdened with making the fateful choice. He worried about public opinion turning against *The Times*, and he recognized the very real possibility that he might wind up serving a jail term for treason. His conscience, however, triumphed over his fears.

"I had but four requests of Abe," Punch recalled. "First, that we share the papers with four of our most senior associates to solicit their input. They were unanimous in their recommendation: Publish. Second, that we cut the material by a quarter. I probably should have said by half. Third, that if the government moved to stop us from continuing publication, we would fight it in the courts but we would honor the orders of those courts as we fought the battle. And, finally, that working with our in-house lawyer, Jim Goodale, we quickly find new outside counsel.

"I had been scheduled to go to Europe with my family on the day following publication. By then I was convinced that one of two things would occur: Either they'd come and take me to jail, or readers of *The Times* would fall back to bed exhausted by the weight of our coverage. Monday morning came and, as I was still a free man, I assumed our readers to be asleep, so I went to Europe. It was a fine visit lasting about three hours. But, ever confident, I told my wife to keep my suitcases and I'd be right back. My clothes had a wonderful holiday."

All of us at the paper applauded Punch's courageous decision. Abe's main concern had been that word of the story would get out before *The Times* ran the first installment of the nine-part series. Knowing the government would try to block publication the moment it learned what *The Times* was up to, he reasoned that the paper would have the legal edge, as well as the scoop, if we could get out at least one or two installments prior to the inevitable injunction. Astonishingly, nobody leaked the story, and Neil Sheehan's first part of the series appeared on page one on Sunday, June 13, 1971. "The aspect of it I can't believe," Abe said later, "is that newspapermen actually kept their mouths shut for almost three months." Curiously, the first article drew little attention.

But after Sheehan's second story ran the next day, a telegram arrived from Attorney General John Mitchell demanding that *The Times* halt further publication and return the documents to the Defense Department. *Times* executive vice president Harding Bancroft replied, "We refuse to halt publication voluntarily."

On Tuesday, June 15, the third of Sheehan's articles appeared, and the Justice Department won an injunction against *The Times* in Federal District Court, temporarily blocking further publication of the series. A trial was set for Friday, June 18. The injunction would expire on Saturday, unless upheld by the court.

Meanwhile, everybody wanted to know the answer to one well-guarded question: Who was Sheehan's source? Sidney Zion, who had left *The Times* in 1970 to start *Scanlan's Monthly*, a muckraking magazine that had recently folded, visited the city room on June 15 to research a piece he was writing for the Sunday *Magazine*. He drifted from desk to desk, asking about Sheehan's source, but no one knew. Some reporters suggested that even Abe was in the dark.

Zion laughed that off in his superior manner. "That's crazy," he told his city-room friends. As he later wrote, "Abe would never go with something this big without knowing the source. I thought Abe looked a little smug today, and he should be smug. He knows something I don't know, and I consider that an outrage. I'll find out, and I'll tell you all tomorrow."

Through *Scanlan's*, Zion had formed knowledgeable connections in the antiwar movement. Three of them said they knew the source and would confirm it if Zion figured it out, but would not tell him outright. The next morning he acquired a list of those with access to the Papers from the *Washington Post*. After one wrong guess, he picked a name that was verified by all three of his contacts—Daniel Ellsberg.

Rather than leaking his hunch to a newspaper, Zion announced he would reveal *The Times*'s source on the Barry Gray radio show, even though he was not absolutely positive he was right. Reporters from all the news services gathered in the studio of WMCA. I had a line held open to the station, so I could speak to Zion as soon as he arrived there.

When Zion got on the phone, I asked him, "What the hell are you doing?"

"I'm going to name the guy who leaked to Neil Sheehan," Zion said.

"Who is he?" I asked.

"Are you kidding? You don't know?"

"I swear I don't know," I said.

"What will you do if I tell you?"

"I'll tell Abe," I said.

"If I'm wrong, will you call right back so I don't make a schmuck out of myself?" Zion asked.

"I can't do that."

"Then listen to the radio," Zion said.

I told Zion I thought he had lost his mind and I waited at my desk to see what he would do. He named Ellsberg.

Abe, of course, was enraged over Zion's "betrayal." He wanted him barred forever from *The Times*. When Murray Schumach, who was at the radio station covering the story for the paper, called in, I told him to tell Zion never to show up in the city room again. Murray conveyed the message, which was Zion's first confirmation that he was, in fact, correct. My warning became a headline in the next day's edition of the *Post*.

The following night, Abe and I were on our way out of Sardi's when Zion came through the door. Abe turned his back on him, and I shrugged at Sidney's idiocy. In years to come, Sidney always insisted he did the right thing, that it was a reporter's calling to tell the facts as he gathered them, no matter who was disturbed by their revelation. His principle, he argued, was that the truth wins out. But his peers didn't see it that way. Article after article appeared in paper after paper, denouncing what he had done, and it took a long time before Zion's newspaper friends stopped treating him like a pariah.

Abe finally thawed after enough time had passed. One night when he bumped into Zion at Sardi's, they greeted each other and talked. Zion told Abe that if he had made his discovery while employed by a newspaper in competition with *The Times*, his story would have made the front page and been hailed as a terrific beat. The problem, he maintained, was that he had disclosed his finding as an independent writer—and on the radio. Besides, he argued, everyone knew Ellsberg's exposure had been hours away; the FBI had already been checking him out. Abe and I renewed our friendship with Zion, who later wrote major pieces for the *Magazine*.

AFTER *THE TIMES* was enjoined from publishing further installments of the Pentagon Papers, Ellsberg offered them to the *Washington Post*, which began running their articles on June 18 in the face of certain government action. Soon, other papers around the country picked up pieces of the documents, in an industrywide nose-thumbing at the Justice Department.

On Saturday, June 19, Judge Murray Gurfein issued his verdict: "I am not going to grant a [permanent] injunction." It was a momentary victory for *The Times*. The government appealed immediately, and the Appeals Court judge issued another temporary stay against the paper. That same day, the *Washington Post* was ordered to cease publication. On Wednesday, June 23, the Appellate Court handed down its decision: *The Times* could resume publication, but only of those sections not deemed a threat by the government to national security.

The Times was faced with a dilemma: Publish the material approved by the government or go for broke and take the case to the Supreme Court. After hours of deliberation, the decision was made to go for broke.

The Times's brief was filed on Saturday, June 26. The court returned its decision on June 30. It stated that the government had not met "the heavy burden of showing justification for the imposition" of a restraint against *The Times* and the *Washington Post*, and the stays were vacated by a vote of six to three. Publication of all the documents was allowed to resume.

In a concurring opinion, Justice Hugo Black wrote that "every moment's continuance of the injunctions against these newspapers amounts to a flagrant, indefensible, and continuing violation" of the First Amendment. "In the First Amendment," he said, "the Founding Fathers gave the free press the protection it must have to fulfill its essential role in our democracy. The press was to serve the governed, not the governors. The government's power to censor the press was abolished so that the press would remain forever free to censure government. The press was protected so that it could bare the secrets of government and inform the people. Only a free and unrestrained press can effectively expose deception in government. And paramount among the responsibilities of a free press is the duty to prevent any part of the government from deceiving the people and sending them off to distant lands to die of foreign fevers and foreign shot and shell. In my view, far from deserving condemnation for their courageous reporting, *The New York Times*, the *Washington Post*, and other newspapers should be commended for serving the purpose that the Founding Fathers saw so clearly. In revealing the workings of government that led to the Vietnam War, the newspapers nobly did precisely that which the Founders hoped and trusted they would do."

We all crowded into Abe's office to celebrate with champagne. Neil made an emotional toast to Abe: "It's easy enough in a crisis like this to be a good soldier if you're well trained, but if you have a general who doesn't have the courage and the wisdom to guide you through the battle all your courage and sacrifice is going to be wasted. In Abe we had a general who made sure our sacrifice and courage were not wasted."

On July 1, 1971, *The Times* began publishing the remaining six installments. The paper received the Pulitzer Prize for "meritorious public service," but I was disappointed that the Pulitzer committee did not include Neil's name on the gold medal along with the name of the paper. (At the instigation of a committee member, Vermont Royster of the *Wall Street Journal*, the vote favored citing only *The Times*.)

Neil had earned the admiration of the entire staff, which knew of President Nixon's vengeful harassment. Nixon, who like Johnson before him could not extricate the country from the war, had encouraged the FBI to make bullying inquiries into the private records and bank accounts of Neil and his wife, Susan, and a grand jury was impaneled in Boston to investigate how he obtained the papers (though the inquiry was dropped after six months). To my mind, Neil is the winner of two Pulitzers, the one he received for his book about Vietnam, *A Bright Shining Lie*, and the one he deserved for his disclosure of the Pentagon Papers, which surely helped bring the Vietnam War to a close.

EVEN THOUGH such national and foreign stories as the Vietnam War and the Pentagon Papers didn't fall under my jurisdiction, I was often asked to participate in editorial discussions about such coverage. And I took as much interest in how we played those stories in the paper as I did in the breaking news of my own metropolitan area—including the biggest running story I was called on to handle in the fall of 1971.

On September 9 of that year, more than one thousand of New York's most hardened criminals staged a revolt at Attica State Correctional Facility thirty miles east of Buffalo, during which they took thirty-three guards and four civilian employees as hostages. Buildings were set on fire, windows smashed, fire hoses cut. Rampaging inmates stormed the prison yard and seized "Times Square," the central guard station at the intersection where the four yards met, giving them control of the catwalks between cell blocks.

Most of the prisoners congregated in "D Yard," where they organized a makeshift government and issued a list of demands: A minimum wage for their work, elimination of overcrowded cells, freedom to practice the religious rites of their choice, an end to censorship of reading material, better rehabilitation services, less pork in the dining hall, complete amnesty from reprisal for the uprising and—least likely to be granted—"speedy and safe transportation out of confinement to a nonimperialistic country."

Fred Ferretti was the first reporter on the scene for *The Times*. I had come to know Fred when we worked as competitors at the World's Fair. He headed the *Trib*'s bureau there, and I often wished he were on my staff, since his coverage sometimes beat ours. After the *Trib* folded, he worked as a political reporter for *Time* and then as producer of the nightly eleven-o'clock NBC news. I hired him in 1969.

Fred was in the first pool of reporters who accompanied State Corrections Commissioner Russell Oswald into Attica for direct negotiations with the inmates. As he entered the prison, he noticed a platoon of policemen armed with rifles and submachine guns, standing ready to rescue the negotiators. When Fred and his group crossed the gated frontier into rebel-held territory, they were met by an escort of prisoners armed with baseball bats and metal pipes whose job, it seemed, was to protect them from other inmates.

Fred alone covered the first day's events for *The Times*, but the next day I dispatched six additional reporters. Soon, we were running a satellite bureau out of Attica—a village with a population of 2,800—under the direction of one of my backfield desk editors, Bill Luce. The village was stretched to its limits under the strain of news crews converging upon it from all over the country. Telephone lines were at a premium and Fred lucked out when he discovered an elderly woman who gave him access to her second phone line. It wasn't long before reporters from other papers figured out where *The Times* was calling from, and his benefactor's parlor, Fred told me, began to resemble a Friday-night queue at a popular movie house on Manhattan's East Side.

By another stroke of luck, Bill Luce managed to rent the front porch of a retired prison guard's house, which became our Attica news desk. That also gave us an additional phone line, and I asked Luce to keep it open to the city room twenty-four hours a day. (The reporters christened it "Arthur's Umbilical.")

By Saturday, September 11, the prisoners had won concessions on most of their constantly changing demands, including the selection of a panel of outside observers to monitor and aid in the negotiations. Among the observers requested were our own Tom Wicker, the lawyer William Kunstler and Bobby Seale. Kunstler, who had demonstrated his value to the anti-establishment cause while defending the Chicago Seven, became one of the chief mediators.

Kunstler announced to the press that agreements on most issues were basically assured. The sticking point, however, was the demand for complete amnesty. But after a prison guard injured in the initial assault on "Times Square" died in a Rochester hospital, the authorities decided they could not ignore or forgive it. "I do not have the constitutional authority to grant such a demand," Governor Nelson Rockefeller stated, "and I would not, even if I had the authority."

By Sunday, Ferretti and Luce told me they sensed time was running out. The prisoners, under stress from their slapdash living conditions and unable to maintain discipline within their ranks, were subjected to relentless pressure from the authorities. Growing ever more agitated, they rejected one deal after another, obstinately holding out for amnesty. The state police waited, weapons at the ready, for their orders. Bobby Seale, who paid a brief visit to the prison on Saturday night, promised to return the next morning. But on Sunday he was barred from reentering. He later said he'd been told he could not speak to the prisoners unless he agreed to encourage them to accept the state's demands. "The position of the Black Panther Party," Seale declared, "is this: The prisoners have to make their own decision. I will not encourage them to compromise their position."

Meanwhile, the hostages continued to be held—often blindfolded—in a wire pen in the middle of the prison yard. Inmates brandished knives, hand-made spearlike weapons, Molotov cocktails, bats with spikes, wire bolos and metal pipes.

As negotiations stalled, it became clear that the state would not allow the prisoners to remain in control of Attica much longer. Kunstler, unlike Seale, encouraged them to accept the state's offer. He had agreed to serve as their legal advisor and told them, "It's the best we could do. If you say it's not good enough, it's your life and your decision." But the inmates continued to believe the hostages were their trump card.

Governor Rockefeller was implored by both sides to go to Attica personally, but he saw the political dangers inherent in his presence in case everything should fall apart, and he stayed in Albany (inviting later accusations that he did not do all he could to resolve the crisis).

Our coverage had been hailed thus far by all sides as exhaustive, balanced and accurate. In addition to Ferretti's fact-studded lead stories on page one, the inside pages contained news analyses, profiles of previously unknown officials, such as Commissioner Oswald and Attica's warden, Vincent Mancusi, sidebars describing the proposals and counterproposals, diagrams of the prison and features about the villagers of Attica.

Then, early on Monday morning, September 13, in response to a state ultimatum demanding the release of the hostages, a number of them were put on public view by the prisoners. Some were dangled over trenches filled with gasoline, others displayed with knives held to their throats. At 9:45, the state troopers were given the signal to move in behind a cloud of tear gas and a storm of bullets, as helicopters hovered overhead. The prison was retaken in four hours—but at a heavy cost. Ten hostages and twenty-nine prisoners lay dead or dying.

None of the reporters had been given any warning of the proposed battle plan. In the stunning confusion, our team of reporters tried to piece together what had happened. Fred Ferretti's lead story, based on official statements, reported that the hostages "died when convicts slashed their throats with knives," and a deputy director of corrections was quoted as saying that two hostages had been killed before the assault, one of whom had been emasculated. But subsequent autopsies revealed that none of the hostages had been slain by knives, nor had any been emasculated. All the hostages, it was determined, had died from bullets fired by the police.

Up until that final fourth day, our reporters had turned in a flawless performance. They now had to amass the confusing facts of the massacre against deadline pressure, and failed to raise doubts about the official reports of how the hostages had died or to label those reports as unverified. To the reporters on the scene, those official accounts had sounded plausible in view of the early-morning public display of throat-slashing threats by the prisoners. It didn't matter that the rest of the news media had also gone along with the first unverified reports of the slayings, or that we promptly set the record straight. We were, after all, *The Times*.

IN THOSE TUMULTUOUS YEARS, as one gripping hard-news story followed another onto page one, I rarely found time to relax. And so I was grateful whenever a compelling cultural development floated into view that promised to lighten the tension. One such event that combined nostalgia and human interest involved a plan to bring Charlie Chaplin back to the United States after his twenty-year exile.

Chaplin, a British subject who, in 1947, had been accused by the House Un-American Activities Committee of having leftist affiliations (a charge he refuted), was denied reentry to the country from abroad. A bitter Chaplin remained with his wife and children in their Swiss mansion overlooking Lake Geneva, and, even when the ban against his return was lifted, he refused to set foot again in the United States.

The impetus to persuade Chaplin to come back arose with Martin E. Segal, founding president of the Film Society of Lincoln Center. At the end of 1971, he told me off the record that his board had decided to honor annually an eminent figure in the movie world and that Chaplin, at eighty-two, was their choice to inaugurate the events. I said it would make a terrific story, and he agreed that if he managed to pull it off he would give it exclusively to *The Times*.

A couple of months later, Marty headed for London, where Chaplin happened to be screening his 1921 silent classic, *The Kid*, for which he himself had written new music. Marty had arranged to be seated behind Chaplin, and when the lights went up he introduced himself. Chaplin impulsively invited Marty and his wife, Edith, to dinner with him and his wife, Oona, during which they finished three bottles of champagne. Marty, who had arrived in America with his parents from Russia in 1921 when he was five, traded "poor-boy stories" with Chaplin, and Chaplin finally accepted his Lincoln Center invitation.

Marty phoned me at two A.M. on February 8 (London time) to announce his coup. I put him on the phone with McCandlish Phillips, who wrote the exclusive story, which was picked up by papers all over the world. On April 3, when Chaplin and Oona arrived, more than a hundred reporters and photographers awaited them at Kennedy Airport.

That next night Marty hosted a small dinner for the Chaplins, to which he invited Barbara and me. I have to say I was awed to be in the presence of the man who had given me such pleasure since childhood. After the dinner and the screening of *The Kid* and *The Idle Class*, Chaplin rose in his theater box, but groped for words to thank the rhapsodic audience. With tears on his cheeks, he said, simply, "It's so very gratifying to know I have so many friends."

D URING THAT EARLY SPRING OF 1972, rumors swirled through *The Times* that Dan Schwarz's retirement as Sunday editor was set for the end of the year. It was no surprise that the rumors ran ahead of any official announcement, since that was ever the way of *The Times*. On the basis of the pledge made by Scotty Reston (and confirmed by Abe when he became managing editor), I was certain the job was mine. I believed I had locked it up the previous September, when, in a successful effort to increase circulation, I had launched the paper's first Sunday suburban supplement, the Brooklyn/ Queens/Long Island Section.

I was so sure of becoming Sunday editor, I began dreaming up projects for the Arts & Leisure section (formerly the Drama Section), the *Magazine*, the *Book Review* and the Week in Review, as well as the Travel section. I even asked my new deputy, Mitchel Levitas, who previously had been a rising young editor on the Sunday *Magazine*, if he wanted to return to the Sunday paper with me or try to succeed me as metropolitan editor. Known as Mike, Levitas was steeped in such subjects as labor and education. He had joined *The Times* in 1965 after jobs at the *Post* and *Time* magazine, and he became my deputy in 1971 when Syl Fox decided to leave *The Times* for a post with the Israeli Foreign Ministry. Mike said he'd be happy with either job.

But later in that spring of 1972, Abe once again gave me some bad news: Scotty no longer wanted me as Sunday editor. Even though he had relinquished the post of executive editor three years earlier and returned to Washington, Scotty maintained an office off the newsroom. He still exerted enormous influence on the Sulzberger family and continued to point out the dangers of an "Abe and Arthur" alliance in control of the entire paper. Sydney Gruson, appointed in March as the publisher's senior vice president and now his closest friend, seconded Scotty. They both lobbied for Max Frankel as Sunday editor, although he did not actively seek the job. In contrast to his failed attempt five years earlier to shunt me aside as metropolitan editor, Scotty this time seemed to be making progress.

To my great disappointment, Punch, in July, named Max to succeed

Schwarz as Sunday editor—to take over the job six months later, in January 1973. Announced as his deputy was Jack Rosenthal (no relation to Abe), who had made his reputation as chief urban affairs correspondent in the Washington bureau. In the early 1960s, before joining *The Times*, he had been special assistant to Attorneys General Robert Kennedy and Nicholas Katzenbach and later became the principal editor of the Kerner Report, the presidentially appointed commission's study of urban riots.

I had no doubt that Reston had trumpeted Max's recent journalistic triumph to secure him the Sunday editorship—and it was admittedly a rare coup. Max had followed President Nixon around China in late February and March of 1972. Nixon, still steaming over *The Times*'s publication of the Pentagon Papers and convinced we were trying to torpedo his reelection, had at first refused to allow any *Times* reporters into his press entourage. He finally relented, permitting *The Times* a single reporter. Over eight days, Max wrote 35,000 words. Nearly every day, he had two page-one bylines, one for a straight news story, another for a new feature called "Reporter's Notebook," initiated by Abe to allow Max to combine fact, analysis and freewheeling commentary. Kept busy running from event to event during the day and writing at night, he had only ten hours' sleep during the entire trip. His prose, brilliantly informative, interwove the present moment with a sense of the history of American–Chinese relations. (It won for him the Pulitzer for international reporting.)

I later learned from Lewis Bergman, who himself had given up hope of succeeding Schwarz, that Reston encouraged the festering fear within the Sunday department of the "Abe and Arthur" alliance. I was angry at what I saw as yet another Reston double-cross, and I seriously considered leaving the paper. But when I came to my senses, I realized how much I still cherished being metropolitan editor. In my heart, I knew there was no job that would ever give me as much pleasure.

BETWEEN THE ANNOUNCEMENT in July 1972 of Max's appointment as Sunday editor and his start in the job six months later, *The Times*'s Washington bureau, which Max continued to head, lost one of the biggest running stories of the century. On June 18, the *Washington Post* published a long, detailed account about the break-in at the Democratic National Committee in the Watergate building. The story was prominently displayed on page one and reported by eight staffers, including Bob Woodward and Carl Bernstein. By contrast, *The Times*'s unsigned, skimpy account of the arrests ran near the bottom of page 30. (The Washington bureau still didn't have the phone number of the D.C. police, I guess.)

In his book, *The Times of My Life and My Life with The Times,* Max beat himself up for letting the Watergate story slip away—an error that infuriated his New York colleagues, especially hard-nosed reporters like Murray Schumach, Nicholas Gage and Marty Tolchin. "Our Washington bureau had no ties to the capital police or courts," Max tried to explain. Woodward and Bernstein continued to stay ahead of *The Times* with embarrassing regularity as they followed the trail from the shoddy break-in directly to the White House.

"We were too sluggish even after the White House was implicated," Max wrote. "Not even my most cynical view of Nixon had allowed for his stupid behavior. . . . For me my habit of hypothesizing my way through a story slowed me down. I was so envious of the [*Washington*] *Post*'s lead that I allowed myself to be skeptical of some of its revelations." Max added, ironically, that he had "better alibis for our Watergate failure than the president had for his."

Abe, meanwhile, fretted like the prisoner of Forty-third Street. Every day he gnashed his teeth when comparing the stories in *The Times* with those in the *Washington Post*. But there was little he could do about it. At one point, he considered sending me to the bureau to head up the coverage as aggressively as my metropolitan staff had investigated the Serpico story. But I believed my going would be of little avail, because once a story as big and complicated as Watergate gets away from you, it's virtually impossible to catch up.

Moreover, Abe realized that sending me to Washington would probably invite an insurrection similar to the Greenfield episode. Nonetheless—as he told me much later—he felt that what he really should have done was remove Max immediately as head of the Washington bureau. Not doing so, he said, was the greatest mistake of his career.

Finally, in the fall of 1972, when Max was about to move to New York, Clifton Daniel was put in charge of the Washington bureau in the faint hope of salvaging what was left of the Watergate story. I wrote him a note, which read in part: "I can't tell you how truly delighted I am with your new appointment. You know I've always been a big fan of yours, and I think with you in Washington, the whole paper will get a big lift." I was sad, though, that a classy newspaperman like Clif had to settle for bureau chief after having been managing editor. A couple of years later the bureau was strengthened further by Bill Kovach, whom Abe sent to Washington to work as news editor under Daniel and who then became bureau chief himself.

Unfortunately, the Sunday editorship was not the ideal job for Max. He had no background in cultural coverage, which was, of course, a major element of the Sunday paper. It seemed to me a case of a first-class journalist placed in a role that simply fell outside the scope of his expertise. Once during his tenure, the critics—John Canaday, Clive Barnes, Vincent Canby, Harold Schonberg, among others—invited themselves to my apartment to voice specific complaints about how their copy was being mishandled for the Sunday section, and asked if I could possibly take charge of the Sunday culture pages as well as the daily. I could only remind them that the Sunday editor reported directly to the publisher. And it wasn't long before Lewis Bergman, unhappy with Max's ideas for the *Magazine*, invited me to lunch to apologize for having opposed me as Sunday editor. Max apparently took the dissension in stride and seemed to bear me no enmity, and I bore him none. Since our early days on rewrite, I had regarded him as a friend, and it was Max, not Abe, who—when he became executive editor—asked me to be his managing editor.

WHILE EVERYONE in the country was debating the identity of Watergate's "Deep Throat," the culture staff at *The Times* was busy discussing the movie of the same name. The film, which opened in New York on June 12, 1972, and grossed $3.2 million in six months, brought porn into the consciousness of the mainstream. Consequently, it faced an obscenity trial slated for late December.

Mayor Lindsay had success in cleaning up the sleazy Times Square area, raiding and shutting down graphic peep shows. When proprietors protested, Federal Judge Charles Brieant ruled that the seizure of peep-show films did not constitute stifling public expression, because the films were shown only to an audience of one, rather than to a full house. The mayor's office then decided to ease its ban on theaters offering soft-core pornography that featured simulated sex.

Deep Throat, however, depicted graphic sex. At our weekly culture department luncheon on December 15, the upcoming trial became the subject of surprisingly intense debate. Since the *Deep Throat* trial was bound to be a major story, I had asked our legal reporter, Lesley Oelsner, to explain the nuances of the obscenity statutes. We had all heard about the movie's sexually explicit theme, but none of us had seen the film. I suggested we cut short our lunch and catch the 1:10 P.M. showing at Broadway's World theater—a legitimate bit of research, we all agreed, albeit a little sheepishly—to acquire a clearer understanding of the forthcoming trial story. Our troupe of seven voyeurs skulked off to the theater, hoping no one we knew would see us buying our tickets.

In addition to Oelsner and me, our party included Grace Lichtenstein, three assistant metropolitan editors—Bill Luce, Marvin Siegel and Les Ledbetter—and Grace Glueck, the newly appointed culture editor. Glueck was the first woman I had promoted to a major editor's post. A bright fixture on the staff since 1952, she had become the art news reporter nonpareil.

We arrived a few minutes late for the movie and someone behind us whispered, "Don't worry, you didn't miss any of the plot." Those in our group with previous porn experience assured us they had never seen anything quite so explicit. "Now I know the reason why we keep the lights out in the bedroom," Ledbetter quipped.

Less than halfway through the film, the theater's loudspeaker blared out, "Mr. Arthur Gelb, metropolitan editor of *The New York Times*, is wanted back at his office." I learned later that it was Fred Ferretti who impishly had called the movie theater's manager. "Mr. Gelb is hard of hearing," Fred told him, "so be sure and page him nice and loud."

It was time, in any case, for me to get back to my desk and I asked Grace Glueck, seated beside me, if she wanted to leave, too. "Oh, no," she said earnestly, "I want to see how it comes out." When my colleagues returned to the city room, Lichtenstein informed me, "You missed the climax." Word spread quickly about our bawdy field trip, and some of the editors viewed it askance. Perhaps, Lichtenstein suggested, they were miffed at not having been invited. Jim Greenfield, for one, asked if he could come along the next time.

At the end of February 1973, Judge Joel Tyler found Mature Enterprises, Inc., which ran the World theater, guilty on obscenity charges and forbade the showing of the film. "This is one throat that deserves to be cut," he said, adding, "I readily perform the operation by finding the defendant guilty as charged."

A few days after our cinema journey, Punch Sulzberger asked me, only half in jest, "Is this the way an editor should be spending his time?"

"I don't plan to make a habit of it," I said, with a straight face, "but I felt I needed some expertise about a much-discussed topic."

I HAD STARTED the Wednesday culture lunches—described by Dick Shepard as my "cooking spoon to stir things up"—when I first took charge of the arts coverage in 1967, and other department heads followed in kind. The lunches, to which we sometimes invited outside guests—an eclectic group ranging from such as George Balanchine, Helen Hayes, Francis Ford Coppola and David Merrick to Mickey Rooney—often prompted offbeat stories. And no forum on the paper was more receptive to the uninhibited airing of our critics' views about *The Times*'s changing attitudes toward social mores. They acknowledged that we were loosening up to a degree. But some of our critics did not think the changes went far enough. At one lunch, a couple of them tried to make a case for relaxing the restrictions against explicit language—when it was part of an interview subject's quote—even if the quote contained what they cautiously described as "that four-letter word."

"Why stop there?" I challenged, playing devil's advocate: "There are more graphic terms. Where would we draw the line?" I reminded them that reporters, after all, weren't stenographers. Editors relied on their good sense to decide what to extract from the facts they gathered. The discussion continued in the elevator, as we glided back down to the city room. Ada Louise Huxtable said she agreed with her colleagues who thought it wrongheaded to ban "that word."

"What word are you talking about?" I prodded. There were eager eavesdroppers in the crowded elevator, and Ada just smiled enigmatically.

"You won't mention the word in the elevator," I said. "Why should we pepper the paper with it?" (And "that four-letter word," now ubiquitous in publications, let alone plays and films, remains banned along with others by *The Times*—for better or worse—as of this writing.)

FORTY-FOUR

D URING THE EARLY 1970s, zeroing in ever more intensely on investigative reporting, I came to rely a good deal on Nicholas Gage. Like David Burnham, he had an uncanny ability to sniff out wrongdoing—as was the case when we were trying to determine if Clifford Irving's purported ghostwritten "autobiography" of Howard Hughes was authentic. Nick was the first reporter to reveal that the book was a fraud. I watched him ferociously pursue his assignments, and it was several years before I learned that the motivation for his perseverance was rooted in a tragic childhood.

Gage had come to *The Times* in 1970, but I first encountered his curious mind eight years earlier, when he was still a student at Boston University.

The editor of his college paper and a theater fan, he lacked the ten dollars to purchase the just published O'Neill biography Barbara and I had written, and so he read it several chapters a day standing at the shelf of a local bookstore. As he came to the end, he discovered that in 1953 a suite in Boston's Shelton Hotel had been the setting for the book's climactic scene in which the dying O'Neill, with his wife's help, tore up his unfinished manuscripts and reportedly burned them in the fireplace. The Shelton, Gage knew, recently had been converted by the university into a women's dormitory.

Gage set out to visit the dorm's reconstructed rooms that had been O'Neill's hotel suite. Since men were not permitted in the dorm above the ground floor, Gage obtained special permission and was accompanied by an escort, who shouted, "Man in the hall! Man in the hall!" as they navigated the corridors. In what had been the O'Neill sitting room, he was surprised to find there was no fireplace. He knocked on the walls, thinking perhaps it had been covered over, but there were no hollow sounds. Since he wanted to be absolutely sure, he looked up the building department's files in City Hall, and found the blueprints of the original Shelton Hotel. No fireplace.

Gage wrote up his findings for the *Boston University News*, and his scoop was picked up by Elliot Norton, Boston's dean of theater critics. The AP put the story on its wire, where I first learned of it. I called Gage to inform him that O'Neill's widow had told me about burning the torn-up manuscripts in the fireplace. He asked if I had ever visited the hotel room in question, and I admitted I hadn't. Gage said he would keep poking around and I said I would check again with O'Neill's widow. We would be in touch as soon as either of us had any more information.

Gage found a maid at the dorm who had worked in the building when it was still the Shelton, and she said she had helped Mrs. O'Neill take the torn manuscripts to the hotel engineer for burning in the basement furnace. At the same time, Mrs. O'Neill told me she had misspoken, now remembering having taken the papers to the basement. The story was corrected for the second printing of the book, and I suggested Gage look me up in New York.

After his graduation, Gage asked my advice about whether to attend the Columbia School of Journalism or accept a job offer from a small newspaper. I remembered the advice Meyer Berger had given me about the inanity of studying journalism, but times had changed. Newspapers now gave considerably more weight to a diploma, and the practice of mentoring young reporters was not as common as it once had been. I told Gage he should consider going to Columbia in the hope of acquiring a good foundation, and he took my advice.

Twice, after graduating from Columbia, Gage asked me to hire him as a reporter. Abe had never before rejected any of my candidates, but he believed that Gage, as a recent graduate, didn't have enough experience to start as a *Times* reporter. So Gage went to work for the *Wall Street Journal,* and, finally, after he had written an impressive series of articles about organized crime in England, I insisted we bring him to *The Times*, and Abe agreed. Gage impulsively asked for twice his *Journal* salary and, to his astonishment, Abe consented.

I wanted Gage to succeed Charlie Grutzner, who had earlier done trailblazing exposures of the Mafia. Grutzner had cultivated sources in local and federal law enforcement agencies, and had produced the most penetrating mob stories in any New York publication. But for his age, he would have continued on the beat.

By the time Gage took over from Grutzner, Joseph Colombo, Sr., a former captain in the Profaci family, had risen to head that powerful Mafia clan. He then formed the Italian American Civil Rights League, part of whose mission was to erase the word "Mafia" from the news media as well as from popular entertainment. The league convinced the producer of *The Godfather* to delete the word from the script, and picketed newspapers that used it. When the issue arose at *The Times*, Gage told me, "If we can't use that word, what's the point of my being here?" I backed him up, and *The Times* became the only local paper not to cave in to Colombo's demands.

After covering Colombo's murder during a rally in Columbus Circle on Columbus Day, June 28, 1971, and writing a series of exclusive stories about the intricate politics of the various crime families, Gage was acknowledged as a foremost investigative reporter. Fully appreciative of his gift for winning the confidence of both gangland and law enforcement sources and persuading them to spill secrets, I thought he was just the man to investigate the murky provenance of an ancient Greek vase, the Euphronios krater, whose acquisition had recently been trumpeted by the Metropolitan Museum of Art. It had all the elements of a great art caper.

I had received a memo on January 5, 1973, from our chief art critic, John Canaday, saying he suspected some illegal behind-the-scenes maneuvering by the Fifth Avenue landmark. The Greek krater, putatively 2,500 years old, used for mixing wine and water, had been purchased by the museum in the late summer of 1972. It was painted by the artist Euphronios, and experts called it "the finest Greek vase there is," the only intact krater among the artist's twenty-eight known to exist. The museum claimed to have bought it from its owner for $1 million—a record price—but refused to identify him.

Canaday's indignant memo followed publication on November 12 of a cover article in *The Times Magazine* by a freelance writer, James Mellow, to whom Thomas Hoving, the director of the museum, had given the scoop. What aroused Canaday's suspicion was the fact that the museum had refused to provide Mellow with any details about where the vase came from, and exactly *when* it had arrived at the Met.

Canaday, distressed that he had been beaten by our own *Magazine* on so major an art story, was convinced that the museum had deliberately bypassed him for fear he would have raised questions about the possibility that the vase might have been smuggled out of Italy. Canaday and his assistant, the art critic and reporter David Shirey, were determined to find out why the museum had cloaked its purchase in mystery. The thirty-year-old Shirey had been on the paper less than two years, and this was his first crack at a big story. He was steeped in Greek and Roman art history from his days at Princeton and had done his graduate work in Rome, where he also had been on *Newsweek*'s staff.

After working on the story for more than a month, they hit a dead end— except for one important fact discovered by Shirey. He had cajoled a source at the museum into disclosing the date—August 31, 1972—that the vase had arrived at Kennedy Airport. I told Canaday we needed Nick Gage's investigative smarts. "Let's see where this takes us," I told Gage as I handed him Canaday's memo.

At Kennedy, Nick sought out the vase's entry papers among 1,600 items that had come through customs on that August 31, and searching for the right documentation took several days. According to the entry papers, the vase had been brought to New York from Rome by a Robert E. Hecht, Jr. Gage began making inquiries about Hecht but got nowhere. Canaday, tapping his own sources, reported to me, in a second memo, that "professional caution" was only part of the reason no one would talk to Nick. "Hecht is feared," Canaday's memo continued, quoting his sources as saying, "He is capable of sending men to beat us up."

Canaday's sources did, however, reveal to him that Hecht was the dealer who had sold the vase to the museum on behalf of an anonymous owner. It turned out that Hecht, an American living in Rome, had arrest records in Italy and Turkey for purchasing illegally excavated antiquities and had been declared persona non grata by the Turkish government. (The Metropolitan Museum, not naming him, had described him as "a reputable dealer.")

I was fascinated that such a lofty institution as the Met would stoop to cloak-and-dagger conspiracies. While Shirey continued to investigate in

New York, I asked Gage to go to Rome, track down Hecht and follow the trail to wherever it led. But, armed with a list of names supplied by Canaday and Shirey, he decided to go first to Geneva and Basel, the principal bases of Swiss dealers in antiquities.

Punch Sulzberger was on the Met's board of directors, and I suspected the board might put pressure on him to soft-pedal the story, but I was certain he would never interfere even if he thought our coverage might embarrass the museum or himself. He was a publisher of grace and class and guts. Nonetheless, I decided it would be best not to speak to him about the story, and he never mentioned our investigation to me.

After Gage's visit to Geneva—which as he learned was the place where the vase had been restored—he managed to persuade Hecht to meet him in Rome. Gage by now had discovered that Hecht, despite his arrest record, was one of the most renowned dealers in Italian and Greek antiquities. Most of the information Hecht gave Nick was evasive, but it was clear that he was describing a pattern of deception with regard to the krater and its owner— and Gage implied as much in his page-one story on February 19, 1973.

Claiming in the interview that he was merely the agent, Hecht said the krater's owner wished to remain anonymous because the transaction might cause him tax problems. He added that the owner's family had been in possession of the vase for more than fifty years and had decided it was time to let it go.

In the meantime, David Shirey, with the flow of information from Gage, began asking Met officials some hard questions about the vase's origins. Dietrich von Bothmer, the Met's curator of Greek and Roman antiquities, tried to deflect the questions, even while admitting that he himself had some questions about the vase's provenance. But, he argued, its intermediate history was not important. "Why can't people look at it simply as archaeologists do, as an art object?" he asked.

The following day, von Bothmer surprised us all by revealing to Shirey that Hecht had sold the vase on behalf of an unnamed Armenian collector who had originally purchased it in London in 1920. It was found broken into about forty fragments, which von Bothmer suggested "might have been kept in a shoebox" by the owner all those years. He said it had taken months to properly restore the vase to its present condition.

A day later, von Bothmer disclosed the name of the purported Armenian seller—Dikran Sarrafian, who lived in Beirut. He showed Shirey two letters, in which Sarrafian testified that his father had obtained the krater fragments from an amateur collector in exchange for Greek and Roman gold and silver coins. "I only authorized its restoration some three years ago," wrote Sarrafian. The restoration, von Bothmer added (confirming Nick's research), was completed in Switzerland during the summer of 1972.

The tale offered by von Bothmer might not have been the true story, but he was more helpful than he had intended to be. As soon as Shirey phoned me from the museum with the name of the purported Lebanese "seller," I called Gage in Rome and told him to get on the first plane to Beirut—which in art circles was known as the city that laundered the provenance of smuggled antiquities dug up in Italy and Greece. Gage met Sarrafian at the bar of the Hôtel St-Georges in Beirut, and the two spoke for several hours. Gage described him as a "loquacious old gentleman who preferred reminiscing about the sins of his youth to talking about the vase."

When Sarrafian finally got around to the matter of the vase, Gage grew increasingly suspicious as he stumbled through his narrative. He said he had never seen the vase intact until he glanced at a photograph of its restoration in the newspapers that very morning. All he had given Hecht, he explained, was "a hatbox [not a shoe box, as von Bothmer had earlier suggested] full of pieces," and he asserted that quite a few fragments were evidently missing. "If anyone looks closely at the Metropolitan's vase," he volunteered, "he should see a lot of painting over."

Sarrafian said his father had willed him the box of shards, to which he paid no attention for many years. One day, in the 1950s, he told Gage, he showed the relics to a now dead friend, who saw the name Euphronios inscribed on one piece. He said that in 1971, after having arranged to sell Hecht the pieces, he shipped them from Beirut.

Many contradictions emerged: Museum officials claimed the vase had come from a European collection; it had not. They originally said they could not name the seller because the disclosure might hurt their chances for further acquisitions from him; but Sarrafian had nothing else to sell them. They had also said they were protecting the seller from potential tax difficulties; but Sarrafian told Gage, laughing, "Income taxes don't amount to much in Lebanon."

He further revealed that most of the money paid by the Metropolitan had gone to Hecht, but that he had no complaints since he never thought the vase would bring such a price. This was a glaring contradiction on Sarrafian's part, since one of the letters he supposedly wrote asked for "one million dollars and over if possible." "Whatever the museum paid," he told Gage, "I am not a millionaire. . . . But I am satisfied with what [Hecht] gave me. . . . Good luck to him. Only the U.S. Treasury may be the loser, and it lost a lot more in Vietnam."

In the meantime, Gage learned, in talks with European art experts and dealers, that a vase that might actually have been the krater had been dug up north of Rome in 1971 by antiquities poachers, known as *tombaroli*. The *tombaroli,* it seemed, had sold the vase to Hecht through a middleman for $100,000.

Gage phoned to tell me of this stunning discovery. Together we tried to make sense of the new facts. Was it possible that Sarrafian's story was a complete fiction, masterminded by Hecht to give the unearthed vase a legitimate Beirut provenance in order to avoid charges that it had been dug up in Italy and smuggled out of the country?

Gage told me he was flying back to Rome, where Italian authorities by now had identified the *tombaroli* who had dug up the vase. It wasn't long, of course, before Gage was able to report to me the name of the illicit digger—Armando Cenere—and his whereabouts. If the vase had, indeed, been discovered in Italy, the Metropolitan Museum could be accused of illicitly receiving antiquities belonging to that country and of causing—at the least—an embarrassing international incident.

Cenere told Gage that he was one of six men who had uncovered a krater in several large pieces in Santangelo, an area rich in Etruscan tombs, about twenty-five miles northeast of Rome. A mason and a farmhand, Cenere pilfered ancient sites when he needed extra cash. His gang dug up the vase and other objects, including a cup and a winged sphinx. His memory of a bleeding man painted on one of the large pieces of the vase matched one scene on the Met's krater, which depicted the hero Sarpedon being carried from a battlefield by Sleep and Death during the Trojan War. The figure was bleeding from wounds to his heart, stomach and leg.

The gang, Cenere said, planted the winged sphinx in a field and leaked word to the police of its existence, hoping to divert attention from the real tomb where they found their trove. The police confirmed that the discovery of a sphinx had been reported at that time by an informant.

After selling the vase, the *tombaroli* leaders split the money among themselves. Cenere said he received about $8,800 but suspected he had been shorted, since his partners were driving new cars and buying homes that they never could have afforded on such a modest payoff. That, he said, was why he was willing to talk to the authorities.

Learning of Cenere's disclosures, Thomas Hoving, who began referring to the vase as the "hot pot" (after Shirey had described it as such), summarily dismissed them. But he admitted having seen a photo of a cup by Euphronios, which Hecht had also offered to sell to the museum. The cup, the Italian police had told Gage, was pulled from the same tomb at the same time as the vase, and was probably the one mentioned by Cenere.

Hecht eventually turned up in Zurich and reiterated his and the museum's story to Shirey by phone. "I believe in God. I believe in decency and integrity. I believe in Sarrafian," he said. "Who is this man Cenere, anyway? Cenere means 'ashes' in Italian. Ashes go into vases. This is like the commedia dell'arte and the opera buffa wrapped into one." He said the Euphronios krater had been in Switzerland ever since the Sarrafian family brought the fragments there in 1920. "It was never in Beirut, to my knowledge," he assured Gage. Not knowing what Hecht had told Shirey, however, both Hoving and Sarrafian contradicted him. They said the vase fragments had been shipped to Switzerland from Beirut.

Soon, Italian authorities issued a warrant for Hecht's arrest as more evidence was discovered that supported Cenere's version of events. Trying to solve the contradictions, the Italian officials now agreed that Hecht had purchased the Sarrafian pieces to create a legitimate provenance for the Euphronios vase that had been dug up illegally by the *tombaroli* and sold by them to Hecht. Sarrafian himself impulsively announced that he could not verify that the vase at the Met was composed of the same shards he had sold to Hecht. One new contradiction followed another.

As chapters of the mystery unfolded day by day, our readers were mesmerized, mailing us their own theories from all over the world. Canaday himself, his dignified persona a model of understatement, was overjoyed that his art specialty was holding its own on page one. "The painter Euphronios," he gloated, "set an all-time international record as the only artist in history to make the front page of *The New York Times* ten days running."

It turned out that regardless of the accusations by the Italian police, the Met was not legally compelled to return the vase to Italy, because it had been declared at customs when it was brought to New York. The Justice Department could not press charges since American laws had not been broken. Hecht stayed out of Italy and thus was never tried on the evidence.

But after the museum conducted its own internal investigation, Hoving and Douglas Dillon, president of the board of trustees, proclaimed on March 6, 1974, that, in their "considered judgment," the vase had not been smuggled. Canaday, Shirey, Gage and I found the museum's defense laughable. And, indeed, the museum, soon after, felt obliged to issue a "white paper" announcing it would alter its transactions policy, making its sales and acquisitions activities subject to public knowledge. I wasn't sure how many people were as skeptical as we were about the Met's excuses, but the Euphronios krater, in our minds, would always be the "hot pot."

There was no way to prove our suspicions that the Met's vase had actually been dug up in Italy and smuggled out of the country. But what about the hatbox of shards that supposedly had been in Sarrafian's possession in Beirut? According to a theory privately advanced by Canaday and Shirey, the Met's krater, after being dug up from a virgin tomb in Santangelo, had been deliberately broken into at least two pieces so that it could be smuggled from Italy to Switzerland, where there were no laws prohibiting the exportation of art objects to other countries. In Switzerland, the vase was put back together and shipped to the Met. Like the Italian officials, Canaday and Shirey believed that Sarrafian's shards were a hoax designed to establish a "legitimate" provenance for the Met's hot pot.

Years later, Hoving himself admitted that the vase had been illegally excavated. In a series of articles for *artnet* magazine in 2001, he wrote that throughout the purchase process he was convinced that the Euphronios had dubious origins. At one point after the museum took possession of it, he claimed, he came to believe the Sarrafian story, but then a light suddenly went on and he realized that the Italian authorities had been correct in maintaining the vase at the Met had been unearthed in Italy.

Hoving went on to describe an encounter he had had with Hecht at the end of 2000: "Last December I bumped into Bob Hecht at the opening of the Hermitage Rooms in London's Somerset House. I asked him directly if he'd switched Sarrafian's documents onto the Met's vase. He turned his face to the side after looking at me intently and said, 'Of course.'" At last, from the source himself, Gage, Canaday, Shirey and *The Times* were vindicated.

WITHIN WEEKS of his return from Italy in early 1973, Nick Gage broke the most nerve-wracking story of my editing career. At one point, I thought it might be the *last* story of my career. Wispy rumors—first brought to my attention by Charlie Grutzner—had been circulating for several years that the popular politician Mario Biaggi, a former police officer who had been elected a congressman from the Bronx in 1968, was involved in shady dealings.

No solid information surfaced until October 1972, when word reached Marty Tolchin that Biaggi had taken the Fifth Amendment numerous times on immigration matters before a federal grand jury the previous fall. Biaggi, however, insisted to Marty that he had testified truthfully and fully.

Everyone has the right to plead the Fifth Amendment against self-incrimination, and grand jury testimony is secret, of course. But Biaggi had recently announced his intention to run for mayor in 1973, and his chances of winning were deemed extremely favorable. If he had indeed lied about invoking the Fifth over questions about dubious dealings, we felt it should be public knowledge, as this might affect his eligibility for the mayoralty. But no one could pin down anything specific and, in March of 1973, Biaggi formally sought the nomination of the Conservative Party, receiving its blessings only after denying unequivocally that he had pleaded the Fifth.

Richard Reeves, trying his own sources, turned up only "hearsay and more rumors." Meanwhile, a reporter from the *Daily News* who was also checking on the report asked Biaggi specifically if he had ever refused to answer any questions before any grand jury. "I testified fully—answering each and every question—to a federal grand jury on immigration matters which was impaneled for that purpose," his statement read. "I presented all my personal and official records that were requested." There was no proof to the contrary, but no one in the press believed him.

Biaggi had often been at the center of controversy. During his years— 1942 to 1965—as a police officer, he had shot a man to death in the back of his personal car while off duty. Biaggi said the man was trying to hold him up. Although he had a record as a brave cop and had earned the department's Medal of Honor, many on the force were not satisfied with his explanation. And the word on the street was that Biaggi and his victim were not strangers to each other.

Also troubling was his recent assertion that the magnitude of police corruption had been blown out of proportion. He said that if he became mayor he would dismiss Police Commissioner Patrick Murphy, Howard Leary's successor, who had taken a hard line against corruption. Many believed a Biaggi mayoral win would knock the Police Department right back to where it had been before the Knapp Commission. And we could only imagine what would happen to the rest of the city's departments.

In addition to Conservative Party endorsement, Biaggi became the front-runner in the Democratic mayoral primary in a year when it seemed a given that whoever gained that nomination would coast into City Hall. Our political reporters believed that Mayor Lindsay would not be a candidate for reelection because he wanted to run for president. He soon switched to the Democratic Party to enter the presidential primaries against Senator George McGovern, but withdrew from the race early. He had been humiliated by his defeat in the Florida primary, where Jewish vacationers and retirees, consistently among his principal supporters since his early days as mayor, now decried his neglect of their problems in New York. They held him responsible for crime and drugs invading their once-safe neighborhoods and, among their other complaints, cited his disparagement of taxi drivers, an occupation then dominated by hardworking Jewish cabbies. This was not a career that should satisfy blacks looking for jobs, he pronounced, advising them to aim higher. The vacationers gloated to see planes flying banners over the beaches proclaiming, "Lindsay Spells Tsouris" (Yiddish for "trouble").

On March 7, 1973, the fifty-one-year-old mayor, having endured months of speculation by the public, announced he would not seek reelection. He said his move was being made for "personal considerations," but our political reporters thought it was unlikely he could have won. As he read his statement to the press at City Hall and defended his record, members of his staff wept. "My love for this city and the work still to be done have tempted me to carry on," he said. "Eight years is too short a time, but it is long enough for one man."

As a last resort, I put Nick Gage on the Biaggi story. He called his close source at the United States Attorney's office and asked him to look at the grand jury transcript. The source said it was evident Biaggi was telling the truth. Feeling confident at this point, Biaggi agreed to meet with Gage. He said he had nothing to hide, and Gage posed the same question in a number of different ways. Biaggi repeatedly asserted he had answered every question before the grand jury on immigration matters on October 29, 1971. Gage was suddenly struck by the fact that Biaggi kept volunteering the specific date.

"What about the second time you testified before a grand jury that fall?" he asked, not certain that there had been a second time. Biaggi brusquely replied that he answered everything that time, too, and he had nothing more to say. An assistant quickly ushered Gage out of Biaggi's office.

Gage phoned his source at the U.S. Attorney's office again, and this time asked him if he could dig up the transcript of Biaggi's second appearance. Nick was told it had occurred a month after the first, on November 26, 1971, an appearance based not on "immigration matters," but on issues of personal finances, including favors he was suspected of receiving in exchange for his political influence. Gage's source said he had, in this instance, taken the Fifth a number of times.

Gage arrived at my desk brimming with excitement, ready to write the story. The disclosure that Biaggi had lied when he said he hadn't ever taken the Fifth was a discovery potent enough to destroy his chances of winning the mayoralty. But we had to be a hundred percent sure. "Hold on," I said, reminding Gage of our policy requiring two sources for verification on such a risky story. "God help us if your source was careless in his checking."

Concerned that the *Daily News* was hot on the trail and might beat him, Gage immediately began hunting for a second source. He knew that the assistant U.S. Attorney involved in the case regularly lunched at Forlini's, a popular restaurant near Federal Court. Each day at lunchtime during the next several days, Gage lingered outside the restaurant waiting for the man to show up. On the fourth day, he and a colleague arrived and Gage followed them into the restaurant, finding a table close to them.

I must say I found it a little hard to believe, but Gage claimed he actually overheard the prosecutor discussing a story that had run in the *Daily News* that very morning, in which Biaggi was quoted, once again, saying he had never taken the Fifth. "Did you see that son of a bitch's lie in the paper today about not having taken the Fifth?" the assistant U.S. Attorney asked his colleague. Gage presumably had his confirmation, wrote the story and gave it to me.

Since it was bound to cause an uproar, I took the story to Abe. As he carefully studied Gage's copy, he asked me questions. "If this is not true," he said, "it will be one of the worst mistakes *The Times* has ever made. Nick will have to leave the paper and so will you, and where it'll leave me I don't even want to think about. There can be no doubt whatsoever about its accuracy."

I took Gage for a drink at the Pantheon, a small Greek restaurant on Eighth Avenue. "You're a young guy," I told him. "People may forget about this one day, and sooner or later you'll be able to work again. But if I give the go-ahead on this and we're wrong, I'm finished. I need to be absolutely certain." I asked him to find one more source, and I said I had to hear the answer with my own ears.

Back at the office, Gage phoned a friend of ours who had certain knowledge of the grand jury proceedings and whose word I trusted as definitive. The man, whose identity I still cannot divulge, was hesitant about confirming or denying anything, since revealing closed testimony carried a five-year jail sentence. I got on the phone and personally explained the situation. "I'll call you back in five minutes," the man said. When he called back, his careful words were, "You are not taking any risks printing that story."

It was getting close to edition time. I bolted to Abe's office and told him we had just received positive verification, and we should go with the story. Abe asked me who the source was, but I wouldn't tell him, and have not to this day. "You have to trust me on this one," I said.

The story made it into the first edition of the paper for Wednesday, April 18, 1973. Once it reached the stands, the *Daily News* scurried to get confirmation before its presses closed, and managed to run a reflection of our account in its final edition.

At a televised press conference in the morning, Biaggi called the stories "a complete hoax." "I categorically deny the charges made against me and will prove them completely false. I charge that this is part of a conspiracy to destroy me." He challenged *The Times* and the *News* to produce their source.

Biaggi's campaign manager, Matthew Troy, the city councilman with close ties to the Patrolmen's Benevolent Association, the man who had once tried to derail the Knapp Commission, said he believed Biaggi was telling the truth, but if he was proved wrong, "then Matty Troy is no longer his campaign manager."

"I personally think Nick Gage is a great reporter," Troy added, "but I hope he wins the Pulitzer Prize for something else." He said he had urged Biaggi to release the grand jury transcripts to the public, to "knock this thing down forever." Biaggi did not want to, he said, because he feared hurting other people whose names came up at the hearings.

Gage's investigation added fuel to the uncivil war between New York and Washington. A petition arrived in the city room signed by most members of the Washington bureau, castigating Gage for revealing the testimony of a closed hearing and exposing the fact that the congressman took the Fifth, to which every citizen had a right. They completely missed the point that Biaggi's mayoral nomination was based on his insistence that he never took the Fifth, and the fact that he lied to get the nomination was the news.

In view of the bureau's attitude toward New York, the petition didn't really surprise us. But we were shocked by the fact that Seymour Hersh, the bureau's most aggressive investigative reporter, who had never allowed legal niceties to get in the way of his probes, was among those who signed the petition. Gage later told me he understood Hersh's reason: "He had to live with all those guys in the bureau."

On April 25, Biaggi requested that a three-judge panel review the transcripts to determine "whether or not I took the Fifth Amendment on my personal finances and assets." U.S. Attorney Whitney North Seymour, Jr., countered, asking for complete disclosure of the transcripts. He felt duty-bound to intercede, since he believed Biaggi's proposal was an attempt to manipulate the court. On the one hand, if the court denied opening the transcripts to any type of scrutiny, the congressman would come off looking honest, whether or not he actually was. On the other, accepting Biaggi's narrow proposal would "tie the hands of the court" if he took the Fifth for any other reason. Seymour cited an "overriding public interest" for a full disclosure.

Judge Edmund Palmieri ultimately sided with Seymour. He denounced Biaggi for asking something of the court that he never expected them to grant, "for the purpose of publicly exploiting the court's denial." The Court of Appeals also ruled against Biaggi and gave him five days to appeal to the U.S. Supreme Court before the testimony was made public.

On May 10, 1973, the evening prior to the transcript's release, Biaggi admitted he had taken the Fifth. He had done so, he said, "because I was angry that I was not allowed to read a statement pleading with the grand jury to leave my daughter alone." (One of the issues being investigated was whether he granted favors in return for getting his daughter a job.) In the article about Biaggi's confession, however, Gage pointed out that the "only constitutional right for refusing to answer [before a grand jury] is the right against self-incrimination provided in the Fifth Amendment." Biaggi claimed the questions he avoided were "insignificant."

The questions were, in fact, directly aimed at exploring his relationships to various businesspeople, from whom Biaggi was suspected of profiting illegally. He refused to identify his own signature on two letters and invoked the Fifth when asked if he knew certain individuals. It was further revealed that the inquiry on "immigration matters" revolved around some two hundred bills sponsored by Biaggi in Congress. None of the bills was likely to pass but, the prosecutor held, lawyers were sometimes paid by their clients for getting a bill onto the House floor through a congressman. The implication was that Biaggi was at the least doing favors for friends, and probably collecting kickbacks from the lawyers.

Gage reaped congratulations, and *The Times* ran an editorial entitled "Discredited Candidacy": "The transcript revealing the truth destroys Mr. Biaggi's credibility as a candidate for mayor of New York City. . . . It would benefit the city and the Democratic Party if the primary race were in effect narrowed to the three other candidates, whose programs and capacities for leadership can now be more calmly weighed by the electorate."

Biaggi remained on the Conservative mayoral ticket. Abe Beame handily won the Democratic nomination. John Marchi ran again as the Republican candidate. In November, Beame won the general election with nearly sixty percent of the vote. After the roller-coaster Lindsay years, New Yorkers, sinking ever deeper into financial trouble, wanted a man who was stable, predictable and—they mistakenly believed—knew how to manage money.

Biaggi went on to serve ten terms in Congress, becoming something of an institution. In the end, however, he was finally exposed as a crook. In 1987, he was convicted of bribery, fraud and conspiracy, having used his influence to aid a company in the Brooklyn Navy Yard that had Navy and Coast Guard contracts. He had received paid vacations at a Florida spa as thanks. Biaggi was fined half a million dollars and sentenced to thirty months in prison.

Just over a year later, Biaggi was convicted on fifteen felony counts—including racketeering, bribery, extortion and obstruction of justice—for helping a Bronx company win no-bid military contracts. Biaggi had demanded five percent of the company's stock for his favors. Years later, Biaggi said, "I maintain I was not a felon. I was a victim." When Gage and I got together every so often, we reminded ourselves that we helped save New York from becoming a den of corruption perhaps even surpassing the days of Jimmy Walker.

In early October 1973, several months after the Biaggi coverage, Gage, still smarting from the Washington staff's criticism of his story, managed to get what he called his "sweet revenge." Since the bureau was still falling behind the *Washington Post* on Watergate developments, Abe asked Gage to go to Washington and "come up with something good that will help save our reputation." When Gage checked in with Clif Daniel at the bureau, he found the mood generally despondent over efforts to catch up on coverage, and Daniel accepted Gage's suggestion that he work independently. Within a couple of weeks, he came up with a blockbuster scoop that led the paper.

Nick had found a source with access to White House documents who let him listen to copies of some of Nixon's tapes, the first such tapes to which a reporter had been given access. On the tapes, recorded in 1971, Nixon was heard ordering Richard G. Kleindienst, then deputy attorney general and later attorney general, to stop antitrust actions against International Telephone and Telegraph. After an out-of-court settlement with the government that was generally considered favorable to the corporation, according to Nick's story, ITT agreed to help pay the cost of the 1972 Republican National Convention in San Diego.

Nick heard Nixon on the tapes castigate Kleindienst for his opposition and address him with a vulgar pejorative, adding, "Don't you understand the English language?" But Sy Topping would not allow the obscene word into the paper. I knew Nick would be disappointed, since he had called me from Washington earlier in the day to report boastfully that he'd heard Nixon on the tape calling Kleindienst a "cocksucker."

Nick kept suggesting that I hire more investigative reporters, such as Lucinda Franks, a Pulitzer winner at the UP. (Soon after arriving at *The Times,* she came up with a scary story about the dangers of red dye additives in food.) In early 1977, Abe asked Nick how he saw his future. What he wanted above all, Nick said, was to head the Athens bureau. Neither Abe nor I quite understood why he chose a beat that would make few demands on his investigative skills, but Abe consented. It took some time to discover the true reason for Nick's choice, which involved the fate of his mother during the Greek civil war thirty years earlier.

In the fall, in Athens, Nick hit the ground running, to reveal in a front-page story that Jackie Kennedy had agreed to take $26 million as a settlement on her claims to the estate of her late husband, Aristotle Onassis. And, during the next three years, the foreign editor sent Nick on assignments outside Greece, covering political turmoil in Turkey, Lebanon and Iran, where, for nine months, he filed stories about the revolution that toppled the shah and brought the Ayatollah Khomeini to power.

Barbara and I twice visited Nick in the land of his birth. He and his wife, Joan, a freelance writer, shepherded us on esoteric tours of the Greek mainland and its isles. Somehow, we never quite made it to the mountain village of Lia, where Nick was born, but we listened in fascination to the stories of his boyhood there.

He was born Nikola Gatzoyiannis in 1939. His father, who had left for Massachusetts to find work, had planned to bring his wife and children over as soon as he was established. But he was cut off from his family when World War II began. After the war, when the Communists occupied Lia and began sending children into Albania for indoctrination, Nick's courageous mother arranged an escape for her eight-year-old son and three of his sisters. The Communists regarded her act as treason, and she was tortured and killed by a firing squad.

From the day Nick and his sisters arrived in America, when he was nine, he vowed to someday avenge his mother's murder. Meanwhile, he struggled to overcome the bitterness he felt toward his father for not having brought his family to America immediately after the war ended. Trying to come to terms with his demons, Nick finally left *The Times* in 1980 to write a book about his mother (which he called *Eleni*), and simultaneously to find the man, Katis, who had given the order for Eleni's execution. It took him two years to corner Katis, who was living comfortably in a town not far from Lia. Nick had brought a revolver, but found himself unable, at the final moment of confrontation, to take the revenge he had long dreamed of.

In *Eleni*, he explained why: "If I killed Katis, I would have to uproot that love in myself and become like him, purging myself as he did of all humanity or compassion."

FORTY-FIVE

WHILE NICK GAGE was busy tracing the history of the shards of an ancient vase, Lacey Fosburgh, one of my desk clerks I'd promoted to reporter, was trying to put together the pieces of a grisly murder—which later became the basis of a best-selling novel, Judith Rossner's *Looking for Mr. Goodbar*.

From her earliest days as a reporter, Lacey had displayed a steely desire to show her skeptical male colleagues that blond good looks did not rule out tough reportorial talent. Lacey's stories often outstripped those of her condescending male competitors in gritty detail and earthy atmosphere. At press conferences, she'd invariably elbow her way up front along with the photographers to be the first to get at her subject.

She once asked me what I considered the most difficult assignment a reporter could be given. There were many, I said, but high on my list would be an exclusive interview with the reclusive J. D. Salinger, who had recently expressed his fury (through his lawyer) about the publication of unauthorized editions of his early uncollected works. A couple of days after our conversation, on November 2, 1974, Lacey managed to reach Salinger by phone at his home in Cornish, New Hampshire. Salinger, who hadn't been interviewed in twenty years, was caught by surprise. He said he would talk to her for only a minute, but she kept him on the phone for half an hour. The interview, played on page one, was memorable for Salinger's comment: "There is a marvelous peace in not publishing. It's peaceful. Still. Publishing is a terrible invasion of my privacy. I like to write. I love to write. But I write just for myself and my own pleasure."

Lacey's first really big challenge was tracing the murder of Roseann Quinn, a Bronx-born twenty-eight-year-old schoolteacher, who was found nude, bludgeoned, stabbed and strangled in her blood-splattered West Seventy-second Street apartment on January 1, 1973.

It was a front-page story and, as in the case of the Wylie–Hoffert homicides a decade earlier, it struck a chord of fear in a city full of sexually liberated young women. Once again, it seemed, random violence had invaded the home of an unsuspecting woman, in this case a teacher who worked with handicapped children. And once again, there were no fingerprints, no apparent clues.

But, as Lacey reported, the police finally learned that Roseann Quinn had met her killer, John Wayne Wilson, on the night of her murder, at Tweed's, a raunchy bar across the street from her apartment. Grass was openly smoked at the tables and cocaine was snorted in the bathroom. Wilson, a drifter in his twenties, confessed to having slashed his victim with a carving knife before leaving her apartment.

Unnerved by the ugly facts, Lacey—in her late twenties and single, like the victim—asked me if she could take a few days to look into the psychological aspects of the story. She wanted to tell it against the background of a recent urban social phenomenon—the search for companionship by often lonely women of Lacey's own age, who had begun venturing into bars unescorted by men, no longer concerned they would be stigmatized as prostitutes. In the post-1960s era, Manhattan's singles bars were crowded with unattached young men and women seeking a good time. Roseann, Lacey learned, habitually drank in such bars, often picking up a man she took home to bed.

Lacey interviewed psychiatrists, detectives on the case, members of the victim's family, her friends, neighbors, her colleagues at school and people she had met at Tweed's, to help her understand Roseann Quinn's pathology. According to neighbors, the men she had usually brought home with her after bar-hopping were physically abusive, and it began to seem that Roseann had, to a degree, conspired in her own victimization.

One of Lacey's early discoveries was that Roseann, who was both intelligent and attractive, had suffered from scoliosis, a genetic malformation that had left her from birth with a twisted back and a slight hump. In her periods of depression, she confided to friends that her father always appeared to shun her, unable to confront her deformity. As a teenager, hoping to have her back straightened, she underwent an operation that required her to lie virtually immobilized for a year. When she found the operation was only partly successful, she lost her religious faith. Soon after, when she became a teacher, she began to display the self-destructive symptoms that eventually led to her death. Although she sampled the city's cultural life and enjoyed reading, she told friends that she felt most at home in Tweed's.

Lacey became obsessed with Roseann's life story and could not let go of it. Eventually she wrote her own nonfiction book about the murder called *Closing Time*, which brought a letter of extravagant praise from Truman Capote (who said the case was in some ways similar to the senseless killings he had portrayed in *In Cold Blood*).

In the weeks before John Wayne Wilson's arrest, many New Yorkers believed Roseann Quinn had been murdered by a deranged street person, who had followed her to her apartment. It was a likely assumption in a time when the city's sidewalks teemed with all manner of mental cases, shouting at invisible adversaries, begging wild-eyed for money, urinating and exposing themselves, sleeping off their drunks on building stoops and in doorways, occasionally riding unmanned elevators in apartment buildings.

In late 1973, I assigned Murray Schumach to report on the anatomy of the problem—to find out, if possible, why so many seriously disturbed individuals were not receiving institutional care, and to assess possible solutions. He wrote dozens of articles on the subject, which appeared throughout 1974.

Schumach learned that between 1968 and 1973, the number of psychiatric patients in state institutions had dropped from 78,000 to 34,000. The reasons were fourfold: first, the adoption by state officials of a new therapeutic theory under which mental patients could be transferred from state institutions to halfway houses in local communities, where they could begin to assimilate and strive toward some semblance of a normal life; second, the realization of cost savings by the state, since the release of patients into local communities made them the city's, not the state's, fiscal responsibility; third, the growing movement for patients' civil rights that advocated minimal— and preferably no—governmental intervention in the lives of the insane; and fourth, the development of new medications that patients could take daily on an ambulatory basis to render them nonviolent (but which patients often refused or forgot to take).

The civil rights movement pointedly questioned the "lifelong warehousing" of mental patients—a situation in which potentially salvageable men and women became permanently lost within a labyrinthine institutional bureaucracy. Unless a person was a proven menace to society, the American Civil Liberties Union contended, he should be released. Once discharged, moreover, the civil rights advocates maintained, he could not be forced to take medication even if it was clinically demonstrated he needed it, nor could he be mandated to live anywhere or be subjected to supervision. Basically, the advocates held that a person had the right to be mentally ill, and it was his right to live on the street if he so chose.

What resulted, Schumach discovered, was a revolving-door system. Patients were initially admitted to Bellevue or Kings County Hospital for evaluation, then sent on to a state institution. They were usually released back into their communities within a week. With few restrictions and scant aftercare, the patients once again roamed the streets. It wasn't long before they were sent back to Bellevue, and the process was repeated. All the while, they were going on and off medication and receiving very little psychiatric treatment.

Most disturbing was that the system was enabling mentally ill criminals to find their way out of incarceration. A new law required the mentally ill who were awaiting trial to be housed in regular state institutions rather than in the maximum-security facility, Matteawan State Hospital. Some criminally insane patients were then mistakenly released. Others simply walked out, as did one man who was awaiting trial for cutting his mother's head off with an ax. Fortunately, most were recaptured within twenty-four hours. But the hospitals sometimes neglected to alert the police, as was the case with an escapee who shot three people and then held his gun to a policeman's head and pulled the trigger (the gun misfired). At the time Schumach wrote his article, the man was still at large.

As a result of Schumach's investigation, many doctors who had initially supported more liberal treatment approaches, began to reconsider. Perhaps in theory it was better for patients to live in communities, they said, but in practice it wasn't working. The "homes" to which patients were released offered little, if any, of the psychiatric care essential to improving mental health. Most were run with the goal of producing maximum profit, staffed by unsympathetic attendants who couldn't care less about the welfare of their residents. The city itself did not have the budget to provide for the needs of its mentally ill, and the street vagrants became one of the symbols of New York's continuing slide into urban decay.

During the summer of 1974, I received a tip that care for the elderly in the city was not much better than for the mentally ill. The source, as it happened, was my mother. At eighty, and convinced she no longer could care for herself in her own rented apartment, my mother decided to enter a home for the aged, where she could be with people of her own generation and not be a burden to her family. Without my knowledge, she and a friend went shopping for a retirement home and eventually she found what she regarded as a well-run facility. But she let me know how upset she was by the conditions she and her friend had encountered earlier in their search. "You're the metropolitan editor of *The New York Times*," she chastised me, "and it's your responsibility to do something about this nursing home mess."

I assigned John Hess, a reporter with a naturally suspicious mind, to look into the questions raised by my mother about the shabby care and unsanitary conditions she had found in her visits to a number of homes. Hess had worked for the *Post*, the *Daily News*, AP and UP before coming to *The Times* in 1954, where he served on the financial copy desk, the foreign desk, night rewrite and in the Paris bureau.

Hess confirmed my mother's observations, finding that the condition of nursing homes had hardly improved since Sydney Schanberg wrote about them in 1966. His investigation culminated in a four-part series in October 1974 that exposed the system for the racket it was. Millions of dollars were overcharged to Medicaid. Applicants found it necessary to bribe managers to get into a decent facility without waiting months or years. Cost-cutting measures left the homes feeling more like prisons than places to retire. A nepotistic hiring and contracting system was rife with kickbacks. And there were signs of Mafia involvement in the operation of some homes. The series resulted in state and city scrutiny of the industry, managerial reform and some criminal convictions.

NEW YORK's proliferating problems in 1974 took a backseat to the drama being enacted in Washington. In the newsroom, even though I loaned members of my staff to help out on national stories and Abe occasionally used me as a sounding board on Washington coverage, I couldn't help feeling a little left out. The metropolitan world seemed somehow dwarfed in comparison with the capital implosion. Evidence of executive misdeeds linked to Watergate was, of course, erupting, in part because of Nixon's desperate efforts to cover them up. His top aides had long since been forced to resign. And Spiro Agnew had already vacated the vice presidency after being charged with tax evasion and bribery.

On August 8, 1974, Nixon, under threat of impeachment, announced his own resignation. House Minority Leader Gerald Ford, who had replaced Agnew, was sworn in as president on August 9 and nominated Nelson Rockefeller as his vice president. Rockefeller had resigned as New York's governor in December 1973, to be succeeded by Hugh Carey, putting both the state and city of New York under Democratic control.

But even a political climate favorable to a Democratic city could not forestall New York's downward spiral. That November 1974, my political reporters began to question whether New York could skirt the looming consequences of a decade of financial mismanagement.

The problems had begun under Wagner, ballooned under Lindsay and were now about to explode under Beame. Each administration had lived beyond its means, creating a widening gap between income and expenditures. As all governments do—whether local, state or federal—New York borrowed money against expected revenues. But to make the budget balance on paper, which was a mayoral duty, revenues were cavalierly overestimated. Hence the city had to borrow to pay off previous loans, in addition to what was needed for day-to-day operations. By late 1974, my staff and I could no longer doubt that New York was balancing on the rim of default, about to face the worst fiscal disaster in its history. There was plenty of blame to spread around. New York had instituted a cornucopia of new social programs with the encouragement—and money—of the federal government under the Great Society banner hoisted by President Johnson. With Nixon in the White House, much of those funds had dried up, but Lindsay felt he could not yank the promised programs for underprivileged New Yorkers, partly out of compassion and partly out of his chronic fear of neighborhood riots. So the city had to pick up the bill.

The issue was made worse by mushrooming labor costs. I well remembered the overwhelming victory of the Transport Workers Union at the start of his mayoralty in 1966, when Lindsay, fearing the consequences of turning down the demands of municipal unions, had agreed to staggeringly generous packages. Some critics of the city lashed out not only at these advancing costs but also at what they saw as other municipal "burdens," among them: free city hospital and university systems, upkeep of zoos and public libraries and funds misdirected to "welfare cheats."

My staff had predicted the crisis in our "Changing City" series in 1969. Aside from noting the rise in the welfare rolls and the steady transfer of the tax base to suburbia, the series referred to the sleight-of-hand tactics employed to fudge the city's chronic budget gap. Besides inflating the estimates of anticipated revenues, some operating expenses were shifted to the capital budget, where they could be paid by loans rather than income. In other cases, certain expenditures were debited against the following fiscal year, making it easier to meet current budgets at the expense of future ones. In the city's budget bureau, the technique was known as "the flimflam."

It seemed to me that if anyone should have understood the stark facts of the city's financial situation it was Mayor Abe Beame, who had, after all, served as controller under both Wagner and Lindsay. Upon becoming mayor himself in 1974, he had pledged to reduce the municipal deficit of $1.5 billion he inherited. The budget gap for the 1974–1975 fiscal year, however, expanded beyond all predictions, and in October 1974, Beame ordered an 8.5 percent cut for each municipal department. But when he was alerted to what that meant on the streets—1,800 fewer firemen, 4,200 fewer cops, 2,100 fewer sanitation workers—he followed the course of denial taken by his predecessors. After performing some creative arithmetic, he concluded that such drastic cuts in service were really unnecessary, and announced more moderate layoffs. He then went back to the banks for more money.

I was now confronted with the most tortuous story I had handled as metropolitan editor. Every aspect of a vast governmental financial maze had to be taken apart and probed each day for our anxious readers. Although my reporters and I gradually became adept at dissecting the multiple strands of political and financial maneuverings behind the ever-worsening municipal debt, we weren't exactly schooled in the exotica of banking and accounting legerdemain, Wall Street transactions and bond-rating methodology.

More than ever, I had to rely on that old journalistic assumption that it was possible for a top-notch reporter quickly to gain expertise on an arcane subject. And, in short order, my City Hall staff managed to do just that, learning on the job. As they handed in their copy each day, my admiration surged for the skill with which they brought clarity to a convoluted story that dominated page one week after week.

Our lead writer was Fred Ferretti, now our City Hall bureau chief, who was assisted by a crew of five: John Darnton and Stephen Weisman (both former clerks on the metropolitan desk); Maurice Carroll, a crack political analyst formerly with the *Trib*; Edward Ranzal, who had years of experience on various city beats; and Ronald Smothers, whom I had recently hired from a black community news service in Brooklyn.

Fred knew the city and its neighborhoods inside and out, having covered them all his journalistic life. He was voracious about news, somewhat hot tempered and forthright in his views. He had had the courage, as producer of the eleven-o'clock TV news at NBC, to transfer the equally hot-tempered Gabe Pressman, against his will, from a nightly in-house commentary segment to a job for which Ferretti thought he was better suited—covering news on the street.

Every morning at eleven, Fred called me from City Hall with a rundown on what was expected to unfold that day. Together we shaped the daily report, assigning a news story, feature or a news analysis article to each member of the bureau, and my night editor, Shelly Binn, then shepherded the voluminous copy into the paper without ever missing a deadline. The staff usually put in ten-to-twelve-hour days, and space for the coverage was virtually limitless—whatever it took to tell so twisted a story.

Every so often Fred agreed to appear on a TV news program to deliver his newly acquired punditry. And once, in an off-the-cuff lecture at the Columbia School of Journalism, his candor got him into trouble. A reporter for the daily college paper, the *Spectator*, happened to attend the lecture and, at its conclusion, he said, "It seems to me, Mr. Ferretti, that what you write is not reflected in *The Times*'s editorials." Fred, who for some time had been quietly complaining to me about what he thought were uninformed editorials on the city's finances, blurted out impulsively that they were basically "trash."

The next day's *Spectator* ran a story on the top of its front page saying that Ferretti had called *The Times* editorials "garbage." Abe summoned Fred to tell him he had received an irate call from the editor of the editorial page, John Oakes, "who wants an apology." Fred was indifferent to the fact that Oakes's influence on the paper stemmed partly from his relationship to the Sulzberger family (he was Adolph Ochs's nephew and Iphigene's first cousin). At first, Fred refused to apologize; but finally he conceded, "Okay, I'll apologize for being indiscreet but not for disagreeing with the editorials."

IN THE MEANTIME, the city's credibility with lending institutions was rapidly eroding. They were no longer willing to blindly accept the estimates of expected revenues, having realized they were exaggerated. Various experts playing the deceptive numbers game both within and outside City Hall offered guesses at the true total of the city's constantly growing debt. It was further discovered that some of Beame's belt-tightening measures were illusory. At one point, he announced layoffs of several thousand employees. But when Ferretti asked Smothers to verify the layoffs, by studying the budget entries line by line, he found that the jobs had been eliminated on paper but not in reality. That story made great reading.

On March 6, 1975, the city attempted a routine $567 million note sale, for which there were no buyers. Governor Carey then grudgingly went to bat for Beame, his old Democratic ally. As a stopgap, he had the state borrow $400 million for the city. But from that point on, the power of the mayor's office was gradually sapped, ultimately reducing Beame to little more than a figurehead. First, the banks and lending institutions united as a group to dictate terms, including the interest rate on their loans to the city. There was no competitive bidding among them, and the cost was high. Somehow, the city still managed to remain solvent.

Beame began to pin his hopes on a bailout by the federal government. He launched the first in a series of appeals to President Ford, and Ford issued the first in a series of rejections, plus a scolding lecture on how to manage money.

Dissatisfied with the steps taken by the city to right its course, the banks pressured the state to protect their municipal investments. In June 1975, the governor and the legislature created the Municipal Assistance Corporation to sell bonds, and Carey placed it under the chairmanship of his friend the investment banker Felix G. Rohatyn of Lazard Frères. MAC became both the broker for city bonds and the overseer of the city's economy, with unprecedented influence over city finances. Since city paper was worthless and the coffers empty, Beame had no choice but to agree to the deal. Investors seemed willing to put their faith in the new corporation. My staff and I took a deep breath, thinking the story would now slow down. It didn't for long, however.

By July, MAC had made a few gains toward solving the crisis, but the city's budget had not yet been sufficiently cut. The deficit continued to bulge and more draconian measures were proposed. These included additional job layoffs, a ten-percent salary cut for all city employees, transit fare hikes, a pause on construction projects, imposition of a budget ceiling and more frequent and detailed reporting by the city to MAC.

In September, none of us were sorry to see Beame yield the last of his diminishing budgetary powers. After acknowledging the magnitude of the city's total debt—$3.3 billion—MAC recommended the creation of an Emergency Financial Control Board. The board was given license to approve all city revenue and expenditure estimates, had sole authority to prolong the wage freeze and could review the city's budget. In effect, it became the budget office.

The emergency board was only one part of an elaborate proposal to keep the city afloat. The rest of the plan hinged on the willingness of the state and of investors to put up the needed cash. Contingency measures were devised to deal with the threat of default, which appeared to be where the city was rapidly heading.

New Yorkers were shocked that words like "default" and "bankruptcy" were being applied to their city. For a decade, City Hall had done a masterful job of glossing over the enormity of its financial shenanigans and, so long as trash was picked up and firemen arrived to put out blazes, no one gave much thought to a balanced budget. Like children who unthinkingly trust their parents to put food on the table, New Yorkers blithely relied on their elected officials to keep the city functioning.

By autumn of 1975, despite MAC's intervention, the city's credit rating was so poor it no longer had access to loans needed just to meet the municipal payroll. In conference with my staff, we concluded that the only hope of averting default was a change of heart by President Ford, and it had to happen quickly. In October, the Senate Committee on Banking, Housing and Urban Affairs, as well as the House Steering and Policy Committee, agreed to consider federal loan guarantees, believing that, if New York were to default, the whole country would suffer. Beame and Carey both went to Washington to lobby for such guarantees, pleading with Congress to introduce a bill that would rescue New York for the benefit of the nation.

We could hardly believe it when Ford, in a speech on October 29, put a brutal end to speculation on whether he would pass the as yet unwritten bill. "I can tell you—and tell you now—that I am prepared to veto any bill that has as its purpose a federal bailout of New York City to prevent default. . . . Responsibility for New York City's financial problems is being left on the front doorstep of the federal government, unwanted and abandoned by its real parents." The president, in fact, recommended that New York declare bankruptcy, and had already proposed a bill that would allow for continuation of vital services in the city after it defaulted.

No matter that *The Times* had the most thorough coverage of the president's decision—including the full text of his speech—journalistically the day was won by the *Daily News*, which summed up the rejection in its now historic headline: "Ford to City: Drop Dead."

There was no question that Ford's stance, shortsighted as it might have been, was politically motivated. He figured to blame the fall of New York on a couple of prominent Democrats, Beame and Carey, and he aimed his message at voters in the American heartland, which had never been too fond of New York. But Ford had not reckoned with the fallout. New York Republicans, for once, backed Carey over Ford, and began hinting they would support Ronald Reagan rather than Ford in the 1976 presidential race. Republican officials in other major cities also strove to distance themselves from Ford's antiurban message, which did not play well with their constituents.

Believing there was still a chance to win federal support if New York took a significant step to solve its own problems, Carey and Beame urged the Legislature to pass a bill that would raise $200 million through new taxes. That action, combined with mounting pressure from within his own party, caused Ford to reverse his course.

On November 26, 1975, Ford pledged to ask Congress for "authority to provide a temporary line of credit to the state of New York to enable it to supply seasonal financing of essential services for the people of New York City." The crisis, as far as default was concerned, was over. New York had staved off bankruptcy by a hair.

But New Yorkers had to adjust to life with less. While taxes climbed, municipal jobs and city services were slashed further. What saddened me especially was that free tuition at CCNY and other City University colleges, which had meant salvation for myself as well as Abe Rosenthal and so many of our contemporaries during the Depression, came to an end.

FORTY-SIX

NOT SURPRISINGLY, *The New York Times* suffered along with the city itself from the wounds of the fiscal crisis. In 1975, advertising plummeted. A major source of *Times* income, the classified Help Wanted ads, nosedived along with the metropolitan area's dwindling job market. Conversely, the price of newsprint continued to soar, as did the cost of the paper's daily operations.

By year's end, we were being told that the grim financial situation was likely to worsen. While the paper had previously confronted similar crises, the severity of this one appeared to throw the hierarchy into a panic. I myself was shocked by the disclosure, especially in view of our efforts in the innovative news department in recent years to enliven the paper with new ideas. Only a year earlier, in January 1974, *Time* magazine in a survey of newspapers had commented: "There is no other U.S. daily quite like *The Times*. Its total news staff [then numbering 856] is by far the largest, its scope and coverage the most exhaustive, its influence on national and world leaders daunting. . . . [It] is still the nation's single most informative paper, and it is commendably blessed with a passion for accuracy in things both great and small."

That same year *The Times* not only had avoided another strike but also won an agreement from the printers' union allowing the long-awaited introduction of automation, and enabling the paper eventually to save enormous costs by the electronic use of "cold type," instead of hot metal. Nevertheless, we appeared to be in deep trouble.

The start of *The Times*'s financial woes could be traced back to late 1968. That was when our middle class readers accelerated their flight to the suburbs, largely because of mounting street crime and deterioration of public schools. At the same time, television was competing more aggressively for advertising dollars, and papers like *Newsday* on Long Island along with New Jersey's *Bergen Record* were expanding their news space and vying for readers and advertising.

To keep *The Times* buoyant, the board decided to go the way of other companies that had diversified. Since it took large amounts of cash to acquire other profitable companies (such as Cowles Communications, which included the magazine *Family Circle* and three Florida newspapers), *The Times* went public at the beginning of 1969, trading its stock on the American Exchange. But advertising and circulation continued to decline, and there were more headaches to come. To avoid a strike in 1970, *The Times* had made a disastrous settlement with the printers' union, caving in to its demand for a whopping forty-two-percent wage hike over three years—which in turn led to spiraling new costs. It was then that extreme cost-cutting measures were first deemed imperative, and a hiring freeze was imposed. For the first time, I began to worry if the paper might go the way of the *Herald Tribune*.

A struggle for survival began. For years, *Times* executives had directed the paper's appeal essentially to the business community. The marketing department, in its promotional ads, complacently envisioned the typical reader as a middle-aged man carrying an attaché case. But now, fighting to triumph over adversity, *Times* executives awoke to the narrowness of their approach. We began to realize that many of our readers wanted news that went beyond the financial, governmental and political. Those readers with leisure time, we came to believe, would welcome livelier service-oriented articles about subjects like travel, sports, entertainment, home design and restaurants. But to expand this coverage on the highest level, extra space and money were required—and that meant engaging in the once forbidden tango with the business department.

We in the news department were apprehensive, fearing we were about to embark on a rocky path. What most concerned us was that the business side might end up calling the shots, in which case our editorial independence would be compromised. For my part, in my years in charge of metropolitan and cultural news coverage, I had never exchanged more than a nod of hello in the elevators with an advertising executive. We didn't regard each other as enemies, but it had been pounded into me since my copyboy days that reporters and editors must keep a distance from the "money people" on those mysterious floors of the building where I'd never set foot.

We started gingerly—concerned about possibly making an irretrievable misstep. But to gain the new strength we sought, everyone at management's top level, led by Punch, concluded that the news and business departments had to find ways of working together. With the delicacy of a UN negotiating team, we did at last hammer out a partnership that we in the news department believed would not compromise our ethics or lower our standards.

As EARLY AS MAY 1969, Abe had asked me for suggestions as to how we could attract new readers in the suburbs, as well as reclaim our old readers who had moved there. It was the start of our effort to widen the reach of the paper. We believed that many of these readers—not only in New York State but also in New Jersey and Connecticut—had grown to rely on their local papers, and we wanted to give them the kind of stories they were not likely to find there. I reshuffled my staff to transfer five reporters to the suburbs, adding them to the six already there. Their instructions were to pounce on big breaking stories and develop investigative and trend ideas, leaving routine coverage of neighborhood news to the 150 freelance stringers who lived in the various suburban communities of the tristate region.

What I stressed in my pep talk to my enlarged suburban staff was basically the following: We are known for the excellence of our national and foreign reports, the prestige of our cultural reviews, our financial and business pages and our Sunday *Book Review* and *Magazine*. While we haven't the staff or space to cover all the local news handled by suburban papers, we can compete—and beat—these papers in special news categories. Suburban papers sometimes take good stories for granted. If we pick our shots, we can do better than they do. Your writing skills and our big-gun specialists can clearly outperform suburban papers. We also have a psychological edge. Many suburbanites seem to think that a local story is not really important until *The Times* reports it—and when we do, they believe we care.

There were some tentative gains in circulation, but we were convinced that our new outlook wasn't sufficiently daring to attract new readers. It wasn't until early December 1971 that the news and business departments jointly came up with the strategy that was soon to catapult *The Times* out of its financial doldrums and change the paper forever. It was an all-encompassing blueprint to be carried out gradually, and it took four years to achieve our bold new reality.

Punch suggested that Abe start by scheduling a series of meetings with all his top editors to examine every aspect of the entire daily paper, assess its strengths and weaknesses and explore fresh ideas. No such undertaking had ever been launched in the history of *The Times*.

The invited editors, in addition to Sy Topping, Harrison Salisbury and myself, included Jimmy Greenfield (foreign), Gene Roberts (national), Max Frankel (Washington), Tom Mullaney (business), James Roach (sports), Charlotte Curtis (style), Henry Lieberman (science), John Morris (photo) and Lou Silverstein (now corporate art director). Abe insisted that the underlying assumption was that we were "not going to change the basic character of this paper but look for ways of making it even better, more useful and more widely read."

He laid out some possible objectives, among them:

Examination into readership interests. Do we offer, as just one example, enough service material to fill the needs of readers?

To present the most accurate image of the world around us—raising questions as to whether our journalistic techniques or traditions or our social values inhibit us from perceiving areas of news of interest to our readers. An obvious example is the consumer affairs field of which we were not really journalistically cognizant until Ralph Nader. What else is there in the world around us that we haven't seen but which our readers see or which affects their lives?

Abe also asked each of us to submit a report sketching our ideas. In my own fifteen-page memo, I pointed out that, while few people read the entire paper, many had a specific interest that we served best and any diminution of this would sap our strength. Two questions to be considered were: Why do intelligent people buy *The Times* or not buy it? What do those who buy it absorb from its news columns?

Even without polls, I emphasized, "we must take care to make our reporters and editors aware they are now writing and editing for a regional and not just a Manhattan newspaper. Daily regional editions in suburban counties should be thoroughly explored. Can we eventually put out a daily *Nassau Times* or a *Bergen Times*—of eight to ten pages—that can be folded into *The New York Times*? I pointed out that the *Los Angeles Times* did something similar for its Orange County readers.

I suggested split runs of the paper so we could get more New Jersey news to New Jersey and more Connecticut news to Connecticut. Could we, at least during the periods when the various legislatures were in session, replate a Jersey legislative story for placement on page one for the papers sent to Jersey and do the same for Connecticut? Each of these would be used in place of an Albany story, which would not be dropped from the paper but be placed inside.

"Ideally," my memo stated, "the plan that will open up most opportunities for *The Times* is the four-section newspaper we have begun discussing. With an open Metro page in a four-section paper, as we've already tried to demonstrate at our previous meetings, city and suburban news can receive the attention they deserve. This is the only way to emphasize our best metropolitan coverage without deemphasizing in any way our foreign and national coverage."

Subcommittees, which included reporters and deputy editors, were created, and we started meeting on weekends at an executive retreat in Westchester, first in White Plains and then in Tarrytown, after which many of our suggestions were gradually put into effect. At one point, Walter Mattson, then *The Times*'s senior vice president, took Abe and me and circulation department executives to California to study the Orange County operation of the *Los Angeles Times,* and, when we returned to New York, I began planning a split run for the New Jersey section as well as a Sunday Jersey supplement.

Abe and Mattson had developed a mutual respect. Mattson was the first person on the business side (except for the paper's vice president Sydney Gruson) that Abe felt he could talk to about news matters and who seemed to understand our problems involving news space and production. I, too, liked Mattson, whom I had known since his arrival at *The Times* in 1960 at twenty-eight, when he became assistant to the production manager. We sometimes found time to chat, and if I occasionally needed a composing-room favor that a foreman wouldn't grant—a rearrangement of space or a little more time to close a story—Mattson somehow found a way. Now and then he would drop in at night to visit the bullpen and banter with Ted Bernstein. He made good friends in the city room.

The printers were uniformly fond of Mattson, who felt at home during his visits to the composing room. It is often said of newspapermen that ink flows in their blood, and, in Mattson's case, it might have been true. He had loved visiting his uncle's small newspaper near Pittsburgh when he was a boy, and, while attending the University of Maine, studying business administration, he worked as a Linotype operator at the *Portland Press Herald*. He was my height but brawnier, and liked to throw a long friendly arm around my shoulder.

AS THE CITY'S FISCAL CRISIS continued to infect the paper's health, Mattson delivered bleak news to Abe Rosenthal—that the unabated rise in the cost of newsprint in 1975 might actually send the paper into the red. For the first time, Abe felt it necessary to caution me about reducing overtime payments, and I stopped assigning reporters to borderline feature stories that might require their working extra hours. I also asked my news assistant to scrutinize expense accounts for overloaded charges. Other cost-cutting measures were proposed, but they did little to change the paper's overall economic picture. The profit margin by year's end was only 1.9 percent, with few positive indicators for future stability.

Punch asked Abe and Mattson to bring together, once again, the key members of the news and business departments to find a way out of the dilemma, and once again we held weekend meetings at Tarrytown. In case any editors still had doubts about the importance of the growing relationship between the news and business departments, Mattson, before our scheduled first meeting, invited all desk editors to the fourteenth-floor boardroom, where he displayed large graphs projecting steadily decreasing circulation and advertising in years to come, and costs rising sharply. The message was unmistakable—the paper was in big trouble. I turned to Jimmy Greenfield and said, "Let's open the window and jump right now." It couldn't have been clearer that quick and dramatic action was needed. The time for memos was past.

Punch finally approved the commissioning of polls to determine the demographic profile of our readers and discover why more in that pool were not reading *The Times*. As we had surmised, our readers were mainly college educated and held responsible jobs with good, steady incomes, the kind of highbrow circulation that attracted splurging advertisers in such fields as high-end retail stores and restaurants, fashion, culture and travel. But how were we to net more readers from that pool? More polls were ordered, and we soon discovered that there were tens of thousands of potential *Times* readers in that group, who were in their twenties, thirties and forties—but chose to get their news from *Time, Newsweek* and television.

One night at the bar at Sardi's, Abe and I discussed the momentous changes that were taking place before our eyes. Our close alliance with the business department still felt strange, but Mattson had demonstrated his willingness to let us have our creative heads. As long as we held our ground and didn't allow advertising to call the shots, we'd be all right.

At our next Tarrytown meeting, Mattson told me how pleased he was with the ongoing success of the Sunday New Jersey Section that I'd introduced the previous year. Circulation and advertising were increasing in New Jersey not only on Sunday but during the week as well, due to the recently inaugurated daily New Jersey page. Another circulation and advertising success, Mattson boasted, was our new Sunday BQLI (Brooklyn/Queens/Long Island) section.

Mattson's optimism prompted me to propose yet another immediate innovation. "As you know," I said, "the reviews and stories in the daily culture report are scattered in a hodgepodge over several pages, Mondays through Saturdays. There's no attempt at any design because there's no anchored open space to introduce the report each day. Is there a way of providing us with a half-page of open space each day for stories and illustrations—a page that would be similar in appearance to the Second Front and would act as a kind of cover dress page for the daily culture report? How difficult would it be?"

"Not at all difficult," Mattson replied genially, suggesting I meet him Monday morning in his office. He'd invite Max Ginsburg, the head of culture advertising, and we'd work out a way of reassembling the space to suit both news and advertising.

On Monday, cutting through red tape, we worked out the new space configuration.

"When can we start?" I asked. "Tomorrow," said Ginsburg. We launched the dress page the next day with effective illustrations—our new daily culture "section." Its layout was striking, and the culture world responded with high praise. Our own critics thought it a miracle. It wasn't long before the foreign desk also requested open space as an introduction to its daily report—and so it went.

At our Tarrytown meetings, the topic more than ever on our minds was whether the daily *Times* should switch from being a two-section to a four-section paper. Mattson had always been a proponent of the four-section paper, maintaining it would allow *The Times* the flexibility to modernize its presentation and possibly initiate separate business, metropolitan and sports sections. Abe initially had questioned the concept, concerned that the traditional character of the paper might suffer. Besides, the two-section paper, with a maximum of ninety-six pages (plus a "caboose" of supplementary pages during peak advertising seasons), seemed, to Abe, to have "just the right feel." But 1975 changed his mind.

One day, Mattson and John Pomfret, assistant general manager of *The Times*, met with Abe and me to urge us to proceed with the planning of the first four-section paper as soon as possible. Things had gotten so bad, Pomfret said, "the company is making less money from its newspaper than from the paper mills it owns." Abe insisted that the only way to draw more circulation and advertising was to create sections so inviting that they would become "must reading"—a goal requiring an investment of added space and a talented staff. "When a newspaper like ours needs help in difficult times," he said, "the best way to nourish it is not by watering the soup but by enriching it with more meat and tomatoes." Mattson assured him that the look and content of the new sections would in no way be tampered with, and that Abe could rely on getting all the space he needed to put out sections we could be proud of.

Abe, Topping and Mattson together worked out the overall format for a four-section paper. The first section would continue to feature foreign and national news; section two, metropolitan news; section four would be devoted to a new approach to the coverage of business and finance that would attempt to rival the *Wall Street Journal* for thoroughness.

It was section three that initially stumped Abe and me and led to our first contretemps with advertising department executives. They suggested it be a daily style section, featuring fashion. Abe, Lou Silverstein and I were dead-set against that concept. In the first place, we insisted there had to be a different third section each day, Monday through Friday—and Mattson and Pomfret finally accepted our plan. We agreed we would introduce the sections one at a time, waiting until each was successfully established, before moving on to the next.

Having rejected a fashion section, we began casting about for broader, more inviting topics that would appeal to the younger educated reader. The newly commissioned surveys confirmed our intuition that our young readers, while acknowledging *The Times* as the authoritative source of news, wanted coverage that would enrich their daily lives, particularly their weekends. Mattson told us that the *Miami Herald* recently had achieved success with such a weekend section.

Abe himself noted that *The Times* lagged in meeting readers' interests in this area. "*Times* people themselves confirm this," he wrote in one memo to Punch. "They turn to other publications, like *The New Yorker*, *New York* magazine and *Newsday* for their needs. These publications not only give them the information but achieve a kind of intimacy and affection with their readers because through this kind of service, they relate to the happy and up-beat part of their readers' lives. Moreover, the service information relates di-rectly to the readers who mean most to us—and to advertisers—the young and affluent."

Thus we decided, in early 1976, that the first of the new sections would appear on Fridays, and would contain commentary, criticism, feature stories, columns and service listings about what the city had to offer on the weekend, hence its name: Weekend. The section would be devoted mainly to the arts and to entertainment events, and Abe asked me to take charge of creating Weekend and the four sections to follow.

It was only natural that Lou Silverstein, as the art department's resident genius, was assigned to design the sections, and for the next few weeks Lou and I were inseparable. Aside from having worked together on the aborted afternoon newspaper, we had recently collaborated on various other proj-ects, including the two completely renovated Sunday suburban sections for which I borrowed some of the best writers and critics on my staff—the New Jersey Weekly, introduced on January 11, 1976, and the Long Island Weekly, on February 22.

While all this planning was under way, Punch thought it expedient to merge the paper's daily and Sunday operations once again under a single ed-itor. Since Scotty Reston's departure as executive editor, the daily operations under Abe and the Sunday department under Max Frankel had continued as separate entities, each reporting to the publisher. Punch, a stickler for or-ganizational order, now viewed this jurisdictional division as untidy.

Clearly, there were but two choices for the top job: Abe and Max. To my mind—as well as almost everyone else's in the news department—Abe out-shone Max in experience and ability. Punch, unwilling to rush to judgment, asked both Abe and Max to present a proposal outlining their visions for the paper.

Punch finally picked Abe, largely because of his experience, partly be-cause of the support that Walter Mattson threw his way. Max had been a critic of the proposed four-section daily, having characterized it as "a bloated package." But virtually every other executive by now viewed the forthcom-ing four-part paper as the lifeboat that would rescue *The Times* and secure its future. Punch named Max editorial page editor to succeed John Oakes, who was designated "senior editor of *The Times*," one of those titles that signaled redundancy. At the beginning of the year, Jack Rosenthal, the assistant Sun-day editor, became the assistant editorial-page editor (and went on to win the Pulitzer Prize for editorial writing in 1982).

Abe kept his title of managing editor, wary of assuming the mantle of executive editor because he was all too aware it had not had the happiest of histories. On the day the changes were announced, April 5, 1976, Topping was promoted to deputy managing editor and I took my place on the masthead for the first time, as assistant managing editor. Although I eagerly approached the job as a new challenge, I felt a sense of loss at giving up the metropolitan desk, where I had basked for the last twelve years—three as deputy to Abe, and nine as the editor in charge of both tristate coverage and the cultural report.

For the time being, Abe wanted me to continue focusing on the creation of the new daily sections and supervising them upon their completion. But he said I would eventually be taking on, as well, the principal supervisory duties for the Sunday department. "I hope you're aware," he said, with a congratulatory hug, "of the irony of your having advanced so far beyond the job of Sunday editor that should have been yours years ago. Your new jurisdiction will include that and much more."

"We have reached the moment," Punch announced to the staff, explaining the merger of daily and Sunday operations, "when there is no longer any conceptual division between the works of the two departments. On the contrary, the free flow of our best stories, the full exchange of ideas, information and personnel, promise a still better product. This merger will enable us to pool the talents of our staff so as to enhance all sections, prepare for new journalistic ventures, and better exploit the new technology, which we are introducing."

Mike Levitas succeeded me as metropolitan editor, and he named Sydney Schanberg as his deputy. Schanberg, who had won the Pulitzer Prize for his reporting from Cambodia on the Khmer Rouge, was a good choice, I thought—but he and Levitas turned out to be ill matched and the metropolitan desk soon descended into chaos. Schanberg fought Levitas's ideas and style of operation, belittling him to the point where Levitas, after only a year, was forced by Abe to leave the job. Schanberg replaced him as metropolitan editor and Levitas went on to become editor of the Sunday Week in Review (and later the Sunday *Book Review* and the Op-Ed page).

Abe decided to remove the culture department from the metropolitan editor's jurisdiction and once again put it under my command, with Sy Peck as culture editor reporting to me. I then asked Abe to move Arts & Leisure from its eighth-floor Sunday department headquarters to the third-floor culture area, so that I could keep a close eye on it—trying to revise and strengthen it, working with William Honan, its editor, and all the critics.

For the first time, the Sunday and daily cultural sections functioned as a single staff under one supervising editor, and my colleagues began referring to me—not without a touch of mockery—as the "culture czar."

WEEKEND MIGHT HAVE BEEN the most audacious addition to *The Times* since the introduction of some of the Sunday sections by Adolph Ochs more than half a century earlier. With my jurisdiction considerably expanded, I named Marvin Siegel as my Weekend deputy, with the idea he'd take over as editor when I started shaping the next section. Marvin, who had been one of my trusted assistants over the years on various metropolitan desk editing projects, was devoted to the arts (and eventually was promoted to culture editor).

As Weekend's debut drew near in early spring, Lou Silverstein and I sensed an aloofness on the part of the top editors. We suspected they were keeping their distance in the belief that Weekend might turn out to be an embarrassing flop. But Mattson kept his word as the days passed, never questioning our requests for the space we needed and asking John Pomfret to make sure the advertising department gave us the most advantageous news-advertising configurations to show off our stories and illustrations. As Pomfret was the only man on the business side familiar with both the news and business areas of the paper, he knew exactly how to smooth the way for us—and he always did. I first met Pomfret in 1962, when he left the *Milwaukee Journal* to join our Washington bureau, and in our new posts we developed a good working relationship that led to quick solutions of production problems.

Although Silverstein and I were exhilarated, there were occasional moments of despair. Once, for example, a bullpen editor told us he was concerned that the section, as he understood it, would be "out of place" for a paper like *The Times*, and was likely to offend traditional readers. Some staffers thought I was risking my career on such a frivolous undertaking, while others complained that the section would soften the paper beyond recognition. Rather than argue the point, I silently vowed to prove them wrong.

I decided to approach Weekend, as well as the sections to come, in the conviction that there were hard angles to "soft news" and that such features as going-out guides, restaurant reviews and reports about Broadway theater and Hollywood films could be newsy as well as entertaining, as *The New Yorker* had been demonstrating for years. Steeped in the traditions of the paper as I was, I thought of the sections as new branches sprouting from, but firmly connected to, the solid trunk of *The Times*.

I called on our critics and reporters in all the arts to submit their most imaginative ideas, and I thought up a few myself. For the inaugural issue, Silverstein's refreshingly innovative design positioned a large opening-page photo of dancers from the New York City Ballet in the middle of the page. Most of the space below the fold was occupied by the new Weekender Guide, consisting of wittily written vignettes by Dick Shepard, my old friend and former culture editor, in addition to capsule recommendations by our critics.

John Corry wrote a column called "Broadway," a smart, breezy resurrection of the old "News and Gossip of the Rialto." He included theater items that were both informative and amusing, quoting, for one small example, Mary Martin, regarding plans to erect a statue in her honor in her hometown of Weatherford, Texas: "It'll be wonderful for the pigeons."

There was a featured restaurant review by John Canaday, who had requested a change of pace from art criticism. Reviews of plays, movies, music, art, dance and television were highlighted, as were a chatty column by Richard Eder called "At the Movies"; a page of film listings; a weekly city walking tour by Paul Goldberger called "Metropolitan Baedeker"; a column by Grace Glueck, "Art People"; and John Rockwell's brief comments on contemporary music, entitled "The Pop Life."

On Thursday night, April 29, 1976, when Silverstein, Siegel and I, all propelled by adrenaline, put the section to bed in the composing room, no other editor, not even Abe, had seen the page proofs. We were convinced we had produced a beautiful baby, and now all we had to do was sit back and accept congratulations.

When the section came off the press that night, Abe pronounced himself pleased. The next morning, however, Lou and I heard not a word from any other editor. We told each other that judgment was probably being withheld until the public reacted. Sydney Schanberg and a couple of metropolitan reporters let us know they didn't think much of the section. And a few reporters grudgingly said it "seemed okay." It was so different from anything that had ever been part of the daily paper that the staff evidently didn't know how to assess it.

Later in the day, I bumped into Sydney Gruson and, when he made no comment about Weekend, I asked what he thought. He said, stonily, that he hadn't yet read it. The general silence was unnerving, but Lou and I clung to our faith in what we had wrought. Our spirits finally rose a bit when Mattson called to congratulate us, saying he and his colleagues loved the look of the section. But I understood that part of what he loved about the look was that it was replete with advertising.

I decided to cheer myself up by arranging a last-minute party to celebrate our new baby. With Abe's encouragement, I booked Sardi's private Belasco Room that evening for a cocktail party, and then flipped through my Rolodex and personally invited as many theater, literary and television personalities as I could reach. At the party, some of the *Times* people had heard that Abe liked the section but I was told by a friend that there were those who had sourly commented that it was just a case of "Abe and Arthur" sticking together again. I went up to Punch at the buffet table and asked him what he thought. "Only time will tell," he said. I gulped.

Apart from Abe, the only two *Times* executives who displayed any optimism were Mattson and Pomfret, who told me they had just learned that all of the 70,000 copies ordered for the extra press run had been sold. Mattson said if Lou and I continued on the same track, the sections to follow would ride *The Times* out of its financial bind. But what really concerned me was whether the reporters and editors as a whole regarded Weekend as a journalistic success.

Finally, from among the murmurs around the buffet table, a voice rose, calling for "everyone's attention for a moment." It was Mike Wallace, the star of *60 Minutes*. "I would like to propose a toast to this amazing new section put out today by *The Times*. I read every word of it, and think it is one of the best things *The Times* has ever done." Joe Papp then raised his glass high, exclaiming in thespian tones, "Our warmest congratulations to Arthur Gelb and his team for presenting the theater world with such a wonderful weekly gift." That was it. The ice was broken, and critical praise at last began flowing through the room.

By Monday, we knew that Weekend was a smash hit. Throughout May, sales of Friday's paper were up by an average of 50,000 copies, eventually leveling to 35,000, a remarkable increase in sales. Theater box offices reported the section was often seen tucked under the arms of people waiting in line for tickets.

Friday became the only day of the week to show an improvement over the previous year's circulation, and the section quickly became a magnet for advertisers. The hope was that people who bought the Friday paper would become hooked as readers for the rest of the paper's content and make *The Times* their regular source for news every day of the week.

FORTY-SEVEN

O N A FRIDAY two months after Weekend's debut, it seemed as though everyone in the city was carrying a copy of the section. That particular Friday issue was designed principally as a guide to the July 4 Bicentennial Operation Sail festivities. Millions descended on New York that weekend to watch fleets of ships sail from the Battery up the Hudson and view the fireworks extravaganza over the harbor.

The section's first page was dominated by a Red Grooms drawing of the Battery jammed with a celebratory multitude. Its inside pages included a cornucopia of service material—detailed maps and charts locating the tall ships from a host of foreign countries as well as our own, the best viewing sites, and a pictorial guide to help identify the different types of vessels.

Both old and new readers let us know they found the section to be the consummate directory to OpSail, and the entire printing of 70,000 extra copies was sold. When Abe and I took the long walk down from *The Times* to the World Trade Center for an OpSail dinner at the Windows on the World restaurant, we were struck by the numbers of people carrying photocopies of the maps and charts in Weekend. To our delight, we discovered that on-the-spot entrepreneurs had been selling them to tourists.

The following weekend was no less of a triumph. Our section featured a special tourist guide, pegged this time to the Democratic National Convention at Madison Square Garden. The entire first page was a street-by-street, building-by-building map of midtown Manhattan, designed to aid the delegates as well as all New Yorkers. There were articles by our experts about restaurants, cabarets and stores, suggestions for walking tours and an article describing "What to Avoid on Eighth Avenue." We scored another hit with readers and, in only three months, Weekend had earned acceptance as a permanent part of *The Times*.

Soon after the Democratic convention that nominated Jimmy Carter, I left my firstborn section in the capable hands of Marvin Siegel. "Don't get too relaxed," Abe told me. "You've pulled off a wonderful job with Weekend, but now we've got to top it." It was typical of Abe to warn against self-satisfaction. There was never a time when he himself was content to rest on his laurels after attaining a particular goal. One of his favorite lines—which I took for my own—was: "What are we going to do tomorrow that will make the paper even greater?" And now he asked if I thought it possible to produce an imaginative section featuring food.

Many papers around the country published Wednesday supplements pegged to food shopping, and Walter Mattson thought *The Times* could profit from this trend. The sections, however, consisted mainly of advertisements and contained little editorial content, and Abe and I told Mattson we would find it humiliating to produce such a section, which would lower the paper's standards and be viewed—with justification—as purely a bid for advertising dollars.

I told Abe I thought the solution was to incorporate into the section the Wednesday cultural news. The first half of the section would feature expertly written articles about gourmet chefs, home cooking and the science of food, followed by a page of staff-written (and, I hoped, witty) columns that would provide a bridge between the food features and the cultural coverage. Abe loved the idea, agreeing it would distinguish our food section from anything published by any other paper in the country.

We explained to Mattson that the section would combine sophisticated articles about wine and food, as well as such subjects as the science of the palate, celebrity cooks in their own kitchens, service columns on health and medicine and offbeat pieces about where to buy the best corned-beef sandwich or the tastiest ice cream cone. The weekly columns preceding the culture report would be written by two of the best stylists on the staff. John Leonard, our literary critic, would write "Private Lives," an intimate essay, sometimes ironic, sometimes poignant, about the world around him, and Charlotte Curtis would write "New Yorkers, etc.," an irreverent sketch about life behind the scenes in what remained of Manhattan's high society. Abe and I christened our new offspring "The Living Section."

Although the emphasis was on food, I tried to keep original nonfood ideas flowing. There was to be a column by Al Krebs called "Notes on People" (celebrated people, of course); a column, "Metropolitan Diary," by Tom Buckley, consisting mainly of short anecdotes and verse contributed by readers ("Publication," we noted, "will be its own just reward—publication and a bottle of champagne"); a column, "Living Abroad," informal jottings by our own foreign correspondents (the first contributed by our London bureau chief, Robert Semple).

I invited prominent authors to contribute articles, starting at the top with John Cheever, whom I persuaded to write about his memories of Thanksgiving dinners; it was to be the lead article for our third issue, appearing the day before the holiday. *The Times* up to then had rarely asked a nonstaff writer to contribute to the daily paper. After seeing Cheever's byline, no writer turned me down.

But to guarantee the section's success, I knew I needed to enlist Craig Claiborne. A year earlier, Craig, to my sorrow, had left his job as *Times* restaurant critic to take life easy at his home in East Hampton, where he and the chef Pierre Franey were producing a newsletter about food. Craig and I had remained friends, and in early 1974 I was able to do him a favor for which he had been grateful. The phone rang in my New York apartment at two o'clock one morning and it was Craig. "You're the only one I can think of with the influence to get me sprung," he said, sounding a bit dazed. He explained he had been arrested in East Hampton for drunk driving. I asked him to let me speak to the desk officer, who told me Craig's blood test revealed a score of twice the legal alcoholic standard. I pleaded with the officer to have Craig taken home, promising he'd be in court when summoned. He later entered a plea of guilty; his license was suspended for six months, but he told the court he would voluntarily give up driving permanently.

When Barbara and I drove to East Hampton so I could convince Craig to return to *The Times* right away, old memories came rushing back as we passed the former inn known as the Hedges. In the late fifties, it had been opened as a summer epicure's oasis by Henri Soulé, the proprietor of Le Pavillon in Manhattan and a friend of Craig's. Barbara and I had been taken to dinner at Le Pavillon a few times in the 1950s by Elza and Berrie and, on one of those occasions in 1959, I encountered Claiborne, who was eager to tip me off to Soulé's bizarre difficulties involving the Hedges. The local residents, he told me, were trying to drive Soulé out of town. That was interesting, I said, but I was a drama reporter. When he added that the locals were trying to shut down an upstart theater as well, I knew I had a story I could write.

East Hampton was still a rural backwater, and its residents wanted it to stay that way, since they'd seen what had happened to Fire Island. They were primarily concerned about a bohemian, homosexual and Jewish influx from Manhattan and believed that the theater and the Hedges attracted an unwanted element.

When I interviewed Soulé, he was almost apoplectic. Choking on his words, he described how, after the Hedges closed for the night, locals spread garbage from his trash bins across his lawn. Here was a man who reputedly ran his kitchen the way General Patton had run his army, pushed to the edge of emotional collapse. He felt profoundly insulted that the great gift he had brought to the residents of East Hampton was unwanted. By the end of our conversation, he was in tears. He said he was closing the Hedges, and swore he would never again open a restaurant on Long Island.

My story, played on page one on January 4, 1960, elicited profuse apologies from East Hampton community leaders, who entreated Soulé to stay, blaming the trash incident on a few "reactionaries." Although mollified, Soulé nonetheless sold the Hedges.

Claiborne and I didn't become close friends until two years later, when he read *O'Neill,* which he had taken with him on a trip to Japan. When he returned, he told me that the story of O'Neill's tragic family life had helped him gain a deeper understanding of his own dysfunctional family. He had grown up in Sunflower, Mississippi, the youngest of three children. Shortly after he was born, a depression struck the region and his father, who was successfully involved in various business ventures, lost everything, including his spirit. Tensions in the home became exacerbated as Craig's mother took charge of the family's affairs and opened their house to boarders. It was during this period of family upheaval that Craig, as a teenager, discovered his homosexuality.

Craig was responsible for a recipe column in *The Times* as well as for reviewing restaurants, and the paper equipped his East Hampton house with a magnificent professional kitchen. On weekends, a few guests would be invited to watch Pierre Franey, Soulé's former head chef, who by now had become Craig's associate, invent recipes. Pierre rarely measured his ingredients, just pouring, sprinkling or pinching them in. Craig observed and took notes on his electric typewriter, which sat on the counter near the stove. When the meal was cooked, the guests sat down to enjoy it, listening to Pierre and Craig assess the product. The recipe was then published in *The Times,* accompanying a story under Craig's byline.

I told Craig his return was important to me personally, that the new Wednesday section couldn't possibly succeed without him as the pièce de résistance. At last, he agreed—if *The Times* would hire Pierre Franey as well. There was no way, he said, that he could do what I was proposing without Pierre as his collaborator. And it was only fair, he added, that Pierre be given a byline on his own weekly recipe column (that Craig said he would help Pierre write). Craig also wanted to submit some articles with Pierre under a double byline, then a practice frowned upon by *The Times.* In addition, Craig said he himself would write critiques of food under his own single byline.

It all sounded like a perfect arrangement, a great coup for The Living

Section. But before calling it a day, I wanted to come to an agreement about the nature of Pierre's new recipe column. Barbara suggested Pierre target his column to the working woman, featuring gourmet recipes that could be prepared in a half hour. "You could call it '30-Minute Gourmet,'" she volunteered. Pierre loved the idea but said he wouldn't want to be hemmed in by only thirty minutes. "That's okay for sautéed chicken," he said, "but not for lamb chops rouennaise." For flexibility, he explained, he needed an hour. And so, "60-Minute Gourmet" was born. It became among the most popular columns in the history of food coverage, and, when the recipes were collected as a book, Pierre dedicated it to Barbara.

I then asked Frank Prial to create a column called "Wine Talk." I had recruited him for the rewrite staff from the *Wall Street Journal* in 1970, and he soon emerged as one of the best all-around metropolitan staff reporters. He was fast-thinking and particularly adept at getting on top of a breaking story. But, to his everlasting regret, he committed the indiscretion of telling me one day about his knowledge and love of fine wines.

Consequently, I loaned Frank from time to time to Charlotte Curtis to do wine stories for her style page. Utterly without pretensions, Frank appreciated the extra cash, but his heart was only with breaking news stories under deadline pressure. There was no one else, however, who possessed such a flair for evaluating wine. After a while he began regarding the work as a burden, and pleaded to be posted as a correspondent to the Paris bureau.

Frank did well in Paris, but our wine coverage deteriorated and our readers communicated their displeasure. When I called Frank, asking him to return home to take over the new wine column for The Living Section, he agreed, albeit halfheartedly. In short order, he became arguably the country's greatest wine critic. Nonetheless, whenever we lunched together in later years, he'd tell me that he'd give up the job anytime for another shot at some major breaking news stories.

The only staffers who complained about contributing to the section were Jane Brody, a down-to-earth science writer whom I wanted for the "Personal Health" column, and Mimi Sheraton, who by now had succeeded John Canaday as restaurant critic for the Weekend section. Mimi didn't particularly like the idea of The Living Section, but she reluctantly agreed to file periodic reports on the food scene.

She soon became a proud staple of *The Times* and second in reputation only to Claiborne. As restaurant critic, she made her rounds disguised in wigs, hats and glasses, and restaurateurs lived in fear of her unannounced visits. Mimi's power was such that when she liked a new restaurant, she could put it on the map overnight, but when a restaurant displeased her, the ruthlessness of her review could put it out of business.

Mimi could also be stubbornly self-righteous. Later that year, she faced off with Jim Greenfield, to whom she turned in her restaurant review on a Thursday morning for Friday's Weekend. Abe had put Greenfield in overall charge of style and food coverage, as I moved on to launch the third of our five weekly supplements, The Home Section. Greenfield found one of her restaurant reviews for Weekend unnecessarily harsh, and suggested a couple of moderating changes that would convey the message without sounding mean. When she refused to change a single word, Jimmy called me in. I supported him, and he told Mimi there was no alternative, that she had to make the changes. She said there was an alternative and she walked out.

I told Frank Prial we needed a restaurant review immediately. Was there anywhere he had dined recently that he could write up for tonight's deadline? No, he said, but he had been meaning to try an attractive little Italian hideaway, Nicola Paone, on Thirty-fourth Street just east of Third Avenue.

"Go eat there and hurry back," I told him. Aware he'd have to taste more dishes than he could manage on his own, he searched for someone to accompany him. It was 1:30 P.M., the middle of lunch hour, and the staff had virtually deserted the city room. On his way out, Frank spotted a young reporter recently hired from the *Post*.

He said to Anna Quindlen, "Have you had your lunch yet?"

"I never eat lunch," she replied

"Today, you're eating lunch," Frank said, grabbing her hand and whisking her away with him. When they sat down to eat at Nicola Paone, they sampled dish after dish, along with two bottles of expensive wine. "The waiters think we're crazy members of the idle rich," Frank whispered to Anna. They were back in the city room in just over an hour.

Frank, looking more than a little pleased with himself, turned in a crisply written, authoritative review at four o'clock. "Real good job," I said. "But now you have to give us a second short review. We have to conform to the format of past restaurant reviews in Weekend. Mimi always wrote two reviews and our readers will expect a second one. Haven't you dined out anywhere in the last couple of weeks?"

Frank said the Four Seasons had recently opened the Grill Room, and he'd been there a couple of times to sample the wine for his column. In those early days, the Grill Room had an abbreviated menu of no more than a dozen dishes. Frank reported he had been particularly taken with the gravlax, the paillards of veal and chicken, the marinated salmon and the dessert of plump fresh raspberries. He wrote a splendid review from memory, pointing out that a complete lunch came to about fifteen dollars. "If the old saw about eating where the truck drivers eat has any validity where roadside diners are concerned, eating where the wine trade eats is a good idea in New York," Frank began. "These days, the importers, the salesmen, the vineyard owners from Europe and California and the journalists who follow them around are among the Grill Room's most ardent fans." Frank gave Nicola Paone two stars and the Grill Room three.

"You are our restaurant critic as well as our wine critic until further notice," I told Frank. But his new post lasted only a couple of days. Mimi was quick to return to work, and her restaurant column appeared the following week. And I was happy to have her back.

Jane Brody, one of the paper's top science reporters, thought that the "Personal Health" column I asked her to write for The Living Section was demeaning. I assured her that I expected her column to be reported and written with the usual high standards she applied to her science stories. As an example, I cited an assignment I had just given Boyce Rensberger, one of the science department's most respected writers. He was exploring the physiology of the palate, to explain why some people were able to discern subtle tastes and others couldn't. I planned to twin that story with an article by Claiborne on his thoughts about his own discerning palate. I told Jane I wasn't asking for soft-headed pieces, but columns of health guidance based on penetrating scientific reporting and expert analysis. I said she could write about any subject, including sex.

Jane really had no reason to mistrust me, for I had backed her when, not long since, she came to me with an article she wanted to run in the daily paper about the new Hite Report, a survey of female sexuality. Her article described the anatomy of the vagina and mentioned "orgasm," "masturbation" and "penile thrusting," and Jane knew she needed highly placed support to get the article into the paper. She'd had prior discouraging experiences with prudish male editors whenever she wrote about sex. Once, for example, she filed a story about the rhythm method of birth control. The paragraph that described the process was cut by the copy desk. Among other facts in the paragraph, Jane had included a way to test for ovulation—by sampling the cervical mucus. Because of the excised paragraph, readers had no idea how to practice the method.

That wasn't Jane's first encounter with the bullpen's prissy standards. In 1966, when Dr. William Masters and Virginia Johnson published their massive study *Human Sexual Response*, Jane was told by Harrison Salisbury that the bullpen believed it was "improper" for a woman to report on sex. John Corry was given the assignment instead, and even he had to rewrite his story six times to accommodate Ted Bernstein's censorship. For example, Corry was permitted to use the word "vagina" (rather than the traditional "female sex organ") but Bernstein insisted "penis" be changed to "male sex organ." Corry wasn't given any rationale and, when I inquired, I got double-talk.

When Jane first approached me with her story on the Hite Report, I admit I hesitated to stand by her, almost certain it would never get past the bullpen. Her lead paragraph bluntly stated that "a large percentage of women do not reach orgasm during intercourse without direct stimulation of the clitoris." An exasperated Jane suggested, "Why don't you take the story home and ask Barbara what she thinks?" When Barbara read the copy, she said The Times had to run the story, because it could probably save countless marriages.

The next day I persuaded the bullpen of the story's merit, and said there was no way we could write responsibly about health if we were not willing to talk frankly about the penis, the clitoris and the vagina. I convinced them that the story was perfectly fit to print, and it ran on October 2, 1976.

But Jane still resisted the "Personal Health" column, and I finally had to order her to write it. I could have asked another reporter, but I sensed that she was the ideal candidate. She proved me right beyond a doubt. "Personal Health" became one of the most popular features in the paper and it turned Jane Brody into a household name. Her first column was not even controversial; it was about jogging.

I wanted The Living Section to make its debut with a splash on November 10, 1976, so I assigned Craig and Pierre to lead off with a story about the restaurant they considered the best in the world. They chose Restaurant Girardet, outside Lausanne, Switzerland, which featured Fredy Girardet's version of nouvelle cuisine. Barbara and I, at Craig's recommendation, had once eaten a celestial lunch and dinner there on the same day, taking time in between to tour Vevey, where Charlie Chaplin made his home.

I wrote the headline for Craig's article: "Cook Along with the World's Greatest New Chef"; and Franey listed some of Girardet's outstanding recipes that he had tested in his own kitchen.

Now that Craig and I were working together again, it was easier to find excuses for showing up in his kitchen in East Hampton. We introduced him to Joseph Heller and his first wife, Shirley, and they hit it off immediately. Craig developed a crush on Heller, who had eyes only for attractive women and who often crankily rebuffed new acquaintances of both sexes. To my surprise, he good-naturedly tolerated Craig's flirting. After enough margaritas and wine, Craig was apt to launch into a routine about his sex life, past and present. He told us once that as a boy in Mississippi he had experimented with various barnyard stock, including chickens. "Tell me, Craig," Heller asked with a typically devilish grin, "is there much foreplay with a chicken?"

In our small, iconoclastic crowd, such conversation was the norm, and the more outrageous, the better. It was anything but the norm, though, among the very proper friends of Abby Catledge, Turner's widow, who, a couple of years later, invited Barbara and me to meet some of them at a small dinner in a private room at the Cosmopolitan Club. Craig was also her guest, and, during a lull in the conversation—after he had as usual drunk too much—he broke the silence.

"When I die and they autopsy my brain," he said, "do you know what they'll find?" I held my breath as Craig answered his own question: "Pubic hair." Barbara and I were the only ones at the table who giggled.

Craig's compulsive interest in sex led to his alerting me, early in 1981, to a mysterious new illness that as yet had no name. While we were having lunch together one day in New York, he showed me a leaflet being circulated in Greenwich Village, warning gay men that they appeared to be the special target of a debilitating and rapidly proliferating infection.

I showed the leaflet to Lawrence K. Altman, the medical doctor on our science staff, who began checking into it. It took some time—longer than Craig, for one, thought necessary—to pin down the details of this baffling report. The story, primarily based on an early account in a medical journal, finally ran in *The Times* on July 3, 1981, under the headline "Rare Cancer Seen in 41 Homosexuals." It was the first detailed story of the AIDS epidemic in any major paper, although it did not yet have a name. The focus, at that time, was on the peculiarly high incidence of Kaposi's sarcoma among gay men. It was not until early 1982 that the suspicion of an immunodeficiency virus was confirmed.

AIDS, more than anything, finally opened the closet on homosexuality at the paper itself. One *Times* man in the vanguard of those who were direct about their homosexuality was Jeffrey Schmalz. In December 1990, when Schmalz, the talented, wickedly funny deputy national editor, was working at his desk, he collapsed with a brain seizure. At the hospital, he was diagnosed with full-blown AIDS.

When Schmalz returned to the paper, he asked to cover AIDS-related topics, and wrote penetrating, frequently moving reports that earned acclaim from both the public and the journalistic community. At his death, he was memorialized as an inspiration to people living with AIDS—as well as to gays at the paper, who saw that Schmalz, a first-rate newspaperman, had been accepted for who he was without discrimination.

PUBLIC REACTION to The Living Section was as enthusiastic as it had been to Weekend. Sales on Wednesdays increased by 32,000 copies, and the section, in its first four issues, attracted 100,000 lines of food-related advertising, more than half of it new. In addition to designing each of the new sections, Lou Silverstein—in cooperation with Larry Hauck, a bullpen editor—fashioned an appealing new format for every page of the daily paper. Starting Tuesday, September 7, 1976, there were to be six news columns to a page instead of eight, as had been the case during the past six decades. (*The Times* had begun with six columns in 1851 and gone to eight in 1913.) Everyone liked the six-column measure, which gave the pages an airier, more open look and made for an easier read.

The paper seemed stronger, its future rosier than ever. Circulation continued to climb and advertising dollars were pouring in. Punch Sulzberger made it all crystal clear when, on December 17, he presented his top team with special Christmas gifts—promotions, raises and bonuses (and additional stock options).

He crowned Abe as executive editor, the title that had been out of use since Reston had relinquished it more than eight years earlier. The position now was that of the active day-to-day operating chief—unlike the tenure of Reston and that of Catledge before him. Punch announced Sy Topping as managing editor and me as deputy managing editor and, in virtually all my areas of responsibility, I continued reporting directly to Abe. Lou Silverstein was elevated to assistant managing editor, and Jim Greenfield was also named an assistant managing editor. For the first time, the art department, under Silverstein, which heretofore had reported to the publisher, now was responsible to the executive editor.

In a public statement saluting the year as a period of enormous growth, Punch said the paper had begun the process of automating news operations that would give it "great flexibility and range in what it will be able to do . . . to introduce innovations that we consider newsworthy and attractive. We will be producing more new sections. We will be starting Sunday weeklies in Westchester and Connecticut. We plan other changes and developments in the daily newspaper and some of the Sunday sections. We will be moving into advanced phases in the computerizing of our news operations. The new organization of the top new management group is designed to handle all this and perhaps more."

With hardly a pause, Lou Silverstein and I pressed on to The Home Section. It was conceived to highlight mainly design and furnishings, and we embellished it with columns and features we thought would appeal to middle-class women. I had no expertise in this area (or, to be truthful, much interest), and after Silverstein and I created the concept for the first issue, I was glad to turn the section over to Nancy Newhouse, whose credentials suited her ideally for the job. Clay Felker, who had given birth to the trendy and widely read weekly magazine *New York*, had met Nancy in Paris in 1970, where she worked part time assisting an art dealer. He offered her the job as senior editor in charge of architectural and home design coverage for his publication. In 1976, she went to *House & Garden* as senior editor, and I hired her away after she had been there only eighteen months.

Nancy and her star writer, Joan Kron, worked frantically to put together The Home Section. They emphasized not only furnishings and design but also gardening, landscaping and home entertaining and, in many ways, it was a sophisticated and expanded version of the once so-called "women's page." We also introduced a column called "Hers," for which highly regarded women authors wrote personal essays. It was Abe's pet idea, and he signed Lois Gould to start it off.

The Home Section made its debut on Thursday, March 17, 1977 and, as with the other new sections, it immediately lured added Thursday readers—in this case 30,000. But even though the Living and Home Sections continued to maintain high writing and design standards, I believed they had taken us far enough in the direction of soft subjects. Abe and I met with Mattson and Pomfret and we all agreed the fourth section should be on the news—sports news. We would approach it as a kind of Monday magazine pegged mainly to analysis and features about Sunday's games. We christened it Sports Monday.

The paper had long been criticized for the haphazard way it covered sports. From its inception, *The Times* had looked upon sports as an uncouth country cousin, acknowledging its existence but treating it as though it didn't quite belong at the same table as "real news." I enjoyed walking, loved fishing, rooted for our New York teams. Ever since childhood, I had attended baseball games, first at the Polo Grounds and then at Yankee Stadium. I showed up as often as possible for basketball at Madison Square Garden. And one of my sons played a good game of tennis. But still, I was no sports maven, so I decided to bone up.

For almost six months I submerged myself in bats and balls and racquets and courts and fields and locker rooms. I learned about drafts and trades, rankings and seeds. I interviewed writers on *Sports Illustrated* and sports writers on other publications, and chatted with freelance sports writers and friends who knew and loved sports, like Gay Talese and Peter Maas, and met with a number of coaches. Soon I could talk sports almost like an expert.

Finally, I felt prepared to hold discussions with the fifty-five members of the *Times* sports staff. While the sports editor, Jim Tuite, tended to patronize me about some of the new ideas I was cooking up, the columnists—Red Smith, Dave Anderson and George Vecsey (who had once been a reporter on the metropolitan staff)—were helpful. They sharpened my viewpoint and gave me sustained guidance. With their generous backing, I was ready to move.

I wanted Sports Monday to feature hard-hitting interviews with major sports figures and analysis pieces that would explore a particular game, strategy, trend or point of view, just the way city reporters wrote about politics or government. I introduced a feature called "Sports Writer's Notebook"— similar to the "Critic's Notebook" I had initiated to allow the culture staff to offer their second thoughts on the arts. Writers on every sports beat would have the chance to tell readers about a player's form, why a manager had made a certain decision, analyze strategy and comment on such topics as sports manners—the kind of items sports writers talked about in the office among themselves but didn't put in their stories.

Once again, I appealed to outside writers to contribute to the section, including Talese and Maas. I invited the popular suspense novelist Dick Francis to comment on a recent scandal concerning switched horses at Belmont. And I urged Joe Vecchione, the sports picture editor (who later became sports editor) to assign more and more pictures to photographers like Bart Silverman—lots of action pictures.

Abe, whose expertise in sports consisted mainly of attending games at Yankee Stadium, offered suggestions now and then, and came up with the Sports Monday slogan: "If you can't hit it, kick it or catch it, forget it." But his principal contribution was to put his stamp of approval on our ideas about content and design. I was happy when he'd offer a suggestion, because the continuing success of the sections was beginning, for the first time in our friendship, to create some slight tensions. *Times* colleagues were referring to the innovations as "Gelb's sections" and several items quoting me about the sections appeared in *Editor & Publisher* and other publications. Though Abe seemed delighted with my triumph, I suspected he might unwittingly have been just a little resentful at my breaking new ground on my own. I even thought it possible that, in spite of his own colossal achievements and accolades, he might have been feeling a bit left out.

When Mattson asked me to address the advertising sales staff just before Sports Monday's launch date, I felt like a cheerleader: "Our aim is to give each 'section three' its own character. Each is an entity in itself. What we have been doing piecemeal will all come together when the final, Tuesday section is born, and a newly designed business section makes its appearance as section four, five days a week."

Sports Monday's inaugural issue appeared on January 9, 1978. Though it was a bitterly cold, snowy day, the paper sold 37,000 more copies than usual. When the next issue appeared on January 16, the day after the Super Bowl, it sold 50,000 extra copies, and was the most successful single day for the new sections since Weekend had made its debut.

Once the section was established, I shocked the sports department by urging Abe to hire a thirty-three-year-old woman to succeed Jim Tuite as sports editor. Le Anne Schreiber had covered the 1976 Montreal Olympics for *Time* magazine, then had taken a job as editor-in-chief of *womenSports*, a short-lived monthly magazine founded by Billie Jean King and her husband, Larry King. Le Anne also found time to play second base in the Central Park Publishers League and right wing for the New York Women's Soccer Club. As *Times* sports editor, she headed a virtually all-male staff of reporters, columnists and editors.

AT *THE TIMES*'s annual stockholders meeting on April 5, 1978, Punch rose proudly to declare, "Let me start my report with some very good news." He announced that "the first quarter of this year was by far the best first quarter in our history." Earnings had risen thirty-two percent over the previous year. The profits were partly attributed to the increases in circulation and advertising of both the daily and Sunday *Times*, and partly to continuing efforts to diversify. Punch reported that the affiliated companies—which now included magazine, book, broadcasting, information and education corporations—"all showed outstanding gains." What was also comforting was that the city itself was beginning to recover from its fiscal crisis. In my own neighborhood on the Upper West Side, young professionals were taking over renovated brownstones and buying co-ops.

I reveled in the success of the new sections, but never in my career had the work seemed more endless. One night I didn't make it home, and napped for a couple of hours at my desk. Even when I slept, my mind kept spinning. I was often wakened by a fresh idea, and kept a pad and pencil close by whenever I dozed off. There were times I worried I might be losing my mind, and I was equally concerned that Barbara was losing her patience. I promised that once the last of the five sections came off the press, we'd unwind in Paris.

Our big challenge now was what to do on Tuesdays, the last of the five sections. When Mattson and Pomfret approached Abe and me with their idea for the section, the goodwill we had nurtured over the past two years abruptly evaporated. Once again, they trotted out the idea of a style section that would emphasize fashion. Abe and I abhorred the idea, and we hit a daunting stalemate. But then Abe rallied, displaying the same stubborn fervor he had summoned during the Pentagon Papers controversy; and I knew he would have his way.

Abe, Lou Silverstein and I were convinced that a style section, in addition to the Living and Home sections, would be redundant. What was needed, we firmly believed, was a serious report—not another "soft" one, no matter how well presented—to keep the five days of sections in proper news balance. After much discussion, we hit upon the idea of a section to be called Science Times.

The Times had the most authoritative staff of science reporters of any newspaper in the country, and science had traditionally been part of the paper's lifeblood. It was *The Times*, after all, that had sponsored Admiral Byrd's polar expedition; Carr Van Anda had insisted *The Times* publish the most thorough coverage of the opening of Tutankhamen's tomb; William Laurence had given us the early exclusive reports about the atom bomb; our front pages often carried the first news of medical breakthroughs.

When the business department resisted our idea, maintaining there was no ready advertising market for a science section, Abe took our case to Punch, who was himself something of a technology buff. Abe's plea was brilliantly argued—and Punch accepted our concept. Abe once again, as he had done on numerous occasions since becoming an editor, praised Punch for his consistent support of the news department. Over the years, Abe had advised aspiring journalists to choose a paper to work for not only for its editor but also for its publisher. "By that I mean," he would say, "the Sulzberger family always gave editors the space and money for staff to do the job we wanted to do. How many editors on newspapers around the world can make that boast?"

Abe, Lou and I took advantage of an eighty-eight-day strike by the pressmen to shape Science Times, and a week after the strike was settled—on November 14, 1978—we introduced the last of the five sections. It grew almost as popular as Weekend, which still had the largest readership.

As the supervisory editor of the new section for the first few weeks, I held frequent meetings and luncheons with our science writers, who were eager to air their ideas, pleased they would now have their own part of the paper to spotlight their stories, with—we promised them—beautifully designed illustrations. I made sure that the stories and the new columns—like "Doctor's World," by Lawrence Altman—were jargon-free, so that readers would have no trouble understanding even the most complex theories being expounded.

The truly remarkable aspect of the section was that it quickly came to be used by elementary and high school teachers as a classroom textbook tool, and yet was written on a high enough level to appeal to doctors and scientists. It wasn't long before we added a pioneering column on computers—which John Pomfret suggested we peg to the growing home-computer market—and the computer ads started pouring in. Within a few years, when the personal computer revolution swept America, Science Times actually became one of the most profitable of our new sections.

THE TIMES WAS GROWING and changing, becoming bigger, financially stronger, more streamlined. Our dream of a four-section paper was finally realized: the first section devoted mainly to foreign and national news; the second to metropolitan news; the third changing daily Monday through Friday; and the fourth devoted daily to greatly expanded coverage of business and financial news, and entitled Business Day.

With Lou Silverstein, I continued working on new projects to improve the paper—the remodeling of Arts & Leisure, the Sunday Travel section, the daily Metropolitan News page, the Sunday *Book Review* and the creation of new Sunday *Magazine* supplements. I was well aware that an irreversible trend had been set, that the paper would continue to adapt to the demands of the future, enabling it not only to survive but also to thrive. New printing presses allowed for greater production flexibility, and soon *The Times* would be able to adapt to any number of sections, including an arts section and a sports section every day.

Although I was on my way up to becoming managing editor, I never felt truly comfortable in the new world I helped create. As the paper prospered, its staff proliferated. The newsroom became more efficient and businesslike.

It was quiet, even serene. Reporters were well educated, some flaunting two or more degrees. Rarely could an editor take a gamble on hiring an inexperienced youth without a college degree just because his instinct told him to. Some of the reporters I most admired who began their careers as copyboys—Mike Berger, Murray Schumach, McCandlish Phillips—might not be given the opportunity to start as cub reporters on *The Times* today. Even if Mike Berger could get onto the staff, he would never get away with his erratic (if entertaining) desktop romps at deadline.

I missed the freewheeling flavor and casual bravado of the old city room, forever lost—the smell of the paste pots, the fires in the wastepaper baskets, Pat Spiegel dressing down recalcitrant rabbis, Edwin James's private bookies, the feel of an inky, warm newspaper fresh off the basement press, David Burnham quixotically tilting at wrongdoers, the brave vanguard of women and black reporters fighting for their opportunities.

When Abe Rosenthal retired at the end of 1985, Max Frankel went from head of the editorial page to executive editor. Sy Topping had also retired, and I became managing editor. In that position, I found myself more removed from the reporters than I would have liked, for I was obliged to concern myself more with overall operations than with the day-to-day management of individual stories. The place where I had spent so much of my life felt less and less like my second home.

FORTY-EIGHT

I UNDERSTOOD, of course, that the changes in which I myself had participated were necessary, and that they had invigorated *The Times*. I believe the choices we made were, for the most part, good choices. But for me—doubtless because I had spent my entire forty-five-year career in the city room—something was lost along the way. What was lost mainly, I think, was that sense of romance that is simply not compatible with the ubiquitous computer—essential as it is (and without which, I must admit, I would never have attempted this book).

When I retired from the paper at the start of 1990, to be succeeded by Joe Lelyveld, I felt a pang of deprivation. True, Punch had offered me the presidency of The Times Company Foundation—a job not without its own rewards. I was given a small staff and a luxurious office in the solitude of the tenth floor (just about the same spot where I had once delivered copy to poor Rachel McDowell).

As reporter and editor, I had known the sort of power and influence that had opened all doors. I had been a dinner guest at the White House, had attended the most envied social events, the most glamorous Broadway opening nights. On jaunts to foreign countries, I was treated like royalty. I had dined with leaders of state, science and letters—and I assumed most of those doors would now be closed.

If nothing else, I had wanted to leave the city room in style. I was not interested in drawn-out good-byes, in speeches, in ceremony of any kind. I truly wanted neither tears nor a charade of gaiety. I had seen the full spectrum of retirements in my years at *The Times*, and to me the most graceful were those that took place without fanfare, those that possessed something of the character of the paper itself—unsentimental, even august. I wanted to leave just as I had arrived, quietly and unnoticed.

Max Frankel graciously invited me to come down to the third floor each evening to sit in on the page-one meetings, as I had done ever since becoming metropolitan editor in 1967. But I told him I thought that would be a mistake. Once you leave the newsroom, it's pointless to hang around as a kibitzer. (When *he* retired, and Joe Lelyveld succeeded him as executive editor, Max, too, declined to sit in on page-one meetings.)

Now, in my latest job as director of The New York Times College Scholarship Program, I've again changed offices. I still delight, however, in being surrounded by my framed photographs. There is Homer Bigart, next to Peter Kihss, both in shirtsleeves, sitting in the front row of the city room. Edith Evans Asbury is there, looking both pert and poised in her pretty hat, as she scribbles in her notepad on a street corner. The whole crew that wrote the HRA investigative series is seated around a table, looking pleased with themselves, as indeed they should. To the side of my desk hangs a large drawing by Al Hirschfeld of Brooks Atkinson and Clara Rotter in the old drama department.

The college scholarship students, who come from New York's most underprivileged areas, and who managed to excel in high school despite almost unimaginable hardships, visit me often. They always ask about the photographs and seem to enjoy my stories of an antiquated newspaper world—unless, of course, they are just humoring a sentimental ancient. But I prefer to think my love for that world is contagious.

Some of the students, roughly the same age as I when I first arrived at

The Times, live in the same Bronx neighborhood where I once lived. They want to know about the old Loew's Paradise, now a vacant landmark building, and what life was like along the Grand Concourse in its glory days. I'm beguiled by the way the city, through such students and their striving families, renews itself. While my friends and I in that bygone era were mainly offspring of hardworking immigrants from Eastern Europe, Ireland and Italy, my Bronx scholarship students are principally children of striving parents from the Caribbean, Asia, Africa and Latin America.

The students ask me for guidance in their search for the right career path, and I find myself offering hope and encouragement the way Mr. Fairbanks and Grover Loud once did, reflexively echoing some of their very same words. In their ghostly presence, I feel I am repaying them for the time and effort they once lavished on me.

AFTER MY RETIREMENT from the newsroom, I was afforded a chance to heal some old wounds incurred during my years as metropolitan editor. One afternoon in the early 1990s, I was at the Century club with Clifton Daniel, long since retired. We were having a late lunch, and there were few people at any of the tables, including the long one reserved for members who were lunching alone. In the midst of our conversation, Clif interrupted himself, pointed to the long table, and said, "Look at that man with his head down on the table."

"It looks like John Lindsay," I said.

"It is Lindsay!" Daniel agreed.

We went over to him, shook him gently by the shoulder, and asked if he was all right. He mumbled something incoherent and pointed to his chest. I opened his shirt, uncovering a medallion engraved with his doctor's phone number.

When I called, the doctor said to phone 911 right away, which I did, declaring, "Mayor Lindsay needs an ambulance!" Within a couple of minutes, some dozen police officers arrived at the club.

Lindsay survived his attack and called to thank me. I invited him to have lunch with Punch and me, and, a few weeks later, he arrived at the *Times* dining room, frail but cheerful in spite of a mild stroke and heart ailment. Lindsay told us how much he loved *The Times*, which caused me a twinge of guilt. But it seemed he had forgiven and forgotten our past enmity. We talked about his days as a congressman, before he ran for mayor, when we used to lunch together at Sardi's or at the Algonquin, and I'm grateful we parted as friends.

At *The Times*, many of the friendships I forged with colleagues are still going strong. I'm often in touch with Abe, although our intimacy hit some turbulence in the mid-1980s, when he underwent a period of profound unhappiness, which I believe was largely due to the pain of confronting his mandated retirement from the newsroom. Running the paper had become such an integral part of his daily existence that giving it up, on October 10, 1985, was tantamount to facing exile. For a time, he seemed to lose his perspective, occasionally clashing with people both on and off the paper. As the day of his retirement neared, and his power waned, he became a target for those who had earlier feared to voice their resentment of what they regarded as his intemperate behavior.

When Abe did retire, Punch—in appreciation for what he had done to bring the paper to its golden era—rewarded him with an Op-Ed column and built him an elegant office on the tenth floor. Having spent his career keeping the personal opinions of his reporters out of the paper, along with his own, Abe now found himself voicing opinions loud and clear twice a week on such topics as human rights, the First Amendment, patriotism, the Dalai Lama, Israel, and female genital mutilation in Africa. Twice a week he sounded off, apparently relishing every word of his frequently pugnacious judgments.

In the fall of 1999, the column (by then reduced to once a week) came to an end. Arthur Ochs Sulzberger, Jr., Punch's son, who had succeeded his father first as publisher in 1992 and then also as chairman of the board in 1997, was not a champion of the column and told Abe the time had come for him to give it up. Although Abe was by then seventy-seven, he was still percolating at high speed and was in no mood for a second retirement. He was dumbfounded by Arthur's message, which negated the warmth with which Punch had always embraced him. Abe, in a fury, cleaned out his desk and left. He swore to me he would never again set foot in the *Times* building. He then did the unthinkable, contracting to write a column for the *Daily News*.

By now divorced from Ann and joyfully married to Shirley Lord, a writer and editor—and gratified by the reception of his new *Daily News* column—Abe eventually pushed his bitterness aside. While still testy on occasion, he managed to recapture much of the wry, mischievous humor that had so engaged me when I first met him in the city room of the mid-1940s, when he, Bernie Kalb and I became an irreverent trio. We still enjoy reminiscing about old times, although we don't always agree about the details of every past adventure. I'm certain my memory about those days is better than Abe's and, if he can't be convinced any other way, well, I'm still bigger than he is. Mostly when we meet, we talk about the days when he and I were turning the metropolitan report upside down, rarely about anything later than that.

Actually, it would be an egregious disservice not only to Abe but to the history of American journalism not to acknowledge his immense contribution to the evolution of contemporary newspaper writing and editing. While he has detractors who would like to see his reputation diminished, he has ardent supporters among the best in journalism, who remember and value— as I do—his brilliance in covering the early days of the United Nations and as a foreign correspondent in India, Poland and Japan, as well as his inventiveness and unflagging integrity as an editor.

NOT LONG AFTER COMPLETING the special sections, I grew somewhat closer to Punch, largely, I think, because his wife, Carol, and Barbara became friends. We often dined out together and we stayed with them in their London flat—and they stayed with us on and off while hunting for a house in the Hamptons. Carol was scrupulously a lady, in the old-fashioned sense. She held firmly to her values in a world that she sometimes complained was growing uncouth and vulgar. And while she was very much a woman of her time, she might have felt more at home in the nineteenth century. She did, in fact, mirror the heroines of Jane Austen and Trollope—whose novels she loved—in her elegance, her taste, her modesty, her sense of occasion.

Carol was as well-informed about current affairs as anyone I knew. And she was a sharp media critic—as I learned when I was managing editor. She sometimes called me at *The Times*, questioning a fuzzy detail in an article, or a slant that seemed to her unfair. I was lucky if it was a story I had read carefully and could defend. She was a rare conservative voice in the *Times* family—often playfully acting the devil's advocate. She sometimes made Punch's life difficult when she hammered at him with her critical appraisals of *Times* personnel and doctrine.

After Carol's death from cancer in 1995, Punch—who became chairman emeritus of *The Times* upon his retirement—settled into a happy marriage with Allison Cowles, whose late husband, William Cowles, had been publisher of the *Spokane Review* in Washington. Allison's devotion to Punch is absolute—as is his to her. Warm, unpretentious and optimistic, she shares Punch's enjoyment of travel and they divide their time between trips abroad, visits to Allison's home in Spokane—where her children and grandchildren live—as well as their homes in Manhattan and the Hamptons.

Among other of my continuing *Times* friendships are those I formed with several extraordinarily gifted members of the younger generation, whose careers I helped nurture when they arrived at the paper in their twenties and early thirties: Maureen Dowd, Michiko Kakutani and Frank Rich. It became something of a ritual for the four of us to lunch together. They were peculiarly compatible, even though their personalities couldn't have differed more— Maureen, with her dreamy, romantic attachment to the forties and her savvy take on today's blatant hypocrisies; Michi, shy and reclusive, and so dedicated to literature she once kept her overflow of books in her never-used oven; and Frank, the dedicated family man and only domesticated one of the three, with his sometime melancholy but essentially buoyant weltanschauung.

Another old friend on the paper was Howell Raines, who took over as executive editor on September 5, 2001, upon Joe Lelyveld's retirement. Tragically, Howell's career at the paper came to an abrupt end less than two years later—shortly after the searing journalistic misdeeds of Jayson Blair, a young black reporter, became known. Blair's errors and flagrant deceptions in the stories he filed over many months included plagiarizing from other publications and concocting quotes from persons he had never interviewed. The problem had gone unresolved by editors, including Gerald Boyd, *The Times*'s first black managing editor, far too long before they took decisive action leading to Blair's resignation.

Gerald had made journalistic history when he was appointed in September 2001. It had taken a little over half a century for the vision that George Streator had described to me at Child's, during my early days at *The Times,* to approach realization. Gradually, over the decades, the hiring of black reporters and editors had become a desirable practice. Gerald had paid his dues—first as White House correspondent, then as metropolitan editor and later as deputy managing editor. During his tenure, he played a leading role with the reportorial teams that won two Pulitzer Prizes.

A caring, conscientious man, he nurtured many young people on the staff. His own and *The Times*'s determined dedication to diversity resulted in great rewards, but in the Blair case the spirit of inclusion was somehow misapplied. Blair, a charming rogue, had been given chance after chance and repeatedly deceived his supporters.

Once the extent of the damage was realized, *The Times* publicly acknowledged Blair's egregious behavior. Publisher Arthur Sulzberger, Jr., characterized the episode as "a huge black eye" and "an abrogation of the trust between the newspaper and its readers." The paper documented Blair's specific deceptions and apologized for its failure to intervene in a timely manner to stop his stories. All to the good. But in what seemed to me—as well as to many of my colleagues both at *The Times* and outside—to be a vast overreaction, the editors elected to run four full pages of explanation and apology on May 11, 2003, about Blair's transgressions (some committed under the influence of alcohol and drugs).

Striving for an even fuller disclosure—and bordering on self-flagellation—the paper followed its published apology three days later with a "town hall" meeting at a leased Broadway movie theater, to which the newsroom staff, from the humblest office clerks to the highest desk editors, was invited. The meeting was chaired by Arthur Sulzberger, Jr., Howell Raines and Gerald Boyd, and attendees were encouraged to vent their opinions about what had gone wrong—and many did so with a venom that rattled their hosts. When the meeting ended, reporters from virtually every major newspaper, wire agency, TV station and online news service—many gleeful at the chance to take a whack at the lordly *Times*—pumped staffers willing to talk about what had been said.

A newsroom committee and subcommittees were quickly organized in an attempt to address the staff's unrest, along with the bad publicity, but they served only to feed the conflagration. The committee was mandated to prepare a detailed report about how and why the top editors had malfunctioned. Day after day, the outside news coverage continued to spiral.

The paper's apocalyptic four-page saga of self-incrimination, and its unrelenting insistence on beating up on itself—including Howell's own defensive cries of mea culpa—licensed a release of pent-up resentment harbored by many on the newsroom staff toward its top management. Washington correspondents had been upset because they believed Howell was trying to replace the popular bureau chief, Jill Abramson, with his friend the chief correspondent, Patrick Tyler. Sportwriters were upset because two sports columns, one written by the highly regarded Pulitzer Prize winner Dave Anderson, had recently been killed for criticizing the paper's coverage of the Augusta National Gulf Club's policy of barring women as members. National correspondents were upset because one of their colleagues, Rick Bragg, a Pulitzer Prize winner, had written a feature story in which the facts were supplied by a volunteer stringer-intern who had received no pay or credit, Bragg's fellow correspondents disputed his claim that what he had done was common practice. And Howell, they maintained, did not rise quickly enough to the defense of his staff.

Once thrown open, the floodgates of criticism overflowed. Some of the anger was justified, some not. I myself was aware that Howell was increasingly being perceived as inaccessible and at times enveloped in hubris. In recent months, several of my talented friends on the news staff who had warmly endorsed his appointment as executive editor complained to me that he was too preoccupied to listen to them, and I tried to alert him to their grievances. There were, of course, extenuating circumstances: it was a period of overwhelming news coverage, requiring Howell's constant daylong attention, from the September 11 World Trade Center horror to the war in Iraq. It was also a period of personal upheaval for him: he buried his elderly mother and father; he fell in love and married.

It should be noted that Howell was by no means the first or only executive of *The Times* to have erred in his judgment or to be resented. I don't think there was ever a time in all my years on the paper that I didn't hear grousing by reporters and editors, especially from my colleagues in Washington. As a reporter myself for fifteen years, I, too, did my share of grousing and was, in fact, taken aback when I became a top editor and discovered that the grousing was sometimes about me. No one groused more about the top editor than Hildy Johnson in *The Front Page,* the play that helped lure me into newspapers in the first place. I suppose that complaining comes naturally to the *Times* newsroom, where so many peerless reporters and editors often become restive, and where any kind of slight, no matter how small, offends mightily.

But in Howell's case, he became more vulnerable and defensive when the Blair affair took on the characteristics of a scandal. The critical onslaught appeared gradually to immobilize him. He lost control of the newsroom. After five weeks of agonizing, Howell and Gerald "resigned." No executive editor or managing editor had ever been forced to resign, and the shock waves reverberated throughout *The Times,* not to mention the journalism world at large.

At ten A.M. on June 5, the publisher called a few of us together in the boardroom to tell us that Howell and Gerald were stepping down that morning. It was an emotional jolt, and I couldn't bring myself, a half-hour later, to go to the newsroom and witness their sorrowful farewells.

Arthur Sulzberger, Jr., asked Howell's predecessor, Joe Lelyveld, to return temporarily as executive editor. There was a tentative sense in the newsroom that the paper might, before too long, emerge in all its former strength. On July 14, after weeks of speculation inside *The Times* and out, the publisher named Bill Keller executive editor. I was delighted that Bill urged the staff to "move on" and put excessive "introspection" (prompted by the Jayson Blair affair) behind them, because, he said, too much of such reflection is "poison." The irony is that Bill, a distinguished Pulitzer Prize–winning foreign correspondent who had been managing editor during most of Joe Lelyveld's original tenure, and who had been Joe's choice to succeed him, had earlier been passed over by the publisher in favor of Howell.

It pleased me too when Jill Abramson, an old friend, was named managing editor for news gathering, the first woman to rise to that position at *The Times* (while John Geddes was appointed managing editor for news operations). What pleased me as well was that in her acceptance speech to the staff, Jill said that one of her objectives was to "recapture" some of the fun, as I had often described it to her, of my old city room.

I WILL NEVER FULLY fathom the twisted ins and outs that led to Howell Raines's downfall. I first met him in 1978, when I was among those who interviewed him for the job of national correspondent based in Atlanta. Three years later, Bill Kovach, the Washington bureau chief, assigned him to cover the White House. During that time, accompanied by Lou Silverstein, I spent a few weeks in Washington to inaugurate a new daily page called "Washington Talk," consisting of columns, profiles and features pegged to life in the capital. It was then that I had a chance to watch Howell in action as White House correspondent and came to appreciate his zest for—to use his favorite phrase—"muscular journalism."

Howell, who won a Pulitzer Prize in 1992 for feature writing, was the first executive editor of *The Times* since Turner Catledge to hail from the deep South—Birmingham, Alabama, in Howell's case. After a two-year stint as head of the London bureau, he returned to Washington at the end of 1988 to take over the bureau and, in 1993, was appointed by Arthur Sulzberger, Jr., to be editor of the editorial page.

On the morning of September 11, only six days after he had become executive editor, Howell found himself mobilizing virtually the entire *Times* staff of reporters and editors to cover the attacks on the World Trade Center, one of the most horrendous and demanding spot-news stories in the history of journalism. The next day's paper was monumental and, for weeks after, the coverage never flagged. Even our most avid competitors acknowledged the propriety of the seven Pulitzers awarded to *The Times*, the most any paper had received in a single year.

When he learned of the Pulitzers on April 8, 2002, Abe called me to share his pride and pleasure in the paper's achievement. He was especially pleased that his son Andrew—whom Howell had promoted from foreign editor to assistant managing editor—was integrally involved in the coverage.

Howell, aware of course of the circumstances of Abe's unhappy departure from *The Times* two and a half years earlier, urged his presence in the newsroom that afternoon for a celebration, explaining that the invitation came from the publisher as well as himself. Abe agreed to be there.

He looked somewhat pale and walked haltingly, the effects of a recent illness, when he picked me up at my tenth-floor office to accompany him down to the newsroom. When we entered the room, already jammed with scores of reporters, editors and people from all over the building, Arthur Sulzberger, Jr., encircled Abe in a welcoming bear hug.

I had participated in overwhelming moments in that room a number of times over the decades, but nothing ever matched the emotions of that day. Abe and Arthur Jr. stood together, along with Punch, Max Frankel, Joe Lelyveld and others formerly in the top echelon, as Howell began speaking. He congratulated the staff for "a performance that will be remembered and taught, remembered and studied, as long as journalism is taught and practiced." Recalling the words of Dizzy Dean, whom he labeled "Mississippi's greatest moral philosopher," Howell added, "'It ain't bragging if you really done it.' Ladies and gentlemen of *The New York Times*, you've really done it."

When Abe's wife, Shirley, decided to celebrate his eightieth birthday on May 1, 2002, Howell thought the occasion would be an appropriate way of erasing any vestiges of animosity. He suggested that he, Punch and Arthur Jr. join her as co-hosts of the event at one of Abe's favorite restaurants, the Grill Room of the Four Seasons. Punch read an endearing poem about Abe, and Arthur Jr. hailed him for his newsroom achievements. "All of us who work for *The Times* know that we are part of a great continuum," Arthur said. "If we're good and if we're lucky we'll take what we've been entrusted with and build on it—reshape it for the world we represent—and pass on to our successors something strong and vibrant.... Our goal is to see that *The New York Times* thrives and adapts as well as it did under the leadership of Punch Sulzberger and Abe Rosenthal. And that's no small challenge."

Abe was visibly moved. When it was his turn to speak, he saluted his former newsroom colleagues and paid tribute to the Sulzbergers, especially to Punch: "I've worked for most of my career for Punch. In all that time only now and then did he try to influence me about what would appear in the paper. Sometimes, when a child or a friend was getting engaged or married, he sent down a little note asking if we could use it. Damn right we could. It was one way we could blow a little kiss to the man who did so much to sustain the best paper in the world and its respect for its readers."

After returning home that night, I wrote Abe a letter, dwelling on the richness of our old city-room partnership and how lost we probably would have felt in the recently rebuilt, sleek two-story newsroom. And I wrote regretfully of how the designation "journalism" had all but lost its original meaning, with many now referring to our treasured newspaper world as "the media," lumping it with celebrity TV newscasters, often reckless Internet reports and snide gossip magazines.

The Times itself now has a group of TV stations, produces documentaries and provides up-to-the-minute reports and features on its Internet website. The company has grown to such a degree that Arthur Sulzberger, Jr., is building a new fifty-two-story tower a couple of blocks south on Eighth Avenue, to which operations will be moved within the next few years.

A FINAL NOTE: The week after I retired as managing editor in 1990 and left my old city room, I began suffering from separation anxiety. What set me on the road to recovery was a long, thoughtful letter from a highly talented deputy news editor, Russell King, who died in 2000 of AIDS-related pneumonia.

"I'm still relatively new here," Rusty wrote in part, "and it's only in the last couple of years that I've been in a position to see you and your influence and ideas at firsthand. What came through to me is that you loved *The New York Times*, that you were excited about working there. And every story and every page had to be right, and penetrating, and interesting, not because the most important people in the country depended on *The Times*, and not because we had to worry about attracting new readers, and not because of lofty devotion to journalistic principles—no, you wanted everything done right simply because it was *The Times*, and you cared about its being the best it could possibly be."

Answering Rusty's letter was a sort of catharsis. I tried to explain myself to him, as well as to myself, and in a way the letter became an outline for my memoir:

When I became a reporter, I realized that what I and my friends on the paper had in common (and openly admitted to) was a genuine love (Yes, love) for the paper. It wasn't easy to earn a byline in those days and when our stories were signed it was like the thrill an actor gets when his name goes up in lights. What could be more glamorous for a kid fresh out of the Bronx? We poured our hearts out for the paper. I guess you could call it insane devotion, but most of us had the fever, and we huddled in Bleeck's after work, with staffers on the *Trib* and *The New Yorker* and elsewhere, to compare thoughts and ideas about our world.

It was in the city room that I first saw the bulletins announcing the end of World War II, and the Hiroshima devastation, and where I experienced Joe McCarthy's villainy and where I saw reporters weep when they learned of President Kennedy's assassination. And then the time I was metropolitan editor. Can you imagine what it was like for an editor to arrive at work each morning, to look up from his desk at a sea of the most talented reporters in the newspaper world? Those were the happiest days of my life.

ACKNOWLEDGMENTS

Chiefly to blame for my writing this book are Phyllis Grann, until recently the superpublisher who ran Penguin Putnam, as well as Scott Berg, the biographer, and Dan Harvey, Putnam's publishing director. During a small dinner party at Phyllis's home, after listening to me go on and on about my love and nostalgia for the bygone days at *The New York Times*, Scott and Dan urged her to sign me to a book contract. If the result in any way lives up to their expectations, I thank them all from the bottom of my heart.

The stories I regaled them with that night began with the raffish city room I found at *The Times* when I entered it as a lowly twenty-year-old copyboy in 1944—a room filled with exacting, tradition-steeped editors and streetwise, freewheeling reporters who gave me the newspaper smarts that helped boost me eventually to managing editor.

With the best will in the world, I could never have written this book had I not been, all my life, a pack rat, who saved letters, memos, official records, newspaper and magazine clippings, notebooks filled with personal jottings and notes of conversations, and other assorted memorabilia—not to mention a complete (if yellowing) file of the *Times* house organ, *Timesweek*, which I cofounded and edited shortly after I joined the paper.

While this enormous accumulation was of considerable value in jogging my memory, I could not have proceeded without the patient and painstaking work by my essential research aide, Michael Benanav, who spent months helping me sort and organize my material, checking facts, acting as a vital sounding board—and, not least, getting me out of maddening difficulties with my computer.

I am also grateful to Howard Fishman and Jenny Allen for their generous assistance with various aspects of research and for helping me get started. And I thank particularly Jeffrey Roth, whose encyclopedic knowledge of *The Times*'s newspaper and photo morgues is unmatched, and who always managed to find the elusive fact I needed.

I am much indebted to friends and colleagues both on and off *The Times* who vetted my manuscript: Linda Amster, John Corry, Maureen Dowd, Bernard Kalb, Michael J. Leahy, Alex S. Jones, Nancy Sharkey, Marvin Siegel, Richard Reeves, my sons Michael and Peter, and Linda Healey, who also gave me encouragement throughout my writing of *City Room*.

For checking the accuracy of various aspects of my recollections, I thank the following (in alphabetical order):

Renata Adler, Arthur Altschul, Martin Arnold, Edith Evans Asbury, Sandra Blakeslee, David Burnham, Ric Burns, Earl Caldwell, Vincent Canby, Deirdre Carmody, Francis X. Clines, Clifton Daniel, John Darnton, Vincent Di Leo, Art D'Lugoff, Dan Edelson, Milton Esterow, Fred Ferretti, Don Forst, Sylvan Fox, Max Frankel, Lucinda Franks, C. Gerald Fraser, Nicholas Gage, Paul Gardner, Bernard Gersten, Grace Glueck, Lewis Gould, James Greenfield, Gil Hagerty, David Harris, Eddie Hausner, Al Hirschfeld, Laurie Johnston, Michael Kaufman, Jean Kerr, Alice Kihss, Lora Korbut, Joseph Lelyveld, Russell T. Lewis, Grace Lichtenstein, J. Anthony Lukas, Linda Feinfeld Magyar, Phyllis Malamud, Nancy Maynard.

Also, Robert D. McFadden, Gerald McQueen, Lesley Oelsner, Guy Passant, Nick Pileggi, Frank J. Prial, Howell Raines, Frank Rich, A. M. Rosenthal, Ann Rosenthal, Vincent Sardi, Murray Schumach, Neil Sheehan, Richard F. Shepard, Trudy Shepard, David Shirey, Allan M. Siegal, Louis Silverstein, Hedrick Smith, Brent Staples, Gay Talese, Martin Tolchin, Lawrence Van Gelder, Patrick Wallace, A. H. Weiler, Steven R. Weisman, Robert Whitehead, Richard Witkin, and Sidney Zion.

My special gratitude goes to Arthur Ochs Sulzberger, *The Times*'s caring, courageous publisher during my long tenure as reporter and editor, and to Marian Wood, my editor at Putnam, for her incisive counseling. And I am grateful to Anna Jardine for her eagle eye.

As for all those warriors, sung and unsung, of the old city room—most of them long gone—they will always be joyfully alive in my memory. I can never repay them for the romance and suspense they brought to my life during my years in the city room.

INDEX

ABOUT THE AUTHOR

When Arthur Gelb joined *The New York Times* in 1944, manual typewriters, green eyeshades, spittoons, floors littered with cigarette butts, and two bookies were what he found in the city room. Gelb, who had just turned twenty, began as a copyboy. He would spend the next forty-five years honing his skills as reporter, rewrite man, and editor. When he retired at the mandatory age of sixty-five, he was managing editor.

On his way to the top, he exposed crooked cops and politicians, mentored a generation of our most talented journalists, was the first to praise the as yet undiscovered Woody Allen and Barbra Streisand, and brought Joe Papp public recognition. As metropolitan editor, Gelb reshaped the way *The Times* covered New York, and while assistant managing editor, he led the launching of the paper's daily special sections.

From D-Day to the liberation of the concentration camps, from the agony of Vietnam to the resignation of a president, from the fall of Joe McCarthy to the rise of the Woodstock Nation, Gelb's memoir of his years at *The Times* reveals his intimate take on the great events of the past half-century.

The raffish early days are long gone, the hum of computers has replaced the clatter of typewriter keys, but the same ambition, passion, grandstanding, and courage that Gelb found at twenty still fill the city room.

On his retirement from the paper, Arthur Gelb became president of the New York Times Company Foundation. He is now director of The New York Times College Scholarship Program.